I0110134

Innovations in Land Rights Recognition, Administration, and Governance

Klaus Deininger
Clarissa Augustinus
Stig Enemark
Paul Munro-Faure

THE WORLD BANK
Washington, D.C.

Copyright © 2010
The International Bank for Reconstruction and Development/The World Bank
1818 H Street, N.W.
Washington, D.C. 20433, U.S.A.

All rights reserved

1 2 3 4 13 12 11 10

World Bank Studies are published to communicate the results of the Bank's work to the development community with the least possible delay. The manuscript of this paper therefore has not been prepared in accordance with the procedures appropriate to formally-edited texts. Some sources cited in this paper may be informal documents that are not readily available. This volume is a product of the staff of the International Bank for Reconstruction and Development/The World Bank. The findings, interpretations, and conclusions expressed in this volume do not necessarily reflect the views of the Executive Directors of The World Bank or the governments they represent.

The World Bank does not guarantee the accuracy of the data included in this work. The boundaries, colors, denominations, and other information shown on any map in this work do not imply any judgment on the part of The World Bank concerning the legal status of any territory or the endorsement or acceptance of such boundaries.

Rights and Permissions
The material in this publication is copyrighted. Copying and/or transmitting portions or all of this work without permission may be a violation of applicable law. The International Bank for Reconstruction and Development/The World Bank encourages dissemination of its work and will normally grant permission to reproduce portions of the work promptly.

For permission to photocopy or reprint any part of this work, please send a request with complete information to the Copyright Clearance Center Inc., 222 Rosewood Drive, Danvers, MA 01923, USA; telephone: 978-750-8400; fax: 978-750-4470; Internet: www.copyright.com.

All other queries on rights and licenses, including subsidiary rights, should be addressed to the Office of the Publisher, The World Bank, 1818 H Street NW, Washington, DC 20433, USA; fax: 202-522-2422; e-mail: pubrights@worldbank.org.

ISBN: 978-0-8213-8580-7
eISBN: 978-0-8213-8581-4
DOI: 10.1596/978-0-8213-8580-7

Library of Congress Cataloging-in-Publication Data has been requested.

Contents

Tables

Figures

Acknowledgments

The World Bank, together with its partners, has a long tradition of organizing an annual conference on land policies and administration to facilitate exchange of experience among practitioners and showcasing innovative solutions to technical and policy issues in this area. This volume contains papers presented at these conferences to make them available to a wider audience interested in this topic. The volume, as well as the conference that underlies it, would not have been possible without the support of members in the Bank's Thematic Group on Land Policy and Administration and other partners (in particular Carlos M. de Souza Jr., Charles di Leva, Daniel Fitzpatrick, Daniel Monchuk, Daniel Stigall, Danilo Antonio, Diji Chandrasekharan Behr, Douglas Batson, Frank Byamugisha, Garo Batmanian, Guo Li, Harris Selod, Helge Onsrud, Iain Greenway, Jonathan Conning, Jonathan Mills Lindsay, Jorge Munoz, Malcolm D. Childress, Martin Adams, Martín Valdivia, Megumi Muto, Michael Carter, Paul Munro-Faure, Paul van der Molen, Quy-Toan Do, Renée Giovarelli, Richard Grover, Richard Trenchard, Rosie Kingwill, Santiago Borrero-Mutis, Shaun Williams, Shenngen Fan, Solomon Haile, Stig Enemark, Timothy Hanstad, Tommy Österberg, Túlio Barbosa, Victoria Stanley, Vincent Palmade, and Willi Zimmerman) who peer reviewed and provided constructive comments on each of the papers and the many partners in bilateral and multi-lateral organizations, research and academic institutions, civil society organizations, and private foundations who are active in this field and who contribute to the sharing of experience embodied in this volume. Our special thanks go to the ARD editorial team (in particular, M. Mercedes Stickler, Sonia Madhvani, Raji Manikandan (DEC), Julie Cannon, Gunnar Larson, and Katie Lancos) which did a marvelous job in steering this publication through on schedule.

Publication of this volume would have been impossible without the material and intellectual support by the Global Land Tools Network, the International Federation of Surveyors, and the Food and Agricultural Organization of the United Nations, as well as the guidance of the ARD management team, led by Juergen Voegele and Mark Cackler. It is our hope that, in addition to providing insights to practitioners, this volume will help to attract other partners to and be followed by many similar publications resulting from the very fruitful partnership that has been established.

Land Governance and the Millennium Development Goals

KLAUS DEININGER, The World Bank, U.S.
STIG ENEMARK, The International Federation of Surveyors (FIG), Denmark

The Global Agenda

The eight Millennium Development Goals (MDGs)[1] form a blueprint that is agreed to by all the world's countries and its leading development institutions. The first seven goals are mutually reinforcing and are directed at reducing poverty in all its forms. The last goal—global partnership for development—is about the means to achieve the first seven. To track the progress in achieving the MDGs a framework of targets and indicators has been developed. This framework includes 18 targets and 48 indicators enabling the ongoing monitoring of the progress that is reported on annually (UN 2000).

The contribution of land professionals to achieving the MDGs is central and vital. The provision of relevant geographic information in terms of mapping and databases of the built and natural environments, as well as providing secure tenure systems, systems for land valuation, land use management and land development are all key components of the MDGs. Land professionals have an important role in directing land administration systems in support of secure property rights, in particular for those who have traditionally been disadvantaged, of efficient land markets, and of effective land use management. These functions underpin development and innovation and form the "backbone" in society that supports social justice, economic growth, and environmental sustainability. Simply, no development will take place without having a spatial dimension, and no development will happen without the footprint of the land professionals.

In a global perspective the areas of surveying and land administration are basically about *people, politics,* and *places.* It is about *people* in terms of human rights, engagement, and dignity; it is about *politics* in terms of land policies and good government; and it is about *places* in terms of shelter, land and natural resources (Enemark 2006).

The key challenges of the new millennium have been clearly articulated. They relate to climate change, food shortage, energy scarcity, urban growth, environmental degradation, and natural disasters. These issues all relate to governance and management of land. Land governance is a cross-cutting activity that will confront all traditional "silo-organized" land administration systems.

Land Governance

Arguably sound land governance is the key to achieving sustainable development and to supporting the global agenda of the MDGs.

Even in terms of standard indicators such as corruption, land has long been known to be one of the sectors most affected by bad governance, something that is not difficult to understand in light of the fact that land is not only a major asset but also that its values are likely to rise rapidly in many contexts of urbanization and economic development. The most authoritative survey of global corruption finds that, except for the police and the courts, land services are the most corrupt sector, ahead of other permits, education, health, tax authorities, or public utilities (Transparency International 2009).[2] Although individual amounts may be small, such petty corruption can add up to large sums—in India the bribes paid annually by users of land administration services are estimated to be $700 million (Transparency International India 2005), equivalent to three-quarters of India's total public spending on science, technology, and environment. Large-scale and serious corruption associated with acquisition and disposal of public lands is more notorious in some contexts. For example, in Kenya "land grabbing" by public officials reached systemic proportions during 1980–2005 and was identified as "one of the most pronounced manifestations of corruption and moral decadence in our society" (Government of Kenya 2004). For private land, bad governance manifests itself in the difficulty of accessing land administration institutions to obtain land ownership information or to transfer property. Together, large- and small-scale corruption will reduce the perceived integrity and, because of high transaction costs, the completeness of land registries; thereby undermining the very essence of land administration systems.

Beyond the negative element of reducing opportunity for corruption and bribery, good land governance is also critical as a precondition for sustainable economic development in a number of respects. First, those who have only insecure or short-term land rights are unlikely to invest their full efforts to make long-term improvements attached to the land and may instead be forced to expend significant resources to defend the rights to their land, without producing benefits for the broader economy. Land rights are particularly important for women (especially in case of inheritance or divorce) and for other traditionally disadvantaged groups such as migrants or herders. Second, secure land tenure facilitates transfer of land at low cost through rentals and sales, improving the allocation of land. Without secure rights, landowners are less willing to rent out their land, something that may impede their ability and willingness to engage in nonagricultural employment or rural-urban migration, reducing the scope for structural change and reducing the productivity of land use in both rural and urban areas. Third, setting up or expanding a business requires physical space, i.e. land. Non-transparent, corrupt, or simply inefficient systems of land administration constitute a major bottleneck that makes it more costly for small and would-be entrepreneurs to transform good ideas into economically viable enterprises.[3] Also, to the extent that easily transferable land titles can be used as collateral, their availability will reduce the cost of accessing credit, thus increasing opportunities for gainful employment and contributing to innovation and the development of financial systems. Finally, economic development increases demand for land, and together with public investment in infrastructure and roads, tends to increase land values. But the lack of well-functioning mechanisms to tax land limits the benefit for society, in particular local governments, as much of the gains end up with private individuals and may fuel speculation. If land institutions function properly, land taxation provides a simple, yet efficient, tool to increase effective decentralization and foster local government accountability.

The need for good land governance is reinforced by three broad global trends. Increased and more volatile commodity prices, population growth, and the resulting increased demand for rural and urban land make it more important to define and protect land resources. Climate change is likely to have particularly pernicious effects on areas traditionally considered to be hazardous or marginal. Adequate land use planning together with land-information based geospatial tools to manage disasters can help mitigate these effects. Global programs that provide resources for environmental protection are more likely to accomplish their objectives if local land rights are recognized and resources are allocated appropriately.

Land governance is about the policies, processes and institutions by which land, property and natural resources are managed. This includes decisions about access to land, land rights, land use, and land development. Land governance is basically determining and implementing sustainable land policies (figure 1).

Land governance and management encompass all the activities associated with the management of land and natural resources that are required to fulfill political and social objectives and achieve sustainable development. Land management requires inter-disciplinary skills that include technical, natural, and social sciences. The operational component of the land management concept is the range of land administration functions that include the areas of land tenure (securing and transferring rights in land and natural resources); land value (valuation and taxation of land and properties); land use (planning and control of the use of land and natural resources); and land development (implementing utilities, infrastructure, construction planning, and schemes for renewal and change of existing land use).

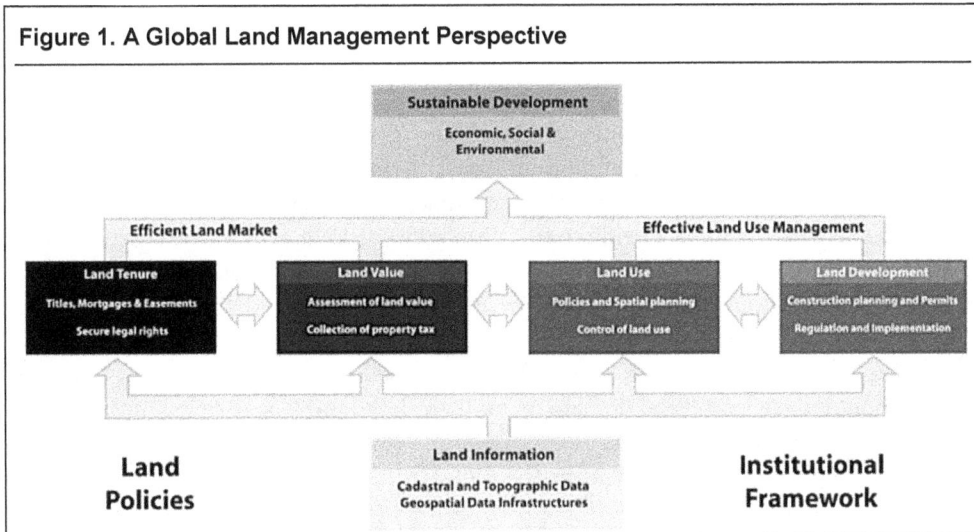

Figure 1. A Global Land Management Perspective

Source: Enemark, 2001.

Land administration systems are the basis for conceptualizing *rights, restrictions* and *responsibilities*. Property rights are normally concerned with ownership and tenure whereas restrictions usually control use and activities on land. Responsibilities relate more to a social, ethical commitment or attitude to environmental sustainability and good husbandry. In more generic terms, land administration is about managing the relations between people, policies, and places in support of sustainability and the global agenda set by the MDGs.

Property Rights

In the Western cultures it would be hard to imagine a society without property rights as a basic driver for development and economic growth. Property is not only an economic asset, however; secure property rights also provide a sense of identity and belonging that goes far beyond and underpins the values of democracy and human freedom that surpasses their economic value. Historically, land rights evolved to give incentives for maintaining soil fertility, making land-related investments, and managing natural resources sustainably. Therefore, property rights are normally managed well in modern economies. The main rights are ownership and long term leasehold. These rights are typically managed through the cadastral/land registration systems developed over centuries. Other rights such as easements and mortgage are often included in the registration systems.

The formalized western land registration systems are basically concerned with identification of legal rights in support of an efficient land market and do not adequately address the more informal and indigenous rights to land found especially in developing countries where tenures are predominantly social rather than legal. Therefore, traditional cadastral systems cannot adequately provide security of tenure to the vast majority of the world's low income groups or deal quickly enough with the scale of urban problems. A new and innovative approach is found in the continuum of land rights (including perceived tenure, customary, occupancy, adverse possession, group tenure, leases, freehold) where the range of possible forms of tenure is considered as a continuum from informal towards more formal land rights and where each step in the process of securing the tenure can be formalized (UN-Habitat 2008b).

Property Restrictions

Land-use planning and restrictions are becoming increasingly important as a means to ensure effective management of land-use, provide infrastructure and services, protect and improve the urban and rural environments, prevent pollution, and pursue sustainable development. Planning and regulation of land activities crosscut tenures and the land rights they support. How these intersect is best explained by describing two conflicting points of view—the free market approach and the central planning approach.

The free market approach argues that land owners should be obligated to no one and should have complete domain over their land. In this extreme position, the government opportunity to take land (eminent domain), restrict its use (by planning systems), or even regulate how it is used (building controls) should be non-existent or highly limited.

The central planning approach argues that the role of any government includes planning and regulating land systematically for public good purposes. In these jurisdictions the historical assumption that a land owner could do anything that was not expressly forbidden by planning regulations evolved into the different principle that land owners could do only what was expressly allowed, everything else being forbidden.

The tension between these two points of view is especially felt by nations seeking economic security. The question is how to balance owners' rights with the necessity and capacity of the government to regulate land use and development for the benefit of society. The answer is found in a country's land policy which should set a reasonable balance between the ability of land owners to manage their land and the ability of the government to provide services and regulate growth for sustainable development. This balance is a basis for achieving sustainability and attaining the MDGs.

Informal development may occur where vacant state-owned or private land is occupied and used for housing or any other construction works without formal permission from the planning or building authorities. Such illegal development could be significantly reduced through government interventions supported by the citizens. Underpinning this intervention is the concept of integrated land-use management as a fundamental means to support sustainable development, and at the same time, prevent and legalize informal development (Enemark and McLaren 2008).

Property Responsibilities

Property responsibilities are culturally based and relate to a more social, ethical commitment where individuals and others are supposed to treat land and property in a way that conforms to cultural traditions and ethical behavior. This relates to what is accepted both legally and socially. Therefore, the systems for managing land use vary throughout the world according to historical development and cultural traditions. More generally, the humankind to land relationship is to some extent determined by the cultural and administrative development of the country or jurisdiction.

Social responsibilities of land owners have a long heritage in Europe. In Germany, for example, the Constitution insists on the land owner's social role. In general, European countries take a comprehensive and holistic approach to land management by building integrated information and administration systems. Other regions in the world, such as Australia, create separate commodities out of land, using the concept of "unbundling land rights," and then adapt the land administration systems to accommodate this trading of rights without a national approach.

The Land Management Paradigm

Land management underpins the distribution and management of a key asset of any society. For western democracies, with their highly geared economies, land management is a key activity of both government and the private sector. Land management, especially the central land administration component, aims to deliver efficient land markets and effective management of the use of land in support of economic, social, and environmental sustainability.

The land management paradigm illustrated in figure 2 below allows everyone to understand the role of the land administration functions (land tenure, land value, land use, and land development) and how land administration institutions relate to the historical circumstances of a country and its policy decisions. Most important, the paradigm provides a framework to facilitate the process of integrating new needs into traditionally-organized systems without disturbing the fundamental security these systems provide.

Figure 2. Land Management Paradigm

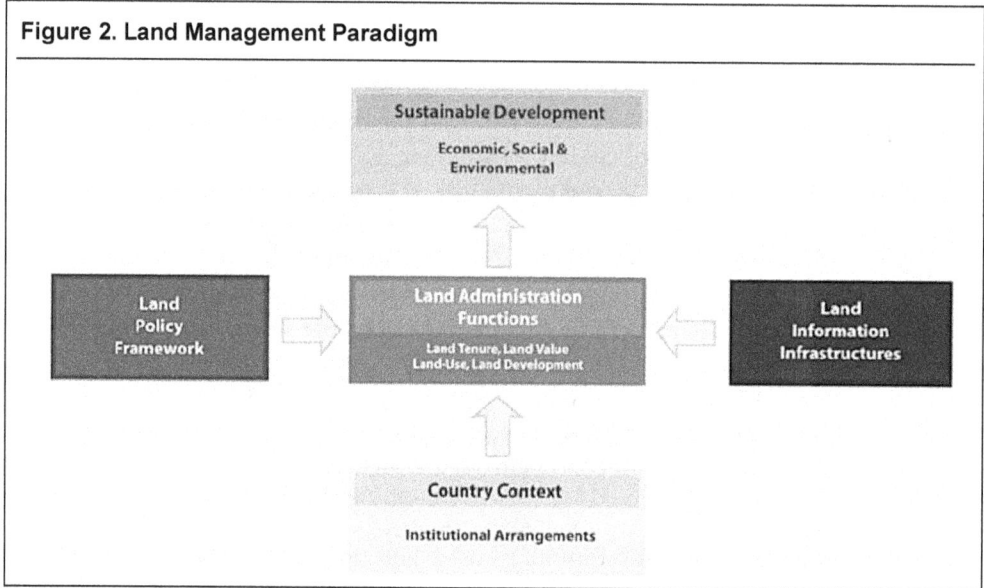

Source: Enemark, 2001.

Sound land management requires operational processes to implement land policies in comprehensive and sustainable ways. Many countries, however, tend to separate land tenure rights from land use opportunities, undermining their capacity to link planning and land use controls with land values and the operation of the land market. These problems are often compounded by poor administrative and management procedures that fail to deliver the required services. Investment in new technology will only go a small way towards solving a much deeper problem: the failure to treat land and its resources as a coherent whole.

How a particular jurisdiction responds to changing needs will depend on how local leaders understand the vision. While the larger theoretical framework described above is futuristic for many countries, they must still design their land administration systems around the land management paradigm. A starting point in systems design is to understand how the components of the paradigm fit together hierarchically (figure 3).

The hierarchy illustrates the complexity of organizing policies, institutions, processes, and information for dealing with land in society, but it also illustrates an orderly approach for doing so. This conceptual understanding provides the overall guidance for building land administration systems in any society, no matter the level of development. The hierarchy also provides guidance for adjustment or reengineering of existing systems. This process of adjustment should be based on constant monitoring of the results of the land administration and land management activities. Land policies may then be revised and adapted to meet the changing needs in society, which will, in turn, affect the way land parcels are held, assessed, used, or developed.

Figure 3. Hierarchy of Land Issues

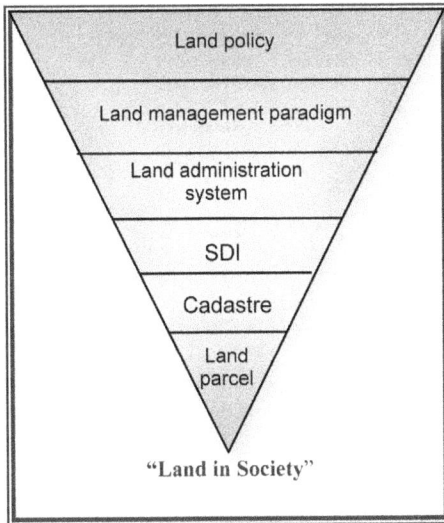

"Land in Society"

Source: Williamson, Enemark, Wallace, Rajabifard, 2009.

Land Policy determines values, objectives and the legal regulatory framework for management of a society's major asset, its land.

Land Management includes all activities associated with the management of land and natural resources that are required to achieve sustainable development. These activities include the core land administration functions: land tenure, land value, land use and land development.

The **Land Administration System** provides the infrastructure for implementation of land policies and land management strategies, and underpins the operation of efficient land markets and effective and use management.

The **Spatial Data Infrastructure** (SDI) provides access to and interoperability of the cadastral information and other land information.

The **Cadastre** provides the spatial integrity and unique identification of every land parcel usually through a cadastral map updated by cadastral surveys. The parcel identification provides the link for securing land rights and controlling land use.

The **Land Parcel** is the key object for identification of land rights and administration of restrictions and responsibilities in the use of land. The land parcel simply links the system with the people.

Spatially Enabled Government

Place matters! Everything happens somewhere. If we can understand more about the nature of "place", and the impact on the people and assets in that location, we can plan better, manage risk better, and use our resources better (Communities and Local Government 2008). Spatially enabled government is achieved when governments use *place* as the key means of organizing their activities in addition to information, and when location and spatial information are available to citizens and businesses to encourage creativity.

New distribution concepts such as Google Earth provide user friendly information in a very accessible way. We should consider the option where spatial data from such concepts are merged with built and natural environment data. This unleashes the power of both technologies in relation to emergency response, taxation assessment, environmental monitoring and conservation, economic planning and assessment, social services planning, infrastructure planning, etc. Merging spatial data with planning information systems requires designing and implementing suitable service oriented IT-architecture so the information is available, accessible, and reliable.

Spatial enablement offers opportunities for visualization, scalability, and user functionalities, which are relevant to a variety of institutional stakeholders, such as Ministries/Departments of Justice, Taxation, Planning, Environment, Transport, Agriculture, and Housing; as well as regional and local authorities; public utilities; and civil society interests such as businesses and citizens. Creating awareness of the benefits of developing a shared platform for Integrated Land Information Management takes time. The Mapping/Cadastral Agencies have a key role to play in this regard. The technical core of Spatially Enabled Government is the spatially enabled cadastre.

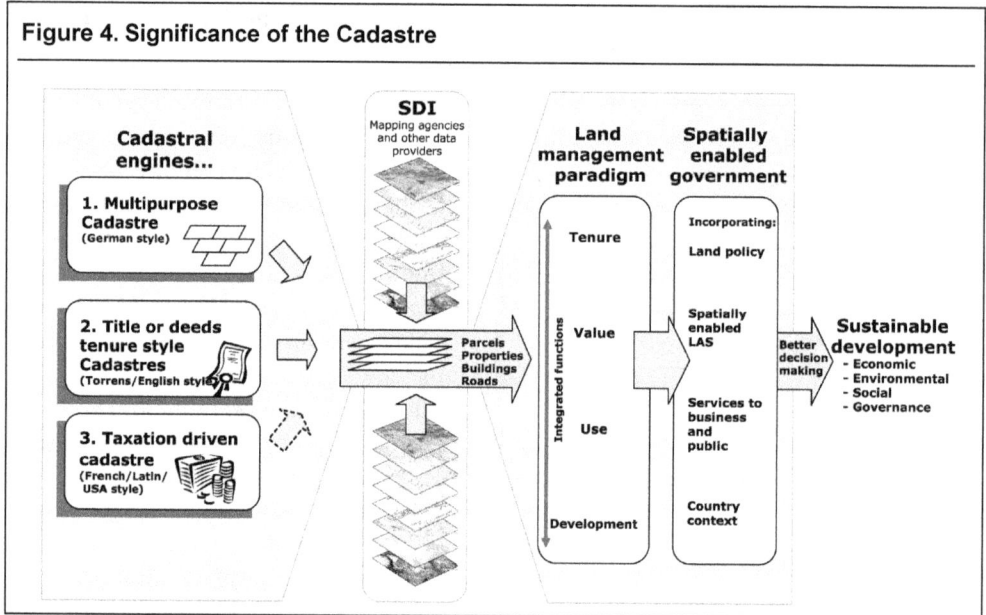

Figure 4. Significance of the Cadastre

Source: Williamson, Enemark, Wallace, Rajabifard, 2009.

The land management paradigm makes a national cadastre the engine of the entire land administration system, underpinning the country's capacity to deliver sustainable development (figure 4). The role of the cadastre is neutral in terms of the historical development of any national system, though systems based on the German and Torrens approaches are much more easily focused on land management than systems based on the French/Latin approach.

The diagram highlights the usefulness of the large scale cadastral map as a tool by exposing its power as the representation of the human scale of land use and how people are connected to their land. The digital cadastral representation of the human scale of the built environment, and the cognitive understanding of land use patterns in peoples' farms, businesses, homes, and other developments, then form the core information sets that enable a country to build an overall administrative framework to deliver sustainable development.

The diagram demonstrates that the cadastral information layer cannot be replaced by a different spatial information layer derived from geographic information systems (GIS). The unique cadastral capacity is to identify a parcel of land both on the ground and in the system in terms that all stakeholders can relate to, typically an address plus a systematically generated identifier, since addresses alone are often imprecise. The core cadastral information of parcels, properties and buildings, and in many cases legal roads, thus becomes the core of Spatial Data Infrastructure (SDI) information, feeding into utility infrastructure, hydrological, vegetation, topographical, images, and dozens of other datasets.

Governance refers to the manner in which power is exercised by governments in managing a country's social, economic, and spatial resources. It is simply the process of decision-making and the process by which decisions are implemented. Government is just one of the actors since the concept includes both formal and informal processes used to arrive at and implement decisions. Good governance is a qualitative term or an ideal which may be difficult to achieve. The term includes a number of characteristics (adapted from FAO 2007):

- **Sustainable and locally responsive**: It balances the economic, social, and environmental needs of present and future generations, and locates its service provision at the closest level to citizens.
- **Legitimate and equitable**: It has been endorsed by society through democratic processes and deals fairly and impartially with individuals and groups providing non-discriminatory access to services.
- **Efficient, effective and competent**: It formulates policy and implements it efficiently by delivering services of high quality
- **Transparent, accountable and predictable**: It is open and demonstrates stewardship by responding to questioning and providing decisions in accordance with rules and regulations.
- **Participatory and providing security and stability**: It enables citizens to participate in government and provides security of livelihoods, freedom from crime and intolerance.
- **Dedicated to integrity**: Officials perform their duties without bribe and give independent advice and judgments, and respect confidentiality. There is a clear separation between private interests of officials and politicians and the affairs of government.

Once the adjective "good" is added, a normative debate begins. In short, sustainable development is not attainable without sound land administration or, more broadly, sound land management.

Climate Change

Climate change, which has been identified as the defining challenge of our time, together with the current global financial crisis, puts all the progress made toward meeting the MDGs thus far at risk. The poor, who contributed the least to this planetary problem, continue to be disproportionately at risk and will suffer the most from it. Climate change increases the risks of climate-related disasters, which cause the loss of lives and livelihoods, and weaken the resilience of vulnerable ecosystems and societies. This is especially relevant to the fact that some 40 percent of the world's population lives less than 100 km from a coast, mostly in big towns and cities. Another 100 million people live less than one meter above sea level.

On the other hand, the global challenge of climate change also provides opportunities. Better land use planning and improved building codes that will allow cities to keep their ecological footprint to a minimum and ensure that their residents, especially the poorest, are protected as much as possible against disaster can help mitigate its impacts. Adaptation to and mitigation of climate change, by their very nature, challenge professionals in the fields of land use, land management, land reform, land tenure and land administration to incorporate climate change issues into their land policies, land policy instruments and facilitating land tools (Molen 2009).

Figure 5. The Interaction between Climate Change, Ecosystem Degradation, and Disaster Risk

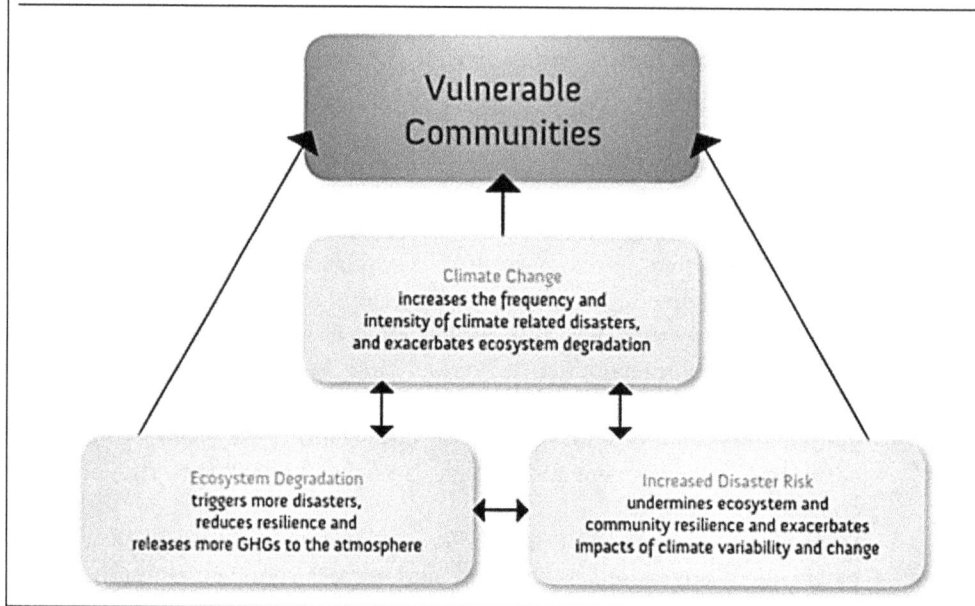

Vulnerable
Communities

Climate Change
increases the frequency and
intensity of climate related disasters,
and exacerbates ecosystem degradation

Ecosystem Degradation
triggers more disasters,
reduces resilience and
releases more GHGs to the atmosphere

Increased Disaster Risk
undermines ecosystem and
community resilience and exacerbates
impacts of climate variability and change

Source: UNEP, 2009.

The interaction between climate change, ecosystem degradation, and increased disaster risk is shown in figure 5.

Climate change mitigation means reducing the anthropogenic drivers such as greenhouse gas emissions from human activities—especially by reducing emissions of carbon dioxide (CO_2) related to use of fossil fuel. These emissions stem from consumption that of course tends to be higher in rich industrialized countries. For example, the megacity of Sao Paulo in Brazil produces one-tenth the emissions of San Diego in the United States, even though the latter is only one-quarter the size of the former (UN-Habitat 2008a). However, the impact of global warming tends to be worse for the poorest countries that lack the resources for protection against the consequences such as possible sea-level rise, drought, floods, etc.

Vulnerable countries such as Bangladesh, and most small island states, therefore often claim to be the victims of climate change "crimes" caused by the richer parts of the world. This issue of global responsibility is the heart of the current climate change agenda. Bangladesh, for example, is one of the world's poorest nations and also the country most vulnerable to sea-level rise. A sea-level rise of 1.5 meters will affect about 22,000 km^2 and 17 million people, about 15 percent of the total population. Similarly, the Himalayan countries like Nepal and Bhutan are facing the risk of short-term climate change disasters, such as glacier lake outburst floods, as well as a long-term projected decrease in water supply.

This calls for mitigation measures to be agreed to by the developed countries, such as setting targets for decreasing the emissions of carbon dioxide (CO_2) related to use of fossil fuel. Although negotiators at the 15th Conference of Parties of the United Nations Framework Convention on Climate Change (UNFCCC) in Copenhagen (December

2009) fell short of agreeing to binding reductions, the meeting did take an important step forward by mandating monitoring of greenhouse gases. Overall, there remains hope that a post-Kyoto Protocol regime will mandate countries to take the bold actions necessary to avert disastrous climate change impacts worldwide.

Building sustainable and spatially enabled land administration systems could identify all areas prone to sea-level rise, drought, flooding, fires, etc., and introduce measures and regulations to prevent the impact of predicted climate change. Implementation of such systems will benefit all countries throughout the globe and does not necessarily relate to the inequity between the developed and less developed countries.

Key policy issues to be addressed relate to protecting citizens by avoiding concentration of population in vulnerable areas and improving resilience of existing ecosystems to cope with the impact of future climate change. Building codes may be essential in some areas to avoid damage caused by flooding and earthquakes. Other issues that must also be addressed relate to plans for replacement of existing settlements as an answer to climate change impacts, such as rising sea levels that threaten to inundate major coastal human settlements like Mumbai and Bangkok.

Therefore, the integrated land administration systems should, in addition to appropriate registration of land tenure and cadastral geometry, include additional information that is required about environmental rating of buildings, energy use, and current and potential land use related to carbon stock potential and greenhouse gases emissions.

This also relates to the fact that climate change is not a geographical local problem that can be solved by local or regional efforts alone. To address climate change, international efforts must integrate with local, national, and regional abilities (Chiu 2009).

Climate change adaptation should link into sustainable development. Economic growth is necessary for poverty reduction and the other MDGs. For environmentally sustainable economic growth and social progress, development policy issues must inform the work of the climate change community so that the two communities can work together on integrated approaches and processes that recognize how persistent poverty and environmental needs exacerbate the adverse consequences of climate change (IPCC 2007).

In short, the linkage between climate change adaptation and sustainable development should be self-evident. Measures for adaptation to climate change will need to be integrated into strategies for poverty reduction to ensure sustainable development.

Natural Disaster Prevention and Management

Sustainable and spatially enabled land administration systems also play a key role with regard to prevention, mitigation, and management of natural disasters, a role that is growing in importance due to the increasing frequency of disasters worldwide. The total number of disasters per year (such as drought, earthquake, flood, slide, volcanic eruption, hurricane, etc.) has increased from about 150 in 1980 to more than 400 in 2000. Much of the increase is probably due to significant improvements in information access, but the number of floods and cyclones being reported is still rising compared to earthquakes, perhaps as a result of global warming. Also, the humanitarian as well as economic impact of disasters is significant. In the United States, for example, more than 90 weather disasters have occurred in the last 30 years, with total costs exceeding $700 billion.

Consequently, international organizations, governments and NGOs, such as the International Federation of Surveyors (FIG), are upgrading the priority of disaster risk management for policy makers and are developing techniques and tools for disaster risk management.[4]

Generally, the disaster risk management process (cycle) is composed of the following main elements:

- Risk identification and vulnerability assessment
- Risk prevention and mitigation measures
- Disaster preparedness
- Disaster event and emergency relief
- Early recovery/transition
- Reconstruction
- Review and ongoing risk reduction

These components represent an ongoing circle of activities related to the situation *before* (risk identification, prevention, preparedness), *during* (emergency relief) and *after* a disaster (recovery, reconstruction), where the results should then feed back into improving the resilience of vulnerable communities and reduce future risks. As noted by Kofi Annan, the former UN Secretary General: "While many people are aware of the terrible impact of disasters throughout the world, few realize this is a problem that we can do something about."

Land Administration Systems in Support of Natural Disaster Risk Management

Sustainable land administration systems should include a range of issues and measures relevant to disaster risk management.

Disaster risks must be identified as area zones in the land use plans and land information systems with the relevant risk assessments and information attached. Such disaster risk zones may relate to sea level rise, earthquakes, volcanic eruption, flooding, drought, hurricanes, etc., and the information should include predicted risks as known through statistics and positioning measurement systems. By combining the disaster risk information with the relevant information on land tenure, land value, and land use, the necessary risk prevention and mitigation measures can be identified and assessed in relation to legal, economic, physical, and social consequences, for example, measures to prevent collapse of buildings in vulnerable earthquake zones. Ideally, disaster risk management should be an integrated part of land use planning and land management.

In disaster zones, relevant measures should be taken to build the preparedness for managing any disaster events. Land issues are an important component in the emergency relief phase. Land is necessary for emergency shelter and protection of displaced persons, and the selection of sites for emergency shelter can lead to long-term conflict or tenure insecurity. Land is also necessary for restoration of livelihoods, and land grabbing after a disaster is a key risk to effective protection and emergency shelter activity. Humanitarian actors are therefore confronted with land issues as they undertake emergency shelter and protection activity.

Sustainable land administration systems provide clear identification of the individual land parcels and land rights attached to these parcels. This information on the people to land relationship is crucial in the immediate post disaster situation. Following the relief and early recovery transition period, where focus is on the overriding humanitarian efforts of saving lives and providing immediate relief, the recovery and reconstruction phase will to a large extent relate to re-establishing the situation of legal rights to land and properties and the reconstruction of buildings and infrastructure. Sustainable land administration systems provide the basis for managing these processes.

Finally, the process of having managed an actual natural disaster should lead to a process of improved risk and vulnerability assessment to be incorporated into the overall land use planning. This should be reflected through the development of ongoing risk reduction measures. Increased sustainability should then be achieved through increasing the resilience of local communities towards the goal of future disaster prevention.

Integration of all aspects of the disaster risk management cycle into the overall land administration system will enable a holistic approach that should underpin the general awareness of the need for being prepared for natural disasters and also being able to manage actual disaster events.

Building the Capacity for Disaster Prevention and Management

The capacity to be prepared for and manage natural disasters will of course include the use of early warning systems that provide timely and effective information which allow for an efficient response.

Another key issue is to establish the necessary political commitment for integrating mitigating measures and disaster risk reduction into general development planning and policymaking across broad sections of the economy; and to implement these policies through organizational structures and regulatory frameworks.

Establishing a general public awareness policy in relation to management of natural disasters is essential. This should lead to information programs, education and training and research in disaster risk reduction.

In the context of disaster risk reduction, capacity building can be achieved through disaster management training and education, public information on disasters, the transfer, provision or access to technology or other forms of technical assistance intended to improve institutional efficiency. The concept also relates to the training of disaster managers, the transfer of technical expertise, the dissemination of traditional knowledge, strengthening infrastructure, and enhancing organizational abilities (UN/ISDR 2004).

To achieve these improvements, the process of capacity development should be addressed at all levels and all sectors. In the twenty-first century, the key issues in capacity-building efforts are strengthening the legal and organizational capabilities of institutions in charge of disaster risk management and the networking between them.

Figure 6. Good Governance and Capacity Building for Disaster Risk Reduction and Sustainable Development

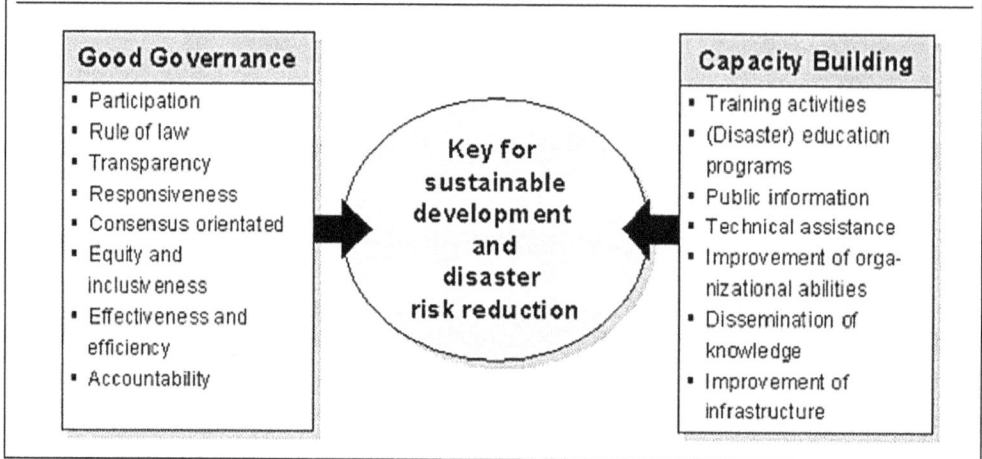

Good Governance	Key for sustainable development and disaster risk reduction	Capacity Building
• Participation • Rule of law • Transparency • Responsiveness • Consensus orientated • Equity and inclusiveness • Effectiveness and efficiency • Accountability		• Training activities • (Disaster) education programs • Public information • Technical assistance • Improvement of organizational abilities • Dissemination of knowledge • Improvement of infrastructure

Source: FIG, 2006.

Figure 6 summarizes good governance and capacity building as a central component regarding the process and implementation of disaster risk management and sustainable development.

Conclusion

No nation can build land management institutions without thinking about the integration of activities, policies, and approaches. Technological innovation provides additional opportunities. Careful management of land related activities on the ground is crucial for delivery of sustainability.

Land administration systems, in principle, reflect the social relationship between people and land recognized by any particular jurisdiction or state. Such a system is not just a GIS. Land Administration Systems are not an end in themselves but facilitate the implementation of the land policies within the context of a wider national land management framework.

Land administration activities are not just about technical or administrative processes. The activities are basically political and reflect the accepted social concepts concerning people, rights, and land objects with regard to land tenure, land markets, land taxation, land-use control, land development, and environmental management.

Sustainable land administration systems provide clear identification of the individual land parcels and land rights attached to these parcels. This information on the people to land relationship is crucial and plays a key role in adaptation to climate change and in prevention and management of natural disasters. No matter the inequity between the developed and developing world in terms of emissions and climate consequences, there is a need to develop relevant means and measures for adaptation to climate change both in both the rich and the poorer countries.

Building sustainable and spatially enabled land administration systems will enable control of the access to land as well as the control of the use of land. The systems should identify all areas prone to sea-level rise, drought, flooding, fires, and potential natural disasters. The systems should also include relevant measures and regulations to prevent the impact of predicted climate change as well as natural disasters and provide preparedness for managing any disaster events.

The land management perspective and the operational component of integrated and spatially enabled land administration systems therefore need high-level political support and recognition.

In short, the linkage between climate change adaptation and sustainable development should be self-evident. Measures for adaptation to climate change and prevention and management of natural disasters must be integrated into strategies for poverty reduction to ensure sustainable development and meeting the Millennium Development Goals.

The importance of good land governance to strengthen women's land rights, facilitate land-related investment, transfer land to better uses, use it as collateral, and allow effective decentralization through collection of property taxes has long been recognized. The challenges posed by recent global developments, especially urbanization, increased and more volatile food prices, and climate change have raised the profile of land and the need for countries to have appropriate land policies. However, efforts to improve country-level land governance are often frustrated by technical complexities, institutional fragmentation, vested interests, and lack of a shared vision on how to move towards good land governance and measure progress in concrete settings. Recent initiatives have recognized the important challenges this raises and the need for partners to act in a collaborative and coordinated fashion to address them.

The breadth and depth of the papers included in this volume, all of which were presented at the Bank's annual conference on land policies, illustrate the benefits from such collaboration. They are indicative not only of the diversity of issues related to land governance but, more importantly, highlight that, even though the topic is complex and politically challenging, there is a wealth of promising new approaches to improving land governance through innovative technologies, country-wide policy dialogue, and legal and administrative reforms. The publication is based on an on-going partnership between the World Bank, the International Federation of Surveyors (FIG), the Global Land Tool Network (GLTN) and the United Nations Food and Agriculture Organization (FAO) to provide tools that can help to address land governance in practice and at scale. It is our hope that this volume will be of use to increase awareness of and support to the successful implementation of innovative approaches that can help to not only improve land governance, but also through this channel contribute to the well-being of the poorest and the achievement of the MDGs.

Notes

[1] These are to (i) eradicate extreme poverty and hunger; (ii) achieve universal primary education; (iii) promote gender equality and empower women; (iv) reduce child mortality; (v) improve maternal health; (vi) combat HIV/AIDS, malaria and other diseases; (vii) ensure environmental sustainability; and (viii) develop a Global Partnership for Development.

[2] In land services 15% of users have had to pay a bribe, putting it after police (24%) and the judiciary (16%), but ahead of other registry and permit services (13%), education and health (both 9%), and tax revenue or utilities (both 7%).

[3] World Bank investment climate surveys indicate that access to land was the main obstacle to conducting and expanding business by 57% of the enterprises interviewed in Ethiopia, 35% in Bangladesh and about 25% each in Tanzania and Kenya.

[4] *See*, e.g. UN/ISDR (2004), FIG (2006), and RICS (2009).

CHAPTER 1

Key Policy Aspects in Selected Countries

1.1: Taking Land Policy and Administration in Indonesia to the Next Stage

JOYO WINOTO, PhD, Head, National Land Agency (NLA),
Republic of Indonesia

Introduction

Land is an important resource for Indonesia. As an agrarian country, its land-based economy contributes significantly to the welfare of Indonesian society. Land is fundamental for development, and has a variety of cultural and social values. The importance of land gives rise to conflicting claims. The government therefore gives serious attention to land development and management.

Indonesia is a large archipelagic country of more than 17,000 islands of which about 6,000 are inhabited. The five main islands are Sumatra, Kalimantan, Java, Sulawesi, and West Papua. Its total area is about 9.8 million km², including a land mass of 1.9 million km² (20 percent of total area) and marine area, including the exclusive economic zone, of 7.9 million km² (80 percent of the total area).

Administratively, the country comprises 33 provinces, 349 districts, and 91 cities. In 2009 the population was estimated to be 231 million. Population density is uneven, with 58 percent living in Java. Average population density is 121 people per km², but it is nearly 134.16 people per km² in Java.

Critical problems facing the Indonesian political economy are poverty, unemployment, inequality in income distribution, and land disputes and conflicts. Around 34.9 million people (or 15 percent) live below the poverty line. Of these, about 66 percent live in rural areas. The agriculture sector employs 56 percent of rural dwellers. Those with little or no land are particularly poor and are typically farm laborers (*buruh tani*) working on other people's land or peasants (*petani gurem*) operating extremely small plots. The agriculture census in 2003 found that almost half of all agricultural households cultivated less than 0.5 hectares.

The unemployment rate is 10 percent or 23.1 million people. In terms of disguised unemployment, the figure is much higher, reaching 30.36 million people or 27 percent of the labor force. The manufacturing sector cannot provide enough employment for newcomers to the labor market. Many unemployed are driven to labor in rural areas, which places stress on the agricultural land to person ratio. Without significant technological improvement, a smaller agricultural land to person ratio results in reduced income per farmer.

In terms of income distribution, the Gini coefficient has steadily increased from 0.31 in 1999 to 0.33 in 2002 and 0.36 in 2005, suggesting a widening gap between income levels of the poor and the non-poor. In terms of agricultural land ownership distribution, the figure is much worse, around 0.6. This is in part due to continuous fragmentation of household agricultural land, and constant issuance of land use rights for large companies that already own 100,000 hectares of land or more. Of the 25 million farm households, 56 percent now own less than half a hectare. Inequality in distribution of land ownership causes serious problems, especially if it is under-utilized, idle, or abandoned, perhaps due to "land hoarding" practices. Surprisingly, the area of idle or abandoned land is estimated to be 7.3 million hectares. This is a problem too large to be ignored.

A growing number of land disputes and conflicts afflict the political economy. In 2007, the number of significant land disputes and conflicts reached 7,491 cases covering almost 608 thousand hectares of land.

The persistence of poverty and unemployment in the period following the Asian Economic and Financial Crisis indicates a fundamental problem. The economy has shown periods of steady growth, yet wealth has failed to trickle down to the poor and unemployed, particularly in rural areas. The major problem appears to be the poor agrarian structure, which constrains access to sufficient areas of land and to other productive inputs, including public services for most peasant and landless farmers. Substantial agrarian reform is needed. From the perspective of the National Land Agency (NLA), effective agrarian reform must be planned and implemented and the delivery of agrarian-related public services must be improved. These reforms will require accurate information and institution and capacity building.

Land Policy

State land policy was set forth in the Constitution of the Republic of Indonesia of 1945. Article 33 sub-article 3 stipulates that land (earth), water, and natural richness are controlled by the state and must be utilized for the welfare of the people. Implementation is primarily through Law Number 5, 1960, the Basic Agrarian Law (BAL). The BAL was put into practice through many government regulations, presidential decrees, ministerial decrees, etc. However in 1970 other laws relating to land were enacted without considering the BAL, resulting in some contradictory regulations. This led to legal conflicts over land ownership, confusion over land use rights and slow implementation of agrarian reform. In response, the House Consultative Assembly issued Provision IX/MPR/2001, on Agrarian Reform and Natural Resources Management, and Decree 5/2003, relating to its implementation.

In early 2006, the NLA began to focus on the extreme disparity of land ownership and utilization in policy development. Presidential Decree 10/2006 relates to land administration at the national, regional, and sectoral levels. The long-term development plan in UU No.17/2007 mandates the NLA to implement efficient and effective land management; to enforce laws dealing with land rights through democratic, transparent and just principles; to reconstruct regulations of land reform for the betterment of occupation, rights, and utilization of land; to identify incentives and disincentives in the tax system according to the size of area, location, and land use; to improve access to land by the poor; to improve the land law system through an inventory; to improve land regulation taking into consideration customary tenure (*adat*) rules; to improve the resolution of land conflicts through administration, justice, and alternative dispute resolution; and to develop human resources.

These changes reformulated land policy based on four main principles:

1. Improvement of the welfare of the people;
2. Distributive justice;
3. Fostering a just and peaceful sustainable system of Indonesian society; and
4. Creation of social harmony (resolved land conflicts and disputes).

These principles were translated into eleven land policy objectives, known as the "eleven NLA prioritized agendas":

1. To build the public trust;
2. To improve land services and land registration;
3. To improve land rights;
4. To resolve land problems in areas affected by natural disasters and ethnic conflicts;
5. To systematically settle land lawsuits, disputes and conflicts;
6. To develop a national land management information system and land document security system;
7. To address corruption, collusion, nepotism and improve participation of the people;
8. To establish large scale land mapping and a land ownership database;
9. To consistently implement all land laws and regulations;
10. To strengthen the NLA organization;
11. To develop land laws and policies.

NLA Strategic Plan

To achieve its policy objectives, the NLA has four strategic plans:

1. Reforming land policy;
2. Reforming NLA's organization and bureaucracy;
3. Developing land administration and service infrastructures; and
4. Improving land services and administration processes.

The quality of governance is critical to achieving the NLA's objectives. Good governance facilitates participatory, pro-poor policies as well as sound land policy and management. It ensures the transparent use of public funds, encourages the growth of the public sector, promotes the effective delivery of public services, and helps to establish the rule of law. Reforming land policy is needed to encourage efficient and productive domestic investment and accelerate growth of agricultural and rural areas to enhance the real income of the poor.

The purpose of land policy reform is to improve land administration for social welfare, sustainability, and social harmony. This reform entails the reconstruction of land laws and regulations and the improvement of land policy for implementation of agrarian reform. Legal reform aims at improving land rights; solving existing land problems; systematically handling and settling land lawsuits, disputes and conflicts; and consistently implementing all land laws and regulations. Agrarian reform is necessary to foster equality in land holding, land ownership, land use and utilization; reduce poverty; create employment; improve access to resources, especially land; minimize land disputes and conflicts; protect and regenerate the environment; and enhance the security of household food and energy.

Reform of the organization of the NLA is directed at its policy objectives: (a) building public trust in improved and honest land services and land registration, (b) preventing corruption, collusion, and nepotism, (c) empowering public participation, (d) consistently implementing land laws and regulations, and (e) strengthening the NLA organizationally. New infrastructure that supports this reform are essential, including large-scale land mapping, a land ownership database for spatial and textual data, a national land management information system (NL-MIS) and a land document security system (LDSS).

Effective and efficient delivery of basic services by the public sector matters the most to the poor, and weak governance hurts them disproportionately. Public sector inefficiency, corruption, and waste leave insufficient resources available to support public services and target antipoverty programs. However, the denial of basic services to the poor is not just a matter of a lack of government commitment or investment. Often, it is the result of institutional structures that lack accountability; domination by local or national elites; widespread corruption; culturally-determined inequality; and lack of participation by the poor. These problems must be met by systemic changes to move ineffective governance towards government accountability to the poor. Change of this kind is difficult to bring about because existing arrangements that exclude the poor reflect prevailing economic and power inequalities. Yet unless these issues of inequality are tackled, it will be difficult to raise the living standards of the poor.

Improvement of land services and administration is also the key to establishing public trust in the NLA. Trust can be earned by improving service delivery and simplifying standard operating procedures in land administration. Setting up mobile land offices (LARASITA) and other efforts toward simpler, faster, cheaper, and more reliable land services are good first steps.

Program Implementation

Land Policy Reform

Disparity in access to land is in part the effect of unnecessary complexity and confusion in the legal framework. A study of land laws and regulations found 585 legal documents, comprising 12 laws, 48 government regulations, 22 presidential decrees, 4 presidential instructions, 243 ministerial/head of NLA regulations, 209 circular letters of minister/head of NLA, and 44 instructions of minister/head of NLA. These include many overlapping, contradictory, or unimplemented regulations. Some efforts to improve this legal framework have been carried out and implemented and others are in preparation.

Efforts to improve land policy include: preparation of an academic manuscript draft on Land Law (*RUU Pertanahan*); preparation of an academic manuscript draft on Agrarian Reform Law (*RUU Reforma Agraria*); a draft government regulation on idle land (*RPP Tanah Terlantar*); and a draft government regulation on government non tax income (Government Regulation No.46).

Some land issues involve many government institutions. NLA has therefore increased its cooperation with other institutions by setting up 14 memoranda of understanding. NLA has also formulated four strategies that focus on land policy implementation: legalization of private and state assets; agrarian reform; idle land management; and land dispute and conflicts resolution.

The Reconstruct Land Regulation Program aims to improve the construction and configuration of existing land laws and regulations. A previous study showed land regulations created a "jungle of law" because many regulations overlap and are contradictory. The activities of this program are:

- Analyzing and reconstructing the land legal framework.
- Improving agrarian reform law.
- Improving land-related laws.
- Improving government regulation of idle land.

The Agrarian Reform Program: Agrarian reform is defined as a significant change in agrarian structure, resulting in increased access to land by the rural poor, as well as secure tenure for those who actually work on the land. It also includes access to agricultural inputs, markets, services and other needed assistance. The official speech of the President of the Republic of Indonesia on 31 January 2007 defined the program as:

> Agrarian reform program … gradually …shall be started in the year of 2007. The implementation is preceded by allocating land, which originates from forest conversion, for the poor, and other land, that is allowed by our land law, to be allocated for the interest of the people. This is that I call the principle of land for justice and people prosperity … (that) I consider must be implemented.

The fundamental political nature of agrarian reform must be recognized at the outset. Agrarian reform seldom involves making only a minor adjustment in the socioeconomic environment. Historically, many agrarian reforms have attempted to fundamentally change social relationships of property ownership, wealth, social status, and political power. These tend to be contested in the political sphere between reformers and those often powerful interests who expect to lose from it.

At the heart of this politically charged reform are differences between land as a resource, and other farm inputs and outputs. Land has certain essential attributes which warrant noting:

- Land is resource in agricultural production, but is ultimately fixed in supply within a nation state. While it can be transferred between uses, meaning that supply for a particular use is seldom completely inelastic, the potential to increase its availability at the extensive margin is either non-existent or involves high costs.

- Land is a stock of capital, a fixed asset or investment, and it is a measure of wealth. It plays multiple roles in these regards. The value of land—the price per hectare—seldom merely reflects the expected rate of return to land as a capital investment in agricultural production. Land is also held as a livelihood security, as a financial security, and as a transfer of wealth across generations.
- Agricultural land ownership involves social and economic relations between, for example, landlord and share tenant, landowner and cash tenant, or plantation owner and wage laborer. Peasants have historically derived their access to land by tenancy or by customary tenure rather than by ownership.

The way land is owned in Indonesia is rooted in the country's colonial past, in government policy, and in social changes which have taken place over time. Once established and consolidated, land ownership tends to remain fixed, with little if any change. In Indonesia, land distribution and later allocation processes produced unequal access. Pressure for agrarian reform arose from the inability of this highly unequal but fixed land distribution to meet the needs generated by rapid changes in society. Population growth, increased mobility, market development, income growth, and changing forms of economic exchange and social interaction are all relevant. When a rigid land ownership structure does not absorb social change, social forces are set in motion.

Based on a study of land laws and regulations, agrarian reform has been mandated in the Basic Agrarian Law 1960, in House Consultative Assembly Decree number 5/2003, and in House Consultative Assembly Provision number IX/MPR/2001. Agrarian reform requires the reform of the land policy and law that was based on *Pancasila*, State Constitution 1945, and Basic Agrarian Law 1960. In practice, agrarian reform is land reform implemented by improving access. In other words, it involves both assets and access to the assets. Many writers consider the absence of supporting policies—price policy, credit policy, input policies and so on—as having contributed to the lack of success of many agrarian reform efforts. The provision of agricultural extension and training services, credit, loans, guarantees, appropriate technologies, markets, and other agricultural inputs and services for small farmers, rural workers and other beneficiaries during the post-agrarian reform period is as crucial as providing them with land in the first place. There are vast differences between regions in their production capacity, levels of rural economy and social provisioning. However, the issue of improvement in post-reform peasants' livelihoods is frequently neglected in agrarian reform. Regular monitoring of general living and working conditions of beneficiaries is also important, especially to ensure that people continue to hold their land, do not enter into a vicious circle of indebtedness, and are able to exploit production potential fully. The objectives and related activities of agrarian reform are presented in table 1.1.

Strategies to implement agrarian reform are: (1) rearrangement of the concentration of assets and idle land by reforming land policies and law based on *Pancasila*, State Constitution, and the Basic Agrarian Law 1960, and (2) allocation of state controlled land directly for poor people. The land area under state control is 9.25 million hectares, much of which can be used to improve the welfare of poor people.

The program target is to create 10.53 million job opportunities and to alleviate poverty in 9.5 million households.

The role of the state is crucial in any agrarian reform, not only for practical reasons (carrying out cadastral surveys, promulgating and implementing relevant legislation, providing technical and financial support, etc.), but also because agrarian reform is inherently a political process. Without the implementation by the state of effective, socially- just land laws, policies and strategies, agrarian reform remains a dead letter, regardless of donor pressure or popular demand for land by the landless. The provision of supporting services by the government to land beneficiaries is also important in guaranteeing the sustainability of the whole process.

The Optimizing Use of Idle Land Program: In Indonesia, an estimated 7.3 million hectares remains idle. Idle land causes social unrest, poverty and lost economic opportunities. The objectives of this program are to increase access to this land, and to increase the economic value of the land itself in a sustainable manner. The idle land program involves:

- Optimizing the use of idle land by strengthening land control in order to improve people's access to land.
- Improving the structure of land use in rural and urban areas.
- Empowering farmers through community development models in order to increase their welfare.

An idle land inventory has been carried out for the entire region. Draft laws have been prepared to support the idle land inventory.

The Program for Minimizing Land Disputes and Conflict: A study in 2007 revealed 7,491 cases of land disputes and conflicts. Handling of these cases is therefore urgent. Dispute resolution has been carried out by developing and implementing programs such as land dispute settlement operations (*Operasi Tuntas Sengketa*) and land dispute investigation operations (*Operasi Sidik Sengketa*). These programs have solved about 1,778 cases. This program is meant to decrease the number of land disputes and keep conflicts to a minimum. The large number of land disputes and conflicts causes social unrest, disturbances, insecurity, and poverty. Land disputes and conflicts also lead to economic losses because they prevent land from being used to produce goods and services. Activities include:

- Mapping land cases and causes of conflict and dispute problems.
- Improving coordination between NLA and the Indonesian Police Department.
- Establishing a civil servant investigator.
- Establishing a desk for reporting land disputes.
- Improving the capacity of the NLA to resolve land conflicts and disputes.
- Carrying out routine activities concerning land conflict and dispute resolution.
- Accelerating land conflict and dispute resolution, through:
  - land dispute settlement operation (*Operasi Tuntas Sengketa*)
  - land dispute investigating operation (*Operasi Sidik Sengketa*)

Implementing the settlement operation has significantly decreased land disputes and conflicts. This program will be continued until a minimum number of cases is reached.

Institutional Reform

Bureaucratic reform started in 2006 with a focus group discussion series on agency functions. As part of the Government of Indonesia, the NLA has goals to take part in creating welfare, sustainability, and social harmony among Indonesian people. The focus group discussion aimed at formulating objectives and strategies to implement state goals. Reorganization was instituted by Presidential Decree 10/2006. In response, the NLA:

- Merged some organizational units and developed new offices, such as the Deputy of Land Survey and Mapping, and the Deputy of Land Dispute Resolution and Management;
- Implemented an incentive system for NLA staff performance;
- Implemented a new merit-based promotion system through competitive selection;
- Implemented a new staff recruitment system guided by the Ministry of Empowerment of State Civil Services, in order to be more transparent and accountable. The success of this system was indicated by the absence of complaints from the test attendees.

Capacity building and strengthening the institution are necessary because land is a strategic resource for Indonesia. As one of the government institutions that deal with land, the NLA must be a strong institution with sufficient management capacity. Strong institutional and management capacity will help NLA to implement the national programs related to agrarian reform, poverty alleviation, land conflict and dispute resolution, etc. The activities of this program are:

- Improving physical resources (buildings, technologies, and support facilities);
- Human resources development and training;
- Improving the standard of public service;
- Developing quality assurance in the organization.

Infrastructure Development

Infrastructure development is necessary to execute the tasks and functions of NLA in land administration and to deliver simpler, faster and cheaper public services. Some activities are:

- Improving the hardware and software used in land administration.
- Developing a detailed base map to support land administration and agrarian reform.
- Digitizing vector maps for 11 million of 80 million land parcels.
- Providing facilities for mobile land services, called LARASITA.
- Developing and improving information and communication technologies used by land offices to support land services on-site and online.
- Developing automatic information services in many land offices.

The Build and Improve Land Mapping and Land Information System Program will apply spatial data and the latest information to support NLA's services. Comprehensive land information is an essential instrument for land policy and administration. A current study shows that the existing land data, based on maps and geodetic network stations, for administration and land policy covers only about 5 percent of total area of Indonesia. Meanwhile land thematic maps are of limited use. Most of them are insufficient in scale and out of date. Improved maps are important to support the formulation of land policy, land administration, space allocation, land-use planning, agrarian reform, land use control and monitoring, community empowerment and development, land conflict resolution, urban and rural planning and development, and GIS public services. Indonesia has very large total land area but a limited total annual budget for mapping (only for about 500,000 hectares annually). Comprehensive and complete maps covering all of the country will not materialize for a long time. To improve access and update data, land maps and other information should be managed within a computerized land information system. Acceleration of this program is essential to support the other programs and to meet national objectives.

NLA plans that all land parcels will be registered within 18 years or less. Both land data based on maps and land thematic maps should therefore be available within 3 to 15 years. To achieve this goal NLA programs comprise:

- Developing cadastral base maps;
- Accelerating cadastral mapping;
- Developing land thematic mapping;
- Establishing a national land information and management system.

Improvement of Land Services and Administrative Processes

Processes and procedures in land offices have often been very complicated and time consuming. Brokerage systems resulted which involved unofficial payments. Land services became very expensive and as a result some NLA offices lost the people's trust. Land services have been improved by:

- Rearranging and simplifying procedures, both in front and back offices, by publishing internal and external standard operating procedures (SPOPP) for land offices. All offices of the NLA have to implement the SPOPP and it must be disseminated to the public. Thus the public are informed of the proper procedures, wait times, and price of land services. Fourteen specific land services must now be finished in not more than 15 working days (Head of NLA Regulation No. 6, 2008).
- Limiting opportunities for brokerage systems by:
  Setting up mobile land services offices (LARASITA) which now cover more than a quarter of the country's area.
  - Mass legalization of private assets that are financed through the public budget (*Prona, Proda, Ajudikasi,* and LARASITA) or that are self-financed (Government Regulation No. 46).
  - Developing a land information system through the internet and short message services (text).
  - Eliminating the opportunity for staff to become a consumer's proxy in land services.

Land services will continue to improve at an even faster rate. The number of published land certificates has nearly tripled since 2005 when 919,319 were issued. There were 1,345,809 issued in 2006; 2,691,167 in 2007; and 2,671,551 in 2008.

Service improvement also contributes to state revenue. Non-tax state revenue increased from IDR 541.12 billion in 2006 to IDR 682.80 billion in 2008. The non-tax revenue target in 2009 is IDR 1,350.00 billion.

The Improve Land Administration Program is intended to provide certainty in the relationship between people and their land. Only about 45 percent of the 85 million existing parcels are registered, but most of these registered parcels are not yet mapped. This increases the number of land disputes and conflicts. The existing archives in land offices are still managed by a manual system. This system is not conducive to improving public service or building public trust. If not managed and organized carefully, manual archives create many problems, including mistaken, overlooked, and lost documents, loss through fire and moisture, and so on. Activities in this program involve:

- Accelerating creation of the land cadastre by improving the land registration system;
- Promoting mass land registration;
- Improving land record management by developing digital archive management and security systems.

Strengthening LARASITA Implementation is necessary in improving land administration and accelerating land registration. Implementation has significantly increased the number of certified land parcels. LARASITA provides mobile land services—cars, motorcycles, and boats—equipped with modern information technologies. The service can reach clients in remote areas. LARASITA is suitable for the specific geographical conditions of Indonesia and has become popular with consumers. LARASITA has received many awards, including from the President of Indonesia and the World Bank. The World Bank recognizes this program as *"Indonesia-Pioneering mobile land information services."* Hopefully, LARASITA will increase its operation rapidly to cover the entire country.

Development of Land Acquisition System for Public Infrastructures Program: Many types of national infrastructure development programs are supported by NLA, for example, the development of the Trans-Java Tollroad for 1,000 km, the 1,000 Towers for housing in urban areas, the Sunda Strait Bridge connecting Sumatra and Java, food security, special economic zones, biofuel, etc. NLA also supports reconstruction and rehabilitation of disaster areas such as those affected by the tsunami in Aceh and East Sumatra, earthquakes and floods. In response to these national infrastructure development programs, the NLA assists with land acquisition and improvements in the valuation system.

Additional priority programs of the NLA are based on the four main land policy and management principles, the eleven NLA prioritized agendas, the four objectives of the strategic plan, and the results of program implementation. Some priority programs involve continuation of existing programs. The four objectives of the strategic plan have discrete activities but they are interrelated to achieve certain outcomes. A matrix of priority programs, expected supports, and line divisions is shown in table 1.1.

Conclusion

A number of national challenges persist for the Government of Indonesia. These include poverty, unemployment, inequality in income distribution, wide disparities in land holding, land ownership, land use and land utilization, a high number of land disputes and conflicts, and other issues related to land. As a government institution, the NLA addresses these challenges through policies that promote harmony, social welfare, and sustainability. To implement change, a number of programs have been designed and implemented. Action must proceed at two levels. Public administration and management of expenditure at the national level must be strengthened to promote pro-poor growth and social development. At the same time, responsibility for the provision of NLA services to the public must be developed at the lowest appropriate level of government. Unfortunately, institutional capacity tends to be weak in local governments and there is danger of capture by local factions. The long-term objectives, however, should be to empower the poor and to develop institutional arrangements that foster participation and accountability until local governments are more effective.

A diverse range of stakeholders are involved in achieving land policy objectives and poverty reduction efforts generally. Apart from the government and the private sector, civil society institutions have an important role to play. Numerous vibrant and responsive NGOs—both national and local—are engaged in development work and in championing the legal rights of the poor. The NLA actively seeks to cooperate with these NGOs and to benefit from their experience and perspectives, as well as to take advantage of their closeness to the poor and vulnerable.

Some programs of the NLA have been successfully implemented with World Bank support. Many programs still need financial and technical support to implement new land policy. Strengthening the relationship between the NLA and the World Bank is important for these programs. With World Bank support, the challenges that face the Indonesian Government can hopefully be gradually overcome.

Table 1.1. Matrix of Priority Programs, Expected Supports, and Line Divisions

No.	OBJECTIVES	PROGRAMS/ACTIVITIES	EXPECTED SUPPORTS BUDGETS		
			GRANT	LOAN	GOI
Land Policy Reform					
1	• To alleviate disparities of land holding, ownership, use and utilization • To alleviate poverty • To create employment • To improve access to economic political resources, especially land • To strengthen national food and energy security	**Agrarian Reform:** • Identification, verification and mapping of Agrarian Reform Land (object) • Identification, verification and registration of Agrarian Reform Subject (poor and landless people) • Identification and verification of Stakeholder related to access reform • Establishment of Institution for Agrarian Reform: • Agrarian Reform Council at National, Province and Regency/Municipal levels • Management and Fund of National Agrarian Reform Office • Agrarian Reform Delivery and Action • Monitoring, evaluation and continuous improvement of Agrarian Reform implementation processes (Quality Assurance of Agrarian Reform Implementation)	√ √ √		√ √ √
2	• To minimize land dispute and conflicts • To improve people access to economic political resources (especially land)	**Minimizing Land Disputes and Conflicts:** • Further mapping and studies on conflict and dispute roots • Further implementation of strategic program to enhance the settlement of conflict and dispute • Strengthening Civil Servant Investigator	√ √		√ √
3	• To increase access to land and improve economic the value of land • To alleviate poverty • To create employment	**Optimizing Use of Idle Land:** • Strengthening land control in order to increase access to productive land; • Improvement of landuse restructurization suitable to land capability in rural and urban areas • Empowering farmers welfare through implementation of community development	√ √	√	√ √
4	• To strengthen land politic system. • To reconstruct Land Regulation	**Reconstruct Land Regulation:** • Analyzing and reconstructing the existing Land Legal Systems • Developing Agrarian Reform Law • Developing Land Related Laws • Improving the Government Regulation on Idle Land	√ √ √ √		

(Table continues on next page)

Table 1.1 (continued)

No.	OBJECTIVES	PROGRAMS/ACTIVITIES	EXPECTED SUPPORTS BUDGETS		
			GRANT	LOAN	GOI
Institutional Reform					
5	• To improve capacity building and strengthen institution	**Improve Capacity Building and Strengthen Institution:** • Improving physical resources (building, technologies, and support facilities) • Human Resources Development and Training • Improving Public Service Standard • Quality Assurance of Institution Development		√ √ √	√ √ √
Land administration and Service Infrastructure Development					
6	• To build and improve land mapping and land information system	**Build and Improve Land Mapping and Land Information System:** • Developing cadastral base maps • Developing thematic land maps for supporting land control, community development, optimizing use of idle land, agrarian reform, land-use control and land dispute resolution. • Establishing National Land Information Management System	√ √ √	√ √ √	√ √ √
Improvement of land service and administration processes					
7	• To improve Land Administration	**Improve Land Administration:** • Accelerating land cadastral mapping by improving land registration system • Promoting mass land registration • Improving Land Archive Management by Developing Digital Archive Management and Security Systems		√ √ √	√ √ √
8	• To enhance land registration • To accelerate people access to economic political resources, especially land	**Strengthening LARASITA Implementation** • Developing Physical Support System (transport, communication, software, hardware etc) • Strengthening capability of staffs to be excellence public services	 √	√	√
9	• To Support Public Infrastructure Development	**Development of Land Acquisition System for Public Infrastructures** • Setting up workable legal document • Development of land acquisition system • Improving land valuation system	√ √ √		√ √ √

Source: Author.

1.2:   Moving Towards Clear Land Titles in India: Potential Benefits, a Road Map, and Remaining Challenges

RITA SINHA, Secretary Department of Land Resources, Ministry of Rural Development, Republic of India

Introduction

On 21 August 2008, India took a historic step to move from the present system of "presumptive" property titles to the system of clear property titles known as the "Torrens system," which is prevalent in countries such as Australia, Canada, Malaysia, New Zealand, Singapore, Switzerland, the United Kingdom, the United States, etc. In India, the Registration Act, 1908, provides for the registration of deeds and documents, but does not confer titles on the property owner, whose title therefore remains merely "presumptive."

Conclusive Titles

A conclusive title may be defined as one that provides conclusive and unassailable proof of property ownership. In order to reach the stage of conferring Conclusive Titles, four fundamental principles need to be in place, namely, that:

1. A single agency should handle property records;
2. The "mirror principle" should be operative, meaning that at any given moment property records should mirror reality on the ground and in real time;
3. The "curtain principle" should apply, meaning that the record of a title should depict the conclusive ownership status, making investigation into past transactions unnecessary; and
4. Title guarantee should indemnify the property holder against any losses that may result from inaccuracies.

Most states in India have two or three agencies handling property records. The Revenue Department usually prepares and maintains the text records. The Survey and Settlement Department prepares and maintains maps. The Registration Department verifies encumbrances and registers transfers, mortgages, etc. A few states have a Consolidation Department in lieu of a Survey and Settlement Department. In some of the states, the local bodies have been empowered to do undisputed mutations. Urban local bodies update property records for the purposes of taxation. Merging these departments into a single agency is, in many cases, administratively and politically difficult.

The tedious manual processes of survey and the system of property record management have resulted in outdated maps and arrears of data entry in a vast number of cases. The result is that the records do not reliably reflect reality on the ground in real time. At present, the registration of deeds and documents in India requires probing into past ownership and property transactions in order to establish non-encumbrance. The need to do so is the result of both the system of presumptive titles and of the arrears in mutation. In the system of presumptive titles, the question of giving title guarantee and indemnification does not arise.

As a result of conclusive titling, the maintenance of property records will cease to be merely a tool for governance and revenue generation. It will also become instrumental to the agenda of citizen services. Computerization will enable property records to be placed in the public domain, allowing property owners easy access to their records. This is in contrast to the present system, in which property records are in the custody of a Revenue Department official, usually known as the *patwari*.

The computerized property records will be real time and obtainable from a single window, thereby saving the citizen time and effort in obtaining them. Litigation, which is the bane of presumptive titling, will be considerably reduced once the titles are conclusive and tamper-proof. The time required to prepare and to obtain real time records, registration, and mutation will be greatly reduced. Because property market values and past titles and transactions will be available on a web site, property transfers and electronic payments of stamp duty and registration fees will be facilitated.

While citizens will likely be the primary beneficiaries of conclusive titling, real time cadastral records will also enable improved governance in areas such as disaster management, land acquisition, rehabilitation, and resettlement, and land use planning. Improved governance will include better management of barren land and watershed programs, and increased revenues as a result of proper valuation of stamp duty and registration fees.

A Roadmap for Clear Land Titles

Conclusive titling involves four major principles: a single-agency property record management, the "mirror" principle, the "curtain" principle, and title guarantee and indemnification. Because the final principle only becomes possible when the first three are in place, the priority in terms of sequences is assigned to the first three.

The Government of India has launched a major program named the "National Land Records Modernization Program" (NLRMP). The Program's activities are designed to foster the establishment of the first three principles of conclusive titling. It has four major components:

1.   Computerization of property records;
2.   Survey and preparation of maps using modern technologies,
3.   Computerization of the registration process; and
4.   Training and capacity building.

India is divided into 28 States and 7 Union Territories. Each State is further subdivided into districts. The districts are sub-divided into sub-divisions known variously as *tehsils*, *talukas*, *blocks*, and *anchals*. Four to six villages in a district are placed in the charge of a village level Revenue functionary usually known as the *patwari*.

Computerization of property records involves the following sub-activities: data entry and entry into the National Code, conversion of textual data into a digitized format, digitization of cadastral maps, integration of textual and spatial data, setting up data centers at sub-divisional, district, and *tehsil* levels, data centers at the state level as part of data recovery and disaster management, modern record rooms at the *tehsil* level, and inter-connectivity among revenue offices.

The survey component consists of fresh cadastral surveys, re-surveys and updating of survey and settlement records, including a ground control network and ground-truthing. The technologies identified for the survey are: (a) pure ground-truthing using total stations and a global positioning system (GPS); (b) hybrid technology using aerial photography along with ground-truthing; and (c) high resolution satellite imagery (HRSI) along with ground-truthing.

Computerizing registration includes computerization of the Sub-Registrar's Office, data entry of property valuation, data entry of legacy encumbrance data, scanning and preservation of old documents and inter-connectivity between the Registration and Revenue Offices.

Training and capacity building and strengthening of training institutions are major activities under the NLRMP to build up cadres well versed with the new technologies and new processes.

These activities are conducted at the district level. The country has a little over 600 districts. Each state government was requested to take up a few districts per year in such a way that the entire state is covered in the next eight years under the NLRMP. The states that are undertaking cadastral surveys for the first time may take a little longer to complete the NLRMP. The eight year Perspective Plans include the numbers, names and details of districts chosen each year, activities proposed to be undertaken, technologies proposed to be used, milestones, timeframes, and expenditures involved. Sixteen state governments have sent their Perspective Plans to the Government of India. The Government, through its Project Sanctioning Committee, has sanctioned Rs.2372.6 million during the current financial year to implement the NLRMP in 56 districts. It is anticipated that the activities in each district will be completed within two to three years.

The total project cost of the NLRMP for eight years has been estimated to be a little over Rs. 56 billion of which the central government will fund around Rs. 31 billion. The state governments will be required to raise the remaining Rs. 25 billion. Even given the combined efforts of the central and state governments, there may be gaps in fulfilling such an ambitious program within the targeted period. Public-private partnerships for the NLRMP have therefore been incorporated as an integral part of the scheme. The state governments can identify areas which can easily be contracted out to private parties, with government functionaries fulfilling only their legal obligations.

The Government of India was expected to prepare guidelines and technical manuals to roll out the NLRMP. The guidelines have already been prepared and are in the process of being implemented. The technical manuals are under preparation. A number of national-level committees had to be set up to monitor the implementation of the Program. An Advisory Committee on the Legal Changes for Conclusive Titling was created to examine the changes that will be required in the legal framework of the country to implement the Conclusive Titling regime. A Core Technical Advisory Group addresses issues relating to technology, the transfer of technology to the states and provides continuous advice regarding technology upgrades. The state governments have been advised to set up similar technical advisory groups and this process is underway. A Program Management Unit monitors and evaluates progress under the NLRMP at the national level. A consultant has been appointed to help set up this body and the state governments have also been advised to set up similar bodies.

The NLRMP will enable India to achieve three out of the four principles which form the basis of conclusive titling. Although it is envisaged that the NLRMP will be completed in eight years, the country need not wait until then to introduce conclusive titling. Appropriate legislation can enable the states to implement conclusive titling in a modular way by introducing it in those districts that have completed the process first.

The Remaining Challenges

The Magnitude of the Problem

The challenge of implementing the NLRMP can be better appreciated if we consider the dimension of the exercise being undertaken, which is probably one of the largest in the world. India has to survey an area of approximately 2.16 million square kilometers. In the rural areas alone, more than 140 million land owners have more than 430 million records. There are about 92 million ownership holdings of four to six parcels of holdings. Not only does the survey have to be done for each plot of land, but a settlement has to be arrived at between the government and each landowner, certifying that the owner is satisfied with the survey. This involves meticulous ground-truthing after using the sophisticated technology of either satellite imagery or aerial photography along with total station and GPS. A similar survey is required for approximately 55 million urban households. Urban areas require door-to-door surveys, which are all the more cumbersome in multi-storied buildings. The technology for surveying urban properties has yet to be finalized.

Considering the size of the country, some 3.29 million square kilometers, the establishment of the ground control point library (GCPL) presents a major problem. The Survey of India has developed a national control frame and the first phase of GCPL of 300 points spaced about 200 to 300 kilometers apart covering the whole country has been provided. The second phase of 2,200 points spaced 30 to 40 kilometers apart, and the third phase with control points at a distance of about 8 to 10 kilometers apart have yet to be established.

India has approximately 640,000 villages. Of these, 140,000 villages, largely in southern and western India, are surveyed by using field measurement books (FMBs) based on data of plot measurements, i.e., the "FMB method." Each village has approximately 300 FMBs. Thus, around 42 million FMBs must be digitized. The remaining 500,000 villages follow the system of "village maps." One village has between 1 to 3 map sheets. Thus, at least 1 million village maps need to be digitized. India has 4,018 registration offices. Of these, 1,896 have yet to be computerized. Except for the State of Haryana, all registration offices have to be inter-linked with the revenue departments of the respective states.

Some parts of the country have never been surveyed and cadastral surveying is under way for the first time. Even in those states where surveys have been carried out, government lands, rural residential areas known as "*abadi* sites" have never been surveyed. Urban areas require fresh surveys as the local urban bodies update data for purposes of taxation but not for ownership.

Constitutional Provisions

According to the Indian Constitution, land is subject to legislation by the state, but not by the central government. State governments will have to usher in laws adapted to local requirements while keeping in mind the overall spirit of conclusive titling. Some central acts may also need modification in which case the central government will have to take the initiative. The latter is developing a "model law" for conclusive titling to provide guidance to those states which may request help in drafting legislation.

National and State Program Integration

Land records in India are maintained by state governments in the local language. India has nine major scripts covering 18 languages. Moreover, in each state, a different terminology is used for describing the record of property rights. India has had to come out with information technology software compatible with the regional languages. The challenge is making the software operational across the country.

Not only do the states have different languages and terminologies for property records, they also have different methodologies for preparing textual and spatial land records. Even within a state there may be more than one method of preparing and maintaining these records, depending upon historical factors in the creation of the state. For example, the State of Andhra Pradesh was created by the unification of the erstwhile Telengana State and some areas taken out of the erstwhile Madras Presidency. Villages within Telengana State continue to follow the pattern of land records preparation and maintenance of the Telengana State, while the rest of the villages follow the pattern of the Madras Presidency. Karnataka State was carved out of four erstwhile princely kingdoms, each of which followed its own system of preparing and maintaining land records. These four methods continue to be followed in Karnataka even today.

It is difficult to have a single software solution for the entire country, and virtually each state has had to evolve software compatible with its land revenue system or systems. Those states doing their first cadastral survey have to evolve their own systems for preparing textual and spatial land records.

In most of the states, the revenue, registration, *panchayati raj*, and local bodies and departments are headed by separate ministers or secretaries. Politically and administratively, it may be difficult to integrate them immediately. Information technology has provided a way out by letting them be inter-linked procedurally without disturbing existing administrative arrangements. However, it will be a challenge to make this integrated system function smoothly within the existing regimen.

The states within the country are at different stages in the modernization process— some of them doing cadastral mapping for the first time while others have already integrated the revenue and registration processes and are just a few steps away from conclusive titling. The challenge for the central government is to bring all the states to the same level of modernization, so that the country moves together towards conclusive titling without disturbing the varied socio-economic systems that prevailing within the states.

Due to variations in languages and terminologies among the states while referring to the property records, the Central Government developed a National Code for data computing and circulated it to all state governments for filling in the data. This will facilitate the creation of a national database of property records and other attributes. The challenge lies in ensuring that each state adopts this National Code and fills it up systematically. The Program Management Unit will monitor and interpret this vast volume of data that will be accessed at the national level.

Technology

The selection of technology is a major challenge for the country as a whole, as well as for each state government. The varied topography of the country requires a judicious combination of technologies for proper survey. A single district may have a variety of terrains such as plains, hills and valleys, and forests. A common, stable technology for use in valleys and forests and urban areas has yet to be developed.

Even where appropriate technologies have been identified, transferring the technology to the field level workers all over the country is a daunting task. It is difficult to organize national level programs and workshops for technology transfer owing to the variety of languages spoken by the field level workers.

Due to variations in technology, issues relating to security of data, redefinition of accuracy standards and a system for 100 percent quality check for errors in computerization and digitization have to be put into place.

Capacity Building

The issue of capacity building is intimately linked with transfer of technology. Where once the knowledge of measuring land by chain and tape was enough for revenue functionaries, they now have to be well-versed with computers, scanning, digitization, total stations, GPS, aerial photography, satellite imagery, and to some extent, with the registration process. Similarly, the Registration Officers now have to be trained in computer technology as well as in land record management. The capacity building involves between 100,000 to 200,000 million *patwaris*, staff for approximately 5,000 *tehsils* and 4,000 registration offices, and over 50,000 survey staff.

The first step would be to build a cadre of master trainers at the state level who would then ensure the percolation of technology to the district level, from where it would be transferred to the village level. This requires time, effort, and financial resources.

Upgrading existing training institutes has become an integral part of the NLRMP. Some states do not have a training institute and a way will have to be found to establish one.

The manual systems of survey, record keeping, registration, mutation, etc. have created a large backlog of work which must be attended to in a mission mode to ensure that records are updated. One way of addressing this challenge could be outsourcing the work or hiring of temporary staff by government agencies.

Conclusion

India has begun the journey towards ushering in the system of conclusive titles with title guarantee. Modernization of the land records management and property registration systems is the first step. The task appears to be stupendous, with monumental challenges at every step of the way. With the unstinted support of the state governments, the Department of Land Resources in the Ministry of Rural Development, which has rolled out the NLRMP, is confident of fulfilling its charter.

1.3:   Improving Land Administration in Ghana: Lessons and Challenges in Moving Ahead

HON. COLLINS DAUDA, Minister, Ministry of Lands and Natural Resources, Republic of Ghana

Introduction

We consider that the achievement of at least three of the Millennium Development Goals depends, among other things, on good governance of land. These are the eradication of extreme poverty, promoting gender equality, and empowering women, and environmental sustainability. Within this broader context, I would like to discuss what we are doing in Ghana under the Land Administration Project.

The Land Administration System Prior to the Land Administration Project

The land administration situation in Ghana prior to the implementation of the Land Administration Project has been aptly described in the National Land Policy of 1999 as follows:

- General indiscipline in the land market characterized by a spate of land encroachments, multiple sales of residential parcels, unapproved development schemes, haphazard development, etc. These have led to environmental problems, disputes, conflicts and endless litigation.
- Indeterminate boundaries of customary owned lands resulting directly from lack of reliable maps or plans, and the use of unapproved, old, or inaccurate maps. This has led to land conflicts and litigation between stools, skins, and other land-owning groups.
- Compulsory acquisition by government of large tracts of lands, which have not been utilized to the full and for which payment of compensation has been delayed.
- Inadequate security of land tenure due to conflict of interests between and within land-owning groups and the state, land racketeering, slow disposal of land cases by the courts and a weak land administration system.
- Difficulty in accessing land for agricultural, industrial, commercial, and residential development purposes due to conflicting claims to ownership, and varied and outmoded land disposal procedures.
- A weak land administration system characterized by the lack of a comprehensive land policy framework, reliance on inadequate and outdated legislation, the lack of adequate functional and coordinated geographic information systems and networks, as well as of transparent guidelines. The system is also characterized by poor capacity to initiate and coordinate policy actions, let alone resolve contradictory policies and policy actions among various land delivery agencies.

The net effect of these constraints is a distorted and dysfunctional land market that is not investor and development oriented and which cannot guarantee security of tenure, resulting in high transaction costs and high incidence of poverty.

The Land Administration Project

The Land Administration Project was designed as the implementation mechanism for the National Land Policy and was intended to address the challenges mentioned above. The Project became effective in October 2003. Its development objective is to undertake legislative and institutional reforms and strategic pilots that will lay the foundation for a sustainable land administration system that is fair, efficient, cost-effective, and that guarantees security of tenure.

The Project's components relate to legal reforms, institutions and their capacity, and information systems. An inventory of lands which have been acquired by the state is intended to inform the formulation of policies that address those outstanding issues that arise out of compulsory acquisition. A number of components relate to reform, and to the capacity of public sector institutions, including the judiciary. The Project supports customary forms of land administration, in part through the demarcation of customary boundaries. Congested land registries have been the source of numerous problems, and these are addressed by a number of components as well. In addition to decongesting the registries themselves, the development of computerized land information systems is necessary for more systematic land titling in order to reform the land use planning system. Improved information systems are also required for the revaluation of properties. Support to academic and research institutions and the use of an effective monitoring and evaluation system will also improve the information that is available to decision makers in the planning system. The Project is also intended to expand participation in policy formulation.

Achievements

Since the inception of the project the following has been achieved:

- All the laws on land and land use have been reviewed and proposals have been made to consolidate and update them.
- Based on an inventory undertaken on some lands acquired by the state, the government has started returning excess lands to the original owners.
- The Judiciary has established six land courts which are being furnished by the Project.
- A new Lands Commission Act 2008 (Act 767) has been passed, merging four of the six public land sector agencies.
- Thirty-eight customary land secretariats have been established to provide support to the customary land owners.
- A Civil Society Coalition on Land (CICOL) has been formed.
- Eight Land Registries have been established in eight regional capitals, reducing the turnaround time for land registration from more than 36 months to less than three months in those regional capitals.
- The Geodetic Reference Network has been reorganized for the southern part of the country.

- Pilot customary boundary demarcation is on-going in two areas.
- Two beneficiary impact assessments have been undertaken on the establishment of the Land Registries. The results found considerable enthusiasm on the part of the populace to register their properties. On average, about 30 percent of the lands registered have been registered by women.

Lessons

Six years into implementation, we are able to catalogue the following lessons:

- Land administration reforms are long term interventions and should be conceptualized and planned as such. This is particularly so in situations where the land sector has been neglected for a long time. Short to medium term one-off projects are not likely to make any significant impact. In fact modest gains made during the project period may be eroded. Development partners who are interested in such interventions should be willing to commit themselves to the long term.
- Expectations must be managed throughout the implementation of a project, which should be modest in its conceptualization and design. Any assumptions that land administration reforms will be widely accepted must be thoroughly tested. Even though there may be widespread dislike for the existing system, implementation of the reforms must be strategically planned and executed to be successful.
- Manageable small to medium sized projects are preferable to a more ambitious, comprehensive program. Scoping studies, pilots and good baseline studies including implementation capacity are essential before launching the project.
- Human capacity should be the core around which a land administration project is designed and implemented, including appropriate remuneration packages. Implementation teams that consist of a mixture of consultants and civil servants working together can be difficult process to manage. Champions for the reform among key stakeholders must be sought before implementation begins.
- A land administration reform project unit must not be an integral part of the mainstream civil service structure. Whereas mainstream activities rely on compliance with procedures and processes, 'projects' are mainly output-oriented. Therefore while compliance with all the rules and procedures would have been met in a mainstream environment, actual project outputs could be minimal. On the other hand, mainstreaming project implementation builds the capacity of ministries, departments, and agencies and helps in assimilating the project into operational activities of the agencies. It therefore provides institutional memory and sustainability when the project ends. The two must be carefully weighed in making a decision as to the implementation structure and what the project seeks to achieve.
- Political and key stakeholder commitment must not be taken for granted. It must be consciously sustained throughout the project.

- Practical and innovative approaches are required in developing methodologies for undertaking key pilots to provide a framework for scaling up.
- Appropriate communication tools are essential for the dissemination of information about project deliverables.
- Access to information about best practices and their adaptability to local conditions is necessary for success.
- Appropriate technology is a vital input to successful land administration reform—LIS development, Geodetic Reference Network, Surveying and Mapping etc.
- Participation and transparent practices are essential to increased ownership of the reform process and to the sustainability of the project.

Challenges

In moving ahead with the implementation and to achieve the objectives of the Project we have to deal with the following challenges:

Management of the change processes and dealing with resistance to change: Managing the change processes to transform agencies that have merely existed for a long time into service-delivery oriented ones is a daunting challenge. It requires a lot of transparency, education, and participation.

Sustaining some of the project deliverables: The establishment of customary land secretariats, nurturing them to grow into proper local land administration institutions and their eventual acceptance by the customary authorities as part of the land management structure require time. More external financial support will be required to enable them function effectively as sources of local information.

Financing the land administration infrastructure: The development of good land administration infrastructure requires a good and accurate geodetic reference system, and accurate and up-to-date cadastral records and land information systems. These are expensive to maintain, especially when annual licenses for software have to be paid. We have decided to use open source software for the national land information system. Where national funds are not available, innovative means for attracting private capital must be developed, such as partnership arrangements between the state and the private sector, build-operate-transfer (BOT) arrangements, turnkey operations, outsourcing, etc.

Power plays: Where the implementing agencies are themselves subject to institutional reform—as is the case with both customary institutions and public sector land agencies—there can be considerable latitude to gain advantage. This must be managed very well.

Participation: The big challenge is to determine when consultation is enough. This can be especially problematic when dealing with large number of stakeholders in a plural environment. Participation tends to lengthen the implementation period.

Integrating project outputs into mainstream activities: Project outputs are still seen as separate results and not part of the routine outputs of the agencies, especially when undertaken by consultants. This should also be managed as part of the change process.

Conclusion

The land administration project is on course after initial delays that resulted from limited capacity. It is still a challenging reform program but the new administration is committed to ensuring that the Project is steered to successful completion and that subsequent phases are developed in time to ensure continuity. While challenges persist, the desire for change and improvement will drive us to achieve the objectives of the program. We have to be innovative and proactive in many respects in handling as sensitive an issue as land administration reform. The commitment of development partners, especially during the initial stages, is essential. There is also the need to harmonize the participation of such partners so as to reduce the effort needed to comply with the different requirements of each respective partner. In complex projects such as the Land Administration Project in Ghana, development partners should strive to agree on a program of basket funding.

CHAPTER 2

Innovative Approaches to Improving Land Administration in Africa

2.1: Registering and Administering Customary Land Rights: Can We Deal with Complexity?

PHILIPPE LAVIGNE DELVILLE, Group de Recherche et d'Echanges Technologiques (GRET), France and L'Institut de Recherche pour le Développement (IRD), Niger

Summary

The opportunity of land rights registration programs is heavily debated. When there is a justification for such programs, there are still two important and related issues, which are crucial where local land rights are complex bundles of rights with more or less collective regulation, as is the case in "customary" land rights. First, *the nature of the land rights recognized through the registration process:* are they only individual ownership rights, or is there room for more complex property rights? Second, *the systems to administer these rights:* can a diversity of land rights be recognized?

This paper highlights these issues, drawing on the case of Rural Land Maps (*plans fonciers ruraux*) (PFRs) in West Africa. It shows that, while ethnography of land rights can help in designing tools for identifying complex land rights, the issue of managing these rights has not yet been taken into account.

Introduction

The debate on poverty has highlighted the fact that, in developing countries, a large share of the population is excluded from access to formal rights because of the law or administrative practices. In his work, which re-launched the debate on the registration of local/extra-legal land rights, de Soto (2000) stunningly describes the "bell jar" that separates the vast majority of the population from the small elite that is protected by the law and administration. This observation is true in particular for land rights: his analyses of how the administrative complexity and cost of legal procedures form a true "obstacle course," imprisoning most stakeholders in an informal status, are convincing. As far as informality is a real problem for them, people's (and especially poor people's) access to formal rights, the legal acknowledgement of local land rights, and the legal and institutional systems that can break this "bell jar" are truly fundamental.

While there is broad consensus on this point today, the question of institutional frameworks and operational methods to truly attain this ambition remains unanswered. The debate is lively on the impact of classic rights registration procedures. The classic scheme under which title-granting operations automatically bring about security of tenure, investment and increased productivity is seriously challenged by numerous empirical studies (Platteau 1996, Durand-Lasserve et Selod 2009, Colin et al. 2009). It seems clear that this scheme is only valid in conditions that are in fact both relatively restrictive and insufficiently explicit. First of all, informality is not equal to insecurity (Lavigne Delville 2006b) and conflicts over land are frequently related to failures in arbitration systems more than to informality (Lavigne Delville 2002). In addition, the assumption that the regularization of rights provides real access to credit (Platteau 1998) and that land markets can operate in favor of the poor is also questioned. The consideration of interlinked markets clearly shows that, when there are significant imperfections in one or the other of these markets (products, credit, labor, etc.), liberalizing the land market runs the very real risk of having counter-productive effects in terms of both equity and productivity (Binswanger et al. 1995). Finally, we know that registration operations are often favored moments for manipulation, corruption, and exclusion to the benefit of political elites and technicians (Shipton 1988).

More broadly, land is not only an asset. It is an issue of *"wealth, power and meaning"* (Shipton and Goheen 1992). Local land rights are frequently embedded in social norms and institutions, and cannot be isolated easily. Issues with land rights registration are not only economic; they also have to do with heritage, identity, citizenship, and governance (Land Tenure Committee 2009). Where local land tenure is not only de facto private ownership, land registration processes based on private ownership will transform the rights in the process of survey and adjudication. Existing regulations will be challenged, family rights holders or secondary rights holders may be excluded, and individuals who hold the land in trust of a family group may legally be seen as individual owners and exclude other right holders. All this is likely to produce exclusions, social costs, and conflict (during or after registration) with few or no economic gains and strong social costs.

Therefore, serious questions about the conditions under which land rights registration can be economically positive for the poor remain. In their pivotal book on land tenure security in Africa, Bruce and Mighot Adholla (1994) questioned whether (systematic or sporadic) registration was still relevant given these numerous shortcomings. Nearly twenty years later, it is quite surprising to see that, while focused on the poor and their legal empowerment, the current debate still seems to ignore most of them. Given this, one could wonder as to the ultimate goal of this discourse: is it truly to work to lift the "bell jar" to allow the poor to benefit from efficient land law and administration, currently reserved for a protected elite, or is it to favor, through land registration, a free market in land rights that, in numerous situations, has every chance of working in the interest of those who are already privileged?

However, even if one cannot expect substantial economic outputs from land rights registration, and formalization in most contexts, there are several possible outcomes which may justify such policies. It can help avoid land conflicts when the local knowledge on land is not efficient, making the balance fairer between poor farmers and urban buyers; have beneficial side-effects on productivity; or establish a basis for fiscal revenue for local governments. The opportunity for land registration is a real issue, which requires strong analysis.

Considering that this opportunity is clear in a given context, there are still two important issues that are rarely dealt with. One, the *nature of the rights* recognized through the registration process: is the explicit or implicit model one of private property, or is it a true attempt to start from local rights and rules as they are and to address their complexity? In this case, how are they addressed? Two, are *systems to administer these rights* capable of ensuring reliable management of these complex registered rights and can land management bodies take into account the local diversity of rights?

Indeed, in numerous places, local land rights are not a de facto private ownership. They build a complex set of property rights to land and to natural resources that may overlap. In places where "customary" rules and rights[1] form the basis of land tenure, is it possible to register land rights as they are, with their diversity and complexity?

The answers to these questions will determine to a great extent the real social and economic impacts of legal empowerment and rights registration policies. Rural land tenure maps (*plans fonciers ruraux*) (PFRs) in West Africa show that, while ethnography of land rights may provide tools to identify complex rights, their administration requires further attention.[2]

The PFR Approach to Securing "Customary" Land Rights through Registration

In French-speaking Africa, the colonial heritage induces a dualism in land law and administration: the law focuses on "Land Titles" generated by public registration procedures (*immatriculation*) as the primary legal form[3]. Customary land rights are disregarded, or barely acknowledged as use rights. All unregistered land (95 percent of the territory, and thus nearly all rural land) is included in the State Private Domain and is supposed to be under state control. In practice, the land is run according to local rules, which are dynamic and reactive to changes in economic and social context, and which have been transformed more or less by public intervention. All unregistered land can thus be called "customary," a term that covers very diverse situations within the countries, with more or less individualized land rights, more or less market land transactions, more or less grazing rights. This situation—which is not necessarily a problem when outside influences are few—leads to a plurality of norms and competition among arbitration bodies, and finally, fosters conflicts and land grabbing (Lavigne Delville 2002; Lund 1998, 2001, 2002).

This unregulated plurality of norms is widely considered as one of the main sources of conflicts. The stake for rural land tenure policies is to thus cut this legal dualism, and propose concrete responses to the problems facing rural populations, with an aim to economic effectiveness, social peace, and citizenship building. For this, the challenge is overcoming the divorce between legality, legitimacy, and practices by building land tenure regulation mechanisms based on shared norms:

- Moving away from the dichotomy between statutory rights and local land systems, and starting from a recognition of existing rights, however determined the state may be to transform these rights;
- Allowing farmers and herders to escape the legal insecurity in which they have been maintained since the colonial period; and
- Proposing a range of securization measures, allowing different types of actors to secure their concrete rights according to their needs, without turning "immatriculation" into the only form of title.

This means changing from a dual, exclusive legal framework, to a plural, inclusive one, built on an articulated diversity of legal statuses. This implies numerous judicial, institutional, or technical innovations. Beyond a simplification of the "immatriculation" procedure, various approaches are proposed, emphasizing the recognition of local land tenure norms, local authorities or bodies for land tenure regulation and arbitration, and/or concrete rights held by individuals and family or residence groups (cf. Le Roy 1998 and Lavigne Delville 2002 for an overview). PFRs are one of these current approaches. While decentralized management of resources emphasizes land and natural resource management *rules* and *bodies*, PFRs emphasize *rights* over land.

Identify and Formalize Local Rights

PFR approaches were experimented with utilizing different scopes and in diverse institutional contexts as early as the early 1990s in Côte d'Ivoire and then Guinea, Benin and Burkina Faso (Gastaldi 1998). In Benin, they have been part of larger projects focused on natural resources management.[4] These field operations were supposed to lead to a reform of the law in order to integrate the approach, define the types of rights acknowledged by the state and give legal acknowledgement to the rights identified in the field. In practice, Côte d'Ivoire passed a new land law in 1999, which is not yet applied due to the political conflicts in the country. Benin passed a new land law in 2007 and implementation within the new legal framework is beginning. Thus, it is too early to analyze concrete impacts of PFRs and land certificates. However, we have enough material to discuss the concept of PFRs and the issue of the registration process.

PFRs are based on an "instrumental" logic, not on law as the starting point (Le Roy 1998). They rely on a will to identify and map the existing rights, at parcel level, whatever their origins may be. At the village level, a systematic survey process, which allows for public contestation of the proposed registration of rights, and a flexible and effective mapping system are set up. This leads to a simplified "cadastre" whose objective is to materialize rights over land that are accepted at the local level on a consensual basis. The methodology is based on parcel-level field surveys in the presence of rights holders and their neighbors. The socio-land survey identifies rights holders and the rights they hold, and the land survey draws parcel limits onto an orthophoto. The survey record (procès-verbal) is signed by the right holder and the neighbors. The process is presented as neutral since it is limited to the materialization of concrete existing rights.

Where the land law makes it possible, as in Benin since the 2007 law on rural land tenure regime, registered plots receive a "land certificate," which is a new legal status. Land certificates can be sold or used as collateral. However, the state does not grant them any authenticity, as opposed to Land Titles. On request, land certificates can be transformed into Land Titles through immatriculation. A specific land administration body is put in place for these certificates, coupling village level committees for the formalization of land transfers (sales, gifts, loans, mortgage, etc.) and public service at commune or district level for issuing new certificates and updating land information.[5] This new land administration body is funded by the commune budget and by taxes on land transfers. It is connected with the classic land administration service, which deals with Land Titles because they share the same maps on which all legal statuses are recorded (Lavigne Delville, Mongbo and Mansion, eds. 2009).

In French-speaking areas, this approach is a real innovation:

- *Conceptually*, with the pragmatic principle of starting from existing and locally acknowledged rights, which is in marked contrast with states' ambiguous (to say the least) attitudes to local rights, and with the legal culture in French-speaking countries for which the only "real rights" are those recorded on Land Titles through immatriculation;
- *Methodologically*, with a land rights survey method that is operational, applicable on the large scale, and relatively inexpensive (approximately US$7-$10 per hectare for field surveys depending on the size of the parcels); and
- In terms of *land law and land tenure administration*, with the creation of a new legal status for land (the land certificates) and of village bodies in charge of updating information.

Made realistic by the low cost of the surveys, the principle of systematically surveying the land allows everyone to obtain a certificate, whereas registration on request usually leads to the delivery of certificates only to wealthy farmers or farmers who have contacts within the government administration.

A Hybrid Approach to Securing Land Tenure

One of the reasons that PFRs raise interest is because they borrow from the two major concepts in securing land tenure:

- The one founded on titles, deeds, and legal acknowledgement of ownership rights, promoting investment and productivity; and
- The one that emphasizes the legitimacy of local/customary rights and the effectiveness of local land management institutions.

On the one hand, the method clearly follows the logic of registration: it is a systematic method of identifying and mapping rights that leads to a register of right holders and a parcel map. Allegedly, PFRs allow farmers to stop relying on the spoken word and enter the domain of written law. PFRs, therefore, aim to clarify the land tenure situation, clearly materializing plot limits, and thus reducing conflicts and acting as an incentive for investment. The land certificates produced by the procedure are accepted as loan guarantees. They are to be managed by a public scheme at sub-prefecture level in Côte d'Ivoire (Bini 1999) and commune level in Benin; the village level having only a technical role in recording changes.

Once a consensus has been reached through the surveys and publicity phase, the identified rights move beyond local/customary regulations and enter a technical updating procedure (inheritance, cession, etc.). Thus, PFRs are a method of registration that aims to *absorb* local rights in the public system: "The specificity of the PFR tool is the desire to capture and 'externalize' procedures to validate observed rights: that is to say, once rights have been identified and recorded, to extract them from local validation procedures and substitute a legal procedure." (Chauveau 2003: 39). This results in rights that are recognized by the state, managed by public institutions, and the subject of a market.

On the other hand, PFRs are also presented as an alternative to immatriculation, which in most French-speaking African countries is the only status of land ownership: "while admitting that PFRs could open the way to land immatriculation, we believe that the legal reach of customary rights confirmed and consolidated by PFRs should provide farmers with sufficient land tenure security in their relationships with the land to avoid the need to rely on land titles" (Hounkpodote 2000: 232). It is a "bottom-up" method of creating property rights based on the acknowledgement of existing rights as they have been forged through history (and may thus be diverse), and not a "top-down" method based on the allocation of rights designed by the state.[6]

Under this second perspective, the ambition is to identify and record rights on which there is a local consensus and to "identify all rights," including—in theory— rights to natural resources and rights delegated to third parties. The rights identified can be individual or collective, and in the latter case, the "administrator"—who manages the parcel in the name of the family group that owns it—is identified and recorded as such. During the surveys, the decision as to which rights are recorded is left to the local stakeholders on a case by case basis. In pilot sites in Benin, the average parcel size varies from a few hectares to several dozen hectares. Individualized rights or the rights of extended families or lineage groups are recorded (in the second case, the internal distribution of rights among rights holders being managed within the group).

In Benin, PFRs are produced at the request of villages. In areas where there are few conflicts or little insecurity, the villages can merely formalize a few local rules and have them validated, and record monetary transactions. The lack of a reliable procedure is one cause of challenges and conflicts. When there is a request for a PFR,[7] local stakeholders can register their heritage, their lineage/family estate, at the scale of concrete local land units or at least at the scale for which they want to mark the difference between the internal affairs of a (more or less extended) family group and that which has an "external" dimension (relationship with the state, third parties, etc.). Nothing obliges them to individualize these rights or foster commercial transactions. Choosing which rules to formalize, individualizing —or not—of heritage during registration, and formalizing agreements between the granter and receiver of delegated rights can generate debate or even conflict among local stakeholders. What has to be recorded and formalized is the balance of power and compromises—even temporary ones—between stakeholders. In addition, the composition of the village committees naturally leaves room for local powers; the fact that all transactions must be run by the village committees can lead one to think that transactions seen as illegitimate would have a hard time being acknowledged and formalized.

Such systems leave thus a relatively large degree of autonomy for the definition of what kind of rights and modes of regulation are to be identified. In this perspective,

PFRs offer a legal and institutional framework that secures local rights and shores up the role of local land management institutions at the village level.

Land certificates do not formalize only standard ownership rights. They are in fact the legal envelope given to individual and/or collective rights that allows land units (village and family) to be better protected from the risk of dispossession by the State and/or third parties and to formalize their relationships with *outside* stakeholders (cessions, agrarian contracts, etc.) while continuing to freely manage their *internal* relations (within the village, extended family, etc.). Far from being a tool for *absorbing* local land rights into private ownership and into a public regulation framework, as in the first conception, PFRs can be a tool to *articulate* local and state land regulation modes.

In this perspective, PFRs work differently depending on the context. In areas where customary regulation is in force and there are few transactions, a village can choose to stay without PFR, and only monetary land transfers will be recorded at the land village committee, avoiding at minimum cost the main source of land conflicts. When a village asks for a PFR, extended family units will register large parcels as collective property while individual owners will register their own plot as a private ownership. As land transfers are not frequent, there will be few changes over time in land certificates and only a small burden on the commune budget for land administration. Village committees would be mainly composed of customary authorities insuring the legitimacy of land regulation and conflict resolution. PFRs do not forbid the commoditization or the individualization of land, nor do they encourage it: they mainly give a legal status to customary rights, protecting them against land grabbing, and formalize individualization when it takes place.

However, in areas where rights are more individualized, and where the market is active and is now the primary mode of access to land, the logic of formalizing transactions on clearly identified and legally recognized plots takes on its full meaning. Many smaller, more individualized plots will be recorded; village committees (more open to a wider range of stakeholders, such as indigenous groups, migrants, etc.) and commune land officers will have more work to register a greater number of land transactions, to issue new certificates and to keep land records up-dated. However, the value of the land allows for higher taxes.

From this perspective, land registration does not intend to provide dramatic changes in land tenure. It aims to provide a legal framework, able to fit with diverse contexts, with more or less complex or more or less individualized land rights. However, it does not impede social and tenure change. Land registration identifies and secures land rights independently of the social relationships that gave them legitimacy, without drastically overturning the long-standing tenure systems that have developed in each local context. In short, it recognizes that social and economic changes more than public intervention are likely to determine, at their own pace, peaceful processes of individualization or commercialization.

PFRs borrow from these two logics. This hybrid logic is one of the method's major strengths. It favors consensus on the political choice of acknowledging local rights. It makes sense in regard to the diversity of land situations in rural areas, and makes it possible to respond to a wide diversity of stakeholders. But these two logics cannot be fully harmonized. They are built on different views about the nature of local/"customary" land rights and about what kind of rights are to be recognized by the law. They lead to different methodological choices in terms of PFR operation implementation and differ even more in terms of legal and institutional frameworks and procedures for land administration.

My argument is that PFRs come from a topographic conception of land rights, which underestimates the issue of the nature of the rights to be recorded, and which may lead to distortion and conflict (though less so than immatriculation). Using recent advances in ethnography of land rights, as well as PFR practical experience, it is possible to design land survey methodologies that fit better with complexity. However, this way challenges a conception of land certificates as recording a "customary ownership" and calls for a more open conception of property rights in the land law and for more complex land administration procedures to administer them.

Formalize "Customary Ownership" or Bundles of Rights?

The PFR method originally relies on a "topo-legal" view of rights. Land tenure insecurity is seen above all as the result of a lack of formal rights and conflicts over limits. The aim is to take a "photograph of rights" and "clarify" them by making them explicit. Emphasis is placed on outlining parcels in the field, and identifying the right holder. The nature and content of local/customary rights are not seen as a problem: implicitly, the concept is one of "customary (individual or collective) ownership" in which all rights are concentrated in the hands of a "customary owner," or "manager" in the case of family groups owning the plot. In such situations, it is sufficient to identify the "owner" or "manager," the other rights holders (people having borrowed, rented in, or taken plots in sharecropping), and the limits of the parcel.

In the early versions of the PFR handbook for survey teams, most of the methodology was devoted to plot delimitation. The socio-land tenure survey was the subject of little detail and few practical recommendations on how to do it. The way in which survey sheets were filled out varied greatly from one team to another, and sometimes even within the same team. Some survey sheets contained detailed information that gave a clear image of the rights beyond the limits of the form, and others merely contained standard, somewhat vague formulas.

Overall, the difficulties in identifying rights and the stakes underpinning identification operations were under-estimated. This led to methodological biases that provoked distortions, which were sometimes very serious compared to the method's ambitions.[8]

Indeed, PFR experiences—as they have been implemented in the framework of pilot operations in various countries—showed certain limitations:

- *They suffered from "agricultural" bias.* Rights over natural resources and common lands were barely taken into account.
- *They started from an overly positivist approach to rights,* implicitly supposing that one parcel corresponds to one "owner" (albeit customary or collective) and thus sometimes generated serious errors in the identification of rights. In fact, the apparent simplicity of the process clashed with the complexity of describing these rights, especially in areas where land systems relied on a range of nested rights. The focus on the mapping exercise has contributed to

neglecting sociological analysis of these bundles of rights (Chauveau et al. 1998; Chauveau 2003; Edja and Le Meur 2003). The different levels of nested rights that existed on the field are, after the survey, boiled down to a mere differentiation between "land managers" and "farmers." Secondary rights (youth rights and women's rights, rights regarding trees or pastures, etc.) were neglected.

▪ *They under-estimated the socio-political stakes behind registration operations and the anticipation strategies that emerge in response to such operations.* Far from making stakeholders more secure and resolving conflicts, PFR operations—like any registration process—excluded people or provoked conflicts, especially when only some of the rights holders were able to have their rights recorded. Thus, PFR operations offered an opportunity to re-negotiate rights, prior to the surveys. In Côte d'Ivoire, some villages, installed several centuries ago by their neighbors, thus saw their rights called into question (Chauveau et al. 1998). In Benin, lineage heads have been recorded as land "managers" of thousands of hectares, even if they had no concrete responsibility in land management which was at a lower level of lineage organization (Edja and Le Meur 2003).

These biases could be more or less marked in function of the region or context in question, based upon, for example, the importance of renewable resources, the social heterogeneity of stakeholders, the complexity of local land norms, and the degree of conflict regarding land tenure. These limitations did not call into question the interest in the method, which was appreciated by farmers (Edja and Le Meur 2003). They did, however, question the underlying concept of land rights and call for more rigor in taking rights into account in the process, and in survey methods[9] in particular.

Land Tenure and Customary Ownership

Tenure research on land rights ethnography and PFR intervention site surveys (Chauveau et al. 1998, for Côte d'Ivoire; Jacob 2009 for Burkina Faso; Edja and Le Meur 2003, Le Meur 2006, Le Meur and Edja 2009, for Benin) clearly show that such a vision of "customary ownership" comes from a disputable concept of customary land rights and local regulations. Customary land rights are embedded in a system of norms (Berry 1989). They are the subject of balance between individual prerogatives and collective regulations. They depend on social belonging, result from negotiations and arbitrations, and in short are fundamentally socio-political in nature (Chauveau 1998).

Different theoretical frameworks attempt to describe the nature of customary land rights. Beyond their differences, these frameworks open the black box of land rights and question the social distribution of the different rights within the social groups concerned. Revisiting and completing the neo-classic analysis of the economics of property rights, Schlager and Ostrom (1992) analyze the rights held by different users by distinguishing between "operational" rights (those that concern human actions directly on resources) and "administration" rights (those that deal with the organization and management of these operational rights).

This approach is nevertheless focused on individuals' rights, which is problematic when dealing with family land estates or common pool resources. Le Roy (1997) made a crucial contribution by introducing the concept of "territorial masterships" (*maîtrises foncières*)[10] which avoids the ambiguity of *propriété* in French (there is no distinction between "ownership" and "property rights") and fits better with endogenous conceptions. He also shows that the social stakeholders holding administration rights may be diverse, depending on the resource at stake and the social norms (individuals, social groups based on family or residence, allied social groups, etc). He proposes a grid containing 25 different cases and showing the weakness of concepts that oppose only private and public property. Recent empirical works (Chauveau, Jacob, Colin, etc.) have enriched the grid and shown that it is operational to identify and describe the "bundles of rights" really held by the various stakeholders, even within family groups holding lineage-based land tenure heritages (see Colin 2005 and Colin 2008).

The Different Types of Land Rights[11]

Operational Rights (rights to operate)

- Access: the right to enter a given space, or to cross it
- Withdrawal: the right to withdraw natural products
- Exploitation or Farming: the right to modify the space or the resource to produce (annual crops)
- Development: the right to sustainably transform the space or the resource (land development, tree plantation, etc.)

Administration Rights (rights to manage)

- Management: the right to distribute and regulate use of the land among rights holders
- Inclusion/Exclusion: the right to determine who receives operational rights
- Transmission: the right to determine how and to whom the preceding rights transmit or are transferred
- Alienation: the right to freely dispose of all preceding rights (including by sale)

The social organization of the territory in the savannas of West Africa is frequently structured within supra-village "territorial masterships", with the founding lineage holding ritual power and the right to allocate clearing rights.[12] Various lineages hold land masterships over the lands they cleared that make up their "estate". Within them, the various production units/households hold more or less extensive rights to cultivate that their chief allocates to members of the farm or temporarily cedes to third parties. Gathering rights, pasturing rights, etc. are overlaid on this layered social organization of the territory (figure 2.1).

Different "bundles of rights" can be held by different individuals or groups on the same space. Figure 2.2 illustrates the fundamental difference between a conception in

Figure 2.1. Multi-layered Rights and Territorial Organization in a Savannah Village

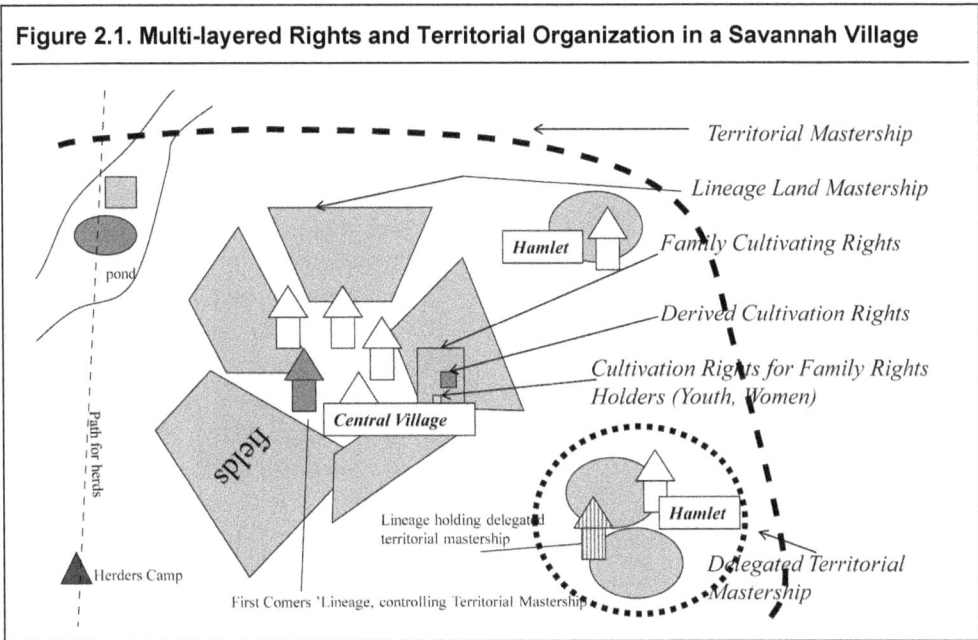

Source: Lavigne Delville.

Figure 2.2. "Customary Ownership" vs. Bundles of Rights and Land Masterships

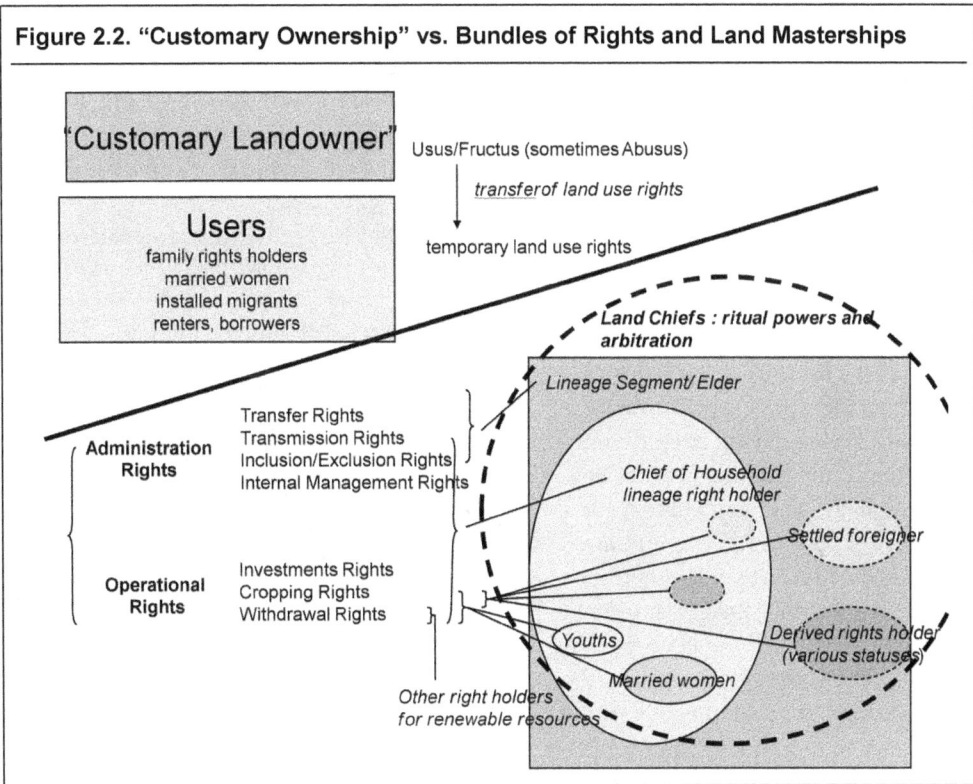

Source: Lavigne Delville.

terms of "customary private ownership" and a conception in terms of bundles on a family land estate, with production units holding transmissible exploitation rights on part of this estate and different stakeholders having various sets of rights.

Table 2.1. Bundles of Rights in a Family in Southeastern Côte d'Ivoire

Rights Held	Family Group Council	Head of Family Group	Right-holder within the Family Group
Operational Rights			
Right to cultivate an individual parcel for annual cropping (but not for tree planting)	–	+	+
Right to cultivate tree crops	–	+	–
Administration Rights			
Right to delegate cultivation rights through a share-cropping arrangement	–	+	+
Right to delegate cultivation rights through renting	–	+	–
Right to lend	–	+	–
Right to allocate parcels within the Family Group	–	+	–
Rights to sell	+	–	–
Rights to bequeath	–	–	–

Source: Soro and Colin, 2004.

In such a configuration, the rights to manage land rights are distributed among different stakeholders (head of household, lineage head, etc.), none of which can claim to be the full "owner" in that no one holds all decision-making powers over the parcel. For example, transfer rights may be held by the head of the extended family or lineage segment, on behalf of this group, while rights to internal management are devolved to the lineage segment or household head, and cultivation rights are allocated to several members of the households (table 2.1). The head of the family group, the "manager" in the name of the group, is supposed to act in the interest of the individual members (as a trustee). He manages the day-to-day distribution of rights among family rights holders and has the right to cede cultivation rights to third parties. But the group of rights holders conserves the monopoly over decisions regarding the family land estate, and in particular the right to sell lands (if such right exists).

Such complex configurations can coexist alongside individually-owned parcels that their owners have cleared, bought, or received as gifts (table 2.2).

Recent work on land tenure and on the "ethnography of land rights" (Colin 2006, 2008) helps to explain the issue of customary rights and allows describing precisely the bundles of rights relevant in a given context. It shows that PFRs' legitimate ambition to record land rights "as they are in the field" is quite contradictory with the concept of rights in terms of "customary ownership" and challenges the current methodologies for land rights surveys.

The apparent simplicity of the PFR method covers, by its

Table 2.2. Ego's Land Parcels and Land Estate

	Ego's land estate		
	Land parcel 1: inherited family land	Land parcel 2: parcel received as a gift from his father	Land parcel 3: purchased parcel
Ego's bundle of rights			
Right to sell	–	-1	x
Right to make inter vivo gifts	–	x	x
Use right	x	x	x
Right to lease out	x	x	x
Exclusion right; right to regulate access to land for other use-rights holders	x	x	x
Family authorities	Family council	Donor (as long as he lives; then: Ego)	Ego
Claimants	Lineage segment	Ego's siblings	Ego's children

Source: Colin, 2006.

very concept, a series of operations to select and translate rights that transforms these rights more or less massively. Hence, the PFR method *"can be read as an 'ethnography applied to rights' that seeks to take exhaustive account of the complexity of land rights but that generates imperfections and biases in and through the mode of describing rights and the translation chain, resulting in a tendency to erase diversity and homogenise categories"* (Le Meur 2006). These distortions are not necessarily serious: not all rights need to be recorded; in addition, not defining *a priori* the types of rights to be identified allows, at least in theory, local stakeholders to decide what level of rights they record (individual, family, groups of heirs) and what they choose to maintain in the family group, thus giving a large degree of flexibility (which has been verified in practice).

A certain amount of simplification is inevitable in all registration operations. Nevertheless, in the way the method was initially implemented these simplifications were the uncontrolled result of a topo-legal reading and not the result of a reasoned method based on the nature of the rights in question. Many of the problems identified during PFR operations can be explained by the inadequacy in the conceptual framework—and thus in the resulting methodology.

The ambition of "photographing" rights demands a rigorous method for collecting, transcribing, validating, and processing land information from the farmers' spoken words during the survey to the registers and certificates (d'Aquino 1998). The method must be able to encompass the diversity of situations and identify, parcel by parcel, the rights holders and the more or less complex bundles of rights that they hold. Research on ethnography of land rights can allow for the development of a more satisfactory approach, reducing the distortions linked to the identification and transcription of rights.

Although the method is not yet fully perfected, a great step toward such improved methodologies has been made in Benin: in 2002-2003, a field study of the effects of PFR (Edja and Le Meur 2003) made it possible to identify the key points that created problems in regard to the identification of rights. Changes were proposed to better identify the approach's "fields of validity" and revise the procedures for identifying and transcribing rights. In 2004-2005, the PGTRN teams reviewed their methodology, demonstrating the capacity to mobilize their field experience to integrate the recommendations formulated. A comprehensive methodology was developed (Hounkpodote 2007) based upon:

- *Land diagnostics*, identifying the major characteristics of modes of access to land and land regulation in the zone, based on a sound grid;
- A *lexicon* of local land terminology, which makes it possible to use local terms when surveying the parcels;
- A repertoire of *local norms* that gives meaning to the rights identified; and
- A new survey grid, which makes explicit both the *origin* and *content* of the rights held by the various rights holders, and avoid confusion between ownership and family estates.

This detailed description of rights has to be written in the survey procès-verbal, and therefore be validated by the people interviewed and the witnesses. It has to be part of the "publicity" stage, where villagers are asked to validate or contest the information.

While some new progress would be necessary, this new methodology allows a sound description of the different rights held on a plot and their holders, while taking into account the links between the rights held by people and the social norms that give them legitimacy.

While every registration process makes a selection in a complex sets of rights, such methodologies make it possible to deal with complexity, and to reason the simplification of rights through survey and registration. They are not able to avoid all problems and risks of manipulation, but they limit seriously the gaps, provided that they are implemented by highly skilled field teams, having enough time in the field to develop a sound understanding of local land rights and issues. Specific training is needed for the teams (Codjia et al. 2008), as well as support during the first months of work, in order to allow them to develop the necessary skills.

Recognizing Complex Land Rights: Implications for Land Administration and Regulation

PFRs lead to land information systems, with a map of the plots and a register of land holders. Once the land certificates have been issued, every change has to be recorded, as in every land information system. Sales, gifts, inheritance, etc. are to be recorded at the village level and then recorded at commune level, for issuance of a new certificate. PFR land information systems face the same issues of sustainability as every land information system. But they also face specific issues related to the nature of the registered rights. Because land laws recognizing land certificates are quite new, it is too early to assess whether land certificates are effectively managed within the new land administration framework. However, it is possible to highlight some issues.

More Sustainable Land Information Systems?

No matter which rights are recorded, a land tenure information system is only meaningful if it is constantly kept up-to-date and if changes are integrated. Registers that are not updated lose their usefulness and the growing contradictions between the rights contained in the registers and real rights generate new conflicts. This requires that:

- Populations have an interest in following the procedures to record changes; and that
- They can do so in practice, at a reasonable cost.

The first point deals with real economic stakes and the reality of problems of insecurity; it also deals with the relevance of the system in relation to the rights lived by the local stakeholders (*cf.* the debate on the conditions of relevance for land rights registration systems; Land Tenure Committee 2009, 61-65). The second deals with the design of the land administration system: proximity, reactivity, transparency, the real cost—both formal and informal—of changes for farmers, etc., with the dilemma of proximity vs. cost containment. These two issues raise serious questions about the conditions where land tenure information systems are relevant and workable/sustainable.

PFRs go along with a highly decentralized system, starting at the village level, making it possible to reduce the use of a complex land administration: village committees are the ones that register and manage every change. They have a copy of the map and of the registers. Registering a rental contract or a land sale is easy and inexpensive, a necessary condition for people writing up their transactions. Only those changes that require a modification of certificates (sales, inheritance, etc.) are treated at commune or district level. The land information is managed by the commune technical services. They have the documentation for every village PFR existing in the commune. They register the changes, and issue new certificates to be signed by the commune head. Although PFRs involve new land administration bodies, these are more decentralized and less costly than the classic public land administration. There are links between them: they have to share the same maps, for example. Land certificates can be transformed into Land Titles, if the owner so requests.. Moreover, the size of the commune-level land management service can vary with the scope of the job, which correlates to the degree of land commoditization: in places where there are few transactions, the communal service will have little work for rural land management, and few agents; where plots are small and land transactions frequent, it will have more work, but also more resources through taxes on land transfers.

Administering Complex Land Rights

The question of the relevance and viability of land administration systems also raises the question of rights: taking into account bundles of rights and levels of co-management is not only an issue for surveying. It has implications for land administration procedures within the public land administration system. If the choice is made to register complex land rights, then the rules and procedures for administering these rights must be coherent with this choice.

In the classical view of lawyers and administrators, formal land rights are ownership rights. Logically, land administration is seen in terms of a public regulation. Customary regulations have neither usefulness nor a place, except for the resolution of certain conflicts, those that are not prevented by the PFR procedure (intra-familial conflicts, conflicts regarding agrarian contracts, etc.). Registration of sales and immatriculation are done on request. The role of the village land management committees is strictly technical: they are the first level of formalization and registration of contracts and changes in ownership. Thus an individual who has his name on the land certificate will be considered as the "owner", whatever the bundles of rights held on the field and recorded through the survey may be. From a legal point of view, he can act freely, cede or sell the parcel, and request its immatriculation in his or her name (table 2.3).

But, in practice, someone having a land certificate in one's own name is not always a full "owner." He may be only the trustee for his family group. Local social norms and rules within the family group (and in particular the extent of the prerogatives entrusted to the "manager") may limit the extent of his prerogatives on the plot to a greater or lesser extent. If nothing in land administration and procedures prevents it, someone who is a "manager" of a family estate will be legally authorized to sell a plot he does not own and that he does not have the right to sell in local norms.

Table 2.3. "Customary Ownership" vs. "Bundles of Rights" in PFRs: Implications for Land Management Procedures

Managing "customary" private ownership	Managing bundles of rights
Once the certificates have been issued, land management is independent of social norms and done through a public technical system. • Village land management committees have, above all, a technical role. • Certificates do not have to take into account the nature of rights. • Each parcel is the subject of a certificate that can be freely sold, registered, etc. • The head of the family acts *de facto* as the owner. Rights are transferred by sale, rental, share-cropping, in function of the autonomous decision of the "owner"..	Even with land certificates, land management falls within local norms which define what can legitimately be done or not (land rights are still partly embedded in local norms). • Village committees have a technical and legal role. • The nature of rights and their distribution must be explicit, either in the certificate, or in the survey procès-verbal, which acts as a reference for this. • Decisions concerning the land estate (sales, inheritance, modification of rights, etc.) are made by the family group. • In particular, sale and registration can only take place if the local norms authorize them, they are compatible with the rights identified, and on the explicit decision of the group of rights holders who mandate their representative to undertake the procedure.

Source: Author.

This will lead to new manipulations and conflicts, as the other family right holders will legitimately contest the sale. If there is a gap between a socio-anthropological approach for survey and registration, and a classical ownership-based land administration, it will create new gaps and space for manipulation and exclusion.

If the PFR approach really aims to acknowledge the rights *as they are*, it is indeed this set of prerogatives and restrictions that the procedure must identify and acknowledge, and that the certificate has to document. First of all, a certificate on a family estate must be issued in the name of the family group (even if it has no legal status) and not the trustee. Secondly, in areas where the right to sell is held by the family council, no sales should be able to take place without the explicit agreement of this council, who has to mandate its representative to act in its name for a sale. The village committee should verify this before agreeing to record a sale. Similarly, for immatriculation or collateral procedures, only plots that truly fall under private property (by being cleared, bought, or received as gifts by the owner) should be able to undergo these procedures directly. For other parcels, a prior procedure with claimants (family authorities or children) validating the transfer of rights should be a prerequisite and a condition (an agreement of rights holders, the creation of a land interest association with the family group as legal body, a subdivision isolating part of the land estate as individual ownership, etc). The legal procedures for managing land certificates should take into account the nature of the rights recorded, and what they authorize or forbid.

When land registration has been made in terms of bundles of rights, it is not difficult to build sound procedures. In this concept, the state offers legal acknowledgement of individual or family land estates, respecting existing prerogatives. The local norms and family groups' internal rules remain in place as long as they are legitimate for the stakeholders. A shift towards individualization, immatriculation, and sales is possible but must be accepted by the rights holders and local land management bodies bear responsibility in this. Hence, they play a role in explicating and changing norms, and not only the management of residual conflicts.[13]

They verify the legitimacy of the changes in land rights that they are asked to formalize and record in regard to both local norms and the content of the certificates. The logic here is one of lasting coordination between local and public regulations, given that, at this pace, changes can tend toward greater formalization, partial individualization, etc. We see that there are two concepts of land administration with PFRs. In both cases, the integration of a new legal status extends the range of legal options (land certificates) and offers legal acknowledgement of farmers' land estates. However, in the first concept, it is a matter of "normalizing" the diversity of rights to produce private, individual, or collective ownership that is subject to public management, with the risk of producing exclusion and conflicts at the same time. In the second concept, it is a matter of formalizing land estates to protect them from third parties, clarify land transactions, while leaving room for local and changing local land regulations. The first concept aims at transforming local land rights through certification to absorb them in a framework of private ownership and bureaucratic regulation. While the "customary ownership" PFR approach fits better to local land rights that classical land registration processes based on immatriculation, it bears the same issues and problems in terms of economical and social impacts and in terms of efficiency and sustainability.[14] The second concept acknowledges the diversity, legitimacy, and efficiency of "customary" rights and seeks to build a sound and affordable public land administration with dynamic articulations between customary and bureaucratic land regulations allowing for a progressive incorporation of local rights along economic and social changes. It provides a broad framework that tries to answer to issues that are different from one region to another.

These two approaches start from the same premise. However, they have different implications in terms of land survey processes and in terms of land administration procedures. While the issue of the complexity of rights has been dealt with in the Beninese case, the issue of land administration does not seem to be clearly raised, at the risk of discrepancies between the rights recorded during the survey and the procedures for land administration. There is a strategic and political choice that does not seem to be addressed at the moment.[15]

Conclusion

This analysis sheds some important light on the debate over the "legal empowerment of the poor" and the economic and social impact of land rights registration. Beyond the principle of legal acknowledgement of local rights, beyond the important debate on the economic justification of registration, which calls for a careful assessment of the opportunity of land registration programs, two fundamental questions are at play and the responses to them determine to a great extent the social and economic results of the process.

The first question is that of the nature of the land rights in question. Do we take the ambition of formalizing populations' rights *as they exist* seriously, even where they are embedded in social norms and networks? If so, there is a first political choice on the approach: do we recognize norms, institutions, and/or concrete rights?[16] Then, if the choice is on registering family or individual land rights, we then need to develop adequate conceptual frameworks and methodologies. Where land is above all a family or lineage heritage, where different uses are superimposed, this can demand detailed in-depth prior socio-anthropological work, to avoid bias and the exclusion effects brought about by inadequate approaches. Moreover, there are places where rights are contested, not clearly established, and with frequent conflicts, and where PFR type approaches are not relevant. Ethnography of land rights gives tools to design sound surveys methodologies, aiming at a sound simplification of rights through registration.

The second question lies in how to incorporate these local rights and arrangements in the formal framework and in land management procedures. Do we accept this diversity of rights and the existence of social regulations, in a logic of articulation between land regulation modes, and count on time to make them converge? Or do we provide a single model of ownership and make people adapt to this model, even if it does not fit local rights, and at the risk of creating new gaps between statutory law and local rights, room for opportunist behaviors, and new conflicts and exclusions? While the first option is more complex to understand and to design, there are strong arguments in favor of it.

However, these two questions are linked and ultimately refer to:

- An analysis of economic opportunities and the social stake of registration: is the "extra-legal" nature of rights really the primary economic constraint for agricultural development, before prices and control of commodity chains? One could wonder if this is really the case in numerous rural zones in developing countries. Are there real problems of insecurity? Is full citizenship for people a real issue? Could providing a sound framework for formalizing and registering transactions over land, without systematic maps, be a more efficient approach, at least where market is not the main mode of access to land?

- Even more of a political decision: about the degree of autonomy left to local societies, about the pace of convergence and national integration, about the economic opportunities offered to poor populations. Clearly, choices in land policies are never only technical and methodological choices. Historically, focusing on immatriculation and Land Titles has led to the exclusion of the majority of the population from access to formal rights and to the rule of law. There are now strong incentives to overcome this colonial legacy and give people an opportunity of formalizing their land rights. This is a great change. But focusing on only "ownership" means cutting social links between individuals. There are good reasons to fear that it will not work and/or lead to new exclusion. Far from being an outdated tradition, the logic of family groups' land rights has an obvious economic logic: it aims to preserve access to land and to subsistence for descendants. It allows preserving their "chances for life" (Jacob 2005). Whenever outside job opportunities are not very evident, the social cost of individualization and privatization should not be understated.

All in-depth field research shows that, in most of rural Africa, the social embeddedness of land rights is a long-term reality, even through social and economic changes (Chauveau et al. 2006). Processes of commoditization are partial and change the balance between individual rights and collective regulations without fully destroying the previous ones (Lavigne Delville 2006a). In places with complex land rights, there are few reasons for imposing a dramatic transformation of rights during registration. One can wonder whether the right strategy should not be to acknowledge the complex reality, and design land registration processes and land administration frameworks which fit with that reality, while using procedures which allow for evolutions, commoditization, and individualization, if wanted by people, at their own pace.

Dealing with complexity is not only a technical and methodological issue. It is much more a political one, or even a polity one, which has to do with the society's very conception of property rights, its will and ability to broaden the set of statutory rights beyond private ownership and Land Titles, and doing so, broaden its will and ability to renegotiate the relations between individuals, social groups and the state in order to build a new social contract and allow for a full integration of rural populations in the nation.

Clearly the answers to these questions are a national political choice which has to be discussed and weighed. A condition for that is that the questions are clearly raised and put on the agenda. Often, the questions relating to the nature of the rights to be recorded seem to have been little identified and taken into account by the experts and policy makers. Or, more exactly, field agents with real practice are aware of the problems but do not have the conceptual tools to solve them, and policy designers often do not identify the problems, because they are not dealt with in policy narratives, or the policy designers do not want to deal with the problems as it would challenge the overall vision of "modernization" vs. "tradition" they bear.

Such decisions are fundamentally society choices, and cannot be made by experts alone. Are these policy choices—and how they are embodied in rules and procedures—not fundamentally a matter for in-depth public debate within the populations themselves and their organizations, and between them and policy makers?

2.2:   Designing and Establishing a Land Administration System for Rwanda: Technical and Economic Analysis

DIDIER SAGASHYA, National Land Centre, Rwanda
CLIVE ENGLISH, HTSPE Ltd, United Kingdom

Summary

Since 2004, the Government of Rwanda (GoR) has been designing and establishing a new Land Administration System, which includes the development of a land policy and a coherent regulatory and institutional framework. This paper gives an overview and a technical and economic analysis of the process, particularly with respect to the Land Tenure Regularization (LTR) element and, based on experiences gained in four trial areas, recommendations for a nationwide roll-out of LTR.

Figure 2.3. General Maps of Rwanda showing District Boundaries

Note: For baseline statistics see tables 2.4 and 2.5.

Introduction

Rwanda is a small country with a gross area of 25,300 km² and a net usable area, excluding lakes and national parks, of 20,635 km². With a total population of 9.9 million, this gives an average population density of 479 people/km², one of the highest in Africa. Limited land area and a rapidly growing population have resulted in almost all areas of land in the country outside of the conserved areas and national parks being cultivated.

The country is divided into 30 districts, three of which make up Kigali City. Districts are divided into sectors and thence to cells. Within the cells, villages (*Imidugudu*) are the smallest unit. There are 416 sectors and 2,146 cells nationwide (see figure 2.3).

The land, though highly productive in many areas, has become fragmented into small holdings numbering some eight million nationwide. The national average land parcel size is 0.35 ha but this varies with population density; in the high density population areas in the West and North-West, average parcel sizes are around 0.17 ha, while in the less densely populated areas in the East, the average parcel size is 0.77 ha.[17] Households usually hold more than one parcel in different locations and grow a variety of crops; the average total land holding (the sum of all parcels held) is 2 ha and may be larger if land is held in different areas of the country scattered over five or six land parcels.[18]

Rapid population growth and successive waves of social unrest, culminating in the 1994 genocide, have weakened traditional land allocation systems. Tenure insecurity has been further compounded by increasing scarcity and marketization of land and, in urban and some rural areas, rapid development driven by a State-led land expropriation process. The latter has gained momentum in urban areas in recent years, driven by a need to provide land for investment.

In the immediate post-war period and following the 1994 genocide, the State was able to easily expropriate individually-occupied land to expand and provide settlement areas, and was only required to compensate for improvements on the land (immoveable property) against a list of gazetted values for buildings and crops. Using these provisions, the Government was able to resettle many internally displaced persons and returnees. Kigali City, in particular, continued to use the expropriation methods applied in the post-war period to acquire land for investments and a modern building program. This usually resulted in land being expropriated in what was considered to be prime sites, displacing informal settlements and individuals on land that had been allocated by the government in the post-war period or land that they had inherited.

Before 2005, land belonged to the State, and citizens only had rights to improvements made on the land. None of the land was formally registered, and rights to land other than those to immoveable property were not formally recognized for occupants. For expropriation, a list of occupants was prepared and compensation provided only for immoveable property. No replacement land was provided, leaving insufficient funds for displaced families to purchase alternative land on the informal land market. No dwellings for displaced persons were provided. This system, against a background of rapidly developing urban areas in Rwanda, resulted in considerable insecurity of tenure.

In rural areas, land is expropriated for land-sharing schemes by resettlement of returnees and the "villagization" (*Imidugudu*) program. Land boundaries are being re-drawn and land expropriated for the purposes of reallocation of land and construction of village settlements. Implementation of radical terracing is also resulting in loss of land and re-orientation of field boundaries for individual land holders. No compensation scheme exists at present for these rural programs, and much of the wider rural population has no banking facilities to handle transactions.

All of these issues continued to generate tenure insecurity. Existing systems of land administration and planning under the old laws were deemed insufficient to meet these challenges. Moreover, the old colonial laws left a legacy of inequality between urban and rural land and a system of land administration that was outdated.

Responding to this situation, in June 2004 the Government approved a new National Land Policy and, following a period of public consultation, in September 2005 passed the *Organic Law N° 08/2005 of 14/07/2005 Determining the Use and Management of Land in Rwanda*, referred to as the Organic Land Law (OLL). This law, aimed at improving tenure security through land registration, facilitates the development of an equitable land market in Rwanda and promotes the sustainable use of land.

After enactment of the OLL, individual and state rights to land were recognized and clarified. The State had specific rights over certain categories of land (State Land in the Private Domain and State Land in the Public Domain) while rights over 'individual land'—whether acquired through custom, gift, sharing, or purchase—were upheld (*Article 11*). The requirement to register all land in Rwanda (*Article 30*) would also require all transactions between individuals and the State in expropriation to be legally registered.

The final version of the Expropriation Law was not published in the Official Gazette until April, 2007. In comparison with the laws governing expropriation (compulsory acquisition) in several developing and some developed countries, this law provided for transparency of the expropriation process and safeguards to landowners against arbitrary and unfair treatment. The Law is consistent with the fundamental right to property guaranteed by Article 29 of the Constitution of the Republic of Rwanda, which provides that the right to property may not be interfered with except in the public interest, subject to fair and prior compensation.

Given the pace of development in Rwanda, the government considered it of prime importance that first the OLL and then the Expropriation Law be effectively implemented on the ground. Research, field consultations, and trials were completed in four areas of the country between 2006 and 2007 to develop a strategy for implementation of the OLL and to test its framework and procedures. This was to provide the necessary details to enable the development of a time-bound and cost effective strategy for implementation of the law, including the design of transparent land use planning and land administration systems and procedures that will enable the country to meet its visions and objectives as set out in Vision 2020 and the Economic Development and Poverty Reduction Strategy (EDPRS).

This paper presents an overview of these developments in the context of the evolution of national formal systems of land administration in Rwanda and a review of some of the challenges ahead for effective and sustainable land reform in Rwanda.

Land in Post-Colonial and Post-Genocide Rwanda

All land not held under written law was nationalized in 1976.[19] This included the majority (as much as 98 percent) of land previously held under customary law; only the small percentage allocated to colonialists and other foreigners under written law (embodied in the Civil Code) prior to Independence was classified as being privately owned, with formal title. Written law was applied mainly to some urban areas, with rural areas regarded as being principally under State management and ownership.

This situation prevailed until 1994. A combination of rapid development, natural population increase, and acceptance of a large number of returnees put increasing pressure on the government to develop land policies, plans, and laws to improve the legislation and provide the effective means for its implementation. Increasingly intensive use and fragmentation leading to greater competition for land required more formal systems be applied to the whole country, rather than the more limited approach that had prevailed under the civil code.

The Emerging Legal Framework

The Organic Land Law

In 2003, the government started a long process of consultation on land tenure, which revealed broad support for land tenure reform. The *Organic Land Law of 2005 (OLL)* anticipated wide-ranging and radical reforms in land administration and planning in order to eliminate the division between informal (customary) rights and formal (private) titles to establish one unified legal and administrative tenure system. This represented a major shift in land legislation and administration in Rwanda from the Civil Code and provided the basis for the current reforms. Key strategic principles of the law are:

- A clear recognition of rights and obligations of both the State and the individual to land. This means that landowners now have rights beyond the exploitation and use of the land but also an obligation to use it well and sustainably.
- A nationwide land registration and titling system accessible to all citizens. Previously open to only a few mainly urban-based land holders, registration will now be extended to all land holders.
- A system for land planning and development control.

The government's first objective with the introduction of the OLL was to eliminate the residual division between urban and rural, customary and formal land allocations created by the civil code so that all Rwandans could hold land under one unified legal and administrative tenure system defined by the OLL and its associated orders and laws.

The OLL aimed to do this by requiring nationwide land registration, converting existing land title instruments, and formalizing customary rights to establish two types of private land tenure instruments,[20] namely:

- Long-term, renewable leases of between 15 and 99 years, depending on the type and use of land, which will remain under grant from the State;[21] and
- Absolute title or full ownership of land, with criteria for allocation still undergoing clarification.

Where land documents and proof of ownership are required immediately, there are provisions for the issuance of interim land certificates.

The State, at national, district, town, and municipal levels, will continue to directly own and manage land in the public domain[22] and in the private domain.[23]

The starting point is the establishment of a national transparent, accessible land registration and titling system combined with a system for land planning and development control. These changes represent a major shift in land legislation and administration in Rwanda and provide the basis for the current reforms.

At the time of its enactment, the OLL was only an enabling legal framework for land tenure reform, requiring other legal and administrative instruments for implementation. There was substantial drafting required both of secondary orders (decrees) and tertiary regulations. Over 20 orders (ministerial and presidential) were required, including detailed orders relating to the leasing and registration of land. The details of these and associated regulations still had to be developed through field research and analysis of existing conditions. Meanwhile, with no formal interim arrangements in place following the enactment of the OLL for completing these tasks, existing land administration and recording systems as used under the Civil Code were temporarily retained and gradually phased out as the main decrees required under the Organic Land Law were drafted and enacted.

The existing legal and administrative documents (letters, forms, contracts and concessions) based on 1940s legislation were all presented in French. These needed to be comprehensively reviewed and revised in terms of the new land law and translated into Kinyarwanda and English, Rwanda's other official languages. For the tertiary regulations that apply to systems and procedures, the language that described them also needed to be simple, succinct, and clear with minimal scope for ambiguity or interpretation. Given relatively low literacy rates[24] and lack of access to written media throughout the country, the passing of the OLL was announced in national media, with particular use made of radio in order to reach as wide an audience as possible. The different orders published subsequent to the OLL set out a series of tasks to be undertaken in the short-term, namely:

- Clarifying the *detailed* status of rights and obligations in land for all citizens and the State;
- Finalizing orders establishing new title instruments and confirming the status of old title instruments;
- Finalizing orders and operational procedures establishing the land registration system in all its aspects;
- Agreeing on principles, guidelines and procedures for first registration of all land holders, including simple guidelines for households to register land;
- Finalizing operational procedures for Land Tenure Regularization;
- Reviewing orders and laws establishing the key governance institutions and their mandates.

Given the short time frame, sequencing was important. Administrative strategies, procedures and systems development, for example, were not entirely dependent on legislative development and did not require legal specialists, leaving scope for development over time based on best practice and field testing.

Careful analysis has provided estimates of the number of land parcels per district, sector, and cell. It is estimated that the country would have to regularize up to 7.9 million land parcels nationwide.

The Expropriations Law

Before the passing of the OLL in September 2005, most land belonged to the State and citizens only had rights to improvements made on the land. During the post-war period up to September 2005, the State was easily able to expropriate individually occupied land. The State only had to compensate for improvements on the land. Using these provisions, after 1994 the government was able to resettle many internally displaced persons and returnees. After 1994, Kigali City, in particular, continued to use the methods applied in the post-war period to expropriate land for investments and a modern building program. This usually resulted in land being expropriated in what was considered to be prime sites, displacing informal settlements and individuals on land that had been allocated by the government in the post-war period, inherited, or acquired by individual purchase on the informal market.

The OLL recognized and clarified individual and state rights to land. Following on from this, the government approved an Expropriations Law[25] in 2007 to govern compulsory land acquisition, which continued to take place for housing development and investment projects. The Expropriation Law requires that any expropriation compensation should take into account payments for the land at the market price in addition to fixed assets on the property. This implies a legal requirement for land transactions, including those undertaken as part of the expropriation process (i.e. transfers between land owners/occupants and the State), to be formally registered with the Office of the Registrar of Land Titles.

There have been an increasing number of complaints arising from the implementation of the expropriations law, and the procedures and practices being followed have come under greater scrutiny. Just as advice is now being developed and made available to the public on land tenure regularization and registration, there is a legal requirement to provide similar advice to persons to be expropriated on rights and obligations under *both* the OLL and expropriation law.

In the context of the OLL and the proposed land registration program for all land in Rwanda, it must be assumed that all occupants of land with a valid claim of right that can be proven through documentation and/or community attestation have full rights to compensation for their land, in addition to immoveable property. This key principle will be incorporated into the overall ongoing process of land registration. Procedures for clarifying and confirming rights in land have been put in place under the *Article 30* of the OLL, detailed in the *Ministerial Order Determining the Modalities of Land registration Order N° 002/2008.*

These positive developments in the legal framework will be realized in the implementation of the overall land registration process by the authorities at local and central level in the land tenure regularization process that commenced in 2009.

The Land Governance Institutions

Land tenure reform is part of Rwanda's wider program of public sector reform and decentralization. Within that framework, the OLL sets out the structure for the governance of land management in terms of the following institutions, moving from national to local level (see figure 2.4):

Figure 2.4. Land Management Organization

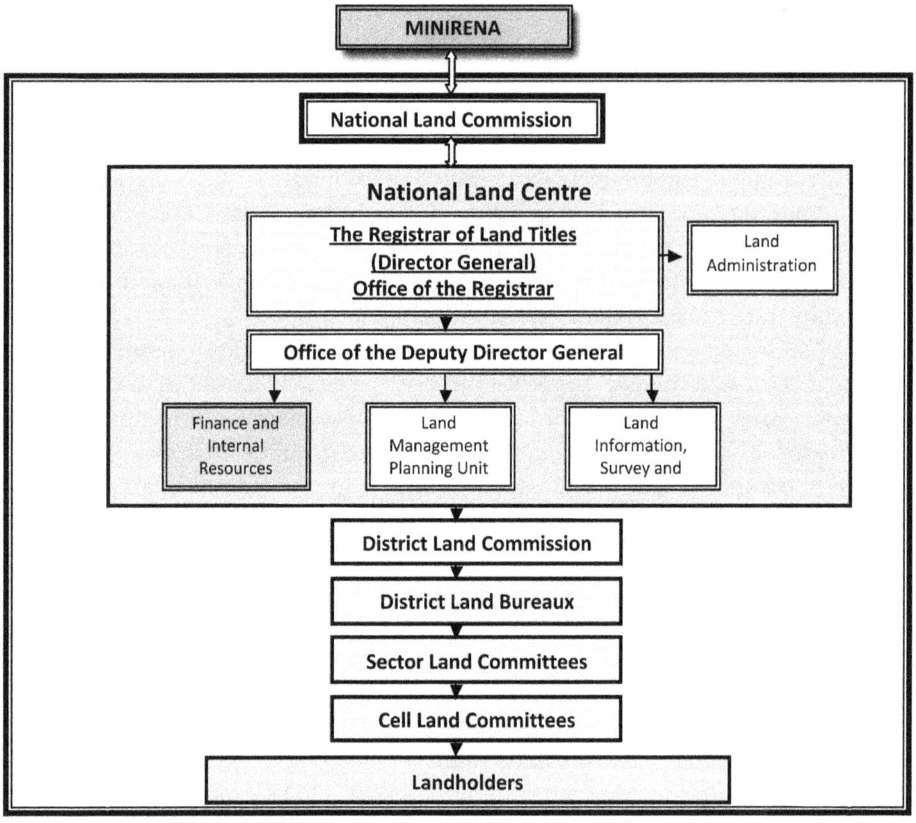

Source: Authors.

- Ministry level: the Ministry of Natural Resources (MINIRENA) has principal responsibility for land and addressing issues of policy, in particular through Ministerial orders and/or orders that set out laws and procedures for the administration, planning, and allocation of land.
- Land Commissions: a new institution, established by Presidential Order at National and District Levels, which bears the principal responsibility for overseeing the implementation of the OLL. The National Land Commission is to be responsible for the strategic direction of the National Land Centre (NLC), answerable and accountable to the Commission, which will act as the Centre's Board of Directors or Governors. The National Land Commission is also responsible for overseeing the District land commissions and bureaus and promoting, by advocacy and consultation, ownership of land policy by the public.
- National Land Centre (NLC): a new institution described under a separate law that makes provision for key land-related functions of spatial planning, surveying, and land administration within a single institution under a single

management framework. Although the NLC is a technical agency, its primary function is to support the delivery of land management services; its proposed mission statement is *"to effectively and efficiently administer lands for the benefit of all Rwandese citizens and national development"*. The NLC is therefore the central implementing agency for Land Reform.

▨ Office of the Registrar of Land Titles: the OLL prescribes the establishment, by Presidential Order, of a "registrar of land titles" housed within the NLC. He/she is supported by five deputy zonal registrars covering each of the four provinces of Rwanda and Kigali City.

▨ District Land Bureaus: the OLL establishes District Land Bureaus (DLB), to be directed by a District Land Officer (DLO), as the focus of land use planning and administration at the district level. The DLBs answer administratively to the District Council and are the public notary for land, i.e. the DLO will certify applications for land and land transactions, maintain the cadastral index maps, and record all land to be registered by sporadic or systematic means on behalf of the Office of the Registrar. The DLO will be authorized to issue leases and prepare records for certificate of registration.

▨ Sub-district organizations: the sectors and the cells will have an important part to play as the first point of contact for land registration and land use planning. Thus, there are sector and cell land committees within all sectors and cells.

Since the passing of the OLL and the local government law in 2006, MINIRENA has put a major effort into the preparation of laws, orders, and regulations needed to implement this new institutional structure. Although these are now largely complete, many have advanced ahead of the legislation that set out the key procedures and functional mandates for land administration and planning for each of the governance institutions. However, the legal vacuum has subsequently been filled by secondary and tertiary legislation.

In addition, a *'Land Tenure Regularization (LTR) Support Team'* is to be established in the NLC to support the Office of Registrar and District Land Bureaus in setting basic standards and regulations for first registration and implementing these through field programs. The LTR Support Team functions are to be both administrative and technical as related to registration processes and procedures on the ground. The intention is for the LTR Support Team to consolidate all District LTR plans into a National LTR plan and support and monitor its implementation.

The LTR support team will also have overall responsibility for training for LTR in the field and assisting implementing institutions such as the DLB and Sector and Cell Land Committees on processes and procedures. The LTR Support Team will be responsible directly to the Registrar and his/her deputies. Plans, priority areas, and targets will be established through the District Land Bureaux, the District Land Commissions, the Mayors, and the District Council (figure 2.4).

Bringing the Laws into Effect—Researching the Issues

All of the above initiatives—the Land Policy, the OLL and related decrees and regulations, and the proposed institutional framework—were framed by the desire to provide tenure security to all Rwandans. To better understand how these laws would be implemented and to help shape the legislation and design, three interrelated tasks needed to be undertaken:

- Field consultations (2006)
- Field trials of tenure regularization (2007-08)
- Field trial evaluation and baseline studies (2008)

Field Consultations

Field consultations were carried out with district and sector authorities and members of the public with the objective of understanding local land tenure practices and issues, devising a feasible consultative and participatory approach to the registration of landholdings, and ensuring that the drafting of decrees and design of the strategy was based on reliable, systematically collected data.

Tenure issues investigated included: means of access to land, the functioning of the informal land market, state expropriations, inheritance, land fragmentation, consolidation and parcel size, boundary demarcation methods, current formal and informal documentation practices, the nature and number of land disputes, and the overall status and strength of local land tenure practices. Over 2,500 people were consulted in rural, urban, and peri-urban settings in one district in each of four provinces (West, North, East, and Kigali City)[26] through focus group[27] discussion with members of the public and structured interviews with local authorities and other local and national stakeholders.

Focus group discussions were conducted in a structured manner incorporating subgroups within: local officials, land users (including: tea, coffee and, pyrethrum commercial food farmers—large and small scale, livestock farmers, urban commercial and residential users, developers and the Church) and sociological groups (including: women's groups, orphans, genocide survivors). Local and international NGOs and Civil Society organizations were also consulted. The majority consulted saw the Government and statutory law, and not 'custom', as the best guarantor of tenure security. However, awareness and understanding of the OLL was low with regard to the nature and legal status of existing land rights. It was also clear that reconciliation of currently existing real and perceived rights with the new arrangements would have to be undertaken through a formal process of regularization based at the local level. Other salient findings are as follows:

- All land users are increasingly reliant on, and demanding, written proof of land ownership to increase tenure security—this may be formally issued by local Sector offices or informally issued through agreement between buyer and seller.
- Increasing land scarcity and population pressure is reducing the availability of land for young people to inherit. At the same time, it encourages the continued growth of the land market in Rwanda, involving sales and rentals of small parcels of land. In most cases, land sales are informally documented, whereas rentals are largely verbally agreed.
- Rights over land are perceived to have improved since the *OLL*, making it easier to buy and sell land legally. However, there is a strong demand for

statutory regulations on sales, to make registering proof of sales and ownership mandatory.

▩ The growth of land sales involving small parcels of land and the continuing importance of land inheritance—traditionally involving subdivision—suggests that land fragmentation is a continuing trend in Rwanda. Small farmers may own several plots, but may sell, buy, or rent them in any one year according to their immediate requirement for staple or cash crops and to reduce risk. The government is concerned that this pattern of land use and fragmentation is inefficient and leaves households with land parcels that are too small to support them. Though evidence does not support this, the OLL seeks to reduce land fragmentation by restricting further subdivision of land of one hectare or less.

▩ It is likely that when effective local registration and titling becomes established the practice of holding multiple land parcels will become more accepted.

▩ The main causes/types of land disputes are inheritance, boundary encroachment, polygamy, and land transactions, with the majority being within extended families. Other, lesser causes of disputes include past land sharing problems and trespassing of livestock on neighbors' land. However, most land disputes that have come before the new sector authorities have been easily resolved.

▩ Those consulted expressed confidence that clarifying rights through tenure regularization leading to land registration and titling will reduce and resolve the majority of land-related disputes in the longer-term, through 'once and for all' recognition of the owners of each and every parcel of land.

Two common strands emerging from these consultations were that land users require clarification of rights and a more formal system through new laws implemented through the State, but that one of the principal causes of tenure insecurity is land planning and State interventions through expropriation, particularly in urban areas. Until the passing of the Expropriation Law, the State was not required to compensate for loss of land, nor was the right of occupancy of those on the land fully recognized. Development plans were drawn up and those displaced were obliged to seek alternative land without the means to pay for it. In addition, expropriation procedures and practices were not being uniformly and consistently applied. This created the conundrum of the State being both the guarantor of rights and a source of insecurity.

The question remains whether the implementation of statutory law and consequent introduction of written title through the regularization of land tenure would alleviate some or all of these concerns. Although there is evidence from similar experiences in Sub-Saharan African countries to suggest that the implementation of statutory law does not necessarily increase tenure security, what emerged from field consultations in Rwanda was that the context and experience may be different. Many local authorities were already establishing *ad hoc* 'registration systems' to meet demand whilst most citizens continued to participate in a thriving and expanding market in land. The development of the secondary legislation and the regulations took into account the best of these systems, which were incorporated into formal drafts of procedures.

Recent history, land pressures and the increasing commercialization and accelerating expropriation of land by the State suggest that the time for change is already overdue. For example, land users considered that a one-off clarification of rights and obligations through tenure regularization would address the very specific problems faced on the land and allow for new titles to be issued. Existing rights under formal law and customary law would be upheld as given in the OLL.

Field Trials of Land Tenure Regularization

The results of consultations provided direction to the field trials. Subject to detailed design and approval through stakeholder consultations discussed above, the systematic clarification of rights and obligations through a program of tenure regularization was the preferred method. Regularization of tenure nationwide would be used to test laws, procedures, and methods for formal, systematic land registration using low-tech, local level methods based on active public participation. Broad principles and detailed methodologies for what has become known as Land Tenure Regularization (LTR) were prepared with regard to field approaches and procedures.

Land Tenure Regularization (LTR) is a set of administrative procedures undertaken for the purpose of recognizing and securing existing rights that people and organizations other than the State have to, in, or over different categories of land; in the case of Rwanda, this includes Individual Land, State Private Land and Private District, and City of Kigali Land. The principle is that a decentralized, transparent, and participatory process of completing LTR would also raise awareness of the law, clarify the situation on the ground, and resolve specific issues. LTR is designed to clarify the rights of the existing owners and occupants of land and, where necessary and desirable, to convert those rights into a legally recognized form that will allow people to legally transact their interests in land and use their titles for mortgaging and credit purposes.

In practice, LTR is a set of procedures that systematically brings land owners to first registration of their land. It requires all land owners in a designated LTR area to participate. There are nine related procedures that have to be followed:

1. Notification of areas for an LTR Program;
2. Local information dissemination-public meetings and awareness raising;
3. Appointment and training of Land Committees (responsible for adjudication and recording claimant detail) and para-surveyors(locally trained photo-interpreters from the villages responsible for marking boundaries on an image);
4. Demarcation of land, marking of boundaries on a photographic image;
5. Adjudication: recording of personal details, issuing a claims receipt, recording objections and corrections simultaneously with demarcation;
6. Publication of adjudication record and compilation of a parcel index map;
7. Objections and corrections period - finalizing the record and disputant lists;
8. Mediation period for disputes; and
9. Registration and titling—preparation and issuance of title documents.

The first six steps are administrative in nature but require a set of transparent procedures using simple documentation and boundary demarcation methods. The remaining three procedures are legal, requiring the results from the other six steps to be completed first, and culminating in formal registration and titling.

Field trials of these procedures took place covering more than 3,500 households in over 14,900 land parcels in the four districts used previously, commencing in March 2007 and concluding in December 2007. The four districts in the trial areas reflect some of the social, economic, and geographic diversity across Rwanda, and this diversity has implications for the implementation of land tenure reform.

Demarcation and adjudication and (if possible) registration was undertaken transparently at the lowest administrative level, 'the cell', with maximum public participation, working systematically through each village (*umudugudu*) in the cell, parcel by parcel. Local Adjudication Committees oversaw the examination of evidence of claims, adjudication, and demarcation that would lead to final registration and titling. This system relies on community attestation and recording, and allows sufficient time for clarification, objection and, where necessary, correction of records.

Low-tech methods were used based on 'general boundaries' principles, incorporating existing accepted parcel boundaries on the ground, which are mostly clearly demarcated by walls, fences, and vegetation, using simple methods of boundary demarcation marked on aerial photography and/or satellite imagery. Boundaries were therefore incorporated as 'social' rather than 'technical' boundaries. The majority of land holders consulted seemed to be generally accepting of what are largely 'general boundaries' principles based on their own existing demarcation methods, and wished to continue using natural boundaries wherever possible. Ownership information was recorded for each parcel and the parcel boundaries recorded on a satellite image. All of the work was undertaken by the community with para-surveyors at village level. Disputes over land were recorded separately for subsequent resolution by village committees (mediators commonly known as "*Abunzi*") or other resolution mechanisms. All of the data was captured in a database for analysis and final registration and titling. Summary procedures are shown in figure 2.5.

In addition to testing procedures and systems for LTR, the field trials were also designed to:

- Quantifiably support and develop the findings of the preparatory field consultations to guide policy and development of the new land administration system.
- Inform the preparation and design of the Strategy for implementation of the National Land Tenure Reform Program.
- Provide a baseline for detailing formal land law in Rwanda with regard to secondary legislation and tertiary regulations.
- Inform the preparation and design of locally based land administration and planning procedures.
- Inform the design and development of local institutions dealing with land and requirements for capacity building.

Figure 2.5. Summary LTR Procedures

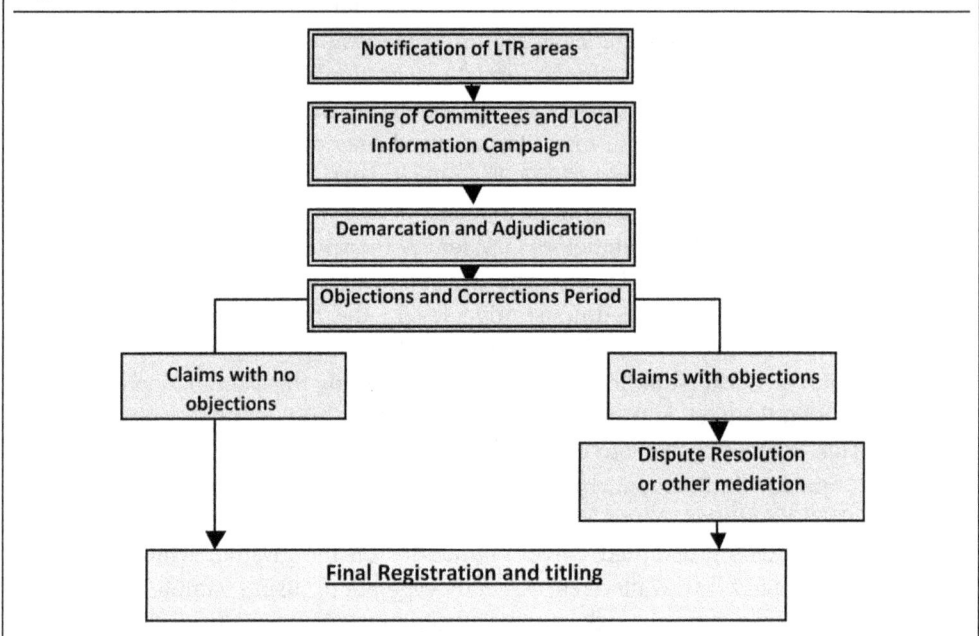

Source: Authors.

Supplementary information was collected regarding the type and number of informal land transfers that had been undertaken in recent years as well as information on persons dependent on, or with an interest in, the land being claimed. In addition to standard information collected for adjudication record (names, ID card numbers, etc.), supplementary data was also collected related *inter alia* to land use, sales, and rental, all of which would be used to ensure that any system of recording and/or registration that would be introduced would not hinder local production and business.

Lastly, the process of completing LTR would also raise awareness of the law and the need to clarify the situation on the ground and resolve specific issues.

Field Trial Evaluation and Baseline Studies

Once the LTR trials were completed, results were used to analyze all aspects of how the land was owned, perceived to be owned, and used to determine how best to apply the OLL with regard to registration and titling. Comprehensive analyses were completed on 15,000 parcels including area, land use, land sales and inheritance, gender balances in ownership claims, and other issues relating to how households used land. Analysis of land disputes was also undertaken.

In addition, a quantitative survey in and around the four trial areas and control locations was designed and implemented to provide impact assessment information on reactions to the field trial intervention activities, and measuring the perceived effectiveness of the communication approach employed during the trials. The survey collected baseline data on a variety of issues important to understanding land reform (factual and attitudinal), as well as impact assessment data associated with the process so far.

Findings suggest that the higher the level of involvement in meetings and activities around land tenure reform, the higher the level of awareness of the process of land tenure reform (figures 2.6 and 2.7).

Overall, the overwhelming majority of respondents in both trial area and control cells had positive attitudes about land tenure reform (see figure 2.8), and felt that it could yield positive impacts, improving transparency and tenure security, easing land transactions, and reducing corruption and the risk of dispossession for widows and orphans.

Figure 2.6. Awareness of Land Reform Program Trial Cells

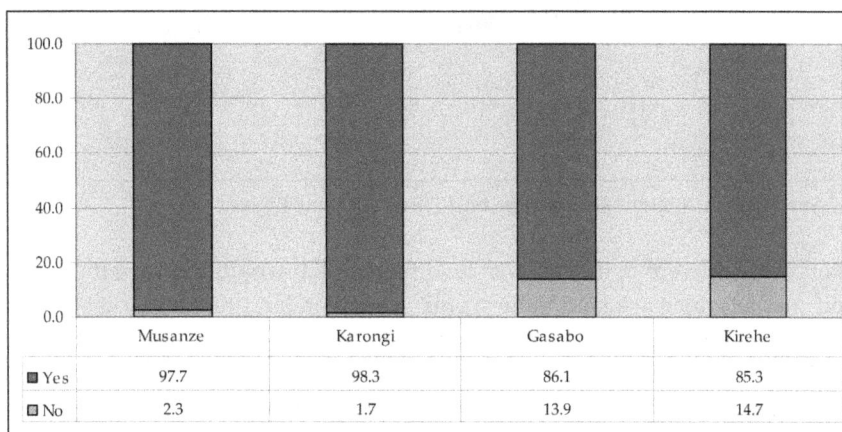

	Musanze	Karongi	Gasabo	Kirehe
Yes	97.7	98.3	86.1	85.3
No	2.3	1.7	13.9	14.7

Source: Annex VII the *Strategic Road Map for Land Tenure Reform in Rwanda.*

Figure 2.7. Participation in Public Meetings

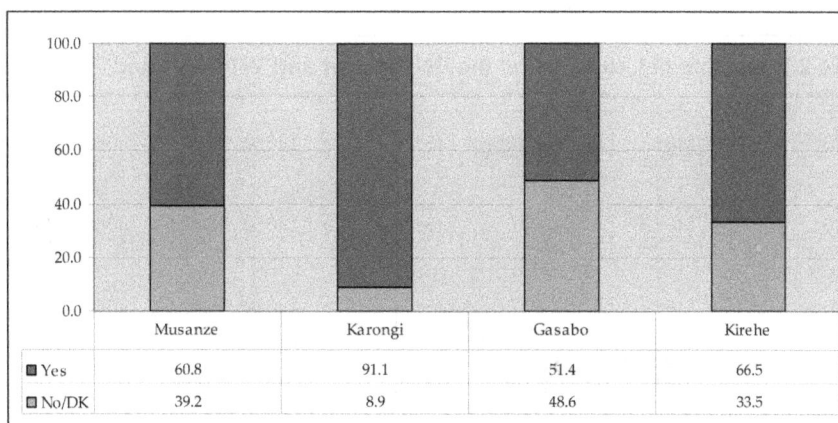

	Musanze	Karongi	Gasabo	Kirehe
Yes	60.8	91.1	51.4	66.5
No/DK	39.2	8.9	48.6	33.5

Source: Annex VII the *Strategic Road Map for Land Tenure Reform in Rwanda.*

Figure 2.8. Attitudinal Scale Statement: "Overall, the land registration process will make us more secure in our landholdings"

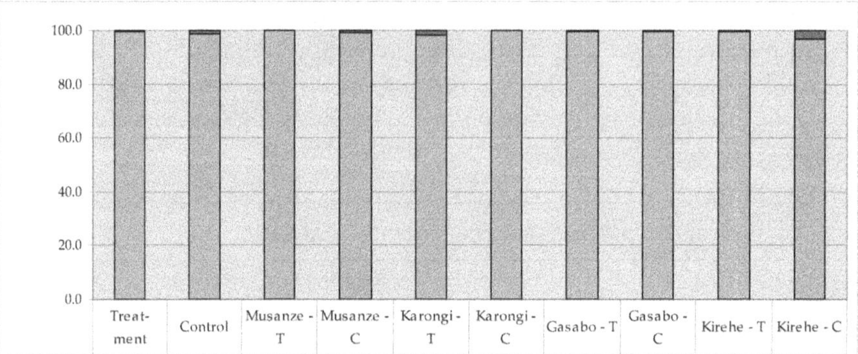

	Treat-ment	Control	Musanze - T	Musanze - C	Karongi - T	Karongi - C	Gasabo - T	Gasabo - C	Kirehe - T	Kirehe - C
Disagree	0.5	1.3	0.0	1.1	1.8	0.0	0.6	0.6	0.6	3.0
Agree	99.5	98.7	100.0	98.9	98.2	100.0	99.4	99.4	99.4	97.0

Source: Annex VII the *Strategic Road Map for Land Tenure Reform in Rwanda.*

Respondents were optimistic that land registration would improve the functioning of land markets, increase land values, and strengthen land rental markets (see figures 2.9 and 2.10). However, many had doubts about the costs associated with land registration (e.g. possible taxes or transaction fees), and the socio-economic consequences of these costs compared to the possible benefits of improved land markets. There were particular concerns about the possible marginalization of poorer households due to land tenure reform, particularly in urban areas as a result of the urban planning processes and widespread expropriation of land. For the rural poor, problems of access to land administration services are an important issue in some of the more remote areas.

Figure 2.9. Impacts of Land Title on the Demand for and Value of Land

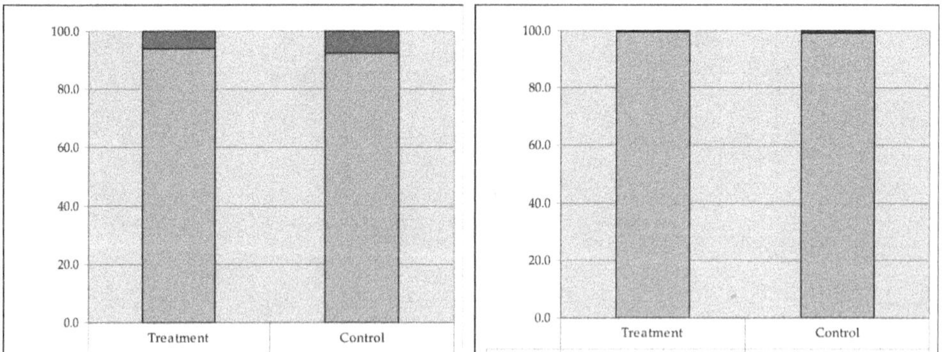

	Treatment	Control
Negative	5.9	7.7
Positive	94.1	92.3

	Treatment	Control
Negative	0.2	0.8
Positive	99.8	99.2

Source: Annex VII the *Strategic Road Map for Land Tenure Reform in Rwanda.*

Figure 2.10: Attitudinal Scale Statement: "With land title, households in this area would be more likely to rent out plots of land"

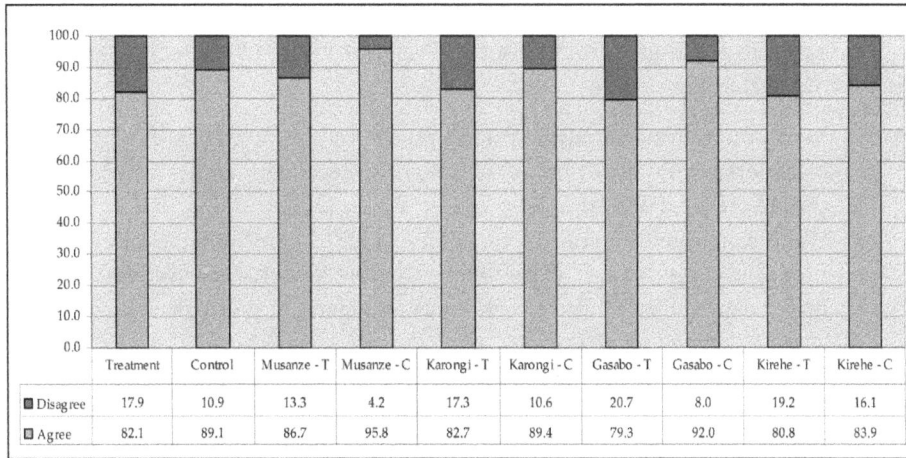

	Treatment	Control	Musanze - T	Musanze - C	Karongi - T	Karongi - C	Gasabo - T	Gasabo - C	Kirehe - T	Kirehe - C
■ Disagree	17.9	10.9	13.3	4.2	17.3	10.6	20.7	8.0	19.2	16.1
□ Agree	82.1	89.1	86.7	95.8	82.7	89.4	79.3	92.0	80.8	83.9

Source: Annex VII the *Strategic Road Map for Land Tenure Reform in Rwanda.*

There are also particular concerns that the uneven roll-out of land tenure reform may mean in-migration to locations where the reform has improved land values. Another concern is that high transaction costs might be an obstacle to selling land as a coping mechanism in times of need. This, coupled with prohibitions against selling subdivided parcels of less than one hectare, may mean there is a risk that poor households may adopt other potentially damaging coping strategies (such as high interest loans).

Although there is some optimism that the land tenure reform process will improve land values and land management, there are some uncertainties about how the process will be managed. These uncertainties include such things as the transparency of the process and institutions, the accessibility of key personnel involved in the process, and possible additional financial burdens on households.

While disputes are not especially common,[28] respondents did not feel that disputes would decline following land registration. However, evidence from the survey suggests that a number of households used the registration process (listing of claimants and persons of interest) to secure a desired inheritance outcome (upon death) and avoid future conflicts within the family.

Respondents were concerned about the possibility of unfair expropriation, especially in urban Gasabo District, and in Kirehe District in the East. This is in recognition of the current dysfunction between expropriation procedures, the expropriation law, and the laws that govern land registration whereby expropriation of unregistered land is leading to non-payment for land or payment below market rates. However, respondents felt that land registration would, in the future, help ensure that fair compensation would be provided for any expropriated land.

Finally, it should be underlined that a number of findings suggest that the land tenure reform process may have varied impacts on single and married women and men. Married couples are required to jointly claim and register land. Women living alone, but who may be in polygamous arrangements, have been able to make claims to register land they occupy even if the husband no longer resides with them or lives with his main wife. Rights of inheritance for children under these arrangements are covered by the Succession Law.

The recommendations for a nationwide roll-out of the LTR process that emerged from the field trials are clear:

- Monitoring and evaluation of land tenure reform activities should be used to consider potentially differential impacts, and land tenure reform activities should respond accordingly.
- Significant attention needs to be devoted to improving awareness of the procedural provisions of the expropriation law that protect people against unfair expropriation, and processes of engagement with affected communities should be developed.
- To the extent possible, the involvement of civil society organizations in the land tenure reform process will enable improved implementation of expropriation law, and should therefore be included in the land tenure reform process.
- Community participation in the process will also need to be treated as an opportunity to assess the performance of personnel involved in land tenure reform.
- More attention will need to be given to the potential for future conflict that may arise from the land tenure reform process and efforts should be made to clarify the rights, rules, and procedures around land tenure reform for beneficiary communities. There is also a need to strengthen dispute resolution systems, increasing training and extension of personnel involved in the process. There is a particular need to ensure that the right of inheritance by females and minors is clear to the community at large but most critically to those involved in dispute resolution.

Developing the Strategy for Reform

Strategy, correctly formulated, shapes both the details required for implementation and the correct sequencing and programming of the reforms. The strategy for reforming Rwanda's land legislation and administration, the so-called Strategic Road Map (SRM), details requirements in six interrelated elements that will be needed to bring the OLL into effect:

- Further development and refinement of policy and legislation: this includes the drafting/refinement of priority orders, regulations, and operational manuals central to implementing the National Land Policy and the OLL.
- A framework for the development of a land administration system for Rwanda: with provision for land administration services, specifically registration of all land in Rwanda.
- A one-off investment program for regularization of land tenure: to systematically bring land to first registration, clarify rights and obligations in land and to allow all citizens equal access to the new systems.

▪ Development of land management organizations: principally the establishment of a National Land Center and Office of the Registrar under a separate law, the District Land Bureaus, Land Commissions at District and National Levels, and land committees at Sector and Cell levels.
▪ A national framework for monitoring and evaluation of the reforms
▪ A national system and program for land planning and development control: to ensure rational use of land and effective development as well as environmental protection.

After the preparatory phase, which terminated in 2008, full implementation is envisaged for the period 2009–2013. The central component of the program is implementation of field LTR for first registration, which will be the driver of the reform process in other components. However, the resources required for its implementation, the manner in which this will be undertaken, and the proposed timeline is, at the time of writing, still under discussion.

The Economic Case for Reform

The strategy for reform was subject to analysis of the wider costs, benefits, and economic justification of the reforms to the national economy. At the same time, detailed cost estimates were made for the 'one-off' investment in land tenure regularization and the longer-term investment in the institutions of land management. These three strands are still, at the time of writing, under review and discussion.

Because of the dearth of data from actual registration and land titling programs and projects, quantifying the long-term benefits remains problematic. In terms of their characteristics and benefits, rural and urban land titling should be treated separately in an economic analysis.

General Benefits of Land Registration and Titling

Although it is not possible to provide accurate quantitative data on the expected benefits of land registration and titling, a brief qualitative review of existing documents and discussion with stakeholders in Rwanda strongly suggests there will be sufficient positive economic impacts resulting from the titling and registration of land to justify the costs. However, the extent of these impacts will greatly depend on the implementation and enforcement of the new legislative framework as well as reforms in other sectors.

Based on the information obtained, it appears that land registration and titling is one of the key reforms required to eliminate existing constraints on credit access and increasing investment, enabling increased levels of agricultural production in rural areas and general economic activity in urban areas, and to improve labor mobility and the efficiency of land markets.[29] The evidence suggests that larger businesses and middle-to-high income earners will almost certainly benefit from the reforms, providing the necessary benefit to cover the economic costs (and possibly earn a significant positive margin).

The economic analysis presented here takes no account of the substantial socio-political benefits of regularizing tenure in a rapidly developing situation such as that of

Rwanda. Such political benefits, which cannot be easily quantified, will be hugely important (Adams and Palmer 2007).

Quantifying the Costs and Benefits

Given the difficulties in quantifying the benefits of land registration and titling, it was agreed that the economic study would consist of:

■ Cost-effectiveness analysis: the calculation of overall project cost (in present values) per unit (hectare or parcel);[30] and

■ Break-even economic analysis: the calculation of the increase in the net value of economic output (gross output minus non-labor costs of production) required to justify the project.[31]

A sensitivity analysis was also conducted in order to demonstrate how the break-even value of production/income changes when project costs over-run or the benefits are reduced.

Cost-effectiveness Analysis

Unit capital costs for rural titling are estimated to be US$35 to $41/ha (RwF 19,075–22,345/ha)[32] and US$9 to $11 (RwF 4,905–5,995) per parcel/title. After the main rural land titling work has been completed in the first five years of the program, the recurrent costs of the subsequent rural land administration activities are estimated to be just over US$2.50/ha (RwF 1,635/ha) and just under US$1 (RwF 545) per parcel.

The unit capital cost for urban titling is approximately US$9 to $10 (RwF 4,905–5,450) per parcel and US$150 to $200/ha (RwF 81,750–109,000/ha). This is due to the greater population density and smaller parcel size in urban areas. After Year 5 of first registration and titling the subsequent recurrent costs are estimated to be less than US$1 per parcel (RwF 545) and US$14/ha (RwF 7,630/ha). Rural people in the trial areas have indicated they are willing to pay up to US$4 transaction costs and up to 2 percent on the values of the land. Values vary considerably within rural and urban areas.

With the scarcity of data on titling costs in other developing countries, it is difficult to draw clear conclusions as to the cost-effectiveness of Rwanda's reform program. However, the unit costs do not, at this stage, seem to be excessive. In fact, these appear to be at a level that could be covered by reasonable fee payments (discussed in the final section). The key factor is how they compare to the potential benefits.

Break-even Economic Analysis

In broad terms, the analysis showed that rural land titling would need to increase agricultural production by between about 1 percent and 2 percent per annum to be economically justified, depending on whether benefits are valued on the basis of value added or net production value.

Value added was taken as a more valid basis for the calculation of benefits at a sector-wide level.[33] Using this measure, the required rates of annual increase in the value of agricultural production would be 1.3 percent if field registration took two years and 1.75 percent if field registration took five years. If costs turned out to be 25 percent greater than predicted, the required rate of increase in the value of agricultural production would be 0.4 percent to 0.5 percent higher.

Achievement of an increase of 1 to 2 percent should be attainable, through the channel of easing access to credit and enabling greater levels of investment, making the rural land registration and titling program economically justifiable. The analysis does not consider the financial and fiscal aspects of the land titling program because it was deliberately confined to economic aspects alone.

Based on the estimates made, the recurrent costs incurred in running the rural land registration system after its implementation (i.e., after 2013) will be substantial, at RwF 3.56 billion (US$6.53 million) per annum. For the program to succeed, the required funding would need to be made available, either through user charges or Government subvention or a combination of the two.

The results for urban land registration and titling are even more encouraging. A very small increase in economic activity of between 0.03 percent and 0.04 percent—as represented by an increase in the level of urban land prices—will justify the costs of urban titling. Furthermore, if land reform results in a 1 percent increase in urban land values (or economic output) then the resulting benefits from urban registration and titling will exceed the *total* cost of land titling (in rural as well as urban areas).

The results are not significantly different under a five-year registration period, suggesting that prolonging land regularization fieldwork would not make the program economically unviable. Indeed, a 1 percent increase in urban land prices would still cover the total costs of land reform.

In the event that the share of urban costs as a proportion of the total was higher than assumed (i.e., more than 5 percent of the total costs), this still makes very little difference to the overall results. If costs unexpectedly overran and were 25 percent greater than predicted, the required rate of increase in urban land prices would be just less than 0.01 percent higher. With recorded informal land prices increasing by as much as 25 percent between 2006 and 2007 in some areas, this estimate is more than exceeded.

Due to the lower number of parcels and smaller area involved, total annual recurrent costs of urban land registration and titling are much lower than in rural areas—RwF 188 million or just under US$345,000—and appear to be sustainable. Furthermore, just as a 1 percent increase in urban output would justify the costs of the whole land reform program, revenue sources that are raised through maintaining the registry in urban areas could be used to "subsidize" the costs in rural areas.

Ensuring the Realization of Benefits

While the accumulation of capital, wealth, and increased investment on the part of higher earners that land reform may facilitate is an important pre-requisite for economic growth, extending these benefits to smaller enterprises and low income earners will require solutions to other problems both within and outside the main financial services through provision of micro-finance. In the context of land reform, it is also important that individuals are not made worse off by the economic impacts.

It is crucial that the laws governing the procedures for expropriation and compensation are fully operational before the land tenure reform implementation program commences. Aside from preventing a Pareto improvement (a re-allocation of resources that makes at least one individual better off without making any other individual worse off), below-market compensation rates, and unregulated expropriation procedures also mean that informal settlements—which should be the main beneficiaries of secure tenure—will continue to grow, at a cost to the national economy.

The baseline survey in the field trials addressed key issues relating to land registration and titling before issuance (but after completion of the LTR from adjudication and demarcation to the claims receipt stage). Subsequent analyses, post-titling, would require data to be collected on current household levels of investment and credit access at fixed periods of time. In this regard, other socio-economic surveys collecting data on the above would be of value to the reform program, as would a mini-survey under the program itself (50-100 households).

To meet these requirements, a framework for monitoring and evaluation has been assembled for inclusion in the strategy. This framework document (Annex VIII Strategic Road Map for Land Reform MINIRENA/DFID/HTSPE August 2008), aimed at 'setting the direction', provides a broad overview of all of the economic, social, environmental and governance parameters that might be measured, accompanied by key measurable indicator clusters under each of these headings.

Information routinely recorded in the land registries conventionally measures and monitors the progress of land registration and titling in terms of the number and type of land transactions, sales, and investment in land. Improvements in systems and procedures will ensure key parameters can be recorded and monitored in real time.

Implementation: Ongoing Challenges, 2009

As discussed earlier, the OLL launched the process of clarifying land tenure and enhancing secure access to land, with LTR identified as a fundamental first step. On a pilot basis, the LTR exercise has been well received at the local and national levels, with perceived benefits in terms of improved land sales, rental markets, and land values. In the meantime, concerns were raised about the costs associated with the registration process and its impact on poorer households.

While the pilot LTR scheme has been carried out successfully, challenges remain in replicating the pilot process on a national scale and in implementing the range of reforms envisaged in the OLL.

Understanding the Issues

The State and its representatives at all levels will need to understand the laws with regard to land issues to ensure they are implemented equitably in all areas, and will need to be fully aware of the consequences and implications for the way they must operate. The public will also have to be fully educated in the new laws and procedures. Until now, there has been general acceptance of the LTR procedures but the details of the possible legal implications have yet to be presented to the public. This will require a carefully structured media campaign and provision of local information provided through a variety of media to both public, District, Sector, and Cell authorities.

Acceptance of the Proposed Changes

Adherence to old procedures in land administration is continuing in the absence of more detailed guidelines from central government on the new procedures. At the present time, some of the Mayors have not recognized the provisions in the new laws and regulations, and continue to apply *ad hoc* procedures, in some cases infringing on the rights of land holders. Implementation of LTR and registration, plus a growing number of challenges from households being displaced, will make it increasingly more difficult for the old practices to continue.

This is leading to inconsistent approaches, bad practices, and confusion in some areas. To reduce risks and adverse impacts of *ad hoc* approaches, the development and dissemination of new procedures is required urgently, backed by strong political support and a program to raise public awareness.

The State itself, at central and local government levels, will have to accept and promote the OLL as enacted by Parliament and abide by the provisions in the orders and regulations. This will need to be consistent with the application of the expropriation law. The State will need to be seen to fully underwrite the process as well as applying the principles to State-owned land. Lastly, there is also a clear need to clarify powers and mandates within and between ministries and agencies with regard to land acquisition, repossession, land allocation and, more importantly, the powers of expropriation.

Capacity Constraints

The National Land Policy and OLL set out the institutional and human resource requirements at the district level, which are modest by international standards but represent a quantum increase for Rwanda's public service in relation to existing resources. Needs center on capacity building and training (formal and informal) of some 100 land professionals for district land bureaus. While the recurrent costs are affordable, maintaining the required levels of staffing will require effective management of income from land-related revenues. Models related to the anticipated levels of service, and hence revenues to offset recurrent costs, have been drawn up for all districts.

Fees, Rates, and Taxes

While some mechanism must be put in place to cover the costs of first registration and the recurrent costs of land administration in order to ensure the system's sustainability, the approach adopted must be considered carefully, taking into account several concerns:

- If rates are set too high, or the procedure for collection too cumbersome, avoidance by landholders will maintain or expand the informal land market, undermining the basis for future revenue collection.
- Any attempt to tailor rates to affordability via means testing or tying first registration fees to the size of parcels is not practicable in first registration where the size of parcels is not known.
- It is important that registration is perceived as a clarification of rights and obligations rather than as a tax collection exercise in order to win public confidence and help to institutionalize the system more effectively.

In response to these concerns, and to ensure that the government obtains an up-to-date land register at the earliest opportunity with the potential for revenue collection further down the line, the principle of free first registration for all has been advanced.

It is suggested that taxes, stamp duties, etc. could come later through development of a fiscal cadastre.

Planning and Development

Economic development, and how this is managed by the state and local authorities with regard to both the acquisition and allocation of land, is currently seen as the single most pressing problem facing the planned land reform process. The rapid pace of development, particularly in Kigali City, and implementation of planning agendas has, to date, proceeded without recourse to registration laws and principles which are seen by planners as a costly drag on development initiatives.

If due process, administration of land rights, and implementation of legal and regulatory procedures are not followed adequately, a loss of public confidence will result. The government is now moving to greatly improve public understanding through field LTR and improved and accessible procedures and services for land.

Pace of Change

While it is important to maintain the momentum of the nationwide LTR exercise, moving too quickly with LTR may mean that the full consequences and outcomes cannot be fully evaluated through effective monitoring and evaluation. The full legal implications and consequences for the national economy, and individuals and households in particular, will require further research and monitoring to ensure *inter alia* adequate social protection.

In addition, if field LTR is implemented too quickly, there is a risk that it will outpace developments in policy and legal procedures and institutional capacity, resulting in compromises in registration procedures and legal outcomes that will adversely affect the outcome for individuals. Changes in procedures and documentation will need to keep pace with developments on the ground.

Vision and Leadership

As the principal implementing agency, the NLC, backed by the Ministry, must provide strong vision and leadership for the reform. Within the NLC, the Registrar and Deputy Registrars are key, and should, as apolitical leaders charged with administering affairs of land, be free from interference. There is a risk that reforms could stall if this leadership and guidance under the laws and regulations is not recognized and allowed to develop.

Table 2.4. Constituency Summary, Population by Districts Sectors and Cells—2007 and 2020

	East		North		West		South		Kigali City		National	
Province	2007	2020	2007	2020	2007	2020	2007	2020	2007	2020	2007	2020
No districts	7	7	5	5	7	7	8	8	3	3	30	30
Av population/ district	277,158	401,810	353,410	498,539	329,325	463,641	288,892	369,251	329,020	662,488	367,894	410,708
Av households/ district	61,591	89,291	78,536	110,787	73,183	103,031	64,198	82,056	73,115	147,219	81,754	91,269
No sectors	95	95	89	89	96	96	101	101	35	35	416	416
Av no sectors/ district	14	14	18	18	14	14	13	13	12	12	14	14
Av population/ sector	20,453	29,703	19,956	28,080	24,190	33,897	23,517	30,009	28,370	57,388	26,464	30,568
Av households/ sector	4,545	6,601	4,435	6,240	5,376	7,533	5,226	6,669	6,304	12,753	5,881	6,793
No cells	502	502	413	413	538	538	532	532	161	161	2,146	2,146
Av no cells/ sector	5	5	5	5	6	6	5	5	5	5	5	5
Av population/ cell	4,026	5,864	4,378	6,132	4,332	6,043	4,447	5,640	6,242	12,604	5,234	6,187
Av households/ cell	895	1,303	973	1,363	963	1,343	988	1,253	1,387	2,801	1,163	1,375
No imidugudu	3,808	3,808	2,742	2,742	3,629	3,629	3,512	3,512	1,185	1,185	14,876	14,876
Av no imidugudu/ cell	8	8	7	7	7	7	7	7	7	7	7	7
Av population/ imidugudu	516	753	651	919	638	893	691	879	835	1,686	753	883
Av households/ imidugudu	115	167	145	204	142	199	154	195	186	375	167	196

Source: Authors.

Table 2.5. Average Number of Land Parcels by District, Sector, and Cell

Province	East	North	West	South	Kigali City	National
No. districts	7	5	7	8	3	30
No. parcels/district	215,567	388,899	512,283	410,868	65,804	318,684
No. sectors	95	89	96	101	35	416
Av no. sectors/district	14	18	14	13	12	14
Av no. parcels/sector	11,229	22,904	27,236	20,904	9,457	18,346
No. cells	502	413	538	532	161	2,146
Av. no. cells/sector	5	5	6	5	5	5
Av. no. parcels/cell	2,286	4,967	4,895	4,016	2,353	3,703
No. villages	3,808	2,742	3,629	3,512	1,185	14,876
Av. no. villages /cell	8	7	7	7	7	7
Av. no. parcels/ villages	286	710	699	574	336	521

Source: Authors.

2.3:   Land Registration Using Aerial Photography in Namibia: Costs and Lessons

DONATHA KAPITANGO, Communal Land Board, Oshikoto Region, Government of Namibia
MARCEL MEIJS, German Development Service, Namibia

Summary

Since 2003, the Ministry of Lands and Resettlement, together with the Communal Land Boards, have administered communal land in Namibia. In this context, new methods using aerial photos have been devised to fast track the process of land registration. By these means the registration process is now proceeding eight times faster, is more accurate, is less prone to mistakes, and is more cost effective. The Namibian Communal Land Administration System (NCLAS) has been concurrently developed to provide an improved means of storing data on communal land rights. The NCLAS is more secure, better accessible, and reduces administration time by half.

Introduction

Access to land is one of the most pressing social and economic issues in Namibia (Malan 2003). It is a concern not only because of the unequal distribution of freehold or commercial land between the people, but also because of growing pressures on the communal land. Uncertainties surrounding land holding on communal land have arisen due to the inability of legally recognized authorities to act in terms of their mandates. There is a need to recognize that everyone is equal before the law in matters of access to communal land. The National Land Policy (1998) states that clear steps need to be taken to remove uncertainties about legitimate access and rights to communal land. The directives given in the National Land Policy have been enacted in the Communal Land Reform Act (CLRA), which is the legislation underpinning access to communal land. If the Act was to provide practical support to communal land users, recording their land rights was recognized as a key outcome. Since 2003, the Ministry of Lands and Resettlement (MLR), together with the Communal Land Boards (CLB), has been given the task to register land rights on communal land. By the beginning of 2008 it was concluded that, although progress had been made, there was a need to hasten the land registration program. In 2008 MLR, together with its supporting organizations, the European Commission (EC) and the German Government through its implementation structures, the German Development Service (DED), German Technical Cooperation (GTZ) and German Development Bank (KfW), commenced activities that are aiming to register all communal land rights before the end of 2012. This paper describes the new methods applied to hasten land registration and presents the way forward envisioned by the Ministry.

The Republic of Namibia gained independence from South Africa on 21 March 1990. It is situated in Southern Africa and is fully covered by desert, semi-desert, and savanna. It has a population of 2.1 million on a total surface of 825,418 km^2. General population density is low (second lowest in the world), with a countrywide population density of 2.5 persons per km². The density of the rural population is highest in the north due to a more favorable agricultural climate and due to past colonial and apartheid interference. It is estimated that 50 percent of Namibia's population lives in the rural parts of the communal lands in the north.

The climate in the northern regions allows for the cultivation of crops such as millet, sorghum, and maize. Most of the country is used for cattle, small livestock, or game farming or is unsuitable for any agricultural activities. About half of the population depends on agriculture (largely subsistence agriculture) for its livelihood.

Namibia's economy consists primarily of mining (diamond and uranium), agriculture, and Tourism. In terms of revenue, mining is the biggest contributor to Namibia's economy, accounting for 25 percent of the country's income. Namibia's economy is tied closely to that of South Africa, which is the source of four-fifths of Namibia's imports.

In Namibia, land is classified for administrative purposes as *state land*, *commercial land*, or *communal land* (Malan 2003). Each of these categories bestows certain rights and responsibilities on the people who are using the land. Both urban and rural land may fall within any of these categories. Figure 2.11 shows the distribution of the different categories:

State land is land that belongs to the State. Under the Constitution, all land, water, and natural resources belong to the State, unless lawfully owned by individuals. The State can decide to allow people to reside on a particular piece of state land, or permit them to rent it out, whilst still remaining the owner of the land. As the owner of the land, the State can also decide what to do with the land, whether to convert it to communal land or to sell it so that it becomes commercial land. Much state land is classified as Protected Areas and named as National Parks, Game Parks, Recreation Areas, Restricted Areas, etc. The boundaries of state land are surveyed and registered within the National Deeds Registry and Cadastral systems.

Commercial land is freehold land that can be bought by private individuals, who then become the owners of the land. Under the colonial government, commercial land allocations were made on racial lines, with the result that there are long-standing grievances with regard to these lands. The Agricultural (Commercial) Land Reform Act of 1995 was enacted to address some of these issues. In particular, this Act gives the State the first option to buy land when an owner wants to sell commercial farm land. While protecting the right of every person to own property in Namibia, the Constitution allows the State to expropriate property according to lawful procedures, if it is in the public interest and if just compensation is paid to the person whose property is expropriated. The Act allows the State to expropriate commercial land where an owner owns a disproportionately large amount, or it has been abandoned or under-utilized for some time. The State has only rarely exercised its right to expropriate commercial farmland. All commercial land is surveyed and transactions are registered within the National Deeds Registry and Cadastral systems.

Figure 2.11. Map of State, Communal, and Commercial Areas in Namibia

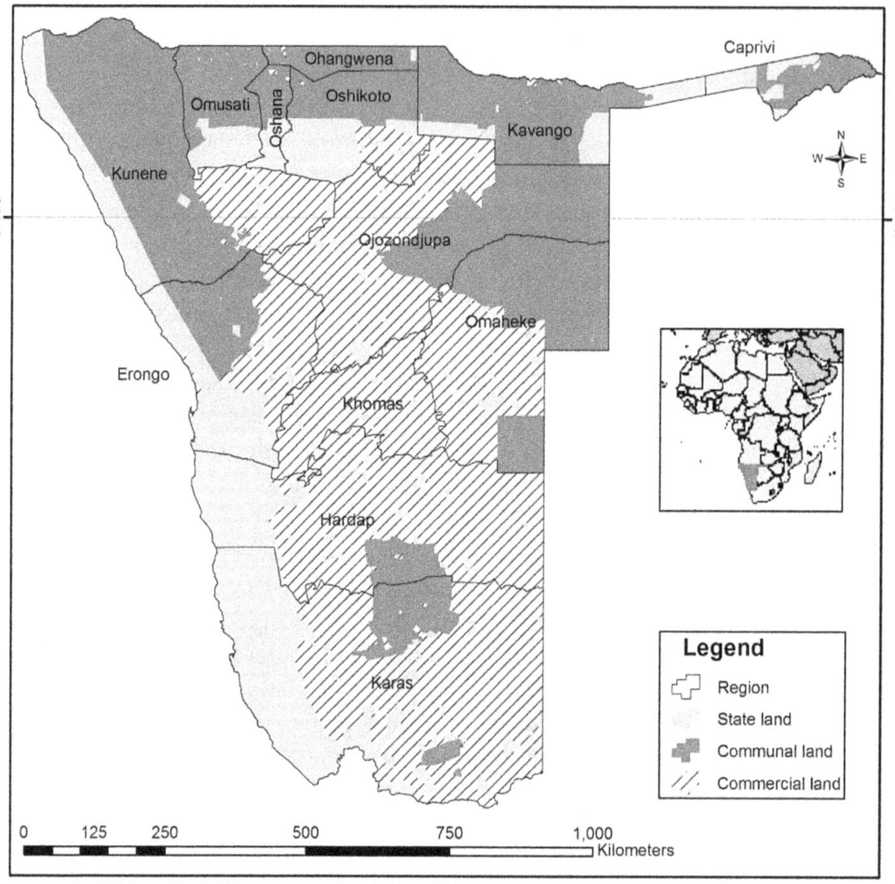

Source: MLR, M. Meijs, 2008.

Communal land is vested in the State by the Constitution. The State has a duty to administer communal lands in trust for the benefit of the communities residing on these lands and for the purpose of promoting the economic and social development of the Namibian people. Communal land cannot be bought or sold, but can be leased out. It can also be transferred to a new owner who then has to pay compensation to the previous owner for the improvements on that land (Malan 2003).

Communal Land Reform

Legal instruments and policies such as the Communal Land Reform Act No 5 of 2002 (CLRA), Traditional Authority Act of 2000, and the National Land Policy empower statutory bodies to administer and allocate land rights on communal land. The State must put systems in place to ensure that communal land is correctly administered and managed. The CLRA legislates this by incorporating the Traditional Authorities in the administrative structure, and by creating CLBs.

Two broad categories of land rights are stipulated in the CLRA, namely: customary land rights and rights of leasehold. The rights that are allocated under customary land rights are rights to residential units and rights to crop farming units. Customary land rights are primarily for small scale and subsistence activities. The second category, the leaseholds, covers all the rights that can be allocated for specific commercial purposes. The rest of the land is referred to as commonage and can be used for grazing by the local community. Grazing rights can also be allocated to outsiders by the Traditional Authorities.

Before the enactment of the CRLA, Traditional Authorities used to allocate land rights in accordance with their customary tenure systems (National Land Policy 1998). These allocations were not documented and were considered biased by some residents of communal land. Results included that some people were allocated large land parcels whereas others received less; some people were allowed to fence around their land parcels, whereas others were not; and there were cases of double allocation of land rights. This biased land tenure system was characterized by many land related disputes, including boundary disputes, self-extensions and illegal fencing, and was operated in the absence of regulatory legislation.

The CLRA was passed with the aim of facilitating a proper and uniform land administration system, with a secure land tenure for all, which will result in the minimization of land disputes on communal land (Communal Land Reform Act, No 5 of 2002). This is the key reason why communal land registration is being carried out in Namibia. Moreover, by having all land rights registered and surveyed, the MLR as well as the Traditional Authorities will be able to improve their means of land administration and ensure that all people have equal access to land.

Communal Land Boards

The passing of the Act gave birth to the CLBs. The Act empowers CLBs and Traditional Authorities to administer and allocate land rights on communal land. Traditional Authorities allocate customary land rights, with CLBs verifying the allocations before they become legally effective. The allocation of leasehold rights is undertaken by the CLBs.

CLBs have been established from 2003 for all the regions that contain Communal Land. The tasks of the CLBs as stipulated by the CLRA are to:

- Control the allocation and cancellation of customary land rights by Chiefs and Traditional Authorities;
- Decide on applications for rights of leaseholds;
- Create and maintain registers for the allocation, transfer, and cancellation of customary land rights and rights of leasehold;
- Advise the minister on regulations to be made to meet the objectives of the CLRA; and
- Give effect to the provisions of the CLRA.

The CLBs are comprised of representatives of all the parties involved in communal land administration. CLBs meet every two months and can form committees to investigate certain issues. This results in CLBs holding six regular meetings a year, which is insufficient for effective land administration in most regions. The CLBs can also request the Minister to give permission to hold an extraordinary meeting, if there are matters that need urgent attention.

The CLBs make decisions on land related administrative issues in communal land. Public servants of the Ministry of Lands and Resettlement are appointed to perform specific tasks such as verifying, mapping, and administering the land rights.

Land Registration

The CLRA required that any person who held a right to communal land for subsistence farming and/or for a residential plot before the commencement of the CLRA should apply for recognition and registration of his or her customary land right before 1 March 2006. It is estimated that about 300,000 land rights will have to be registered, of which 24 percent is estimated to be allocated in the central and Southern regions, whereas 76 percent will be allocated to the Northern Regions (see table 2.6).

Table 2.6. Estimate of Communal Land Rights Allocation per Region

Northern Regions	Estimated number of Communal Land Rights	Central and Southern Regions	Estimated number of Communal Land Rights
Kunene	14,373	Erongo	1,875
Omusati	45,000	Otjozondjupa	21,875
Oshana	37,500	Omahake	43,750
Ohangwena	31,250	Khomas	0 (no communal land)
Oshikoto	21,875	Hardap	1,125
Kavango	50,000	Karas	1,375
Caprivi	25,000		
Total	**224,998**	**Total**	**70.000**
		Overall Total	**294.998 ≈ 300.000**

Source: Roadmap Registration Communal Areas 2009–2013.

The registration of communal land rights will have to be done according to a set procedure. The applicant will first have to get a letter of consent for his land right from his village headman. He then fills out an application form and submits it with the letter of consent and N\$25 (€2.5) to the Traditional Authority (TA). After the approval of the TA, the letter is forwarded to the CLB for verification and ratification.

It is estimated that on 1 March 2006, less than 15 percent of the land users had applied for registration and still fewer of the land parcels had been mapped and registered. Hence, the deadline was extended by three years to 1 March 2009. The reasons for the non-application of right holders are many, but most can be attributed to communication issues and slow processing of applications. The CLRA can only become effective if it is introduced to all people in an appropriate way. The Guide to the Communal Land Reform Act was made and the act itself was translated in local languages but these are only made available for MLR, CLBs, and TAs. In reality, very little information on the CLRA is available for the people affected by the CLRA. This absence of information led to speculations on the content of CLRA, especially in the more remote areas where information is scarce. The slow processing of the applications can only be attributed to the MLR who have opted to register in a precise but time consuming way without having the necessary capacities.

Status of Registration of Communal Land Rights in January 2008

Mapping Parcels

After a hesitant start in 2003, it was decided by MLR that communal land had to be surveyed in order for CLB to approve its registration. Although there are few legal reasons why parcels were to be surveyed, MLR saw many additional benefits of surveying all communal land, amongst which were that it:

- Provides a record of occupants on communal land;
- Enhances security of tenure over the land for these occupants and therefore reduces disputes;
- Enables land to be more readily managed sustainably and equitably;
- Reveals areas that are legally and illegally fenced;
- Supports the upgrading of communal land towards a freehold status, as may happen in the future.

The CLRA states that CLBs can only approve customary land rights up to 20 ha and right of leaseholds up to 50 ha in size. Any land right outside these limits should be approved by the Minister of Lands and Resettlement. Therefore, the extent of each parcel must be known by means of surveying the parcels as well.

It was then decided that communal land parcels would be surveyed with the use of hand-held GPS units (Garmin V), which was the fastest and most economical method available at that time. From 2003 until January 2008 a total of 1389 parcels were registered, less than 1 percent of the estimated number of parcels that need to be registered on communal land.

From the experiences in the first five years of land registration, the following main lessons were learned:

- A maximum of 10 parcels could be mapped by one team of two persons a day using hand-held GPS. Our experiences are from areas where parcels are relatively small, therefore a country wide average is more likely to be around *five* parcels per team per day. The number of parcels that can be surveyed a day is limited by the size of the plots and the accessibility. Most parcels are bigger than 10 ha, and to walk around these parcels with a GPS is a tedious job, especially under the burning Namibian sun. Additionally, most of the village headmen, who accompany the field teams, are elderly people. These headmen cannot be expected to walk around fields the whole day and therefore limit the number of plots that can be surveyed.
- A faster and less strenuous way to register parcels needed to be found, and more people needed to be employed to be able to finish the work in a realistic time frame.
- A new method should also ensure that fewer mistakes will be made. Mapping using hand-held GPS units has a number of weaknesses, including the following:
  - Waypoints can be taken before a 3D position fix is acquired by the GPS hand held unit, which decreases the absolute accuracy of the record.

- Often, too few waypoints are taken for an accurate outline of the parcel, such as when a boundary deviates from a straight line that is not visible through vegetation.
- Incorrect notes are taken in the field, resulting in confusion in the office. A common mistake is to take a waypoint for a house or other feature in the parcel. Later, if not properly recorded, this point mistakenly is used as one of the boundary points of the plot.

Registering Land Parcels

Data on parcels, owners, and land rights were not registered in an organized manner. A parcel's boundaries would be digitized with ArcView 3.2, using a separate shape file for each parcel. A map showing the boundaries of the parcel was then produced in ArcView 3.2, saved under the applicant's name, and printed on the reverse of a certificate paper. The front of the certificate was made in MS Word and printed on the opposite side of the paper. In this way an average of ten land right certificates could be produced a day. Approved certificates were given a number and were recorded in a paper-based land register book.

In this system, errors could be made but remain undetected and some valuable information from the application forms was not copied in the registry book or onto the certificates. This system provided no logical means to find data. All CLBs used a different format, making it practically impossible to incorporate the regional data into one national database.

- After evaluating the way the land and the land user's data were registered, the following lessons were learned.
- Any land registration system should enable information to be found on a specific land right (including the owner, the right, and the parcel) by as many means of entry into the system as possible. These means would include by personal identification number, by name of applicant, by parcel identifier, by village name, and by certificate number.
- Parcels must be checked for overlapping areas before they are sent for approval, as conflicts will arise in the doubly allocated areas of parcels otherwise.
- A Unique Parcel Identifier (UPI) system should be used to make sure that each parcel in Namibia is uniquely numbered.
- The digital system of communal land registration should be as similar as possible to the national Cadastre and Deeds Registry system where commercial land is registered.
- All CLBs should use the same system for registering communal land parcels. This will enable future integration of all regional databases into one National Database of land parcels
- The system should be easy to use, at least for the people who enter the data.
- A digital system should have a secure backup. There should also be a backup paper-based system that can be searched by a person's name (or company's name), by UPI, by village name, or by certificate number.

Accelerating Communal Land Registration

In summary, there were two main challenges in facilitating the communal land registration program. The first was the need to hasten the process and complete the registration of existing land rights within a reasonable timeframe. The second challenge was to safeguard the collected information in an organized and easily administered manner.

Accelerated Mapping and Field Verification

The process of field verification of land rights required improvements to enable the Ministry to finish the registration of existing land rights on communal land within a limited amount of time. Increasing the number of personnel by outsourcing the work to contractors would improve the rate of progress, as would making the mapping process easier and faster. In Namibia, a combination of both options has been tried by means of initiating outsourcing and by using aerial photography to hasten the rate of field verification.

Aerial photos and/or satellite images (Quickbird) have been used in various countries for mapping as well as for the registration of land rights (e.g. in Ethiopia (Lemmen et al. 2009), in Rwanda (Sagashya and English 2009), and in Thailand (Rattanabirabongse et al. 1998)). The main reasons to use aerial photos for the registration of land rights is because it has proven to be a relatively inexpensive and efficient method. This is particularly the case in Namibia, where good quality aerial photography is available for a large part of the country. In order to test and to compare the methods of using aerial photos with the regular method of land registration (by using hand held GPS units) under Namibian circumstances and conditions, the Olukonda Project (in Oshikoto region) was undertaken. This project provided much needed experience of using aerial photos for land registration, and gave scope for improving methods and techniques. The project was followed by three further projects that tested the speed and the costs of the new methods. Three of these projects were carried out in the north central regions; namely the Oshikuku project in Omusati Region, the Oshikango project in Ohangwena Region, and the Sibinda project in the far North East in Caprivi region.

The aerial photos were acquired for 275,000 km², covering all of Namibia north of 20⁰ south latitude (see figure 2.12). The financing of the photography was made available through the European Commission funded Rural Poverty Reduction Program (RPRP), which is supporting land reform measures across the country. The air photo coverage is of 75 percent of all communal land in the country.

The photographs were acquired between September 2007 and April 2008, and were taken from 8900 meters by a Beechcraft King Air B200 aircraft flying a digital Vexcel Ultracam X aerial survey camera with 14,330x9,420 CCD. The quality of the digital air photos in terms of visibility was extremely good, due to the favorable climatic conditions with low humidity and minimal air pollution. The nominal pixel size of the photographs was 85 cm. The photos were rectified using ground control point data obtained every 50 km across the entire survey area, which was then covered with seamless digital orthophotographs (orthophotos), in true color and near infra-red with a pixel size of one meter (see a sample in figure 2.12). All this data was provided to MLR in a digital format and was ready to be used.

Figure 2.12. Sample of an Orthophoto

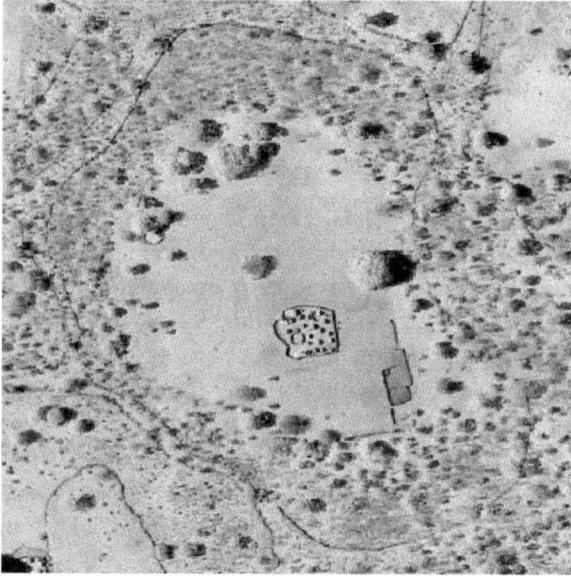

Source: RPRP, funded by the European Commission.

The intended use for these aerial photos was to update the cartographical maps for the north of the country, but their high quality and digital format has ensured their worth for many other development purposes. This includes the registration of communal land rights.

What is used from the available data are the digital orthophotos; these were printed on A1 sized photo paper at a scale of 1:5000 and used as such in the field. At the end of 2008, a tool within ArcGIS mapping software was written to export all tiles automatically to PDF to facilitate their printing and save time.

In the preparation stage of the project a comparison was made between the orthophotos and Quickbird satellite images. It was concluded that both can be used for the mapping of communal land rights. This means that for areas which are not covered by aerial photos, Quickbird images will be obtained.

Communication with the Stakeholders

The most important part of the project, and a critical factor and key to the success, was communication, organization, and planning. The key player in this respect was the team leader. All contacts between different actors and stakeholders in the project went through the team leader. This was necessary to ensure good coordination, good progress, and good results.

The communication consisted of four steps:

1. Workshop with village headmen/headwomen and stakeholders;
2. Radio messages before and during field work;
3. Visit the headman/headwoman of a village;
4. Visit all homesteads within the village with key informant.

In step 1, the goal of the registration and the way forward were explained to the village headmen and other stakeholders (representatives of CLB, Regional Council, and Traditional Authority). This was supported by radio messages in step two to ask the people for their participation, to apply for their land rights, and to cooperate during field work. The radio messages were always broadcasted in local language and in cooperation with the Traditional Authority (TA). In step 3, the village headman was visited before the start of the field work in his village. The course of the project and the planning for his village were explained and he was asked for his cooperation and to appoint key informants. Once he agreed, the people of the village were informed on the start of the project in their village and asked again for their cooperation. Again, this was done by radio messages which were coordinated with the TA. The last step was to visit every homestead with the key informant. The purpose of the registration was explained before the boundaries of the parcel were mapped.

The pilot projects were well covered by the media, which added to the success of the communication campaign. Rural Poverty Reduction Program (RPRP) created an information Folder and German Technical Cooperation (GTZ) financed a film on the Registration of Communal Land in Namibia (DVD available through GTZ). This film will be used in the upcoming registration campaign and is planned to be broadcast on national television.

The Verification of Land Rights

After the procedures and activities were explained and understood by the land users, the team started mapping the individual plots using the orthophotos, beginning with the village headman's parcel and progressing outwards until all land rights in the village were verified. A field team consisted of at least two experts. At least one should have had experience in the mapping of land rights with orthophotos and one should have spoken the local language. The field team was then joined by the appointed key informant.

Each parcel was mapped on the orthophotos following three steps:

1. First, the team wrote the names of the land right holders onto the orthophotos in such a way that they could be sure that they would not disturb the mapping of the boundary. These names were cross-checked with the names on the application forms when available.
2. Then, with the help of the key informant and the landowners, the team systematically mapped all parcels for which the boundaries could be recognized on the orthophotos (by using features such as fences, roads, footpaths, individual trees, and natural depressions). Mapping was most easily undertaken on completely fenced parcels. This could be done during a village gathering or by visiting individual land owners.
3. Finally, the team visited land parcels containing boundaries that were not clearly recognizable on the orthophotos. Frequently, by careful interpretation of the orthophotos, it was possible to identify indistinct features that were key waypoints around parcel boundaries, and to use them to complete the boundary maps. If not, then GPS points were taken where necessary.

Team members were instructed to pay special attention as they mapped boundaries on the orthophotos. The act of putting pen to paper was the moment of recording the boundaries of a land parcel, and was done with great care and the agreement of all concerned stakeholders.

Disputes

Land related disputes that could not be resolved by the field team were documented and reported to the team leader whenever they were encountered. They mostly involved conflicts over the exact boundaries of two neighboring parcels. The disputes were then investigated by the team leader, who tried to solve them in the field. The team leader reported disputes that could not be resolved to the relevant traditional authority for further action.

Advantages and Disadvantages of Using Orthophotos

Large scale orthophotos proved to be particularly suitable for the *systematic survey* and registration of customary land rights. This approach was different from the sporadic approach to survey and registration that was applied until 2008 in Namibia. In that earlier approach only the parcels of

Figure 2.13. Field Work in Action, putting the pen on the photo

Photo: R. Witmer, 2008.

people who had applied for customary land rights were verified and registered. The remaining parcels were left unmapped until applications for their registration were received. Compared to the sporadic survey method, the advantages of the systematic survey method include:

- It was more efficient and cost effective, because transport and logistical requirements were lower through the area only being traversed once.
- It was more productive, because all parcels were verified at the same time, permitting boundary issues to be resolved in the field.
- It enabled a better overview of a whole project area, and so facilitated a more thorough analysis.

One of the biggest advantages of using orthophotos is that they supported the What You See Is What You Get (*WYSIWYG*) principle. The lines demarcating parcel boundaries that were drawn on the orthophotos could be seen and agreed to by everyone present. This resulted in:

- The land registration applicants being able to check that their certificates really indicated the land parcels that they were entitled to use. The orthophotos were available to serve as a background to the survey diagram printed on the back of the certificate. This gives the land holders good overviews of their parcels relative to those of their neighbors and/or the features visible in the field.
- The village headman being able to check that no one was claiming more than their entitlements.
- The village headman being able to draft a village land use plan, indicating where new parcels could be demarcated but also ensuring that there was space for movement of cattle and people where needed. For this purpose, village maps were produced.
- The whole community being able to check that important communal resources and areas used communally, such as water ponds and trees, were not claimed by individuals and were kept outside registered parcels.

- Disputes being more readily resolved. People could identify the location of the disputed area on an orthophoto. It was also easier to determine the owners of different fields and where fences and features were located. In many cases, the disputing parties, village headman, and MLR employees could resolve the dispute with the help of the orthophotos on the spot. In fact, during the Olukonda project, all except three conflicts over boundaries were solved by a mediating process involving the two conflicting land owners. Two disputes were solved by interference from the local headman and only one dispute could not be solved in the field and is still pending TA and CLB judgment.
- Field team members from MLR making fewer mistakes in mapping the boundaries.
- Checking the size of a parcel, while in the field, with the aid of a transparent grid overlay marked with squares representing one hectare at 1:5000 scale. The number of squares covering a parcel was counted and, if the area equated to more than the maximum 20 ha permitted, the applicant could be advised on what to do. Either the size should be reduced to below 20 ha, a motivation letter sent to the minister requesting permission to retain more than 20 ha, or part of the land could be allocated to a relative.

Accuracy: The aerial photos were delivered with an accuracy report and were all reported to be within an absolute accuracy of two meters. When digitizing parcel boundaries, they are as accurate as the locations of the features used to identify these boundaries. In cases where fences were used, the accuracy was high, but when the middle of a pond was indicated, or a similar vaguely defined area, than the accuracy was lower. With a ground resolution of one meter, a final accuracy of the land register of better than 10 m could be easily manageable. Presently the orthophotos are being used to update the parcels digitized with hand-held GPS units, as it is being shown that the points surveyed with these units are sometimes not as accurate as expected. There is a study going on to compare a (professional) survey with kinematic Digital Global Positioning System (dGPS) with the survey using the orthophotos; unfortunately no results are available yet.

Speed: Previous experiences in the Omusati region have shown that with hand held GPS survey an average of 10 land rights a day can be mapped in the densely populated areas in the North. In less densely populated areas, parcels are often bigger, which means there is more time needed to walk the premises of the parcel. Parcels in those areas are also located further apart increasing traveling time in between. All in all the average number of parcels mapped a day by using GPS is estimated to be five parcels per day.

By using orthophotos, a survey of up to an average of over 40 parcels a day can be completed (see table 2.7). The Olukonda project has a low number of parcels mapped a day since this was the first project in which we had some startup problems. The Sibinda project has a lower average value because the area is less populated and the land tenure system is different and includes shifting cultivation and parcels being far from the homesteads.

Table 2.7. Number of Parcels Mapped a Day during the Four Pilot Projects

Project	Nr of parcels	Nr of field days (approximation)	Parcels per day
Olukonda project	2,137	60x2 teams 120	18
Oshikuku project	2,352	30x2 teams 60	39
Oshikango project	3,422	40x2 teams 80	43
Sibinda project	951	30x2 teams 60	16
Total	**8,862**	**320**	

Source: Authors.

The high rate of 40 parcels per day will only be achieved in the more densely populated areas; this is expected to be true for 40 percent of the land rights. A lower rate of 15 parcels per day is expected to be realistic for the rest of the country. Therefore the overall average for the whole country will be:

$$40\% * 40 \text{ (high)} + 60\% * 15 \text{ (low)} = 25.$$

It can be concluded that working with orthophotos is not only faster but also easier. This is because most parcels can be mapped while standing at their centers, from where identifying features around their boundaries can be recognized both on the ground and on the orthophotos.

Cost: A number of variables were used to calculate the likely *costs* of the whole land registration program in Namibia using orthophotos.

- 300,000 land rights are estimated as awaiting registration.
- Approximately 40,000 A1 tiles are required to be printed, at an average cost of €10 each. Forty tiles can be printed a day by a team of two if the work is carried out in-house in the Ministry of Lands and Resettlement (MLR).
- Assume that six teams each of two persons are employed by the program, and the salary on average is €50/day/person. Assume also that €50/day is required for transport for each team. The total cost of each team is then €150/day.
- We determined that for GPS survey, five and for orthophoto survey, 25 parcels per day per team are realistic averages for the entire country.
- All other costs are assumed to be the same for both survey methods.

> **Cost calculation for GPS survey:**
> 300,000 land rights / 5 parcels a day = 60,000 days * €150
> Total €9,000,000
>
> **Cost calculation for aerial photo survey**
> *Printing of orthophotos*
> 40,000 tiles * €10 + 40,000 tiles / 40 prints a day = 10,000 days * €150
> Sub Total €550,000
>
> *Field work*
> 300,000 land rights / 25 parcels a day = 12,000 days * €150
> Sub Total €1,800,000
> Total €2,350,000

From these calculations it is apparent that the cost of mapping a plot with hand held GPS units is 3.8x more expensive than mapping a plot with orthophotos.

The orthophotos were provided to MLR free of charge. Nevertheless, for planning purposes, we need to know if buying aerial photos or satellite images is still economically viable.

The complete cost for the aerial photos for the North was €1,696,000 (which includes the aerial photographing of National Parks including Etosha and the Skeleton Coast, and also significant commercial farming areas).

The communal lands not covered by the orthophotos are around 120,000 km². Quickbird images cost US$23.00 - per km², thus it will cost €2.1 million (1US$ = €0.75) to cover the remaining communal lands. If the cost for the orthophotos and the Quickbird images is added to the above costs, then the costs for an aerial photo survey will be €6,146,000 (2,350,000 + 1,696,000 + 2,100,000) which is still 32 percent cheaper than surveying with hand held GPS.

Improved Land Parcel Registration

In the beginning of 2008, it was concluded that there was a need for a comprehensive recording system for communal land rights. Such a system had to be easy to use but also able to accommodate future developments in technology and the opportunity for integration of the commercial and communal land registration systems. The system that was developed was tested during the Olukonda and Oshikuku projects and was implemented in all regions in November-December 2008. It was termed the Namibia Communal Land Administration System (NCLAS).

As shown in figure 2.14, the NCLAS consists of two parts, termed the Communal Deeds and the Communal Cadastre. The Communal Deeds part was developed to resemble the structure of the Cadastre and Deeds Registry systems covering commercial areas. It was based on Microsoft Access, since this software is readily available on most computers and since it is also the software for which expertise is the easiest to find in Namibia. The Communal Cadastre part of the system was based on ArcGIS, as this software was made available by a donor, GTZ, to all MLR offices that support CLB activities.

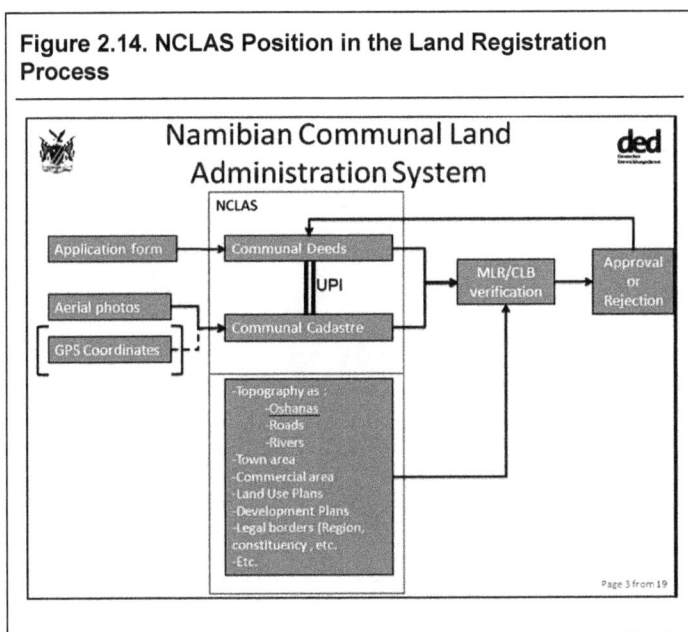

Figure 2.14. NCLAS Position in the Land Registration Process

Source: M. Meijs, 2008.

This was also the software on which MLR staff members have received training in recent years.

The two separate Deeds and Cadastre parts of the NCLAS are linked by a Unique Parcel Identifier (UPI) system. The UPI is a coding system that is being finalized to ensure that every land parcel in the country will have a unique number. This will enable the exchange of information, not only within the NCLAS but also between the NCLAS and the commercial Cadastre and Deeds Registry systems.

Four different types of output are created out of the NCLAS. These are Certificates, Village maps, Registers, and Index Cards. The certificate (see figure 2.15 for an example) describes the land right in full detail with the official description on the front and a diagram of the parcel on the back.

The village map(s) are maps at a scale of 1:10,000 and display all parcels for a particular village with the aerial photo on the background. A village map is used in the paper based backup system to provide a spatial entry into the data. The village map is also a useful tool for land management, since it is easy to see which areas are occupied and which areas are still unoccupied.

Registers are printed to provide easy access to the paper based system by UPI and village. Index cards provide access through the individual owner names.

Figure 2.15. Example of a Certificate (front and back)

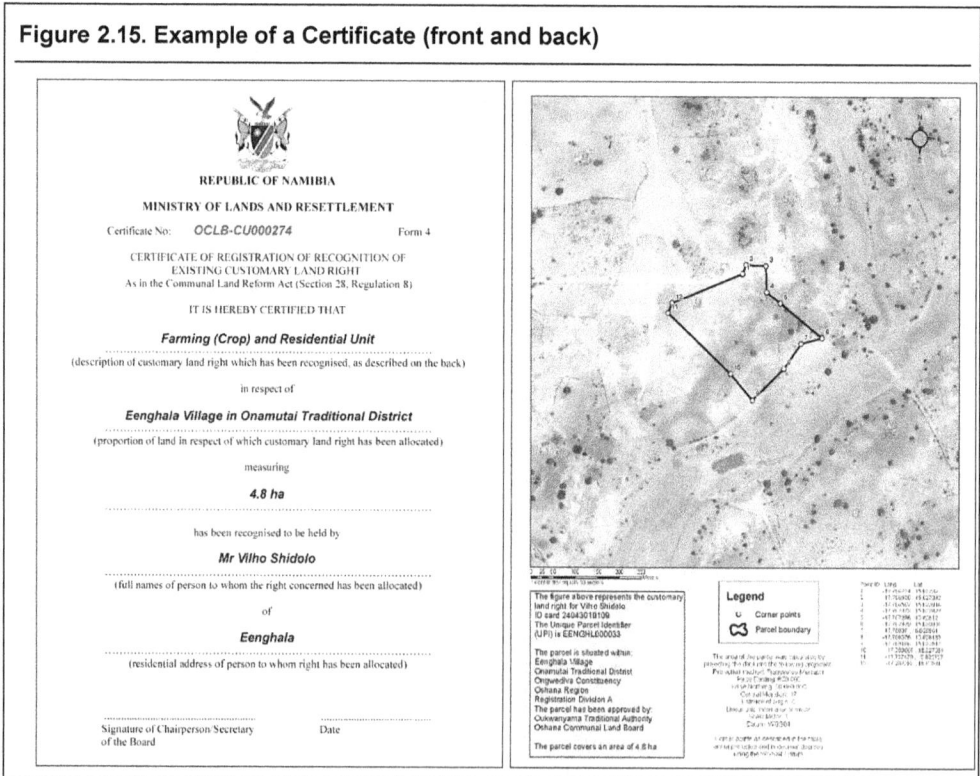

Source: MLR, M. Meijs, 2008.

Accuracy

The NCLAS has features that enable the checking of the quality of the data. The most important are the checks for overlapping parcels and the check that ensures that the right person is allocated the right parcel. With the aerial photo printed on the certificate, owners can verify the boundaries of their parcel.

Speed

Entering the data into the Communal Deeds part of the NCLAS is the slowest part in the registration process. Data from about a hundred parcels can be entered on one computer in a day, provided that personnel are rotated to counteract the tedium of the task. Checking and correcting data is also time consuming, depending on the quality of the original data entry. The process of creating certificates in the Communal Cadastre part of the NCLAS is automated through ArcGIS by the use of the VBA programming language. Experience showed that it takes approximately the same amount of time to survey the data as it takes to enter, check, and print the data. This is still a big improvement on the speed of work, as before an average of about 20 certificates were prepared in a day, whereas now this rate of progress has been doubled to 40 certificates per day.

Status of Registration in January 2009

The Roadmap

At the end of 2008, around 13,000 land rights were mapped and registered. This is close to 5 percent of the estimated number of communal land rights. A draft plan for the communal land registration work has been prepared with the assistance of the RPRP for the period 2009-2013. Currently arrangements are being put in place to implement the processes described in this roadmap. A summary of the roadmap is given below:

Orthophotos will be used to complete the registration of existing communal land rights by the end of 2012. Where areas are not covered by digital air photos, satellite images from Quick Bird or Ikonos will be purchased. Within the next four years, all land-related spatial data will be stored in a central database of the MLR. The plan is that it will then be possible to view the rights of communal as well as commercial areas in one integrated system. For this to be realized, it is necessary to first agree on a series of IT measures regarding the standardization of data, the form of the IT infrastructure, and the security of IT management.

As soon as a land parcel is registered, its records are open to being changed. Parcels can be amalgamated or divided, and in both cases updating of the registry records is required as new UPI numbers and owners are recorded. The registry also has to be maintained in good order, with its records readily accessible to inquirers. Additional MLR staff members, termed Land Officers, are required to be placed in each region with communal land. They will have the responsibility of maintaining and updating the communal land registers in their region.

The success of communal land registration depends very much on the quality of an intensive publicity campaign explaining to all stakeholders the value to them of communal land registration. Communication will have to target important stakeholders as the TAs and Regional Councils as well as the rural population in general.

The Ministry of Lands and Resettlement does not have human resources to manage this substantial work. Private companies will therefore be contracted to execute the activities as Executing Organizations. A competent Project Organization with sufficient authority and responsibilities has first to be convened within the Ministry to direct the program.

Consultants should be contracted that will be responsible for developing the program and financial management components, designing the necessary IT measures, and addressing issues such as the registration of common and Government parcels, the registration of parcels larger than 20 hectares, and the possibilities of upgrading communal rights, through leaseholds and possibly to freehold status.

The Challenges

Challenges being faced by MLR, as it takes forward the Namibian communal land registration program, are comparable to those found elsewhere. Many are management related, whether they concern financial or human resources, project management, or logistical support. Some of the challenges are specific to the conditions found in Namibia. They deal with the local legislation, responsible authorities, and the young history of the country.

Legislation

The CLRA is being implemented with different levels of effectiveness. In the north-central areas, it is largely being applied as intended and is strengthening the security of tenure over individual land parcels. In other areas, the CLRA appears to confuse the land administration with its inflexibility and inability to address local land tenure problems. A large part of these problems does come from the regulations rather than from the act itself.

For instance, according to the regulations, customary land rights can only be registered for land used for residential and crop production purposes. Registering residential plots is not a priority, as the ownership of these areas is rarely contested. Crop production is only feasible in the higher rainfall north central and north east areas of the country; elsewhere it is irrelevant and the land is used solely for extensive livestock grazing. This leaves the much larger and more important commonages unregistered but still open to tenure abuse. Such land, used mostly for cattle grazing, can only be registered to an individual as leasehold under the present legislation. Where the commonage remains unregistered the cattle grazers use it as communal grazing areas. The regulations are also inflexible in handling shifting cultivation. According to the regulations, each plot that the farmer crops has to be separately registered, and the registration cancelled when it is abandoned for any reason. Group rights are not mentioned in the regulations, but will be a valuable addition. Both the method using orthophotos and the NCLAS are ready to be used for the registration of group rights.

The CLRA describes the general legislative framework and calls for regulations to be made. These regulations are to be reviewed and adjusted whenever there is a need. While the authors believe that this was the intention of the Act, reality is that regulations were made just after the enactment of the CLRA and were never revised. The reasons are believed to be a high staff turnover, including Ministers and Permanent Secretaries as well as the fact that the standard document on the CLRA, the Guide to the Communal Land Reform Act, does not clearly distinguish the Act and its regulations.

The CLRA was passed with the aim of facilitating a proper and uniform land administration system with a secure land tenure for all, which will result in the minimization of land disputes on communal land (Communal Land Reform Act, No 5 of 2002).

The results from fieldwork show that the number of disputes in the Olukonda pilot area is very low. Within the 2,137 land rights mapped, there was only one dispute that could not be solved immediately. Results from the other projects show that this is the general trend in all areas.

Most known longstanding disputes are between TAs, villages, and in the so called previously underutilized areas. In those underutilized areas, different ministries, companies, as well as individuals, see opportunities for development. These developments are not coordinated which calls for land use planning complimenting land registration.

Responsible Authorities

The CLRA and regulations endorse the fact that much of the ultimate power and responsibility for communal land management rests with the MLR Minister. For purposes of effective land tenure and sustainable land use, it would be beneficial for this power and responsibility to be transferred to lower levels of the administration. What is required is the strengthening of the combined forces of Traditional Authorities and CLBs. Traditional Authorities are authorized by the Act to manage and allocate communal lands. However, at present they are frequently faced by inconsistencies, where the local land uses and cultural requirements are ignored and the Act and regulations do not permit flexibility in its interpretation. The CLRA has created CLBs to provide diverse bodies of stakeholders who can address communal land affairs, and are given powers overarching the Traditional Authorities. However, CLBs have been ill-equipped to handle those responsibilities. Their role makes them ideal for resolving land disputes but less capable of addressing the legal and procedural matters that are assigned to them by the Act.

Skills

Namibia is a young country that only started to develop recently. It is also a country where much of the expertise needed for land management is taken away by the private mining companies. In addition, Windhoek being the economical centre of the country is the preferred living place for many Namibians. Finding skilled people to work in the remote regional offices is becoming a challenge for which no permanent solution has been found yet. For the upcoming registration of existing land rights, outsourcing will solve part of the problem since a first registration has to be done only once. The maintenance of the NCLAS will be the challenge of the future. We will only be able to face that challenge if we start recruiting and training the people needed today.

Notes

[1] The term "customary" is very ambiguous. It may evoke historical, fixed, or "traditional" rights. Numerous studies show that local/customary rights are dynamic and evolving. Le Roy (2003) speaks of "so-called customary rights." Some scholars speak rather of "local land rights", to avoid an essentialist view of "custom." But the term "local" is also ambiguous. I use the term "customary" to describe contexts where current access to land is linked with social norms and networks, and where local powers play an important role in land rights regulation and conflicts resolution (Chauveau 1998; Lavigne Delville 1998, 19; Le Roy 2003). In such contexts, land rights themselves can be individualized or not, commoditized or not; land authorities may have historical legitimacy or be the product of colonial and/or postcolonial public policies, either active or passive (leaving people with no alternative than local authorities regarding land issues).

[2] While drawing on the Beninese experience, this paper will not evaluate PFRs in practice or their impact. For further reading on PFRs and their impact, *see* Bassett 1995; Chauveau et al.1998; Chauveau 2003; Ouedraogo et al. 2005; Le Meur 2006; Lavigne Delville 2005a; Le Meur 2006; Le Meur and Edja 2009; Jacob, 2009.

[3] "Land Title" refers here to Torrens inspired legal procedure in French-speaking Africa, with ownership warranted by the state and being impossible to contest.

[4] PGRN: natural resources management project (1992-1997); PGTRN: village territories and natural resources management project (1998-2005).

[5] How to update topographic information after plot division is still being debated.

[6] *See* Comby (1998) for a comparison of these two property creation modes.

[7] Of course, the question of what a "village request" means, the conditions necessary for informed decision by the stakeholders, and the balance of power among diverging interests leading to this request should be examined.

[8] *See* Edja and Le Meur 2003; Le Meur 2006.

[9] In the case of Benin, the new methodology defined by the PGTRN in 2005 in response to the observations and proposals of the study conducted in 2002-2003 is a good response to these stakes.

[10] The concept of *maîtrise foncière* was proposed by Le Roy (1996, 1997) to describe customary forms of appropriation and control of land and natural resources. Le Roy identifies five major types of "masterships" with successive degrees of the exclusivity of rights ranging from free access to exclusive use by individuals or groups.

[11] Chauveau, according to Ostrom. The typologies vary from one author to the next and may need to be given context. *Cf.* the case of the lower Côte d'Ivoire, table 2.1 below.

[12] This is clearly a simplified conceptual framework. Concrete situations are very diverse and require study.

[13] Let us note in addition that the certificate can also and without difficulty cover common lands (ponds, water supply points, woodlands, etc.).

[14] *See* Durand-Lasserve and Selod 2009, and Colin and al. 2009, for good assessments of titling programs, in urban and rural areas.

[15] The PFR logic itself is currently under debate in Benin, as the Ministry of urbanism and land reform builds its strategy on immatriculation and sees PFR as tool for generalizing it. See Lavigne Delville, forthcoming.

[16] *See* Le Roy 1998 on this issue, and Fitzpatrick 2005, for an overview of different strategies.

[17] *National Land Tenure Reform Programme, NLTRP Statistics 2007.*

[18] *Annex I to Strategic Road Map for Rwanda – Field consultations.*

[19] Law No. 09/76 of 4th March, 1976.

[20] Articles 25, 3, 4, 5, 7 and 11.

[21] Article 3 of the OLL states that the State has the supreme right to manage the land in the general national interest. While this cannot be construed as declaring that the State is the ultimate owner of all land in Rwanda, it is intended to clarify that all title to land now lies in grant from the State. This would include all existing registered titles acquired under the written law before 2003 as well as titles to be granted under the OLL in the future.

[22] Land reserved for organs of State or for environmental protection.

[23] Vacant land: land expropriated for public purposes or purchased by, or donated to, the State; land occupied by State forests; swamps suitable for agricultural use; and land previously part of the public domain that has been re-classified in accordance with law (Article 14 of the OLL).

[24] Less than 78% in 2000 (UNESCO Institute for Statistics in EdStats, 2009).

[25] Law No. 18/2007 of April 19, 2007.

[26] Districts of Karongi (West Province), Musanze (North Province), Gasabo (Kigali Province) and Kirehe (East Province).

[27] Focus groups were selected to reflect a range of geographical and social groups, including women and orphans, associated and non-associated farmers of different scales and producing a range of crops.

[28] Only 8% of the households interviewed had been involved in disputes around the land reform process.

[29] *See* K. Deininger and G. Feder (2008), S. Pagiola (1999), G. Payne et al. (2007) and R. Smith (2004).

[30] This analysis enables an assessment of whether the level of project cost is "reasonable" and whether the project stands a reasonable chance of being economically viable.

[31] If the resultant production (and income) increase required is small, the likelihood of the project being economically justified can be considered to be reasonably promising. This level of analysis avoids the need for detailed data to estimate the impact the project will have on key parameters in the future.

[32] Using an exchange rate of US$1=RwF 545.

[33] Value added calculates the gross value of production minus only the non-labor costs of production, while the net economic value of production removes both *non-labor* and labor costs from the gross value of production. In the case of a sector-wide analysis, it is difficult to argue that all the labor used to produce the country's crop and livestock output has an opportunity cost that can be factored into the calculations.

CHAPTER 3

Technology for Low-Cost Land Administration

3.1: Positioning Infrastructure and Its Relevance for Sustainable Land Governance

MATTHEW HIGGINS, International Federation of Surveyors (FIG) and Queensland Government, Australia

Summary

This paper is designed for professionals and managers working on land governance projects, such as those carried out for the World Bank, United Nations organizations, and aid agencies. It explains the evolution from the traditional concept of a geodetic datum to the more recent concept of positioning infrastructure and its relevance to the parallel evolution from the concept of land administration to that of land governance. A geodetic datum describes positions in three dimensions and underpins all of what we now call geospatial information. The concept of a positioning infrastructure is based on Global Navigation Satellite Systems (GNSS) such as the Global Positioning System (GPS) and extends to the ground infrastructure used to improve the accuracy and reliability of GNSS positioning for the most demanding users. A key focus of the paper is to outline three broad roles for a modern positioning infrastructure, from the traditional function of supporting surveying and mapping processes underpinning spatial data infrastructure, to enabling the monitoring of global processes like climate change and extending to real-time precise positioning in new industrial applications like precision farming. Experts argue that land governance officials can make a far more compelling business case to higher-level decision makers for the establishment of positioning infrastructures when these three broad roles are fully considered. This paper also outlines how positioning infrastructures can enable new approaches to land governance in the future and contribute to United Nations and World Bank goals such as reducing hunger and poverty, improving environmental sustainability, managing disasters, and responding to climate change.

The Traditional Concept of a Geodetic Datum

Historically, in fields such as surveying and cartography, the term geodetic datum has been widely used. A geodetic datum enables accurate location of features anywhere on

Earth through a mathematical model that describes the origin, orientation, and scale of coordinate systems (see figure 3.1). In its broadest sense, a geodetic datum describes positions in three dimensions, which are often expressed as latitude, longitude, and height.

The geodetic datum is now widely recognized as the most fundamental layer of any Spatial Data Infrastructure (SDI). A commonly agreed upon definition for the term SDI has been given by the Global Spatial Data Infrastructure Association as

> The Global Spatial Data Infrastructure supports ready global access to geographic information. This is achieved through the coordinated actions of nations and organizations that promote awareness and implementation of complimentary [sic] policies, common standards and effective mechanisms for the development and availability of interoperable digital geographic data and technologies to support decision making at all scales for multiple purposes. These actions encompass the policies, organizational remits, data, technologies, standards, delivery mechanisms, and financial and human resources necessary to ensure that those working at the global and regional scale are not impeded in meeting their objectives.
>
> (GSDI Association—www.gsdi.org)

As the fundamental layer of a SDI, the geodetic datum underpins all of the other layers, including what are often called the foundation layers of an SDI. One such foundation layer is the property boundary layer, or cadastre, which in turn underpins effective land administration.

In practice and again, historically, most usage of the term geodetic datum differentiates between the horizontal datum for latitude and longitude and the vertical datum, for heights. For many practical purposes, such as topographic maps and engineering projects, vertical datums need to depict heights above mean sea level.

Figure 3.1. Mathematical Model for a Geodetic Datum

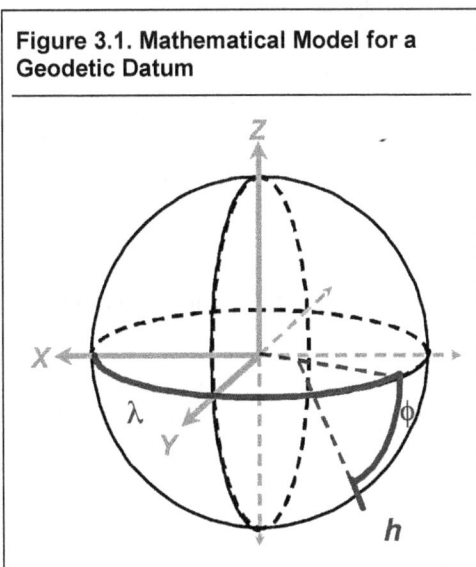

Source: Author.

From a user's perspective, the typical public face of a traditional geodetic datum is a set of so-called permanent survey marks spread across the ground in the area of interest, along with a set of published latitudes, longitudes, and heights for those marks.

Note that the scope of geodetic datums can vary from quite local in nature to national and regional in nature. An increasingly important trend is to refine existing national and regional datums to be compatible with or even coincide with a global geodetic datum.

The widespread use of the Global Positioning System (GPS) has led to the geodetic reference frame used for GPS, known as WGS84, being seen by many as a proxy for the global geodetic datum. However, an approach based on a particular satellite system from a particular country has problems in a global context. Therefore, in modern geodetic best practice, a global geodetic datum is realized as closely as possible to the definition of the International Terrestrial Reference System (ITRS). A realization of the ITRS that is now widely recognized by the scientific community and an increasing number of national mapping organizations is the International Terrestrial Reference Frame (ITRF) (see Altamimi et al. 2007).

The characteristics of the typical approach to geodetic datums up until recently can be summarized as follows:

- Coverage was initially characterized by very local coordinate and height systems giving way over time to more national and continental coverage;
- Measurement processes historically involved ground-based, labor-intensive geodetic surveying techniques, giving way in recent decades to increased use of satellite positioning techniques, such as the U.S. Global Positioning System and its forerunners. The use of GPS has led to significant productivity increases in establishing and maintaining geodetic datums. Note that GPS is now becoming part of a system of systems under the umbrella term of Global Navigation Satellite Systems. GNSS includes GPS but extends to Russia's almost complete system, GLONASS, and planned systems from Europe (Galileo) and China (Compass). For a recent comprehensive description of GNSS developments see Rizos 2008;
- Outcome was typically focused on producing coordinates and heights on permanent survey marks in the ground with subsequent surveys using those marks to propagate coordinates. When GPS surveying came along, it was simply applied as a measurement tool inside the existing approaches, focused on permanent survey marks as the outcome;
- Data capture and maintenance was initially done in a very analog way. That has moved over time to be more and more digital. That more digital approach not only involves computerized data bases about the geodetic survey marks but also adheres to the typical structure of a SDI, with components such as well-defined data access mechanisms, standards, policies, and institutional frameworks. This more digital approach to the geodetic datum can be seen in the concept of eGeodesy, which is being developed in Australia and New Zealand (see Picco et al. 2006).

The Role of Geodetic Datums in General

Some typical traditional roles for a geodetic datum (excluding those in support of land administration) include

- Mathematical control of local mapping projects and a broadening of scope over time to supply control for national topographic mapping on land and hydrographic charts in coastal waters and waterways;
- Control for other land surveys for cadastral, engineering, and topographic applications extending to regional and national infrastructure projects requiring consistent heights and coordinates;

◩   Support to the emerging concept of SDIs and the need to underpin the many other geospatial data sets involved.

The Role of Geodetic Datums in Land Administration Systems to Date

The initial, and still typical, role for a geodetic datum in land administration was in support of cadastral surveying and mapping. In some jurisdictions, the influence of the geodetic datum on cadastral surveying has been minimal and limited to the cadastral mapping process, while in other jurisdictions the geodetic datum has been more integral through concepts such as the coordinated cadastre.

The variability in the level of influence of the geodetic datum has been closely related to how well cadastral surveys were connected to the geodetic datum. The ability to make the necessary connections between the geodetic and cadastral layers of an SDI in a cost-effective way was typically dictated by the density of geodetic survey marks available in the area of interest. Before the advent of satellite positioning, supplying the necessary density of geodetic survey marks was often an expensive exercise, and in areas with rapid and expansive land development, the creation of cadastral parcels often quickly outstripped the creation of a sufficiently dense network of geodetic survey marks.

In countries where a strong connection between the geodetic and cadastral layers was not economically viable, the management of land administration typically had to rely on small-scale cadastral mapping. In such cases, the role of the geodetic datum was more about achieving overall uniformity, and high levels of accuracy and reliability were not possible at the level of an individual cadastral parcel. In sparsely populated developed countries (such as Australia) and in many developing countries, this has hampered the ability to move to more digital processes for land administration. In such cases, the only choice was to digitize small-scale cadastral maps, and the resulting Digital Cadastral Data Bases (DCDBs) have not had sufficient accuracy to be used for other purposes, such as the management of engineering and utility information.

This lack of accuracy and reliability in key layers of an SDI, due in large part to the expense of creating a sufficiently dense geodetic datum, has been recognized as a significant impediment for effective land administration in many countries. For example, the Bathurst Declaration on Land Administration (UN/FIG 1999) states the following:

> The availability of reliable information about land and its resources emerged as a vital issue. If relevant and good decisions are to be made by public authorities, private resource users, or community bodies, they must be based on sound information about the land and environment in order to contribute to sustainable development.

This has also been recognized in the Aguascalientes Statement in the context of developing countries in Latin America (UN/FIG 2005):

> There are difficulties being faced by many States in the region when designing appropriate spatial data infrastructures to support effective land administration, and in integrating cadastral and interoperable topographic spatial data.

A key point for policy makers to realize is that the advent of GPS and GNSS has significantly reduced the time and cost of propagating the geodetic datum as well as the time and cost to connect cadastral, topographic and other surveys to the geodetic datum. Before GNSS, propagating highly accurate coordinates may have taken days or even weeks for a single new geodetic survey mark. Using a modern positioning infrastructure based on GNSS, those days or weeks can be reduced to minutes or even seconds, using so-called real-time precise positioning.

This revolution in the ability to accurately and reliably propagate the geodetic datum can therefore remove what always has been seen as a significant inhibitor to the creation of an accurate and reliable SDI in support of land administration.

From Geodetic Datums to Positioning Infrastructures

In recent years, the concept of a positioning infrastructure has developed based on the widespread availability of GNSS receivers for geodesy, surveying, and for geospatial data capture. A positioning infrastructure has two main components.

The first and most essential component of the positioning infrastructure is the GNSS "system of systems" itself. The GNSS systems have a number of subcomponents including the space segment (the satellites) and the ground segment. The ground segment typically includes a sparse network of tracking stations across the globe sending data to a central control station, which maintains the satellite constellations and creates the orbital and positioning information that is made available to the user's receiver.

A single-point position using a standalone GNSS receiver has a typical accuracy of a few meters to tens of meters. Unlike other infrastructures such as water, transport, energy, or telecommunications, the same basic level of GNSS service is available globally to users in every country, rich or poor. As such, GNSS could be considered as the most truly global infrastructure.

While single point positioning using GNSS has revolutionized humanity's ability to navigate and locate features, the basic accuracy can be worse than ten meters under the wrong conditions. Therefore, many GNSS users require improved accuracy or improved reliability and many require both. Such improvement requires the second component of positioning infrastructure, referred to as an augmentation system, which uses additional ground infrastructure in the form of Continuously Operating Reference Stations (CORS) to improve accuracy and/or reliability. A reference station uses a high-quality GNSS receiver at a known location to calculate corrections for factors such as the satellite orbits, the ionosphere, and troposphere. Those corrections can then be applied to the user's receiver, which can then be more accurately positioned relative to the reference station.

Therefore, the term positioning infrastructure used in this paper includes both the fundamental GNSS (with its space and ground segments) and the CORS networks that augment those systems as shown in figure 3.2.

Figure 3.2. Components of Positioning Infrastructure

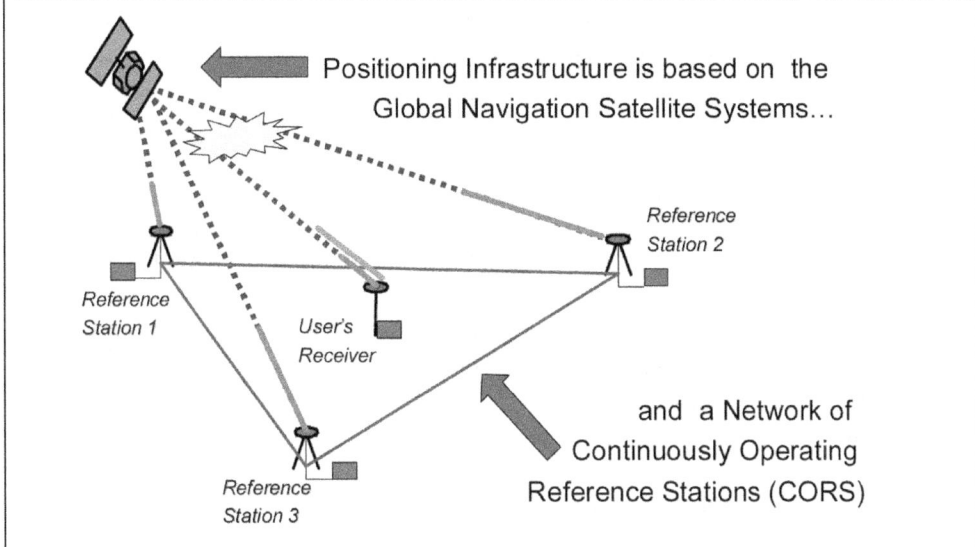

Source: Author.

The Broadening Role of Positioning Infrastructures

The concept of a modern positioning infrastructure still supports the activities traditionally associated with a geodetic datum but extends to much broader roles on the global stage. The roles of a modern positioning infrastructure can be grouped into three main categories:

1.   A continuation of the traditional role of a geodetic datum as the fundamental layer of a Spatial Data Infrastructure by underpinning surveying and mapping activities;
2.   The realization of the value of a stable geodetic reference frame for precise measurement and monitoring of global processes such as sea level rise and plate tectonics; and,
3.   An extension of the concept of a true infrastructure that underpins the explosion in industrial and mass-market use of positioning technology.

An important issue for land-related policy makers to grasp is that the positioning infrastructure has a role that is much broader than simply being a sub-layer of the SDI. This is not to say that the role in SDI is not important, but land related policy makers can make a far more compelling business case to higher-level decision makers when all the applications for a positioning infrastructure are fully considered.

Continuation of the Traditional Role of a Geodetic Datum

There is a need to support the traditional roles of a geodetic datum in surveying and mapping. However, the role is extending beyond supporting the traditional professional domain of a surveyor or cartographer to supporting more and more industries and even the general public, who are becoming more and more spatially aware and spatially enabled.

Traditionally, the geodetic datum has been realized through the placement of permanent survey marks and carrying out surveys to generate accurate latitudes, longitudes, and heights for those marks. A global trend during the last decade has been to establish CORS using GNSS technology. CORS networks are complementing and/or replacing permanent survey marks as a means of realizing and delivering the geodetic datum.

A significant issue for current and future geodetic datums is that traditional and new users of geospatial data have a never-ending hunger for better and better quality. That requirement for better geospatial data applies across several aspects of quality, including accuracy, reliability, and access. The requirement for increased accuracy has ramifications for the geodetic datum role because the accuracies required of the data in many end-user applications are reaching the centimeter level. If users need centimeter accuracy then the underpinning geodetic datum needs to be defined, realized, and maintained with millimeter accuracy.

Requirements for centimeter accuracy often do not come from cadastral surveying but from engineering construction and new applications such as precision agriculture. This can lead to a significant institutional issue because the people responsible for the geodetic datum are typically in agencies responsible for cadastre, land administration, and SDI, where the in-house, core business need for such high accuracy is less acute. In such cases decision makers need to realize that a modern positioning infrastructure has broad applications across the economy. Ironically, recognizing that broader role not only improves the business case for the positioning infrastructure but can also enable the agency's role in SDI and land administration to be more effective.

Achieving high levels of accuracy across broad coverage areas and servicing many diverse applications is a challenging task but can be achieved using modern satellite positioning technology. High quality networks of CORS enable efficient establishment and maintenance of the geodetic datum at the millimeter level. The GNSS data from CORS networks in any country can now be processed with data from the global CORS network run by the International GNSS Service (IGS) (Dow, Neilan and Rizos 2008). Connection to IGS enables the local geodetic datum to achieve excellent internal and external accuracy, as well as global compatibility through links to the ITRF.

In the context of developing countries, establishing a positioning infrastructure can mimic a telecommunications infrastructure where it is possible to leap from a limited and unreliable infrastructure based on landlines to a state of the art digital mobile phone network. Such a leap-frog approach would see a developing country using CORS networks to enable rapid establishment of a high quality geodetic datum linked to the ITRF that can also deliver enhanced positioning services to users across many parts of the economy.

Measurement, Modeling, and Monitoring of Global Processes

Enemark (2008) summarizes the key challenges of the new millennium as climate change, food shortage, energy scarcity, urban growth, environmental degradation, and natural disasters. Enemark also states that this requires

> high level geodesy to create the models that can predict future changes and modern surveying and mapping tools that can control implementation of new physical infrastructure and also provide the

basis for the building of national spatial data infrastructures; and finally sustainable land administration systems that can manage the core functions of land tenure, land value, land use, and land development.

Against that background, the second role of positioning infrastructure considered here is the enhancement of our ability to measure, model, and monitor global processes.

Figure 3.3. GNSS and CORS for Monitoring Sea Level Rise

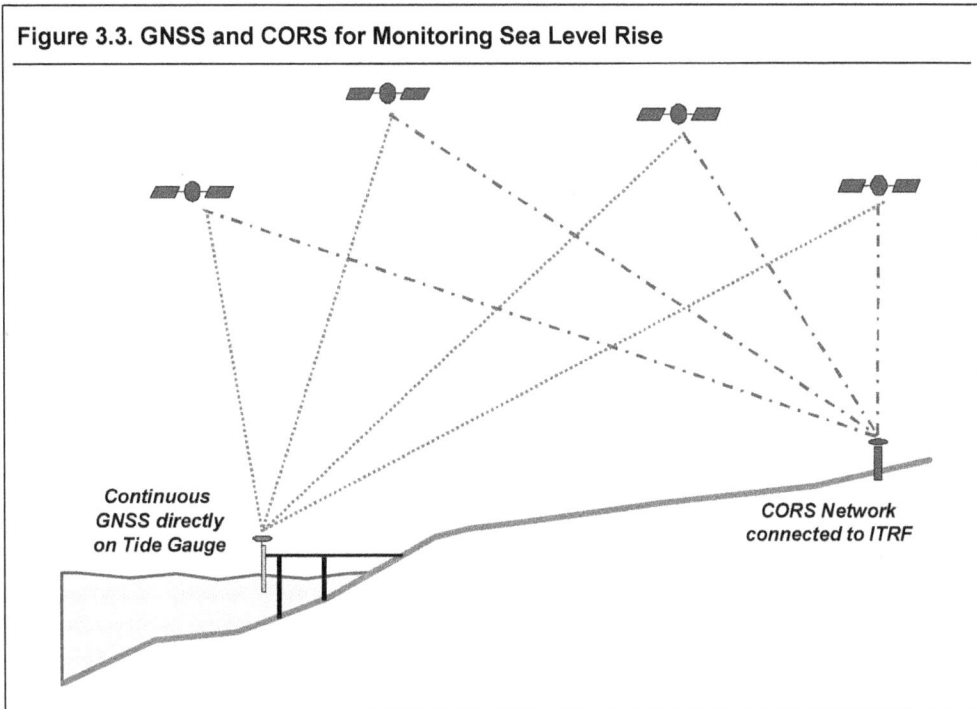

Source: Author.

A simple example of this second role for the positioning infrastructure is that it is difficult to be confident of millimeter quality measurements of sea level rise using a tide gauge, when the wharf on which the tide gauge is mounted could be subsiding. The question arises whether sea level is really rising or is it simply the wharf sinking? To address this problem, the state of the art approach to monitoring sea level rise is to use continuous GNSS measurements at the tide gauge to monitor its height relative to a reference frame that is highly stable over time. That long-term stability is achieved by connecting the GNSS measurements at the tide gauge to the national and global CORS network (figure 3.3).

Thinking more broadly, the role of modern geodesy in understanding global processes is typified by the concept of the Global Geodetic Observing System (GGOS) (see Rummel et al. 2005). GGOS is being developed under the auspices of the International Association of Geodesy (a sister organization of FIG). The ability of GGOS to measure, model, and monitor global processes is illustrated in figure 3.4.

GGOS is enabling greatly improved measurement and monitoring of global processes such as:

- Changes in sea level due to global warming;
- Changes in various layers of the atmosphere over the short term (e.g., assisting weather prediction) and over the long term (e.g., greenhouse gas concentrations or ozone depletion);
- Changes in the planet's overall water storage, either as liquid in the oceans, as vapor in the atmosphere, or as ice at the poles;
- Changes in ground cover through desertification or deforestation;
- Changes in the earth's crust as motion, uplift or deformation and including plate tectonics.

These change detection capabilities can then be applied to disaster monitoring and management of, for example, earthquakes, tsunamis, floods, cyclones, and hurricanes.

For land governance to effectively support sustainable development, a much better understanding of the global processes outlined above and the ability to set, monitor, and adjust policies about the land accordingly is required. The scope of this paper does not extend to a detailed examination of such policies but several examples arise in the coastal zone. Policy decisions about existing and new developments in the coastal zone will need to be based on a strong understanding of the effects of climate change such as sea level rise and increased frequency and severity of extreme weather events.

Such policy decisions will need to be based on high-quality measurements at a given instant and on the ability to regularly repeat such measurements over long time scales into the future. Therefore, those measurements will need to be based on a highly and accurate stable geodetic reference frame, which is best realized in a given area through a positioning infrastructure based on GNSS and CORS and its strong connection to the global reference frame.

Figure 3.4. Global Geodetic Observing System

Source: www.iag-ggos.org.

An Extension of the Concept of a True Infrastructure

The third and most recent role comes from the growing trend to think in a more systematic way about addressing the issues outlined herein in terms of a true infrastructure. In the coming years, positioning infrastructure will come to be seen as the fifth infrastructure after water, transport, energy, and telecommunications. Like them, the positioning infrastructure will increasingly be seen as a critical to society's triple bottom line.

To understand this trend to a true infrastructure, revisiting the stages in the evolution from geodetic datum to positioning infrastructure is worthwhile.

The use of GNSS reference stations to enable real-time precise surveying began in the mid-1990s and has become a well accepted technique for highly efficient and accurate surveying tasks. In its simplest form, real-time GNSS surveying involves establishing a high quality GNSS receiver at a known location and referring all measurements to that reference station. The reference station calculates corrections to the orbits, ionosphere, and troposphere and then broadcasts those corrections to the user's receiver, which is measuring the points of interest for the survey. Such systems often use dedicated radios to broadcast the corrections from the reference station to the user's receiver. Due to the mathematics required to derive the corrections, reliable centimeter accuracy from a single reference station is typically limited to users within a maximum radius of 20km.

After the single reference station approach, the next logical step was to develop a CORS network and calculate the corrections based on the multiple stations surrounding the users (as depicted in figure 3.2). In the real-time network approach, data from all the reference stations are brought together in a central computer, which models the errors in the orbits, ionosphere, and troposphere across the entire network area. The mathematics behind deriving those models with centimeter accuracy currently requires placing reference stations across the area of interest at a maximum spacing of 60km to 70km. Therefore, the network approach can cover large areas of land with fewer reference stations compared to the 20km radius limit with the single station approach. Real-time surveying using a CORS network has also been found to be more accurate and more reliable than using a single station (Ong Kim Sun and Gibbings 2005).

While positioning infrastructure described here is designed to deliver centimeter accuracy to users, it can also deliver lower accuracies (e.g., decimeter to one meter), depending on the level of sophistication of the equipment employed by the user. This is analogous to one type of mobile phone allowing only voice and text messaging capability while another has those plus other capabilities such as internet browsing, but both phones connect to the same underlying telecommunications infrastructure.

The ideal way to transport the data required in modern real-time precise positioning is to link the positioning infrastructure to a modern telecommunications infrastructure:

- In the case of retrieving the reference station data to the central control and processing centre, Broadband Internet is required, and;
- In the case of delivering correction data to the users, wireless mobile phone technologies based on Internet protocols are ideal.

Therefore, the development of a positioning infrastructure can be synergistic to the development of telecommunications infrastructure.

An interesting byproduct of directly connecting users of the positioning infrastructure to the Internet and reliably locating users is that possibilities open up for all sorts of data exchange in both directions. Such information could be tailored not only to the user's application but also to their location.

Another important characteristic is that in many countries we see a mix of government and private sector involvement, such as a government deploying the reference stations and the private sector delivering value added services to users. Higgins (2008) outlines a model for understanding and agreeing on the respective roles of various organizations, from specifying and operating the positioning infrastructure to delivering the services to users.

While the above description of positioning infrastructure with its roots in surveying is useful background, the most important influence in recent years has been the rapidly growing market for precise-positioning outside surveying.

Precise positioning enables heavy machinery to be guided in a way that delivers significant productivity gains in key industries such as agriculture, construction, and mining. Higgins (2007) gives details of some examples from Queensland, Australia, demonstrating the economic benefits that can accrue to those industries from precise positioning:

- A 30 percent productivity increase in several key activities in the mining industry;
- A significant increase in yield and reductions in input costs through precision agriculture using GNSS enabled auto-steer and controlled track-farming techniques. For example, recent studies in Australia have demonstrated fuel savings as high as 52 percent from controlled track farming;
- A 30 percent time reduction in major civil engineering and construction projects, along with 10 percent reduction in traffic management costs and a 40 percent reduction in lost-time injuries.

Allen Consulting Group (2008) has found that in agriculture, construction, and mining alone, productivity gains from machine guidance have the potential to generate a cumulative benefit to the Australian economy of between AUD$73 billion and AUD$134 billion during the next twenty years.

The study also found that a coordinated rollout of a national network of GNSS and CORS across Australia (as opposed to leaving it solely to market forces) would increase the total uptake and the rate of uptake, providing additional cumulative benefits of between AUD$32 billion and AUD$58 billion (gross) to 2030 (figure 3.5). Allen Consulting Group helped develop a submission to the Australian government that estimated the cost of establishing a national CORS network for Australia at approximately AUD$300 million with an annual operating cost of around AUD$30 million. A study by Lateral Economics (2009) building on the Allen Consulting Report (2008) and supporting the submission to the Australian government stated the following:

Figure 3.5. The Effect of a National Network on GNSS Adoption in Australia

CONCEPTUAL ADOPTION MODEL FOR GNSS

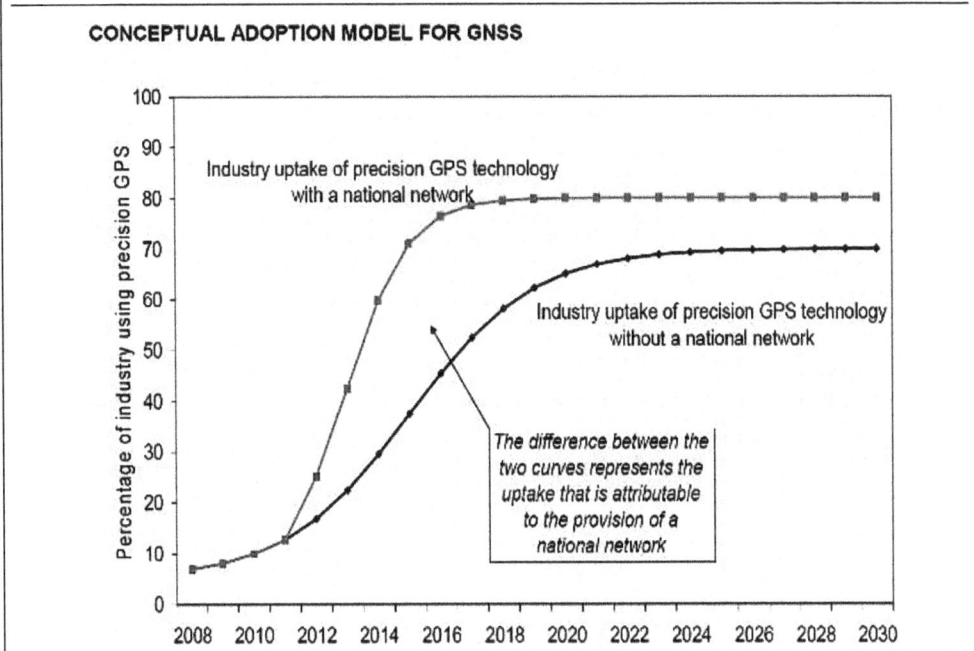

Source: Allen Consulting Group, 2008.

By way of illustration, if a system costing $300 million accounted for only 1 per cent of the estimated benefits outlined above, the benefit to cost ratio would still be between 2-4 to 1.

(Lateral Economics 2009)

A positioning infrastructure can result in significant potential environmental benefits because many of the efficiency gains in agriculture, construction, and mining come through fuel efficiency. For example, in controlled track farming of wheat, fuel efficiencies have been estimated to reduce the carbon footprint by 89kg of CO_2 equivalent gases per hectare. Significant amounts of carbon are also produced in the manufacture of fertilizers and pesticides. Therefore, reduced fertilizer and pesticide usage, along with unreleased carbon through less soil disturbance means that controlled track farming could reduce overall emissions of CO_2 equivalent by as much as 300kg/Ha (Tullberg 2008). Besides the carbon footprint, there are also significant additional environmental benefits through minimization of fertilizer and pesticide use.

The economic and environmental benefits outlined above are not considered if the business case for a positioning infrastructure is based on the benefits for land administration and SDI alone. However, even if a positioning infrastructure is best justified on the significant and broad benefits across the economy and the environment, a positioning infrastructure may still deliver the benefits to land administration and the SDI outlined elsewhere in this paper.

The Role of Positioning Infrastructures in Sustainable Land Governance for The Future

This section outlines future trends to expect in the development of positioning infrastructures and examines what effects they may have on the future of land governance in the context of developing countries. There are two key trends to expect in the next five to ten years:

- The key overarching trend will be the move from reliance on the U.S. GPS to a GNSS system of systems with several more global systems, including Russia's GLONASS, Europe's Galileo and China's Compass, as well as regional systems from India and Japan;
- A significant implication for users from the evolution to a GNSS system of systems will be that two and three frequency signals from many more satellites will be readily available to civilian users. This will allow high accuracy positioning using significantly more cost-effective hardware than is currently possible. Companies such as Nokia have already demonstrated the ability to do centimeter accuracy positioning using existing mobile phone handsets. Mobile phone manufacturers are now also developing standards to take advantage of the increasing availability of positioning infrastructure based on CORS networks (Wirola 2008).

These two points will have several implications for the future of land governance in developing countries:

- The facilitation of much broader spatial enablement across society through trends such as the rapid uptake of GNSS capabilities in mobile phones. Global sales figures for GNSS capable mobile phones are estimated to reach 400 million by 2011. This trend is already particularly evident in countries such as India and China and will likely extend to many other developing economies in the coming decade;
- The strong synergy between telecommunications infrastructure and positioning infrastructure to enable the possibility of real-time processes in land governance. It is conceivable, for example, that within a decade mobile phones with embedded GNSS and imaging technology and a mobile connection to the Internet will enable accurate positioning, adjudication, and recording of property rights to be carried out in real time;
- The positioning infrastructure will greatly increase the accuracy and efficiency of construction and maintenance of hard infrastructures such as water, transport, energy, and telecommunications. This is especially true for large projects in rural and remote areas and is significant for the World Bank, given that the development of rural infrastructure constitutes a substantial and growing component of World Bank activities (World Bank 2009). Accelerated infrastructure development will also place significant demands on land governance to respond with equally efficient and spatially accurate processes;
- Practices like precision agriculture may greatly increase profits and yield and decrease fuel, chemical, and water use. Therefore, the positioning infrastructure can underpin and contribute to broader United Nations and

World Bank goals such as reducing rural hunger and poverty, responding to climate change, and improving environmental sustainability. A secondary effect for land governance is that increased spatial enablement in agriculture will create increased expectations of land administration and the SDI in rural areas;

  ▣ Finally, an increased understanding of global change and disaster management issues enabled by the positioning infrastructure will be factored into long-term decision making on land use, planning, and tenure security. The positioning infrastructure will also allow much more effective monitoring of and response to the impacts of those decisions into the future.

Conclusion

The term positioning infrastructure as used herein includes both the fundamental Global Navigation Satellite Systems and the Continuously Operating Reference Stations that augment those satellite systems.

Three main roles have been proposed for a modern positioning infrastructure:

1. Continuation of the traditional role of a geodetic datum as the fundamental layer of and SDI by underpinning surveying and mapping activities;
2. Realization of the value of a stable geodetic reference frame for precise measurement and monitoring of global processes such as sea level rise and plate tectonics, and;
3. Extension of the concept of a true infrastructure that underpins the explosion in industrial and mass-market use of positioning technology.

Also outlined herein are future trends to expect in the development of positioning infrastructures and what effects these innovations may have on the future of land governance.

The three roles outlined above and the associated applications can be used to build a broad and comprehensive business case for the development of a modern positioning infrastructure. The relevance of the three roles proposed will vary depending on factors such as geography, population distribution, industrial base, and economic position, but the issues presented will have relevance in most countries.

Most land governance officials would typically be comfortable with the first role and the traditional link between the geodetic datum and the SDI. However, the benefits to SDI related activities alone are often not sufficient to justify the expenditure required to move from a traditional geodetic datum approach to one based on a positioning infrastructure. That is especially true in sparsely populated areas where one must maximize the number of users of the infrastructure. Spreading the user base for a positioning infrastructure across more industries also helps to justify and/or recover expenditures for ongoing maintenance and operations.

However, the second and third roles above link the positioning infrastructure to key political issues such as climate change, environmental sustainability, and economic development. While it can be challenging to mount such a broad business case, success can influence the effect by enhancing the importance of the SDI and land administration activities in the eyes of high-level decision makers.

Land governance officials can make a far more compelling business case to higher-level decision makers for the establishment of positioning infrastructures when the three broad roles presented are taken into consideration and all of the associated applications are fully considered.

3.2:   A Statewide Land Information System for Natural Resource Management and Disaster Mitigation: Scope for Land Administration

DR. YELISETTY V. N. KRISHNA MURTHY, Indian Space Research Organization, India

Summary

The economic growth of any developing country is often linked to the sustainable use of natural resources, mainly land and water. Developmental planning with an integrated approach has been widely accepted for optimal management of natural resources for which timely inflow of appropriate and reliable information is a prerequisite. Satellite remote sensing, by virtue of its potentials, plays an important role in generating a spatial information base for integrated developmental planning. Integration of such spatial information with local expertise helps in developing appropriate action plans for land and water resources development. The Land Information System (LIS), which is comparable to a Geographic Information System (GIS), but more focused on spatial information on land resources, supports decision making for developmental planning at various levels.

The Indian space program, in its pursuit of taking the benefits of space technology to mankind and society, has taken up many application projects and thus evolved a standardized methodology for georeferencing village cadastral maps using satellite images for creating LIS. This methodology is being adopted in many operational application projects taken up at the national level.

This paper discusses the requirements for the creation of LIS and for its application potential in various fields including micro-level planning, implementation of a holistic watershed program, revenue collection, assessing the impact of various actions at parcel level, e-governance, crop damage assessment, etc.

Introduction

Across the world, land is considered a critical resource and the foundation of human civilization. In India, land continues to be of enormous economic, social, and symbolic relevance. The way in which access to land is obtained and the rights to it documented are at the core of the livelihood of the large majority of poor, especially in the rural and tribal areas, and determines the extent to which increasingly scarce natural resources are managed. Land has been one of the most sought after possessions in the way that social security and status are linked to the extent of an individual's land property. The details of the land property belonging to an individual are recorded in the form of land registration records, which are maintained by the Land Revenue Department. Currently, due to the difficulty in handling conventional records, cost implications in maintaining them and rapid technological developments, traditional cadastre and land registration systems are undergoing major changes worldwide.

Many countries, particularly developing countries, are facing challenges on the issues of land administration. Traditional systems are no longer adequate to support sustainable development as they were designed to satisfy the limited needs of the past.

Today, the diverse needs of land information and technological advancements have driven the necessity of changes in land administration systems (Williamson et al. 2000). There is an urgent need for the development of a Land Information System (LIS) that is efficient, reliable, cost effective, scale independent, interoperable, capable of adopting information from various sources, and compatible with other information systems. The LIS should also address the individual farmers and/or other stakeholders with parcel (survey) numbers as the unique identity derived from the cadastral map and should integrate the corresponding thematic maps and action plans generated in other information systems. The integrated LIS should act as a planning and developmental tool for addressing all the issues of a national-, regional-, and local-level planning exercise, its implementation and subsequent temporal monitoring of the impact of developmental programs (Krishna Murthy et al. 1996, 2000).

A commitment to the alleviation of poverty has been a defining characteristic of the Indian state from the time of independence to the present day. The Indian state that has emerged after independence is deeply committed to industrialization and economic growth. In terms of poverty alleviation, the state was involved in an early attempt at improving agricultural productivity through implementation of land reforms, agricultural cooperatives and local self-governance. The government of India through the 73rd Amendment to its constitution created the legal conditions for local self-rule (*Panchayati Raj*) that empowers the rural administrative bodies of the government of India (*Panchayats*) at the village level. The Eleventh Schedule of the 73rd Amendment identifies 29 areas over which Panchayats can legitimately have jurisdiction such as agriculture, minor irrigation, animal husbandry, fisheries, social forestry, small-scale industries, and implementation of land reforms (GOI 1985).

An integrated approach to developmental planning has been accepted worldwide to optimally manage and better utilize natural resources toward the goal of improving living conditions and meeting the growing demands of an increasing population. Timely inflow of appropriate and reliable information is a prerequisite for integrated developmental planning. Satellite remote sensing, with its wider and nearly simultaneous view of the Earth's resources from space and its timely, accurate, and cost-effective data, is an ideal tool for generating such a spatial information base. The pragmatic action plans for land and water resource development are prepared with due consideration of conservation and development. Further, to meet the people's requirement and incorporate local wisdom in the action plans, the integration of the information available at the parcel level (land information) with the spatial information base (Geographic Information System) on natural resources is a prerequisite.

Land Information System

Land information refers to physical, legal, economic, or environmental information. It can also refer to characteristics concerning land, water, and sub-surface resources. The information has been used in a variety of systems over the years from registers' of deeds indexes to surveyors' tie sheets, or soil surveys. Today, many organizations are moving land information into Geographic Information Systems (GIS).

The Land Information System (LIS) is similar to GIS but more focused on land records. GIS and LIS provide tools that support many types of record keeping, analyses, and decision making. GIS and LIS techniques facilitate the fulfillment of broader social obligations by helping decision makers make more effective decisions for using natural resources in an optimal way. The International Federation of Surveyors defines LIS as a tool for legal, administrative, and economic decision making, and an aid for planning and development. LIS consists of a database that contains spatially referenced land-related data for a defined area and procedures and techniques for the systematic collection, updating, processing, and distribution of the data. An ideal LIS should be (1) comprehensive enough to cater to all the information requirements of the community with respect to the land resources, (2) sound enough to be financially self-sustaining with structured business models, (3) robust enough to accommodate newer technological developments, and (4) capable enough to preserve the integrity of the data: format, completeness, security, audit, and history. LIS should also address the issues related to disaster management and mitigation at grass-root levels.

Analyzing the status of existing cadastral maps is essential to understanding the importance of integrating them with LIS. The elements such as archiving, updating, retrieving, surveying and settlement, scale, accuracy, parcel definition, projection, and elevation, etc., need to be analyzed to understand the status and limitations of the existing cadastral system in India. In addition to the deficiencies in the above parameters, the traditional cadastral systems fail to meet requirements connected with supervision, management, decision making, forecasting, and developmental planning. The most significant problems in the traditional cadastral systems are (a) a low geometric precision of data/low quality of data, (b) protracted data acquisition techniques (terrestrial for the most part) and speed of data access, (c) a divergence between the map and the register, and (d) a lack of supervisory tools. These shortcomings have led to the improvement of the cadastre in many countries. A modern cadastral system can be referred to as a multitask cadastre with a possibility of linkage with other subsystems, leading to their integration within the frame of LIS and GIS (Dhal et al. 1994, Gopala Rao 2000).

LIS in Indian Context

The creation and maintenance of information pertaining to land related activities is a state subject in India and is generally under the control of more than one entity, such as the following:

1. The Survey and Land Records Department, which conducts cadastral surveys and creates and maintains basic records for each revenue village.
2. The Revenue Department, which manages land records by way of updates of titles as required.
3. The Registration Department, which undertakes the registration of deeds pertaining to transactions of land involving sale, purchase, gift, etc.
4. The urban and rural local bodies, which maintain ownership information necessary to collect taxes, and undertake planning and developmental activities within Panchayat and municipal towns.

The Need for LIS

The importance of LIS cannot be overemphasized because the land records provide the basis for

- Recognizing an owner's title, boundaries, and usage,
- Collecting all land- and property-based levies, like property taxes, vacant land taxes, water taxes, etc.,
- Developing and maintaining a Geodetic Control Network for referencing maps, maintaining all records in integrated digital form in a central repository, and making the database available to various governmental and nongovernmental users, and
- Planning by governmental agencies to provide value-added services in areas like development planning, welfare activities, and implementation of livelihood sustenance programs.

The main driving forces influencing the development of LIS in India are (1) the status of natural resources, (2) sustainable development, (3) globalization, (4) microeconomic reforms, (5) technological reforms, (6) changes in the planning process, (7) legislation for local-level planning, (8) the implementation of developmental plans, and (9) monitoring mechanisms. These drivers do not exist in isolation, but are related and have an integrated impact. An understanding of all these forces is vital in developing a framework for facilitating consideration of the substantive components of the popular rhetorical "holistic" approach.

LIS basically consists of cadastral maps as the base layer to which various thematic maps are added. The thematic maps on natural resources are generated using satellite images in the GIS environment, which are then linked to LIS. The basic requirements for creation of LIS are (a) accurate, up-to-date and standardized cadastral maps in a digital environment, and (b) a geodetic control framework for the georeferencing of cadastral maps.

Methodology for the Georeferencing of Village Cadastral Maps

An approach has been developed to georeference the cadastral maps using high resolution satellite data like LISS III and Cartosat-1, thereby providing a seamless mosaic of the cadastral maps at a *taluka* level (a *taluka* or *tehsil* is the administrative division of some countries in South Asia that exercises certain fiscal and administrative power over the villages and municipalities in its jurisdiction).

The analog cadastral maps, in a 1:4,000 or 16" = 1-mile scale, available from the land revenue department are scanned using a raster scanner at 200 dots per inch (DPI). Indexing and coding schemes are used to arrange the maps properly. To make the scanned map orient perfectly north and remove all the rotations and internal distortions caused during scanning, the maps are properly tiled using a mathematical grid developed at the sheet level to reduce distortions. The gridded map is then vectorized using software tools. Topology is created for point, line, and for polygon features, and attributes are linked to these features. The codes for each sheet and village files are standardized for unique identification in a given state. The features are codified based on the standards designed for the point, line, and polygon features. Vectorized village (cadastral) maps are mosaicked to generate bigger maps and a GIS database is created for these vectorized maps. A projection and coordinate system, which induces lesser distortions in terms of angular, linear, and area distortions, is identified and adopted to facilitate a seamless mosaic of georeferenced satellite data or cadastral maps at different hierarchies and to establish a one-to-one correspondence between different information systems such as GIS and LIS.

The standard products of the Indian Remote Sensing (IRS) series of satellite (IRS 1C/1D PAN & LISS III or LISS IV, and Cartosat-1 and Cartosat-2) images are used for georeferencing. From these standard products, precision products are generated using ground control points from a reference map base or Differential Global Positioning System (DGPS) surveys. Merged products are generated using digital image processing techniques for better feature depiction and recognizability. Linking the spatial and nonspatial information at the village level adds value to the georeferenced cadastral maps. The sequence of steps involved in the georeferencing of cadastral maps is shown in figure 3.6. The deliverables mentioned in this figure consists of raster scanned files of cadastral maps, digitized files, village-level raw coverages and georeferenced coverages, mosaic coverages of village cadastral maps at the taluka level village boundary covering up to the district level and various intermediate files. Georeferenced satellite images with village cadastral overlays are the value added products for natural resource management and disaster mitigation.

A well-defined set of procedures is established for quality assurance of the database. The quality check procedures are both qualitative and quantitative. They consist of checking the scale of the georeferenced cadastral map with that of the corresponding analog map, ensuring that all the available parcel boundaries have been vectorized in the same shape and aspect as that of the original map; identifying the wrong entries, like duplicate parcel numbers, parcels with no numbers, etc.; checking the topology of the vectorised cadastral map; and getting the vectorized maps certified by the land records department as to the correctness of the map and its content, etc. All coverages or hard-copy maps of the project generated by various agencies are subjected to quality-check procedures before acceptance. Figure 3.7 depicts two village cadastral maps, on A4 size, with duplicate parcel identifications and parcels with no identifications, and duly signed by the concerned officers.

Utilization of Cadastral Maps and LIS

LIS, generated from the georeferenced village (cadastral) maps has a high potential to address the issues related to the parcels at a large scale using high-resolution, panchromatic sharpened multispectral satellite data. The dynamic information provided by the satellite images compatible with the cadastral maps has applications in crop identification, monitoring the impact of developmental programs at the parcel level, land-value assessment using multiple themes and their potentials, and content updates of cadastral maps such as new transportation networks, drainage networks, land treatment measures, and surface-water harvesting structures, etc. A breakthrough was made using the parcel-based thematic maps and action plans in reaching the landowners, understanding their requirements, modifying, wherever necessary, and finalizing the action plans for land and water resource development as per local needs.

Figure 3.6. Flow Chart Showing the Methodology for Georeferencing of Cadastral Maps

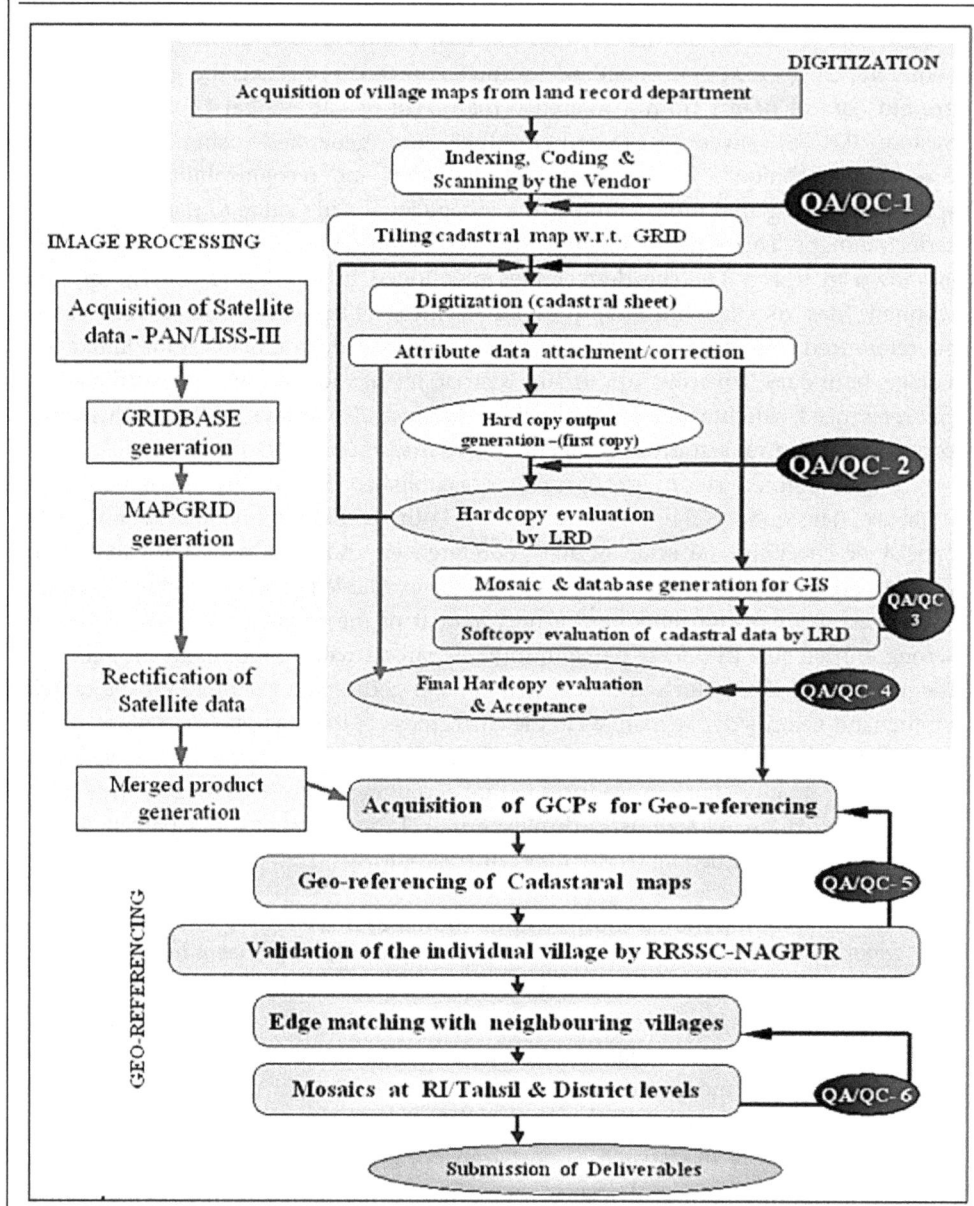

This breakthrough has also facilitated the monitoring of the impact of the plan implementation at the watershed level and at the individual farmer level. Some of the applications of LIS are mentioned below.

Figure 3.7. Quality Checking of the Digital Cadastral Maps—Quality Assurance of the Features

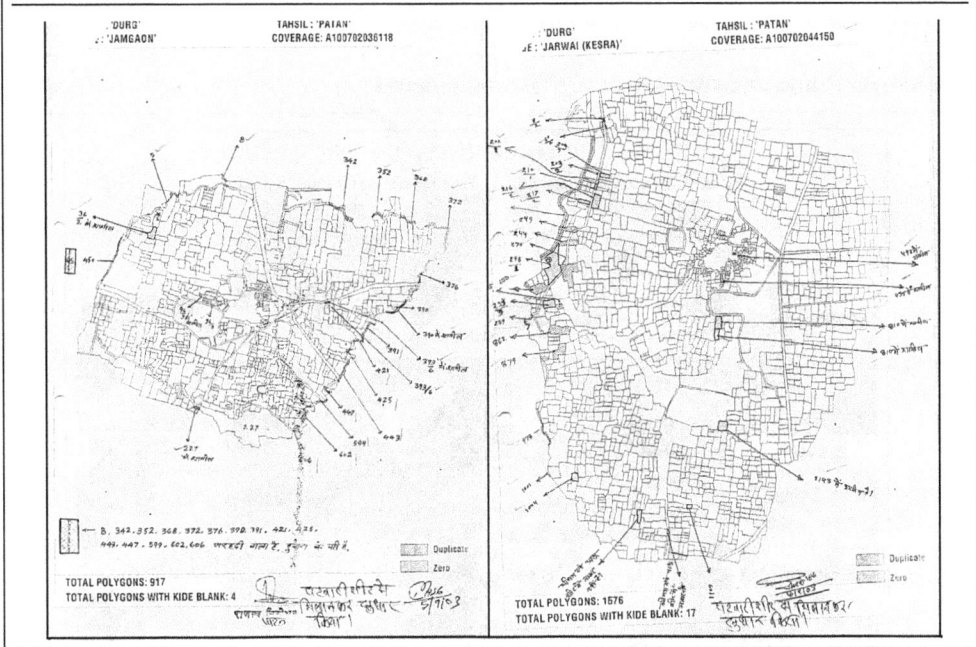

Micro-Level Planning

The Department of Space (DOS) and the Integrated Mission for Sustainable Development (IMSD) project initiated and funded the creation of thematic maps of natural resources and action plans for land and water resource management at the watershed level on a 1:50,000 scale. For pinpointing the location for a specific activity, action plans on the cadastral scales (1:8,000 to 1:4,000) with survey numbers and landowner details (private, government, etc.) are needed for an effective implementation. A simple methodology to transfer the action plans from the 1:50,000 scale to the cadastral maps in the Uma-Gani Nadi watershed of the Chandrapur district, Maharashtra, India, with the participation of the farmers, nongovernmental organizations (NGOs), and state machinery has evolved. The action plans at the village level with the cadastral boundary overlay formed the base for project planning, implementation, and subsequent monitoring of the impact in the watershed. This study has resulted in the successful utilization of cadastral maps, geo-referenced with high resolution satellite images for micro-level planning in pilot areas.

Implementation and Monitoring the Impact

An awareness program for all stakeholders (officers involved in plan preparation/ implementation and monitoring, NGOs, women's organizations, village assembly (*Gram Sevaks*) and farmers) involved in the project, i.e., the Uma-Gani Nadi watershed in the Chandrapur district of Maharashtra, has been carried out through village level meetings and block level interactions. Using satellite data to detect change, the watershed is being monitored for changes in terms of land use/land cover and field studies to establish the increase in crop yield, status of groundwater, and reduction of runoff (see figure 3.8 and figure 3.9).

Figure 3.8. Land and Water Resource Development Plan

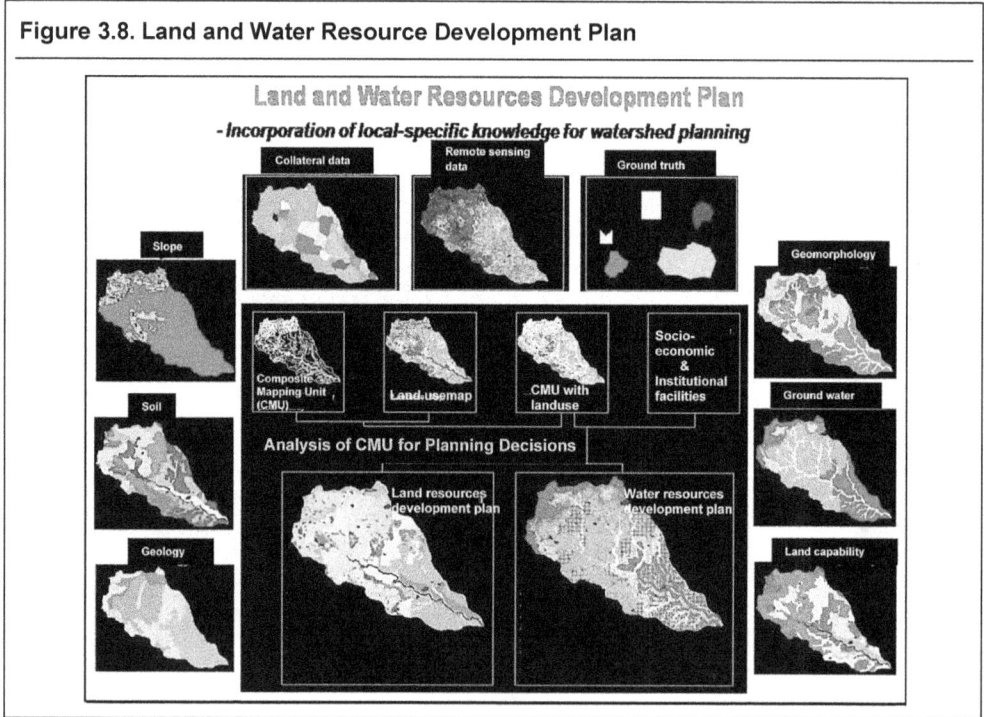

Figure 3.9. Village Panchayat Meeting to Discuss Problems and Solutions

Satellite data for the years 1989, 1995, 1996, and 2007 are evaluated for changes in land use/land cover and their impact. After five years of plan implementation, the cropping intensity increased from 107 percent to 127 percent (see figure 3.10). Figure 3.10 depicts the satellite data of the watershed for the years 1989, 1995, 1996, and 2007, respectively. The average yields of crops like rice, wheat, and cotton have increased from 1.6, 0.65 and 1 ton/ha to 2.4, 1.1 and 2.1 ton/ha, respectively. The areas under horticulture have also increased considerably. With the increase in the groundwater level, the drinking water problem has been solved in watershed areas using groundwater conservation and recharge measures. Although rainfall for the year 1996–97 was around 60 percent of the average annual rainfall, the cropping intensity and yields had increased significantly, showing trends of sustainable development.

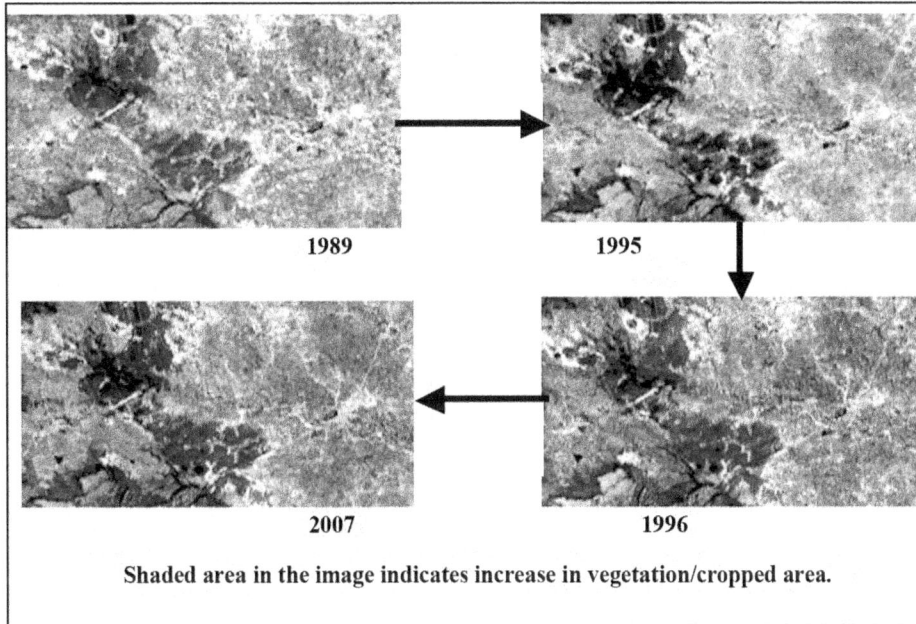

Figure 3.10. Satellite Images Showing Increase in Vegetation/Cropped Area With Year

1989   1995

2007   1996

Shaded area in the image indicates increase in vegetation/cropped area.

The results also show that, on a sample basis, farmers have achieved good economic returns: ten-fold in marginal lands ($100 to $1,000 per farmer per year); four-fold in moderately developed lands ($300 to $1,200); and more than two-fold in developed lands ($600 to $1,400). The availability of LIS has facilitated impact evaluation at parcel level.

Revenue Collection

Revenue targeting is an important application of LIS and helps the irrigation department collect applicable levies from farmers.

The georeferenced village cadastral maps integrated with the crop maps from satellite images have facilitated the identification of parcels where respective crops are grown. Village-wide crop area statistics provide revenue targets for the field officers enabling them to identify farmers and to collect levies. Crop maps in the LIS environment enable the irrigation inspector to verify the information given by the farmer and to assess the water levy (see figure 3.11).

Figure 3.11 depicts the overlay of a cadastral map on the satellite data and classified image of the study area. This information helps farmers with crop planning at the parcel level and helps them use water judiciously. The Maharashtra Krishna Valley Development Corporation (MKVDC) has successfully used georeferenced village cadastral maps for sugarcane crop identification and revenue targeting in command areas. The Maharashtra Engineering Research Institute (MERI) at Nasik and the Maharashtra Remote Sensing Application Centre (MRSAC) at Nagpur are periodically carrying out the project, in operational mode, in the command areas of the Krishna and Godavari river basins in Maharashtra, India.

Figure 3.11. Cadastral-Level Sugarcane Crop Identification in Canal Irrigated Area

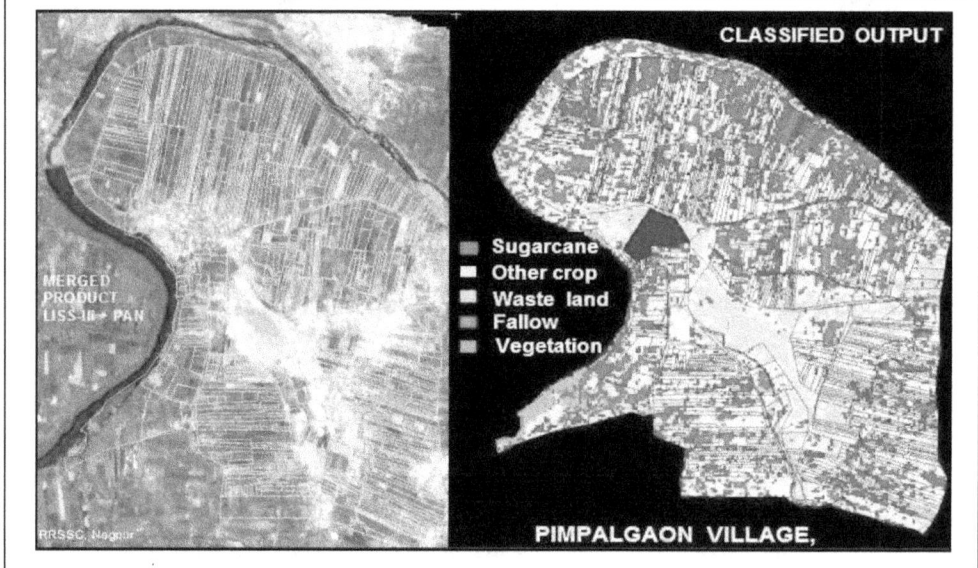

Note: Government revenue collection increased by 3-fold due to water assessment collection.

Impact Assessment at Parcel Level

Impact assessment is another important application of LIS. Impact assessment enables personnel to monitor the impact for mid-course corrections, if necessary, and to assess the cost-benefits of the measures, such as monitoring of salt affected and water-logged areas. Farmers increase the area under farm ponds to bring more area under irrigation and reap the benefits (see figure 3.12), but this degrades the adjoining fields by increasing salt concentration thereby causing a decrease in crop yields. LIS is periodically updated using satellite data, which helps to monitor such land use changes and provide timely advisories to farmers.

Figure 3.12. Impact Analysis of Increasing the Area under Farm Ponds

State-Level Developmental Plans Using LIS and GIS

Developmental planning by a state whose goals are to provide better living conditions to the people has to operate within the framework of physical attributes, biological attributes, socio-economic conditions, and institutional constraints. The physical and biological attributes are composed of baseline data on geology, hydrology, soil, land use/land cover, climate, demography, flora, and fauna. Socioeconomic conditions relate to information on the basic needs of people, input-output relationships, marketing and transportation arrangement, and developmental incentives and facilities (technologies, equipments, labor, material, energy/power, etc). Institutional constraints relate to laws, regulations and ordinances, governmental policies and priorities, political acceptability, traditional customs, beliefs and requirements of the people, and administrative support.

Understanding the importance of natural resources as well as the cadastral database for the developmental planning of the state, Chhattisgarh Infotech and Biotech Promotional Society (CHiPS), an autonomous organization under the government of Chhattisgarh, India, is playing a major role in generating a database for the State of Chhattisgarh on 1:50000 scale and developing a spatial database for a road network and for the georeferencing of village (cadastral) maps (20,000 villages, covering 44,000 cadastral maps) using high-resolution satellite data like LISS IV, Cartosat-1, and Cartosat-2. With $4 million in funding from the government of Chhattisgarh, CHiPS, in collaboration with the Regional Remote Sensing Service

Centre (RRSSC) and the Indian Space Research Organization (ISRO) at Nagpur, implemented the project within a twenty-four month time frame. National Natural Resource Management System (NNRMS) standards and a codification scheme have been adopted for the digital databases (GIS) for seamless data retrieval across the state through the district, taluka, and village, and are further linked with the georeferenced village (cadastral) maps (LIS).

The natural resource databases thus generated are used to derive land and water resource development plans up to the micro-watershed level for implementation by the state government. To assist in implementing such plans and identifying the beneficiaries, the action plans have been transferred to cadastral maps. Since the watershed is a natural management unit, the villages falling within a watershed have been georeferenced using high-resolution Cartosat-1 data and mosaicked to identify the beneficiaries from ridge to valley. The prescriptive measures in the developmental planning include area specific activities like dam checks, stream bunds, Continuous-Contour-Trenches (C.C.T.), and social forestry, etc., and locale-specific activities like tube wells, farm ponds, paddy bunding, and agroforestry, etc. Funding for plan implementation emphasizes the involvement of individual farmers and benefits a certain strata of society, i.e., the landless population, the below the poverty-line population, small and marginal farmers, and target group populations, etc. Depending upon the socioeconomic status of the farmer, the associated beneficiaries, and the nature of the activity, funding norms will vary. Ownership of land under study is a pre-requisite to identifying the individual farmer, his/her socioeconomic status, and willingness to participate in developmental programs, which play a major role in the successful implementation of the action plan in the field. The cadastral maps that have parcel boundaries that define the land ownership, do not have any geodetic coordinates. The georeferencing of the cadastral maps with high resolution satellite data provides seamless access to the databases, and the resultant action plans from the regional level to the local level have taken significant strides in terms of public consultation that can lead to refining the action plans of land and water resource development to reflect local expertise. Further, this process has also facilitated monitoring of the impact of plan implementation at the watershed level as well as monitoring the economic benefits accrued to individual farmers. This technique has facilitated the monitoring and quantification of the impact of the developmental activity in the watershed on a temporal basis.

The overlay of georeferenced village (cadastral) maps on the satellite data also provides invaluable information for better planning of rural development programs. Many examples have been demonstrated to the officials of the state government, NGOs, and other related institutions on the effective use of this technology for better management of rural resources. Some of the observations include:

- Delineating microwatershed boundaries even in relatively flat areas;
- Updating the village (cadastral) maps based on recent land use/land cover changes;
- Showing drainages, which are vital for soil and water conservation, by high resolution satellite data, that are not shown in the existing maps and cadastral maps;

- Mapping and monitoring inherent soil moisture along drainages in different kinds of terrains;
- Prioritizing silted small- and medium-water bodies and village tanks for de-silting purposes;
- Identifying eroded lands in upstream water bodies that need to be treated;
- Identifying suitable wastelands for energy plantation in the catchments of village tanks;
- Identifying survey numbers (farmers) affected by natural calamities for compensation;
- Identifying waterlogged and salt-affected lands, survey number-wise for treatment and reclamation; and
- Collecting water levies for the water being provided through various irrigation schemes to farmers growing cash crops.

The customized GIS solutions for watershed characterization, watershed prioritization, run-off modeling, demand-based irrigation scheduling, and the decision support system for water resource and land resource development plans have been achieved through software like Samruddhi, Nris-Geolawns, Gardss, Geomorsis, Varun, etc. Indigenous softwares like Bhuinyan, which facilitated the viewing and printing of cadastral maps with ownership and crop details for obtaining agricultural loans from banks (see figure 3.13), and from Gramin Yojana Suchana Pranali (GYAN), which enables the visual display and query of natural resources and socioeconomic data (see figure 3.14), contributed greatly to the developmental planning of the state.

The advantages to establishing digital databases on natural resources have been optimally realized for the priority requirements of various departments of the state of Chhattisgarh. Some of the major applications accomplished include:

- Prioritizing watershed and water resource development plans for the Department of Panchayat and Rural Development;
- Providing rural road connectivity through forests to villages by the Twelfth Finance Commission;
- Identifying suitable sites for horticulture, floriculture, and vegetable crops;
- Providing Urban amenities in Rural Areas (PURA);
- Providing a Forestry Management Information System (FMIS), for the forest department;
- Creating a Hydrology Project in the Water Resources Department;
- Identifying suitable areas for siting industries in the state of Chhattisgarh through the State Industrial Development Corporation (CSIDC);
- Optimizing high power transmission lines for the Chhattisgarh State Electricity Board;
- Improving development planning in the new Raipur City, for Town and Country Planning, Raipur.

Figure 3.13. Village Cadastral Mapping Using Buinyan

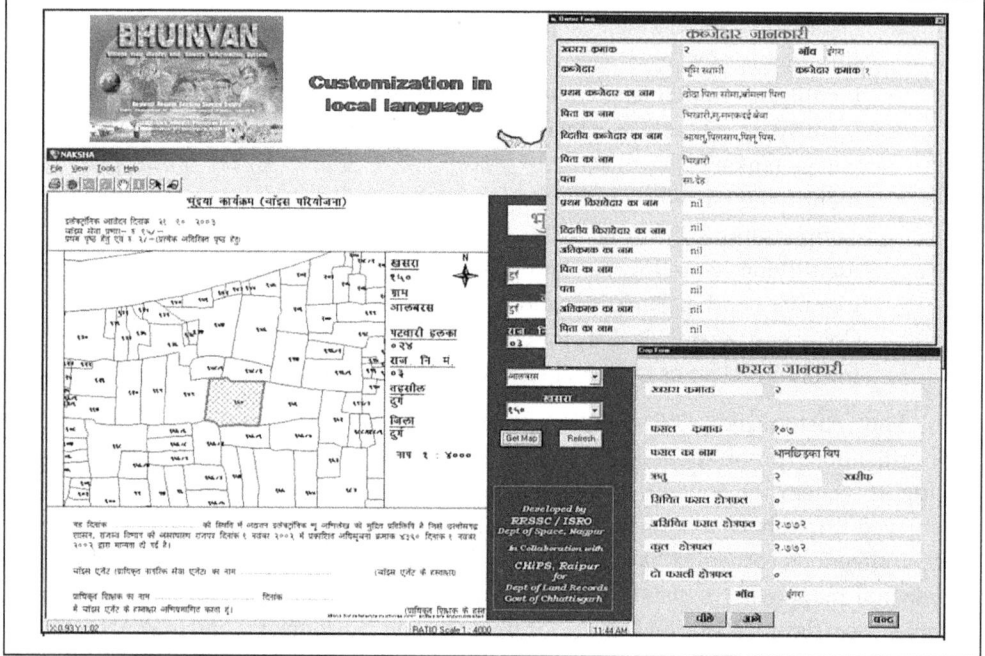

Figure 3.14. Natural Resource Display and Query using GYAN

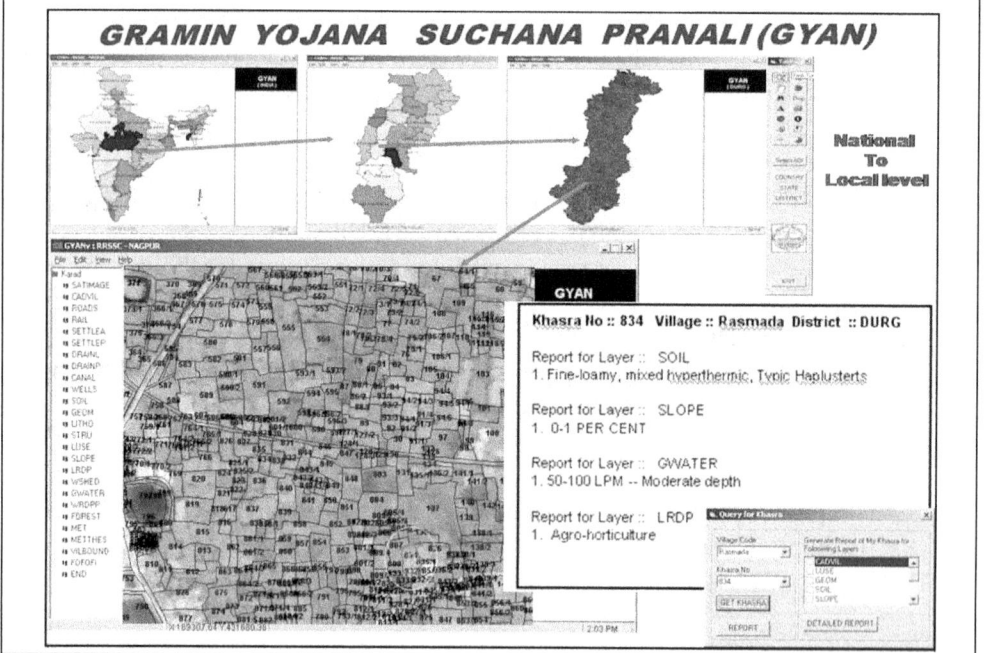

Watershed Development Program by Financial Institutions

The National Agricultural Bank for Rural Development (NABARD) has undertaken a holistic watershed development program in thirty-six village clusters covering about 90,000 hectares of the most drought-affected areas of the agricultural belt under the prime minister's package for the rain fed region of Maharashtra, India (see figure 3.15). The program envisages parcels/survey-numberwide planning locally referred as the Gat-level planning-Net level exercise. The main goal of the program is to enhance the capabilities of the Resource Support Organizations (RSOs), Project Implementing Agencies (PIAs), and Self-Help Groups (SHGs) to use LIS and georeferenced village cadastral maps and corresponding natural resource information to prepare the action plans with the participation of the villagers.

Figure 3.15. NABARD Supported Holistic Watershed Development Program (For Six Districts of Vidarbha, Maharashtra)

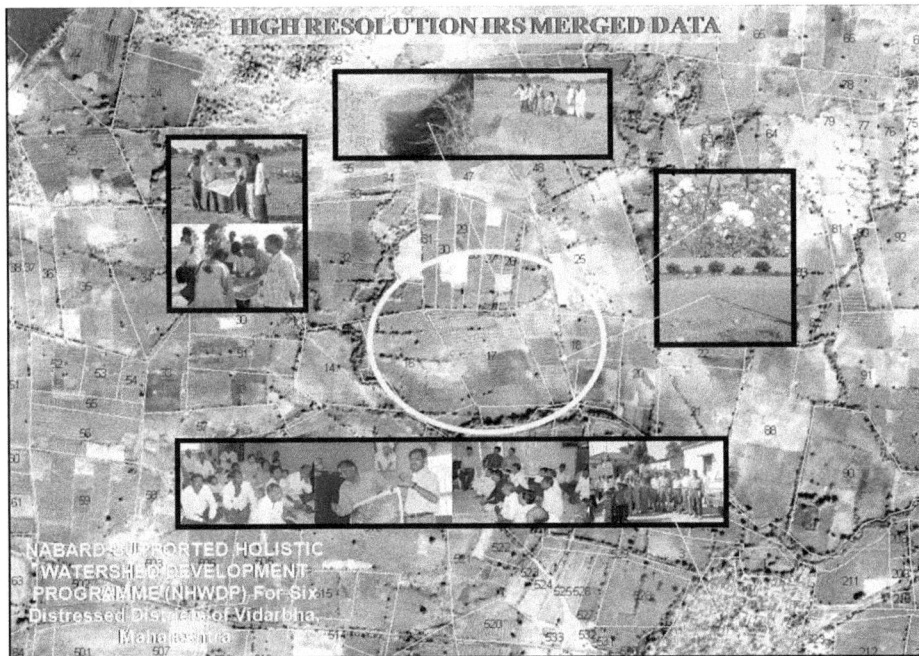

This can be successfully achieved through capacity building by the stakeholders at various levels and through investment by NABARD of less than one dollar per hectare. The stakeholders, through participatory research, could effectively prepare detailed maps on soil (see figure 3.16), groundwater, land capability, and slope, etc., to arrive at actionable maps on land and water resource development and soil conservation and drainage treatment (see figure 3.17). Plans are in the process of being implemented through NGOs and concurrent monitoring to evaluate the impact of such programs of livelihood sustenance through LIS.

Figure 3.16. Soil Map Updation Using LISS-IV and Carto-1 Merged Product

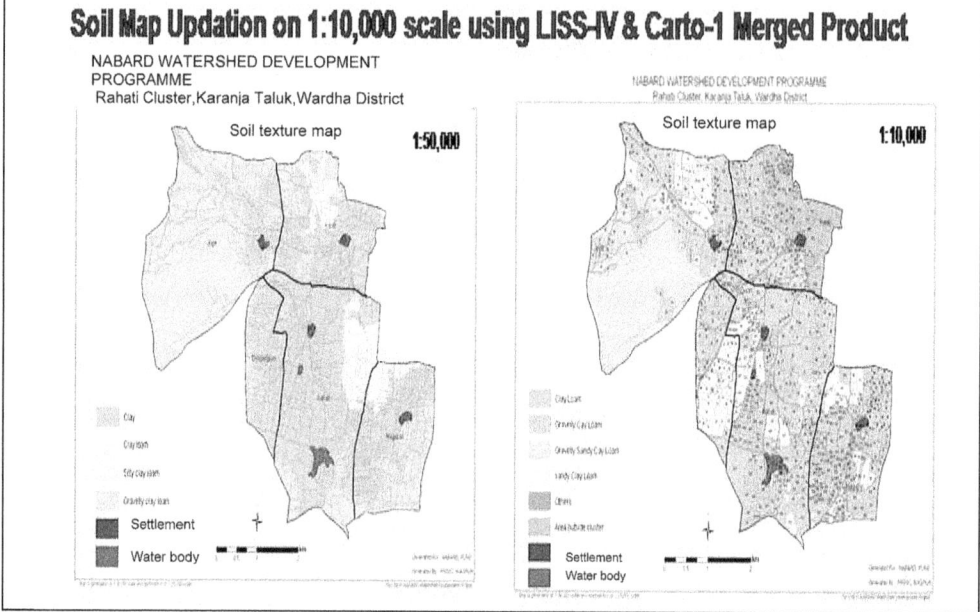

Figure 3.17. Drainage Treatment Map

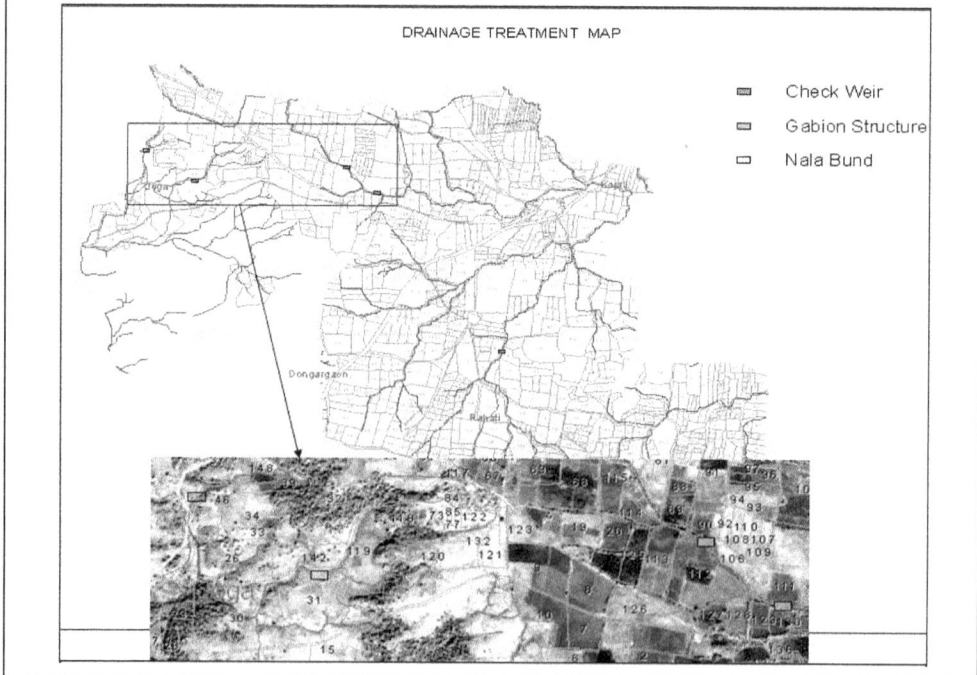

Figure 3.18. Use of Cadastral Map for Crop Damage Assessment Due to Natural Calamities

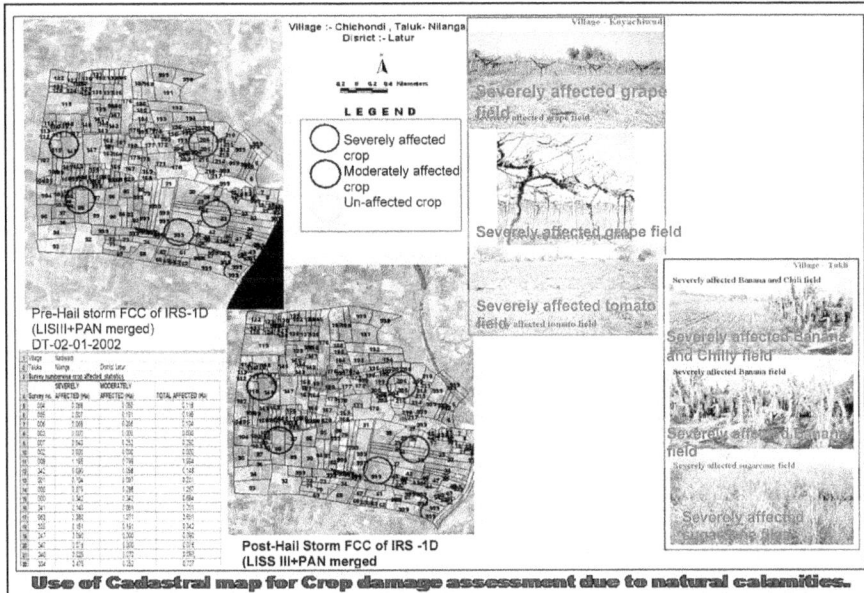

Crop Damage Assessment Using Cadastral Maps and LIS

High resolution data with cadastral overlay was used to assess the damage caused by the hail storms in the agricultural fields. Value added products were useful in parcel-wide exact damage assessments and in providing proper distribution of compensation and relief during the rehabilitation measures for the farmers concerned (see figure 3.18). The end beneficiary-landholder has been identified through a hierarchical database from district to cadastral in the Latur district of Maharashtra, India.

Conclusion

The development of LIS through the georeferenced village (cadastral) maps has facilitated a number of applications in the areas of micro-level planning and impact assessment. Studies have shown that the participation of industries and NGOs with government agencies has enhanced the timeliness and outcomes of the program. The addition of georeferenced village (cadastral) maps has been carried out using indigenously developed software packages like Gyan, Naksha, and Gramins for delivering interactive LIS products. Such databases are available for about 100,000 villages covering an area of almost 500,000 square kilometers. The georeferencing of cadastral maps has been completed for the States of Maharashtra, Chhattisgarh, and Gujarat and is in progress for the States of Karnataka and Jharkhand. The States of Andhra Pradesh, Orissa, Tamil Nadu, and Uttar Pradesh have already taken up pilot projects while the States of Assam and Bihar are in the process of preparing the project proposal.

The technological developments in space-based remote sensing in India are providing timely high resolution data and Digital Terrain Models (DTMs) from the Cartosat series of satellites and are generating ortho-corrected products for precise mapping and development of LIS. Multispectral data products from the ResourceSAT series of satellites are useful in cost-effective periodic updates of databases required by LIS both for monitoring and modeling. Georeferenced multispectral high resolution satellite data and the derived thematic information provide an excellent database for understanding the carrying capacity of natural resources and for suggesting alternative strategies for land and water resource development planning. Such high resolution data also enable the georeferencing of village (cadastral) maps, which are useful in different developmental planning at the micro-level. Additionally, this facilitates the participation of local stakeholders in site-specific action plan preparation and in the implementation of various beneficiary-oriented programs.

The major applications of georeferenced village (cadastral) maps and LIS by different states are in the areas of:

- Micro-level planning and implementation of developmental activities with people's participation;
- Monitoring and evaluating developmental programs,
- Reclaiming and monitoring of sodic and saline soils and degraded lands;
- Finding suitable sites for bio-fuel plantations;
- Prioritizing village tanks for desiltation, restoration, and improving groundwater recharge mechanisms;
- Identifying encroachments in forest land and mangroves;
- Implementing holistic watershed programs for sustaining livelihood;
- Preparing developmental plans for towns and cities;
- Efficiently implementing the National Rural Employment Guarantee Program (NREGP);
- Establishing National Resources Advisories for farmers at village resources centers;
- Estimating crop acreage for evaluation of the performance of irrigation commands;
- Designing feasibility studies for implementing infrastructure projects like road, rail, and pipeline alignments;
- Rationalizing wildlife habitat boundaries in national parks and wildlife sanctuaries;
- Locating suitable sites for new industries and townships;
- Identifying crops and water levy assessments;
- Efficiently settling compensation claims due to crop damage;
- Identifying cotton farmers for effective procurement mechanisms; and
- Rehabilitating and providing relief to Tsunami affected villages.

Other application projects under active consideration by state governments, a few of which are in pilot mode, include:

- Ready references for tax assessments;
- Carbon credit assessments;

- Citizen services providing boundary (*chatursima*) maps with record of rights information for agriculture loans;
- Identification of mine lease areas for environmental planning;
- Preparation of soil health cards;
- Crop Insurance;
- Land acquisition and rehabilitation in infrastructure projects; and
- Smart cards for farmers to facilitate e-governance and e-banking.

Georeferenced cadastral maps overlaid on high resolution satellite data also help to identify, both quantitatively and qualitatively, the changes within the cadastral boundaries, thereby identifying priority areas for update graphically, if the changes are minimal, or by using DGPS if changes are more extensive.

3.3:   First Experiences with High-Resolution Imagery-Based Adjudication Approach in Ethiopia[1]

CHRISTIAAN LEMMEN, University of Twente, Netherlands
JAAP ZEVENBERGEN, Delft University of Technology, Netherlands

Summary

Great progress has been made with rural land certification in Ethiopia. This process, however, has been mainly confined to the first phase certificates—those without a georeference. In 2008, a team conducted a simple field test using high resolution imagery. On-site tests were performed to determine if Quickbird satellite imagery could be used to establish parcel index maps in selected villages. The data collection in the field was performed with the help of land rights holders and local officials. The image quality of the plots at a scale of 1:2000 was sufficiently high to allow the parties to easily understand the images and contribute input, making the process very participatory. Many land rights holders were not able to present their certificates, suggesting updating issues. Even though the test was not well prepared, it yielded useful experiences and data. This limited data set was processed initially with ArcGIS and later with the first prototype of the Social Tenure Domain Model (STDM), which is open-source software. Processing the limited graphical display of the boundaries was relatively easy, but trying to link the data to Global Positioning System (GPS) coordinates (collected, at the same time, with hand-held GPS) was not immediately possible due to offsets caused by a number of reasons. Nevertheless, the approach seems very useful for lower land value areas where coverage is more important than (absolute) accuracy.

Introduction

Since the beginning of the 21st century, great progress has been made with rural land certification in Ethiopia. Several Ethiopian states have introduced land administration systems for rural areas aimed at issuing land use certificates at an affordable cost for all (sedentary) farmers in that state. Unlike many similar initiatives in other countries, the implementation of this quickly caught on in Ethiopia, and by 2005 data had been collected on about six million households, about half of which have actually received their "first phase" certificates. These certificates identify the landholders (by name, etc., and with photographs), but are weak on the description of the land plots, which include neither a map nor any kind of spatial reference (except for a list of neighboring landholders) and only give a roughly measured or estimated indication of acreage.

To gain more of the benefits that land administration can bring, graphical and/or geometrical data on the spatial units to which the landholders have their (eternal) use rights need to be collected. After adding such spatial plans, some speak of second phase certificates, although very few have been issued to date. In practice, it is possible to combine the issuance of first and second phase certificates.

The fact that large areas are being covered (and soon all rural landholdings in several states) makes it possible to have a real effect on the way land is administered and managed in those states. This differs from the "advanced" cadastral and registry approaches that, even after many years, often only extend to certain pockets of territory. For details on the procedures applied and the effects see e.g., Deininger et al. 2006 and Deininger et al. 2008.

In a number of places, with support from different donors (Swedish International Development Agency (SIDA) and the U.S. Agency for International Development (USAID)), the regional land administration authorities have used GPS and Geographic Information System (GIS) to collect and process boundary surveys. In July 2008 a team (partly overlapping with the authors of this paper), did a first simple field test in the Tigray and Oromia states using high resolution satellite imagery as a base for data collection. This limited data set was later processed using ArcGIS software, and has been re-processed using the first prototype of the Social Tenure Domain Model (STDM). In early 2009, further testing was done by the Environmental Protection Land Administration and Use Authority (EPLAUA) in Amhara as part of the Cadastral Index Mapping piloting (Belay 2009). Comparable work includes earlier doctoral research in Ethiopia (Haile 2005), ongoing doctoral research in Pakistan (Zahir 2009), as well as pilot projects in Rwanda (Sagashya and English 2009) and Namibia (Kapitango and Meijs 2009).

The field tests of July 2008 in Ethiopia, the processing of the data collected, and some recommendations for ways forward are described in the next sections.

Data Collection

Acquiring Imagery

Using satellite imagery for cadastral applications is not new.[2] Only of late are images available with resolutions that make them useful for standard-size land parcels (spatial units). Satellite images have, for a long time, been used for applications on large pastoral ranges and forest reserves. A quick scan of Quickbird satellite images led to the conclusion that it would be possible to acquire satellite images for a number of villages (*kebelles*), the lowest level of local government, in four different regions at 60 cm resolution which were nearly cloud free. We chose the true color, with pan sharpening (see figure 3.19).

Given the size of the data set (as well as the costs), it was important to acquire only the images covering the area needed. Digital contours of the *kebelles* were obtained from the Central Statistic Agency of Ethiopia (CSA) and could be used to select and order the required images from a private company (Digital Globe). This still amounted to 5.8 Gb of data. The base price was US$17 per km^2, and the original choice led us to acquire 26+32+39+61 km^2.

Overview plots of each region were made and used to define the exact test area, making sure a mix of terrain and land use modalities were incorporated. For a part of the *kebelles*, large scale plots representing a size of 1 x 1 km in the field were plotted on a 1:2000 scale on paper of sufficient quality for field data collection. The 1 x 1 km grid square was then drawn in red on the paper plot. The real area represented on the paper plot was bigger to allow for drawing in parcel boundaries (spatial units of lands in use by persons) intersected by a grid line (see figure 3.20).

Figure 3.19. Quickbird Image Fragment

Source: Digital Global.

Figure 3.20. Raster Data of Hanigodu-Megelta with Parcel Boundaries, Identifiers and Names of Parcel Owners

Source: Digital Globe, including field observations from Klaus Deininger and his field team.

Informing Local Communities

The local communities were informed in advance of the data collection exercise. Individual rights holders, as well as community representatives, were asked to be available on site. The rights holders were also asked to bring their (first level) certificates.

Fieldwork

Fieldwork was carried out in early July 2008. Local district (*woreda*), the second level of local government, staff accompanied the team members to different locations (Hanigodu, Megelta, and Alengu) to aid with data collection. Land rights holders present in the field were invited to identify the boundaries of the land in use both in the field and on the paper plots. Land rights holders, neighbors, and community representatives participated in boundary identification.

The spatial units of boundaries were drawn on the plots by pen (see figure 3.21). Additional information collected included the name of the land rights holder of the parcel (or spatial unit), the certificate identification, the area, and the names of neighboring land rights holders to the north, east, south, and west. This additional information was to be used as administrative data and was written on (nonstandardized) papers. Different methods were used by different teams for the identification of spatial units and for linking the identified spatial units on the plot:

- By writing the name of the land user (this name was used as a link to the administrative data),
- By plot identification as given on the certificate, and
- By coordinate identification combined with a coordinate list (for the teams using hand-held GPS devices).

Figure 3.21. Drawing Boundaries on a Satellite Image

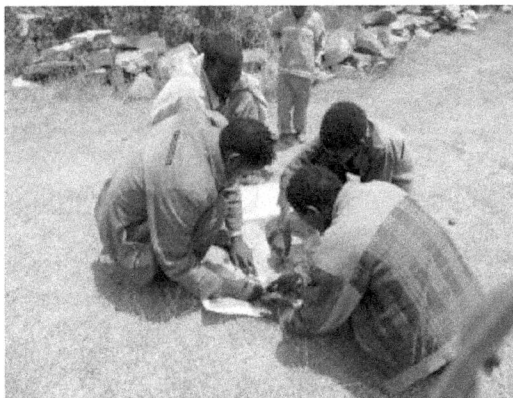

Photo by Christiaan Lemmen.

Figure 3.22. "General Boundaries": Easy to Identify on the Enlarged Satellite Image

Photos by Christiaan Lemmen.

Local *woreda* staff took over the fieldwork activities for one of the teams after about an hour. It was evident that most of the participants quickly understood the images. They recognized where they were and even noticed changes between the present field situation and those at the time the images were made. For example, when looking for a small, irrigated plot in Tigray, the trees were counted, then people started to laugh when they realized that one tree had been chopped down in the meantime. Similarly, a number of water storage facilities that had appeared black (full) on the image, were now empty.

Although, during the informing of the local communities, land rights holders had been asked to be present with their land certificates, many of them did not show a certificate to the teams. Some said they did not have one, or that it was in an office for updating. Others mentioned that the family member who held it was presently not living on the land, etc.

In some areas, the boundaries were easy to recognize on the enlarged plots. These types of boundaries appeared as paths and looked like "general boundaries" (see figure 3.22). In other areas, the boundaries were more difficult to identify. They looked as if the boundaries had "moved" when compared to the image. Creative ways to plough may have been the reason (see figure 3.23).

Figure 3.23. "Moving" Boundaries

Photo by Christiaan Lemmen.

Lack of Absolute Accuracy

The images were not related to ground control points. This implies that the absolute accuracy is (according to Digital Globe, the provider of the images) up to 14 meters horizontal accuracy (root mean squared error) and 23 meters vertical. Orthorectification would improve this, but for "absolute pixel accuracy," ground control points are needed. A small sample orthorectified afterward showed differences of -20 meters on mountains and +40 meters in valleys. The NASA Shuttle Radar Topographic Mission (SRTM) was used as a digital elevation model for this. According to NASA, for regions outside the United States, the latest SRTM set is sampled at 3 arc-seconds, which is 1/1200th of a degree of latitude and longitude, or about 90 meters (295 feet).

Lessons from Similar Recent Tests

Similar tests held in Rwanda and Namibia concluded positively on the use of satellite images and aerial photos for land administration purposes. Sagashya and English (2009) performed a field test in Rwanda using satellite images and aerial photos. They refer to the simple methods of boundary demarcation on satellite images and aerial photos, which is a low-tech approach that costs about US$10 per parcel. After year five of first registration and titling, the subsequent recurrent costs are estimated at less than $1 per parcel in urban areas and $3 in rural areas. Kapitango and Meijs (2009) report on land administration in the communal areas of Namibia by the Ministry of Lands and Resettlement (MLR), together with the Communal Land Boards (CLB). In their paper, they present an approach where aerial photos have been used to fast-track the process of land registration. They conclude that by these means the registration process is now proceeding eight times faster than when undertaken with hand-held GPS units. They further conclude that the method is also more accurate, less prone to mistakes, more cost-effective, and more accessible. It also saves processing time.

Data Processing

Processing of the data involved scanning, georeferencing, digitizing, and feeding the fieldwork attribute data to the digitized parcels.

Figure 3.24. Georeferenced Images from Hanigodu-Megelta Overlaid on Original Image

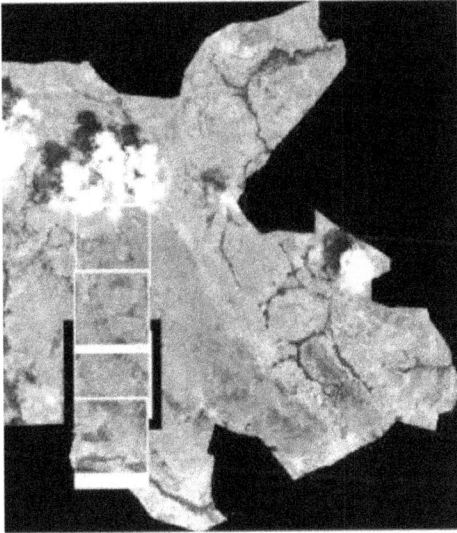

Source: Prepared by Monica Lengoiboni in ArcGIS.

Figure 3.25. Georeferenced Images from Alengu Overlaid on Original Image

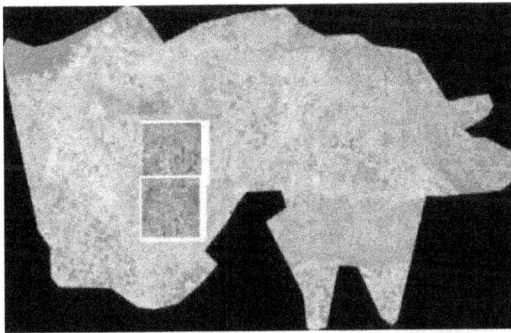

Source: Prepared by Monica Lengoiboni in ArcGIS.

Scanning

This resulted in six analog images, each containing the identified boundaries and parcel-identifiers, which were scanned using a Cougar 36 scanner with 30 dpi resolution as a first step in transforming the field information in to a digital environment. Scanning resulted in six raster data sets in JPEG format. Necessary corrections such as rotations were carried out in order to ease the following processes.

Georeferencing

The six raster data sets contained undefined spatial references. Spatial references were defined by importing the coordinate system and projection of the original image. After defining the reference system, georeferencing was then performed by identifying and matching the coordinates of the new images (marked at the edges of each scanned image) with the original image. Control points such as road intersections and other identifiable features were also used. Figures 3.24 and 3.25 show an overlay of the scanned and georeferenced photographic images against the original image.

Digitizing

Once the images were georeferenced, on-screen digitizing was performed in ArcGIS. Parcel boundaries were extracted by pointing and tracing the cursor along the parcel boundaries drawn on the image. Each parcel was created as a closed polygon. The polygons do not share boundaries with neighboring parcels and are, therefore, independently identifiable. The digitizing process tried as accurately as possible to avoid overlaps between boundaries, especially where parcels bordered each other (see figure 3.26). This process resulted in parcel boundaries in shapefile[3] format. Two shapefiles were created: one from Hanigodu-Megelta, and another from Alengu.

Figure 3.26. Digitized Parcels Shown in Red Lines in ArcGIS

Source: Prepared by Monica Lengoiboni in ArcGIS.

Linking Field (Administrative) Data to Spatial Units in ArcGIS

A database containing administrative data about the attributes of the parcels was created in Microsoft® Excel® and was exported and joined with the attribute table of the parcel's shape file.

The results were that parcels (geometric data) now also contained administrative records, i.e., the names of the land rights holders of the parcels, their certificate identifications, the area, and the names of neighboring land rights holders to the north, east, south, and west (see figures 3.27 and 3.28). The information was successfully uploaded into the STDM prototype.

Figure 3.27. Attributes of the Parcels Are Linked to Parcels

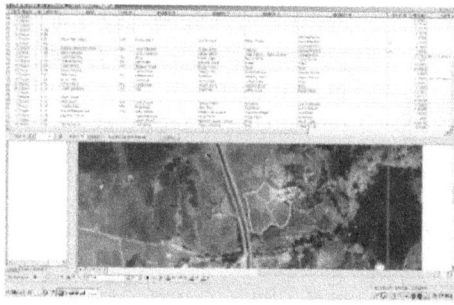

Source: Prepared by Monica Lengoiboni in ArcGIS.

Figure 3.28. Parcels and Attributes Identified Using "Identify" Icon in ArcGIS

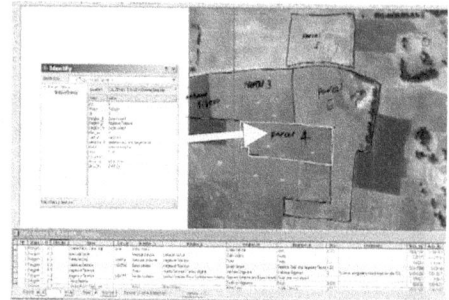

Source: Prepared by Monica Lengoiboni in ArcGIS.

Using GPS Positions to Collect Evidence from the Field in Identification of Locations of Parcel Boundaries

GPS points consisting of survey points from the edges of various parcels in the field were uploaded and superimposed on the shape files. They were examined for mismatches between the GPS positions and corresponding parcels (see figures 3.29 and 3.30).

It was observed that the

- GPS positions displayed suffered from both vertical and horizontal offsets,
- Vertical offsets were greater than the horizontal offsets, and the
- Parallel/diagonal offset is about 200m.

Figure 3.29. GPS Positions Overlaid to Image

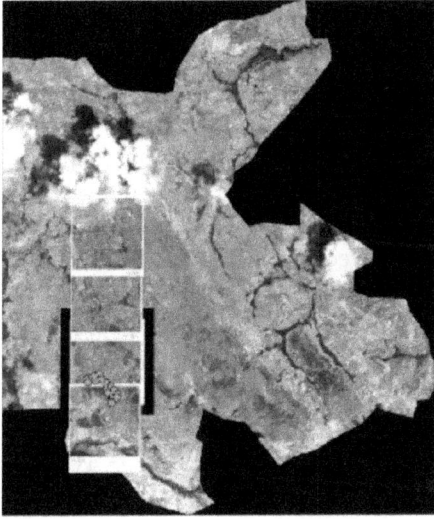

Figure 3.30. Offset of GPS Positions from Parcel about 200m

Source: Prepared by Monica Lengoiboni in ArcGIS, with field observations from Tony Burns and his field team.

Source: Prepared by Monica Lengoiboni in ArcGIS, with field observations from Tony Burns and his field team.

Figure 3.31. Scanned and Original Image

Source: Prepared by Monica Lengoiboni in ArcGIS.

Source: Prepared by Monica Lengoiboni in ArcGIS.

These offsets are likely caused by the fact that the images were not orthorectified and by errors introduced during scanning and georeferencing processes (see figures 3.24, 3.25 and 3.31), as well as by relief distortion resulting from the differences in elevation of the aerial images and the GPS observations as described above. A more comprehensive analysis for more and less mountainous areas has been recently undertaken in Pakistan (Zahir 2009).

Reprocessing with the STDM Prototype

In the same period as the data processing just described, the first author was heavily involved in work on the prototype of the STDM. The STDM is a pro-poor land administration tool intended to cover land administration in a broad sense, including administrative and spatial components. Conventional land administration systems relate names and addresses of persons to land parcels (or spatial units) via rights. In the STDM, an alternative option for this is to relate a personal identifier, such as fingerprints, to a coordinate point inside the land in use by that person, via a social tenure relationship. Depending on the local conditions, there can be a variety of social tenure relationship types and other rights. The STDM thus provides an extensible basis for an efficient and effective system of land rights recording. The STDM is seen as a specialization of the Land Administration Domain Model (formerly known as the Core Cadastral Domain Model) of the International Federation of Surveyors (FIG). (See Augustinus et al. (2006) and Lemmen et al. (2007)) It is based on the principles of Free/Libre/Open Source Software.

The STDM development so far entails the making of a conceptual, functional, and technical design, and starting software development with a prototype.[4] When the STDM prototype became available for testing in the beginning of 2009, the data collected in July 2008 was entered as a first test, resembling a field test.

In STDM-enabled land administration, data coming from diversified sources is supported based on local needs and capabilities. This pertains to both spatial and administrative (nonspatial) data. For example, it may be used in informal settlements, sufficient as a start, to relate people-land relationships to a single point. Then attributes such as photographs and fingerprints can be attached to the records. In areas of high market value, a traditional cadastral map and register may be required, while elsewhere land administration needs may entail using a map derived from satellite images, combined with formal descriptions of rights and rights holders. The STDM encourages and caters to all these variations.

High resolution satellite imagery is one of the emerging and promising sources of spatial data for this type of land administration. A large-scale plot of such images can be used to identify land over which certain rights are exercised by the people themselves, i.e., in a participatory manner. The data collected in July 2008 fits this approach. This data has been inserted into ArcGIS as previously described and has been reprocessed in the STDM prototype in the beginning of 2009 for internal testing. Even with this limited amount of data, the reprocessing was done successfully (see figure 3.32). The testing was continued in a more

Figure 3.32. Presentation of Parcels (Shown in Dark Lines) in ILWIS/Postgres5 Based STDM

Source: Prepared by Monica Lengoiboni in ArcGIS.

Note: Postgres5 is free open source software that can be used to create and store GIS and remote sensing data.

extensive field test in late August 2009 in Bahir Dar, Amhara. The STDM's user interface proved to be simple and the prototype could be used in a flexible way. The software requires improvements to be more stable, which, in principle, is outside the scope of prototyping and a step toward real systems development. During the field test, a proof of concept for using satellite images for land administration based on open source software was delivered.

Lessons Learned

From the field test and processing done in 2008, the following was learned:

- People can read the satellite images easily. Almost without exception, the local people could easily recognize on the paper plot the area and buildings where they were living and the land they were using. For the data collectors, it was easy to record the location of the boundaries of land in use as agreed between the neighbors on site directly onto the printed satellite images. In some cases, when neighbors were not on site, data collectors observed that people tended to claim extra land. An alternative approach may be to bring a Personal Digital Assistant (PDA) to the field to present the satellite image on a screen (see Palm 2006). This implies that the screen data must be readable even in sunshine. Costs could be saved because there would be no need for plotting and scanning as the parcel boundaries could be vectorized[5] directly onto the orthoreferenced satellite image using the PDA. Whether such an approach has the same perception of validity as collecting evidence from the field or not should be tested.
- The approach is a participatory approach. The paper plots are attractive, and people are surprised by how much they see and recognize. The paper plots are something "to sit around and to work with," especially for illiterate people. The same may be valid for an alternative setting where a village community is invited to identify boundaries in a room where the satellite image is projected on a wall, as was tested in early 2009 in Amhara (Belay 2009). But this will not produce the same level of evidence from the field as walking around the land in use.
- In most cases, boundaries can be easily identified on the satellite images, especially when small paths are in use to access the lands, which creates a type of general boundary. Sometimes people demarcate the boundaries, but this is not always the case and in some areas the boundaries are "flexible" and move during the different seasons. Clear differences between the boundaries observed on the images and the field situation have been observed in cases of such "flexible boundaries." The ease of identifying boundaries on the satellite images may depend on the weather conditions present on the day of the satellite observation in mountainous areas (see Zahir 2009). Of course, clouds present during when the images were captured will affect the clarity of the images and their usability for this methodology.
- The data are available in a homogeneous reference framework. However, the accuracy may not be comparable to conventional systems in, for example,

Europe. The approach allows for the reconstruction of individual points within a certain standard deviation in case of boundary disputes later in time.

▪ It is easy to get lost in some field environments: GPS for orientation purposes may be a requirement to be investigated.

▪ Relatively speaking, checking administrative data takes a lot of time. Data collected during the fieldwork was incomplete and contained many errors, especially where the names of people are concerned. The same names were collected several times resulting in data duplication and interpretation errors because the same names appeared in different spellings. If no spatial data can be produced, this method is an option to describing the location of a spatial unit, but there is a risk of errors and extra processing time because of this.

▪ In some cases, the ink disappeared from the images used in the field. A good marker and other equipment is vital. For a comprehensive test, the following issues need to be tackled in time:

• Paper type (costs and volume in large scale applications)
• Paper size (e.g., A3); overlap areas are presented on paper
• Ink to draw boundaries in relation to weather conditions
• Thickness and pen color (to draw straight lines on the image using a thin pen point)
• Possible impact for archiving, such ason scanning the images of the images and then vectorizing the collected spatial data in post processing
• Symbiology in drawing (e.g., to mark a deleted line)
• General approach in identifying objects, such as using lines around the parcel, this means no individual point identifications. Name of the user directly drawn on the image? Or a temporal plot identification (related to the data collector)?
• In short, a more systematic approach, but we are aware of that, of course, and much can be learned from earlier work with aerial photographs.

Conclusion

The use of satellite images to support the collection of spatial data for land administration is participatory, produces field evidence, and is relatively easy to process. There are processing concerns about scanning images with drawn boundary data on it, georeferencing and digitizing the boundary data, and referring administrative data to spatial units.

Accuracy depends on the quality of the image, whereby very mountainous or cloudy areas result in reduced accuracy. Accuracy further depends on the plot structure, whereby visible boundary features, and a coherent parcelation to improve accuracy.

The approach fits with land administration concepts like those behind the Social Tenure Domain Model and affordable Cadastral Index Mapping, as well as when coverage is more vital in the short- and medium-term than decimeter precision (as it was identified by the relevant government officials during the fieldwork reported in Zahir 2009).

The earlier identified lack of updating of rural land certificates was noticeable through the fact that many land rights holders did not have their certificates with them in the field. Most likely, second-level certification work will largely include re-doing the first-level work to some extent as well. Even the current digitalization of first-level certificate data includes a new posting for public inspection after the entry of each kebelle. First- and second-level certificates could be easily combined in a non-certificated area.

Notes

[1] This work would not have been possible without the contribution and support of Dr Clarissa Augustinus, Dr Solomon Haille and Ulrik Westman from UN Habitat, Nairobi, Kenya; Monica Lengoiboni, Gerard Reinink, Chris Paresi, and Martin Schouwenburg from the International Institute for Geo-Information Science and Earth Observation, ITC, Enschede, The Netherlands; Mrs Liliana Alvarez and Co Meijer from Kadaster International, Apeldoorn, The Netherlands; Dr Klaus Deiniger, World Bank, Washington DC, US; and Tony Burns, Wollongong, New South Wales Australia.

[2] Kansu and Sezgin (2006); Konstantinos (2003); Paudyal and Subedi (2005); Tuladhar (2005); Ondulo and Kalande (2006).

[3] A shapefile is a commonly used data format for GIS software that spatially describes features depicted on a digital map as geometric shapes (e.g. points for water wells, lines for roads, polygons for parcel boundaries).

[4] This prototype is developed by the International Institute for Geo-Information Science and Earth Observation in a project in co-operation with UN Habitat. This project was announced during the fourth session of the World Urban Forum, held in Nanjing, China, November 3–6, 2008.

[5] Recorded digitally using vector-based GIS, which is comprised of lines or arcs and depicts features on the map using their boundaries (see the footnote on "shapefile" above).

CHAPTER 4

Assessing the Impact of Efforts to Improve Tenure Security

4.1: Hindu Inheritance Law, Land Bequests, and Educational Attainment of Females in India

Aparajita Goyal, The World Bank, U.S.
Klaus Deininger, The World Bank, U.S.
Hari K. Nagarajan, The National Council of Applied Economic Research, India

Summary

Using disaggregated household-level data from India, this paper examines whether changes in inheritance legislation impact the socioeconomic status of females. The states of Andhra Pradesh, Tamil Nadu, Maharashtra, and Karnataka amended the Hindu Succession Act in 1986, 1989, and 1994, respectively, granting daughters coparcenary birthrights in joint family property denied to daughters in the past. We show that the amendment significantly increased the probability of females inheriting land, but that even after the passage of the amendment, significant bias against females persists. Our results also indicate a significant increase in educational attainment for girls, suggesting an alternative channel of wealth transfer. Furthermore, females achieved better outcomes in the marriage market, such as marrying at a later age, marrying a more educated spouse, and being more able to make favorable reproductive decisions, which suggests that the legislative changes in inheritance rights have a significant effect on the status of females in India.

Introduction

With 185 countries having ratified the convention on the elimination of all forms of discrimination against women (CEDAW[1]), there are few goals that have been as broadly subscribed to as that of gender equality. The global consequences of gender inequality transcend all aspects of human welfare, including poverty, disease, education, and income earning opportunities (World Bank 2001). Women continue to have fewer rights, lower access to resources, and weaker decision-making power than men. As a result, improving the status of women has been identified as a necessary condition for improving lives worldwide. Indeed, increased female autonomy has been shown to confer benefits like long-term reduction in fertility, higher investments in children's education and health, and better outcomes at the community level (Thomas 1990, Anderson and Eswaran 2009).

Yet, in many cases, ground reality remains far removed from this ideal and gender inequalities either persist or show little sign of narrowing over time. In fact, in the political sphere, affirmative action in favor of females has come under criticism for being potentially costly and of limited effectiveness (Munshi and Rosenzweig 2008). Similarly, Duflo and Topalova (2004) find that even though villages reserved for female leaders have more high-quality public goods with less corruption, residents of villages headed by females are less satisfied with the public goods, suggesting perhaps a significant cultural barrier to recognizing females as competent policy makers. Although the underlying cultural and social dynamics are complex, legal change to improve women's inheritance rights could thus provide a low-cost means to reduce gender discrimination and improve a wide range of socioeconomic outcomes for females.

However, empirical study on this topic in developing countries is almost nonexistent. Apart from a number of descriptive accounts noting that constitutional changes to establish the equality of women before the law had little impact on real-world outcomes (Walker 2002), possibly because of low awareness, studies on inheritance rights are few and focus mainly on the distribution of wealth among different descendants (Arnold 2001, Behrman and Rosenzweig 2004). In a recent study, changes in Muslim family law have been shown to affect household behavior in terms of marriage (Ambrus, Field, and Torero 2009). A number of studies have recently highlighted the potentially far-reaching impact of legislative provisions on individuals' or households' behaviors. Divorce laws that imply an implicit change in the terms of the marriage contract have been postulated to change incentives for the accumulation of marriage-specific capital and thus female labor-force participation (Chiappori, Fortin, and Lacroix 2002)—a hypothesis supported by empirical analysis (Stevenson 2007).

The fact that modifications in divorce laws in the United States had large and far-reaching impacts on female labor supply and asset accumulation, as well as on intra-marital violence, suggests that exploring the impact of legal changes on inheritances, especially for females, may be an area where further study could yield significant insights of potentially high policy relevance far beyond India.

India has had a long history of legal activity to overcome a historical legacy of discrimination and high inequality with varying levels of success. To deal with the roots of gender inequality in inheritance rights, the states of Andhra Pradesh, Maharashtra, Karnataka, and Tamil Nadu amended the 1956 Hindu Succession Act in 1986, 1989, and 1994, respectively, to establish that the daughter of a coparcener does by birth become a coparcener in her own right and equal to a son. The phrasing of these amendments, which applied to all unmarried daughters present in the household at the time of the promulgation of the amendment, was identical across the states (Agarwal 1994). In fact, in 2005 the Hindu Succession Act (HSA) was amended nationally (the Hindu Succession Act Amendment, HSAA), across all states, along the same lines. To the extent that females were aware of the amendment and its implied redistribution of property rights to assets, especially land, within the household and confident of their ability to enforce it, this awareness should have an immediate impact on females' behavior.

We use changes of inheritance legislation that aimed to put females on an equal footing in four Indian states to explore whether these changes affected the endowment of females with physical and human capital. This is of relevance for two reasons. First, methodologically, information on all females in a household allows us to test for the significance and magnitude of changes but also to explore the extent to which these compensate existing disadvantages or interact with other initial conditions. We can also try to identify mechanisms underlying the change and explore the robustness of our results on the impact of legal changes on female empowerment. Second, as India has recently amended the Hindu Succession Act on a national basis, our results potentially provide insights to the effects that might be expected on a national scale.

Using data from the 2006 nationally representative Rural Economic and Demographic Survey of approximately 8,100 rural households in sixteen major states of India conducted by the National Council of Applied Economic Research, we find that females whose fathers died after the amendment came into force had a significantly higher propensity for inheriting land but that the change in legal arrangements failed to fully eliminate the gender gap in asset endowments. The same is true for the education levels of girls comparing young and old cohorts in treatment and control states. Girls who started their education after the amendment came into force had 0.5 years more of educational attainment in 2006 in treatment states than those who had completed an elementary education at that point. Stronger inheritance rights are likely to improve a woman's marital outcome and have been shown to have significant effects on her subsequent life outcomes. For instance, characteristics of her spouse and her age at marriage have been shown to have significant effects on maternal mortality and reproductive decisions, as well as her status or autonomy in her husband's home (Jensen and Thornton 2003, Panda and Agarwal 2005). Indeed, we find that females who married after the reform in treatment states were associated with better outcomes in the marriage market, such as marrying at a later age, attracting a more educated spouse, and making favorable reproductive decisions as measured by the number of children. In the Indian context, better dissemination of the 2005 legal changes to the law could significantly increase the potential impact on females' economic and social outcomes, suggesting that greater attention to inheritance laws in other countries may be warranted.

Background

India's Hindu Succession Act Amendment

On a national level, the Hindu Succession Act (HSA) 1956, which was established to codify the law of intestate succession, governs the property rights of Hindus today.[2] There are two main schools of Hindu law, *Mitakshara* and *Dayabhaga*. *Dayabhaga* is largely confined to Bengal and Assam, while *Mitakshara* enjoys dominion over the rest of India (Carroll 1991). The *Mitakshara* system identifies two types of property: separate property and joint family property.[3] All Hindu individuals are free to give their separate property to a desired beneficiary by will. However, in the absence of a will, as a legal matter, the laws of succession are applicable and govern the inheritance of property.

Under the HSA 1956, the separate property of a Hindu dying intestate (without a will) devolves to class I heirs—first to surviving children (both sons and daughters) and spouse, followed by the heirs of the spouse. For joint property, the coparcenary is comprised of the father and his male lineal descendants. Female heirs, daughters and widows, are not considered coparceners in *Mitakshara* joint family property, do not receive a share, and cannot demand partition. Therefore, sons receive two shares of the property, while daughters and spouses receive only one.[4]

Thus, although India's constitution provides for equality before law, the females' ability to inherit equally to males in case of intestate succession[5] was historically limited by the fact that, under the *Mitakshara* system, the right to ancestral or joint family property, which includes land and the majority of family assets, is limited to a narrower body of (male) descendants within the dynasty called the coparcenary. All coparceners share equally in the joint property of the family by birth, but coparcenership is limited to males. The 1956 HSA establishes the right of females to inherit but failed to make them coparceners. Thus, upon the intestate death of the head of household, each of the male coparceners first receives his share of the joint property and only afterward will the head's notional share of the joint property be distributed equally among all male and female heirs. Letting m be the number of (male) coparceners and f be the number of additional females who are entitled to an equal share, intestate succession of a Hindu head of household would have each of the former receive a share of $[(1/(m+1))+(1/(m+1))/(m+f)]$ whereas each of the latter will receive only $(1/(m+1))/(m+f)$ with the difference being the coparcener share.

To deal with the roots of gender inequality, the states of Andhra Pradesh (in 1986), Tamil Nadu (in 1989), Maharashtra (in 1994), and Karnataka (in 1994) amended the 1956 HSA to establish that the daughter of a coparcener does by birth become a coparcener in her own right and equal to a son. The phrasing of these amendments, which also applied to all unmarried daughters present in the household at the time of the promulgation of the amendment, was identical across the states.[6] In fact, in 2005 the HSA was amended nationally along the same lines. To the extent that females were aware of the amendment, and its implied redistribution of property rights to assets, especially land, within the household, and confident of their ability to enforce it, this should have had an immediate impact on the behavior of females.

However, the proclivity of India's bureaucracy to try to legislate certain undesirable practices out of existence as reflected in the large amount of legislation on social issues (e.g., dowry), which cannot be enforced and are largely ineffective (Anderson 2003), cautions against premature conclusions. The purpose of our paper is to use household data to explore whether amendments to the HSA had an impact, to test for the magnitude of its impact, and to explore the channels through which it may have materialized. The key challenge is to not confound the HSAA with that of other effects that may be occurring at the same time. To fix ideas and highlight the importance of this topic, we review other studies that have explored similar subjects.

Importance of Female Rights to Property and Inheritance

A significant and growing body of literature from developing countries highlights the importance of the way in which assets are distributed within the household. The ability of females to control and access resources, such as land, credit, and earned income is increasingly recognized as being of great importance to a wide range of social and economic outcomes (Anderson and Eswaran 2009). This ability has been shown to affect spending patterns within the household, the level of investment in children's education and health, lower fertility rates, and to result in better outcomes at the community level. For instance, in South Africa, pensions received by women had a significant impact on the anthropometric status of girls as compared to pensions received by men, which is reflective of the differential preferences of the two sexes (Duflo 2003). After controlling for total household income, an exogenous increase in female income among lower castes significantly increased investment in schooling, particularly for girls in India (Luke and Munshi 2007). Thomas (1990) finds that income in the hands of a mother has a bigger effect on a family's health than under the control of the father. An increase in females' bargaining power is shown to reduce fertility and child mortality rates (Dyson and Moore 1983, Eswaran 2002). Qian (2008) finds that following the agricultural reform in rural China, an increase in the female income increased the survival rates for girls. At a more descriptive level, studies in a range of countries find that children's well being is strongly correlated with women's income relative to men's, as women devote a higher proportion of their income to family needs than do men (Strauss, Mwabu and Beegle 2000) and that, in India, women owning immovable property face a lower risk of marital violence than property-less women (Panda and Agarwal 2005).

In rural societies, at low levels of development, large parts of a household's endowment of physical capital is in the form of land—a key asset that serves not only as a source of livelihood but also as a source of old-age support and status (Agarwal 1994). Restrictions on women's land rights and tenure security not only affect their bargaining power but have also been shown to lead to significant productivity losses (Udry 1996, Goldstein and Udry 2008). In many customary systems, inheritance, which often constitutes the main avenue for acquiring land, remains heavily biased against females (World Bank 2001, Platteau and Baland 2001) and is often considered a key reason for the persistence of gender bias over time (Deere and Doss 2006).

Despite a significant and growing body of literature from developing countries highlighting the importance of the way in which assets are distributed within the household, evidence on the impact of legal changes aimed at improving the status of females and asset ownership remains largely mixed. This is in marked contrast to evidence from developed countries where legal changes, particularly divorce laws, have been shown to be quite effective. For instance, Stevenson (2007) uses quasi-experimental variation in state-level changes in divorce laws in the United States to investigate the incentives of couples to invest in their marriages. Controlling for a rich set of state-level, time-varying factors, Stevenson finds that regardless of the prevailing laws for property division, a state's adoption of unilateral divorce laws reduces investment in several types of marriage-specific capital. In a recent study by Ambrus, Field, and Torero (2009), constitutional amendments to the Muslim Family Law in Bangladesh have been shown to affect household behavior in terms of marriage where the value of both dowry and prenuptial agreements increased after legal barriers to polygamy were enacted and decreased after additional divorce costs were imposed on men.

The state-level amendments to the HSA in India present an interesting natural experiment to directly investigate whether changes in inheritance legislation contribute to females' ownership of assets and consequently to their socioeconomic status. The main source of bias comes from joint family property, where sons enjoyed rights by birth to an independent share but daughters did not. However, both sons and daughters had equal rights of inheritance to the separate property that their father accumulated during his lifetime. Due to the fact that a considerable amount of property, especially land in rural areas, is still jointly owned, such biased rights are likely to have adverse effects on the status of females in India. This paper exploits the natural experiment relating to the amendments undertaken by the four states of Andhra Pradesh, Tamil Nadu, Maharashtra, and Karnataka, to correct the inherent gender bias by granting daughters equal share in the joint family property just like sons.

Roy (2008) also studied the impact of state-level amendments to HSA using the National Family Health Survey (NFHS) data on never-married females. Roy compares three self-reported indicators of social and economic freedoms of Hindu females with non-Hindu females who married before and after the reform and finds that endowing females with inheritance rights equal to males increases the females' autonomy within their marital families. While the underlying question is similar, our paper differs from Roy's study mainly because we were able shed light on the mechanisms underlying an improvement in the socioeconomic status of females. Observing the amount of inheritance endowed by the father to his children at the time of his death enables us to directly examine whether changes in inheritance legislation have had any impact on the amount of property endowed to daughters, and consequently, on their socioeconomic status.

Data and Empirical Strategy

We use a nationally representative 2006 survey of approximately 8,100 rural households in sixteen states of India conducted by the Indian National Council for Applied Economic Research.[7] The Rural Economic and Development Survey (REDS) collects comprehensive information on the demographic characteristics of all household members and patterns of asset ownership over three generations of individuals, allowing us to examine intergenerational transfers. The data are unique because the head of the household is specifically asked how much land each of his brothers and sisters inherited at the time of his father's death. To our knowledge, this is the first attempt, using disaggregated household-level data in India, to directly investigate whether changes in inheritance legislation improved the ability of females to inherit land and subsequently improve their socioeconomic status.

Table 4.1 shows summary statistics. Based on the details of the HSA amendment, we classify the states of Andhra Pradesh, Tamil Nadu, Karnataka, and Maharashtra as treatment states, and the remaining as control states. The non-Hindu households

Table 4.1. Summary Statistics

	Total Sample	Treated States	Non-Treated States	
Panel A: All Households				
Household size	5.07	4.85	5.34	**
Hindus	0.94	0.97	0.92	**
Head's Age	50.7	50.15	51.43	**
Head's Years of Schooling	4.89	4.4	5.51	**
Land Ownership	0.71	0.77	0.65	**
Share of Land in Asset Value	0.59	0.54	0.61	**
Head's Father Passed Away	0.72	0.74	0.71	*
Education Attainment by the Head's Father	1.12	0.78	1.57	**
Number of Siblings of Head	3.39	3.48	3.29	**
Proportion of Head's Sisters	0.51	0.51	0.52	
Number of Children of Head	3.03	2.96	3.15	*
Proportion of Head's Daughters	0.46	0.46	0.46	
Value of Assets of Land Owning Households (2006 Rs.)	488,378	465,314	523,576	
Value of Assets of Landless Households (2006 Rs.)	108,392	75,062	136,254	**
Number of Observations	8,190	2,574	5,616	
Panel B: Head's Sisters				
Age	50.39	49.65	50.71	*
Years of Schooling	3.24	3.7	3.19	
Married Post HSAA	0.11	0.11	0.08	*
Inherited Any Land	0.06	0.09	0.05	**
Share of Land Inherited	0.036	0.043	0.03	
Age at Marriage	15.5	13.9	16.2	*
Number of Children	2.9	3.08	2.58	*
Spouse's Education	4.08	3.93	4.43	*
Number of Observations.	13230	3868	9362	
Panel C: Head's Daughters				
Age	24.3	24.48	23.89	*
Educational Attainment	4.03	4.7	4.58	
Number of Observations	7762	2036	5726	

Source: 2006 NCAER REDS survey.

Notes: The last column denotes significance of difference in means between treatment and control states. ** significant at 1%; ** significant at 5%

(6 percent) were dropped from the total sample used for our analysis because the inheritance act applies only to Hindus. The average household size is five members; on average, the head of the household is 51 years old with five years of education. Approximately 71 percent of the households own land; the average share of land in total assets of land-owning households is 59 percent.[8] Panel B provides descriptive data on 13,230 sisters of the household head. There are significant differences in the ability to inherit land between females in the treatment and control states. For instance, while only 9 percent of females in treatment states inherited land, this proportion is much smaller (only 5 percent) in the control states. Changes in inheritance legislation could be a cost-effective way of increasing female asset endowments and empowerment, thus bringing about some of the positive socioeconomic outcomes that the literature has generally associated with such changes. Several studies demonstrate the effectiveness of legal changes in increasing a wide range of gender-specific outcomes and the far-reaching impacts of inheritance legislation. Recent gender-specific changes in India's inheritance legislation thus provide an ideal setting to explore the extent to which legal arrangements could provide a low-cost means to increase female asset ownership and the potential implications of such a shift.

This paper uses the variation in the timing of amendments to the Hindu Succession Act across the four states of India to identify the effect of the HSAA on the ability of women to inherit property, become better educated, and consequently, improve their socioeconomic status. We use the fact that the Indian states of Andhra Pradesh (AP), Tamil Nadu (TN), Karnataka (KA), and Maharashtra (MA) amended the act in the years 1986, 1989, and 1994, respectively, to perform three types of analysis. First, since we observe data on the amount of land each of the sisters of the household head inherited at the time of her father's death, we examine the intergenerational transmission of land assets to children. Information on inheritance-related land transfers to all sisters of the household head at the time of their father's death is used to assess whether, in these four states, passage of the amendment affected the females' propensity to inherit land. We use the inheritance of land for a number of reasons. First, in contrast to other assets, land is mostly joint family property so its inheritance follows the (amended or original) HSA, which cannot be modified through a will. Second, information on whether or not land was inherited by individuals is easily obtained via recall and will be less intrusive than obtaining information on other variables relating to inter-generational asset transfers. Moreover, in rural India, land continues to be the main asset and source of livelihood, status, and social security; in fact, for land-owning households in our sample, it accounts for almost two-thirds of total asset value.

The sample used for the analysis contains only those land-owning Hindu households where we observe the date of the father's death. Since the HSA was amended nationally in 2005, we dropped all women whose fathers died on or after 2005. Out of 13,230 sisters of the head used to perform the analysis above, we lose approximately 30 percent (because the father does not own land) and an additional 25 percent because the father is still alive. This leaves a sample of 6,562 sisters of the household head to we can use to perform the analysis regarding patterns of inheritance. We start by estimating the following equation:

$$Y_{iks} = \alpha_0 + \alpha_1 D_{iks} + \alpha_2 X_{iks} + \mu_{ks} + \varepsilon_{ijks} \tag{1}$$

where the dependent variable is an indicator variable for whether daughter i, born in year k, belonging to state s inherited any land.

D_{iks} is an indicator variable for whether the father (of the daughter) died after the amendment of the act. This variable takes that value 1 if the death of the father occurred after 1986, 1989, and 1994 in the states of AP, TN, MA, and KA, respectively, and is zero otherwise.

X_{iks} is a vector of parental characteristics such as the father's educational attainment and land holding. We include a complete set of state-year of birth fixed effects (μ_{ks}) to control for time and for varying aggregate factors affecting outcomes for all daughters separately in each state. The coefficient of primary interest is α_1, which represents the estimate of the amendment-induced increase in the likelihood of females to inherit land. The difference in differences estimate can be interpreted as the causal effect of the legal amendment under the assumption that in the absence of the reform, the likelihood of females' inheritance would not have been systematically and significantly different between the treatment and control states.

Second, while the use of land inheritance as an outcome variable has many advantages, including that it is this variable that the HSAA aimed to modify, it has the disadvantage of being irrelevant for the large number (some 30 percent) of landless households. To be able to include these households, we examine the effect on the educational attainment of girls because investing in the education of children could also be considered a way of transferring wealth by households. For rural households, bequeathing land and providing an education are the main ways in which parents assure the future welfare of their children. But parents do not necessarily invest in these valuable resources equally for both sons and daughters. Decisions about how to allocate wealth to children can have a profound impact on the pattern of income inequality between males and females over time. If parents educate and bequeath land favorably to their sons, for instance, women will soon be worse off than men. Thus, knowing how men and women acquire land and education is key to allocating scarce resources and planning for a better future (Estudillo, Quisumbing, and Otsuka 2001). Since females whose fathers are still alive and landless households have been excluded from the previous analysis, it will be of interest to complement the focus on land with an analysis of the HSAA on alternative measures of assets.

Moreover, even compliance with the HSAA will translate into an improvement of females' welfare only if parents do not decide that, to comply with the HSAA requirement, they will reduce the amount of non-land bequests transferred to girls. In fact, as human capital has been identified as one of the most important bequests, and because females have a comparative advantage in using human capital rather than land, one could easily imagine a situation where perfect compliance with the HSAA could, through a reduction of the amount of education transferred to girls, result in a situation that does not improve the status for females. To account for such possibilities, we focused on daughters of household heads and compared relative changes in the level of education between cohorts who completed educational decisions before and after the implementation of the HSAA as the relevant indicator. In view of India's high levels of landlessness and the fact that poverty is disproportionately concentrated in such households, such analysis will also be of considerable interest for policy makers.

As the educational decisions for sisters of the household head had all been completed by the time the HSA had been amended, the only viable way of exploring the potential human capital effects was to focus on the educational attainment of the daughters of the household heads whose (expected) inheritance has not yet been realized. We compared the elementary educational attainment of younger and older cohorts of girls in the treatment and control states. Specifically, we compared the educational attainment of girls who were less than six years old at the time of the amendment so that their decisions would have been affected by the HSAA as compared to those who were 13 years or older at the time of the amendment of the HSA, implying that, since they were supposed to have completed their elementary education by then, their schooling decisions were not affected by the HSAA. Girls who were between six and 12 years old at the time the act was amended were excluded to avoid contamination of the results. Table 1 shows that the household head has, on average, three children of which 46 percent are female. The average education attained by the household head's children is 4.13 years; the educational attainment of daughters is not statistically significant between the treatment and control states.

A third way of exploring the impact of the HSAA is to focus on female bargaining power in the marriage market. Even in cases where actual inheritance has not yet occurred, the expectation that a woman can inherit land or other property from her parents may make her more able to attract a more educated or more affluent partner, or to assert herself more once in marriage. A female's right to property has been shown to strengthen her fallback position, increase her independence, and lower domestic violence. Three variables are used to capture outcomes in terms of bargaining in the marriage market, namely (i) the spouse's education as a proxy of the ability to attract a more educated partner; (ii) the number of children in the household, and (iii) age at marriage. In India, marrying at an early age is reflective of lower bargaining power, which is unambiguously associated with lower educational attainment, maternal mortality, and child malnutrition in developing countries (Caldwell et al. 1983, Marimuthu 2008). In fact, the high prevalence of child marriages in rural India is demonstrated in our data (Table 4.1.1) where the average age at marriage in our total sample is 15.5 years, and the average age in the untreated states is 16.2 years as opposed to 13.9 years in the treated states. In fact, exploring the age at marriage by calendar year of marriage reveals that in the treatment states, the average age at marriage for females whose marriages occurred before HSAA was 12.67 years; this jumps dramatically to 19.78 years for females who married after the amendment to the HSA, with no correspondingly dramatic jump in untreated states. How much of this can be attributed to the HSAA as compared to broader social trends is a question that requires econometric analysis. The estimation equation then becomes:

$$Y_{iks} = \alpha_0 + \alpha_1 U_{iks} + \alpha_2 X_{iks} + \mu_{ks} + \varepsilon_{iks} \tag{2}$$

The dependent variable measures various outcomes of woman i, born in year k, in state s. U_{iks} is an indicator variable for whether a woman married before or after the amendment of the act. This variable takes that value 1 if the woman married after 1986, 1989, and 1994 in the states of AP, TN, MA, and KA, respectively, and the value zero otherwise. Since the

Hindu Succession Act was amended nationally in 2005 along the same lines as the earlier state-level amendments, we drop all females from the sample who were married on or after 2005. X_{iks} is a vector of background characteristics such as a father's educational attainment and a father's land holding. We include a complete set of state-year of birth fixed effects (μ_{ks}) to control for time varying aggregate factors affecting females' outcomes separately in each state. The coefficient of interest is α_1, which captures how the impact of the inheritance law on females varies by state. The difference in differences estimate can be interpreted as the causal effect of the legal amendment under the assumption that in the absence of the reform, the change in female status would not have been systematically and significantly different between the treatment and control states.

Results

Land Inheritance

Table 4.2 shows our results from estimating equation (1) above. The dependent variable is an indicator variable for whether the daughter inherited any land. Columns 1 through 4, show that the likelihood of daughters inheriting land is between 8 to 9 percent higher if the father died after the amendment of the act in the states of AP, TN, KA, and MA, after controlling for state specific year of birth fixed effects. The results point toward a clear and relatively large impact of the HSAA on increasing females' probability of inheriting land while implying that the legal change alone was insufficient to bring about full gender equality in the probability of land inheritance.

Table 4.2. Effect of the Hindu Succession Act Amendment on Inheritance of Land

Dependant Variable:

	Any Land Inherited				Share of Land Inherited			
	(1)	(2)	(3)	(4)	(5)	(6)	(7)	(8)
Father's Death Post HSAA	0.077	0.089	0.094	0.098	0.021	0.024	0.026	0.028
	[0.040]*	[0.046]*	[0.050]*	[0.054]*	[0.008]**	[0.008]**	[0.009]**	[0.010]**
Father's Death Post HSAA* Father's Land Holding		−0.001	−0.001	−0.001		0.001	0.002	0.003
		[0.001]	[0.001]	[0.001]		[0.000]	[0.000]	[0.000]
Father's Death Post HSAA* Father's Education			0.009	0.008			0.003	0.003
			[0.007]	[0.006]			[0.003]	[0.003]
Married Post HSAA* Father's Death				−0.025				−0.012
				[0.016]				[0.014]
Observations	6562	6562	6562	6562	6562	6562	6562	6562
R-squared	0.17	0.17	0.17	0.17	0.17	0.17	0.17	0.17

Source: Authors.

Notes: All regressions include state specific year of birth fixed effects. Standard errors in brackets are clustered at the state level. * significant at 10%; ** significant at 5%; *** significant at 1%.

To explore the extent to which estimated effects may be driven by parental background, we included interactions of the level of education and land endowment of the father with the death variable in columns 2 and 3. While greater awareness of legal changes and quicker learning by the more educated, might lead one to expect reform effects to increase with the father's level of education, the regression does not support such a relationship in the data. In contrast, reform effects are estimated to be slightly more pronounced for households whose head owned less land although the magnitude of the estimated interaction are not statistically significant. Furthermore, legal provisions state clearly that the HSAA only applies to females who married after the amendment, but not earlier. To test the extent to which this has been enforced, we included an indicator variable for whether or not the women were unmarried at the time of the amendment of the act. In column 4, we find no differential effects on a daughter's inheritance with respect to her date of marriage, suggesting that the effect is uniform across all daughters in the household. At the same time, the coefficient on father's death variable remains virtually unchanged, suggesting that asset ownership is affected more by actual inheritance than by a hypothetical entitlement.

In columns 5 through 8, the dependent variable is the share of land inherited by daughters. We find that fathers who died after the amendment of the act tended to bequest approximately 2 to 3 percent more to their daughters after controlling for state-year of birth fixed effects. In columns 6 and 7, we examine the heterogeneous effects of the reform by the father's background. Interestingly, the effect of reform is greater for households where the father owned lower amounts of land, although again the coefficient is not significant. Column 8 shows no differential effect based upon the daughter's date of marriage, suggesting that asset ownership is affected more by actual inheritance than by a hypothetical entitlement and that there are not too many *inter vivos* transfers.

Educational Attainment

Columns 1 and 2 of Table 4.3 indicate that girls whose educational decisions were made after the amended inheritance regime came into force had 0.37 to 0.59 more years of elementary schooling than their older cohorts after controlling for state specific year of birth fixed effects. Columns 3 and 4 show that girls who were less than six years old at the time of HSAA and who belonged to landless households in treatment states also achieved similar levels of education. Columns 5 and 6 show that the effect on educational attainment of girls belonging to landholding and landless households is reasonably similar, suggesting that effects are relatively uniform across the socioeconomic spectrum. There could be two potential reasons why we find a positive and significant effect of HSAA on the educational attainment of girls. First, to the extent that girls' asset ownership and educational attainment are complements rather than substitutes, parents may have an incentive to provide them with both assets and education in equal measure. Second, improved educational outcomes by younger girls could be the result of the increased ability of women to control and access resources. Unfortunately, neither the data on the mother's level of asset ownership nor whether her paternal grandfather was still alive (or when he passed away) were available, which prevents us from exploring the underlying mechanisms more directly.

Table 4.3. Effect on Educational Attainment of Head's Daughters

Number of Years of Education

	All Households		Landless Households		Land Owning Households	
	(1)	(2)	(3)	(4)	(5)	(6)
Young	0.373	0.59	0.396	0.493	0.358	0.653
	[0.059]***	[0.094]***	[0.088]***	[0.131]***	[0.154]**	[0.224]**
Father's Education		0.079		0.058		0.088
		[0.008]***		[0.008]***		[0.010]***
Young* Father's Education		−0.022		−0.026		−0.028
		[0.015]		[0.020]		[0.016]
Observations	7,762	7,762	2,550	2,550	5,212	5,212
R-squared	0.13	0.16	0.21	0.23	0.13	0.17

Source: Authors.

Notes: All regressions include state specific year of birth fixed effects. Standard errors in brackets are clustered at the state level. * significant at 10%; ** significant at 5%; *** significant at 1%.

Interestingly, the estimated effect is reasonably similar to what has been in the literature on other programs. For instance, several school feeding, deworming, and conditional cash transfer schemes in developing countries which, due to a randomized rollout, have been amenable to rigorous evaluation, have been shown to increase educational attainment by between six months and 2.5 years. That is, children would stay at school for between one-half year and 2.5 years longer as the result of such programs. Although adjustment is required to account for the fact that the educational impacts of inheritance reform will not be instantaneous, the estimated effects, together with the limited cost of such reform, imply that changing inheritance legislation is a potent mechanism to improve not only asset ownership by women but also human capital accumulation by the next generation.

Marriage Market Outcomes

Table 4.4 shows the results from estimating equation (2) above. In columns 1and 2 of Table 4.4, the dependent variable is the age at marriage. We find that women who were married post HSAA are 1.5 years older, after controlling for state specific year of birth fixed effects. Furthermore, columns 3 to 6 indicate that post-HSAA marriages seem to have an effect on both the number of children and the spouse's education. For instance, women married after HSAA tend to have significantly fewer children (columns 3 and 4) and better educated spouses (columns 5 and 6). For females, marriage post-amendment is associated with a decline in the number of children by 0.86 and an increase in a spouse's education by 2.9 years. Overall, the findings suggest that an improvement in the inheritance rights of females has a significant effect on the socioeconomic status of married women. A woman's marital prospects have important implications for her subsequent life outcomes. Characteristics of her spouse and his family and her age at marriage have been shown to affect socioeconomic outcomes for

Table 4.4. Effect of the Hindu Succession Act Amendment on Marriage Market Outcomes

Dependent Variable

	Age at Marriage		Number of Children		Spouse's Education	
	(1)	(2)	(3)	(4)	(5)	(6)
Married Post HSAA	1.502	1.861	−0.863	−0.861	2.944	2.972
	[0.516]***	[0.533]***	[0.146]***	[0.144]***	[0.737]***	[0.726]***
Married Post HSAA*Father Owns Land		0.003		0.001		0.002
		[0.000]		[0.000]		[0.000]
Married Post HSAA*Father's Education		−0.372		0.016		−0.25
		[0.231]		[0.041]		[0.17]
Observations	13,230	13,230	13,230	13,230	13,230	13,230
R-squared	0.2	0.2	0.2	0.2	0.27	0.36

Source: Authors.
Notes: All regressions include state specific year of birth fixed effects. Standard errors in brackets are clustered at the state level. * significant at 10%; ** significant at 5%; *** significant at 1%.

the woman and her children, including the likelihood that she will have to endure domestic violence, her social status in her husband's home, her school attainment, her health status, and her control over reproductive choices (Bloch and Rao 2002, Jensen and Thornton 2003). Indeed, in line with previous literature, we find that granting inheritance rights to women on par with men is associated with better outcomes in the marriage market, such as marrying at a later age, attracting a more educated spouse, and being able to make favorable reproductive decisions as measured by the number of children.

Conclusion

This paper investigates the effect of changes in inheritance legislation on the ability of females to inherit property, on their educational status, and on their marriage market outcomes by exploiting a natural experiment in the form of an amendment to the original Hindu Succession Act in the states of Andhra Pradesh, Tamil Nadu, Maharashtra, and Karnataka. That amendment gave daughters a birthright to an independent share in joint family property, equal to sons, which daughters were deprived of earlier.

We use a difference-in-differences strategy to estimate the impact of the amendment of the Hindu Succession Act, comparing the likelihood of bequeathing land to daughters whose fathers died before and after the act's amendment in treatment and control states. We find that the HSAA significantly increased the probability of females to inherit land, although it did not bring about full gender equality. At the same time, the finding of a significant increase in the level of education of girls can be attributed to the HSAA, which suggests that the act led to genuine improvement in the socioeconomic status of women, rather than complying with the legal requirement in terms of physical asset transfers only while reducing the human capital transfers to their daughters, thus creating a substitution effect whereby parents did not change the total amount of (human and physical capital) assets transferred to their daughters. Moreover, this finding also implies that the impact was not limited to landed households. Furthermore, we find that granting inheritance rights to women that were on par with men is associated with better outcomes in the marriage market, such as marrying at a later age, marrying a more educated spouse, and being able to make favorable reproductive decisions as measured by the number of children.

Our results suggest that expansion of the HSAA to all of India in 2005 could have considerable potential to bring about greater access to physical and human capital assets by women. In view of the fact that full equality in land inheritance still remains a distant goal, and possibly because increased awareness is likely to be one of the driving factors underlying a greater impact, efforts at disseminating these legal provisions would be of great importance and might merit further support. Although changes in inheritance legislation have to confront multiple cultural norms, doing so beyond India, is not impossible and could provide a cost-effective means of increasing the ownership of assets by women. Further micro-level research exploring the potential mechanisms that can be used to hasten such change and help in enforcing legal arrangements, as well exploring the impact of such arrangements on tangible outcomes in other contexts, would be of great relevance.

4.2:   Gender, Low-Cost Land Certification, and Land Rental Market Participation in Ethiopia

STEIN T. HOLDEN, Norwegian University of Life Sciences, Norway
KLAUS DEININGER, The World Bank, U.S.
HOSAENA GHEBRU, Norwegian University of Life Sciences, Norway

Summary

There is renewed interest in whether land reforms can contribute to market development and poverty reduction in Africa. This paper assesses the effects on the allocative efficiency[9] of the land rental market of the low-cost approach to land registration and certification of restricted property rights that were implemented in Ethiopia from the late 1990s. Four rounds of balanced household panel data collected from 16 villages in northern Ethiopia are used. After controlling for endogeneity of land certification and unobserved household heterogeneity affecting land market participation, it was found that land certification enhanced land rental market participation of female landlord households.

Introduction

The empirical evidence on the impact of land titling and land certification reforms in Africa is mixed and there exist few rigorous studies assessing their impact. While most studies have focused on investment impacts, few have controlled for endogeneity of land rights (Brasselle et al. 2002).[10] There are, however, hardly any rigorous studies of such impacts on the allocative efficiency of land sales and land rental markets. Place and Migot-Adholla (1998) find no evidence of increased land market activity after land titling in Kenya. Jacoby and Minten (2006) also find no significant effect of titling on land leasing in Madagascar. The main novel contribution of this paper is therefore to provide a rigorous assessment of the impact of the recent low-cost land registration and certification reform in the Tigray region in Ethiopia on the land rental market activity of potential landlord households.

Bliss and Stern (1982), Bell and Sussangkarn (1988), and Skoufias (1995) have made important contributions to the analysis of allocative efficiency of land rental markets. Holden et al. (2008) provide new evidence of the emergence of land rental markets in Africa. Several of the case studies from Ethiopia, Kenya, Malawi, and Uganda revealed that land rental markets are good for poverty reduction because they enhance access to land for the poor but also revealed that there are significant transaction costs undermining the potential of these markets given that these transaction costs are reducible. Access to a unique balanced household panel data set allows us to combine two novel approaches based on Holden et al. (2009) to control for endogeneity in the allocation of certificates and on Wooldridge (2005) to control for time-invariant household heterogeneity in probit and tobit market participation panel data models. This builds on earlier work by Arellano and Carrasco (2003), Honoré (1993), Honoré and Kyriazidou (2000), Blundell and Bond (1998).

We developed a theoretical model that shows that asset poverty enhances and tenure insecurity suppresses female landlord households' land renting activity, while land certification that strengthens their tenure security should enhance such activity. The empirical findings are consistent with the theoretical model.

The Ethiopian Land Policy: A Brief Historical Overview and Recent Reforms

Civil war and border conflicts have had severe negative impacts on development in Ethiopia and land disputes and land policies have played a central role in these disputes. A military regime (Derg) took power from Haile Sellassie in 1974 and made all land state property. No household was allowed to have more than 10 ha. of land and the landlord class was excluded from leadership positions in local peasant associations that were given the responsibility for land distribution, organization of collective agriculture, collection of taxes, and production quotas. This effectively eliminated the earlier, highly powerful elite that dominated in Southern Ethiopia in particular. The regime followed up with frequent land redistributions, and land allocations based on family size was practiced to maintain an egalitarian land distribution (Rahmato 1984, Holden and Yohannes 2002). All land transactions were prohibited and so was the hiring of labor because markets were considered to be "evil capitalistic creatures." Another dimension of the "land-to-the-tiller" ideology was that households unable to cultivate their land could not feel tenure secure and risked that the land could be reallocated to other households demanding additional land (Holden and Yohannes 2002).

After a long civil war in northern Ethiopia, the military government was overthrown and a new government formed in 1991. Eritrea was separated out and a more market-friendly policy introduced. Some authority devolved from the federal to the regional governments. This was also the case for land policies where a new federal land proclamation was introduced in 1995 and followed up by regional land proclamations at different points in time after that, allowing for some variation in the land laws across regions as long as these did not violate the federal land law. These land laws retained the state as owner of all land, prohibited all land sales and mortgaging of land, and restricted the duration of land rental contracts. However, these laws strengthened the user rights of farm households by making them perpetual and inheritable and by declaring that land redistributions should stop. Such redistributions had been a commonly used tool under the previous regime to prevent landlessness from occurring and to maintain an egalitarian land distribution. However, the land redistributions created tenure insecurity and the new land laws imposed stronger restrictions on such redistributions (Alemu 1999, Holden and Yohannes 2002, Deininger and Jin 2006 Deininger et al. 2008).

The Tigray region was the first to start a land certification process in 1998–99 and used simple traditional methods in the implementation. More than 80 percent of the population in the region had received land certificates when the process was interrupted by the war with Eritrea. This was, at the time, a unique large-scale, low-cost approach that could set a new standard for land reforms that involve much lower costs than the traditional titling upon demand approach that has dominated in most countries until recently (Deininger et al. 2008).

The land registration and certification reform providing rural households with written documentation as proof of their user rights was, therefore, a welcome undertaking. The key elements of the low-cost reform included:

- Using staff with limited training to organize the local land registration;
- Using only local tools for demarcation and measurement of farm plots;
- Covering all land in a village through a sweeping survey where households walked the fields together with the organizers and agreed on the plot demarcations and ownership of the individual plots;
- Listing all plots on forms through identification of the name of the owner, the name of the location, the size of the plot, the land-quality class, the names of the neighbors to the plot, and with the neighbors as witnesses of the plot borders;
- Writing all the information into registry books that were kept at the community level and with a copy at district level; and
- Finally, issuing certificates in the name of the head of the household, where information on all the plots of the household was listed.

Deininger et al. (2008) assessed the early impacts of the Ethiopian rural land certification program and its possible implications for other African countries. The Ethiopian reform was characterized as having a low-cost compared to land titling programs in other countries and had been rapidly implemented, providing certificates for more than 20 million plots and 8 million households within a few years. While the reform had many weaknesses, it was still highly cost-effective as a first-time registration and provided important lessons.

Female-headed households (widows, divorced, and single women) also received certificates in their name for land in their possession. Traditionally, women move to the home of the husband upon marriage (patrilocal residence system), the husband is in charge of land management and only men can cultivate with oxen. Female-headed households, therefore, face problems with land management and commonly rent out much of their land (Ghebru and Holden 2008). Their relatively weak position makes them more tenure insecure because of their limited ability to till the land (the "land-to-the-tiller" philosophy) and because of the demand for land by in-laws and blood relatives. Their receipt of land certificates is likely to have strengthened their position and ability to rent out land without losing it. Land certificates likely enhance tenure security more for female-headed households than for male-headed households.

The approach gives hopes that the poor may also benefit from land reforms especially since they have been most often excluded in countries where the conventional land titling upon demand method has been used (Besley and Burgess 2000, Cotula et al. 2004, Deininger 2003). This is, therefore, an excellent opportunity to study one of the possible benefits and related poverty implications of this low-cost approach.

Other regions in Ethiopia have already learned from the Tigray experience and have started to implement similar land registration and certification programs (Deininger et al. 2008). The Amhara Region started land registration and certification in 2003 with some donor support; it used and tested more-modern equipment. The Oromia and Southern Regions started this process in 2004, after the Amhara Region, and the process is not yet completed in any of these three regions. The variation in the methods of the reforms across regions and communities provides excellent opportunities for research that can give useful insights about costs and benefits of alternative low-cost reform designs. The lessons from Ethiopia may also be highly relevant in some other poor countries characterized by high land pressure, tenure insecurity, severe rural poverty, and land degradation (Deininger et al. 2008).

Even though the 1975 land reform in Ethiopia contributed to an egalitarian land distribution, land rental markets are very active and are dominated by sharecropping arrangements (Teklu and Lemi 2004, Holden and Ghebru 2006, Holden and Bezabih 2008, Pender and Fafchamps 2006, Deininger et al. 2008, Tadesse et al. 2008).

Important policy concerns are whether the land reform in the form of registration and certification has contributed to increased tenure security, especially for the poor, including women. Anecdotal evidence from Tigray (Haile et al. 2005, MUT 2003) that women think differently about their land certificates than men do as women's tenure rights have been less secure than those of men, may imply that the certificates have a higher value to women than they have to men. Furthermore, the cultural rule against women cultivating their land causes single women to depend on assistance from men or to rent out, or to sharecrop their land. This cultural taboo often causes female-headed households in Tigray to be landlords and among the poorest of the poor (MUT 2003). Having a certificate may strengthen the bargaining power of these female-headed households in the land rental market and this may have a poverty-reduction effect.

Ghebru and Holden (2008) found the land rental market in Tigray to be characterized by substantial transaction costs and asymmetries due to rationing on the tenant side. Many tenants and potential tenants failed to rent as much land as they wanted to (Ghebru and Holden 2008). A large share of the contracts was among kin, and kinship ties appeared to improve access to land in the market (Holden and Ghebru 2006). Another study in the Amhara region (Deininger et al. 2008) also found signs of high transaction costs in the land rental market. Similarly, Tikabo et al. (2007) found significant transaction costs in the land rental market in Eritrea.

MUT (2003) suggested that land certificates may not be important for land rental contracts and found no sign of changes in the land rental markets due to certificates. Their qualitative evidence from tenants indicated that tenants did not care whether the landowner has a certificate or not. What was more important was that they could trust the other party. With trust the certificate is unimportant. They also made the point that high enforcement costs may reduce the value of the certificate as an instrument to enforce contracts through the social court. Our data allow us to make quantitative assessments of whether certificates enhance participation in the land rental market. Trust and enforcement possibilities are clearly important determinants of the transaction costs and have implications for the extent to which land certification can enhance the allocative efficiency of the land rental market.

Theoretical Model

Early studies of transaction costs and adjustment in the land rental market include those by Bliss and Stern (1982), Bell and Sussangkarn (1988), and Skoufias (1995) who developed static models for analysis of land rental market participation in the presence of transaction costs. These early studies relied on cross-section data and could not control for unobserved household heterogeneity. We develop a theoretical model of landlord behavior in the land rental market building on these earlier contributions, taking tenure insecurity into account.

Tenure insecurity is captured as an asset loss probability that may reduce future income. Renting out of land today will increase the probability of losing the rented land in the future. The probability of losing the land in the future (ξ) depends on gender (g), where $g=\{1=female, 0=male\}$. Female-headed households are more tenure insecure than male-headed households[11], $\xi_g>0$. Tenure insecurity also depends on whether the household has a land certificate for the land, ⊚. The basic idea of the land certification is that $\xi_⊚<0$, $\xi_{⊚g}<0$; that is tenure insecurity is reduced for households having a land certificate, and tenure insecurity is reduced more for those that are initially more tenure insecure, like female-headed households receiving a land certificate.

There is a transaction cost (c) in the land rental market and this transaction cost is non-decreasing in area rented out[12]. It is lower the more land the household rented out in the previous period since contracts typically are renewed (Fafchamps 2004, Holden and Ghebru 2006); therefore, $c=c(R,R_{t-1}), c_R \geq 0, c_{Rt-1}<0$. Established landlords are likely to face lower transaction costs in the land rental market because they have already established trade relationships with tenants. This implies that we assume there are non-convexities and entry barriers in the land rental market that may hinder market participation for those who are not yet in the market. These non-convexities and barriers may also constrain the ability to expand market participation for those inside the market.

Land is rented out through a sharecropping contract. We assume that the share of the output that the landlord gets, ($1-\alpha$), is fixed and nonnegotiable in the short to medium run that the model covers[13]. For simplicity, we assumed that the returns in the land rental market are linear in area rented out, $q_R=1, q_{RR}=0$ (where q is output). For simplicity, we also ignore production risk, which possibly could be one reason for the preference for sharecropping contracts. Production on owned land (q) is a function of owner-operated land area, ($A-R$), a tradable factor (L), and a non-tradable factor (N). These are assumed to be complements in production. There is a significant difference in the endowment of the non-tradable factor for male- and female-headed households, $N=N(g)$, $N_g<0$, as female-headed households typically are poorer in non-land resources like oxen, male labor, and skills. This is because acquiring farming skills is culturally the responsibility of men and because cultivating land using oxen can be done only by men. However, oxen rental markets are missing in the setting we are studying.

The standard assumptions apply for the functional forms of the value and utility functions. The landlord's optimization problem is formulated with a Bellman equation:

$$V(A_t) = \underset{R,L}{Max} U \left[\begin{matrix} pq(A-R, L, N(g)) + p(1-\alpha)q(R) \\ -c(R, R_{t-1}) - wL \end{matrix} \right\} + \beta V\{A - \xi(\mathbb{C}, g)R\} \right] \qquad (1)$$

The Kuhn-Tucker conditions, allowing nonparticipation in the land rental market are

$$V_R = U_Y\{p(1-\alpha) - pq_A - c_R\} - \beta V_{At+1}\xi \leq 0 \perp R \geq 0$$
$$V_L = U_Y\{pq_L - w\} = 0 \qquad (2)$$

A simple inspection of the corner solution indicates that nonparticipation in the land rental market is more likely the lower the share of the output the potential landlord gets; the higher the marginal return under owner-cultivation, the higher the marginal transaction cost, the higher the tenure insecurity of the rented out land, and the higher the discount factor (β). If females have less of non-tradable, non-land resources (N), they are likely to have lower marginal returns on their own land and should be more likely to rent out land. On the other hand, if they are more tenure insecure, they are less likely to rent out their land and the consequence may be that they cultivate their land but have lower land productivity as found by Holden and Bezabih (2008) in the Amhara region of Ethiopia.

By comparative statics, assuming that the second order conditions for maximum are satisfied, we get the following gender response in area rented out:

$$R_g = |H|^{-1} \left\{ \begin{array}{l} U_Y p q_{AN} N_g - U_{YY} p q_N N_g \left(p(1-\alpha) - p q_A - c_R \right) - \beta \left(V_{At+1,At+1} R - V_{At+1} \right) \xi_g U_Y p q_L \\ -(U_Y)^2 p^2 q_{LN} q_{AL} N_g \end{array} \right\} \quad (3)$$

This expression is positive if the endowment effect of gender dominates; that is, female-headed households rent out more than male-headed households because they have less non-tradable endowments. On the other hand, the expression will be negative if the tenure insecurity effect dominates; that is, the female-headed households rent out less because they are more tenure insecure.

The effect of receiving a land certificate on area rented out by landlords becomes

$$R_C = |H|^{-1} \left\{ \beta \left(V_{At+1} - V_{At+1,At+1} R \right) \xi_C U_Y p q_{LL} \right\} \quad (4)$$

The result is unambiguously positive when $\xi_\bullet < 0$. If this tenure security enhancing effect of land certification is particularly strong for female-headed (potential) landlord households, they may have responded more strongly than male-headed households by renting out more land after receiving certificates.

Hypotheses

The following hypotheses are tested:

- Female-headed households are more likely to rent out land and rent out more land than male-headed households (due to their poverty in non-tradable, non-land resources), versus
- Female-headed households rent out less land than male-headed households because they are more tenure insecure.
- Landlords who received certificates rent out more land after the reform (due to increased tenure security).
- Female landlords who received land certificates rent out more land as a response to getting land certificates than compared to male landlords who received land certificates (because female landlords initially were more tenure insecure and land certificates increased their relative tenure security more).

Data and Descriptive Statistics

Data

We have used a unique household panel data set covering the five main zones of the Tigray region in northern Ethiopia. The data are from 400 households in 16 different communities located in 11 districts covering the major variation in agroecological, market access, population density, and access to irrigation. Within each community, we have a random sample of 25 households who were interviewed in 1998, 2001, 2003, and 2006. The first survey round took place just before the land registration and certification program was introduced. The need to have balanced panel data made it possible to include only 303 households. The households have been surveyed four times, covering the years 1997–98, 2000–01, 2002–03, and 2005–06 while land certification was implemented in all Tigray region communities in 1998–99.

Descriptive Statistics

The baseline survey in 1998 revealed that 51 percent of the sample households feared losing their land due to future land redistributions, indicating a high level of tenure insecurity based on the land policy where land redistributions within communities have been an important element. Typically, households with more than average land in the communities feared such land redistributions because they were likely to be among the losers. The other half of the population, rather, was expecting to gain land in the next redistribution; many of them, therefore, hoped for a new redistribution (Hagos and Holden 2003).

   The survey in 2006 included questions to households about their perceptions about the effects of the land certification; 84 percent of the households stated that they perceived the risk of being evicted from their land to have been reduced due to the land certification and 78 percent of the households stated that certification increased the probability that they would get compensation in case of land takings.

   Key summary statistics are presented in Tables 4.5 and 4.6. Table 4.5 presents change in means over time for all key variables, including their standard errors. The percentage of households renting out land increased from 24 percent in 1997 to 27 percent in 2000 and to 26 and 29 percent in 2003 and 2006. Average area leased out increased from 0.52 *tsimdi* (1 *tsimdi*=0.25 ha) in 1997 to 0.73 *tsimdi* in 2000, 0.80 in 2003 and down to 0.74 *tsimdi* in 2006. The percentage of the households with certificates increased from 0 in 1997 to 95 percent in 2000 and to 89 percent in 2003, and declined to 89 percent in 2006. The reasons for the reduction may be that some households lost their certificate and/or a change in head of household through inheritance, which also may have involved a subdivision of the land holding, without receiving new certificates. The share of female-headed households increased from 13 percent in 1997 to 31 percent in 2006. This could partly be explained by the Ethiopia-Eritrea war in 1998–99 and the aging of the household sample where male heads of households who are typically older than their wives may die before their wives.

Table 4.5. Summary Statistics for Land Rental Market Participation and Land Certificate Distribution by Year

Year	Statistics	Landlords, percentage	Land rented out, tsimdi	Land certificate, percentage
1997	Mean	0.24	0.52	0.000
	Se(mean)		0.08	
2000	Mean	0.27	0.73	0.951
	Se(mean)		0.09	
2003	Mean	0.26	0.80	0.892
	Se(mean)		0.10	
2006	Mean	0.29	0.74	0.889
	Se(mean)		0.09	
Total	Mean	0.26	0.70	0.683
	Se(mean)		0.05	

Source: Holden et al. (in press).
Note: se(mean) is the standard error of the mean. 1 *tsimdi*=0.25 ha.

Table 4.6 characterizes the landlord households versus all households. Landlord households were significantly poorer in oxen, other livestock, male labor, and female labor, while they were not poorer in terms of land endowment. This pattern remained fairly stable during the years the data covered. Oxen are crucial for land cultivation and a pair of oxen is needed for that. Households with one ox may pair their ox with another household also having one ox. Households without oxen typically face severe difficulty in accessing oxen for land cultivation because the market for renting oxen is almost nonexistent. The basic rationale of the land rental market is, therefore, that households poor in non-land resources rent out land to households with relatively more non-land resources. Female-headed households are typically poor in non-land resources and cannot plough with oxen; therefore, they are more likely to be landlords. The 1975 land reform and the follow-up land redistributions have maintained an egalitarian land distribution, and a consequence is this "reverse-tenancy system" with poor landlords and slightly more wealthy (but still poor) tenants.

Table 4.6. Summary Statistics for Key Endowment Variables of Landlord, Non-participant and Tenant Households

Household type	Statistics	% female headed	Adult females	Adult males	Oxen	Other livestock	Farm size, tsimdi
Landlord	Mean	0.42	1.23	0.97	0.40	1.14	4.48
	Se(mean)	0.03	0.04	0.06	0.04	0.10	0.17
All	Mean	0.20	1.27	1.34	0.85	2.19	4.27
	Se(mean)	0.01	0.02	0.03	0.03	0.07	0.10

Source: Holden et al. (in press).
Note: Se(mean) is the standard error of the mean. Other livestock measured as tropical livestock units (tlu). 1 *tsimdi*=0.25 ha.

Econometric Issues and Estimation Approach

Econometric Issues: Attrition and Endogeneity

Attrition bias was tested and corrected for using Deaton's approach of including a polynomial form of the predicted probability of households being in the balanced household sample from the attrition model (Deaton 1997). Due to multicollinearity only the third polynomial was retained in the final regressions after having removed the first and second polynomials due to their higher variance inflation numbers.

Possession of land certificates is potentially endogenous. An empirical investigation of the process of registration and certification revealed the following reasons why some households did not have land certificates: (a) administrative failures causing incomplete registration and certification in some communities, (b) some households may have been left out of the registration because they were absent at that time, (c) some households did not receive the certificates because the administration ran out of certificates and failed to obtain additional ones, (d) some households did not collect their certificates because they may not have considered them to be important at that time, and (e) some households lost their certificates after they received them or, if there had been a change in the head of the household, the new head of the household had failed to take over the certificate or to get a new certificate. The administrative failures appear to have affected households and communities quite randomly and are not likely to create any endogeneity bias. Reasons (b) and (d) above may have the potential to create this bias.

Finding good instruments for identification of the potentially endogenous land certification variable was not possible. A novel approach proposed and tested by Holden et al. (2009), and found to give more robust results than alternative approaches, is therefore used. This involved using a linear probability model with household fixed effects on the panel data in the instrumentation equation to clean out all possible observable and unobservable time-invariant household, farm, and village determinants of allocation of certificates, while the residual was used to estimate the impact of random certification. A large positive residual implies that the household has a certificate but is predicted not to have one, and a large negative residual implies that the household does not have a certificate but was predicted with a high probability to have one. While the random certification residual variable was included to test for the effect of random certification, models with and without the predicted certificate variable were run in combination with the Wooldridge (2005) approach described below to control for unobserved household heterogeneity in the random effects panel probit and tobit models. Inclusion of the predicted certificate variable from the linear probability model with household fixed effects may be seen as an additional control for unobserved household heterogeneity in the renting out models. Bootstrapping, by re-sampling households was used to obtain corrected standard errors.

Econometric Estimation: Dynamic Panel Data Modeling Approach

An approach to dynamic probit and tobit models suggested by Wooldridge (2005) has been used. The dynamic panel data models with binary and censored response variables included controls for unobserved time-invariant heterogeneity. The probit form was used for the binary land rental market participation models and incorporated a lagged dependent variable along with strictly exogenous variables with standard random effects, following Wooldridge (2005).

The dynamic probit model is specified as follows:

$$P\left(y_{it} = 1 \mid y_{i,t-1}, \ldots, y_{i0}, z_i, c_i\right) = \Phi\left(z_{it}\gamma + \rho y_{i,t-1} + c_i\right) \tag{5}$$

where y is the dependent variable conditioned on the lagged dependent variables, exogenous variables (z_i), and unobserved household heterogeneity (c_i). The unobserved heterogeneity is assumed to be additive inside the standard normal distribution function (Φ) (ibid.). The model allows us to test for state dependence. Previous participation in the land rental market may matter for current participation. This is modeled as an AR1 process. This is considered acceptable when there are three years between each year observed.

The unobserved heterogeneous effect is modeled as (Wooldridge 2005)

$$c_i = \alpha_0 + \alpha_1 y_{i0} + z_i\alpha_2 + \alpha_i \tag{6}$$

on the initial condition and exogenous variables to get a likelihood function that does not depend on the unobserved individual effects. This allows deriving the likelihood function by integrating over the distribution of α_i, and we get the same structure as the standard random effects probit model, except that the explanatory variables at time period t are

$$x_{it} = \left\{1, z_{it}, y_{i,t-1}, y_{i0}, z_i\right\}$$

The dynamic Tobit model with unobserved effects is specified as follows (Wooldridge 2005):

$$y_{it} = \max\left[0, z_{it}\gamma + g\left(y_{i,t-1}\right)\rho + c_i + u_{it}\right]$$
$$u_{it} \mid y_{i,t-1}, \ldots, y_{i0}, z_i, c_i \sim \text{Normal}\left(0, \sigma_u^2\right) \tag{7}$$

for $t = 1, 2, \ldots, T$ time periods and $I = 1, 2, \ldots, N$ households in the cross section. The $g(.)$ function is formulated to allow the effect of lagged y to be different depending on whether it was a corner solution or not.[14]

The dynamic corner solution model controlling for time-invariant unobserved heterogeneous effects for land rented in or rented out can therefore be modelled as a random effects tobit model where the explanatory variables at time t are $x_{it} = \left\{z_{it}, g_{i,t-1}, r_{i0}, z_i\right\}$, where $g_{i,t-1} = g\left(y_{i,t-1}\right)$ and $r_{i0} = r\left(y_{i0}\right)$[15].

Dependent variables in the analyses of land rental market participation are dummy variables for participation in the land rental market as landlords or tenants and land area rented out or rented in. Lagged dependent variables and initial year participation were included to test for state dependence and to correct for time-invariant unobserved heterogeneity, based on the new approach proposed by Wooldridge (2005) and described above.

An interaction variable between the sex of household head and the random certificate residual variable was created and included to test for the gender impacts of land certification. The owned-land farm size variable was included to test for allocative efficiency in the land rental market (Bliss and Stern 1982, Skoufias 1995, and Holden et al. 2008). The variable is considered to be exogenous to households because selling of land is prohibited. Other household endowment variables were not included because they are potentially endogenous, but the key results of the paper were not significantly affected by their inclusion.

Results and Discussion

Land Reform and Participation in the Land Rental Market

The results of the land rental market participation probit models are presented in Table 4.7. The sex-of-household-head variable was highly significant (at 0.1 percent levels) in both models and with a positive sign, supporting hypothesis H1, indicating that the endowment effect strongly dominates the tenure insecurity effect. The random certificate residual variable was insignificant in both models but the interaction variable between the random certificate residual and the sex of household head was significant at 10 percent level in both models and with a positive sign. Hypotheses 4 and 2 cannot, therefore, be rejected. Households with larger land endowment were significantly (at 5 percent level) more likely to rent out their land, but the coefficient was close to zero, which is indicative of high transaction costs in the market. Together with the lagged participation variable, this indicates that there are initial entry costs for households that have not participated in the market before.

Table 4.7. Determinants of Participation in the Land Rental Market

Variables	Landlord 1	Landlord 2
Landlord dummy, lagged one period	1.422****	1.421****
	(0.15)	(0.15)
Landlord dummy, initial year	0.588**	0.605***
	(0.23)	(0.22)
Random certificate, residual	0.047	0.066
	(0.40)	(0.37)
Years since certification	0.016	-0.002
	(0.02)	(0.03)
Sex of household head	0.560****	0.566****
	(0.14)	(0.15)
Sex of household head*Random certificate, residual	1.822*	1.687*
	(0.95)	(0.93)
Own farm size	0.031**	0.031**
	(0.02)	(0.02)
Predicted certificate, control for unobservable household heterogeneity		0.234
		(0.18)
Attrition bias test	-0.276	-0.271
	(0.26)	(0.24)
Constant	-1.445****	-1.556****
	(0.19)	(0.18)
Lnsig2u _cons	-12.827****	-13.039****
	(0.18)	(0.16)
Prob > chi2	0.000	0.000
Number of observations	1212	1212

Source: Holden et al. (in press).

Note: Bootstrapped standard errors in parentheses, re-sampling households, using 300 replications. * significant at 10%; ** significant at 5%; *** significant at 1%, **** significant at 0.1%.

Land Reform and Degree of Participation in the Land Rental Market

The results of the household random effects tobit panel data models are presented in Table 4.8. In order to test all our hypotheses and assess the robustness of the findings with respect to possible endogeneity of certificate, we specified four alternative models without and with the random certificate residual and sex-of-household-head interaction variable and without and with the predicted certificate variable as an additional control for unobserved household heterogeneity. Hypothesis H1 is strongly supported by all models as the sex-of-household-head variable is highly significant (at 0.1 percent levels) and with a positive sign meaning that female-headed households rent out significantly more land than male-headed households. Controlling for unobserved household heterogeneity by inclusion of the predicted certificate variable in addition to doing so by inclusion of the initial areas rented out and initial period landlord dummy variables did not change this. Inclusion of the actual certificate variable rather than the predicted certificate also gave the same basic results.

Table 4.8. Area Rented Out Models with Gender and Certificate Interaction Variables

Variables	Area rented out 1	Area rented out 2	Area rented out 3	Area rented out 4
Lagged land area rented out	0.231**	0.237**	0.232**	0.237**
	(0.10)	(0.11)	(0.10)	(0.11)
Land area rented out, initial year	0.542****	0.548****	0.551****	0.556****
	(0.15)	(0.16)	(0.15)	(0.15)
Landlord dummy, lagged one period	3.008****	3.046****	3.028****	3.060****
	(0.34)	(0.36)	(0.36)	(0.33)
Landlord dummy, initial year	-0.008	-0.035	0.043	0.02
	(0.42)	(0.42)	(0.40)	(0.41)
Random certificate, residual from prediction	0.839	-0.213	0.913	-0.065
	(0.70)	(0.73)	(0.68)	(0.75)
Years since certification	0.069**	0.071**	-0.021	-0.011
	(0.03)	(0.03)	(0.05)	(0.04)
Sex of household head	1.471****	1.411****	1.475****	1.414****
	(0.26)	(0.26)	(0.24)	(0.24)
Sex of household head* Random certificate, residual		4.264**		3.874**
		(1.71)		(1.61)
Predicted certificate, control for unobserved household heterogeneity			1.118****	1.025***
			(0.34)	(0.36)
Own farm size	0.163***	0.160***	0.166****	0.163***
	(0.05)	(0.05)	(0.05)	(0.05)
Attrition bias test	-0.772	-0.784	-0.754	-0.763
	(0.48)	(0.53)	(0.49)	(0.56)
Constant	-4.182****	-4.154****	-4.667****	-4.603****
	(0.47)	(0.51)	(0.53)	(0.57)
Sigma u _cons	0	0	0	0
	(0.17)	(0.17)	(0.16)	(0.17)
Sigma_e _cons	2.774****	2.752****	2.750****	2.732****
	(0.18)	(0.17)	(0.17)	(0.16)
Prob > chi2	0.000	0.000	0.000	0.000
Number of obs.	1,212	1,212	1,212	1,212

Source: Holden et al. (in press).

Note: Bootstrapped standard errors in parentheses, re-sampling households, using 300 replications. * significant at 10%; ** significant at 5%; *** significant at 1%, **** significant at 0.1%.

The random certification residual variable was insignificant in all models while the interaction variable between the random certificate residual and the sex of household head was significant (at 5 percent level) in the two models where it was included. It had a positive sign indicating that female-headed landlord households who received land certificates increased the area they rented out due to the certification. The random certification residual variable changed sign from positive to negative (although insignificant) when the interaction variable was included, indicating that landlord households in general, and male landlord households especially, did not rent out more land after receiving land certificates. This result implies that hypotheses H4 and H2 cannot be rejected while hypothesis H3 is partly rejected. Land certification has made female landlord households more willing to rent out their land, probably because they have become more tenure secure. This finding is also supported by perception-data collected from the households in the last survey round in 2006.

The farm size variable was also highly significant (1 percent level in three of the models and at 0.1 percent level in one specification) but with a low parameter value in the range 0.16–0.17—a sign of significant transaction costs and limited adjustment. This finding is consistent with the finding of highly significant (0.1 percent level) state dependency for the lagged landlord dummy variable and the significant (5 percent level) lagged area rented out variable, both having positive signs. These findings are consistent with potential landlords facing high initial transaction costs (entry barrier) in the land rental market.

Conclusion

The analysis of the panel data from Tigray has demonstrated a significant and positive effect of the low-cost land certification that took place in the late 1990s on the amount of activity in the land rental market. The reform appears to have reduced transaction costs in the land rental market by making poor female (potential) landlord households more willing to rent out their land.

The analyses demonstrate that transaction costs in the land rental market remain high and there should be scope for further reducing them by facilitating land rental transactions at the local level. However, care should be exercised when reforming land rental markets to ensure that the benefits from the reforms are higher than the costs. A system for voluntary registration of land rental contracts may be better than the system with compulsory registration of all land rental contracts that has been included in the most recent revisions of the regional land proclamations in Ethiopia.

Another important contribution of this paper was to apply a new approach to generate a random policy variable for unbiased impact assessment in a situation where endogeneity is a potential problem and no good instruments for identification are available. This approach deserves wider application and may reduce the need for randomized experiments to tease out the impact of policy reforms particularly in limited dependent panel data models.

Notes

[1] Adopted in 1979 by the United Nations General Assembly.

[2] The Hindu Succession Act applies to Hindus, Buddhists, Jains, and Sikhs, but excludes Christians, Muslims, Parsis, or Jews.

[3] According to Roy (2008), the most important distinction between these two schools was in terms of their classification of property. The *Mitakshara* system made a distinction between joint family property and separate property. Joint family property consisted principally of ancestral property (that is, property inherited from the father, paternal grandfather, or paternal great-grandfather), plus any property that was jointly acquired or was acquired separately but merged into the joint property, while separate property included that which was self-acquired (if acquired without detriment to the ancestral estate) and any property inherited from persons other than his father, paternal grandfather, or paternal great-grandfather (Agarwal 1994). Under *Mitakshara*, three generations of male members became joint heirs or coparceners to the joint family property by birth while females had no such rights. The *Dayabhaga* system, on the other hand, treated all property as separate property, and does not recognize a coparcenary right to property.

[4] Historically, among the patrilineal Hindu groups, the inheritance rights of both widows and daughters were extremely limited, with those of the daughter being weaker than widow's (Agarwal 1994). On the other hand, under the *Dayabhaga* system, no distinction is made between separate and joint property with the owner maintaining absolute control over it. Upon a man's death, property went in the first instance equally to his sons. Widows and daughters could inherit only in the absence of male heirs. This meant that the probability of a widow or daughter inheriting some property was somewhat greater under *Dayabhaga* than *Mitakshara* (Agarwal 1994).

[5] To keep things simple and for purposes of clarity, we limit our discussion below to the case of intestate inheritance. This is justified on the one hand by the fact that in rural India formal wills are very rare. More importantly, as discussed below, the key innovation of the HSAA is to make females coparceners by birth, implying that their share cannot be willed away.

[6] Kerala abolished joint family property altogether in 1976 (Agarwal 1994) in favor of an arrangement where all family members hold their shares separately.

[7] We use data on the states of Maharashtra, Karnataka, Andhra Pradesh, Tamil Nadu, Orissa, West Bengal, Bihar, Chhatisgarh, Gujarat, Haryana, Himachal Pradesh, Jharkhand, Madhya Pradesh, Punjab, Rajasthan, and Uttar Pradesh.

[8] Value of assets for each household is computed from current (2006) values (in rupees) of all residential and commercial property, land ownership, jewelry, livestock, consumer durables, mechanized, nonmechanized assets, and savings and investments in financial institutions as reported by the household head.

[9] Allocative efficiency may be defined as the possibility of combining factors of production in optimal ratios through trade of these factors. If the markets for non-land factors of production are imperfect or missing, the market for land can compensate for this if it is efficient.

[10] Exceptions in Africa include Besley (1995) in Ghana; Carter et al. (1994), and Place and Migot-Adholla (1998) in Kenya; Jacoby and Minten (2007) in Madagascar; Moor (1998) in Zimbabwe; and Holden et al. (2009) in Ethiopia.

[11] This is a widely held assumption, especially in patriarchal societies.

[12] An initial fixed transaction cost for searching and negotiating with potential partners will always exist, and there is likely to be an additional variable transaction cost element with a marginal transaction cost that may go towards zero as area rented out increases. The transaction cost function can be more complex if the household has several geographically dispersed plots, see Holden, Otsuka, and Place (2008) for further elaboration on this.

[13] The share takes values like 0.5, 0.33, or 0.25 going to the landlord with the highest share on good-quality land and the lowest share on poor-quality land and that these shares have been constant for many years.

[14] In our analysis, we only used two alternative specifications: first we included the lagged variable directly since we have a small T and there is three years between each observation. In the second specification, we included a dummy for whether the lagged variable was positive or not. We treated the initial value for the dependent variable in the same way. *See* note 15 below.

[15] We use two alternative specifications: the first is $g\left(y_{i,t-1}\right) = y_{i,t-1}$ and $r_{i0} = r\left(y_{i0}\right) = y_{i0}$, the other also includes dummies. Table 4 contains models with the second formulation. For Table 3 the response variable is binary, leading also to inclusion of only binary lagged variables.

CHAPTER 5

Land Governance for Rapid Urbanization

5.1: Improving Access to Land and Shelter

CLARISSA AUGUSTINUS, Global Land Tool Network and the United Nations Human Settlements Programme (UN-HABITAT), Kenya

Introduction

One of the key challenges of the twenty-first century is to move away from chaotic cities toward sustainable urbanization. Addressing the land and shelter agenda is crucial to achieving sustainable urban development. Land and shelter encompass a range of other factors, such as infrastructure, land administration, economic growth, and finance. This paper reviews some of the key issues in regard to the land and shelter sectors, including the Millennium Development Goal 7 on slums, and the lessons learned, in regard to the delivery of land and housing globally. It also identifies policy and implementation gaps and outlines the priority actions necessary to address these gaps.

Urban Challenge: Background and Context

Half of humanity now lives in cities, and within the next two decades 60 percent of the world's people will reside in urban areas. By the middle of the twenty-first century the total urban population of the developing world will more than double, increasing from 2.3 billion in 2005 to 5.3 billion in 2050. "Urban growth rates are highest in the developing world ... [which is] responsible for 95 per cent of the world's urban population growth" (UN-HABITAT 2008). However, many cities will be characterized by urban poverty and inequality, and urban growth will become virtually synonymous with slum formation. Indeed, Asia is already home to more than half of the world's slum population (581 million), followed by sub-Saharan Africa (199 million), where 90 percent of new urban settlements are taking the form of slums. The latter region also has the highest annual urban and slum growth rates in the world, 4.58 percent and 4.53 percent, respectively, which are more than twice the world average (UN-HABITAT 2008). As shown in figure 5.1, at least one third of the urban population in the developing world lives in slum conditions.

In regard to the poverty profile of urban areas, Baker (2008) states that "on average the urban poverty lines are about 30 percent higher than the rural lines, though this differs from region to region, ... [with] approximately 750 million people living in urban areas in developing countries below the poverty line of $2 a day in 2002 and 290 million using the $1 a day line. This represents about one third of all urban residents ($2 a day) ... and one quarter of the total poor in developing countries. Also, "in many countries the gini coefficient within urban areas is substantially higher than in rural areas, ... and inequality in access to ... housing [and] land ... can have ... political repercussions" (Baker 2008).

Figure 5.1. Estimated Urban Population Living in Slum Conditions between 1990 and 2001

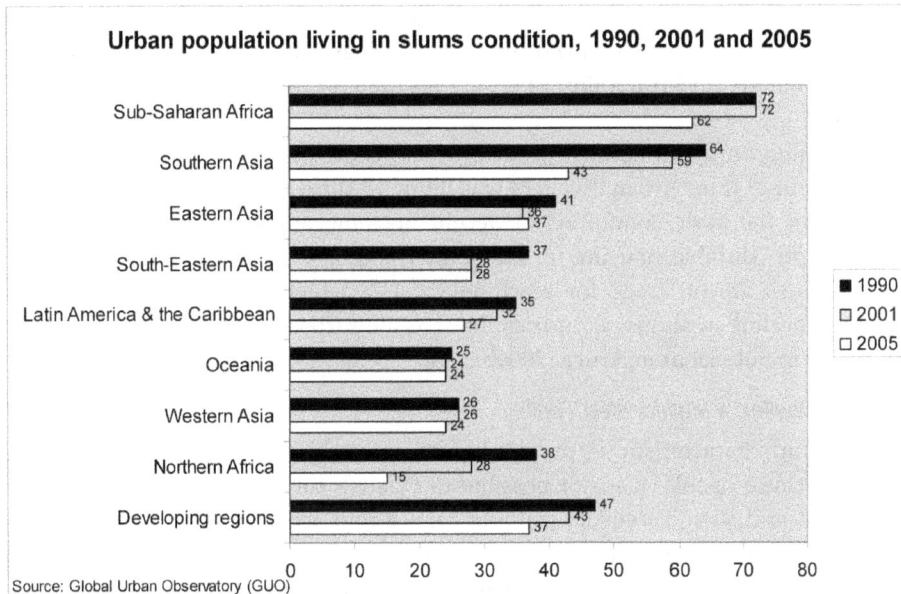

Urban population living in slums condition, 1990, 2001 and 2005

Source: Global Urban Observatory (GUO)

Source: Moreno: Forthcoming.

Note: The drastic reduction of the percentage of urban population living in slums, particularly in Sub-Saharan Africa between 2001 (72 percent) and 2005 (62 percent) is largely explained by the change in slum definition which now includes the use of pit latrines.

From another angle, the space taken up by urban localities is increasing faster than the urban population itself. Between 2000 and 2030, the world's urban population is expected to increase by 72 percent, while the built-up areas of cities of 100,000 people or more could increase by 175 percent. The land area occupied by cities is not in itself large, considering that it contains half the world's population. Recent estimates, based on satellite imagery, indicate that all urban sites (including green as well as built-up areas) cover only 2.8 percent of the earth's land area. This means that about 3.3 billion people occupy an area less than half the size of Australia (Angel et al. 2005, cited by UNFPA 2007).

Over the next 25 years, over 2 billion people will be added to the growing demand for housing, water supply, sanitation and other urban infrastructure and services. What is critical when considering this number is the order of magnitude. Close to 3 billion people, or about 40 percent of the world's population, will need housing and basic infrastructure and services by 2030. This translates into the need to complete 96,150 housing units per day (UN-HABITAT 2005). There is an acute housing shortage around the world, but it is more severe in developing countries. For example, 40 million housing units are needed in India, 735,000 in Indonesia, 709,000 in Malaysia, 700,000 in Angola, 659,000 in Bangladesh, 650,000 in South Africa, 240,000 in DRC, 73,000-151,000 in Ethiopia, and 70,000 units in Cameroon (UN-HABITAT 2006).

Millennium Development Goal 7, Target 11, commits the international community to achieving a significant improvement in the lives of at least 100 million slum dwellers by the year 2020. Attaining even this very limited goal is not likely. A slum household is defined as a group of individuals living under the same roof lacking one or more of the following conditions: access to improved water; access to improved sanitation facilities; sufficient living area (not more than three people sharing the same room); structural quality and durability of dwellings; and security of tenure (UN-HABITAT 2008).

Reporting on the attainment of Goal 7, the United Nations (2007) stated that "in 2005, one out of three urban dwellers was living in slum conditions—that is, lacking at least one of the basic conditions of decent housing: adequate sanitation, improved water supply, durable housing, or adequate living space." UN-HABITAT states that few countries are on track for reaching Goal 7, which would imply a rapid and sustained decline in slums. Countries that are the furthest from the slum target goals are mostly in Sub-Saharan Africa (2006b).

Land and Shelter: a Multifaceted Topic

A key urban characteristic is proximity and concentration of activities, assets, and people. Because of this, it is not possible to create a robust analytical framework for urban land and shelter delivery without taking into account other activities that are integrally linked to, and often in the critical path of, the supply of land and shelter. These activities include, among others: politics (political economy, strategy and priorities, culture, social capital within communities, corruption, vested interests), planning, law (regulations and enforcement), and governance (national government, municipalities, civil society, private sector, and partnership approaches). They also include factors such as services (trunk infrastructure and individual connections, water, sanitation, electricity, roads), housing and land markets, finance (investment, subsidy, mortgage, fiscal flows, land tax, valuation), economic growth and poverty reduction (including employment and livelihoods), as well as community facilities (public transport, schools, clinics, etc.), environmental management (including building technologies), land information management, land administration and land management, institutional strengthening and capacity building (public and private sector, all stakeholders), types of urban settlement (formal and informal). These factors also play out, albeit differently, within post-disaster and post-conflict environments. Practitioners in the shelter sector know that working holistically with the complexity and multiple linkages of the sector is integral to the success of delivering shelter at scale.

Key United Nations Conventions

A few of the United Nations key conventions are highlighted here. The right to adequate housing is laid down in Article 11(1) of the International Covenant on Economic, Social and Cultural Rights (General Assembly Resolution 2200 A (XXI), adopted 1966). The right to property is a human right that is laid down in the International Covenant on Civil and Political Rights. Together with the Universal Declaration on Human Rights (General Assembly Resolution 217 A (III), adopted 1948), these two International Covenants form the 'International Bill of Human Rights.' All human rights apply equally to women and men, and discrimination on the basis of sex is prohibited by the International Bill of Human Rights and other international human rights instruments, such as the Convention on the Elimination of All Forms of Discrimination Against Women (CEDAW) (United Nations General Assembly 1979). Women's equal rights to adequate housing, land, and property are firmly entrenched in international law.

The Habitat Agenda is the key comprehensive international convention in the United Nations system which outlines international responsibilities for land and shelter. Adequate shelter for all is the key focus of UN-HABITAT, which draws its mandate from this agenda. In regard to land and shelter it states

> Access to land and legal security of tenure are strategic prerequisites for the provision of adequate shelter for all and for the development of sustainable human settlements affecting both urban and rural areas. It is also one way of breaking the vicious circle of poverty. Every Government must show a commitment to promoting the provision of an adequate supply of land in the context of sustainable land-use policies. While recognizing the existence of different national laws and/or systems of land tenure, Governments at the appropriate levels, including local authorities, should nevertheless strive to remove all possible obstacles that may hamper equitable access to land and ensure that equal rights of women and men related to land and property are protected under the law. The failure to adopt, at all levels, appropriate rural and urban land policies and land management practices remains a primary cause of inequity and poverty. It is also the cause of increased living costs, the occupation of hazard-prone land, environmental degradation and the increased vulnerability of urban and rural habitats, affecting all people, especially disadvantaged and vulnerable groups, people living in poverty and low-income people. (Habitat Agenda 1996, 75)

In regard specifically to shelter, the Habitat Agenda states

> The formulation and periodic evaluation and revision ... of enabling shelter policies, with a view to creating a framework for efficient and effective shelter delivery systems, are the cornerstone for the provision of adequate shelter for all. A fundamental principle in formulating a realistic shelter policy is its interdependence with overall macroeconomic, environmental and social development

policies. Shelter policies, while focusing on the increasing demand for housing and infrastructure, should also emphasize the increased use and maintenance of existing stock through ownership, rental. and other tenure options, responding to the diversity of needs. These policies should also encourage and support the people who, in many countries, particularly developing countries, individually or collectively act as important producers of housing. Policies should respond to the diverse needs of those belonging to disadvantaged and vulnerable groups. (Habitat Agenda 1996, 65)

After the 2nd United Nations Conference on Human Settlements (HABITAT II) held in Istanbul, which produced the Habitat Agenda in 1996, the next major milestone for UN-HABITAT was 2001 at the United Nations Special Session of the General Assembly for an Overall Review and Appraisal of the Implementation of the Habitat Agenda, ("Istanbul + 5 conference", at which the General Assembly adopted the Declaration on Cities and Other Human Settlements in the New Millennium. In adopting this declaration, the General Assembly gave recognition to this new strategic vision and its emphasis on UN-HABITAT's two global campaigns on secure tenure and urban governance as strategic points of entry for implementing the Habitat Agenda. In 2007, these campaigns were merged into one *Sustainable Urbanization* campaign.

Importantly for this conference, in 2004 the General Assembly adopted a resolution encouraging governments to support the Global Campaigns for Secure Tenure and Urban Governance, as important tools for *promoting the administration of land and property rights* (Resolution A/59/484).

UN-HABITAT is the focal agency for Millennium Development Goal 7, Target 11, which aims to significantly improve the lives of at least 100 million slum dwellers by the year 2020.

In essence, UN-HABITAT strives to achieve adequate shelter for all, especially for the urban poor, through creating an enabling approach to the development and improvement of shelter that is environmentally sound. This means working with Member States, Habitat Agenda partners and all shelter stakeholders, to improve the production and delivery of land and shelter, and support national housing policies and enabling strategies.

Finally, note that for the purposes of this paper, adequate shelter

means more than a roof over one's head. It also means adequate privacy; adequate space; physical accessibility; adequate security; security of tenure; structural stability and durability; adequate lighting, heating and ventilation; adequate basic infrastructure, such as water-supply, sanitation and waste-management facilities; suitable environmental quality and health-related factors; and adequate and accessible location with regard to work and basic facilities: all of which should be available at an affordable cost. Adequacy should be determined together with the people concerned, bearing in mind the prospect for gradual development. Adequacy often varies from country to country, since it depends on specific cultural, social, environmental and economic factors. (Habitat Agenda 1996, 60)

For the purposes of this paper, adequate housing is defined by drawing on the International Covenant on Economic, Social and Cultural Rights (1966), General Comment No. 4 (1991) on the Right to Adequate Housing (Article 11 (1) of the Covenant. "A number of factors ... must be taken into account in determining whether particular forms of shelter can be considered to constitute "adequate housing," such as legal security of tenure, availability of services, materials, facilities and infrastructure, affordability, habitability, accessibility, location, cultural adequacy.

General Status of Urban Land and Shelter

Where are We?

Land in General

Much policy work has been done on land, but much remains to be done. However, this area, compared to other parts of the land agenda, is quite well covered. Conventional land administration and land titling approaches are also fairly well covered. In regard to pro-poor land tenure and land administration tools, we are much better off than we were six years ago, when the seminal study was produced by Deininger (2003) on land policy for economic growth and poverty reduction. Thanks to the work of the Global Land Tool Network's partners (www.gltn.net), there is an agreed agenda to address pro poor large-scale land tools and work has started. However, this is a huge agenda that could take many years, and a lot more work and resources are needed to go to scale globally. Some of the key areas in which there has been success in the global discourse: rural and urban land are much more closely tied together; land governance has now been mainstreamed; the range of land rights, rather than a focus only on individual title, is embedded in the discourse; and there is a first set of viable evaluation framework criteria for gender in regard to large scale land tools.

Urban Land

The statements above hold also for urban land. In addition to this, while we have some knowledge here and there, in general there is insufficient knowledge about how urban land markets in the developing world really work, which impacts housing finance and other issues.

Shelter

In general there is a need for a new concept of shelter policy, as there is a lack of commonly accepted conceptual frameworks for systematic shelter interventions that work at scale. Government, Bank, and bilateral support for shelter solutions for the urban poor have dwindled in the past decade, shifting the burden to the private sector (formal and informal), local governments, community groups, and individual households. There is no general model for social housing that works, to support the difficult task of integrating large groups of migrants, often poor, into existing cities. For sustainable cities to become a reality, the concept of social housing, along with other subsidy options for housing the poor, needs to be re-invigorated. The market alone has not been able to provide affordable adequate shelter, including services, for all segments of society. There has been a general failure of both welfare-oriented and market-based low-income housing policies and strategies in many (but not all) countries. There has been insufficient coordination between the shelter policy and other policies, such as for economic growth and poverty reduction. This has meant that shelter has not been prioritized within the context of national economic frameworks and/or Poverty Reduction Strategies Papers (PRSPs). (UN-HABITAT 2003 and United Nations Economic Commission for Europe 2008). Of course, the biggest gap relates to the issue of climate change and rising sea levels and their impact on cities, as 65 percent of urban populations live in coastal areas (UN-HABITAT 2008a).

Shelter and Land

While some knowledge exists in a few countries about how land and buildings are linked, there is insufficient global knowledge about how shelter and land are linked, either conceptually or at the level of implementation.

Slum Upgrading

Even in Europe with all its resources, as the seminal work by the United Nations Economic Commission for Europe on informal settlements states, there is no ready-made, 'off the shelf' solution, and there are no accepted "slum upgrading approaches which are holistic and not fragmented" (2008). Slum upgrading approaches have to be integrated into broader slum prevention shelter policies, and appropriate shelter policies, as indicated above, need to be better developed. Baker writing for the World Bank when undertaking a global review states that a "major area requiring substantial analysis is the impact of slum upgrading, infrastructure, and poverty reduction programs and policies in urban areas to help determine how these can be better designed to maximize impact and cost effectiveness" (2008).

The above statements are generally recognized views of the sectors rather than definitive. They are merely intended to identify gaps and point us in the right direction to take the sectors forward. The shelter gaps identified, as with many other aspects of shelter, need to be much more thoroughly researched.

What are the Key Issues for the Land and Shelter Sectors?

In regard to land and shelter delivery, it is not useful to take a narrow view of the sector. Instead it is important to see the sector holistically with all its linkages. The reason being that, for example, it is likely that serviced land for low-income housing cannot be delivered because there is insufficient infrastructure, and there is insufficient infrastructure because of a lack of financial capacity in the municipality, and so on. The issues highlighted below should be understood within this broader framework. Also, even though there is not always a one-to-one correspondence, for the purpose of this paper, land linked to shelter will be treated the same as land on its own. This paper will only briefly refer to the key land issues, as most of them are already known to this audience, but will instead elaborate more on the shelter issues.

Land

Some of the key land issues that impact the delivery of shelter at scale are outlined below. First, it is likely that in the developing world less than 30 percent of the country is covered by the cadastre. This leaves at least 70 percent not covered, which has major implications for land administration, governance, and land information management. This in turn has implications for slum upgrading and prevention, city management, corruption, state capture, and the operation of the land market, among other things. Also, if societies have become used to working off-register and illegally, this becomes a way of life. One of the key indicators of the cause of slums is that slums are already a way of life (Sietchiping 2008).

Second, less than 2 percent of the registered land rights in the developing world are held by women, which has implications for democracy, governance, conflict, and sustainability. The Global Land Tool Network, led by the International Federation of Surveyors and the Huairou Commission, a grass-roots international umbrella civil society organization of women, have developed a set of criteria for the evaluation of gender in regard to large-scale land tools. These criteria can also be used to design more gender responsive land tools (www.gltn.net).

Third, there has been a lack of political will and focus at national level about going to scale, in terms of budgetary allocations, political strategy, planning, and implementing. Also, there has been a lack of prioritization of land in government budgets, which is sorely needed for institutional strengthening of a wide range of land actors, both public and private, improved delivery, and innovation.

Fourth, there has been an over emphasis in many global programs on the delivery of individual land titles. This has meant that few countries have been able to go to scale on the delivery of land documents. More important, this has left little room or resources for innovation on how to deliver security of tenure at scale to the poor. The Global Land Tool Network partners' work (www.gltn.net) is one of the few focused on this area. There has been an over emphasis by some leading organizations on conventional land administration, when addressing the land issues in country. In countries with social inequity and poverty, a sustainable land agenda needs to focus also on land governance issues, such as the management of conflict over land and the issue of land redistribution, rather than just on the creation of an efficient land administration system, too often captured by the political elites and middle class.

Fifth, land, as a key asset, has attracted large-scale corrupt practice by private individuals, political elites, and government officials (state capture). In many parts of the world this has led to gross inequity of land distribution, which in turn continues to impact political stability and economic growth (South Africa, Brazil, and Kenya). Dysfunctional urban land markets exist also as a result of these factors, which in turn impact delivery of sufficient land and in terms of the types required, such as roads, residential, services, and community facilities. This affects not only efficiency but also affordability, especially for the poor. Well-located land with adequate infrastructure is scarce and often hoarded for future profit. Many cities in developing countries have serviced land zoned for housing development, which remains vacant for years, while areas with little or no services are densely populated by the urban poor. This is a result of structural failure in the land market.

Sixth, land governance has become a new way of thinking about land in the past few years because of the lack of good governance in this sector. "Fundamentally, land governance is about power and the political economy of land. Land tenure is the relationship among people with respect to land and its resources. The rules of tenure define how access is granted to rights to use, control, and transfer land, as well as associated responsibilities and restraints. These rules reflect the power structure of society. They develop in a manner that entrenches the power relations between and among individuals and social groups. The quality of governance determines how the following questions are addressed: Who benefits from the current legal and policy framework for land? How does this framework interact with customary... (and informal) ... institutions? What are the incentive structures for diverse stakeholders, and what constraints do they face? Who influences the way in which decisions about land are made? How are decisions enforced? What recourse do the less powerful members of society have?" (Food and Agricultural Organization and UN-HABITAT, forthcoming).

Seventh, most countries have incomplete land registration or land records systems, incomplete and non-interoperable land information systems and ineffective control due to inadequate institutional capacity are characteristic of most cities and countries. Long delivery processes are more the norm than the exception.[1] These encourage people to move into informal acquisition of land, especially in times of rapid urbanization. Therefore after war, disaster, or major changes in the political sphere, large-scale informal land subdivisions can emerge rapidly.

Finally, there are insufficient pro poor land tools to implement the good land policies that many countries have already. The Global Land Tool Network partners are focused on the production of some of these critical tools, but it is a slow process that takes years rather than months.

Shelter

Turning to the key shelter factors, there is a broad range of issues, many of which are in the critical path of successful shelter delivery at scale. First, issues differ from country to country, and the issues identified here will manifest differently in different countries. For example, different configurations of slum types can be found in different countries, such as squatter settlements on public or private land; inner-city slums in dilapidated buildings; illegal subdivisions on private or public land; settlements for refugees; upgraded/partially upgraded slums; formally built buildings; and informally built buildings (including houses and buildings up to 10 stories).

Second, ideally the need for land and shelter delivery should build up steadily over time, allowing cities to cope. However, the reality is different, and in general, planning and affordable land and shelter delivery has to catch up with the people. Many cities have not addressed the buildup of illegal buildings that have developed over decades and find themselves in a situation in which, in some regions and countries, the city is already more than 70 percent informal, and a major shelter backlog has to be addressed. Other cities experience rapid demand because of conflict (national and/or regional)—such as in the Balkans and the Eastern Democratic Republic of the Congo (DRC), and natural disaster—such as Sri Lanka and Indonesia post-tsunami, leading to rapid movements of people. Other countries that experience large-scale political economy change have also seen major migration to the cities—such as post-apartheid South Africa and post-communist Albania. Aside from the size and pace of the migration, the political economy particularities—foreigners, poverty profile, and so on—linked to the migration streams, also have to be addressed for successful city management.

Third, despite the growth of slums, for many years there has been very little political will or prioritization in regard to the shelter sector, both at the global and country levels. Adequate shelter for all, particularly for the poor, is difficult without subsidies and complex financing packages. Shelter has not featured seriously in public expenditure priorities, also because shelter has not been recognized as a key aspect of economic growth and poverty reduction for the country. Also, shelter development has often been passed on to the private sector, which has not produced formal affordable shelter for the low-income population at scale. The informal sector continues to be one of the biggest providers of shelter in the developing world, where, for example, it delivers 70 percent of all housing in Sub-Saharan Africa—in the form of slums. A successful shelter strategy at country level requires political and budgetary commitment by government over the long term.

Fourth, there is insufficient recognition that slum settlements are already part of the housing solution and that the informal sector has already housed hundreds of millions of people. The role of the grass roots in housing provision and the development of informal settlements and neighborhoods, and grass-roots involvement in slum upgrading and prevention, are key to sustainable urban development (Mangin 1967 and Mitlin and Patel 2005). An appropriate environment is needed to harness the potential of all actors, including the grass-roots and the private sector (formal and informal).

Fifth, while the idea of *in situ* slum upgrading, and not evicting people and/or resettling them, has been generally accepted, the focus has been on upgrading individual slums instead of tackling the issue systemically across the city. Sometimes a project has focused only on legalization of the slum—giving people legal tenure—and not the full upgrade that is required to ensure social inclusion. Systemically means to include all the cities' systems from finance to land to shelter to planning and so on, at a citywide scale, within an overarching shelter policy. Instead, the approach has often been project-based in a few areas, instead of systemic, and this has meant that the approach has been fragmented geographically and/or thematically instead of being integrated. Many existing good practices for shelter and service delivery rarely get past the demonstration pilot phase and tend not to be replicable (UN-HABITAT 2002). Too often slum upgrading is done without developing and implementing any systematic slum-prevention policy. Moving from reactive to preventative approaches is a much needed paradigm shift. A lack of slum prevention policies has negatively impacted the ability of cities and countries to go to scale in regards to the provision of adequate shelter for all.

Sixth, rental housing is critical in most cities for low-income groups. Hundreds of millions of tenants live in the cities of Africa, Asia, and Latin America. Newly arrived migrants rely at least temporarily on rental housing. For others, renting is a semi-permanent state, because ownership, whether in the formal or the informal sector, is not affordable to them. Despite this, few governments have formulated any kind of policy to help develop or regulate this form of housing, even though few would deny that a healthy rental sector should be an integral component of a well-functioning housing system (UN-HABITAT forthcoming).

Seventh, often the focus is too narrow to be able to address the issue. "Responses to the housing question often remain very technical" (United Nations Economic

Commission for Europe 2008). A narrow technical understanding of shelter delivery, based on planning and land administration imperatives, does not provide a sufficiently comprehensive framework to deliver adequate shelter for all, because of the social inequality and unequal distribution of wealth commonly found in the cities. Governments need to guarantee basic human rights and social protection for the poor in regard to shelter. This should be done by linking shelter policies to the broader public policy framework to ensure that they integrate the poor and the slums into broader urban structures and society.

Eighth, analytical work from the World Bank identifies common weaknesses in the state that lead to problems in the shelter sector, namely: the absence of a recent 'regulatory plan' (land use plan) and approved local regulations for land use; the lack of funded municipal programs to build primary infrastructure; the difficulty of acquiring undeveloped land, officially and legally, for construction; high transaction costs in the formal sector; complex processes and unresponsive institutions (World Bank 2007, quoted in United Nations Economic Commission for Europe 2008). Other common weaknesses include unrealistic standards and inappropriate planning and poor enforcement and/or implementation of regulations. Also, the dichotomy of land and housing delivery in various shelter strategies further limits delivery at scale. In regard to the infrastructure issue, UN-HABITAT argues that

> government should provide equal access to basic infrastructure since this is fundamental to the delivery of equal and affordable access to shelter. Investments in the citywide infrastructure are a precondition for successful and affordable upgrading of deprived neighborhoods (or settlements), as the lack of such provision can reinforce the exclusion of the urban poor and prevent their access to affordable shelter. Yet in reality there are large-scale infrastructure deficits in the developing world. (2003)

In regard to the regulatory framework issue, appropriate enabling regulations are needed to regulate housing, land and other property, including access, use, and supply, at various levels, for a range of economic and social groups, to deliver affordable housing for all. Such regulations need to be enshrined in national shelter policies.

Ninth, local authorities are in the critical path of delivery of affordable shelter for all. Too often they have insufficient financial capacity, as their mandates and functions are too large for their revenue base and they are overly dependent on financial transfers from central government. Instead of being able to plan ahead preventatively in the face of large-scale urbanization, they are often forced into *ad hoc* project-based crisis management interventions. Generally they cannot fund the development of citywide trunk infrastructure, a key provision for the creation of affordable shelter. Often infrastructure provision is passed on to developers, leading to houses that the poor cannot afford and fragmented infrastructure that cannot be maintained by the local authorities. An infrastructure deficit is one of the results of municipal financial weakness. From another angle, the backlog of slums is probably ten times more expensive to formalize than if preventative development had been done, also because of the low-density sprawling nature of slums and the need to compensate owners for land acquired for service provision. The municipal revenue base is further undermined by the large-scale illegal connections to infrastructure that are part and parcel of slum settlements. All these costs make it even less likely that the shelter agenda will be addressed adequately. Municipalities also suffer from numerous human resource constraints that also impact their ability to deliver in the face of urban growth.

Tenth, the regulation of buildings has its own challenges. Even in parts of Europe, the detection and registration of illegal buildings is too expensive, time-consuming, and complex to be practical. Often there are outdated building codes, which impact negatively on the delivery of small underfunded municipalities, which struggle to cope also with the delivery of building permits. Frequently the 'as built' environment does not conform to the law and national plans. This creates problems for planners, who do not have adequate information about the reality on the ground when they do their planning, which then causes knock-on problems to those who are delivering land, planning permissions and building permits, and enforcing them. All these gaps create opportunities for delays and a cycle of corruption.

Finally, the economic dimension has to be taken more seriously by all players, not just in terms of finance but also in terms of land and housing markets. Understanding how land and housing markets work, both formal and informal, is critical, and as Martine, McGranahan, Montgomery, and Fernandez-Castilla argue, "proactive action requires decision-makers to better understand the slack created by urban land market distortions and other 'institutional discontinuities' that are filled in by informal activities" (2008). Mixed market approaches, whereby the social market and the private market are both used to provide shelter, are being examined more carefully in the light of the 2008 credit crunch. The approach whereby the private formal shelter market was expected to cater for all urban residents has not delivered the required results. The United Nations Economic Commission for Europe (2008) argues that the "pro-ownership" and "pro-private housing market," which has been the dominant genre over the last decade, has squeezed out other options like renting, leading to a lack of alternative shelter and tenure options, including group rights, social housing, Islamic land tenure types and so on. This range of tenure options approach, within an incremental framework, has also been advocated by the Global Land Tool Network partners.

Promoting the delivery of adequate housing for all cannot be done by any one global organization on its own. UN-HABITAT's approach is to work with partners and to try and build strategic networks, partnerships, and think tanks to tackle some of the key issues and gaps. The Global Land Tool Network is one such network of partners (www.gltn.net).

A Few Lessons: Implementing Shelter and Land Delivery

National Governments Have Been More Successful Than Local Governments in Delivering Shelter

Despite the frequent statements that land and shelter functions need to be devolved to the local government level to improve delivery, a review of shelter delivery for low-income people (including upgrading) shows that national governments have been more successful than local governments in delivering at scale (UN-HABITAT 2006b).

Fully Subsidized Housing Estates for Low-Income Groups Have Not Worked

Governments started trying to address the shelter issue through the direct provision of housing estates funded by their investment budgets. Often houses have been delivered through fully subsidized government plans, or through some form of cost recovery plan that is partially subsidized. The acquisition of land for these plans was subsidized or partially subsidized, linked to partial cost recovery from the household. Too often these plans were turned into housing for civil servants and neglected other segments of the urban population. Also, generally they were too slow and too small to meet the demand and were fraught with problems in regard to maintenance, leading to public housing estates becoming slums.

New thinking is that locally based sources and cross-subsidy policies need to be more thoroughly explored. The impact that infrastructure and land use planning have over land values could be used to finance adequate shelter. A wider variety of sources of income should be used and aligned with city objectives, such as property tax, value capture, financial transfers to local governments, housing subsides, micro-financing and community-based plans, and flexible mortgage systems. There was also a tendency in slum upgrading toward the use of subsides from government budgets, sometimes linked to international donor funds. However, this did not prove scalable, so other financial approaches have also become more common in the last two decades, such as the use of community saving plans and cost recovery.

Inappropriate Planning Standards Can Block Upgrading and/or an Incremental Path to Property

The settlement pattern of slums seldom conforms to the minimum plot sizes, road widths, gridiron design, etc., laid down in planning regulations. Often the allocation of legal land tenures requires that the property conform to the planning regulations. Upgrading slums so they fit with planning standards is problematic because of their high densities and nonstandardized settlement patterns and because of the cost of the upgrades. Often this means that upgrading is not attempted at all or that the upgrade is partial. In some cases, partial upgrades are done without the allocation of legal land tenure (Indonesia), and in others the whole slum area is isolated from the national planning standards and some upgrading is done with a weaker land right being allocated (Zambia). In some countries, a weaker form of property right is allocated to the slum properties, but it is not possible to climb the property ladder at all unless the whole area is "properly planned" (Tanzania), which usually involves the resettlement of some of the slum residents. One solution is to undertake a full upgrade, including security of tenure, by applying local, rather than national, planning standards, in regard to plot sizes or road widths. These local standards would be based on the 'as built' environment as much as possible, to limit disruption to people's lives and property, and at no stage would the land registry require full national planning standards to be applied (Albania). This would facilitate an incremental path to property. Equally the lack of a building permit may prevent a household climbing the property ladder incrementally. Georgia allows the registration of a parcel of land without the requisite building permit showing that the building is in compliance with regulations.

Land Use Planning of De Facto 'as Built' Environments at Scale Remains Unsolved

The allocation of formal land use rights at the parcel level remains fraught with problems in cities characterized largely by informal rights to land and buildings, both for residential and high rise use. Planners conventionally rely on cadastral information to assist them to make new urban plans, and in some countries the changing of land use rights is monitored by using the cadastral records in the surveyor general's office. Given the absence of cadastral information in large parts of most developing countries' cities, as well as the large-scale informal developments, this approach does not work. In some situations, planners have tried to use recent aerial photography to identify illegal buildings. This has been only partially successful, as it is not possible to identify the informal land boundaries and therefore the land being claimed by the households occupying the buildings. New land and land use information systems, which do not rely on data reflecting only the legal situation, need to be developed. These need to facilitate planning, land use and building regularization and the allocation of formal land use rights, which make it possible to merge the de facto with the de jure, also for use during slum upgrading. The Social Tenure Domain Model, funded by the Global Land Tool Network, is one such tool that would have to be accompanied by institutional strengthening. This tool is being developed by a number of GLTN partners working together, namely the International Federation of Surveyors (FIG), the International Institute for Geo-information Science and Earth Observation (ITC), UN-HABITAT and the World Bank, which is leading on this in Ethiopia.

The Path to Legalization of Properties and Buildings Can Be Made More Efficient

In many countries individual households acquire land and buildings illegally and then spend years going through the process of legalizing them, by making incremental adjustments, paying bribes, and spending the time and money to get the right permits (Turkey, Greece, Egypt). Some countries have found a more efficient way of doing it. In South Africa, using a developer driven exercise, special planning boards were set up to examine the de facto planning standards of existing slum settlements, to ascertain to what extent they need to be changed to be able to be legalized, while simultaneously avoiding the adverse effects of poor planning, such as overflowing sewers. In Albania, a special Ministry has been set up to do the slum upgrades systemically and then move the paper work into the line ministries, such as the Registry.

Harmonization, Alignment, and Coordination Could Be Key to Delivery at Scale

In countries with multiple multilateral and bilateral donors operating, middle level government officials who drive development programs can become overwhelmed with work. The Paris Declaration on Harmonization, Alignment, and Coordination (HAC) of donor aid created a new aid architecture meant to address this issue. Donors funding the land sector can have very different approaches that can easily cause contradictions in government programs (e.g. titles or deeds, standards, accuracies, reference networks). HAC is critical to ensuring that contradictions are limited. The urban sector—to which shelter is tied, is much more complex than the land sector, because it is by nature fragmented across a range of government departments and different levels of government, as well as parastatals, and tends to be embedded in donor programs, rather than being a stand-alone program. This implies that, to go to scale, the creation of an urban sector within a HAC framework should be considered key in countries using donor budgets for shelter development.

Housing, Land and Property Issues in Post Conflict Need a Fresh Approach

A particular set of approaches applies in post conflict environments that are dominated by a United Nations presence. Essentially, even where land is at the centre of the conflict, the emergency, or first phase, is dominated by emergency issues and short termism. It is only in the second, or reconstruction phase, that housing, land and property rights are treated within a medium to long term framework. Too often there is little funding for the second phase by comparison to the first phase. This means that housing, land, and property issues in post conflict situations are not always addressed adequately. UN-HABITAT, through its role in the Executive Committee of Humanitarian Affairs which oversees the emergency system, is trying to improve the way the issue is dealt with, by advocating for longer term measures to be put in place from the outset.

New Approaches to Land Administration

There has been a major paradigm shift globally in regard to our understanding of land issues. Whereas a decade ago individual land titling was considered the only robust way of delivering land, today a range of rights has been introduced by many governments and is considered a much more pro poor approach. The range of rights approach has meant that new ways of constructing land administration, as well as land information systems and their management, have had to be developed. The Social Tenure Domain Model is one such answer to the challenge. This type of pro poor tool will also facilitate post conflict and post disaster situations better and provide a stronger foundation for peace building.

Another positive development in the land field has been the embedding of land governance into the land discourse of land administration actors, and the World Bank and FIG are to be congratulated on choosing this as their conference theme. Previously there was too little recognition of the role of land governance, also in regard to land administration systems. An enormous amount of slippage exists in land administration projects because of land governance issues, which is not risk managed in project management, and this needs to be much more thoroughly documented to improve success rates. From another angle, there is still too little emphasis on capacity building in the land sector to ensure successful outcomes at scale. Much more work needs to be done on this aspect to embed it as part of projects and programs, as well as when preparing for the implementation of land policy.

Conclusion

The urban challenge is enormous. Cities are already struggling to cope with the impact of urbanization and this is set to increase in many countries, especially in Africa. Managing the expected increase in the geographic area of cities will require large-scale investment to ensure that urban development is not chaotic. The amount of shelter and land delivery needed over the next few decades to ensure adequate housing for all, and for the world to move to sustainable urbanization, is daunting. Yet a review of the global position in regard to shelter delivery indicates that the agenda is nowhere and urgent action is needed to get a focus back on this sector. While the implementation of pro poor large scale land tools has started, much more needs to be done to go to scale.

A few UN-HABITAT recommendations to meet these challenges:

- Revitalize the shelter agenda and put it back on the global and national agendas, also by integrating it with the economic growth and poverty reduction strategies.
- Develop and undertake an agenda of research, documentation for learning, dialogue, and advocacy for shelter (including land).
- Link land and housing more robustly, in terms of both conceptual approaches and country-level implementation.
- Move from slum upgrading to systemic slum prevention (including upgrading), especially learning lessons from the few countries that have already gone to scale on this issue.
- Take opportunities for implementing better regulations. The current financial crisis, and its linkage to the housing and mortgage markets, has created enough concern about regulations, and their role in curtailing undesired market behavior, to give a window of opportunity for this.
- Continue to develop pro-poor and gender responsive land tools and scale up – support the Global Land Tool Network, as an alliance of partners, which has an agreed agenda.

Both the World Bank and the International Federation of Surveyors are key active partners in the Global Land Tool Network. Other international organizations should also consider becoming part of the network to advance the Global Land Tool Network agenda.

Finally, we need to aim at strengthening national and local shelter policy development and implementation to better meet the goals of the Habitat Agenda and the Millennium Development Goal 7, Target 11, with a particular focus on the poor.

5.2:   Land Information Updating, a De Facto Tax Reform: UpDating the Cadastral Database of Bogotá

MARIA CAMILA URIBE SÁNCHEZ, Cadastre of Bogotá, Colombia

Summary

Efforts to reduce lags in the Cadastral database of Bogotá raise the base for the property tax, which property owners perceive as a change in the rules of taxation. This has given Cadastral Updating processes the same political economy of a tax reform. This paper describes the Cadastral Updating Project of Bogotá implemented in 2008 and focuses on the key elements behind its success. They include improved management of human resources, implementation of a Taylorist approach, introduction of information technologies, improved massive assessment techniques, mitigation of the project's impact on the property tax, engagement of stakeholders and career civil servants, and openness to reviewing the project's results. The paper ends with an overview of the current reform agenda for the Cadastre of Bogotá and a closing remark.

Introduction

With around seven million inhabitants, a 384 km² urban area and more than two million real properties, Bogotá is the capital and the largest city of Colombia. Its government is divided into twelve administrative sectors.[2] The Cadastre of Bogotá belongs to the finance sector. Its mission is to keep the city's geographical information up-to-date. All parcels—of formal or informal origins—are included. From a fiscal perspective, the most useful part of the information that the Cadastre administers is the cadastral value of each parcel, which is the base for the property tax. This means that efforts to reduce a lag in the agency's database will raise the base for the property tax, which property owners will perceive as a change in the rules of taxation. In the last decade, attempts to reduce the lag in cadastral information have been few and far between. This has turned recent Cadastral Updating processes into full-fledged tax reforms at the local level. Thus, these processes in Bogotá have had the same political economy of a tax reform and have come under the same public scrutiny. In 2008, property tax represented 19.8 percent of Bogotá's tax revenues, generating the second largest amount of resources of all local taxes, after the business income tax.

This paper focuses on the Cadastral Updating Project of Bogotá (CUPB) implemented in 2008, the first successful effort since 2004. This Project generated a 10.2 percent increase in property tax revenue—approximately $37 million.[3] In addition to its fiscal impact, the data produced are allowing urban planning authorities to review the city's land use master plan using reliable information of the city's physical reality.

The study of this project provides insights into public administration and governance at the local level and institutional reform and tax management in a developing metropolis.

The first section introduces the context in which the Cadastral Updating takes place. The second section describes some of the technical innovations, political strategies, and main results of the CUPB. Finally, the paper ends with an overview of the current reform agenda and a closing remark.

Cadastral Updating in Bogotá

Weak Inter-Institutional Linkages and Heavy Reliance on Fieldwork

Beyond providing the base of the property tax, the Cadastre's information must reflect the building, usage, and ownership dynamics of the city. In Colombia, as in most developing countries, the task of keeping cadastral information up-to-date is not a question of a periodic review of administrative records and a systematic crossing of databases. The shortage of sources of robust information and the lack of interagency synergies prevent automated or simpler processes from developing.

The agencies in charge of the official registry of property in its different aspects (e.g., transaction registration, construction permits) fulfill their missions in an independent manner. The lack of communication is even more severe between national and local agencies. No system links all the real estate information coming from different sources within the city. In many cases, the differences between the agencies' plans for collecting and storing information further hinder the possibilities for exchange and analysis. The National Registry Office (*Superintendencia de Notariado y Registro*), the city's Planning Department and the urban curators, the National Statistics Department, the Department for Emergency Management, and utility companies have independent systems with crucial information about the city's parcels.

In addition to this lack of interoperability, the real estate market is opaque. The costs of property transaction registry are proportional to the transaction amount and thus prompt evasion; buyers and sellers declare lower values of transactions. As a consequence, reliable information on sale and purchase values of real property between agents in the secondary market is hard to obtain.

This is why in Bogotá—as in many other developing metropolises—building and keeping up-to-date a robust parcel inventory requires a series of burdensome processes with a heavy component of fieldwork in which the Cadastre must survey hundreds of thousands of parcels.

Legal Constraints

Resolution 2555 of 1988 of the National Geographical Institute—the policy design and regulatory agency of cadastres in Colombia—governs Cadastral Updating processes and restricts the methods the cadastres can use to calculate the values of each parcel.

The resolution establishes that the cadastral value of a parcel is, in all cases, the sum of the individually estimated values of its land and its building(s). It also defines the method to determine the value of land: neighborhoods are divided into Physically Homogeneous Zones (ZHF) and then into Geoeconomically Homogeneous Zones (ZHG). Finally, the Resolution stipulates that statistical methods—that consider physical characteristics of the parcel and its location—are to be used to determine the value of construction.

On the one hand, the ZHF are constructed through the study of a neighborhood's land use bylaws, the access to utilities and roads, topography, and the actual land use. Neighboring real properties sharing these characteristics will define the polygon of the ZHF. Variations in the actual value of land within a ZHF will further divide it into

ZHGs—i.e., areas that share the same value of land. Figure 5.2 shows an example of a cadastral sector, its ZHFs and its ZHGs.

Figure 5.2. Example of ZHF and ZHG: Cadastral sector 008412—Santa Barbara Central

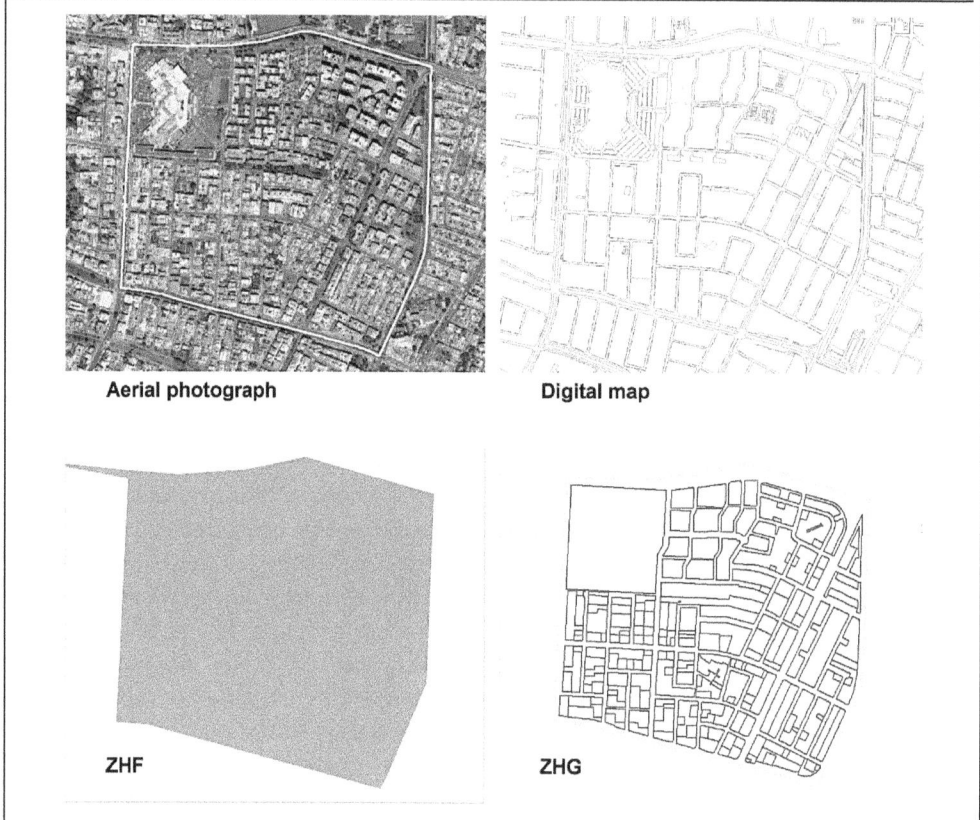

Aerial photograph

Digital map

ZHF

ZHG

Source: Cadastre of Bogotá, 2009.

On the other hand, to use statistical methods to calculate the value of the building, Bogotá's Cadastre has developed tools to register its main physical characteristics. Under the mandate of Resolution 2555, every updating process must include a parcel survey, that is, a visit to every parcel of the neighborhood being updated to capture information on the physical features and age of its building(s) and the area of its land and building(s). The parcel survey's main tool is the Parcel Form (*ficha predial*). Designed in 1984, with over 60 fields, the form is used to collect information on myriad variables—e.g., upkeep of the structure, construction materials, quality of the bathrooms and the kitchen.

When compared to methodologies used elsewhere, this methodology stands out as obsolete and labor intensive. Despite the fast development in the past decade of geographical information systems (GIS), database management, and data modeling software, Colombian mass valuation methodologies have remained unchanged. The pressure of two stakeholder groups accounts for this lack of change. First, professional assessors linked to cadastres and Cadastral engineers trained to apply these methodologies are in short supply. This scarcity generates rents that entice them to defend the status quo.[4] Second, large property owners—rural (large cattle ranchers) and urban (merchants)—put pressure on government to maintain low cadastral values, which in turn provides little incentive to improve mass valuation methods.

The Failed Process of 2006

In 2006, the Cadastre outsourced the updating process to a consortium of private firms. The great increases in some parcels elevated the political pressure, which led to a tight review of all the process's technical and legal aspects. During an audit from the city's control agencies, the practice of impersonation of professional contractors by non-technical personnel surfaced. The scandal grew until April 2007, when the mayor withdrew the results of the process from the official database.

Beyond reducing tax property revenue, the failed process undermined the Cadastre's legitimacy and the confidence in its technical capacity and ultimately affected the city's tax culture.

In 2007, during a period of harsh criticism of the Cadastral Updating process in Bogotá, several studies and evaluations ended, detecting recurring flaws in past processes. Building on this diagnosis, in the first semester of 2008, the current administration conducted an evaluation and overall revision that defined the group of activities and processes to be improved that are described below:

- Weak contract relations between the Cadastre and fieldwork personnel: The contracting plan did not demand full-time involvement of personnel or make them accountable for the quality of the information collected. This generated a lack of commitment and a breach of responsibilities, time lags, allowed subcontracting, and did not provide job stability for contractors.
- Inadequate plans for personnel selection: The professional profiles required specific experience on previous updating processes, which severely restricted the options of candidates and prevented new professionals to train. This trapped the Cadastre in an asymmetrical plan that forced it to hire the same few contractors—who grew in their expertise—and prevented other professionals to train for future processes.
- Ample discretion of personnel: The lack of adequately detailed technical and operational manuals allowed—and in some cases forced—discretionary decisions that were not in line with a coherent massive process.
- Excessive transport and handling of information: The fact that one group of people would fill out the paper forms in the field and a different group would later type their contents into the system generated many mistakes that translated into total or partial loss of data and high supervision costs.
- Inadequate use of statistical techniques: The lack of a full-time quantitative analysis support group lowered the quality of massive valuation tasks: the error of samples and econometric models was high. In particular, the design of independent samples for the valuation of land and buildings increased the risk of inconsistencies in total values. Additionally, the unskilled handling of econometric models affected drastically the models' predictive capability and their performance when applied to the universe of parcels.

Figure 5.3. Sectors Included in the CUPB

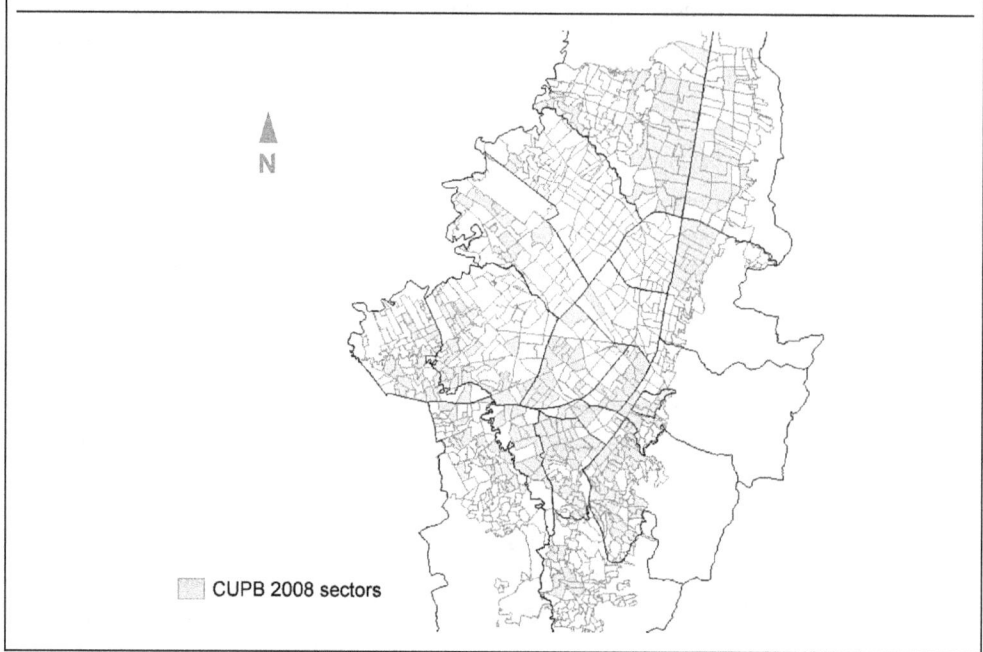

☐ CUPB 2008 sectors

Source: Cadastre of Bogotá, 2008.

■ Lack of communication with stakeholders: Given the magnitude of the fieldwork and the impact of the Cadastral Updating process on the local property tax, the lack of a clear and stable communication plan with the stakeholders of the process tended to generate anxiety and nervous reactions from the citizenry.

Cadastral Updating Project of Bogotá (CUPB)—Fiscal Year 2009

The CUPB updated during calendar year 2008 the geographical information of over 827,000 properties, out of 2 million properties, in 357 cadastral sectors, out of 1,014 (see figure 5.3). This section describes the technical innovations, political strategies, and main results of this updating project.

Short-Term Technical Innovations

The CUPB implemented many short-term changes and allowed the administration to study in-depth the implications and challenges of mid- and long-term reforms.

Management of Human Resources

Innovations started with the selection of personnel based on professional merits and contracting them under a more binding plan (for both the contractor and the agency). First, a call for candidates was open to the public and did not require experience in previous processes, just a compatible background (e.g. civil engineering, architecture). To compensate for the lack of specific experience, preselected candidates took training courses and had to pass a test to enter the list of eligible candidates. As a result, the

Cadastre was able to select the project's personnel from a list of candidates arranged by scores. Second, the Cadastre hired the project's personnel as temporary local government employees (*supernumerarios*). This made them as accountable for their work as any civil servant and established a direct and exclusive relationship. In this hiring method, quality and time commitment rules were clear from the beginning and wages and conditions were more favorable for workers (e.g. severance payment, bonuses).

Taylorist Approach

The project used to be divided by sectors, not processes. Thus, one professional would be in charge of carrying out all the processes for his assigned neighborhoods. In 2008, the project was divided into specialized tasks within a production chain plan, easing direct monitoring, and allowing the formation of specialized teams. Technical manuals were revised and the level of detail for each task was increased. These changes reduced the level of discretion in decision making and facilitated the homogeneity of criteria throughout the project.

Introduction of Hardware and Development of Applications

On of the biggest innovations of the CUPB was the inclusion of portable digital devices (PDAs) into parcel survey processes. The use of PDAs reduced the errors of data transcription and provided a direct and permanent link between the cadastral information system and fieldwork personnel. It also allowed the Cadastre to conduct online control and monitoring of the information collected on the ground, of the performance of employees, and of the time taken collecting information and traveling to the parcels. These devices included information validating algorithms that automated a part of quality control process.

Beyond the PDAs, web-based applications were developed for citizens to review and correct the ownership information of their parcels, forms were created for professional assessors (see below) to systematize their real-estate market research, and protocols were developed for map digitizing and database-crossing with other city agencies. These technological developments made fieldwork more efficient and provided a centralized, homogeneous, and controlled storage of the project's information.

CUPB—Economic Component

Given the impact of the Cadastral Updating on the property tax, the economic component—in charge of setting cadastral values—required careful monitoring throughout the project. This led to technical and methodological innovations that improved the precision of parcel value assessments.

To understand the importance of this component, it is necessary to go into some detail.

Robust Reference Information: the Key to an Equitable Outcome. First, to maintain a principle of equity and to establish the differences in value between parcels, it is crucial for the updating project to have robust reference information on the real-estate market. The goal of the Cadastral Updating is not to equate the cadastral value to the market value as much as to assign cadastral values that reflect the behavior of the market—i.e., similar predictive errors and the same difference between cadastral and market value for all parcels. In this manner, the goal is to avoid overestimation of some values and biases in a given area, stratum,[5] or group of parcels. Therefore, to ensure an equitable outcome, the database with market information of the Cadastral Real Estate Observatory was strengthened with a two-pronged strategy. First, the observatory's field team collected—under clearly defined protocols—all the real-estate offers in the neighborhoods that the CUPB covered. To attain values closer to the real market, trained technicians posing as prospective buyers negotiated by phone the price of an eventual transaction. Second, data on transactions and commercial valuations were obtained through outreach to actors of the real-estate sector (i.e. guilds, online realtors, city agencies, banks, and other mortgage institutions).

Collection of Parcel Information. Cadastral values result from the sum of estimations of the value of land and building for each parcel. To estimate the values, professional assessors are hired to valuate a statistical sample of parcels.

The interpretation of regulations in previous updating projects led to the design of two samples of valuated parcels to estimate the value of land within a ZHG and the value of buildings. For the CUPB, a single sample was designed to fulfill the needs of the two processes while abiding by regulations: the sample was representative at the levels of building uses and ZHF. The unified sample allowed for a unified fieldwork and reduced costs.

To ensure quality standards in the assessors' market value estimations of the sampled parcels, a quantitative analysis team compared them with other sources of information, namely, the database of the Real Estate Observatory and individual studies of prominent assessing firms.

In the past, the assessment of each parcel was reviewed separately. The lack of overall consistency of this discrete approach was overcome by introducing one of the main innovations of the Economic Component: the experts committees. In these committees, assessing experts used statistical analysis and general descriptive tables to take massive decisions based on high-quality information and reduced risks associated with discretion in decision making, and in definition of values and methodologies. In this manner, the Cadastre took direct control over the definition of each value guaranteeing coherence in the overall behavior of values at the neighborhood, use, and stratum levels.

Econometric Models. Historically, work teams dissociated from other cadastral tasks were in charge of generating the econometric models to estimate the value of buildings. The lack of interaction with the other areas of the updating process resulted in static models that depended on few variables. Additionally, the assessors seeking consistency at the micro level would manipulate the models, getting a better fit to the reality of the neighborhoods they were in charge of. This affected the statistical soundness of the models and hampered the possibility of reconciling, within a broad framework, the model's results with reality on the ground.

Previous projects built models for each one of the eighty cadastral uses without statistical evidence that supports such a separation. This practice made it harder to establish the value of multiple-use parcels. Some of these models also used spatial factors in their market value estimations. Nevertheless, the employed geographical references were artificial partitions of the city that did not represent the dynamics of the real-estate market and were incapable of adequately capturing price variations. For example, even though a citizen may accept neighborhoods and districts (*localidades*) as geographical units, the limits that separate them (e.g., political, topographic, social) do not always translate into variations in the value of parcels.

The revision of technical processes of the CUPB defined the need to use statistical methods to model the behavior of continuous variables affected by their location. This led the Cadastre to contact the Geoda Center at Arizona State University, to engage specialists in the construction and application of spatial econometric models. With the support of the Geoda Center, the Cadastre was able to estimate the value of a parcel using not only its physical characteristics but also a spatial component that links the value to its location within the urban perimeter.

This vision of the real-estate market underscores the interrelation between parcels that share physical characteristics or location. The latter was captured by calculating Euclidean distances between each parcel in the city and real-estate landmarks. The data were stored in large matrices that accurately reflected the interaction between a parcel's location and its proximity to others. These matrices also allowed the Cadastre to mathematically represent a path in a certain direction: two parcels will be near only if all distances to landmarks are similar, while a movement in any direction will be reflected on the matrices as a continuing increase in the distance to one or several landmarks.

The landmarks used include: mass-transportation infrastructure, schools, parks, hospitals and clinics, commerce (shopping centers), red-light districts, country clubs, cemeteries, temples, amusement parks, coliseums and stadiums, museums, water bodies, airports, penitentiaries, police and military buildings, landfill, forestry reserves. Beyond these physical landmarks, proximity to other strata, locations of crimes committed in 2008 (muggings, murders, bank or store robberies) and the state of nearby roads were also included.

Abating Political Pressure

Beyond its technical shortcomings, the collapse of the failed 2006 project was a consequence of political pressure from different groups. In addition to adjusting the technical aspects of the project, strategies were implemented to abate the political pressure. They included mitigating the project's impact on the property tax, engaging stakeholders and civil servants, and maintaining an open stance for reviewing the project's results.

Mitigation of the Project's Impact on the Property Tax

Historically, the lag of the cadastral database's information has had a heavy impact on the property tax, turning every updating project into a tax reform which put heavy political pressure on the process and the agency as a whole. In this line, in 2008 the Cadastre implemented two measures to weaken the link between Cadastral Updating and increases in the property tax: capping increases for the property tax and setting cadastral values as a lower fraction of the commercial value.

Since Cadastral Updating processes do not cover all neighborhoods and, by definition, take several years to update the entire city, the value of non-updated parcels tends to lag behind. To counter this lag, the Cadastre applies the Urban and Rural Real-Estate Valuation Index (IVIUR), a price index establishing the percentage change in the real-estate market from one year to the next. The IVIUR is calculated using statistical methods for groups of parcels (by use and stratum for residential parcels). The results of the statistical process are submitted to a committee chaired by the mayor. In most years, the committee has reduced the percentages to be applied and thus increased the lag between the cadastral database and the real-estate market.

Table 5.1 summarizes the differences between the statistical studies to calculate the IVIUR and the final percentages that the committee has set since 2004 (the year of the last large updating effort).

Table 5.1. Urban and Rural Real Estate Valuation Index (IVIUR): Comparison between Results of Technical Study and Official Percentages Assigned in the Committee

FY	2004		2005		2006		2007		2008		
Use	Study	% set	Study	% set	Study	% set	Study	% set	Study	% set	Cumulative lag
Residential stratum 1	−5.7	−5.7	11.9	2.5	8.8	4.5	7.5	5.9	6.8	3	21.6%
Residential stratum 2	−2.3	−2.3	5.1	5.1	9.5	4.5	5.8	5.9	9.8	4.5	11.9%
Residential stratum 3	−4.7	−4.7	5.3	5.3	4.9	6.5	7.9	7.9	12	5.5	5.6%
Residential stratum 4	5.5	5.5	6.4	6.4	7.5	6.5	10.1	10	14.6	6.5	12.2%
Residential stratum 5	10.4	10.4	8.2	8.2	6.8	6.5	11.4	11	13	6.5	10.2%
Residential stratum 6	8.3	8.3	14.4	14.4	6.5	6.5	11.5	11	15.5	6.5	13.9%
Commercial	1.7	1.7	5.8	5.8	8.2	7.5	5.4	5.9	15.5	6.5	11.3%
Industrial	−6.4	−6.4	6.1	6.1	5.5	5	5.9	5.9	13.3	6.5	8.1%
Empty plot	3.3	3.3	−0.4	0	5.6	5	3.4	3.5	7.1	3	4.7%
Others	11.6	11.6	−6	0	5.5	5	0	0	7.5	3	−1.7%
Storage & Parking	0	0	0	0	10.9	10	6.9	7	11.6	3.5	10.5%
Rural	0.3	0.3	2.5	2.5	4.5	4.5	4.5	4.5			0.0%

Source: Planning Department of Bogotá (SDP) 2008.

The committee has tended to benefit lower strata with milder increases in their cadastral valuation than the ones the statistical studies suggested. Over the years, this has worsened the lag for these strata. Since an updating process eliminates the lag in one year, it has a regressive effect on the tax base, which goes against the progressive rates of the property tax. In 2008, the Cadastre and the Finance Secretary presented before the City Council a project to mitigate the impact of large increases in the cadastral value on the property tax. The project passed and became an agreement that imposes a limit on increases that range from 8 percent for the poorest in the city to 80 percent for the most affluent.[6] As seen in figure 5.4, the agreement preserves the progressive rate structure of the property tax.

Figure 5.4. Comparison between Increases for FY2009 with and without the Ceilings

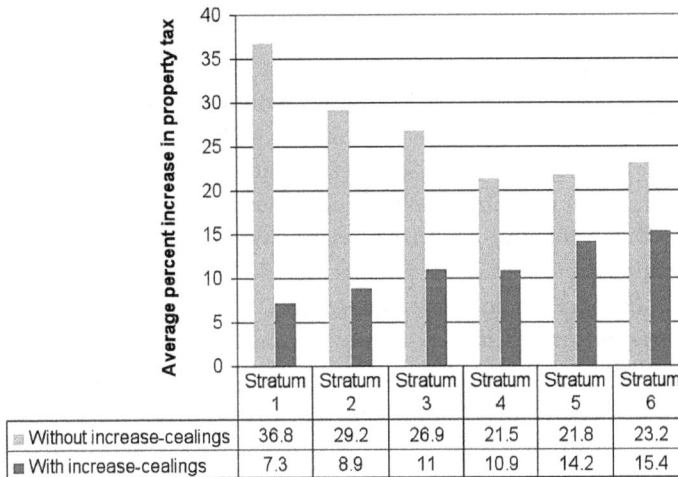

	Stratum 1	Stratum 2	Stratum 3	Stratum 4	Stratum 5	Stratum 6
Without increase-cellings	36.8	29.2	26.9	21.5	21.8	23.2
With increase-cellings	7.3	8.9	11	10.9	14.2	15.4

Source: Cadastre of Bogotá, 2009.

As a result—despite large increases in cadastral values (many over 100 percent)—89 percent of residential parcels will observe increases of less than 20 percent in their property tax.

This agreement will keep this and future updating efforts from being perceived as tax reforms. This was by far the most important strategy to abate political pressure.

Additionally, mass valuation methodologies are founded in statistical techniques with a measurable error, and therefore the cadastral value must be a fraction of the market value to prevent any parcel from being overvalued. Historically this fraction had been established at 80 percent for previous updating efforts. Nevertheless, the lack of updating processes and the yearly upgrading of the database through the IVIUR led this fraction to fall to an average of 57 percent reaching in some cases 35 percent. For FY2009, the Cadastre decided to apply a homogeneous criterion for all parcels included in the CUPB to preserve the equity of the process. After estimating the process's statistical error, the cadastral value was set at 70 percent of the market value on average.

Engaging Stakeholders

Unlike previous Updating processes, the Cadastre was in touch with the public throughout the project. This effort included visits to neighborhoods to present and explain the main implications of the project and to introduce the fieldwork processes that were to take place. In addition, the Cadastre conveyed a Citizen Participation Committee in which stakeholders (property owners' organizations, professional guilds, control agencies, and academics) were able to have their say and have in-depth discussions on key aspects of the Project. This Committee was instrumental in the continuing betterment of the CUPB.

Merchants, most notably those having stores in shopping centers, are one of the strongest groups of stakeholders. Parcels within shopping centers have been among the most undervalued properties in the cadastral database, and their affluent owners have strong political leverage.

For these reasons, the CUPB paid special attention to this group of parcels to understand fully the main aspects that shape their market value. CUPB personnel interacted with shopping center developers and store owners in different scenarios throughout the second semester of 2008. Additionally, in the first four months of 2009, the CUPB was open to review some of the results of the process to provide each parcel with an adequate cadastral valuation. This interaction combined with a review of the academic literature on the subject helped the Cadastre draw key lessons that allowed it to build sound econometric models to assess more accurately the value of parcels within each shopping center. These lessons include the importance of the participation coefficient and the anchor and semi-anchor status.

The differences among market values of commercial parcels within a shopping center reflect their development status. At first, when the shopping center is just a project, the developer seeks the presence of major brands that will secure an appropriate flow of shoppers—i.e., cinemas, supermarkets (anchors), fast-food chains, large popular garment stores (semi-anchors). These parcels are different from others: they require larger areas, and they have the lowest price per square meter of the shopping center. Once the developer has sealed deals with the *anchor(s)* and *semi-anchors* and the project's viability is secured, thanks to the retail demand externalities they provide (Eppli and Benjamin 1994). The developer sells at higher price the remaining smaller parcels to other merchants and real-estate investors.[7]

The price differences tend to remain over time but can change due to location within the shopping center (i.e., floor, type of corridor, proximity to escalators, and entrances), parcel characteristics (i.e., area, front's length), and participation coefficient (i.e., share in the shopping center's common properties and expenses). This last variable is key in the determination of prices within the shopping center. It reflects initial conditions of negotiation, and co-owners accept it widely as an equitable mechanism of burden distribution (i.e., care, upkeep and surveillance costs). In a broad sense, the participation coefficient is a good proxy for several of the characteristics that influence market values of commercial parcels within shopping centers.

Additionally, the Cadastre became aware of the impact of restrictive use easements on the value of retail properties: co-ownership bylaws that set limitations on the use of retail properties (e.g., shoe store only) translate into a limited demand, which lowers its value.

Finally, in several shopping centers there are adjacent parcels joined physically forming a single space that has the same characteristics as an anchor or semi-anchor. Nevertheless, given the current regulations, these parcels cannot be considered as a single parcel, which means a higher cadastral value. Therefore, the best option for owners is to formalize the encompassing of these parcels to be considered an anchor or a semi-anchor.

Engaging Career Civil Servants

In the first stages of the project, there was a clear divide between the newly appointed managing team and the agency's career civil servants. The differences went beyond the fact that the first had been there for only a couple of months and the latter had worked for decades within the agency. The new managers lacked the technical expertise and experience in this kind of project while the agency's servants had worked under several administrations that had had myriad approaches to this process. They were skeptical about the feasibility of the project and resistant to change. Few volunteered to participate, and many were transferred directly to the project without seeking or consenting to the transfer. The managing team kept busy planning and trying to avoid making the mistakes that hampered previous efforts. This polarized initial landscape had changed dramatically by the last stages of the project. Civil servants held most of the senior positions of the project and were committed and empowered in their task, working hand-in-hand with members of the managing team. What were the conditions that allowed this change to take place?

- **Taylorist Approach:** Dividing the project into specialized processes allowed a professional to be in charge of hierarchically organized teams performing a single process for all the sectors included in the project. This empowered the people in charge of the processes, to direct their teams and to become accountable for their results.

- **Empowering Lower-Rank Professionals:** Within the agency's career civil service is a highly hierarchical structure of positions and ranks. Theoretically speaking, higher ranks are assigned to more capable and experienced professionals, which in turn allow them to be trusted with greater responsibility and earn higher wages and benefits. Nevertheless, in practice, the rules and procedures to promote a professional within the agency are muddy. After years under this scheme, the resulting structure of ranks is unbalanced when not openly unfair: professionals having higher skill levels and more experience can have lower ranks. In the course of the project, several of these lower-rank professionals were put in charge of specific processes. Ignoring the established structure allowed highly skilled professionals to access higher positions, which, in addition to working under a committed management team responding to their needs, empowered them. At the end, they were responsible for the success of the project on many fronts, and their contributions were openly recognized as instrumental.

- **Gradual Incorporation of the Agency's Professionals into Planning/ Decision-Making Processes:** Before this incorporation could happen, two parallel processes took place. On the one hand, the scandals and legal problems of the 2006 project left career civil servants fearful of participating in a new project and closed their perspective about the possibilities of change and success of a new venture. Some even feared that the true intentions of the new administration were to fail again, to close the Cadastre, and contract with private firms all of the city's cadastral needs. They had to be convinced that the new administration not only wanted but also needed a successful updating process and that the new managing team was capable of implementing it. On the other hand, after having a clearer idea of what the project and its processes were about, the directive team became more open to incorporating the servants' experience and know-how.

Openness to Reviewing Results

Since the CUPB was a massive process that covered 827,000 parcels, errors were expected. Since inefficiently attended requests for revision could jeopardize the political stability of the process, Bogotá's Cadastre defined customer service plans that allowed citizens to have their revision requests answered swiftly. By mid-March, when this revision and adjustment process started, owners had filed just over 1,400 value revision requests, almost half of them being retail parcels within shopping centers. Nearly 1,200 were answered before June 5 and the rest before the property tax payment deadline (June 30, 2009). Beyond a rapid resolution of filed requests, Cadastre officials were available to answer owners' queries on methodologies used, always willing to verify and double-check results.

Main Results

The CUPB updated the information of 827,000 parcels out of the city's 2 million parcels. This means that the information in the cadastre's database reflects physical, legal, and economic reality of the city's parcels, which allows for a more equitable distribution of the tax burden. On the one hand, the tax will be based on the actual value of properties, therefore accounting for changes in the city in the past five years. On the other hand, it reassures owners that they pay a tax proportional to the value of their property within a progressive plan.

From an organizational perspective, the success of the project gave back to the Cadastre the legitimacy that it had lost in the failed 2006 process. The District Comptroller ranked the Cadastre as the second best public agency of the city. This legitimacy will help the administration bring about profound technical and administrative reforms. Additionally, the momentum of the CUPB will facilitate politically and institutionally a larger updating effort during 2009: our goal is to update the remaining 1.2 million urban parcels. Furthermore, the CUPB provided civil servants—who will remain within the agency long after the current administration has left—with an experience that will enrich future updating processes.

From a fiscal perspective, property tax revenue increased around 10 percent. Figure 5.5 summarizes the fiscal benefit of the CUPB in FY2009 and the cost of the lag in the cadastral database between FY2005 and FY2008.

Future Improvements

Given that this year's effort will complete the updating of the entire cadastral database, the next few years will be an ideal time to implement reforms that will both strengthen and simplify the Cadastre's organization and methodologies.

To understand better the scale of this endeavor, it is important to remember that currently the National Geographical Institute's Resolution 2555 splits cadastral methodologies into two complementary processes: updating and upgrading. In the former, the city government surveys entire parts of the city registering changes in the physical characteristics and ownership of parcels and establishes cadastral values through massive assessment techniques. In the latter, the owner informs the Cadastre of changes in his parcel and the agency verifies and incorporates this new information into its database. Even though they are two distinct processes, their goal is the same: to keep a cadastral registry that reflects the dynamics of the city.

Figure 5.5. Property Tax Revenue 2004-2009: Costs of Lag and Benefits of Updating

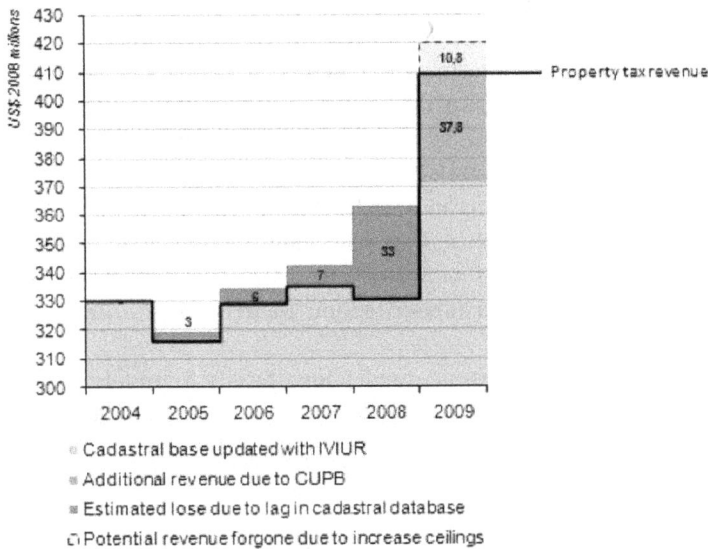

- Cadastral base updated with IVIUR
- Additional revenue due to CUPB
- Estimated lose due to lag in cadastral database
- Potential revenue forgone due to increase ceilings

Source: Revenue calculated using the total cadastral value of the city and the effective rate of the property tax estimated by the Finance Department taking into account evasion and elusion rates. The latter explains the fall in actual tax revenue in FY2005 and FY2008.

The introduction of ceilings on increases led to a 22.2 percent reduction in the additional tax revenue that CUPB generated; that is, 2.6 percent of total property tax revenue.

In the mid-term, the Cadastre seeks to join the two processes into a single one that—while maintaining the definitions that the law provides—holds a unit test that homogenizes the Cadastre's actions on its database. In this manner, the Cadastre will be able to efficiently register information; permanently and systematically overseeing the urban and real-estate transformations while the city experiments. To do this, the Cadastre must create and maintain administrative synergies to obtain the parcel information that other agencies and private firms register. Once the Cadastre has a full picture of the real-estate behavior in Bogotá, it will be able to target its efforts on those parcels that need adjustments in their cadastral information while ratifying the registered information of non-surveyed parcels. In this way, the information of all the parcels in the city will be up-to-date every year.

To reach this level of analysis and understanding of the city, the Cadastre's information system must maintain stable contact with other sources of information such as the National Registry Office, for changes in ownership and transaction values; the Urban Curators, to anticipate changes in street numbering, parcel subdivisions, and new buildings; the Departments of Habitat and Planning, to estimate the impact of changes in land use regulations and informality in general. Additionally, this information system will be founded on a mapping base with aerial photographs and satellite images to establish—through object-recognition and restitution technologies—changes in buildings and to monitor available land within the urban perimeter.

Beyond these institutional synergies and use of new technologies, the Cadastre of Bogotá must bring about profound changes: from overhauling its technological platform to implementing permanent staff training in information analysis.

While updating the physical information can be addressed through reference information analysis, legal information depends on a close and permanent relationship with the National Registry Office, the official custodian of this information. In addition, the current value assessment system must be restructured. Instead of modeling professional assessors' interpretation of the real estate market, a new massive assessment system will monitor and model directly real-estate market information (i.e., offers, transactions, leases, etc.). This plan calls for the Real Estate Observatory to consolidate a detailed census of real-estate offers and a permanent registry of the values of sale and rent transactions. Hedonic models will be directly built from real-estate market information.

This kind of massive assessment will allow the city to update cadastral values on a yearly basis replicating the dynamics of the real-estate market and eliminating the arbitrary surges in property tax generated by the elimination of lags in the cadastral database due to updating processes. This will reduce the political pressure described in previous sections.

On the one hand, the periodic development of models will provide insights into the parcel attributes upon which the market forms its prices, the city's submarkets, and the elements that determine value growth or lack thereof in the different areas of the city. On the other hand, it will generate incentives for the Cadastre to innovate in the data collected during parcel surveying.

The full development of this complete yearly updating of the Cadastre's database will require a deep institutional redesign to improve and simplify its methodologies and processes and improve its human resource management. It will also require an overhaul of the Cadastre's entire computational infrastructure, which will be done with the support of the World Bank.

And finally, it will be crucial to encourage regulatory changes. Values must be calculated as the sum of the independent assessments of building and land. Nevertheless, in the context of a large urban center full of horizontal properties, calculating independent values for building and land is burdensome and technically slack. The Cadastre will promote regulatory independence for decentralized cadastres to set the methodologies that better suit the particularities of their cities. In this environment, the Cadastre will promote forums for technical discussions to promote the continuing improvement of cadastral methodologies.

Conclusion

The technical aspects of the cadastral updating in Bogotá were strengthened and will be further improved. Nevertheless, implementing what is seen as a de facto tax reform generates enormous political pressure. A significant lag on a Cadastre's database calls for the implementation of plans such as increase ceilings to break the link between the cadastral value and the property tax. Without them, the cadastres in charge of these processes will come under pressure that will prevent them from becoming suppliers of vital information for the city's planning and thus from becoming true multipurpose cadastres.

5.3:   Ensuring Access to Land for Private Investors

PATRICK MCAUSLAN, Birkbeck College, London University, United Kingdom

Introduction

An important question in relation to developments in land tenure in developing and transitional countries is the extent to which foreign investment in and ownership of land,[8] particularly agricultural land, in such countries is accepted, encouraged, discouraged, or limited in one way or another. Few such countries have sufficient internal capital to invest in agriculture to increase its diversity and quality and so propel it into becoming a major source of exports and contributor to the country's gross domestic product (GDP). It follows then, that some foreign investment in agriculture will likely be needed if a country's policy is to improve agricultural productivity and quality. Investment in agriculture will usually involve acquiring rights to occupy and use land. The first decade of the twenty-first century has seen a very sharp increase in the interest that foreign investors, both state and private, have shown in acquiring land in countries in Africa, both for purposes of growing crops for biofuel and for purposes of growing food crops for their own national consumption.[9] This trend lends topicality to this issue and this paper highlights several policy and legal issues surrounding the question of foreign ownership, occupation, and use of land, namely:

- Limitations on foreign ownership;
- Alternatives to ownership: rental and other forms of land holding in land and other real estate;
- International legal instruments for protecting foreign investment in property;
- Effects of foreign investment on local and indigenous populations and national and international protection regimes for vulnerable populations;
- Prospects for a uniform land law.

These issues do not seek to exhaust the topic but they are important legal policy matters that need to be considered when advocating or seeking to facilitate such foreign investment.

Limitations on Foreign Ownership

It is usually assumed that limitations on foreign ownership of land is a developing country phenomenon that has also, unfortunately, been copied by some transitional countries not yet fully attuned to the needs of a globalized land market. Nothing could be further from the truth. Concern about and controls on foreign ownership of land are a world-wide phenomenon, rooted in history. Some examples from North America, Australasia, and the European Union (EU) may be given.

Concerned by an apparent excess of foreign ownership of real property, some 30 states in the United States have imposed strict guidelines on foreign ownership or even prohibited it in an effort to protect family farms.[10] For instance, nonresident individuals in Kansas and Wyoming, who are not eligible for U.S. citizenship, cannot acquire or own real estate unless that right is granted by treaty. In New Hampshire, nonresident ownership is fully proscribed, while Missouri limits non-agricultural land ownership by nonresidents to five acres or less. Oklahoma prohibits a nonresident from acquiring land, and if a resident landowner subsequently leaves the state, any real property owned by the departing taxpayer reverts to the state unless disposed of within five years. At the federal level, the government responded to concerns about the apparent growth of foreign ownership of land by enacting the U.S. Agricultural Foreign Investment Disclosure Act (AFIDA) of 1978, which requires foreigners to register the acquisition of any interest (except a security interest) in agricultural land larger than 10 acres within 90 days. Annual figures from that date show that foreigners own around 1 percent of privately owned farm- and forestland in the United States.

Provinces in Canada—e.g., Alberta and Manitoba—prohibit ownership of certain types of land—principally agricultural—over a certain amount; in Alberta, it's a parcel of land over 20 acres, in Manitoba, it is 10 acres. States in Australia—e.g., Queensland—require foreign ownership of any land over a certain amount to be registered in a public register. New Zealand, in response to considerable foreign—especially Australian—acquisition of land during this decade, has recently tightened the rules on foreign acquisition of land with unique cultural and natural heritage attributes and provided that the Crown would have first refusal over foreshore and seabed land.

EU rules require that there should be no restrictions on ownership of a member's land by nationals from other countries within the EU. This provision, however, was one of the main sticking points when countries from East and Central Europe were negotiating for membership at the turn of the century. The reasons for this were both political and economic.[11] Poland and the Czech Republic feared the security implications of German attempts to "reclaim" land that had been lost in the forced relocation of Germans from those two countries after the end of World War II. Hungary was concerned about renewed Austrian attempts to acquire farmland and so recreate the land-holding patterns that existed in pre-World War II Hungary. The Slovak Republic was concerned about Hungarian attempts to acquire land, thus increasing the large numbers of Hungarians in the country. Economically, too, these countries were concerned about the considerable disparity in farmland prices between them and Western Europe, which, quite apart from political issues, would have made acquisition of their land very attractive to Western European investors. All these countries negotiated waiting periods before unrestricted access to their land was permitted. Restrictions also exist among several longstanding members within the EU. Denmark, Finland, Greece, and Ireland, for instance, restrict foreign ownership of specific areas of land or impose residence requirements on foreigners wishing to acquire land. Some—e.g., Ireland and Spain—require foreign investments in land either generally or over a certain amount to receive prior approval from the government. Switzerland also requires prior approval from cantonal authorities for the acquisition of land by foreign nationals unless they have residence permits. Among candidate members, Turkey has updated its real estate foreign ownership law, which is based on the principle of reciprocity.[12]

It should be no surprise that developing countries have followed Australasian, European and North American practices and laws in restricting and regulating foreign ownership of land and for the same reasons. As was once said to the author by a belonger[13] in the British Virgin Islands, "Without land, a man is not a man." A fortiori with a country: without owning its own land, a country is not a country. The overwhelming majority of developing countries were once colonies, and colonies from the time of the Crusades in the twelfth century onward were founded, au fond, on foreigners appropriating land from the indigenous populations. At independence, ex-colonies were and are not going to allow, under the mantra of a free market in land, the same situation to arise again. This concern applies to countries long freed from colonialism such as Brazil as much as it does to those more recently freed as with many countries in Africa.

It is no accident that Ireland, which was a colony for over 700 years and suffered grievously from laws favoring the colonizers over the colonized, has some of the strictest laws on the consents required by foreigners for the purchase of non-urban land in the EU, or that Poland, which has suffered over the centuries from being dismembered by Russia and Germany, is so fearful of the implications of large-scale foreign ownership of land. Similarly, countries that were never colonies—i.e., Ethiopia,[14] Saudia Arabia, and Thailand—learning from the experiences of their neighbors also have restrictions on foreign ownership.

It is important to understand that in virtually all cases, restrictions on foreign ownership do not amount to a ban on foreign investment in land. The restrictions are of three broad types. First are restrictions on *ownership of land*; that is, on owning the freehold of land. In countries where no one can own freehold and the radical title to land is vested in the state—e.g., Tanzania—foreigners are restricted from holding land under a right of occupancy, the highest form of land holding allowed by the law in Tanzania. Foreigners in countries that do restrict ownership or its equivalent are, however, allowed to lease land or acquire a usufruct of land, where a usufruct is a higher interest than a lease—e.g., in countries where land is regulated by Islamic law. The length of a lease may be quite short and less than what a citizen is allowed to obtain, and restrictions may apply on how much land may be leased.

This restriction may appear at first sight more limiting than it is in practice. Twenty-five-year tourist leases for foreign investors in Maldives have not stopped an enormous level of investment from Europe and Asia in tourist resorts there since the mid- to late 1970s. These leases are likely to be extended up to 50 years. Thirty-year leases did not inhibit Korean and Taiwanese investment in building factories in Lesotho to take advantage of the U.S. African Growth and Opportunity Act (AGOA). Foreign investors may not want to burden themselves with long leases and the obligations that such property interests might entail.[15] Short lengths of interest too are likely to reduce possible political opposition to foreign "ownership" of land. The issue here is not so much the length or the nature of the property interest permitted to foreign investors as the quality of the host government's land management arrangements and the welcome accorded to foreign investors. Here one may contrast Mozambique with Zimbabwe: the former country welcomes foreign investment in agricultural land; the latter has for some time been intent on driving it away. In Mozambique, foreign investors are required to consult with local stakeholders before obtaining land, but they may then obtain 50-year renewable land use rights that are the same terms on which domestic investors may acquire land from local stakeholders. The land use right is conditional on the implementation of an agreed investment plan.[16]

The second restriction is on the *types of land* that may be acquired. This is a very common restriction and occurs all over the world. Brazil, Mexico, New Zealand, and South Africa (proposed)—to name a few—and many countries in the EU restrict foreign ownership of land variously called recreational land, heritage land, coastal land, and land within "n" meters of an international border. Some countries may allow land in such areas to be leased or held in a trust (as in Mexico, where the owner may be a bank); other countries impose an outright ban.

The third restriction may be seen more as *regulation* than restriction. Many countries require a potential foreign investor to obtain various permissions from a range of public agencies before the investment is allowed. This may include an investment promotion agency, a license from a ministry involved with land or natural resources, or the environment or all three if they are separate ministries. In addition, permission may be required from a local authority or where the land involved is wholly or partly customary tenure under the control of a traditional authority or a community, from those authorities[17]. Third, registration in a special register for foreign land ownership (as is the case in Queensland) may be required. Some of these permissions may be the same that local investors have to acquire; some are specific to foreign investors and may be designed, in fact, to ease the investor's path through the local bureaucracy.

No purpose would be served by detailing all the individual restrictions that exist in countries throughout the world or the reasons for them, but one general matter that may be highlighted is the various ways in which the concept of a "foreigner" is provided for. Nationality is an obvious and widely used test, but many countries also make use of residence; a foreigner who has been a resident or permanent resident (as defined in immigration laws) for a certain number of years may be permitted to acquire land. Residency is itself likely to be restrictively applied; being resident in a country for less than half or even two-thirds of a year would not qualify as being a resident for the purposes of obtaining property. In rare cases, ethnicity is a qualifying criterion: Fiji limits land ownership to indigenous Fijians and denies it to Indian Fijian citizens howsoever long they and their forebears have lived in Fiji. With respect to foreign companies and partnerships owning land, the test again varies. At one end, in some countries, even one partner is enough for the partnership to be regarded as foreign or any foreign shareholding to convert a company into a foreign company. More tolerant regimes permit companies with 49 percent foreign ownership to acquire land. AFIDA sets the limit at 10 percent foreign owned for a company to be required to register its ownership of agricultural land in the United States. Alberta sets the limit at 50 percent or greater.

The fact that developing and transitional countries are following the example of North American, Australasian, and EU countries has not stopped the latter countries from endeavoring to persuade or pressure the former countries to remove or emasculate such barriers as exist. The EU, as has already been noted, requires members to allow a free market in land ownership and has made this a condition for candidate members to comply but has been prepared to accept a waiting period before the rules apply fully.

Of wider import, and with more serious implications for the countries concerned, are some of the multilateral trade and investment agreements made between the United States and countries in the developing world. AGOA, first enacted in 2000, and its various amendments and additions since, requires countries in Africa that wish to participate in the trade concessions on offer under the law to eliminate barriers to U.S. trade and investment in their countries; the language of AGOA is wide enough to embrace equal treatment for investment in land. The North Atlantic Free Trade Agreement (NAFTA) between Canada, Mexico, and the USA protects investments in real estate by the partners in one another's countries. The Caribbean Basin Initiative is also drawn sufficiently wide to embrace land.

The Protection of Foreign Investments in Land

For any foreign investor, one issue of great concern is the legal framework governing the protection of that investment. With respect to investment in land, in addition to the "normal" avenues of protection—i.e., national courts and international dispute settlement bodies (which are discussed below), an important matter is that of expropriation of land. All states provide for governments to expropriate land in the public interest, and many states have provisions in their constitutions permitting expropriation on payment of compensation.[18] A fairly standard expression is that there must be "prompt payment of fair compensation," and increasingly, the accepted international best practice is that fair compensation means the market value of the land being acquired. There is no universal measure of market value, however, as different countries use different approaches on the factors to take into account or omit in assessing the market value of land.

If a state's laws provide for expropriation in accordance with the above standards and no special rules apply to land leased to foreigners, then foreign investors cannot complain if their land is expropriated. If special and disadvantageous rules apply to the expropriation of foreign leased land that do not apply to locally owned or leased land, then foreign investors might be justified in alleging discriminatory treatment before national or international tribunals. A notable case in Namibia on this issue is worth a brief discussion.[19] Namibia's Agricultural Commercial Land Reform Act permits expropriations—particularly in an effort to remedy Namibia's stark disparities in property ownership. A detailed process is set out under the Act, including various forms of consultation and assessment that government is obliged to undertake. Guenther Kessl and two other German settlers alleged that the Namibian government simply drew up a list of foreign-owned land holdings and then moved to acquire certain ones without complying with the provisions of the Act. The high court agreed with the claimants, holding that the government had omitted to follow key portions of the Act, as well as the Constitution. The claimants also complained that the government's singling out of their landholdings on the basis of their being foreigners violated the investment protection treaty with Germany. On this, the high court observed that Namibia was duty-bound to comply with the treaty: "As German citizens, the three applicants are entitled to the same treatment as Namibian citizens in terms of the Encouragement and Reciprocal Protection of Investments Treaty which was entered into by the Republic of Namibia and the Government of the Federal Republic of Germany."

A trickier situation is one that is alleged to be the case in Ghana (Blessings 2009) in which the government has, in disregard of the constitution, sold unfettered ownership of land to a foreign investor in the course of selling a public utility to that foreign investor. A future government might seek to alter the terms of such a sale on the grounds that it was unconstitutional, but the foreign investor might then have a good case for seeking compensation because it was entitled to rely on the government complying with the constitution and should not be expected to suffer losses for the government's noncompliance with the constitution. It would be otherwise, however, if such a transaction had been tainted by corruption.

However, the use of the word "might" in the above paragraph is deliberate. Consider a rule that gave special protection to land owned and occupied by indigenous peoples or pastoralists that had the effect of causing governments to prioritize the expropriation of land in commercial as opposed to traditional or subsistence use. Even if much of that land was leased to foreign investors, this would not necessarily be a rule that discriminated against foreign investors, as such, compared with a rule that discriminated against land held for commercial purposes in which foreigners dominated the market.

More difficult are cases that arise out of an international treaty that appears to give foreign land holders *better* protection than is accorded national landowners. A case that has been the subject of considerable debate is *Metalclad Corp v United Mexican States*,[20] which arose under the NAFTA treaty and permits commercial entities in the treaty states to bring actions directly against a treaty government other than their own alleging breach of the treaty. A U.S. corporation had purchased a landfill site in the municipality of Guadalcázar. The company failed to get permission to operate the site from the municipality, sued the Government of Mexico, and an arbitration panel determined that Mexico had breached its treaty obligations to provide fair and equitable treatment and to refrain from taking action "tantamount to expropriation." The impugned action was the making by the municipality of a permissible decision under environmental law. On appeal to the Supreme Court of British Columbia—the relevant appeal body provided for by NAFTA—the decision was scaled down and criticism was made of the breadth of the panel's approach to expropriation. But the point being made remains valid: It may be queried whether it would be to the long-term benefits of foreign investors in land if it were known that their government had won concessions from the host government not available to local landowners—i.e., exemption from local environmental and planning regulations.

Turning to judicial proceedings more generally, two matters should be highlighted. First, a general rule of international law is now enshrined in the Brussels Convention of 1968, widely applicable in Europe, that

> in proceedings which have as their object rights *in rem* in immovable property or tenancies of immovable property, the courts of the [state] in which the property is situated [have exclusive jurisdiction] ... (Sparkes 2007).

This rule is based on practical considerations; local courts know about local land and have powers to ensure that local officials enforce their judgments against the land. Where, however, the treaty does not apply, it is open to a private foreign investor or a state on behalf of such an investor to conclude an agreement for some other rule to apply—i.e., that the courts of the state of the investor or an international body are to have jurisdiction.

This leads to the second point: the existence and operation of international dispute settlement rules and bodies separate from dispute settlement bodies established under a specific treaty such as NAFTA to handle interstate commercial disputes that may include land disputes. International arbitration under the auspices of a body established by treaty goes back well over 100 years but has become much more widely used under treaty provisions in the last 20 to 25 years. United Nations Commission on International Trade Law (UNCITRAL) issued a Model Law on International Commercial Arbitration in 1985 that has formed the basis of many national and international arbitration panels since then. Regional conventions covering the OAS, Arab states, African states, and European states provide for regional frameworks for arbitration. Probably the most used system is the International Centre for the Settlement of Investment Disputes (ICSID), established in 1966 by the Convention for the Settlement of Investment Disputes between States and National of Other States. The center is a member of the World Bank Group but is administratively separate with its own governance structure. As of September 2007, 156 countries had signed up to the Convention.

The ICSID has been involved in several cases arising out of land disputes and, more recently, these disputes have arisen from land reform programs—e.g., a dispute between the UK's Vestey Group and the Government of the República Bolivariana deVenezuela[21] and the challenge to Zimbabwe's land reforms by 15 Dutch farmers, the decision on which was handed down in April 2009.[22] It is of considerable importance and merits a brief review. In the words of Peterson (2009):

> The Dutch claimants turned to ICSID in 2003, alleging that they had been forcibly dispossessed of their properties thanks to violent land invasions by so-called War Veterans, as well as various acts and omissions of the Zimbabwean authorities. An [ICSID] tribunal … held that Zimbabwe breached a requirement of the Netherlands-Zimbabwe investment protection treaty to provide just compensation in case of expropriation. The arbitrators ordered Zimbabwe to pay some £7.3 million to the affected landowners for their lost property, other moveable assets (such as tractors and vehicles), and for the "disturbance" suffered as a result of the dispossessions.

As Peterson notes, this decision opens the way for many more foreign nationals with whose governments Zimbabwe concluded investment protection treaties to claim compensation for the loss of their farms. The reasoning in the decision would apply to other land reform programs that resulted in the dispossession without compensation of foreign nationals covered by foreign investment protection treaties.

There is, then, a plethora of international dispute settlement forums used by foreign investors wishing to challenge national decisions about their land rights. These bodies are independent of any treaty provisions establishing special bodies to settle disputes arising under that specific treaty so that it must be queried whether such provisions are necessary. AGOA has not established such a specific body but relies on substantive provisions in the treaty that there must be "the elimination of barriers to United States trade and investment, including by—(i) the provision of national treatment ..." Where it is alleged that this provision has been breached, it will be possible to bring a case to the ICSID.

Effect of Foreign Investment on Local and Indigenous Populations

The phrase used in AGOA—the provision of national treatment—is now the accepted terminology in international commercial treaties to impose an obligation on the host nation not to discriminate against a foreign investor. Those countries that restrict foreign investment in land to leases or usufructs as opposed to ownership or rights of occupancy would as a matter of strict interpretation of a treaty such as AGOA be infringing on the treaty. But there is another aspect of restriction that must be considered: the impact of foreign investment on the local and indigenous population. Under what circumstances might or are such restrictions imposed and what justifications are there for these?

A good and relatively straightforward example is provided by Maldives. Foreign investors in the tourist industry may bid for leases of uninhabited islands to develop them as tourist resorts. Foreign investment is not permitted in inhabited islands while national investment is. There is a strict policy of separation of tourist investment and investment in islands inhabited by citizens in an endeavor to stop citizens being "contaminated" by the lifestyles of tourists. The effort may be in vain, but it would be difficult to argue that that was an unreasonable restriction on foreign investors when they still have over one thousand uninhabited islands in which to invest.

More problematic is foreign investment in lands held by customary tenure and occupied by indigenous peoples. A recent study undertaken for the Foreign Investment Advisory Services (FIAS) of the World Bank Group on investment in Community Land in Southern Africa (Adams et al. 2004) drew attention to the difficulties of obtaining a clear title to such land in South Africa and similar problems that exist in all other countries in that subregion. This is a problem that applies to all would-be commercial investors in countries—principally but not exclusively in Africa—in which part of the land is under the control and occupation of persons living and using land in accordance with customary tenure. Some countries—e.g., Indonesia and Sudan—adopt or are alleged to adopt heavy-handed tactics when faced with opposition by customary communities to losing their land to foreign investors, and in the case of Sudan, this was a major cause of the civil war that wracked that country for so many years.[23] Other countries—e.g., Tanzania—have imposed provisions on consultation with local stakeholders on foreign investors to acquire agricultural and other rural land controlled by villagers and governed by customary tenure for commercial investment and have been criticized by the World Bank[24] and others for so doing. Other countries yet again—e.g., Mexico—have altered their laws and opened up hitherto reserved (*ejido*) land to commercial investment including foreign investment, but this has contributed to considerable internal turmoil in parts of the country.

The issue of involvement of local stakeholders and landowners occupying land under customary tenure has come into sharp focus with the current drive by foreign state and private investors to acquire land in countries in Africa for biofuel and agricultural investment. There is evidence that in the rush to obtain both land and local partners—usually members of local political and business elites—there has been a lack of transparency in many of these arrangements and this spills over into a lack of involvement by civil society and inadequate consultation with local rights holders. Cotula et al. make the point that while article 32 of the United Nations Declaration on the Rights of Indigenous People provides for the principle of free, prior, informed consent (FPIC) on land matters, "consultation tends to be a one-off event rather than an ongoing interaction" and is formalistic rather than substantive.[25]

There is a clash here of laws and cultures. At the formal national and international level, it is the culture of globalization that impels the development of laws and policies based on the free and equal opportunity to invest in land so as to facilitate land being used to its highest and best purpose without regard to such irrelevant matters as the nationality of the user. This sees land as an economic and only as an economic asset. At the informal, local, popular, customary, or traditional level (which exists as much in Europe and the USA as in the developing world), it is the culture that sees land as a social and political as much as an economic asset that resists land being parceled out to whoever can pay for it to exploit it as is seen fit. A government that ignores the social aspect of land—however retrogressive it may seem to devotees of the market—does so at its peril. At best, there will be clashes on the ground between investor and locals: at worst, ignoring local beliefs and attitudes to land can lead and has led to widespread local violence and civil wars.

Toward a Uniform Land Law for Foreign Investment?

This, then, leads to the final issue that must be addressed. There exists a strand of thinking, writing, and policy making that hankers after the development of an international or transnational land law or the development of homogenized national land laws similar to the development of international or uniform commercial and intellectual property laws that are designed to advance international trade, the uniform enforcement of contracts, and the common protection of property rights. Two authors have put the matter thus:

> Uniform laws promote economic development by making it easier for those engaged in commerce to expand beyond jurisdictional boundaries. Uniform laws simplify transactions. ... While the need for uniform laws in commerce is most pronounced in the field of commercial law—*e.g.*, sales of goods, commercial paper and security interests in personal property—the increasing sophistication of real property financing has accentuated the advantages of uniformity in land laws as well. (Schreiberg and Levy 1993)

UN-Habitat, too, via its Habitat Agenda, the Global Plan of Action, and the followup Global Land Tools Network, is urging a measure of international uniformity on land laws (for although the agency focuses on urban land, most land laws apply nationally) with specific reference to such matters as land registration and land transactions. Treaties such as NAFTA and AGOA with their references to "national treatment" may also be seen as tending toward that end. The World Bank, too, has exhibited some moves in this direction. The FIAS development of Accessing Land Indicators for Foreign Investment is clearly based on the assumption that one uniform set of land laws based on a Western model would facilitate foreign investment in land. Two further examples are its requirement for reforms in Tanzania's mortgage law to accord with the wishes of the international banking community (Bruce 2006) and its funding of a project to substitute the common law Torrens system of title registration for the Austro-Germanic Land Book system in Serbia.

It is doubtful whether any attempt to develop or encourage the development of some standard national land law would be either practicable or desirable. On the first point, despite the best efforts of lawyers in the United States, attempts at developing and introducing a Uniform Land Law similar to the Uniform Commercial Code (UCC) throughout the States have achieved absolutely no success. In Europe, the EU is 50 years old: a recently published book notes that while there are a significant number of areas in which EU rules, whose bulk is significant, have had a significant and substantive effect on property law, "they have not coalesced into a coherent form and … are unlikely to do so and neither are national property systems likely to converge" (Sparkes 2007, 153).[26] If these two economic and political unions cannot develop a uniform land law, it is unlikely that a wider political grouping would be able to.

The second point is that in many countries, there is a plurality of land laws and systems at the national level; and as has been shown only too recently, people within such countries are prepared to fight to maintain their systems and laws and the land rights they have under them. There is a growing recognition that rather than attempting to impose a uniform national land law in such countries, an approach that recognizes the strengths and benefits of diversity is more likely to encourage social stability and economic development.[27]

Conclusion

The conclusion, then, must be that foreign ownership and investment in land in developing and transitional countries is fraught with specific and particular circumstances so that each country's special characteristics must be well understood and taken into account by a potential investor. National laws are important but of equal, if not more, importance, in many cases, are local laws, cultures, and social practices. It would be counterproductive for a foreign investor or its government to attempt to assert and impose the provisions of a treaty requiring "national treatment" with respect to access to and occupation of land when there really is no "national treatment" as such even for local investors.

Even within such old and sophisticated countries as exist in Europe, there are clear national differences between countries: the UK may not mind that an iconic shop such as Harrods is owned by a foreign national; France, on the other hand adopts a much more nationalistic approach to such matters. Ditto with the ownership of agricultural land: It is much easier as a matter of law for the Irish to buy agricultural land in England than for the English to buy agricultural land in Ireland. So it is with land in most developing and transitional countries; having reasserted national and private rights over land after a long period when neither were possible, governments and their peoples are understandably reluctant to allow a free market in land to start the process of losing land all over again.

Rather than working toward eliminating all restrictions on foreign investment in land, it would be more constructive to ensure that such restrictions as do exist are transparent, operate fairly, and permit a review when an adverse decision is handed down. Countries such as Ghana, Mozambique, and Tanzania have written into the law the need to consult with local stakeholders as a part of the process of acquiring their land. More effort must be made to ensure that these laws are enforced. First, full publicity should be given to applications to acquire land via using all forms of media, especially those commonly accessed by agricultural communities—e.g., local radio stations. Second, where consultations are required, there may be a need to set out in some detail how these are to be undertaken and which groups of people are to be consulted. Such provisions are often written into the law dealing with applications to develop land in towns and cities and in laws dealing with land adjudication: there is no reason why such provisions should not be applied to applications to acquire and develop land in rural areas. Third, a further step could be to invite local stakeholders to form part of an ongoing advisory group to be consulted on a regular basis during the currency of the project. Finally, local communities could be beneficiaries of a project via investments in local infrastructure for the benefit of local people by the foreign investors.

Overall, the aim should be to develop a partnership approach with local stakeholders, as many foreign investors will be familiar with in respect of investment in their own countries, rather than attempting to ride roughshod over local sensibilities and concerns. Ignoring local concerns and short-circuiting local consultative processes may appear to enable investments to get underway more quickly, but whatever might have been the case in the past, local stakeholders are now more knowledgeable about their rights under the law and more willing to assert them (Gauri and Brinks 2008). The existence of a fair law and compliance with it is not, then, a burden to be circumvented if possible; it is the essential first step in a successful project of foreign investment in land.

Notes

[1] *Doing Business* Survey: World Bank.
[2] The twelve administrative sectors are: planning, habitat, education, health, social integration, public management, government and security, economic development, culture and recreation, environment, mobility, and finance.
[3] In addition to this extra revenue, it is estimated that the city lost another $48 million between 2004 and 2008 due to the lag in its cadastral base.
[4] For example, they are fierce defenders of *Apportionment*—the necessity to separate land and building values—when assessing a property. This practice has been proven to have severe technical shortcomings (*see f*or example Hendriks 2005).
[5] The city's Planning Department assigns a stratum to every parcel according to its physical configuration (entrance, garage, yard, length of front) and the quality of the building (material of facade and ceiling). There are six stratums, one being the lowest and six being the highest. This plan allows the city to structure its utility fees and tax obligation structures in a progressive manner.
[6] Before this project was approved, the ceiling for increases was 100% for all strata.
[7] For more on the impact of anchors on prices of parcels within shopping centers *see* Ingene and Ghosh (1990), Gatzlaff et al. (1994), and Ghosh (1986).

[8] The topic of foreign investment in land is both contentious and has generated an enormous volume of literature, both academic and official. This paper inevitably can be no more than 'one view of the cathedral'. It addresses topics which in the author's experience and knowledge—gained both from work as a consultant and as an academic researcher—are of considerable moment to countries in the developing world, particularly in Africa where a good deal of the author's consultancy and research experience has been.

[9] *See* L. Cotula et al. (2009) for an up-to-date survey and analysis of the current state of play.

[10] Luttrell (1979) states bluntly that "much of the opposition to foreign ownership of land is the result of emotional factors rather than economic factors. The objections are imbedded in utopian views with respect to the structure of agriculture...there is little chance of foreign interests obtaining control of a large percent of US farmland." p.9.

[11] *See* Lynn M. Tesser (2004) for an excellent study of the issue. The Appendix to her paper lists restrictions imposed by 12 EU states.

[12] The law contains lists of countries whose nationals may and may not purchase real estate in Turkey. Thus, a citizen of Israel may but a citizen of Kuwait may not purchase land in Turkey.

[13] The term "belonger" is used to describe people of British Virgin Island (BVI) parentage or birth who are BVI citizens. In contrast to "non-belongers," who are descendents of parents from other Caribbean countries, belongers have unrestricted landownership rights.

[14] Strictly speaking Ethiopia was a colony of Italy for six years between 1935 and 1941. However, the fundamental difference between Ethiopia and other states in Sub-Saharan Africa is that Ethiopia was an independent state, recognized as such, before its temporary conquest by Italy (whose 'colonisation' was not recognized by the international community) whereas all other states were created as such by colonial powers. They didn't exist in the form and with the boundaries they have now before the onset of colonial occupation which was regarded by the international community as a perfectly legal form of the exercise of power by one country over another.

[15] When the U.S. changed its rules on the permitted origins of foreign clothing entering the country, Chinese and Taiwanese investors just walked away from Lesotho almost overnight, leaving empty factories and large-scale unemployment in the wake of their departure.

[16] Articles 17 and 18 Land Act 1997. L. Cotula et al. (2009), 72, 76.

[17] Evidence however suggests that while laws may mandate such consultation with local stakeholders, it tends to be a matter of form rather than substance; Cotula et al. (2009) 72, 73.

[18] *See* A.J van der Walt (1999) and T. Allen (2000), chap. 6 for two comprehensive legal surveys on this matter. For an up-to-date overview, FAO (2009).

[19] *See* S. L. Harring and W. Odendaal (2008). This paper contains the full judgment of the High Court of Namibia and an excellent discussion of its implications for land reform in Namibia.

[20] *Metalclad Corp v United Mexican States*, Award ICSID Case No. ARB(AF)/97/1papr 131 (Aug 30 2000) 16 ICSID Rev-Foreign Investment LJ 168 and *United Mexican States v Metalclad Corp* [2001] 95 B.C.L.R. 3d 169.

[21] Vestey Group Ltd v. Bolivarian Republic of Venezuela (Case No. ARB/06/4) registered on March 14, 2006. Not yet concluded.

[22] *Funnekotter et al. v Republic of Zimbabwe (ICSID Case No. ARB/05/6) Decision of 22 April 2009 Washington D.C. ICSID.*

[23] Issues over land proved so contentious during the negotiations which led to the ending of the civil war that they were, in effect left unresolved by the Comprehensive Peace Agreement in 2005. The provisions on land in the CPA were transposed almost verbatim into the Interim National Constitution, articles 186−189. They required, inter alia, the establishment of a National Land Commission, two State Land Commissions in the 'transitional states' of Blue Nile and Southern Kordofan and a Southern Sudan Land Commission; the renewal of land rights under

customary tenure and a commitment to restitution of land to customary right holders in the transitional states. Four years on and no steps have been taken to establish the NLC, either of the two SLCs, officially recognize customary tenure or commence any process of restitution of land. Some state governments in North Sudan are however recognizing customary tenure, dealing with those occupying land under customary tenure and accepting that so doing is a necessary requirement for ensuring that foreign investment in land can take place. Evidence for this is derived from the author's participation in an FIAS mission on administrative barriers to foreign investment to four states in North Sudan in 2008 and work in the two transitional states for a USAID project on land administration to further the CPA in 2006. See Law and Development Partnership (2009) for the FIAS mission report.

[24] Financial Sector Assessment Report (2003) para. 6. Washington D.C. World Bank.

[25] Cotula, op. cit., 74. *See* also Sulle (2009).

[26] *See generally* Sparkes (2007), chap. 3 on the difficulties to create a European land law.

[27] For Africa *see* J.W Bruce and Shem E. Migot-Adholla (1994) and McAuslan (2006).

CHAPTER 6

Land Governance in the Context of Climate Change

6.1: Deforestation Alerts for Forest Law Enforcement: The Case of Mato Grosso, Brazil

CARLOS M. DE SOUZA JR., Amazon Institute of People and the Environment (Imazon), Brazil
SANAE HAIASHY, Imazon, Brazil
ADALBERTO VERÍSSIMO, Imazon, Brazil

Summary

We have developed a near real-time deforestation monitoring system, called the Deforestation Alert System (*Sistema de Alerta de Desmatamento*) (SAD) to monitor the Brazilian Amazon states. In this paper, we demonstrate how SAD works and how it has been used for monitoring deforestation in different types of forest reserves in the state of Mato Grosso, Brazil, as well as the potential use of this information to stop illegal deforestation in these reserves. The types of forest reserves we have been monitoring are located in protected areas (i.e., indigenous lands, conservation units), agrarian settlements, private lands registered with the state government licensing system, and on unclaimed public land. Using SAD, a total of 19,442 km^2 of deforestation was detected in Mato Grosso state from August 2005 to July 2008. Of this total, 70 percent (13,550 km^2) was detected in the Amazon biome, and the remaining 30 percent (5,892 km^2) in transitional forest types. We estimated that 85 percent of the total deforestation detected by SAD from August 2004 to July 2008 would be classified as illegal. This information is being widely disseminated to authorities and to the public through the media to support law enforcement, which has been the weak link in the fight against illegal deforestation, to implement the forestry code for protected private and governmental forest reserves. As a result of this forest transparency initiative—which combines near real-time detection of deforestation with the strategic dissemination of the information—the debate about deforestation has been kept alive each month by the media. The deforestation information generated by our monitoring system serves as reference to verify official governmental statistics, to create positive pressure on the state and federal governments to act against illegal deforestation, and to release official numbers and maps of deforestation to the public.

Introduction

The annual average deforestation rate in the Brazilian Amazon from 2000 to 2009 was 17,500 km² per year, with the second highest peak occurring in 2004 and reaching 27,400 km² of deforestation, according to the Brazilian National Institute of Space Research (*Instituto Nacional de Pesquisas Espaciais*) (INPE). The average for the last decade was 6 percent higher than the average deforestation rate in the prior decade (that is from 1990 through 1999), which reached 16,300 km². Since 2005, annual deforestation rates have been decreasing as a response to the expansion of protected areas, law enforcement campaigns, and the restriction to rural credits imposed by new policies. However, average annual deforestation rates from 2005 to 2009 are still high at 12,800 km² (figure 6.1) (PRODES 2009). According to the Program for the Estimation of Deforestation in the Brazilian Amazon (PRODES), which is highly accessible to the general population, from 2000 to 2009 the state of Mato Grosso had the highest average annual deforestation rate in the Brazilian Amazon at 6,200 km² per year (that is 36 percent of the deforestation average for that period, see figure 6.1). Pará is in second position accounting for 35 percent or 6,000 km² per year, followed by Rondônia (14 percent or 2,400 km² per year). The other six states (Acre, Maranhão, Tocantins, Roraima, Amazonas, and Amapá) contribute a combined total of 15 percent of the total deforestation in the Brazilian Amazon.

Figure 6.1. Annual Deforestation Rate in the Brazilian Amazon from 1988 through 2009

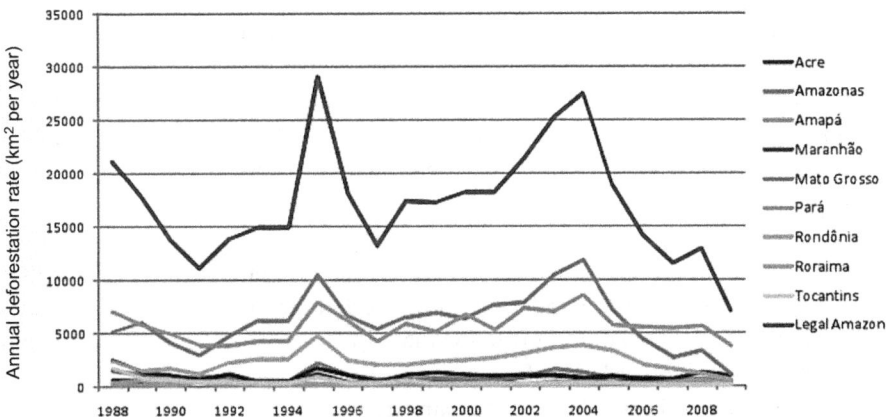

Source: INPE @ http://www.obt.inpe.br/prodes/.

Recent official estimates of deforestation rates in the Brazilian Amazon point to 2009 as having the lowest rate in the past 22 years, reaching 7,000 km² of deforestation. Even though the Brazilian government has implemented several strategies to stop illegal deforestation and decrease deforestation rates in the region, economic drivers have been considered to be the main cause of the fluctuation of deforestation rates from 2000 to 2008 (Ewers et al. 2008). For example, the region's response to the growing domestic and international demand for meat, agricultural products, timber, minerals, and energy supplies from 2000 to 2005 is considered to be the major driver that took deforestation rates to high levels. In 2007, the drop in annual deforestation rates can be partially explained by the ongoing economic crisis, which is creating poor market conditions for the agriculture sector in Brazil, but a preliminary analysis reveals that command and control by the federal government may be the main reason for the recent decrease in deforestation.

There are other deforestation drivers that can push the deforestation rates to high levels, even in an unfavorable macroeconomic scenario. For example, the expansion of biofuel production in other parts of the country—particularly in the southeast—is pushing ranching and agriculture from their original areas to the Brazilian Amazon frontier (Nepstad et al. 2006, Morton et al. 2006). Moreover, the Brazilian government has restarted several development projects in the region, including paving roads, opening waterways, issuing licenses for mineral research and exploitation, and planning the construction of major hydropower plants to accelerate development in the region. Complex land tenure arrangements, the low level of land tenure titling (which accounts for only 4 percent of private lands), and weak law enforcement have also created a culture in which public land can be freely occupied (Barreto et al. 2008). These land tenure factors have kept deforestation relatively high in new deforestation hot spots where public lands are under dispute.

The Amazon Institute of People and the Environment (*Instituto do Homem e Meio Ambiente da Amazônia*) (Imazon)[1] developed and made operational the first nongovernmental deforestation alert system, known as Deforestation Alert System (*Sistema de Alerta de Desmatamento*) (SAD), with the objectives of monitoring the impact of governmental policies, increasing transparency in forest use and land cover change in the Brazilian Amazon, and reducing illegal deforestation by improving forest law enforcement. SAD has been operational since September 2006 in Mato Grosso and was expanded to six other states of the Brazilian Amazon (Acre, Amapá, Amazonas, Pará, Rondônia, and Roraima) in August 2008. Maranhão and Tocantins were not included because deforestation baseline maps for these regions are not as precise as for the other states due to transitional and second growth forests (less than 30 years old), and a long history of forest degradation by selective logging and fires. Our near real-time deforestation monitoring system is being used to generate trend statistics for deforestation and forest degradation in protected areas, indigenous lands, rural settlements, and private lands, and to evaluate the degree of illegal deforestation and the effectiveness of forest law enforcement in the Brazilian Amazon. These statistical results are presented in the Forest Transparency bulletin on a monthly basis (see as an example, Haiashy et al. 2009). Besides PRODES, the Brazilian government also has its near real-time monitoring system that is similar to SAD, named Deter (INPE 2008).

In this article, we present how SAD works and has been used to monitor deforestation in different types of lands in the state of Mato Grosso and discuss SAD's potential for supporting forest law enforcement in the Brazilian Amazon. We chose Mato Grosso because it has the best information on different land categories and has the most advanced rural land parcel cadastral system in the region (Fearnside 2003). Next, we present the land categories and the types of forest reserves of Mato Grosso, then the SAD methodology as compared with the official monitoring systems (PRODES and Deter), followed by the application of the information generated by SAD to enforce forest law. We conclude by pointing out the future challenges and development of this system.

Land Categories and Forest Reserves

The state of Mato Grosso is located in the central-western region of Brazil; it has an area of 903,357 km². Most of its territory is in the Legal Amazon² region. The Amazon biome covers 47 percent of the state, followed by the *Cerrado*³ or savannas (39 percent) and natural grasslands (14 percent). A tropical-humid climate predominates in the region with high precipitation levels of 2,000 millimeters per annum. The Mato Grosso economy is largely based on ranching, mechanized agriculture (especially soybeans and cotton), and logging.

Five types of land categories can be found in Mato Grosso (figure 6.2). The legally protected areas consist of indigenous lands, which cover 14 percent of the total area (128,216 km²) and conservation units which cover a further 5 percent of the state (41,089 km²). Rural settlements for agrarian reform also cover 5 percent (42,161 km²) of the state's territory. Private lands are obliged by law to be registered with the State Environmental Licensing System of Rural Properties (SLAPR). As of July 2008, 21 percent (191,347 km²) of the state of Mato Grosso was covered by private lands registered in SLAPR. The remaining 55 percent (500,543 km²) of the state are either private lands not registered in SLAPR or lands that belong to the federal or state governments that have not been assigned to particular land uses or protection categories.

Figure 6.2. Land Categories Found in Mato Grosso State

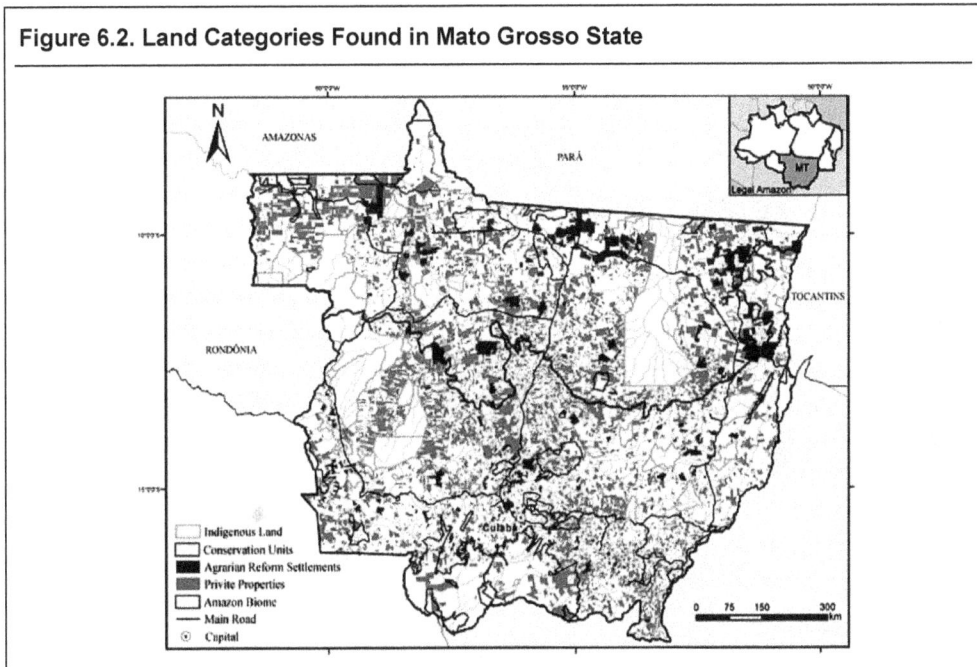

Source: Private Properties: SEMA-MT; Conservation Units: Ibama; Agrarian Reform Settlements: Incra; Indigenous Lands: Instituto Socioambiental (ISA).
Notes: White regions outside of Indigenous Lands and Conservation. Units are undesignated governmental lands.

The SLAPR system began to be implemented in 1999 and became operational in 2000 with the aim of supporting environmental licensing, enforcing the Brazilian Forestry Code, and supporting land tenure regularization (Fearnside 2003, Souza and Barreto 2001, ISA 2005). By 2007, 9,700 private properties with an average property size of 2,350 hectares each had been registered with SLAPR (SEMA of Mato Grosso). The total extent of all registered properties covers an area of 191,000 km², representing 10 percent of all properties in the state of Mato Grosso and 28 percent of the private lands and undesignated governmental lands in the state. The annual adherence rate to SLAPR is about 1 percent. At this pace, according to the Ministry of the Environment (*Secretaria Estadual de Meio Ambiente*) (SEMA) of Mato Grosso, it would take 70 years to register all properties.

Forest reserves are existing forested areas in different types of land categories reflecting different degrees of protection as defined by law. The first type is the forest reserve in protected areas (i.e., indigenous territories and conservation units). Deforestation in most types of conservation units is illegal according to Brazilian law, but can be legally allowed in indigenous land, extractive reserves, and in sustainable development reserves at a small scale only for subsistence practices by the local population (MMA SNUC 2000). Unprotected forest reserves are subject to the Brazilian Forestry Code, which establishes legal reserves (Legal Reserves)—the second category of forest reserve—on private lands. In the Amazon biome, the Legal Reserve legislation requires that 80 percent of the private land be maintained with native vegetation (except in areas where ecological-economic zoning indicates 50 percent), and 35 percent of the private land in *Cerrado* be maintained with native vegetation (ISA 2005). Private properties in transitional forests between the Amazon biome and the *Cerrado* should maintain 50 percent of the original vegetation according to state of Mato Grosso law (Fearnside 2003). The third type of forest reserves, Areas of Permanent Protection (APP), are those along rivers, steep slopes and watershed divisors, and atop hills.

SAD—Sistema de Alerta de Desmatamento

We developed a deforestation change detection technique based on Moderate Resolution Imaging Spectroradiometer (MODIS) daily image composites, called the Deforestation Alert System (*Sistema de Alerta de Desmatamento*) (SAD). The SAD algorithm has three main steps: (1) temporal composite, (2) spectral mixture analysis, and (3) forest change detection (see figure 6.3 below). These steps are detailed below.

Temporal Composite

SAD is based on a temporal composite of 10 to 15 daily acquisitions of MODIS images, using MODIS products MOD09GQK at 250 m (bands 1 and 2) and MOD09GAV5 at 500 m (bands 3 to 7) to build a temporal composite. First, we select a time period (of 10 to 15 days) and run a cloud-screening algorithm to remove cloudy pixels of each MODIS product. Next, we perform a data fusion of the MODIS products using a geostatistical algorithm developed by our research team (Sales et al. *in review*).

Figure 6.3. Imazon's Deforestation Alert System

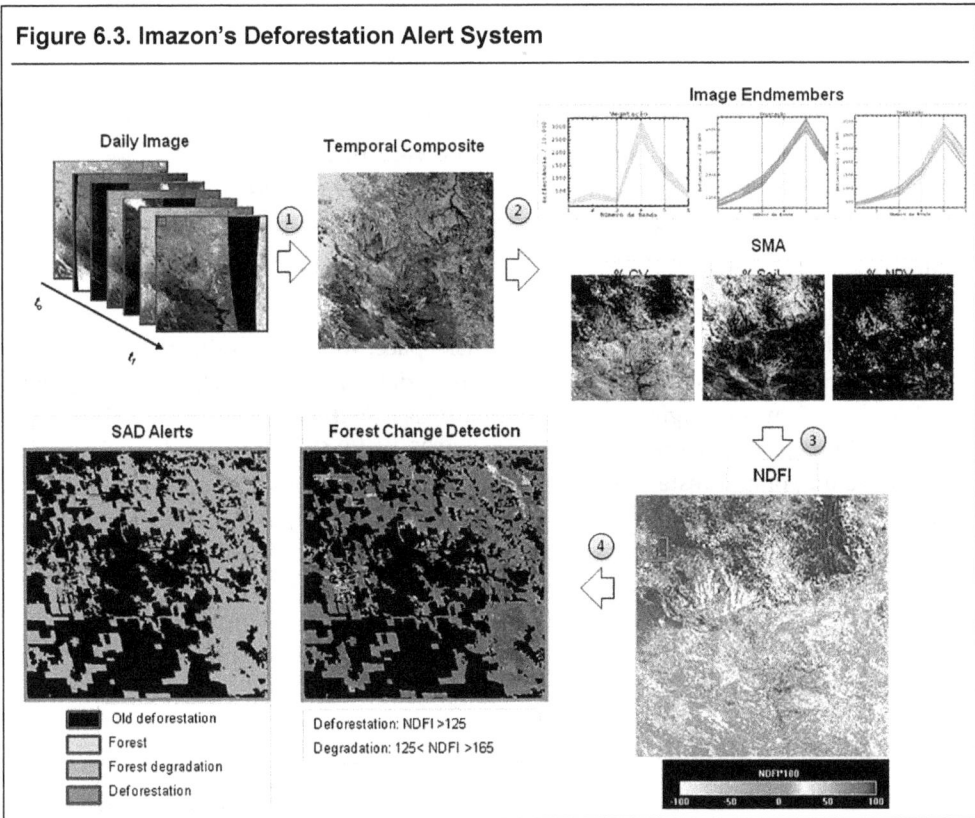

Source: Imazon.

This procedure is necessary to convert the five original bands from 500 m pixel size (MOD09GAV5) to 250 m resolution (MOD09GQK), preserving the spatial structure of the higher spatial resolution bands. As a result, we end up with seven spectral bands at 250 m spatial resolution to be processed in order to detect deforestation and provide forest degradation alerts.

Spectral Mixture Analysis (SMA)

After obtaining the temporal composite with seven MODIS bands at 250 m spatial resolution, we apply spectral mixture analysis (SMA) using a protocol originally developed for Landsat images (Souza et al. 2005). Fraction images of green vegetation (GV), soil (Soil), and non-photosynthetic vegetation (NPV) are obtained with the SMA procedure. A novel spectral index combining the information from these fractions, the Normalized Difference Fraction Index (NDFI) (Souza et al. 2005), was used to more accurately detect deforestation and forest degradation. The NDFI is computed as

$$NDFI = \frac{GV_{Shade} - (NPV + Soil)}{GV_{Shade} + NPV + Soil}$$

(1)

where GV$_{shade}$ is the shade-normalized GV fraction given by,

$$GV_{Shade} = \frac{GV}{100 - Shade}$$

(2)

NDFI values range from -1 to 1. For intact forests, NDFI values are expected to be high (i.e., about 1) due to the combination of high GV_{shade} (i.e., high GV and canopy Shade) and low NPV and Soil values. As the forest becomes degraded, the NPV and Soil fractions increase, lowering NDFI values relative to the intact forest (Souza et al. 2005).

Forest Change Detection

Deforestation and forest degradation detection is performed based on a novel NDFI (Souza et al. 2005). For the sake of saving disk space, we rescaled the NDFI to a range of 0 to 200 in order to store these images in byte data type. All pixels showing NDFI < 125 (i.e., <0.25 in the original NDFI scale) are classified as deforestation, while those with NDFI values between 125 and 165 (i.e., 0.25 and 0.65) are forest degradation. To guarantee that only forested pixels are monitored in each monitoring period, we use a mask of old deforestation events and a non-forest mask.

The deforestation polygons detected with SAD are validated using higher resolution satellite images when available (at least 50 percent of these cases are validated every month). All newly deforested areas are incorporated into the deforestation mask so that in the next change detection period only newly deforested areas are mapped (figure 6.3).

SAD Results for Mato Grosso

Because of the coarse resolution of MODIS, deforestation detected by SAD represents a fraction of the total deforestation detected by PRODES (the Brazilian government deforestation monitoring system). In Mato Grosso, SAD detected 93 percent of the deforestation detected by PRODES for the period of 2004 through 2009 (figure 6.4). The total deforestation detected with PRODES in this period was 30,275 km² while SAD detected 28,082 km². These monitoring systems differ in terms of spatial and temporal resolutions. PRODES is based on Landsat images with a spatial resolution of 30 m, and uses one image acquisition per year to map annual deforestation increments with a minimum mapping unit (MMU) of 6.25 hectares. SAD, as explained in detail above, is based on MODIS at 250 m spatial resolution, MMU of 12.5 hectares and was designed to generate deforestation and forest degradation alerts on a monthly basis. Because individual deforestation clearings in Mato Grosso are usually greater than 25 hectares (Souza et al. 2006), similar results were obtained for these two monitoring systems.

SAD allowed us to keep track of deforestation on a monthly basis in Mato Grosso. The annual aggregated deforestation statistics shown in figure 6.4 point to a trend of decreasing deforestation in Mato Grosso from 2004 through 2009. The information generated by SAD is released through the Forest Transparency Bulletin (Haiashy et al. 2009), as part of our dissemination strategy of placing the deforestation polygons and statistics in the hands of key stakeholders who have the power to stop illegal deforestation in the Brazilian Amazon. Additionally, all deforestation maps and ranking statistics of deforestation in protected areas, settlements, private lands, municipalities, and states are available on the Web portal named ImazonGeo at www.imazongeo.org.br (Souza et al. 2009).

Figure 6.4. Deforestation Detected with SAD and PRODES in the State of Mato Grosso from 2004 through 2009

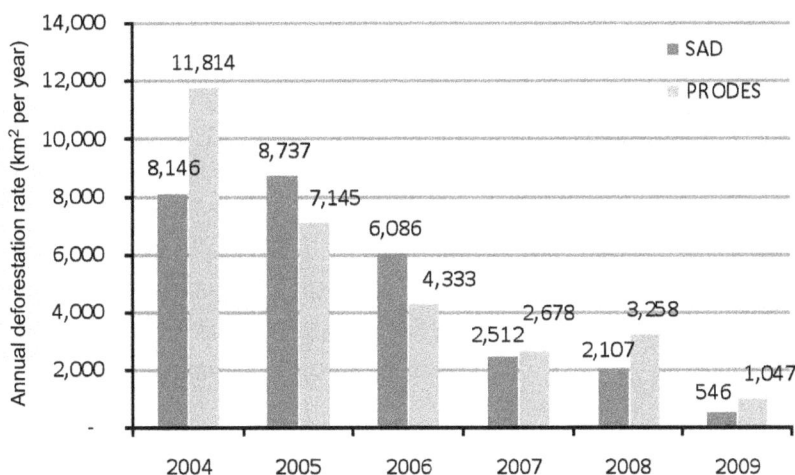

Source: Imazon and INPE, respectively.

Monitoring Forest Reserves in Mato Grosso

In 2006, an agreement was signed with the state environmental agencies (SEMA) of both Mato Grosso and Pará to give them full access to SAD deforestation polygons prior to the release of the Forest Transparency Bulletin. Other formal partners included the Federal Environmental Agency (IBAMA) from the Mato Grosso state office and the public prosecutor's offices in Pará and in Mato Grosso. As part of this agreement, the state environmental agencies also provided access to their rural property cadastral and licensing database and to a GIS database with several geographical data layers (such as deforestation, vegetation, protected areas, zoning maps, and the number of properties registered per month, among others). Access to these databases allowed us to evaluate the quality of the data and to perform detailed geographical analyses of deforestation including deforestation by classes of deforested areas, deforestation in protected areas, deforestation in legal reserves and in areas of permanent protections, and unauthorized deforestation (such as outside the cadastral licensing system).

Access to these digital maps provided a means of qualifying deforestation in terms of legality, in the state of Mato Grosso, by combining SAD deforestation with these databases. This spatial analysis encompassed the period from August 2005 to July 2008 (table 6.1).A total of 19,442 km² of deforestation was detected with SAD during this period in the state of Mato Grosso. Of this total amount 70 percent (13,550 km²) was detected in the Amazon biome, and the remaining 30 percent (5,892 km²) in transitional forest types. Less than 2 percent (431 km²) of deforestation occurred inside protected areas, mostly in indigenous lands (354 km²).

The amount of deforested area within each private property in the Amazon biome cannot exceed 20 percent in order to respect the legal reserve law. Additionally, any deforestation on private lands that are not registered in the rural licensing system

Table 6.1. Deforestation Detected with SAD from August 2004 to January 2009 in Different Types of Lands and Biomes of Mato Grosso State

Land Categories and Biomes	Aug04-Jul05 Area (km²)	Aug05-Jul06 Area (km²)	Aug06-Jul07 Area (km²)	Aug07-Jul08 Area (km²)	Total
Amazon Biome	6,387	4,167	1,722	1,274	13,550
Rural Settlements	876	663	416	177	2,132
Indigenous Land	187	55	39	73	354
State Conservation Unit	17	31	9	10	67
Federal Conservation Unit	3	2	4	1	10
SLAPR	2,110	1,333	394	376	4,213
Outside SLAPR	3,194	2,083	860	637	6,774
Transitional Forests	2,350	1,919	790	833	5,892
Total Deforestation	8,737	6,086	2,512	2,107	19,442

Source: Imazon.

(SLAPR) is considered illegal. We estimated the amount of illegal deforestation on private lands by combining three spatial analysis results. First, we estimated the amount of deforestation detected with SAD inside SLAPR that violated the legal reserve law (that is, more than 20 percent of the property size deforested). To do that, we needed to combine SAD from August 2004 to July 2008 with cumulative deforestation detected by PRODES before 2004 to estimate the amount of legal reserve deforestation detected by SAD in that period. Secondly, we identified deforestation outside SLAPR—not in protected areas, which is also considered illegal because deforestation permits require registering the property into this licensing and control system. Finally, we estimated the amount of illegal deforestation detected with SAD in protected areas. All these three estimates resulted in 85 percent of the total deforestation classified as illegal and detected with SAD from August 2004 to July 2008 (figure 6.5).

We went beyond deforestation detection and monitoring with SAD. First, in November 2007, we signed a formal technical cooperation agreement with the state and federal public prosecutor's offices of several Amazonian states (i.e., Mato Grosso, Pará, Amapá, and Roraima). Through this technical agreement, Imazon provided detailed information on deforestation detected in protected areas so that public prosecutors could commence official enforcement processes. The information provided by Imazon required three steps. First, we use SAD to identify the deforestation cases in the protected areas. The second step consisted of validating the deforestation detected by SAD with more detailed satellite imagery and/or field information (if available) and gathering information about the creation of the protected area (such as the decree creating the protected area, the date of creation, and the type of protection). The last step was to present all the information acquired about the deforestation in an official document (*representation*) to the public prosecutors. All this information is available on the GIS Web site, ImazonGeo (www.imazongeo.org.br) (Souza et al. 2009).

Figure 6.5. Illegal Deforestation Identified by Combining SAD Data with Properties Registered in the Mato Grosso Environmental Licensing System (SLAPR) and Maps of Protected Areas, for the Period of 2004 through November 2007

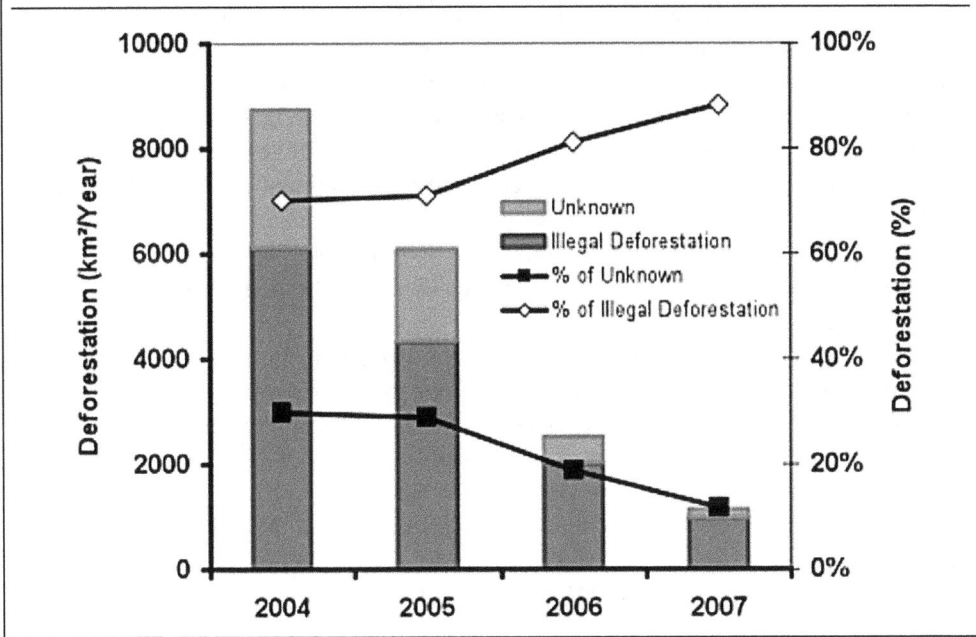

Source: Private Properties: SEMA-MT; Deforestation Alerts: Imazon.

Note: Because information on deforestation permits is not available, the remaining deforested areas outside SLAPR and protected areas were classified as unknown with respect to legality, since permits are required for forest clearing.

The second strategy to support forest law enforcement was to create partnerships with the SEMAs from the Amazonian states. As part of this collaboration, we submitted SAD results to these environmental agencies to support field enforcement campaigns. In January 2009, SEMA from Mato Grosso announced on its official Web site[4] that land owners had received environmental fines based on SAD information. Even though this represents great progress toward forest law enforcement, the effectiveness of these fines is compromised by the low efficacy of the Brazilian judiciary system in judging these types of cases (Brito and Barreto 2006). The formal agreement with SEMA also provided access to the rural property cadastral and licensing database, and to a GIS database with several geographical data layers (such as deforestation, vegetation, protected areas, zoning maps, and the number of properties registered per month). Access to these databases allowed us to evaluate the quality and credibility of the SLAPR data and to perform detailed geographical analyses of illegal deforestation as shown in figure 6.5 above.

Third, we established a strong dissemination strategy to inform the Brazilian population about deforestation threats in Amazon forest reserves to encourage support for enforcing the forestry code. The dissemination strategy had two components. The first, through ImazonGeo, aimed to provide geographical information about the different kinds of threats to the Brazilian Amazon forests, such as deforestation, fires, roads, and logging. Additionally, we released a monthly report, the Forest Transparency Bulletin, with deforestation statistics, trends, geographical hot spots, and spatial analysis. Examples of deforestation analyses include (1) the identification and estimation of illegal deforestation in protected areas (that is conservation units and indigenous land) and outside SLAPR (figure 6.5), and (2) the identification of critical deforestation hot spots in terms of deforestation rates and pressure on remaining forests. Our analyses have shown that most of the deforestation in Mato Grosso is concentrated in rural properties not registered in the SLAPR system. The analyses also revealed that in Mato Grosso illegal deforestation is frequent in areas of permanent protection and legal reserves within the private properties registered into SLAPR. This information is being used to guide law enforcement actions to fight illegal deforestation in the area, and to question the efficacy of the SLAPR system in fighting illegal deforestation.

The second component of the dissemination strategy included a strong connection with the news media aimed at keeping the public informed about deforestation threats in the Amazon region. Since the release of the first Forest Transparency Bulletin in August 2006, more than 800 news items have appeared in the media (TV, radio, newspapers, and magazines). For example, the main headline during the first quarter of 2008 was that deforestation had doubled during that period compared to the previous year. As a result, 30 media insertions were obtained in this period, 10 of which were in newspapers, 7 on TV, 13 on the Internet.

Conclusion

Our near real-time deforestation monitoring system, SAD, is being used as a tool for monitoring forest reserves in the Brazilian Amazon and for contributing to and augmenting transparency in the forest sector in the region. In the state of Mato Grosso, which has the most advanced cadastral and licensing system of private lands (SLAPR), SAD has been used to qualify deforestation in terms of legality. Most of the deforestation detected in private lands in this region is illegal, according to SAD and the spatial analyses that combine property boundaries and maps of protected areas and private properties. This information is being widely disseminated to authorities and the general population through the media to support law enforcement, which has been the weak link in the fight against illegal deforestation, in an effort to implement the forestry code for protected forest reserves. As a result of this forest transparency initiative—which combines near real-time detection of deforestation with strategic dissemination of the information—the debate about deforestation has been kept alive each month by the media. In the past, deforestation statistics were at least one year out of date and the national debate on this issue surfaced only about once a year. This initiative puts positive pressure on the states and federal governments to act against illegal deforestation in the region and keeps up the current level of transparency by releasing official statistics of deforestation and maps to the public. For example, as a result of our monthly deforestation report published September 2007 showing an increase of deforestation in Mato Grosso state, the Ministry of the Environment (SEMA) announced a more in-depth review of the current governmental plan to reduce deforestation. And, more recently, the Brazilian government announced a tighter plan to control illegal deforestation by targeting the top 43 municipalities with the highest deforestation rates in the last three years (2005–2007). Access to rural credit from the private and governmental sectors is suspended in these municipalities and strong field enforcement campaigns were implemented, resulting in lower deforestation rates over the last two decades in these regions. Our current efforts are to encourage the effective use of deforestation maps and statistics for law enforcement and planning at the municipal level.

6.2:   Land Tenure and Climate Change Mitigation in the Brazilian Amazon

PAULO BARRETO, Amazon Institute of People and the Environment (Imazon), Brazil
BRENDA BRITO, Amazon Institute of People and the Environment (Imazon), Brazil
MALCOLM D. CHILDRESS, The World Bank, U.S.

Summary

Several measures aimed at climate change mitigation are closely linked to land use and land tenure in the Brazilian Amazon. In this paper, we review the potential linkages of such measures to the land tenure situation in the Brazilian Amazon by first describing the current situation and then identifying trends in land management and administration that are contributing to the agenda to avoid deforestation. We focus mainly on the linkages of land tenure to avoiding deforestation through the creation of protected areas, the definition of public land, and the regularization and environmental management of private land. While each of these linkages poses specific challenges, a review of the evidence provides cause for optimism that progress toward better land tenure management is contributing to curtailing current deforestation and limiting it further in the future.

Introduction

Public responses to climate change are playing a larger role in influencing how land is allocated, used, and transferred. Through the United Nations Framework Convention on Climate Change and other vehicles, nations are negotiating how to reduce greenhouse gas emissions to mitigate drastic climatic changes and the measures needed to adapt to moderate climate changes. As the world moves to a new, post-Copenhagen phase of negotiations in 2010 about how to deal with climate change characterized by considerable uncertainty about global programs, considering the potential implications of existing policy choices becomes especially important. One area of great concern is the implications of existing land use and land tenure patterns as a basis for evolving policies to mitigate and adapt to climate change. Land issues form an important element of global carbon emissions. Twenty percent of the total greenhouse gas (GHG) emissions comes from changes in land uses (principally from deforestation but also from land degradation). Thus, measures employed to mitigate global climate change will have to address land use directly and indirectly, creating new costs and benefits for different constituencies of land users. These measures primarily include the adoption of biofuels, afforestation, deforestation, and avoided deforestation.

In this discussion, we review the ways in which the existing tenure framework shapes the conditions through which climate change adaptation and mitigation measures will likely play out in the Brazilian Amazon. Our approach focuses on describing measures for avoiding deforestation and on the complex land tenure policy context that will have to be accommodated and strongly administered for significant progress to be made in reducing historical rates of deforestation during the medium term. By focusing on these measures, we have chosen to largely bracket the biofuel debate and the potential consequences of a major expansion of cropped areas for biofuels on Amazonian land use and land tenure. This means our findings must be interpreted with a degree of caution. With this caveat, our conclusion is that Brazil is taking important steps to put in place a tenure and land management structure sufficient to support a significant and lasting reduction in the trajectory of historical deforestation patterns. The actual implementation of this land management and land tenure reform, however, is still in an early stage, varies across a vast region, and still suffers from some remaining incentives toward continued deforestation; creating a measure of uncertainty about the scope and sustainability of its outcomes. Our analysis underlines the need for continued innovation and intensification of institutional efforts, and monitoring of the implementation of the recent land policy reforms across the large region to ensure that they will fully accomplish their stated goals of contributing to the long-term goal of no net deforestation and the sustainable management of the land resource.

Spanning an area of slightly more than 500 million hectares, the region offers compelling examples of the complexities involved in dealing with climate change, land use, and land tenure issues on a large scale. The region harbors about one-third of the world's remaining tropical forests. Deforestation is a major problem, accounting for more than 50 percent of Brazil's GHG emissions[5]. The region will likely benefit from the Bali Action Plan (UN 2007), signed by more than 180 nations in December 2007, which calls for "policy approaches and positive incentives" for reducing emissions from deforestation and forest degradation in developing countries. This could involve compensating farmers who forgo deforestation (avoided deforestation) or who invest in reforestation. Plans for such a scheme are under development through the creation of the Amazon Fund, which will be assisted by a substantial grant from the government of Norway. The Brazilian government is also seeking to create new protected areas to avoid deforestation, in addition to the approximately 200 million hectares currently under protected or indigenous land status. A number of new areas have been proposed. While likely to reduce deforestation, these measures could also lead to further increases in land prices and, potentially, to increased conflicts over land.

At the same time, the continued expansion of Brazil's sugarcane plantations to increase ethanol production could contribute to further deforestation in the country. Brazil is the world's main producer of sugarcane ethanol, which is the cheapest source of biofuel to reduce fossil fuel emissions. The expansion of sugarcane plantations in Brazil could lead to the displacement of cattle ranching from other regions to the Amazon, which, in turn, could lead to increased deforestation, appreciating land prices, and new conflicts if well-formulated land management arrangements are not in place. By virtue of its size, the Brazilian Amazon's land use outcomes will have an important impact on future GHG scenarios. Thus, the Brazilian government's policy approaches in the Amazon will continue to be an important determinant for global climate change mitigation and adaptation outcomes.

In the following sections of this paper, we first review the options for mitigating climate changes that depend on land use and land tenure, with a focus on the set of approaches being taken or being discussed in the forest sector. We then review the current status of land tenure in the region, highlighting the significant expansion of protected areas and the demarcation of indigenous lands in the last 15 years, but also pointing out the continuing uncertainties about who owns the land in large portions of the region and the difficulties this creates for consolidating policies for avoiding deforestation. Next, we discuss in detail the challenges of managing the protected area system for achieving sustainable reductions in net deforestation. In the last section, we present the emerging linkage of commodity certification with good land management as a new instrument for reducing deforestation and describe our conclusions.

Options for Mitigating Climate Change via Land Use Modification in the Brazilian Amazon

Scientists have recommended limiting global warming to less than 2°C because beyond that limit, the risks of serious negative impacts, such as falling crop yields, water shortages, and the frequency and the intensity of extreme weather events, are higher. To avoid such warming, specialists project that global annual greenhouse gas emissions must be reduced by 30 gigatons (Gt) by 2030—which is roughly similar to current emissions and close to 50 percent of the projected emissions—by 2030 (CEA 2007, IPCC 2007a).

Studies indicate that current technologies could be used to reduce about 80 percent of the total emissions that should be abated by 2030 (CEA 2007). Options for reducing greenhouse gas emissions include measures such as improving building insulation, increasing energy efficiency, using biofuels, and avoiding deforestation (Enkvist et al. 2007). Table 6.2 shows mitigation options that may affect land use, land value, and consequently, land tenure. While each of these options is relevant in some way to the land management debate in the Brazilian Amazon, the avoided deforestation option is the focus of this section.

Table 6.2. Mitigation Options Related to Land Use

Sector	Some Key Mitigation Technologies and Practices
Agriculture	Improvement of crop productivity; Improvement of crop and grazing land management to increase soil carbon storage; restoration of degraded lands; cultivation of energy crops (bio-fuels)
Energy	Biomass
	Energy efficiency: reduction of demand for bio-fuel may reduce or delay demand
Forestry/forests	Aforestation, reforestation, avoided deforestation, forest management,
Transport	Biofuels: ethanol (sugar cane, corn); biodiesel (soybean, palm oil, others)

Source: IPCC, 2007a.

Figure 6.6 below outlines the major pathways through which climate change and land use are related in the context of the Brazilian Amazon. In this paper, we focus primarily on the mitigation pathway through avoided deforestation, while acknowledging that the pathway of biofuel expansion is a topic which could have significant consequences on land use in the Amazon, particularly through the displacement of cattle ranching into the Amazon in the absence of strong enforcement of the land management regime now coming into force.

Figure 6.6. Flowchart Depicting the Major Pathways through which Climate Change and Land Use Are Related in the Context of the Brazilian Amazon

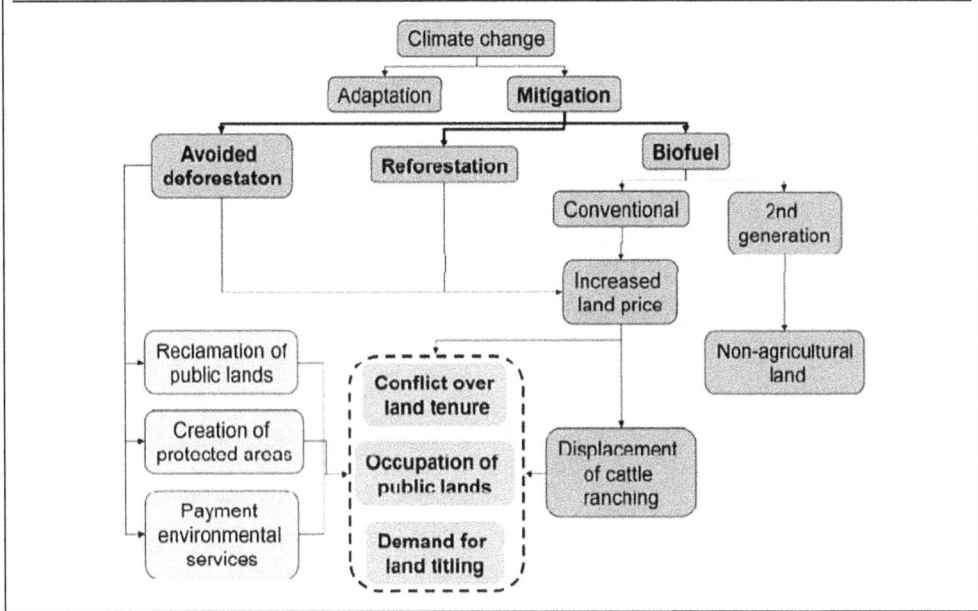

Source: P. Barreto (author).

Focusing on this nexus of relationships between avoided deforestation and land use/land tenure, the next section offers a typology and a discussion of land tenure in the region which reveals both the progress to date in reducing deforestation through land management and tenure reform in the region, and the main factors which complicate this task.

Current Status of Land Tenure in the Brazilian Amazon: A Typology and Discussion for Understanding Land Use Change[6]

A simple typology and discussion of land tenure modalities in the Amazon helps to explain the situation in which climate change adaptation and mitigation measures interact in attempting to influence land use, particularly to reduce deforestation. Land tenure in the Amazon is a mosaic of different types of private and public property rights, all overlayed by sets of environmental and social restrictions and supported by an incomplete and unreliable set of official information. This typology differentiates the following five categories of tenure types and main restrictions.

Occupations (Posseiros)

These are the claims of land users to a certain area based on physical possession and use of the area. This type of tenure is deeply protected by Brazilian law, but has been taken advantage of by private interests on a widespread basis to exploit forests and dedicate land to short-term, unsustainable uses such as pastures. Occupants have strong rights to use forests, make investments, carry out agricultural production, and have their land regularized into fully legal property rights under certain conditions. Legally, occupants must also follow environmental legislation. Legally registered occupations account for a little less than 40 million hectares or 7 percent of the overall area. But an unknown quantity of "existing but undocumented" occupations occur within the roughly 130 million hectares of the region that have not yet been demarcated and officially allocated. The nature of occupations varies greatly in size and use, from smallholder colonists producing subsistence crops to large-scale ranching operations. Occupations may overlap with new protected areas, and nondesignated public lands, complicating the management of these areas. The right to occupation has been a traditional driver of new frontier expansion as occupants lay physical claim to public lands and deforest and convert land to pasture, often selling the land shortly thereafter. New policies (discussed below) toward the regularization of existing occupations and limitations on new occupations, which have been strongly influenced by the climate change debate, hold both promise and risk for decreasing historical rates of deforestation in the Amazon.

Private Properties

Approximately 138 million hectares or 28 percent of the Brazilian Amazon is registered as private property. However, only about 30 million hectares have been confirmed under the re-cadastering exercise underway since 1999. Another 70 to 100 million hectares of ostensibly private area is under title which derives from legally questionable sources. In the Amazon, private property in forest areas is subject to the forest code and its environmental licensing requirements. To date, these requirements, in particular the requirement that 80 percent of the property area be managed as a forest reserve, have often remained unenforced (below we discuss how and why this is changing). Data depict a large concentration of private holdings in the largest size classes across the region. In some regions, like many parts of Mato Grosso, private land hosts some of Brazil's most productive agricultural holdings. But the prevalence of informal markets and weaknesses in the cadastral and land registration system are also blamed for the proliferation of private holdings in many areas that are underutilized from all perspectives, held mainly for speculative purposes, and associated with questionable documentation and frontier deforestation. Underutilized private properties may be eligible for expropriation as part of Brazil's agrarian reform process and some large land holdings, particularly in Pará, have been occupied by land reform activists advocating for expropriation and redistribution as land reform settlements. These are often contentious processes.

Conservation Units

Conservation units in Brazil consist of both private lands subject to environmental management plans called environmental protection areas (*areas de proteccao ambiental*) and public areas which belong to the National System of Conservation Units (SNUC), which is a formal, unified system for federal, state, and municipal forests, extractive reserves, environmental research areas, and parks created in 2000. Until 2006, the protected area system included about 93 million hectares of land in the different types of conservation units, or 21 percent of the region's area. Data show drastically lower deforestation rates within the protected area boundaries than in surrounding areas, even in areas with relatively sparse enforcement, suggesting that the designation of protected areas in itself is a large deterrent to land clearing (presumably because of the diminished expectation that the land can subsequently be regularized and sold). A second generation of protected areas is currently being planned. The existing protected area system includes the areas most likely to be included in the schemes being proposed to provide compensation for avoided deforestation. The map (see figure 6.7) depicts the main protected areas and indigenous lands, while the chart that follows (figure 6.8) depicts the cumulative area of state and federal protected areas over the period 1970-2006.

Figure 6.7. Map of Main Protected Areas and Indigenous Lands in the Legal Amazon

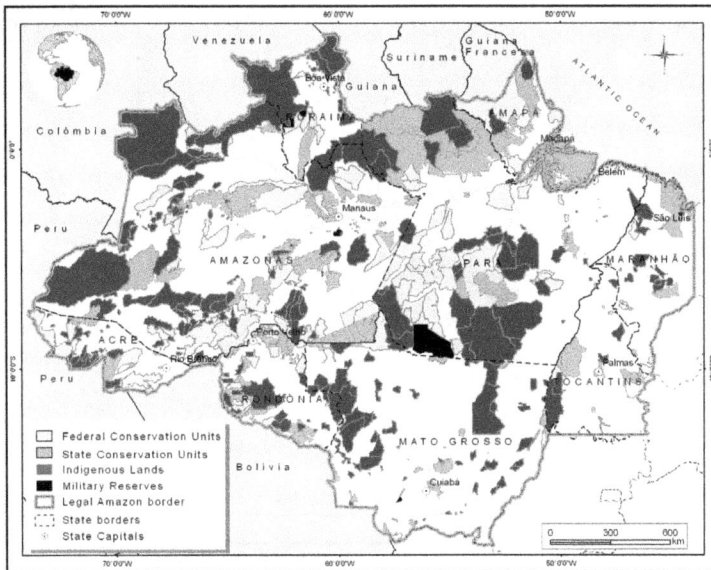

Source: IMAZON's Geoprocessing Lab.

Figure 6.8. Cumulative Area of State and Federal Protected Areas in Brazil (1970-2006)

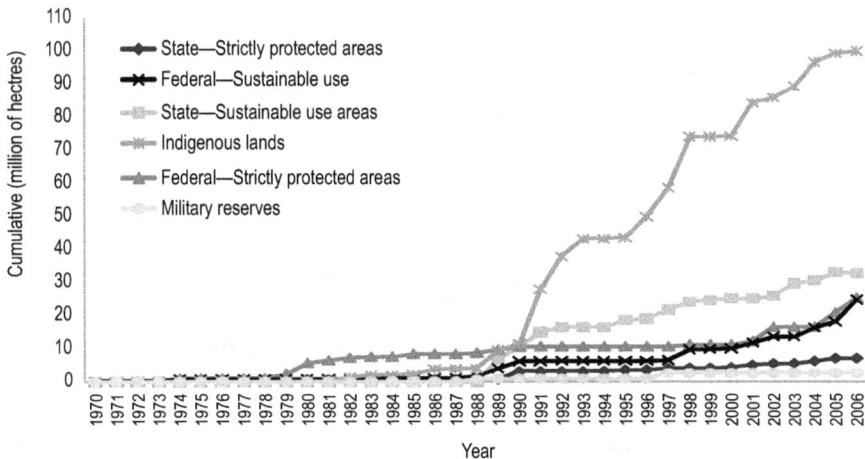

Source: IMAZON's Geoprocessing Lab.

Figure 6.9. Simulation of Cattle Price Gradients as Proxy for Economic Accessibility under Three Scenarios

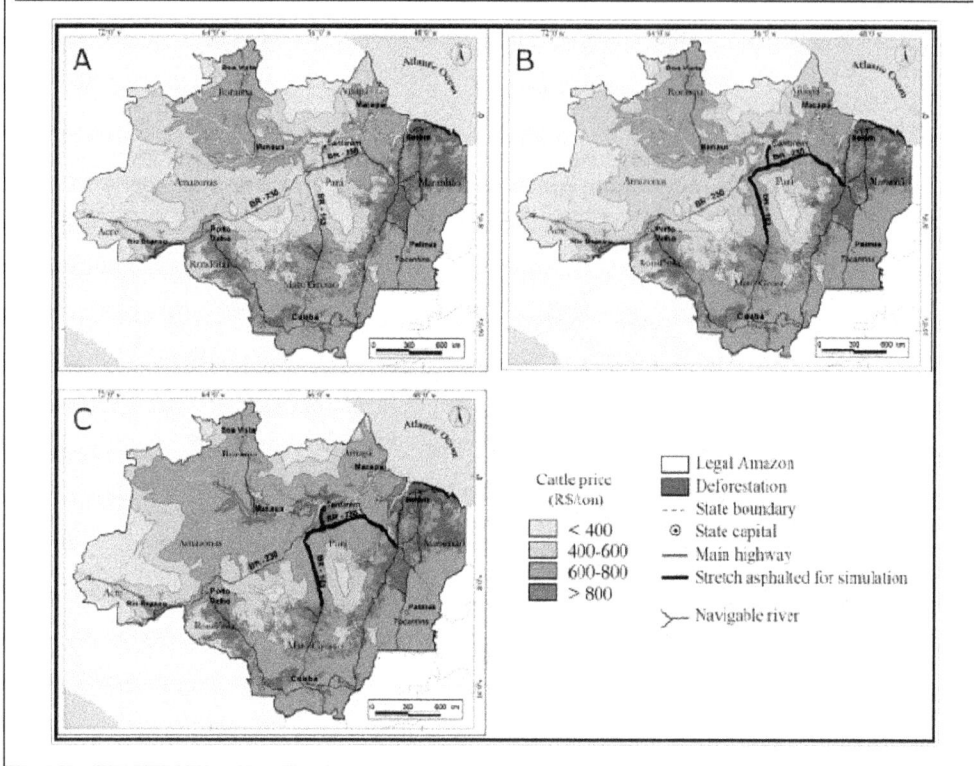

Source: Arima et al 2006.

In many cases the creation of protected areas has deterred new occupations (ISA 2006). A recent study of protected areas created before 1995 demonstrated that the risk of fires in protected areas, including indigenous lands, was 30 percent lower than outside protected areas in the Amazon (Arima et al. 2007). Note, however, that until recently most protected areas were far from the reach of economic activities and passive protection was sufficient. At present, 84 percent of protected areas are within the reach of economic activities and face increasing pressure due to the growth of infrastructure (e.g., roads, electrical grid) and the rise of commodity prices (timber, minerals, meat, and soybeans) (see figure 6.9).

Unrestricted economic pressure has led to illegal harvesting of timber and to rural settlements within some protected areas (Ribeiro and Veríssimo, in press). Economic pressure has even led to the legal reduction of the size of Cristalino State Park in Mato Grosso.

Federal and state agencies responsible for managing protected areas face enormous challenges for the effective protection and sustainable use of these areas. Implementation of protected areas requires (1) the preparation of management plans, (2) the establishment of advisory councils who are responsible for reviewing management plans and for their implementation, (3) the installation of basic infrastructure and allocation of public officers, (4) enforcement against illegal activities (e.g., deforestation and illegal logging) within protected areas, and (5) short- and long-term financial support mechanisms.

Within the impressive size and scope of the protected area system, these specific implementation goals have been hard to reach. In 2006 more than 90 percent of the conservation units in the Amazon lacked management plans (Ribeiro et al., in press). The project Protected Areas in the Amazon (ARPA) and the fund for protected areas (Environmental Compensation Fund–EFC)[7] are expected to provide part of the necessary funds to fill the gap. Nevertheless, about half of the total area of conservation units (e.g., national/state forests, APAs, as well as fully protected areas created without public consultation) is not eligible to receive ARPA funds and the ECF is still incipient. Only 15 percent of the national forests in the Amazon (19 million hectares) have management plans (SFB 2007). New staff working mostly in state environmental agencies have not yet developed the expertise to prepare and implement management plans for conservation units. This is particularly critical because 53 percent of the area covered by conservation units is now under state control while 47 percent is under federal control (Ribeiro et al., in press). For example, only 15 state government staff members are in charge of more than 22 million hectares of state conservation units in Pará.

Indigenous Lands and Quilombolo Lands

Accounting for about 100 million hectares or 20 percent of the land area of the Amazon, indigenous lands are public lands assigned in perpetual trust to the indigenous groups who are their traditional occupants under collective management. Indigenous lands cannot be sold or transferred. Indigenous lands have some of the lowest deforestation rates in the Amazon. Quilombolo lands are the lands traditionally occupied and used by the quilombolo communities who are the descendents of escaped slaves. Quilombolo lands are recognized in a similar fashion as the indigenous lands. They account for a small fraction of the total landholding in the region.

Nonallocated Public Land

Undesignated public land (*terra devoluta*) is believed to account for about 120 million hectares or 24 percent of the Brazilian Amazon's area. Undesignated public land is a reflection of the sheer size of the area and its history as a sparsely populated frontier. The lack of clear management plans for these areas and their susceptibility to occupation and predatory logging make this type of a land problematic for limiting deforestation.

New investments in land in the Amazon, either to avoid deforestation or to expand agricultural production, and policy measures to affect land use are confronting the serious land tenure problems engendered by this situation, chief among them a lack of clarity about ownership and boundaries of large areas caused by the absence of a unified cadaster and a history of informal occupation and land fraud.

These weaknesses in the land tenure system result in a poor understanding of who owns the region's land and complicates efforts to manage land use and mitigate climate change through reduced deforestation (figure 6.10). Given a large amount of documentation fraud, the federal land agency (INCRA) has asked land owners to re-register several times since 1999. However, as of October 2006, INCRA has been able to validate the status of only about 20 million hectares—about 11 percent of the privately held land. The remaining private area includes informal settlers (about 42 million hectares), some of whom have had their informal land registry (*cadastro*) cancelled by INCRA, and large documented areas that INCRA has not been able to finish reviewing. Possession continues to exist on a large scale mainly because the government has accepted requests to regularize informal occupations, but has not responded. The lack of response is the result of an unclear policy to formalize large possessions and a lack of priority to deal with this issue.

During the second Lula administration in Brazil there have been renewed efforts to clarify and regularize the land tenure situation in the Brazilian Amazon. In January 2008, the Brazilian government called for a new re-registering (*recadastramento*) of rural properties from the 36 municipalities with the highest historical and recent deforestation rates. According to INCRA (Brasil 2008), these municipalities account for 80,000 properties or the equivalent of about 100 million hectares. Less than 20 percent of landowners, however, responded to this call (Lima 2008). In this and other instances, many landowners and *posseiros* did not respond to re-registering calls due to a combination of factors: (1) their titles may be illegal and therefore they fear expropriation or condemnation; (2) they hold more land than the government can or is willing to title (that is, more than 2,500 hectares in federal lands[8]); (3) re-registering requires presenting a georeferenced map of the landholding that would allow the detection of nonconformity with the forest code (that is, a minimum of 35 percent to 80 percent of the landholding covered with native vegetation, depending on the original forest cover type); and (4) in the case of larger landholdings (greater than 1,500 hectares), landholders may fear invasions from landless groups that may result in expropriation or condemnation of the land to be allocated to official land reform projects.

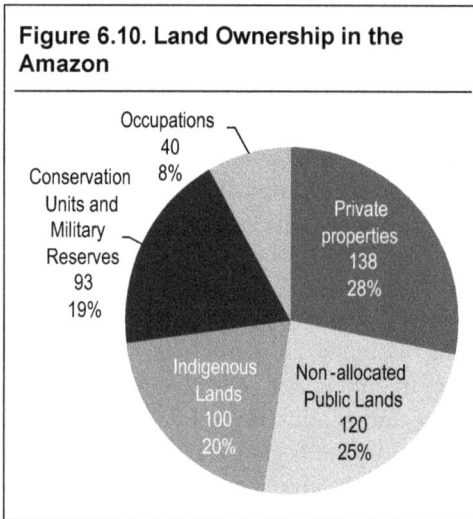

Figure 6.10. Land Ownership in the Amazon

Occupations 40 8%
Conservation Units and Military Reserves 93 19%
Private properties 138 28%
Indigenous Lands 100 20%
Non-allocated Public Lands 120 25%

Source: Adapted from Barreto et al. 2008a.

The most recent effort at land regularization was launched in 2009, called *Terra Legal* (Legal Land), based on Law 11.952 of June 25, 2009. This effort aims to regularize good-faith land occupants with plots up to 2,500 hectares in size. Plots up to 100 hectares will be given without charge to their occupants. Larger parcels from 100 to 2,500 hectares will be sold to occupants using a variety of pricing schemes. Parcels greater than 2,500 (the ostensible legal size limit for agricultural holdings) are to be reclaimed by the government. This effort is recent, but critics (see Brenda and Barreto 2009) have raised concerns about the program's design, in particular:

- The provision for granting land up to 100 hectares without charge, which may generate incentives to occupy further public land;
- Provisions which permit the eventual regularization of occupations after 2004 (creating continued incentives to new occupations);

- The refund of land payments to users whose titles are revoked due to violation of land use rules (which incentivizes the violation of land use regulations);
- The inconsistent treatment of environmental rules in the regularization process (special environmental licenses are to be awarded by INCRA); and
- The fact that the regularization program is moving ahead before the Ecological-Economic Zoning plans are completed or disseminated at useable scales in the Amazonian states, creating the likelihood that areas will be regularized in private status which are actually zoned for public use and protection.

Finally, the actual treatment of illegal occupations greater than 2,500 hectares is still unclear and may become entangled in litigation. Some large holdings will likely be sold to current occupants. These reservations notwithstanding, Terra Legal has ambitiously launched fieldwork in 2009 and 2010 and in some cases, such as in the state of Pará, the program is working closely with state-level land regularization efforts. In Pará the Terra Legal program is sharing an integrated database by digitizing property ownership information and descriptions held by the immovable property registries (*cartorios*).

Ecological-Economic Zoning *(Zoneamento Ecologico-Economico—ZEE)*

The above typology refers to tenure and ownership rights. Overlaid on top of these rights, each Amazonian state, and important road corridors like BR-163, are required by law to have a "macro" land-use zoning plan for the entire state or corridor called Ecological Economic Zoning (*Zoneamento Ecologico Economico*) *(ZEE)*. While the zoning plan does not itself preempt property rights, the zoning plan is intended to guide the siting of protected areas and the allocation and regularization of public lands and in the planning of public investments in transportation and other infrastructure. To date, only Acre, Pará, and Rondônia have completed their zoning plans. Roraima is in the process of concluding its plan. However, even in the states with completed plans, the translation of the macro-zoning plan into operational guidelines at sub-municipal levels has been slow, and coordination in the application of the zoning plan with federal authorities such as INCRA is only incipient. Making the zoning plans operational at a local landscape scale is a key step in ensuring the consolidation of existing protected areas, the siting of additional ones, and the management of private forest areas and legal reserves, all of which are important measures for avoiding deforestation in the future.

Challenges for the Creation and Implementation of Protected Areas

The informal or illegal occupation of public lands discussed in the previous section creates significant challenges to the creation and implementation of protected areas in the Amazon. Informal and illegal occupations limit the possibility for creating protected areas or force the creation of protected areas that are less strict than the ideal. When the government creates protected areas in zones with previous occupations, it faces all the major hurdles for the cancellation of illegal titles and for the eviction of illegal occupants described earlier in this paper. Government agencies must also deal with the concession of land use rights for the populations that are entitled to remain within conservation units or are entitled to be resettled. These and other issues are discussed below.

In 2003, IBAMA created a program to deal with land tenure issues within conservation units that has faced enormous challenges (*Programa de Consolidação Territorial*). According to Boris César from IBAMA (ISA 2006), IBAMA must still clear land tenure problems for at least 10 million hectares within conservation units. César acknowledges that IBAMA is ill equipped for this task due to a lack of resources and experience. He also highlights that IBAMA's approach to land regularization is based mostly on payment for expropriated land and for improvements (*benfeitorias*) and that IBAMA lacks sufficient resources to adequately implement this approach.[9] Reflecting the occasionally contradictory nature of agrarian reform legislation and forestry law in Brazil, most of these "improvements" such as deforestation were implemented illegally and are also the subject of proceedings against environmental crimes. However, the Brazilian Supreme Court has ruled that IBAMA cannot discount environmental fines owed for the payment of improvements and expropriation (ISA 2006). Since the conclusion of judicial and administrative environmental proceedings is slow and inefficient (Brito and Barreto 2006), environmental violators may in some cases continue benefiting from the illegal occupation of public lands within conservation units. Therefore, there have been cases in which IBAMA had to compensate for illegal improvements. In other cases, however, IBAMA has managed to administratively deduct the value of fines from the compensation (Boris César, personal communication, April 19, 2007).

Another problem is that IBAMA has not established rules to use with other approaches for reclaiming lands such as the cancellation of illegal titles (ISA 2006). In fact, IBAMA depends mostly on other institutions such as the judiciary and land agencies for reclaiming full public authority over lands within conservation units. Even in the simplest cases, such procedures tend to be slow. To overcome these problems, IBAMA's attorney general (*procurador geral*) has stressed the need to use expedited procedures for reclaiming legal control of lands within conservation units (ISA 2006). One of these procedures is the administrative cancellation of illegal titles as has been applied by the State Court in Amazonas. Another is to request a judicial expedited custody (*tutela antecipada*) of illegal areas within conservation units. In this case, environmental agencies must demonstrate the evidence of illegal occupation and that expedited custody would avoid damage that is difficult to repair. A final decision on land tenure would depend on a final judgment by the court.

In order to gain full legal control of conservation units, IBAMA also depends on cooperation from the institutions that had jurisdiction over lands prior to the creation of protected areas. For example, the regularization of a federal conservation unit created on land under state jurisdiction requires the state assembly to transfer the land to the federal government, which must then transfer it to IBAMA. In the case of conservation units created on federal land, INCRA and/or the Bureau of Federal Endowment (*Serviço de Patrimônio da União*) must transfer the land to IBAMA. Cooperation is not easy to achieve, however, and according to César (ISA 2006), in some cases INCRA has created settlement projects and state land agencies have issued land titles for land within federal conservation units. This situation is facilitated by the lack of a unified and transparent land cadastre and reduces the government's credibility with regard to the implementation of conservation units.

IBAMA and other environmental agencies must also work intensively to regularize the land use rights of traditional populations (such as Brazil nut gatherers and rubber tappers) within conservation units. In the case of fully protected areas, they are entitled to receive compensation for improvements and should be resettled. Resettlement may only occur after formal agreement is reached between environmental agencies and traditional residents. IBAMA is working in 10 conservation units to reach agreements on resettlement. In the meantime, traditional populations are entitled to remain in the area according to rules aimed at harmonizing conservation and livelihood objectives. According to IBAMA (ISA 2006), *posseiros* other than traditional populations are not entitled to receive compensation but have been resettled. Environmental agencies depend on land agencies to resettle both types of populations. However, IBAMA and INCRA have no general agreement for resettlement despite some local agreements. INCRA has a national agreement with FUNAI to resettle *posseiros* from indigenous lands (ISA 2006).

Traditional populations are entitled to continue in sustainable-use protected areas. Environmental agencies and the forest service must arrange concession use rights for these populations. According to IBAMA (ISA 2006), the challenge is to balance the demands of these populations and the carrying capacity of conservation units.

Another problem for the definition of land use rights in protected areas is the need to prepare a management plan for the entire conservation unit before the concession of use rights. The management plan is supposed to be based on biophysical and socioeconomic information as well as on negotiations to define land use zones within the conservation unit. In the absence of such plans, traditional populations may be precluded from legally conducting activities such as timber harvesting. This may reduce the traditional population's commitment to the implementation of the conservation unit.

Public sector credibility in the maintenance of protected areas is a critical issue for the long term and will determine whether the rapid expansion of nominally protected areas during the past 20 years will last. This short review indicates that land tenure issues will place even more pressure on scarce resources for the implementation of protected areas. This raises serious concerns for the long-term maintenance of these areas.

So far, indications are that the commitment to protect areas varies significantly among states and between states and federal agencies. In Mato Grosso the credibility of the state government's commitment to conservation has been weakened by the legislative assembly's decision to reduce the area of one state park. In 2006, the Assembly again voted to reduce a state-administered conservation unit. However, this action is now being reviewed by the courts.

In Rondônia, deforestation in conservation units raises questions about the commitment to enforcement in these units (Ribeiro et al. 2006). Between 1997 and 2004, deforestation rates grew to 1.5 percent annually in state-administered Conservation Units (while in federal conservation units the rate also grew but remained under 1 percent (figure 6.11). In the same period, annual deforestation was nearly zero in the indigenous reserve areas.

Figure 6.11. Deforestation Rates in State and Federal Conservation Units and Indigenous Lands in Rondônia

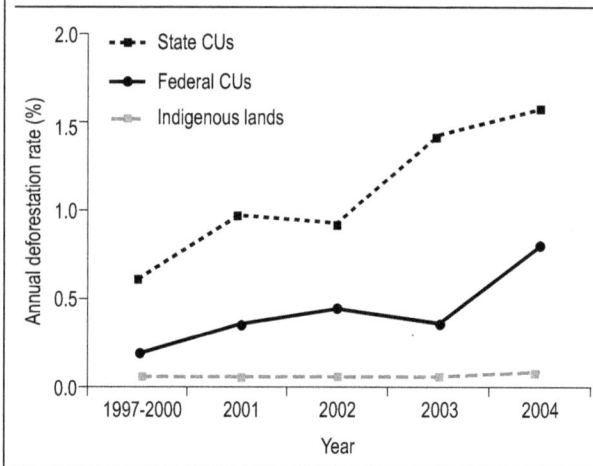

Source: Ribeiro et al 2006.

Implementation problems in some federally protected areas may also be interpreted locally as a lack of long-term commitment to protection. In 2003, federal institutions accepted an agreement to reduce about 350,000 hectares of the Baú Indigenous Land in western Pará due to local protests against its demarcation. According to our interview with *posseiros* in western Pará, this case gave hope that the reduction of other protected areas might also be possible. The Bom Futuro National Forest lost 8 percent of its forest cover between 1997 and 2003 due to illegal logging followed by deforestation (Barreto et al. 2006). *Posseiros* remain in the Tembé Indigenous Land in eastern Pará, although the occupation is already considered illegal. INCRA has not been able to resettle the occupants.

In summary, the long-term conservation of protected areas will require consistent evidence that all levels of government are committed to safeguarding them. Cases of poor enforcement, lack of implementation investments, and the legal reduction of protected areas may signal to current occupants and candidates for invasion that protected areas are likely to be dismantled in the long term.

The new forest management law of 2006 (*Lei* 11.284/2006) may help to change the situation. The new law attempts to put forest concession management on a more secure and sustainable footing and changes incentives to encourage producers to maintain protected areas. However, the lack of consistent rules on land occupation and regularization is threatening the implementation of the law as it was intended.

In 2007, the Brazilian government proposed the creation of a voluntary international fund to be financed by developed countries. Disbursements to a given country would be contingent upon effective emission reductions. In order to implement this idea nationally, in August 2008 Brazil created the Amazon Fund, expecting to raise $1 billion in the first year (Ecodebate 2008). However, up to May 2009 only Norway has pledged to disburse $110 million during 2009 and 2010 out of a total that is expected to reach $1 billion by 2015 (Norway 2009, Lopes 2008) and no other major donation has been announced. The lack of additional donations is likely a result of the absence of a new international climate agreement, put further in doubt by the failure of the Copenhagen summit[10] to reach a final agreement on REDD (reduced emissions from deforestation and degradation).

Potential Implications of Mitigation Options in the Brazilian Amazon

Overall, one can expect that mitigation in the forest sector is likely to develop slowly in the Amazon given existing land disputes and the absence of land titling and georeferencing in extensive areas. Given that REDD and reforestation programs requires monitoring land cover in each property, the implementation of such programs in the Amazon would require targeted investment in georeferencing rural properties where land title is clear. Moreover, it would be necessary to invest in clearing land tenure where informal and illegal occupation is widespread.[11] So using existing protected areas is the logical starting place for REDD programs (table 6.3).

Table 6.3. Potential Implication of REDD and Reforestation Programs on Land Tenure in the Amazon

Situation	Problems	Implications of REDD and Reforestation Programs
Informal settlers within sustainable use conservation units (SUCU).	Deforestation and forest degradation are frequent. Conventional solution to conservation could involve removing settlers or restricting land uses in a way that could endanger the livelihoods of the poorer settlers.	Granting land use rights to settlers to be involved in REDD and reforestation programs within SUCU would be an alternative compatible with conservation.
Informal landholders of public lands.	Landholders are unwilling to seek land titling to avoid costs of complying with forest law.	Complying with the forest code could become financially attractive. Therefore, landholders would be willing to seek land titling.
	Landholders are unwilling to seek land titling because the landholding is larger than the maximum size that the government can or is willing to title.	Larger informal holdings could become the target of landless group invasions in order to pressure government to establish land reform project based on REDD and reforestation programs.
Extensive "unclaimed" public forests.	There is a lack of control of unclaimed public lands. Rules for regularizing informal settlements in public land favor new occupations.	Immigrants could move to "unclaimed" public forest hoping to benefit from REDD. Conflicts could arise among immigrants and between immigrants and indigenous and other local populations.

Source: Authors.

Commodity and Financial Linkages to Land Management: An Incipient Approach to Reducing Deforestation

In August 2009, a series of changes in the commercialization of beef and agriculture finance demonstrated that a new linkage between commodity certification and land management may hold out major new prospects for reducing deforestation on privately held lands. In June 2009, the Federal Public Prosecution Service (MPF) in Pará and IBAMA began legal proceedings against 21 ranches (20 for not fulfilling environmental legislation and one for being located in an Indigenous Land) and another 13 meat-packing plants that purchased cattle from those ranches. Next, the MPF recommended that 69 companies that were consuming products obtained from those meat-packing plants cease acquiring them in order to avoid lawsuits. The MPF action was strengthened by a Greenpeace report that demonstrated the illegal source of raw material for the meat-packing plants and the rest of the productive chain, including supermarket chains, tanneries and sporting goods and clothing factories.

Less than a month after the beginning of prosecution by the MPF and the Greenpeace campaign, 35 retail chains and industries suspended contracts with the meat-packing plants involved in the lawsuit. To avoid continuation of legal proceedings and be able to recommence operations, in August 2009 three meat-packing plants and the ranchers' representative signed a Consent Decree (*Termo de Ajustamento de Conduta*—TAC) with commitments to environmental and land title regularization. The meat-packing plants committed themselves as of the date of signing the TAC, not to acquire cattle from ranches belonging to areas listed as embargoed by IBAMA and for slave labor by the Ministry of Labor, or which carry out new deforestation in the next two years. The meat-packing plants also committed themselves, beginning in January 2010, to buying only cattle from suppliers who present proof of having requested the Rural Environmental Cadastre (*Cadastro Ambiental Rural*—CAR) from the Pará State Environmental Secretariat (SEMA) and who beginning in July 2010 present a request for environmental licensing with SEMA. By July 2011 the producers will have to present the final environmental licensing, and by August of 2014, they must have concluded land title regularization of their ranches.

Faced with those pressures, on October 5, 2009, four of the country's principal meat-packing plants do signed a voluntary commitment for zero deforestation with Greenpeace. Besides the commitment not to buy cattle coming from deforested areas after signing of the agreement, the meat-packing plants will demand land title and environmental regularization from suppliers on terms similar to those of the TAC signed in Pará.

While still an incipient measure, producers who have filed to come into compliance since these measures began number more than 22,000 in August 2010. Strongly influenced by the climate change debate, these measures appear to have changed the incentives around deforestation for cattle ranching in Pará state and may have a far-reaching impact on avoiding future deforestation.

Conclusion

This paper describes the relationship between the main land tenure and land use categories in the Brazilian Amazon and policies aimed at avoiding deforestation as a way to mitigate climate change. The paper focuses on the creation of the protected area and indigenous lands system in the region as a major advance toward limiting future deforestation. However, it points out a series of weaknesses in the land tenure system prevalent in the region, particularly the large amount of informal occupation of public land outside of the protected area system and the problems with the regularization of privately occupied areas both for enforcing requirements for maintaining forest cover on private land and for the management of existing and planned protected areas. The paper ends with a description of recently instituted legal sanctions on the meat-products producers whose products are sourced from illegally deforested land and suggests that this incipient policy could have far-reaching consequences for improving land management in the region for avoiding deforestation by changing the incentives to cattle producers to manage their lands in accordance with legislation.

6.3:   Property Rights to Carbon in the Context of Climate Change

GRENVILLE BARNES, University of Florida, U.S.
SHERYL QUAIL, University of Florida, U.S.

> *[I]f property involves a bundle of rights, it is not at all clear that all the sticks in the bundle fit comfortably together. (Singer 2000: 3)*

Summary

In this paper we review the pools, flows, and fluxes of carbon at a global level and the markets that have emerged since the Kyoto Protocol[12] as a means of identifying the characteristics of carbon and the context behind the need for defining carbon property rights. We examine who has rights and interests in forest carbon emphasizing the extent of community rights. We recognize that a new set of property rights can be conceptualized in a number of different ways, and to that end we discuss different lenses for viewing a property right to carbon. Finally, we consider the basic property information that would be required to support these property rights in some form of carbon cadastre. In this discussion we draw on field experience and the de jure situation in the Amazon areas of Bolivia, Peru, and Brazil.

Introduction

Several years ago we were interviewing a rubber tapper (José) in the Brazilian Amazon state of Acre as part of a project to analyze the dynamics of communal land tenure (Ankersen and Barnes 2004). While wandering down one of José's rubber trails, we came across a magnificent cedar tree that must have been well over 100 years old. José informed us that a timber company had recently offered him $500 for the tree and, given the poor market prices for rubber, he was seriously considering selling the tree to make ends meet.

On the drive back to town we contemplated raising the $500 ourselves to purchase the timber rights to José's cedar tree in order preserve it. At first glance this appeared to be a simple transaction, but on further reflection we began to ask several searching questions:

- What rights did José have to the tree given that the state owned the land?
- How could the transaction be legally formalized?
- What would prevent José from selling the development rights to a number of other unsuspecting gringos?
- How could our rights be enforced if José turned around and logged the tree for its timber value?
- Is $500 a fair market price for the tree given its ecological function as a carbon sink?

All of these fundamental property rights questions arose with respect to a single tree. These questions stretch to a whole forest of trees if forest carbon is to play a critical role in addressing climate change. And the success or failure of attempts to reduce carbon emissions impacts many different levels—from the local to the global level.

Land tenure, and more specifically property rights to carbon stocks, is increasingly recognized as an integral part of the climate change debate. Property rights issues have been raised with respect to communally held land (Randrianarisoa et al. 2008) including indigenous lands (Griffiths 2007); insecure tenure leading to deforestation (Porrua and Garcia-Guerrero 2008, OCC 2008, Parker et al. 2008); legal conceptions of a carbon property right (Allen and Baylis 2005; Boydell, Sheehan, and Prior 2008; Basnet-Parasai 2007; Takacs 2009); and the need to clarify who will be the beneficiaries of carbon payments through mechanisms such as REDD (Forests Dialogue 2008). Property rights to forests and/or carbon have been recognized as a key issue in almost all the major climate change reports, such as the Eliasch (OCC 2008) and Stern reports (Stern et al. 2007) and the various IPCC reports (IPCC 2001, IPCC 2003, IPCC 2007).

Where is carbon currently located? The short answer to this question is "almost everywhere."[13] However, beyond the ocean and earth's crust (where most carbon is stored), scientists usually point to the carbon pools located in tree biomass, vegetation, roots, forest litter, dead wood, and soil (Pearson, Walker, and Brown 2008: 139). For the purposes of this paper, we will focus primarily on tree biomass and the property rights to forest carbon.Other than in a few countries, such as Australia, a carbon "right" has not been distinguished from rights to the entire tree.

We begin this paper with a review of carbon dynamics and the markets and other mechanisms that have emerged since climate change rose to prominence as an international policy issue. These sections clarify both the object (carbon) to which property rights pertain as well as the broader climate change context that is driving the need to clarify carbon property rights. We then link to the major stakeholders—those who control or own forest resources at the global level with emphasis given to the Amazon. We recognize that a new set of property rights can be conceptualized in a number of different ways and to that end we discuss different lenses for viewing a property right to carbon. Finally, we consider the basic property information that would be required to support these property rights in some form of carbon cadastre. In this discussion we draw on field experience and the de jure situation in the Amazon areas of Bolivia, Brazil, and Peru.

The Life and Times of a Carbon Molecule

Understanding the nature and characteristics of the resource—in this case carbon—is a necessary first step in examining carbon within a property framework. Carbon dioxide is most commonly emitted to the atmosphere by the combustion of coal for electrical power, the burning of petroleum products for transportation, the removal of carbon during the production of cement, and the clearing of forests, typically, for agricultural expansion. Once combusted, oxidized carbon enters the atmosphere where it is sequestered by plants, via photosynthesis, or by the oceans where it resides as a carbonate or bicarbonate ion. Should the molecule be sequestered by a tree through a leaf stomata, the molecule will be incorporated into a growing stem and exploited to fuel the synthesis of energy molecules to carry out various cellular functions.

This tree may be set on fire to clear land for a biofuel farm, immediately liberating the carbon in the stem and causing the carbon to re-enter atmospheric circulation. If the tree is harvested for timber, the wood will decay and return its carbon to the atmosphere at a slow, steady rate. The root mass left below ground will decompose and the resulting carbon will eventually migrate to rivers and oceans. Most importantly, the growing tree will no longer exist to grow leaves and biomass to sequester carbon. Aged leaves will no longer fall to the ground to form soil carbon. In summary, unless the carbon is locked in forest biomass over the long term, it will contribute to the growing greenhouse gases in the atmosphere with long-term climate change consequences.

Terrestrial biomass and the oceans are transient reservoirs for CO_2 and serve as stopping points before a carbon molecule reaches its final destination in carbonate rocks. The amount of time a molecule resides in a particular reservoir before transferring to the next varies for CO_2. After roughly 300 years, 70 to 85 percent of CO_2 will have entered the oceans or terrestrial biomass, and even after 100,000 years, a small amount (3 to 7 percent) of fossil fuel carbon may remain in the atmosphere (Archer 2005).

The IPCC (2007) currently estimates anthropogenic CO_2 emissions at 32 billion tonnes per year; 47 percent of this remains in the atmosphere until sequestered over longer periods of time; approximately 20 percent is sequestered by oceans; and 15 percent by terrestrial systems (figure 6.12). A recent study has found that tropical forests alone sequester 18 percent of anthropogenic carbon, representing one-half of the terrestrial carbon pool (Lewis et al. 2009).

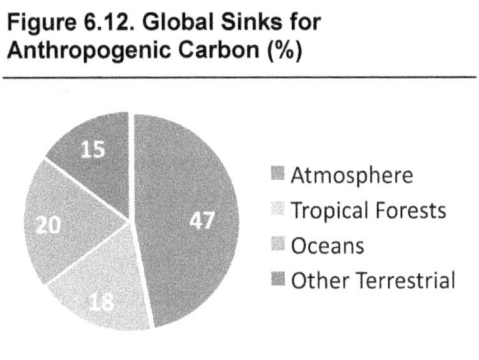

Figure 6.12. Global Sinks for Anthropogenic Carbon (%)

- Atmosphere
- Tropical Forests
- Oceans
- Other Terrestrial

Source: Lewis et al. 2009.

With growing evidence of anthropogenic climate change, identifying the sources of emissions, as well as sinks, is important. There are two approaches to accomplishing this: the "top down" method, which utilizes atmospheric data and transport models; and the "bottom up" method, which draws from forest inventories and land-use change models (Houghton 2007). The largest source of carbon emissions has been from fossil fuels followed by land-use change. In recent times, land-use change has stemmed predominantly from the conversion of forests to agriculture.

Climate Change Mitigation Strategies

It is often claimed that climate change is a market failure requiring a market solution. In terms of pollution, a market failure is described as a negative externality that is an underpriced by-product of human activity that does not fall under any ownership or regulatory regime. According to environmental economic theory, pollution to water and air often occur in open access systems where social restraint is absent and is not subject to private ownership (Goldstein 1995). Proponents of this theory suggest establishing property rights to carbon and using market mechanisms to internalize these externalities so that its price provides the incentive to reduce emissions.

Countries that ratified the Kyoto Protocol agreed to reduce emissions through the Clean Development Mechanism (CDM) in developing nations, and to a lesser extent through Joint Implementation (JI). However, project development under the CDM is time consuming and can take one to two years to emerge from the development and approval pipeline.

The largest emissions trader, the EU ETS (European Union Emissions Trading System) began implementing its cap-and-trade scheme in 2005. Under a cap-and-trade system, a limit or allowance is set on the amount of carbon a company can emit. If the allowance is exceeded, the company then buys an allowance or credit elsewhere, or faces heavy fines. The seller, in turn, is rewarded for having reduced emissions. Other emissions trading regimes under the formal markets include New South Wales and UK ETS.

The value of the formal carbon markets has achieved momentous growth every year—rising steadily from $10 billion in 2005 to $117 billion in 2008 (World Bank 2009; Ecosystem Marketplace 2009; Environmental Leader 2009). Of this, the voluntary CCX (Chicago Climate Exchange) and Over the Counter (OTC) trades, which include companies that offset emissions for corporations and individuals, captured $99 million in 2006, $335 million in 2007, and $705 million in 2008 (Ecosystem Marketplace 2009). Unfortunately, the fantastic growth in the carbon markets has been constrained by the global economic downturn and declining industrial production, causing the price of carbon to collapse. Nevertheless, the carbon market is predicted to rebound and voluntary markets to grow to $50 billion by 2012 (Phillips and Razzuk 2007).

Despite enormous sums of money transacted for emissions reductions, forests have captured very little of this. The EU ETS excludes carbon offset forestry projects at this time, and under the CDM (which only allows afforestation and reforestation (A/R) projects), only 10 projects have thus far been implemented, up from one in 2008 (UNFCC 2009). Stringent CDM project development guidelines raise transaction costs making these projects less financially viable. Additionally, because the permanence of forestry projects are at higher risk, they capture short-term emission credits worth less money, making these projects less attractive relative to the energy sector. As a result, forestry projects have been streamlined into the voluntary markets where, again, the price of carbon is less (Robiedo and Ok Ma 2008). Relative to the voluntary markets, UNFCC regulated CDM/JI offsets are perceived as higher quality due to strict project development guidelines and procedures, and consequently capture a higher value (Ecosystem Marketplace 2009). While obtaining information on pricing in voluntary markets is difficult (see Ecosecurities 2009 for further discussion), a recent survey of off-setters revealed that investors are willing to pay a premium for co-benefits to carbon forestry projects that prioritize biodiversity conservation and sustainable development for communities (Ecosecurities 2009).

At the 2007 UN Climate Conference in Bali, REDD (reduced emissions from deforestation and degradation) was introduced as a mechanism to compensate countries for conserving tropical forests. While REDD has not been formalized due to numerous concerns over policy and technical hurdles, it is expected to be implemented by 2012. In preparation for REDD, the UN and World Bank devised various funds to assist with capacity building and project planning. The World Bank Biocarbon unit, in conjunction with conservation groups and local NGOs (nongovernmental organizations), combines reforestation, agroforestry, and forest conservation and has three REDD projects underway (Woods Hole Research Center 2008), although the bulk of activities are reforestation projects. The World Bank's Forest Carbon Partnership Facility assists countries in REDD preparations and designing a large-scale system for incentive payments (World Bank 2009). In a similar vein, the UN-REDD Programme, in partnership with FAO, UNDP, and UNEP established a multidonor fund in 2008 to provide funding for REDD activities (UNDP n.d.).

Who Controls the Major Forest C Pools?

White and Martin (2002, 22),[14] in their global survey of forest tenure, revealed that 22 percent of forests worldwide are either reserved for (via usufruct rights) or owned by community and indigenous groups (see table 6.4). They found that forests were home to approximately 60 million indigenous people. In the two decades preceding 2002, White and Martin estimated that tenure rights to 149 million hectares[15] were transferred to communities in just four countries, namely Brazil, Bolivia, Colombia, and Peru.

Table 6.4: Global De Jure Ownership of the World's Forests—2002

| CATEGORIES | EXPRESSED IN PERCENT OF TOTAL | | | |
| | PUBLIC | | PRIVATE | |
	Administered by Government	Reserved for Community & Indigenous Groups	Community/ Indigenous	Individual/ Firm
Global Forest Estate	77	4	7	12
Developing Countries	71	8	14	7
Developed Countries	81	1	2	16
Countries with Tropical Forests	71	6	13	10
Top 17 Megadiverse Countries	65	6	12	17
Top 5 Roundwood Producers	80	7	6	7

Source: White and Martin (2002).

A follow-up study in 2008 found a continuing shift from government ownership and administration to all other categories (Sunderlin, Hatcher, and Liddle 2008). There are significant regional differences. Whereas almost all African forests (99.7 percent) are administered by government, in Latin America this figure drops to 34.3 percent.

One important difference between the "Public" and "Private" categories is that the land in the former category is "owned" by the government. Usufruct rights are usually granted to communities on this public land, but the government maintains the "entitlement to unilaterally extinguish local groups' rights." (White and Martin 2002: 4). Legally, usufruct rights allow the holder to profit from the resources on the land without "altering the substance" of it (BLD 1979: 1384). On private land, government may still control the usufruct rights to the forest if it is used for commercial purposes (such as logging companies or local communities). As Monterroso and Barry (2008: 3) warn, government is "never out of the picture."

Both the 2002 and 2008 studies of forest ownership show that, despite the trend away from government control, governments still have de facto control over the large majority of forests. Government departments that approve forest management plans and annual operational plans are often hard-pressed to keep up with the demand. Measured purely by the volume of management plans, governments would seem to be doing a good job of managing the forests. Unfortunately, without enforcement or engagement with local actors, management plans often remain merely words on a piece of paper. Behind the blur of plans, deforestation continues unabated, much of it through illegal logging. This is a major challenge for carbon payment schemes like REDD.

Government should also not be viewed as a single homogeneous entity. Agencies that administer land are usually in completely different ministries than the government entities that manage resources on the land. In Latin America land is typically administered by a national institute of land and/or agrarian reform while resources fall under a ministry of natural resources. During the past several decades, agrarian reform and land titling efforts have focused almost exclusively on the land (and disproportionately on agricultural land). Similarly, forestry departments have been almost entirely concerned with the extraction of timber from the forest and have paid little attention to such resources as non-timber forest products (NTFPs) (Pacheco 2007).

Who controls the forest often depends on where one asks the question. In the capital cities you will usually be directed to the de jure situation as it appears in laws and policies. On the other hand, if you are in the forest the de facto situation is much more complex, often with a range of local actors—communities, firms, or individuals—making use of forest resources with little government presence.

Property Rights to Carbon

How property rights to carbon are defined will depend largely on how immovable property in general is conceptualized. Western property concepts have been shaped historically by a number of well-known western philosophers and legal theorists, such as John Locke, William Blackstone, Jeremy Bentham, and others. These scholars refined the argument that private property rights were the rational outcome of a modern society where the supply of land is limited. Locke, in particular, developed the idea of acquiring individual property through labor. This concept can still be seen today in most countries where private property (including titled land) can be acquired through adverse possession or prescription. In the 1950s, Garret Hardin's much-quoted article on the "tragedy of the commons" added to the argument for private individual property rights if societies were to avoid the degradation of natural resources through overuse (Hardin 1968). Today, economists like Hernando de Soto (2000) continue to advance the private (individual) property rights agenda arguing that property should be treated as a fungible commodity in order to facilitate its role in economic development.

The common property resources (CPR) and commons literature has significantly broadened the property debate and provided a useful counter to the private property school. In fact, most of the earlier works on CPR use Hardin's tragedy of the commons as an initial point of departure and then through case studies demonstrate that many so-called open access "commons" are, in fact, subject to a complex set of formal or informal rules (Ostrom 1990, McCay and Acheson 1987, Agrawal 2001). "Subtractability" and "measurability" are identified as primary attributes of common pool resources (Ostrom et al. 1999). Is carbon subtractable—does the use by one individual reduce the common resource pool available to others? In the case of forest carbon, logging reduces both the stock of carbon (sink) and the forest's capacity to sequester carbon out of the atmosphere. The measurability (the ability to quantify the resource over time) of forests, particularly the level of deforestation and degradation, has been a debatable issue, but with the advent of higher resolution satellite imaging systems is no longer viewed as a major obstacle. But measuring carbon within a forest is a lot more challenging, as it varies with tree diameter and height, specific gravity of the wood, and the type of forest (Chave et al. 2005). Furthermore, whether forest carbon is the property of an individual or community or government remains a complex question (see discussion of two cases in the Case Studies section of this paper below).

Property is commonly conceived as a bundle of rights, divided into public and private rights. The public part of the bundle (rights of the state) generally includes eminent domain (also known as expropriation), the right to tax landholders, and the right to regulate land use (also referred to as "police power"). The last right is particularly relevant to the question of carbon property rights because it can convey significant power to the government over the control of the use of resources such as forests. In Latin America the social function doctrine also gives the government the right to take property from a landowner who is not fulfilling this function (not utilizing the land in a productive manner).

The private part of the bundle of rights may include such rights as access, inheritance, alienation (through sale or donation), use, develop/improve, mortgage, subdivision, exclusion, etc. Formal property systems generally focus on land as opposed to resource rights, such as water or timber rights. As pressure mounts to better manage resources on the land (such as forest carbon), there is an increasing emphasis not just on the definition of land rights, but of individual and communal rights to resources such as trees, wildlife, water, and carbon. Although the bundle of rights conception of property is uni-dimensional and does not capture the richness of property relationships, nor the duties and responsibilities associated with these rights (Singer 2000), it remains the most popular conception of property when it is "unpacked" beyond general regimes such as communal, private, and state.[16]

We have found it useful to visualize complex bundles of rights by identifying the layers of rights and interests attached to above-ground natural resources, the land and sub-soil resources like minerals and oil (figure 6.13). Distinct property regimes generally apply to these categories of resources and land cadastres almost never identify rights to above-ground or sub-soil resources on cadastral maps. This separation has been institutionalized by charging different government entities with the management of rights and interests pertaining to different resources. In Peru, for example, the mining cadastre is handled by the National Institution of Concessions and Mining Cadastre (INACC), while rural land titling was until recently carried out by the Ministry of Agriculture. Forestry concessions and resource information, on the other hand, are the responsibility of the National Institute of Natural Resources (INRENA), which manages a cadastre of protected natural areas.[17]

The case of the eastern department (state) of Madre de Dios in Peru illustrates the diversity of different bundles of rights (see figure 6.13 below). The three resource categories (natural resources, land, sub-soil) are crossed with the major classes of de jure property rights—state, indigenous and private—to illustrate how rights are bundled. This provides a picture of all possible bundles across these different resources. It also exposes the complexity within which carbon property rights must fit.

A number of REDD studies conclude that "clear and secure property rights, either at the individual or the community level, are a necessary to establish PES systems." (Angelsen 2009: 135). For the most part these studies refer to security of *land* rights, and in some cases rights to trees. But what about carbon property rights that are separable from land or timber rights? Takacs (2009) distinguishes between five different types of carbon property rights: sequestered carbon, carbon sinks, carbon sequestration potential, carbon credits, and usufruct rights. Several Australian states have defined a carbon property or "carbon sequestration right" that can be registered (Larson et al. 2008). This right is treated as a type of English common law easement (profit *a prendre*) that allows the holder to take or use the soil or products of the land. However, questions have been raised about this interpretation (see Boydell et al. 2008) and practical experience with these rights is minimal.

Figure 6.13. Bundles of Rights and Interests (Peru)

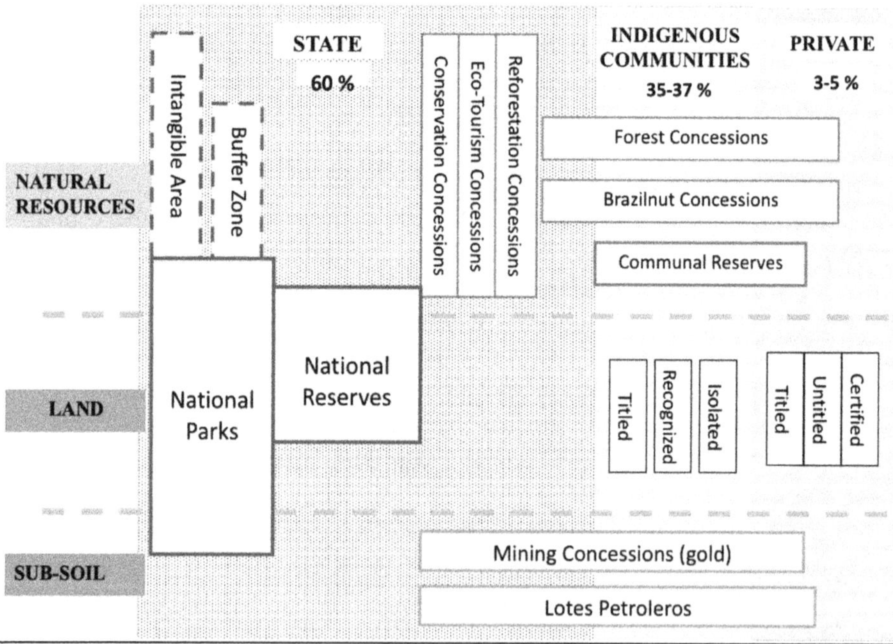

Source: Barnes (2006).

To further understand the tenure environment within which carbon property rights must fit, we describe two case studies: one in northern Bolivia and the other in southwestern Brazil.

Case Studies

Campesino Communities in Pando, Bolivia

In 1996 a new land law (Ley INRA) was passed in Bolivia, which established a new institutional structure and procedures for distributing and adjudicating land. The law defined six types of land tenure: family holdings, small properties, medium properties, agroindustrial holdings, indigenous territories, and communal properties designated for peasant farmers (*campesinos*).[18] We will focus only on the last category within the northern department (state) of Bolivia, where 31 percent of the total area has been titled to *campesino* communities, and where approximately 80 percent of the total area of the department is still forested.

Although these communities have received a title and are regarded as private property, they do not possess all the usual rights in the bundle of rights. Specifically, the property is inalienable, indivisible, not attachable (no mortgages), irreversible, immune from prescription (adverse possession), and must be held collectively. The "ownership" of the trees is attached to the "ownership" of the land in Bolivia and so these communities "own" their trees. If a community wishes to commercially log their forest, they are required to obtain a management plan and permission from the Forest Superintendency. Traditional and domestic use of the forest for subsistence purposes does not require authorization.[19] This part of Bolivia provides most of the world's Brazil nuts and constitutes the main source of livelihood for community members.

Historically, the forests in Pando were controlled by wealthy family-based rubber companies called *barracas*. Even though most barracas disappeared with the decline in the rubber market, they reemerged in the struggle for access to land and Brazil nut trees in Pando (de Jong et al. 2006). With a mere 5 percent of Pando now titled to private individuals, it is clear that the *barraceros* have lost this round although unassigned state land ("fiscal land") is still available and some *barraceros* have pursued land rights through the formation of a community with their previous employees. A 2004 presidential decree that gives peasant families the right to 500 hectares of land per family has also altered the land tenure dynamic in Pando.

Within communities, Brazil nut trees are either harvested communally or the community divides them into family-specific groves. Although these fall under the Forest Law and therefore legally require management plans, this has not progressed beyond the formulation of technical norms and the initiation of communal mapping to inventory the trees (Cronkleton et al. in press). What is clear in this case is that the trees are the property of the community and the state is attempting to extend its police power (right to regulate resource use) over NTFPs under the forest law.

The land titles issued by the national land reform agency (INRA) are registered in the property registry (*registro de derechos reales*), signaling the start of the community's tenure. Provided communities meet the social function of the land as required in the Bolivian constitution, their rights have no temporal limits. Since very few formal rights existed prior to the titling efforts in Pando, most communities acquired their rights as first owners directly from the state. Community boundaries are determined through adjudication with neighboring communities, physically monumented, and surveyed using GPS. These rectilinear boundaries are drawn on a cadastral plan (with a list of plane coordinates for all vertices) that is attached to the title. No internal boundaries, parcels, or natural resources are shown on the plans and subsequent mapping of Brazil nut trees has exposed overlaps between the title's boundary and the de facto resource rights to NTFPs (Cronkleton et al. 2007).

Land and resource tenure immediately to the north of Pando in Brazil, while sharing some of the same history, has evolved in a quite different direction.

Extractive Reserves in Acre, Brazil

In response to the rubber boom in the late 1800s, rubber barons created expansive rubber estates (*seringais*) in the western Amazon and imported workers, mainly from Northeast Brazil, to carry out the labor-intensive job of extracting latex from the rubber trees. With the decline in the rubber market, and increased competition from Malaysia, the rubber barons lost interest in their estates and left the workers to their own devices. Many *seringueiros* stayed on the land and, in addition to continuing to extract latex, they began to harvest Brazil nuts and other forest products. Extractive reserves (ER) are built around these former rubber estates[20] and, although there has been out-migration, the *seringueiros* encountered in today's extractive reserves are largely the descendents of these earlier pioneers (Melone 1993).

The federal[21] or state government owns the land underlying extractive reserves (ERs), while the community acquires a 20- or 30-year concession[22] for joint usufruct rights over the entire extractive reserve. Use rights within the ER are transferable by inheritance. The government controls resource use through requiring a utilization plan as part of the concession (ELI 1995). Generally, deforestation is limited to 10 percent of the area.

Extractive reserves are composed of a complex distribution of de facto individual and community rights that are most often dictated by the spatial distribution pattern of the resource (rubber trees) as opposed to a homogeneous rectangular pattern that characterizes other tenure regimes. Each family on the former rubber estates occupies an area known as a *colocação* that contains the rubber trails or *estradas de seringa*. The resource rights in this case are therefore defined initially by the location of the rubber trees and then by the trails that link them. The *seringueros* allow others to pass freely through their *colocação*, but the areas encompassed by the trails are regarded as relatively exclusive.

In addition, each family has a cleared area where they live, cultivate a few subsistence crops, and raise small animals (Murrieta and Rueda 1995). Brazil nuts constitute the second most important extractive product and the trees are generally regarded as being the "property" of a particular *colocação*. The same is true for individual trees with value, such as cedar and mahogany. The *seringueros* also exercise hunting rights over particular areas of the forest.

Government ownership of the land means that the state has a much stronger interest in forest carbon within the ER than in the Bolivian case discussed above (where the land is owned by private communities). Given the 10 percent deforestation limit, the state is explicitly withholding the use rights to the other 90 percent, at least for use as timber. However, as our interaction with José (discussed at the start of this paper) indicated, members of the ER feel they have a strong claim to the trees in their family *colocação* and, as de facto stewards of the forest, they have a strong claim to any benefits flowing from REDD and other PES schemes.

The spatial dimensions of ER challenge almost all of our conventional notions of property. Family-level use rights are anchored to the ground via the rubber trees and related trails that formed the original *raison d'être* of the system. The length and shape of rubber trails vary widely, but, on average, a family will work three rubber trails, each of which could contain as many as 150 rubber trees. The rule of thumb that is used in Acre is that each trail is equivalent to 100 hectares, although the exact location of this area is not defined and likely overlaps with neighboring *colocações*. Finally, as livelihood dependencies shift from rubber to Brazil nuts, so the trails through the forest begin to change to facilitate access to the Brazil nut trees. In the process, the historical use-rights patterns begin to shift as well.

Table 6.5. Summary of Property Rights Attributes

	Campesino Communities (Bolivia)	Extractive Reserves (Brazil)
What Rights?	Titled to the community with restrictions of inalienable, indivisible, not attachable (no mortgages), irreversible, immune from prescription (adverse possession), and must be held collectively.	Community holds usufruct rights that are transferable via inheritance. The state or federal government continues to own the land under the extractive reserve and controls the use through a utilization plan.
Whose Rights?	Community with de facto division of forest resources to household in some instances. State regulates use of forest resources for commercial purposes.	Government holds the land rights, while community has usufruct rights over land resources.
Time and Duration?	Initiated on registration of title and no restriction on duration.	Usufruct concession usually stipulates 20 or 30 years
How Acquired?	Communal title from government.	Federal or state governments grant a usufruct concession. No title issued.
Spatial Dimensions?	Field adjudicated rectilinear boundaries with physical monumentation. Cadastral plan shows dimensions of outside boundary.	Family-level use rights are tied to location of rubber trails and trails that link them.

Source: Authors.

Towards a Carbon Cadastre

While remote sensing technology now promises "near real-time" monitoring of deforestation (Souza et al. this volume), cadastral information describing the spatial extent of individual parcels and who holds the bundle of rights is still difficult to ascertain. This means that the tenure "landscape" is absent from our models, making it impossible to identify those whose land use practices have led to deforestation. A cadastre is classically used to provide this information.

Given our muddied experience with land titling and cadastral systems during the past several decades, expecting carbon property rights to be easily defined and accommodated within existing legal systems, particularly those with legal pluralism, is not realistic. The challenge is to look for ways to simplify carbon interests. Using trees as a proxy for forest carbon is a first step towards such simplification. Second, the initial emphasis should be on larger tracts of forests, involving multiple landowners (figure 6.14).

Figure 6.14. Carbon Property Tracts within a Leakage Monitoring Area

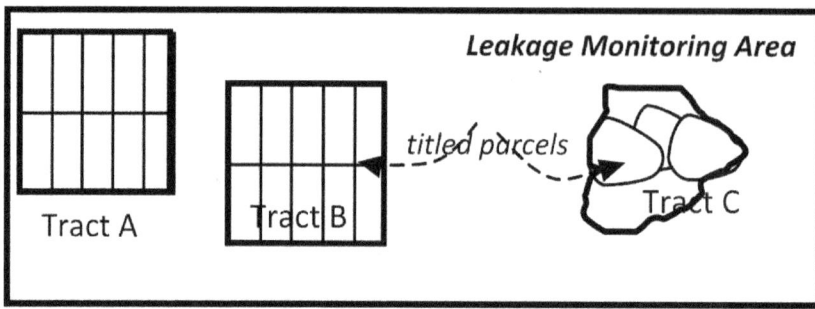

Source: Authors.

REDD is based on the principle of paying landholders for environmental services (carbon sequestration) provided that deforestation and/or degradation are reduced when compared with a certain baseline. In other words, payment should only be made if improvement is demonstrable. In addition, it is anticipated that forest conservation in one area (through REDD) may lead to increased deforestation in other areas. This is known as leakage. For the system to operate, there will need to be reliable information on (a) carbon stock at a certain baseline date, (b) improvement in carbon stock over time within tracts as well as more broadly in "leakage monitoring areas," (c) owner or usufruct holder of carbon property rights and payment for environmental services (PES), and (d) the location and boundaries of the carbon property "tracts."

REDD programs should reduce transaction costs by providing incentives for groups or individual landowners to form associations (carbon cooperatives?) that would create a common pool of forest carbon on the land of its members. Models for such meso-level associations already exist for other purposes, such as Brazil nut processing cooperatives in Bolivia, wildlife conservancies in Namibia, and various innovative governance structures that are emerging in the Brazilian states of Mato Grosso and Para (Stickler 2009).

The question of "Who owns the carbon?" is particularly relevant to REDD initiatives as it identifies the major stakeholders and potential "beneficiaries" of REDD payments. On communal land, are trees (and the encapsulated carbon) the property of the community, the government, or some third-party concessionaire? If REDD programs are designed to also address poverty alleviation, will the poorest rural communities be excluded from the program because they do not have land titles? Addressing these questions requires an effective strategy supported by a robust legal framework and a transparent cadastral information system that links forest tenure to land tenure.

Conclusion

Carbon is a highly dynamic resource that occurs predominantly in the atmosphere, ocean, earth, and biomass. The open access problems associated with air and sea carbon pools, make it difficult to target this carbon. However, we have suggested that the initial focus should be on forest carbon, which avoids this problem. The market value of carbon has increased steadily since carbon markets emerged, but like most markets, it has been severely depressed by the global economic crisis. We highlight the need to recognize that many forests are home to indigenous and other forest people living as communities and suggest that they, not governments, may be the ultimate stewards of these forests. As such, they should be regarded as key stakeholders in the development of climate governance structures that try to link global carbon payments to national governments and ultimately to local users and rights holders in the forest. We believe that forest carbon property rights that are clearly defined (especially for above-ground biomass), are pro-poor, and that respect the rights of indigenous people will reduce the risk of failure for forest carbon projects and increase investor confidence in the forestry sector.

Much of the property literature and efforts to formalize property rights have focused on land without much attention to the natural resources growing on the land. Recent research in the southwest Amazon has shown that participatory mapping of Brazil nut tenure has led to improved tenure security (Duchelle 2009). Carbon, and the demand to clarify these rights, has hastened the need to look beyond land titling to also mapping and documenting rights to resources. We have suggested that one way forward is to create common pools of carbon property tracts across adjacent parcels with all of the carbon "business" under the control of a cooperative or group association with cadastral information maintained in a carbon cadastre. This will enable us to answer the fundamental property questions raised by our proposed transaction with José (see start of paper) and add the human element that is so often lacking in deforestation models.

Notes

[1] A non-governmental research organization based in Pará state, Brazil.

[2] The Legal Amazon describes the socio-geographic area covered by the Amazon Basin in Brazil. It officially includes all seven states in the North region (Acre, Amapá, Amazonas, Pará, Rondônia, Roraima, and Tocantins), as well as Mato Grosso state in the Center-West region and most of Maranhão state in the Northeast region.

[3] The *cerrado* biome is a tropical savanna ecoregion unique to Brazil that is characterized by considerable plant and animal biodiversity.

[4] SEMA announcement can be found at http://www.sema.mt.gov.br/noticia/mostraInforme.aspx?cod=1696. Accessed January 2010.

[5] Some sources state that about 75% of Brazilian greenhouse gas emissions are from deforestation (Brasil 2004). However, this number refers only to CO_2. When considering all the other gases and their relatively higher contribution to climate change, deforestation and land use changes together contribute to roughly 50% of emissions.

[6] This section is largely based on Barreto et al. 2008.

[7] Firms must contribute to this fund in order to compensate for the environmental damages associated with their activities.

[8] According to the Brazilian Constitution, the alienation of public land greater than 2,500 hectares requires an authorization of the national Congress.

[9] IBAMA uses two major sources of resources for land acquisition and compensation of improvements. One is the national budget. The other is the environmental compensation fund which receives money from any activity that requires environmental licenses. To date, 60 to 70%

of the funds received by the environmental compensation fund have been allocated to land regularization within conservation units (Boris César, oral communication, April 19, 2007).

[10] 15th Conference of Parties of the United Nations Framework Convention on Climate Change (UNFCCC) in Copenhagen (December 2009).

[11] One of the authors (Paulo Barreto) recently heard reports from two reforestation investors about the difficulties in finding titled land to buy or to lease in Pará. In one case, the investor decided to change the investment to China and Indonesia.

[12] The Kyoto Protocol is an international agreement linked to the United Nations Framework Convention on Climate Change that aims to combat global climate change. It was adopted in Kyoto, Japan in December 1997.

[13] Almost 20 percent of the human body is composed of carbon.

[14] Their findings are based on official tenure data from 24 countries, which together represent about 93% of the world's natural forests.

[15] Equivalent to the total area of Spain, Portugal, France, and Germany.

[16] See, for example, the "tenure box" that has been developed by Barry and Meinzen-Dick (2008).

[17] See http://www.inrena.gob.pe/ianp/ianp_catastro.htm.

[18] Art. 41 of the land law (Ley INRA) of 1996.

[19] Art. 32 of the Forest Law (Ley Forestal) 1700 of 1996.

[20] The Chico Mendes Extractive Reserve, for example, incorporates 19 former rubber estates.

[21] Either through INCRA, the agrarian reform agency, or IBAMA, the environmental agency.

[22] Concessão do Direito de Uso.

CHAPTER 7

Making Land Governance Real

7.1: The Land Governance Framework: Methodology and Early Lessons from Country Pilots

KLAUS DEININGER, The World Bank, U.S.
HARRIS SELOD, The World Bank, U.S.
TONY BURNS, Land Equity International, Australia

Summary

This paper describes how, as a result of increased emphasis on measureable outputs rather than inputs, and a recognition that outside support will be more effective if the policy and institutional framework is appropriate, empirically-based indicators of aggregate governance are now widely applied as tools for decision-makers and to point to specific areas for reform. Following a review of the challenges to be confronted in developing such indicators in the land sector, we review the extent to which existing land indicators meet these requirements and draw conclusions as to the nature (policy and diagnostic combined with quantitative and fast-moving), coverage (broad to avoid that we provide the wrong answer to the wrong question), and process (empirically-based but with ample involvement by civil society) that would characterize efforts in this field.

Introduction: The Importance of Good Governance in the Land Sector

It is now increasingly recognized that, in practice, establishment and maintenance of institutions to define such rights and make information on them available freely is an important public sector role. Awareness of the importance of institutions has increased attention in governance, broadly defined as "the manner in which public officials and institutions acquire and exercise the authority to shape public policy and provide public goods and services" (World Bank 2007). As described in the Introduction to this volume, land has long been known to be one of the areas most affected by bad governance. In the public sector, this can be tracked through standard corruption indicators. In the private sector, bad governance manifests itself in the difficulty of accessing land administration institutions to obtain land ownership information or transfer property. Together, large- and small-scale corruption will reduce the perceived integrity and (because of high transaction cost) completeness of land registries, thereby undermining the very essence of land administration systems.

The effects of weak land governance will be particularly harmful for the poor in developing countries, for whom land is a primary means to generate a livelihood, a key vehicle to invest, accumulate wealth, and transfer it between generations, and an integral part of their identity. All over the world, land and real estate are a main component of household wealth.[1] Because land comprises such a large share of the asset portfolio of the poor, giving secure property rights to land they already use can increase the wealth of poor people who are not able to afford the (official and unofficial) fees needed to deal with the formal system. It also implies that improved land governance has great potential to benefit the poor directly and indirectly.

Good land governance is critical as a precondition for sustainable economic development in a number of respects. For example, good land governance can encourage long-term investments in land; protect the livelihoods of vulnerable groups, such as women and migrants; facilitate low-cost land transfers to improve land allocation; encourage private sector development through the use of land as collateral for loans; and increase government revenues through land taxation to support effective decentralization and foster local government accountability. Furthermore, the need for good land governance has recently been reinforced by three global trends, namely, increased demand for rural and urban land as a result of higher and more volatile commodity prices and population growth; climate change, which will require careful land use planning to help communities mitigate and adapt to its effects; and global programs that compensate the providers of environmental services, such as reduced deforestation, whose success will depend crucially on the recognition of local land rights to enable the rights holders to benefit from these opportunities.

Recognizing the importance of good land governance, a number of recent initiatives have started to formulate common principles at the political level. For example, in 2009 the Heads of State of the African Union agreed to a framework and guidelines for land policy in Africa which, among other things, calls for the development of benchmarks against which countries' performance can be measured (African Union 2009). This political endorsement has led an increasing number of countries to implement far-reaching programs to improve land tenure, often with significant support[2] by multi-lateral[3] and bilateral institutions[4] and with investment in the sector by various organizations. Finally, FAO, in partnership with other UN institutions, is launching a broad-based process of consultation that is expected to result in a set of voluntary guidelines for good governance of land and associated natural resources (FAO Land Tenure and Management Unit 2009, Palmer et al. 2009). The land governance assessment framework presented below can provide an important technical input into these initiatives and help to take them forward.

How Good Land Governance Is Being Measured

The literature has developed numerous governance indicators that can be categorized into rule-based and outcome-based (Kaufmann and Kraay 2008). *Rule-based* indicators assess whether institutions generally presumed to be associated with good governance such as anti-corruption commissions are in place. As long as it is possible to identify relevant measures that are clearly linked to positive outcomes and easily observed by outsiders, the reference to discrete measures makes assessment of governance status and progress easy. However, a frequently mentioned drawback is that a large number of indicators may be needed to approximate the complexity of real world situations. Moreover, having rules on paper often says little about the extent and quality of their implementation, although it is clearly the latter that counts and is desired.[5] *Outcome-based* indicators, by contrast, focus on either broad citizen perceptions, the extent to which (potential) users found public services to be easily accessed and responsive to their needs, or expert opinion about the de facto implementation of rules. While they provide a more differentiated picture, they are normally more costly to collect and less actionable from a policy perspective. In practice, output- and rule-based indicators can complement each other.

In the land sector, indicators based on opinion by experts who are presumed to be intimately familiar with the sector have been most frequent. The way in which opinions are assessed often includes a large number of individual dimensions for which scores are assigned and then aggregated, e.g. to decide on allocation of resources across competing efforts. At the multilateral level, indicators to determine overall resource allocation, including the World Bank's country policy and institutional assessment (CPIA) and IFAD's performance-based allocation system (PBAS) make implicit or explicit reference to land and property rights as one element.[6] An advantage is that such indicators are rather cheap to collect and, with appropriate explanations, can be actionable. At the same time, the relevance of rankings depends on the qualifications of experts and, especially if there is doubt about experts' skills or subjectivity, credibility may be affected. Also, the ability to compare across countries or over time may be limited, especially if the experts involved change over time.[7]

While *representative surveys* of households, users, or intermediaries (e.g. lawyers) in accessing public services do not suffer from these drawbacks and thus may provide a better assessment of the quality of outcomes that can be compared over time, the size of samples required to obtain estimates that capture variations within a country can be quite large, making such efforts very costly. This is true even if, as in the case of the 'Doing Business' indicators, a sample of experts is asked to provide responses for a hypothetical case, thus limiting potential bias, and cases are chosen to be highly actionable in one or two dimensions. The World Bank's 'doing business' indicators (World Bank 2009) aim to accomplish this by asking experts to identify the actions required and the associated costs for a stylized hypothetical situation frequently encountered by entrepreneurs. Regarding property, focus is on registration of a plot of given size and free of conflict and other encumbrances for industrial use in the surrounding of the country's capital. While this exercise has been effective in drawing attention to the topic and prompting policy reform, the meaning of 'registration' and thus the associated requirements differ across legal systems, and failure to adjust for these differences can greatly reduce relevance and usefulness of such indicators (Arrunada 2007).[8] This may fail to appropriately capture the country-specific nature and nuances of land administration systems (Arrunada 2007) or give more nuanced policy recommendations. They have been highly effective empirical backing for efforts that focus on policy reform in one or two areas such as the reduction of transaction costs and transfer fees. At the same time, the relevance of these indicators in situations such as Africa, where often more than 90 percent of land holders are not registered, may be limited.

Local observatories to monitor land rights along a number of dimensions, often run by civil society groups and linked to advocacy or educational efforts, aim to respond to this gap as a third way to monitor land governance. Experience suggests that these can be very effective tools to build capacity and to create broad awareness about an issue that is of great relevance to the majority of the population. This can be done more effectively if a common and agreed framework that provides a point of reference not only within a country but also beyond it is available. The land governance framework could provide such a framework.

The Challenges of Addressing Land Governance

The high demand for land governance from various sides raises the question: why has there not been more progress thus far? Three reasons relating to:

1. The technical complexity of land administration and the need to make trade-offs;
2. The political sensitivity and in many cases institutional fragmentation of the land sector; and
3. The location-specific nature of land tenure arrangements that makes simple institutional transplants impossible.

Land administration is technically complex and cuts across many disciplines, such as law, information technology, geodesy, geomatics and surveying, economics, urban planning, anthropology, and environmental, social, and political sciences. Some of these fields such as IT are rapidly advancing, making it important to not stick with outdated solutions but rather design systems in a way that anticipates future improvements. A key challenge is the ability to make tradeoffs to improve overall system performance rather than focus on over-engineered approaches that may be appropriate from a disciplinary perspective but make the system unsustainable.[9] While these trade-offs are ultimately a policy decision, a framework for the land sector can help to identify key areas of concern and guide support for developing an integrated strategy.

As control of land is a key determinant of economic and often political power, the land sector is intensely political. This explains institutional fragmentation whereby, contrary to sectors such as education or health, responsibility for formulation and implementation of land policy is dispersed among ministries and institutions in different sectors (e.g. agriculture, environment, urban, mining, lands). Division of responsibility between central and local governments and institutions adds further complexity that often results in uncoordinated actions and high transaction costs. To deal with this, it is critical to take a holistic view and focus on objectively measurable information based on technical issues rather than value judgments and subjective perceptions that can be interpreted as politically motivated.

Land rights and tenure arrangements have evolved over long periods of time and space in response to ecological conditions and resource endowments, and are often reflective of societies' values and norms. Attempts to assess land institutions that fail to draw on local knowledge and instead try to impose 'one size fits all' solutions are unlikely to be effective because they may not be appropriate to the specific characteristics of a given location. Initiatives undertaken without local knowledge or out of sequence (e.g. surveying or titling without a policy framework to secure rights and ensure an accessible and transparent process) often have undesirable impacts.

As a result, rather than just combining existing governance indicators in innovative ways (as done by the de Soto property rights initiative), it was felt that a more specific approach was needed if one was to come up with a tool to assess land sector governance that can serve both as a basis for diagnosis and policy dialogue and to generate data in a replicable and cost-effective way. Ideally, this should be characterized by: sufficient standardization to allow at least qualitative comparison across countries and, more importantly, identification of good practices that could be transferred between countries; the use of quantitative information as much as possible to provide ways to eliminate subjectivity, verify information, and compare over time and even space within a country; comprehensive coverage of relevant issues and a link to actionable policy prescriptions; and a tool that can be applied at sufficiently low cost to generate debate and consensus among stakeholders to allow follow-up measurement and contribute to substantive harmonization and coordination.

The Substantial Content of the LGAF

Before trying to assess or measure land governance, one has to clearly understand the roles to be fulfilled by public institutions in the land sector. Based on the literature, these are essentially three-fold: First, there is need for a legal and institutional framework that clearly defines the rules for allocation of property rights to land and, by allowing their enforcement in a cost-effective way, encourage land-related investment. Second, reliable and complete information on land rights needs to be made available freely to interested parties so as to allow low-cost verification of land ownership status, which in turn forms the basis for low-cost land transfers to more productive use(r)s and the use of land as collateral in financial markets. Finally, there is need to perform a regulatory function to avoid negative externalities that may arise from uncoordinated action by private parties. Weak governance of the land sector and a failure to perform these functions effectively and in an efficient manner will negatively affect development by reducing investment levels, land transfers, financial sector activity, and the scope for meaningful decentralization. At the same time it will contribute to elevated levels of conflict and possibly irreversible degradation of natural resources. Because the poor lack other assets, access to land is more important to them, and consequently bad land governance will have undesirable distributional consequences and disproportionately hurt the poor.

The above functions led us to identify five key areas of good land governance, namely:

- A *legal, institutional, and policy framework* that recognizes existing rights, enforces them at low cost, and allows users to exercise them in line with their aspirations and in a way that promotes the benefit of society as a whole.
- Arrangements for *land use planning and taxation* conducive to avoiding negative externalities and supporting effective decentralization.
- Clear identification of *state land* and its management in a way that provides public goods cost-effectively; use of expropriation as a last resort only to establish public infrastructure with quick payment of fair compensation and

effective mechanisms for appeal; and mechanisms for divestiture of state lands that are transparent and maximize public revenue.

- *Public provision of land information* in a way that is broadly accessible, comprehensive, reliable, current, and cost-effective in the long run.
- Accessible mechanisms to authoritatively *resolve dispute and manage conflict* with clearly defined mandates, and low cost of operation.

Justifications for each of these, as well as ways to make them operational, are discussed below.

Legal and Institutional Framework

A good legal and institutional framework implies that long-standing rights of existing land users are recognized (not necessarily formally but eligible for compensation in case of expropriation) and that the state has institutions and policies in place that allow right holders to easily enforce their rights and exercise them in line with their values and aspirations and in ways that will further the benefits of society as a whole.

Recognition of rights (LGI-1): As failure to recognize existing rights will create tenure insecurity, curb investments in land, increase the potential for conflict, and divert resources that can be more productively deployed elsewhere to the defense of property claims, legal recognition of existing land rights is a key element of good land governance. Failure to clearly identify or define land rights, by either individuals or groups, can reduce the ease of making transactions, blocking movement of land to more efficient uses and possibly its use as collateral. In traditional systems, rights held by women, children, and vulnerable groups such as migrants or herders are often insufficiently protected, come under threat as land values increase, or are in danger of being appropriated by the better-off or well-informed. In a dynamic environment there is thus a need for special safeguards to ensure that such rights are protected. The fact that in practice within a given country or jurisdiction different rights are likely to co-exist and evolve over time implies a need for flexibility in the type of rights that can be recognized and ways in which these can be upgraded. At the same time, it is important that rights be administered transparently, cost-effectively, and in a way that enjoys local legitimacy. In particular, as long as the choice in favor of collective or communal ownership arrangements is made by users based on careful and informed consideration of the advantages and disadvantages of different arrangements, there is nothing inferior about such choices. To the contrary, if rights are not formally recognized but accountable structures within communities exist, and arrangements can be revisited as circumstances change, identification and registration of community boundaries is a very cost-effective way to cover large areas with limited time and resource requirements.

Enforcement (LGI-2): To allow effective protection against competing claims, legal recognition needs to be backed by rights holders' ability to unambiguously identify land boundaries, and call upon the powers of the state to defend their rights if they are challenged. If increased frequency of transfers makes it more likely for competing claims to arise, a phenomenon generally observed as land becomes more valuable, registration to put existing rights—as well as transfers of these rights—on public record is normally worth the cost, especially if locally accepted and low-cost mechanisms are employed to do so. If rights are assigned to groups, regulations on how such groups can organize themselves, decide on internal rules, interact with outsiders, and call on external agencies to enforce rules, will be needed.

Mechanisms for formalization (LGI-3): Although it will not miraculously transform an economy through a sudden emergence of credit markets, putting rights to land on record is often justified if land values and frequency of transactions increase. However, if existing land rights are unclear or weak, using a sporadic or on-demand approach for first-time registration of rights will often carry a significant risk of land grabbing by well-connected and powerful elites. Systematic registration efforts that include ways to (i) inform all potential claimants about process and criteria used to decide between competing rights; (ii) make claimants come forward; and (iii) adjudicate rights at one point in time can significantly reduce these dangers, in addition to often achieving significantly lower unit cost than sporadic registration, especially in sparsely populated areas. Even where a systematic process of registration has been adopted, ways to upgrade tenure on a demand-driven basis will be needed, and mechanisms to do so should be affordable, transparent, and consistent with existing tenure practices.

Restrictions on rights (LGI-4): While user groups or society at large can impose limits on the type of rights or ways in which these can be exercised by individual rights holders, these should be based on a careful assessment of the cost and benefit of different options, aim to achieve certain (environmental, health, security or other) effects at low cost, and not disproportionately affect certain groups of rights holders. Restrictions that are beyond the reach of large portions of rights holders will give rise to high costs of evasion and can lead to highly discretionary enforcement that is not consistent with principles of good land governance.

Clear institutional mandates (LGI-5): Public sector functions on land are normally performed by different institutions and routine administrative tasks should, as long as capacity is available, best be decentralized. Unclear or overlapping mandates and functions increase transaction costs and can create opportunities for discretion that undermines good governance and can push users into informality. They can also create confusion or parallel structures that threaten the integrity and reliability of documents and information provided by land sector institutions, rendering policy implementation difficult.

Participatory policy framework (LGI-6): The legitimacy of land sector institutions and actions performed by them depends on the extent to which the policy framework guiding their activities is backed by social consensus, rather than being perceived as being captured by special interest groups. Land policy is thus most appropriately developed in a participatory and transparent process that clearly articulates policy goals, identifies different institutions' responsibilities, and includes an assessment of the resources needed for quick and effective implementation. It is important that ways to measure progress towards achieving land policy goals be well defined, and that responsibility for monitoring and publicizing progress towards meeting them—in ways that can be understood by the affected and feed into the policy dialogue—is clearly assigned, either based on administrative information by relevant ministries or an independent institution.

Land Use Planning and Taxation

Identification and in many cases recording of land rights is essential to provide sound management incentives. At the same time, rights come with responsibilities and obligations, and there is a clear social interest to have land utilized in a way that allows cost-effective provision of public goods and avoids negative externalities. Moreover, especially at low levels of development, where other sources of revenue may be limited, land taxation can help support decentralization in a way that encourages effective land use.

Existence of justified and transparent plans (LGI-7): While land use planning is justified to allow effective provision of public goods in a way consistent with resources available, three areas are relevant for good governance. First, land use plans and regulations should allow coping with future land demands, avoid unrealistic standards that would force large parts of the population into informality, and be implemented effectively. They need to be designed keeping in mind the affordability of compliance, the resources needed for effective enforcement, and the availability of mechanisms to bring reality in line with existing regulations. Planning or building standards that are beyond the reach of the majority of the population, even if sound from an engineering perspective, may hurt good governance without leading to better land use.

Effective planning process (LGI-8): While changes in the ways land is used or managed are a side-effect of development, they should provide benefits to society at large rather than only specific groups, be made in a transparent fashion, and be implemented accountably. Re-zoning, especially at the peri-urban fringe, can lead to large changes in land values. Having insider information on planned regulations or construction of infrastructure ahead of their actual implementation can allow those 'in the know' to acquire land in anticipation and capture potentially huge rents. To prevent speculative land acquisition along these lines, and the associated dangers of corruption, changes in zoning regulations and major infrastructure construction should be decided transparently with broad participation, be well advertised before their actual imposition, and be combined with measures (e.g. capital gains taxes or betterment levies) that would allow the public to capture a significant part of the surplus generated. Damages, which imposition of land use restrictions imposes on those who acquired land rights in good faith, should be compensated. Good governance also requires that conflict of interest arising from the fact that the same government institution or individual imposes land use plans and regulations, hears appeals, and possibly even acts as the ultimate land owner, be avoided.

Permit processing and allocation (LGI-9): While there is a social interest in having land use adhere to certain minimum standards to avoid negative externalities, routine requests for building and development permits should be handled promptly and predictably (and can in fact be contracted out). Slow and opaque processes can lead to inefficient resource allocation and hinder investment and economic development by imposing uncertainty and costs on potential developers.

Land taxation (LGI-10 & 11): The ability to raise revenue and decide on the desired level of service provision at the local level is a key for effective decentralization. Taxes on land and property are one of the best sources of self-sustaining local revenues. However, political considerations often imply that this instrument is not used to its full potential. This can encourage speculation, e.g. via idle holding of land in anticipation of large capital gains in the future and rent seeking. Allowing local governments to retain a large part of the property tax revenue they collect, providing them with the technical means (e.g. cadastres) to do so, and establishing clear principles for valuation and regular updating of rolls to avoid arbitrariness, all will make land taxation more attractive. While none of these measures pose technical challenges, they may be resisted by those who would be required to pay significant amounts of taxes.

Public Land Management

Public land ownership is justified if public goods are provided (e.g. infrastructure or parks) or if land is used by public bodies (schools, hospitals, defense, state enterprises). At the same time, the way in which state land is managed, acquired, and divested often poses serious governance challenges. To minimize such risks, it is important that (i) state land with economic value be clearly identified on the ground; (ii) expropriation be used as a last resort to provide public goods if direct negotiation is not feasible, and be implemented promptly and transparently with effective appeals mechanisms; and (iii) public land that is no longer needed (or that should not have been public in the first place) be divested in a way that maximizes public revenue and uses transparent mechanisms.

   Inventory of public land (LGI-12): Effective management of public land is virtually impossible if there is no inventory of such land of if its boundaries are defined ambiguously. Having an inventory of economically valuable state-owned land that includes identification of the boundaries of such land is a *sine qua non* to allow for proper management of this important public asset. Absence of such an inventory provides opportunities for well-connected individuals to try and establish land rights through informal occupation and squatting, often with negative environmental impacts. Also, information on revenues received from public lands and costs incurred to manage them should be open for public scrutiny and adequate capacity to staff in the relevant institutions will need to be built.

   Expropriation (LGI-13 & 14): To prevent inappropriate use of the state's powers of expropriation, pose serious challenges to good governance, acquisition of land by the state will need to be carefully proscribed, regulated, and monitored. While expropriation can be justified to prevent moral hazard and holdout problems by private owners, using it too widely runs a risk of public officials using powers in a way promoting private interests rather than public goods. Given the often slow and unpredictable nature of actions by the public sector, and the risk of cases being dragged into politics, private sector operators may be better off acquiring land through a negotiated process.[10] Where appropriate, expropriation procedures should be clear and transparent with fair compensation in kind or cash at market values made available expeditiously. Those whose land rights are affected will need to have access to mechanisms for appeal that can provide authoritative rulings in a swift, independent, and objective manner.

   Divestiture of state land (LGI-15): In cases where, for example due to historical reasons, the state owns more land than it should or can effectively manage, transfer or lease of such land can be an important tool to increase the supply of land or to use the revenue thus generated to provide public goods. In many contexts, *divestiture* of government land is one of the most egregious forms of 'land grabbing', bad governance, outright corruption (e.g. bribery of government officials to obtain public land at a fraction of market value) and squandering of public wealth. Avoiding these will require that such processes be clear, transparent, and competitive, that any payments to be received and the extent to which they are collected be publicized, and that the institutions involved be subject to regular and independent audits.

Public Provision of Land Information

Cost-effective provision of land information through registries has traditionally been at the heart of titling and registration programs. While such programs have often contributed to positive outcomes, examples where they failed to reach their objectives in terms of outreach, equity, and sustainability, point towards a need to ensure that registries provide broad access to comprehensive, reliable, up to date information on land ownership and relevant encumbrances in a cost-effective way. A regular assessment of the extent to which they do so can be an important element to help improve land governance.

Completeness and reliability (LGI-16 & 17): As they cannot be sure whether any gaps that might exist in the registry could be of relevance for their interests, potential investors will derive few benefits (in terms of eliminating the need for checking on land ownership information on a case by case basis) from land registries that do not provide complete, geographically exhaustive, and reliable information. The most extreme form of ensuring reliability of land registries is for the state to indemnify anybody for losses suffered from deficient information by the registry, an institutional innovation that has enabled the Australian Torrens system to quickly spread around the world and that continues to provide the basis for the attractiveness of this system to this day.[11] It is thus critical that registry information be accessible to interested parties quickly, complete, up to date, and sufficient to make relevant inferences on ownership or any economically relevant encumbrances.

Cost-effectiveness, accessibility, and sustainability (LGI-18 & 19): Even if documenting land rights and the boundaries of such rights has clear benefits, sustainability of land registries[12] and their ability to reach out to those with limited resources will critically depend on this being done in a low-cost manner. Failure to choose designs with low cost of operation has often led to establishment of registries that either failed to achieve full coverage or that became outdated as soon as subsidies to their operation stopped. The reason is that users unwilling to pay large amounts of money to register transactions failed to do so and reverted back to informality.[13] Ensuring that operations can be sufficiently efficient to be justifiable in terms of land values and land users' wealth is of great importance to prevent a registry from becoming quickly out of date. A necessary condition for this is that running costs are kept reasonable and that fees are determined and collected in a transparent manner. At the same time, rather than trying to squeeze cost of operation to unrealistically low levels---a measure that could create governance challenges of its own,[14] costs should be kept low through adoption of appropriate technology, especially with regard to the precision required from ground surveys.[15] The fact that in some countries such efforts were opposed by a few surveyors who, by controlling entry, maintained a de facto monopoly on the market points to the important governance issues underlying these rather technical issues.

Dispute Resolution and Conflict Management

Given the secular forces affecting land values, the magnitude of the resources and the vested interests at stake, and the rapid pace of social and economic change experienced by many developing countries, it may be naïve to assume that conflicts over land can be avoided. What is more important from a land governance point of view is that potential sources of conflict be dealt with in a consistent fashion, rather than on an ad-hoc basis, and that institutions to resolve dispute and manage conflict are accessible, have clearly defined mandates, and work effectively.

Clarity of assignment (LGI-20): To prevent either large-scale opportunistic behavior and erosion of authority or a high level of persistent conflict that might escalate with socially disruptive consequences, it is important to have conflict resolution institutions that are legitimate, accessible to most of the population, and legally authorized to resolve conflicts. Failure on any of these counts can lead to 'forum shopping', whereby those with better knowledge or connections choose channels of dispute resolution that are most likely to yield an outcome favorable to them, or even pursue conflicts simultaneously in multiple forums. In many cases efforts to avoid this will require giving recognition to the verdicts reached by local bodies for conflict resolution, possibly subject to them not violating basic norms of equity, transparency, those making decisions have basic legal knowledge, and decisions can be appealed against relatively quickly.

Effectiveness (LGI-21): Continuing dispute that cannot be resolved authoritatively can impose huge cost not only on individuals, but also on society as a whole, as it will 'sterilize' land from investment and development. Therefore, although the wide variety of potential conflicts and the differences in legal and social norms make it difficult to assess the effectiveness of legal institutions (which would be a subject of more detailed analysis under justice reform programs), a minimum criterion is that the share of land users or plots affected by pending conflicts is low and decreasing.

The Methodology for Applying the LGAF

To make sector-specific indicators of land governance policy relevant in a specific setting, a methodology and process are needed that would allow using land governance indicators as a diagnostic tool to assess a country's situation and, on the basis of the shortcomings identified, ideally come up with a set of policy recommendations or areas for future research. This section describes the overall framework used to guide the assessment, the different ways to assemble background information, and the process adopted to come up with a consensus ranking that is sufficiently robust to be presented to policy makers.

The Ranking Framework

To summarize information in a structured way that is understandable by policy makers and can be compared across countries, we chose to build on the methodology used by the Public Expenditure and Financial Accountability assessment tool (PEFA).[16] We follow PEFA by using the five thematic areas as a basis for 21 land governance indicators (LGIs). Each indicator relates to a basic principle of land governance as illustrated above and is then further broken down into between two and six "dimensions" for which objective empirical information can be obtained at least in principle. The result is a LGAF with a total of 80 dimensions. It is based on experience in various countries, and can be assessed based on objective information. Each dimension is ranked by selecting an appropriate answer among a list of pre-coded statements that have been drafted based on extensive interaction with land professionals and refined through the pilot country case studies.

While the general framework for using local knowledge to come up with comparable indicators is adopted from PEFA, the specific challenges of the land sector as outlined in chapter one above led us to introduce four key differences.

First, to ensure that the nuances of local legislation and practice are adequately captured, main responsibility for the conduct of the exercise is with the country coordinator, a local expert in law or land administration. This person is critical to the success of the exercise and will have to be well qualified and carefully chosen. Responsibilities include the compilation of relevant background studies to be made available to those who will actually rank indicators as described below.

Second, dimensions to be ranked are grouped into sets of about ten. Panels of three to five members, with experience in the relevant topic matter, are then formed to come up with consensus rankings for the indicators in their area, drawing on their own experience, informal interviews with experts, and background information provided to them by the experts through the country coordinator.

Third, there is no intention to aggregate across indicators to come up with an 'overall' score of land governance or for individual thematic areas. At this point such aggregation does not seem to be warranted and it will be better to use individual dimensions to compare countries and draw lessons from good practice.

Finally, in contrast to the PEFA assessment tool which is commonly applied during a two-week mission by a joint government donor team that may be dominated by expatriates, the LGAF is applied over a three to five month period under the guidance of a local coordinator in a structured process that involves assembly of key background information on key aspects of land governance, followed by meetings of diverse groups of stakeholders with first-hand knowledge or experience of the issues at stake to come up with a consensus ranking and elaboration of a country report. This helps in obtaining more in-depth background information, capturing regional differences and local realities as perceived by different local stakeholder groups, thereby getting buy-in beyond government and the donor community. Eventually, it may lead to reduced costs.

Compilation of Background Information

In an area as complex and potentially controversial as land tenure, any exercise not based on rigorous review of available information and analysis is likely to be challenged. It is thus critical that rankings are based on a proper understanding of the underlying issues and that all participants start off with the same amount of information. To accomplish this, the country coordinator him/herself or with assistance from a legal expert, puts together a 'tenure typology' that is intended to provide an exhaustive listing of the legally recognized tenure types in the country, their physical size and the number of land holders involved, and policy issues that are likely to arise in their application. In addition, the coordinator recruits one local specialist each in the areas of land tenure, land use policy, public land management; and land administration. These specialists are tasked with putting together relevant studies and administrative or 'unofficial' data, to be obtained through personal contacts or phone calls to the relevant institutions. These are documented and used as a basis for a subjective ranking of the set of LGAF dimensions corresponding to their area of expertise, together with a justification for these rankings. Tenure typology, expert rankings, and a summary of the justifications provided by the experts, and results from any sampling that may have been undertaken, serve as an input into the determination of the consensus ranking for each of the dimensions.

Although the systematic involvement of experts as detailed above may be a significant improvement, issues such as the currency of registries, extent of female rights, collection of taxes, adherence to rules in case of expropriation, transparency of public land dispositions, nature, area, and age of disputes are nearly impossible to assess with any degree of confidence, even for individuals who are very familiar with a country's land tenure system, partly because they are likely to vary significantly over space. While expert opinion may provide a general order of magnitude, making inferences on inter-regional or -temporal variation in these makes reliance on hard data mandatory.

To demonstrate the feasibility and usefulness of having such data available, small surveys of key issues were undertaken in most pilot countries. Although samples were too small to approach representativeness, the exercise confirmed that, given their variation even within a country, such indicators are very meaningful and that their collection does not pose any conceptual difficulties. In fact, combining such data with other administrative data (e.g. on costs of service provision) or with socio-economic information at district level (e.g. on levels of poverty) will provide opportunities for making inferences on the outreach, client responsiveness, and potential poverty-impact of land administration services and the cost effectiveness with which they are provided. As such data refer to administrative functions that are performed routinely by different parts of the land administration system, their collection can easily be built into existing business processes. In light of this, spending significant resources on a separate data collection effort in the context of LGAF application is not cost-effective, and a clear recommendation from the pilot country experiences, which we will return to below, is that collection and publication of such data on a routine basis should be part of any future donor efforts to aid land administration systems.

Expert Panels

While systematic collection of information before any ranking is undertaken is an important innovation by the LGAF, its core is to provide rankings through panels, each including a diverse set of individuals who are exposed to different aspects of services in the area explored. Panel members typically include lawyers, academics, members of business chambers, banks, NGO representatives, government officials, land professionals and others (e.g. builders requiring permits) who interact with relevant institutions and thus have an empirical basis to assess performance. Experience suggests that 3-5 members who will bring together a variety of user perspectives and substantive expertise needed to provide a meaningful ranking can be selected for each of these panels and be provided with a small honorarium for their participation. To ensure that panel members only assess areas they are familiar with and to prevent overload, the 80 dimensions were distributed among eight panels on (i) land tenure; (ii) institutional arrangements; (iii) urban land use, planning and development; (iv) rural land use and policy; (v) land valuation and taxation; (vi) public land management; (vii) public provision of land information; and (viii) disputes resolution.

To provide the basis for a meaningful discussion, panel members are briefed by the country coordinator on the objectives of the exercise, provided with the background material assembled previously and asked to provide any additional information that might be relevant for the topic. This informal briefing (which often also entails a meeting) is then followed by the panel gathering in a workshop-like setting the length of which can range from a few hours to an entire day, depending on the amount of prior preparation. The purpose of this meeting is to jointly discuss and review the material prepared, add specific cases and experience, and on this basis, come up with a panel consensus ranking through debate and aggregation of individual members' rankings.[17]

One advantage of this approach is that, based on their experience in the sector, panel members will in many cases be able to not only identify cases of good or inadequate performance but also identify reasons leading to such performance. In the case of good performance, this can hold lessons for other countries. If performance is unsatisfactory, experts will be able to point to either policy changes or identify issues that will need to be studied in more detail to provide a sound basis for recommendations. Based on discussion in the various panels, the country coordinator can then use this to identify a prioritized list of policy interventions and/or gaps in available evidence in selected areas that can be a basis for recommendations to improve land governance, thereby making the exercise a highly constructive one.

To accomplish this, the country coordinator will summarize results from the panel discussion in an Aide Memoire that is made available to all participants for review and approval. Aide Memoires from the eight panel sessions will provide the basis for, and be annexed to, a country report, the compilation of which is the responsibility of the country coordinator. The country report thus consists of three elements, namely:

- The tenure typology;
- The consensus ranking arrived at for each of the dimensions, together with a summary of the evidence and materials used to come up with a consensus ranking by the panels; and
- Priority recommendations for policy and areas where more evidence might be needed.

Conclusion and Next Steps

Based on lessons regarding the extent to which pilot application of the LGAF in five countries (Ethiopia, Indonesia, Kyrgyz Republic, Peru, and Tanzania) lived up to expectations, this section assesses the usefulness of the framework and the scope for using it as one input, to be developed and improved upon in the course of implementation, into a 'land governance partnership' that would not only explore land governance in other countries but also establish ways of measuring it on a more continuing basis.

Methodological and Process Lessons from the Pilot

A key underlying hypothesis was that a sector-specific approach to governance was required and that, the differences in historical context notwithstanding, a framework that is identical across countries will have many benefits. These include comparison of rankings in specific areas and the use of these to point to good practice and policy reform. This has been fully vindicated. Technically, pilot cases demonstrate that a structured diagnostic review of the land administration system in a given country is feasible without imposing value judgments. Although not all cases were a resounding success, the pilots helped refine the framework and provided lessons regarding implementation and refinements that are already reflected in the LGAF. While not all elements are equally relevant everywhere, there is a general feeling that coverage is broad enough (without becoming too complex) and that there is sufficient scope to adapt to country-specific conditions in the inception stage for the LGAF to be ready for roll-out to other countries with an expectation of producing useful results.

A key decision that made the LGAF deviate from other tools such as PEFA was to put strong emphasis on involvement of local experts and users who interact with the system in a wide range of contexts. This has proved to be critical to draw on the range of experience required to document and identify areas for policy action. At the same time, two areas for improvement can be identified. First, there was little coherence in the way and extent to which government was involved in the process, something that could affect the extent to which policy recommendations will be acted upon. Although the wide range of potential arrangements makes it difficult to make general recommendations, it seems to be desirable to have a general agreement with government that would include access to whatever data are available as well as an arrangement for obtaining official comments and disseminating results through a joint workshop in the end, but leave the extent to which officials are involved up to the country coordinator.[18] To achieve this, a formal mandate to conduct these assessments as an input into making the AU LPI or the FAO voluntary guidelines operational in a country context could be very useful. Second, as experience on implementation of the LGAF accumulates, ensuring that country coordinators have access to procedural and substantive lessons from other countries will be important to make the process as effective as possible and prevent costly learning by trial and error. Mechanisms to do so can involve workshops with country coordinators before starting up the work and involvement of a global coordinator throughout the process and the overall team in dissemination workshops.

Although it is unrealistic to expect the LGAF to be useful for providing cross-country comparisons, we did expect that use of an identical structure for a very heterogeneous set of countries would allow for identifying good practice that could potentially be transferred across countries as well as areas which, because they are problematic in a number of instances, would warrant more analytical efforts. Indeed, results suggest that even in the pilots, there were many lessons and good practices that could be transferred across countries in each of the five main areas. These are critical to feed back into the policy dialogue to show that innovative solutions are indeed feasible and could in turn provide the basis for a vigorous South-South exchange of experience.

Where to Go from Here?

It will be desirable to roll out the LGAF as a diagnostic tool. In all of the countries studied, the LGAF was useful as a diagnostic tool to identify gaps in policy and the way in which institutions function or responsibilities between institutions are assigned. The benefit of having a framework to identify issues in a way that can be compared across countries is that good practice that has been identified in one setting can help to identify possible options for policy reform in another, and in particular illustrate ways in which elsewhere solutions to seemingly difficult policy areas have been identified, something that can also help to gain momentum for policy reform. If applied in a way that draws on existing expertise and broad participation by relevant stakeholders (including governments) from the beginning, the LGAF can not only help to broaden the range of issues to be covered in such analysis but also the relevance of the resulting analysis and the credibility of resulting recommendations for policy or further study. Beyond this, there are three areas that might be addressed jointly by development partners.

First, the LGAF can also provide a basis to monitor discrete (rule-based) indicators of policy reform and, in doing so, provide an opportunity for a broad-based coalition of actors (including NGOs, the private sector, and academics) to monitor to what extent recommendations are followed through. In fact, in Peru, panel members suggested a structure be put in place that could provide such follow up with modest resources; discussions along these lines are ongoing. This is very similar to the 'land observatories' that have already been established in various contexts and, where these are available, could build on this structure to work towards establishment of a broad-based 'land working group'. Such a group could provide regular input into national fora such as the CAADP roundtables to provide specific operational guidance to policy. This could be linked to agreement on specific steps and reporting on progress made towards these in response to multilateral initiatives such as the AU's land policy guidelines or other initiatives.

Second, beyond the discrete indicators, the LGAF points towards a number of areas that change relatively quickly and where thus the design of quantitative indicators to monitor land governance on a more frequent basis will be useful. While more work will be needed to agree on the specific definition of variables, the LGAF experience suggests that key areas of concern include (i) the coverage of the land administration system (i.e. the extent to which primary or secondary rights by groups or individuals are recorded) and the extent to which different types of transfers are registered, with particular attention to women; (ii) the amount of land tax revenue raised; (iii) the total area of public or private land that is mapped with information publicly available; (iv) the number of expropriations and the modalities with which compensation is paid (including amounts and delays in receipt of payment); and (v) the number of conflicts of different types entering the formal system. The fact that each of these indicators is related to one or more core areas of the land administration system suggests that collection and publication of these indicators on a regular basis, and—to accommodate wide variations of these indicators over space—in a way that can be easily disaggregated by administrative units, should be a routine in any land administration system and be integrated in future donor support to this area. In fact, the two elements discussed above taken together, i.e. discrete measures of policy and specific quantitative indicators would not only reinforce each other but could also provide the basis for a more results-based way of providing support to the land sector that could help to increase accountability at the national level and sharing of experience and collaboration across countries to effectively address some of the challenges involved in improving land governance.

Table 7.1. LGAF Dimensions Ordered by Thematic Areas

THEMATIC AREA 1. LEGAL AND INSTITUTIONAL FRAMEWORK		
LGI-1. RECOGNITION OF A CONTINUUM OF RIGHTS: The law recognizes a range of rights held by individuals as well as groups (including secondary rights as well as rights held by minorities and women).		
1	i	Existing legal framework recognizes rights held by most of the rural population, either through customary or statutory tenure regimes.
	ii	Existing legal framework recognizes rights held by most of the urban population, either through customary or statutory tenure regimes.
	iii	The tenure of most groups in rural areas is formally recognized and clear regulations exist regarding groups' internal organization and legal representation
	iv	Group tenure in informal urban areas is formally recognized and clear regulations exist regarding the internal organization and legal representation of groups.
	v	The law provides opportunities for those holding land under customary, group, or collective tenure to fully or partially individualize land ownership/use. Procedures for doing so are affordable, clearly specified, safeguarded, and followed in practice.
LGI-2. ENFORCEMENT OF RIGHTS: The rights recognized by law are enforced (including secondary rights as well as rights by minorities and women).		
2	i	Most communal lands have boundaries demarcated and surveyed/mapped and communal rights registered.
	ii	Most individual properties in rural areas are formally registered.
	iii	Most individual properties in urban areas are formally registered.
	iv	A high percentage of land registered to physical persons is registered in the name of women either individually or jointly.
	v	Common property under condominiums is recognized and there are clear provisions in the law to establish arrangements for the management and maintenance of this common property.
	vi	Loss of rights as a result of land use change outside the expropriation process, compensation in cash or in kind is paid such that these people have comparable assets and can continue to maintain prior social and economic status.
LGI-3. MECHANISMS FOR RECOGNITION OF RIGHTS: The formal definition and assignment of rights, and process of recording of rights accords with actual practice or, where it does not, provides affordable avenues for establishing such consistency in a non-discriminatory manner.		
3	i	Non-documentary forms of evidence are used alone to obtain full recognition of claims to property when other forms of evidence are not available.

	ii	Legislation exists to formally recognize long-term, unchallenged possession and this applies to both public and private land although different rules may apply.
	iii	The costs for first time sporadic registration for a typical urban property is low compared to the property value.
	iv	There are no informal fees that need to be paid to effect first registration.
	v	The requirements for formalizing housing in urban areas are clear, straight-forward, affordable and implemented consistently in a transparent manner.
	vi	There is a clear, practical process for the formal recognition of possession and this process is implemented effectively, consistently and transparently.
LGI-4. RESTRICTIONS ON RIGHTS: Land rights are not conditional on adherence to unrealistic standards.		
4	i	There are a series of regulations regarding urban land use, ownership and transferability that are for the most part justified on the basis of overall public interest and that are enforced.
	ii	There are a series of regulations regarding rural land use, ownership and transferability that are for the most part justified on the basis of overall public interest and that are enforced.
LGI-5. CLARITY OF MANDATES AND PRACTICE: Institutional mandates concerning the regulation and management of the land sector are clearly defined, duplication of responsibilities is avoided and information is shared as needed.		
5	i	There is a clear separation in the roles of policy formulation, implementation of policy through land management and administration and the arbitration of any disputes that may arise as a result of implementation of policy.
	ii	The mandated responsibilities exercised by the authorities dealing with land administration issues are clearly defined and non-overlapping with those of other land sector agencies.
	iii	Assignment of land-related responsibilities between the different levels of government is clear and non-overlapping.
	iv	Information related to rights in land is available to other institutions that need this information at reasonable cost and is readily accessible, largely due to the fact that land information is maintained in a uniform way.
LGI-6. EQUITY AND NON-DISCRIMINATION IN THE DECISION-MAKING PROCESS: Policies are formulated through a legitimate decision-making process that draws on inputs from all concerned. The legal framework is non-discriminatory and institutions to enforce property rights are equally accessible to all.		
6	i	A comprehensive policy exists or can be inferred by the existing legislation. Land policy decisions that affect sections of the community are based on consultation with those affected and their feedback on the resulting policy is sought and incorporated in the resulting policy.
	ii	Land policies incorporate equity objectives that are regularly and meaningfully monitored and their impact on equity issues is compared to that of other policy instruments.
	iii	Implementation of land policy is costed, expected benefits identified and compared to cost, and there are a sufficient budget, resources and institutional capacity for implementation.
	iv	Land institutions report on land policy implementation in a regular, meaningful, and comprehensive way with reports being publicly accessible.

		THEMATIC AREA 2. LAND USE PLANNING, MANAGEMENT, AND TAXATION
		LGI-7. TRANSPARENCY OF LAND USE RESTRICTIONS: Changes in land use and management regulations are made in a transparent fashion and provide significant benefits for society in general rather than just for specific groups.
7	i	In urban areas, public input is sought in preparing and amending changes in land use plans and the public responses are explicitly referenced in the report prepared by the public body responsible for preparing the new public plans. This report is publicly accessible.
	ii	In rural areas, public input is sought in preparing and amending land use plans and the public responses are explicitly referenced in the report prepared by the public body responsible for preparing the new public plans. This report is publicly accessible.
	iii	Mechanisms to allow the public to capture significant share of the gains from changing land use are regularly used and applied transparently based on clear regulation.
	iv	Most land that has had a change in land use assignment in the past 3 years has changed to the destined use.
		LGI-8. EFFICIENCY IN THE LAND USE PLANNING PROCESS: Land use plans and regulations are justified, effectively implemented, do not drive large parts of the population into informality, and are able to cope with population growth.
8	i	In the largest city in the country urban development is controlled effectively by a hierarchy of regional/detailed land use plans that are kept up-to-date.
	ii	In the four major cities urban development is controlled effectively by a hierarchy of regional/detailed land use plans that are kept up-to-date.
	iii	In the largest city in the country, the urban planning process/authority is able to cope with the increasing demand for serviced units/land as evidenced by the fact that almost all new dwellings are formal.
	iv	Existing requirements for residential plot sizes are met in most plots.
	v	The share of land set aside for specific use that is used for a non-specified purpose in contravention of existing regulations is low
		LGI-9. SPEED AND PREDICTABILITY OF ENFORCEMENT OF RESTRICTED LAND USES: Development permits are granted promptly and predictably.
9	i	Requirements to obtain a building permit are technically justified, affordable, and clearly disseminated.
	ii	All applications for building permits receive a decision in a short period.
		LGI-10. TRANSPARENCY OF VALUATIONS: Valuations for tax purposes are based on clear principles, applied uniformly, updated regularly, and publicly accessible.
10	i	The assessment of land/property values for tax purposes is based on market prices with minimal differences between recorded values and market prices across different uses and types of users and valuation rolls are regularly updated.
	ii	There is a policy that valuation rolls be publicly accessible and this policy is effective for all properties that are considered for taxation.
		LGI-11. COLLECTION EFFICIENCY: Resources from land and property taxes are collected and the yield from land taxes exceeds the cost of collection.
11	i	There are limited exemptions to the payment of land/property taxes, and the exemptions that exist are clearly based

		on equity or efficiency grounds and applied in a transparent and consistent manner.
	ii	Most property holders liable for land/property tax are listed on the tax roll.
	iii	Most assessed property taxes are collected.
	iv	The amount of property taxes collected exceeds the cost of staff in charge of collection by a factor of more than 5.
THEMATIC AREA 3. MANAGEMENT OF PUBLIC LAND		
LGI-12. IDENTIFICATION OF PUBLIC LAND AND CLEAR MANAGEMENT: Public land ownership is justified, inventoried, under clear management responsibilities, and relevant information is publicly accessible.		
12	i	Public land ownership is justified by the provision of public goods at the appropriate level of government and such land is managed in a transparent and effective way.
	ii	The majority of public land is clearly identified on the ground or on maps.
	iii	The management responsibility for different types of public land is unambiguously assigned.
	iv	There are adequate budgets and human resources that ensure responsible management of public lands.
	v	All the information in the public land inventory is accessible to the public.
	vi	Key information for land concessions is recorded and publicly accessible.
LGI-13. JUSTIFICATION AND TIME-EFFICIENCY OF EXPROPRIATION PROCESSES: The state expropriates land only for overall public interest and this is done efficiently.		
13	i	A minimal amount of land expropriated in the past 3 years is used for private purposes.
	ii	The majority of land that has been expropriated in the past 3 years has been transferred to its destined use.
LGI-14. TRANSPARENCY AND FAIRNESS OF EXPROPRIATION PROCEDURES: Expropriation procedures are clear and transparent and compensation in kind or at market values is paid fairly and expeditiously.		
14	i	Where property is expropriated, fair compensation, in kind or in cash, is paid so that the displaced households have comparable assets and can continue to maintain prior social and economic status.
	ii	Fair compensation, in kind or in cash, is paid to all those with rights in expropriated land regardless of the registration status.
	iii	Most expropriated land owners receive compensation within one year.
	iv	Independent avenues to lodge a complaint against expropriation exist and are easily accessible.
	v	A first instance decision has been reached for the majority of complaints about expropriation lodged during the last 3 years.
LGI-15. TRANSPARENT PROCESS AND ECONOMIC BENEFIT: Transfer of public land to private use follows a clear, transparent, and competitive process and payments are collected and audited.		
15	i	Most public land disposed of in the past 3 years is through sale or lease through public auction or open tender process.
	ii	A majority of the total agreed payments are collected from private parties on the lease of public lands.

	iii	All types of public land are generally divested at market prices in a transparent process irrespective of the investor's status (e.g. domestic or foreign).

THEMATIC AREA 4. PUBLIC PROVISION OF LAND INFORMATION

LGI-16. COMPLETENESS: The land registry provides information on different private tenure categories in a way that is geographically complete and searchable by parcel as well as by right holder and can be obtained expeditiously by all interested parties.

16	i	Most records for privately held land registered in the registry are readily identifiable in maps in the registry or cadastre.
	ii	Relevant private encumbrances are recorded consistently and in a reliable fashion and can be verified at low cost by any interested party.
	iii	Relevant public restrictions or charges are recorded consistently and in a reliable fashion and can be verified at a low cost by any interested party.
	iv	The records in the registry can be searched by both right holder name and parcel.
	v	Copies or extracts of documents recording rights in property can be obtained by anyone who pays the necessary formal fee, if any.
	vi	Copies or extracts of documents recording rights in property can generally be obtained within 1 day of request.

LGI-17. RELIABILITY: Registry information is updated, sufficient to make meaningful inferences on ownership.

17	i	There are meaningful published service standards, and the registry actively monitors its performance against these standards.
	ii	Most ownership information in the registry/cadastre is up-to-date.

LGI-18. COST-EFFECTIVENESS AND SUSTAINABILITY: Land administration services are provided in a cost-effective manner.

18	i	The cost for registering a property transfer is minimal compared to the property value.
	ii	The total fees collected by the registry exceed the total registry operating costs.
	iii	There is significant investment in capital in the system to record rights in land so that the system is sustainable but still accessible by the poor.

LGI-19. TRANSPARENCY: Fees are determined and collected in a transparent manner.

19	i	A clear schedule of fees for different services is publicly accessible and receipts are issued for all transactions.
	ii	Mechanisms to detect and deal with illegal staff behavior exist in all registry offices and all cases are promptly dealt with.

THEMATIC AREA 5. DISPUTE RESOLUTION AND CONFLICT MANAGEMENT

LGI-20. ASSIGNMENT OF RESPONSIBILITY: Responsibility for conflict management at different levels is clearly assigned, in line with actual practice, relevant bodies are competent in applicable legal matters, and decisions can be appealed against.

20	i	Institutions for providing a first instance of conflict resolution are accessible at the local level in the majority of communities.

	ii	There is an informal or community-based system that resolves disputes in an equitable manner and decisions made by this system have some recognition in the formal judicial or administrative dispute resolution system.
	iii	There are no parallel avenues for conflict resolution or, if parallel avenues exist, responsibilities are clearly assigned and widely known and explicit rules for shifting from one to the other are in place to minimize the scope for forum shopping.
	iv	A process and mechanism exist to appeal rulings on land cases at reasonable cost with disputes resolved in a timely manner.
LGI-21. LOW LEVEL OF PENDING CONFLICT: The share of land affected by pending conflicts is low and decreasing.		
21	i	Land disputes in the formal court system are low compared to the total number of court cases.
	ii	A decision in a land-related conflict is reached in the first instance court within 1 year in the majority of cases.
	iii	Long-standing land conflicts are a small proportion of the total pending land dispute court cases.

7.2:   Applying the Land Governance Assessment Framework in a Middle-Income Economy: The Case of Peru

VICTOR ENDO, Administracion del Territorio, Peru

Introduction: The Peruvian Pilot Program

The Research Group of the World Bank chose Ethiopia, Indonesia, the Kyrgyz Republic, Peru, and Tanzania to field-test[19] the group's new Land Governance Assessment Framework (LGAF) to see how it held up under diverse social and economic situations. Designed as a diagnostic tool for evaluating the recognition, administration, and governance of land rights at the national level, the LGAF provides governments with an objective assessment tool for identifying the areas where improvements are needed. The overall diagnosis results from an assessment of 21 Land Governance Indicators (LGIs) grouped into five main topics: (1) legal and institutional framework, (2) land use planning, management and taxation, (3) management of public land, (4) public provision of land information, and (5) dispute resolution and conflict management. The 21 indicators are, in turn, broken down into several sub-indicators or "dimensions" that sum up 72 ways to measure different aspects of land governance.

This paper summarizes the findings of the LGAF pilot program in Peru—based on discussions involving a series of seven panels of Peruvian experts on issues related to land rights. Following LGAF guidelines, the panels were comprised of five to nine members, involving a total of 38 specialists, 22 of them from the public sector—selected on the basis of the relevance of their respective government agencies to LGIs. Private sector participants included 16 lawyers, architects, and representatives from private sector professional associations and NGOs with an acknowledged track record in the required fields.

Why is the LGAF important even to a middle income country such as Peru? In recent years, Peru has experienced a burst of economic growth that has caught the eye of the world's multilateral agencies and private investors. In 2007, Peru's real GDP growth was 8.3 percent, the highest in Latin America; and the following year it was an astonishing 9.8 percent, the highest in the world. With the developed world's economies trying to move out of reverse gear in 2009 the Peruvian economy was still growing. Exports in commodities and agricultural products have been booming. Peru has signed Free Trade Agreements with the United States, Canada, Singapore, and China. In 2008, Peru won international investment upgrades from Fitch and Standard and Poor's, and in December 2009, Moody's followed with its own upgrade.

Key to Peru's current success and microeconomic stability were Government efforts over the past 20 years to extend legal property rights to more Peruvians. In fact, most of Peru's laws related to land now seem adequate, even progressive: they broadly recognize rights for most of the types of land tenure; they describe the roles of public agencies, including decentralized bodies as well as the central government, in providing safety and basic public services as well as protecting the environment. Legislation and on-going initiatives are also promising. Implementation, however, has been a problem.

Why? The LGAF pilot program has shined a bright light on a number of answers to why Peru is still struggling with land rights issues. Against the measure of LGAF indicators, a number of striking shortcomings in existing law emerge; suggesting that in many areas Peru has been developing so fast that the legal system, despite its recent reforms, has been unable to keep up. And while government agencies can point to impressive land governance successes in urban and rural areas throughout Peru, there are plenty of problems, on-going conflicts, and potential crises that have not received enough attention.

One of the LGAF pilot's clearest findings is that Peru's land rights reform efforts as well as the nation's economic prospects in the near future would benefit significantly from having an LGAF solidly in place—alerting government and independent experts of the aspects of land governance that are working, those that aren't, and where the ticking time bombs are hidden.

Peru is now an astonishingly dynamic society, and rapid changes no matter their blessings are bound to bring unintended consequences. The country's high level of urbanization and entrepreneurial activity in the cities coupled with agricultural innovations and the flight of international investors to Peruvian commodities have made Peru increasingly attractive to local and foreign investors—in several development sectors:

- Urban Construction: The massive growth of informal human settlements and urbanization that shaped the growth of Peru's major cities since the 1960's has been overshadowed by the current boom in the formal construction sector. Promoted by State-driven finance and private sector builders, this surge in legal building is driving job creation and economic growth, while spawning a new middle class. In the face of these rapid socio-economic changes, the hierarchy of articulated planning instruments for organizing and controlling development has been quickly outdated. Worse still, the best land governance plans are limited to the nation's largest cities—and in only a handful of affluent municipalities. In Lima, for example, home to one third of Peru's total population, the development plan on the books dates back to 1992, and is updated only in an *ad hoc* manner and mainly in reaction to economic and political pressures.

- Non-traditional Agriculture: Peru is now the world's number one exporter of asparagus—beating out in recent years such formidable competitors as China and the United States, thanks to strong public-private alliances and leadership. Major investment projects are also underway for expanding the agricultural frontier along the coast through irrigation and private initiatives to use desert land to produce bio-fuels.

- Mining in the Andean Sierra: Rich in such commodities as gold, copper, and zinc, the area has attracted intense outside investment that has emerged as a major and sustained driver of Peru's economic growth. This success, however, is also a new source of conflict in Peru, between the peasant communities of the Andes and eager investors.

- Valuable natural resources in the Peruvian Amazon: Vast forests of potential lumber, gas reserves, areas of land with potential to develop agro-industrial crops, bio-fuels, and "environmental services" (e.g. organic produce, eco-certified wood, and eco-tourism), have earned the attention of international investors eager to take advantage of Peru's Free Trade Agreements. Lack of consultation with native Amazonian communities ignited violence, which only further polarized the discussion about the use of natural resources, an issue that must eventually be resolved fairly and objectively.

Economic progress has obvious benefits and hidden challenges. Twenty years ago, one of Peru's main economic and legal challenges was to formalize the property held in the nation's growing shadow economy. Thanks to a strong formalization effort based on well designed institutional reforms that took into account socially accepted practices, today the nation's growth is taking place in the formal economy—with its own challenges: urban areas are growing, but not all have adequate regulations and controls for containing sprawl and collecting taxes; new Free Trade Agreements and international investor upgrades provide opportunities for Peruvian companies to profit and politicians to take a bow, but they also bring new competition for the nation's resources—and new risks for social conflict. Private and multinational investors may be eager to invest in mines in the Andes or benefit from the natural gas reserves in the Peruvian Amazon, but local indigenous groups are demanding their share, too. Last June, 39 Peruvians died in a clash in the jungle between indigenous groups and the national police over property rights and the presence of investors perceived as unilaterally encouraged by the government to take advantage of provisions in the US-Peru Free Trade Agreement.

How to deal with all these different conflicts is a puzzle that is not easily solved. Indeed, their very nature is not always clear. Are the current conflicts confronting private investors and local communities about merely enforcing already recognized rights, or are new land tenure categories emerging that are not easily captured by the legal system? Past formalization efforts in the Andes and Amazon, for example, established a number of tenure typologies and then created a legal framework to cover them. Peru, however, has an estimated 1,400 indigenous communities, and it is not unusual for a mining or lumber company to enter into a remote area with the Government's blessing —and run into a group of people who claim that their land has been illegally invaded. In some cases, these people may actually be part of a traditional community whose boundaries have not being clearly defined; a natural growth of an existing community eager to establish new settlement or migrants from the Andes—not recognized as a legitimate land tenure group in the Amazon—looking for opportunities.

How do you tell if they are genuine legal parties to a dispute? How do you anticipate their arrival? How does the government or investor deal with this problem or anticipate it? The LGAF pilot program in Peru made it clear that the *status quo* cannot answer these questions. And that is why if LGAF didn't exist, we Peruvians would have to invent it to deal with our current land governance challenges.

What the LGAF pilot in Peru found was clear to all stakeholders in the land sector: the lack of a unified vision regarding land issues. The efforts of the many different government agencies—including a myriad of central government agencies, 28 regional governments, plus 194 provincial municipalities and 1,834 district municipalities throughout the country—are not articulated; worse still, their many different agendas often times end up in conflict. This study also reveals that there is a lack of strong, accountable, and transparent land administration agencies to make sure that the good intentions of law are implemented.

In short, we found that while there are many good and progressive laws related to land issues, there is no overall guiding policy vision that can deal with the current conflicts on the Government's plate, never mind the problems that are not yet agency priorities or the ones that might pop up seemingly out of nowhere in the future. A land sector vision could guide policy in a way that cuts across institutional silos. With such a vision, the different agencies dealing with land and natural resources could establish priority actions together with quantitative measures that can be monitored and used to establish outcomes that can be assessed to hold institutions accountable.

We have concluded that the kind of objective indicators generated by an established LGAF could be a very powerful tool to identify sectors of population that are not yet recognized and protected by the law; verify whether policy objectives are being seriously pursued; and transcend the very distinct viewpoints on all sides of these issues now fueled largely by ideology rather than practical or objective measures.

The LGAF indicators do not have the power to bring vision to narrow-minded politicians or private players guided only by dollar signs. What they can achieve, however, is an understanding of the problems and a set of goals based on objective data and other information that all sides can agree upon, no matter their political agenda. Too often, government officials and various stakeholders try to solve land issues through the prism of their own ideologies—so disparate that they cannot even agree on the problem, never mind the solution. One side, for example, is eager to build more housing, to develop the local economy, or to mine valuable commodities, while the other points to the importance of preserving the cultural identities of indigenous peoples or the environmental impacts of increased deforestation, population density, and transportation.

The LGAF tools sidestep such dilemmas by capturing the facts of the situation and the attendant data so that all sides can see the (objective) problem and then begin thinking about the (objective) solution. Policy ideas and recommendations will emerge from the facts and data, not from the political or economic biases of the parties involved. New solutions—with appropriate safeguards—can emerge from a new agenda based on a new understanding of the problem; all generated by a good-faith interpretation of the LGAF indicators.

The LGAF-Peru Process: The Challenges of Getting the Right Experts and Data

The main mechanism to score the dimensions of each of the indicators was the opinion of experts from government, academia, NGOs and industry who met in a series of seven separate panels convened in Lima. Finding the right people willing to share their time and expertise to work toward an objective consensus regarding Peru's land rights problems generated from the LGAF indicators was no easy task.

The process began with a preparation phase to ensure that participants had a common understanding of the issues and were familiar with the available legal and statistical data. Crucial to facilitating and informing the discussions regarding the

LGAF indicators was the challenge of identifying the relevant stakeholders and building institutional networks of experts from different levels of government (national, regional, and local), NGOs, and academia. The success—and objectivity—of the indicators depended on finding experts who brought their technical expertise (and not their politics) to the panel discussion. The process required semi-structured interviews with private practitioners and government officials, along with a comprehensive review of the secondary literature that provided grist for a "context document" prepared for the panel participants.

Given that the LGAF indicators have been designed to apply to countries with very different historic, socio-economic, and legal land tenure traditions, shaping the indicators to the Peruvian reality involved more than translating them into Spanish. There was a constant effort to identify the relevance of each indicator to the land rights situation in Peru; for certain indicators, the panel had to interpret them in the Peruvian context to make the discussion significant.

Some LGAF components suggest a general valuation based on the quality of the law or on a score of certain organizations' performance (e.g. generally or generally audited). For other dimensions, ranking requires a quantitative estimate (e.g. more than 70 percent of properties formally titled or registered). In most cases, each dimension of the indicators was given a score, open to verification and monitoring. In a limited number of cases, the panel members decided not to give a ranking because in the Peruvian context, such a score would be arbitrary: For example, the panel passed on setting a figure for how expensive individual formalization was because costs were different depending on whether formalization was in the urban or rural sector, whether it was judicial or administrative. It was not even possible to come up with an "average cost": in jungle areas, the size of the parcel would be different than in a coastal area. The panel decided that whatever number they chose would be arbitrary; instead, they proposed that the best strategy for comparative purposes was to use an average parcel size.

During panel sessions, participants were asked to agree not just on the applicable rankings but also provide hard evidence for them—i.e. available statistics, official reports, or trustworthy unofficial studies that would make it possible to audit and monitor the scores over time. During panel sessions, participants often pointed to new sources for information or offered complementary data compiled by their own organizations.

After the panels, there was a data compilation phase: *aide de memoires* were prepared and circulated to each panel member to confirm accuracy, collect further comments, and follow up on data offered or pointed to during the discussions. To facilitate feedback, individual meetings with participants were also held. In addition, field trips for the pilot study were organized in Lima, Chiclayo, and Cusco, including surveys and semi-structured interviews that covered four areas: updating property registries, local government enforcement of land use regulations, property tax collection procedures, and dispute resolution mechanisms.[20]

One important lesson from the pilot was the significant variation in the field samplings. For example, the survey to assess how up to date registration files were entailed contrasting actual registration files with the situation on the ground. Although registration files for dispersed properties are easily obtainable in Peru, the cadastral maps that make it possible to actually find those properties are still incomplete—thus biasing the pilot sample. Similarly, there were inevitable variations in the survey's sample of judges: urban courts handled property conflicts resulting from population density, while property and boundary conflicts predominated in rural courts. The rural-urban divide also affected the sample of municipal governments, revealing significant differences in land planning and taxation.

One clear conclusion emerged from the pilot process. The type of data required for significant monitoring of the indicators should come from administrative data regularly collected by or reported to government agencies rather than the kind of sporadic, *ad hoc*, underfinanced field samplings collected in this pilot study. In fact, the ideal would be to collect data in an on-going fashion, fed from existing agencies and NGOs regularly collecting land rights related information as a result of their own specialized work.

Indentifying and engaging the right group of experts for the panels—to participate in a technical discussion rather than foment political debate—also poses a formidable challenge. The experts with the kind of in-depth operational knowledge crucial to the survey's success are top technicians and practitioners, those who "know things because they do things." As "the experts in their respective fields", they are, by definition, scarce, with limited time to spend on a temporary project like the LGAF pilot in Peru. Equally challenging is creating the conditions for a forum of experts to reach a consensus on real situations where the evidence is not always comfortable. There is also the problem that government agencies tend to be run by politicians hesitant to commit to a study that might end up questioning their competence. They have to be convinced that the process will find ways to make their agencies more successful in the long run. They also have to be persuaded to free up their best *technical* people to participate in the panels, those dealing day-to-day with the data or know the person in an obscure office who is collecting it.

The guiding focus for these panels must be on the technical issues at hand. The goal should be to create a picture of the problem that everyone in the room can agree with, in order to move towards a consensus on what an equally objective solution might look like.

Key Results

Legal and Institutional Framework

The LGAF contains six indicators broken down into 24 sub-indicators or "dimensions" to measure the extent to which land tenure rights are recognized in the text of the law and how they are implemented in practice (LGI-1, 2 and 3); the legal restrictions on land use, ownership or transferability (LGI-4); the clarity in the distribution of institutional mandates among land administration agencies (LGI-5); and citizen participation and equity considerations in land policies (LGI-6).

Recognition and enforcement of rights (based on LGI-1, LGI-2 and LGI-3)

Two panels were convened to focus separately on urban and rural land tenure issues. Both panels agreed that Peruvian law grants extensive recognition of property rights for the most relevant tenure typologies, including individual and group rights. In urban areas, the law explicitly recognizes squatter settlements, housing associations and cooperatives that bought agricultural land legally but developed it without complying with urban regulations, as well as informal land development in traditional unplanned towns (*pueblos tradicionales*). The law for rural areas recognizes peasant farming communities (in the Andes mountains) and native indigenous communities (in the Amazon region); and the regulatory framework includes clear provisions that govern the communities' internal organization and representativeness before the law. In all cases, Peruvian law is significantly advanced in recognizing the equal rights of women.

This expanded legal framework regarding property rights has materialized to a large extent from the Peruvian State's active efforts to formalize property through a number of programs over the last two decades. Key to this success is that the legal framework accepts non-documentary evidence to acknowledge rights based on local practices, as well as economies of scale accomplished through mass formalization campaigns organized routinely and free of charge. On the demand side, close to 70 percent of individual property in urban and rural areas has been granted ownership titles. Property titles have been granted in 5,000 out of 6,000 existing peasant farming communities covering some 23 million hectares. Out of the total of 1,510 native communities in the Peruvian Amazon, 1,260 have been provided titles to their lands.

It is important to note that unlike most of the urban beneficiaries of formalization programs, the Andean and Amazonian communities find that their property rights are still difficult to enforce because of two main reasons: lack of adequate parcel demarcation and problems of representation.

Data from COFOPRI—Peru's land formalization agency—reveals that only 1,959 Andean peasant communities (out of a total 6,000) still suffer from ill-defined boundaries, resulting from unclear, ambiguous metes and bounds descriptions without digital maps. Native communities in the Peruvian Amazon, however, pose a greater problem: only 85 out of 1,510 have official digital maps of their territories. The inability to clearly define their boundaries prevents communities from effectively exercising their rights and creates numerous conflicts with neighboring communities and with settlers (*colonos*) occupying community land. Boundary disputes have also emerged as a major source of conflict with the State over the exploitation of natural resources in the Amazon region, as recent violent episodes have proven.

Regarding representation, these communities face numerous obstacles to complying with all the formal requirements established by law to appoint representatives and enforce their agreements. Without proper representation, the communities' relations with the State are limited. In fact, this is a major hurdle to completing the titling of the rest of the communities—as well as an impediment for negotiating rights of way with private operators who need to transport materials across native lands, build roads, enter into other business arrangements, or develop natural resources through concessions granted by the State. Private sector actors often complain that. "We don't know who to talk to." As a result, uncertainty created by opportunistic behavior is very frequent. This issue also affects the ability of communities to decide on their own if their members can hold individual properties. Although legal provisions set forth clear rules to prevent fraud and ensure transparent decision making over such fundamental issues as disposing of community land, in practice these rules are hard to enforce and often just ignored.

Another problem regarding recognition of group rights is the fact that mass-scale land regularization efforts—successful as they generally have been—have become an open-ended process that is undercutting their main objective, which is getting people into the legal system. On the urban side, new informal settlements appear over time, and governments have historically extended the deadline for recognizing new groups in order to add them to the formalization roster. On the rural side, the priority put on formalization of individual rights and the decades long delay in formalizing the land rights of Andean and Amazonian communities are creating acute problems: demographic growth and the pressure for the use of resources is generating new indigenous groups struggling for recognition. Some are the new generations of "comuneros" who migrate and settle in unoccupied areas, while others are urban migrants looking for opportunities. To make things even more complex, some others are groups organized by speculators and are "planted" in areas where the State has plans for investment projects or where private investors have been granted concessionary rights; large companies and ambitious local entrepreneurs have been known to "plant" settlers in a concerted strategy to deforest the area and then seek adjudication to declare it valuable agricultural land.

The result is an increase in conflicts in areas with abundant forests and other natural resources that attract mining, drilling, cutting, and bio-fuel production. How should the law deal with this? Should these new groups be given the same status as traditional Andean and Amazonian communities—ignoring the fact that they do not originate ethnically from this area or have the same traditional ties to land? And while in the eyes of an anthropologist, a group of *colonos* is not technically a traditional community; from the land policy perspective these new communities that pop up in the region pose a significant legal challenge.

Restrictions on Land Rights (Based on LGI-4)

Both panels also agreed that Peruvian law places few restrictions on land ownership and conveyance. The 1993 Constitution enshrined free ownership and cancelled existing barriers to ownership imposed by the 1960's and 1970's agrarian reform, such as the ban on corporate land ownership, plot size limits and prohibition of certain types of land-related contracts. The Constitution also established the rural land policy objective to increase productivity by creating a free market in land and suppressing restrictions on ownership.

Nevertheless, a number of regulations exist for using property, based on common interest principles. In urban areas the main restrictions include zoning and urban development regulations; in rural areas, there are regulations dealing with natural protected areas, reserve zones and forest areas. Throughout Peru, there are also regulations to protect the nation's historical or archaeological heritage.

The panels agreed that these regulations, although clearly defined, are not enforced with standard criteria and are too often left to the discretion of the respective government oversight agency. Few local governments have the institutional capacity to prepare and approve urban development plans or effectively monitor compliance with urban land use regulations. Nor does the National Institute of Culture (INC) have a cadastre of the historical or archaeological areas, which is bound to limit its ability to ensure the protection of heritage land. To ensure compliance, urban land use changes and building permits require the INC's prior review. However, according to interviews with investors, such oversight is effective only for formal building projects that are not the rule in the cities. Similarly, the National Protected Areas Service (SERNANP), responsible for overseeing officially protected zones of Peru, such as national parks and natural protected areas, suffers from insufficient funding and trying to deal with forest areas that are not properly demarcated.

Clarity of Institutional Mandates (Based on LGI-5); Participation and Equity in Land Policies (Based on LGI-6)

We found that the institutional mandates on land administration in Peru are relatively clear. However, although the mandated responsibilities of the various authorities dealing with land administration issues are defined with a limited amount of horizontal overlap (i.e. with those of other land sector agencies) and vertical overlap (i.e. among different levels of government), there remain problems at the implementation level.

Peru's transition to decentralization partly explains the vertical function overlaps. A complex distribution of roles among levels of government (central, regional, provincial and district), legal voids and poor technical skills in decentralized government agencies are a source of conflict among the agencies and confusion for citizens. Interviews with public officials and private investors revealed, for example, that regional governments often decline making decisions or refer to the central public land management authority regarding issues that have already been transferred to their purview. Competition among agencies for scarce resources or turf wars among various political players further aggravates the transition process towards effective decentralization. In an effort to create a standardized, national mechanism whereby local governments could all issue the same kind of permits, the central government passed a regulation establishing a hierarchy of territorial plans to set the rules and limits for urban land. Soon thereafter, Lima's Metropolitan Municipality, invoking its autonomy to regulate territory planning, issued another regulation introducing specific rules within its jurisdiction, thus disregarding national law. Our interviews with experts include other examples of how district governments similarly ignore land use changes decided by their provincial authorities, along with cases of the central government itself developing housing projects with total disregard for the regulatory powers of a given municipality.

The panels also noted that land policy-making in Peru is not systematic. Policies may spring from a presidential statement, as was the case in 2007 when President Alan Garcia published a controversial article in Peru's most respected daily newspaper charging that the country had too many resources "that are unable to be transferred, cannot receive investment and do not generate jobs."[21] The President proceeded to denounce the fact that huge tracks of the territory in the Peruvian jungle and the Andes belonging to indigenous communities remained dormant and non-productive.

Garcia's vision later was followed by a number of Legislative Decrees establishing mechanisms to promote better use of natural resources—forest, mining and hydrocarbons—through private investment. Not surprisingly, this initiative sparked a highly politicized national debate, massive demonstrations, violent conflict between indigenous communities and the police that soon forced the Garcia Government to abrogate the laws.

In other cases, the land policies are included in legal provisions governing specific land administration areas. For example, the Land Law (Law 26505) and urban and rural property formalization regulations (Legislative Decrees 667 and 803) explicitly set forth public-policy objectives, create the corresponding stewardship entities, declare the reasons behind their decisions, and set the expected outcomes. In other cases, isolated land policy components appear in ministries' plans. For instance, the Ministry of Housing[22] and the Ministry of Agriculture[23] have published their multi-annual plans, including an explicit diagnosis, expected outcomes, and the means to accomplish them. However, in neither case is it clear to what extent citizens were involved in preparing those policies or if indicators were monitored.

We also found that although government agencies regularly publish their progress reports and are subject to transparency regulations, their accomplishments are not measured against a baseline, do not include key performance indicators, or follow pre-established reporting and accountability schemes. In many instances, although such information has been collected and registered, it is not available to the public.

In Peru, equity is on the agenda of several land administration organizations. In fact, formalization rules grant direct benefits and free services to residents in urban and peasant settlements, as well as to Andean peasant farmers and to native communities in the Amazon. However, the lack of coherent policies—largely because of the actions of State agencies—has made these equity goals unsustainable over time. For example, the very modern services offered by the property registry are not accessible to many beneficiaries of formalization programs who in fact are stepping back to informality.

Land Use Planning, Management and Taxation

Land Use Planning and Exceptions from Land Use Restrictions (Based on LGI-7, LGI-8 and LGI-9)

Regulations dealing with land planning establish the need to have planning tools at central, regional, provincial and district government levels, and for appropriate coordination that will ensure the orderly occupation and sustainable use of available resources. Consequently, district-level plans must comply with provincial plan provisions that are, in turn, governed by regional and finally national plans.

According to Peruvian law, such plans should be drafted involving public participation. In practice, however, such coordination is not enforced. We found that in the four major cities in the country, while a hierarchy of regional/detailed land use plans is specified by law, in practice urban development occurs in an *ad hoc* manner with infrastructure provided some time after urbanization.

Interviews with municipal urban planning officials in 13 municipalities in Lima, Chiclayo and Cusco revealed that provincial plans are outdated, while regional-level plans are typically too general. Experts consulted during the pilot study revealed that apart from a handful of district municipalities in Lima (dubbed by urban planners as "the five ladies," referring to their well-heeled residents) and a few more in the provinces, updated development plans are either largely non-existent or outdated. The inevitable result is that land use changes, zoning and building licenses are made on an arbitrary basis, with regulatory gaps that provide ample room for official discretion in decision-making.

In fact, by looking at Peru through the prism of urban planning you see an upside-down picture of the country. In high-income districts, strict building controls and municipal oversight are hard to evade. In low-income districts, controls are almost universally absent, and buildings are constructed without the required permits. The result is that Peruvian cities have sprawled every which way, without regard for existing plans and with very little oversight. Although such chaotic growth has permitted Peru's poor to have a home, it has also created major problems for supplying public services, as well as degrading the soil and the environment, populating hazardous areas, etc.

According to interviewees, the causes for this disconnect between the law and reality are exponential urban growth in recent years and the inability of existing tools and institutions to anticipate unforeseen circumstances; disjointed interventions by government and private land-related organizations (providers of public services, housing, property regularization and registration, etc.); and the lack of national policies with a comprehensive view of land use.

Transparency and Efficiency in the Collection of Land / Property Taxes (based on LGI-10 and LGI-11)

Property taxes are the only means available in Peru to capture surplus from increased land value. According to the panel convened to discuss tax issues, clear regulations distribute fiscal functions between the central and local governments, identify taxpayers accurately, and lay down the mechanisms to compute the amount of property taxes they owe.

Although the property tax value mechanism is updated regularly, the way it is calculated does not reflect the true value of a given property for two reasons: 1) components of the formula used to calculate a building's value do not match market values but respond to political criteria; and 2) no consideration is given to the building's economic use, and thus a private house may be levied a higher tax than a similar property used for commercial purposes.

In principle, the regulation determines the property tax to be paid. In practice, however, municipalities fix the fee schedules. The average Peruvian taxpayer hardly has access to the official gazette where property tax schedules are published. Further, most taxpayers, particularly in rural areas, cannot afford the cost of traveling to the municipal office to check on their tax bill.

Regulations also include a number of tax breaks, some "subjective" (relating to the owners' status, such as pensioners and retirees), while others are "objective" (relating to the status of the properties, part of a forest concession, for example). Overall, these exemptions are coherent, based on legal principles of equity and efficiency. Nonetheless, panel experts considered them excessive and, in many cases, unnecessary.

Actual tax collection is much lower than potential tax revenues because 95 percent of Peru's 1,834 municipalities lack a cadastre to manage collections;[24] and municipalities do not enforce collections and payments – usually because they lack the resources to enforce collection of back taxes (some municipalities even lack resources to collect the taxes). Because poor municipalities provide very few services to their citizens, they cannot justify the taxes they may charge. In some areas, community pressure is very strong and impedes local governments from enforcing legal collections.

Management of Public Land

Justification of Public Land Ownership and Management Clarity (Based on LGI-12 and Justification and Transparency of Public Land Transfers (Based on LGI-15

According to the LGAF, State ownership of land is warranted by the cost-efficient provision of public goods. Therefore, it is important to understand how the Peruvian system governing State-owned goods functions.

In Peru, "State goods" can be classified as such in both the public and private domains. Public domain goods may be used by all citizens without restriction, such as beaches, squares, and parks;[25] they cannot be transferred to private individuals or be acquired through adverse possession schemes. The State's private domain goods are those that remain State property, but are not for public use (arid wasteland, real estate belonging to Ministries, land confiscated from drug traffickers). For this reason, the corresponding managing body holds all ownership rights over those goods, including the option to convey them to private individuals. A rule characteristic of the Peruvian State-owned goods system is that properties over which there are no impending private, peasant or native community rights fall under the State's domain,[26] making the State the default owner of vast undefined portions of the territory.

The LGAF revealed that management of State-owned goods in Peru is distributed across a number of bodies under the National State-owned Goods System (*Sistema Nacional de Bienes Estatales*), which is comprised principally of the branches of the National government (executive, legislative and judicial, along with independent government agencies) and the regional and local governments. The entire system is governed by the National Superintendent of State Owned Goods (*Superintendencia Nacional de Bienes Estatales(SBN)*), charged with issuing the corresponding regulations and overseeing the purchases of State-owned goods, as well as issuing rights of various types (rentals, sales, etc.) on behalf of private citizens.[27]

Peru's constitution enshrines the State's role as guarantor of private initiatives, and gives the important economic role of promoting job creation, health, education, security, public services and infrastructure. This principle is reflected in State policies aimed at deregulating the land market, enforcing individual titling programs (without prejudice to community-based property ownership arrangements), as well as laws regulating and sponsoring transfer of public domain property to private citizens.

The panel concluded that public land is generally divested at market prices in a transparent process irrespective of the investor's status (e.g. domestic or foreign). As a rule, the State's private domain land transfers must take place in a public auction with the property's commercial value as the benchmark price.[28] The law requires buyers to pay for the title in advance; ensuring that the total payment of most auctioned properties is effectively collected.

Against this background, is State property in Peru meeting the LGAF guideline of being justified by the cost-effective supply of public goods? The local government's management of parks and squares is fully justified, as is the protection of the national coastline by central government entities, such as the Coastguard Service. Nevertheless, effective management is hampered by weak land sector institutions. Not infrequently, riverbanks, areas reserved for parks or the buffer zones for natural areas are occupied by squatters or put to alternative uses. And though responsibilities for State-owned goods are distributed among several government levels, and there has been significant progress in setting up a system for their effective management, there is still much to be done. Experts pointed to insufficient resources and lack of a thorough inventory of State-owned goods.

Over time, the SBN has built experience and trained skilled staff, but it still lacks sufficient resources to perform its oversight role. In addition, devolution of land management to regional governments is in an early stage. At this writing, only one regional government had received those rights. Both regional and local governments lack the funding to effectively manage their lands, while officials have only limited technical skills to do so. In most cases, regional and local government officials are not even aware of the regulations governing the management of State-owned property, leading to inefficiencies and increasing the risks of too much discretion beyond SBN's oversight.

According to the panel, less than 30 percent of public land is clearly identified on the ground or on maps. Peru's State-owned goods inventory (*Sistema Nacional de Bienes del Estado (SINABIP)*) has been designed as a SBN database to facilitate managing State-owned goods. However, progress has been slow and the rule establishing the State's property "by default" makes it impossible to ascertain with any accuracy the percentage of State properties that have not been registered. To the extent that the universe of State property remains largely unknown, it is not possible to determine the registration backlog. Clear rules mandate agencies charged with managing State-owned property to complete such an inventory. Despite regulations enacted in 2001 to title unregistered State-owned properties and SBN's efforts to fulfill its mandate, Peru is still far from the goal of a complete inventory of property.

In Peru, the key information regarding land concessions (i.e. the locality and area of the concession, the parties involved, and the financial terms of the concession) is recorded and publicly available. Peruvian regulations provide for transparency and public access to any information flowing from government agencies.

Renewable natural resources (e.g. forests) and non-renewable resources (minerals and hydrocarbons, for example) are legally considered part of the national patrimony and can be developed through concessions awarded by the State. Owners of the surface property cannot freely dispose of natural resources on or under it, and must accept development by those who hold the concession and negotiate compensation for the use of the surface land.

Justification and Fairness of Expropriation Procedures (Based on LGI-13 and LGI-14)

Expropriations in Peru are warranted only for the public benefit. Constitutional rules have set forth a number of mechanisms to guarantee private ownership and prevent government from abusing its expropriation powers:[29] Expropriations can only be carried out for reasons of national security or public need (e.g. expropriating lands to build a road or bridge). Peru's 1990 Constitution explicitly removed the "social interest" rationale from the previous Constitution that had been used to justify land reform expropriations during the Agrarian Reforms of the 1960s and 70s.

Expropriations must be authorized by Congress in a law explicitly spelling out the future use of the expropriated good, thus ensuring public scrutiny and debate of individual expropriations. Moreover, the expropriations law expressly mentions that expropriations are not valid when the State is not the direct beneficiary.

Expropriated owners have the right to a cash payment reflecting the good's market value, in addition to remediation for the damage suffered. To ensure impartiality, the value of the property is assessed in a court proceeding.

Expropriations must meet certain mandatory deadlines: They will expire if the process before the Judiciary has not started within six months of the expropriation's approval, or if the court proceedings last longer than two years. In addition, the property will revert to its owner if the expropriated good has not been used for the planned purpose within one year of the court's proceedings.

Information obtained by the panel members—and supported by the analysis of six dockets during the LGAF survey—reveals that the above rules have actually been enforced on the ground.

However, a recent law[30] declared that the expropriation of private land squatted on before December 2005 is for public need (e.g. to build a road or bridge). This law has stirred up much debate and criticism against the government, because, contrary to prevailing interpretations, the concept of "public need" has been stretched to include specific groups of citizens as beneficiaries, in this case private land squatters.

Existing regulations set forth a number of measures to limit the scope of the law. Only "consolidated" settlements are embraced by these regulations, and expropriations are warranted only when all other ways to solve the problem have been exhausted. Moreover, explicit mechanisms are set forth to ensure payments. Critics pointed out that "locks" to prevent abuse do not guarantee enforcement free of political motivations: enforcement is in the hands of government officials susceptible to pressure from the Executive Branch.

As of this writing, not one single expropriation has been carried out by invoking this law.

As noted above, the expropriation proceedings must meet certain payment deadlines and assessment criteria. The law authorizes property transfers through a direct deal with owners, a frequent scheme used in infrastructure projects to speed up remedy. Payments at market value do not guarantee the injured parties can be restored to their condition before the expropriation. In the case of road building projects, for instance, the commercial value of a rural house is frequently very low, and the remedy payment to the owners will not allow them to build a similar house.

By law, only registered owners or occupants recognized by a competent authority can be paid remediation. However, to prevent delays, road building companies negotiate with and pay to non-eligible occupants who may have no right to such legal compensation.

Informal land appropriation and scarce capacities among State-property management bodies thus hamper land titling and significantly increase costs to public land franchisees. Another frequent practice is speculation by squatters who invade

State-owned land targeted for development in the expectation they will be paid by those who will eventually gain the concessions to State land.

Public Provision of Land Information

Reliability of Land Registries (Based on LGI-16 and LGI-17)

The National Public Registry Superintendent (SUNARP) is comprised of several registries created by law,[31] one of which is the Property Registry (*Registro de Predios* (RP)). Since its inception in 1994, SUNARP has consistently worked to modernize its infrastructure, introducing new technology and improving customer service.

The LGAF has indicated that copies or extracts of documents recording rights in property can generally be obtained within one week of the request. New technologies have been introduced to automate internal processes, thanks to computer systems, digital registry files, and online customer service. Registration offices ensure that deadlines and service quality targets are met. As a result of these improvements, records are provided with very short delays or even online.

Panel experts found that published service standards were significant, and the registry actively monitors its performance against these standards. Nevertheless, according to interviews with users, registration procedures (i.e. applications for registering a purchased property, subdivision, mortgage, etc.) are still slow and troublesome. Applications are often turned down, and it is not easy for users to anticipate the outcome of the registrars' assessments. This happens primarily because large city registration offices are understaffed. Heavy workloads prevent meeting deadlines.[32] A secondary cause is the complexity of regulations governing transactions, which results in cumbersome and poorly compiled property registration dockets. And because of the complexity and wide scope of the required tasks, registrars never acquire expertise in all areas, and many do a poor, protracted, and inefficient job of assessing files.

An important consideration for establishing a registry's reliability is the quality of the information provided about a registered property's physical features. In Peru, registry information is parcel based; property information can be retrieved only if you have the owner's name or docket number.[33] Figures obtained during the study show that out of eight million properties in the Property Registry, only 43 percent can be identified on a map, because traditionally Peru's registration system was not attached to a cadastre. Maps were added to the system as a result of the massive scale of property formalization programs begun in 1990. Lack of a cadastre base for most registration dockets creates frequent rights' overlap issues. As a result, uncertainty about the physical match of property rights leads to frequent boundary conflicts, particularly in rural and peri-urban areas, thus increasing transaction costs and impairing the public perception of the security of the Registry.

To tackle this issue, SUNARP has set up cadastre units specifically devoted to checking rights overlaps. The cadastre offices are currently preparing a mosaic of existing registration dockets for which no maps are available. To prepare this mosaic, a specialist draws a polygon based on the actual recorded descriptions (metes and bounds) in property titles. Then the draft is digitalized and linked, to the extent possible, to known physical landmarks. Because text descriptions were not drafted with measurements, the mosaic reflects the "legal truth" of registrations but does not necessarily match what may be found on the ground. At this writing, SUNARP's mosaic covered 50 percent of the country.

LGAF also suggests assessing a registry's reliability by determining if restrictions to property transactions emanating from contract terms or government provisions are public. The panel established that relevant public restrictions or charges are recorded consistently and in a reliable fashion but the cost of accessing them is high. Most liens and encumbrances on private property must be registered before the title holder can claim them against third parties. To the extent registries are open to the public, users have easy access to encumbrance-related information. Nevertheless, Peruvian courts have decided users should not only check registration records but also the title deeds supporting them.[34] Such in-depth property title scrutiny significantly increases the costs to users who wish to ascertain a property's encumbrances.

However, limits to property disposal imposed by public entities—the National Institute of Culture (INC), Peru's watchdog for protection of the nation's historical heritage, or the National Natural Protected Areas Service (SERNANP) charged with preserving the environment—need not be registered in the Property Registry to be enforced. As a consequence, citizens and investors must pick up the cost of determining whether any restrictions on their potential ownership rights are in place.

The central culprit here is the lack of a network linking institutions that generate land-related information in Peru. The State agencies charged with territory stewardship would operate more efficiently if they could share a standardized cadastre base. Users would more easily identify the scope of their rights, while government agencies could save resources and benefit from information-sharing synergies. Little wonder that LGAF indicators revealed that less than 50 percent of the records for privately held land in the registry are readily identifiable in maps in the registry or cadastre.

The National Cadastre System Law (2004) deals with registry issues and established a strategy and schemes to create and preserve an updated registry cadastre that includes these links, which should enable them to standardize criteria, share information, determine the role of notaries public and private practitioners and other system players, etc. However, five years after the law was passed, no significant progress has been made, principally because of trouble involved in coordinating initiatives across organizations and insufficient technical and budget resources among local governments.

Finally, LGAF suggests assessing registration reliability by examining whether register information is regularly updated. In Peru, inscription in the Property Registry is voluntary; a rightful owner may decide not to update the property's record, without breaking the law. The result is that State bodies lack information on outdated registration. Field sampling organized in Lima, Chiclayo and Cusco revealed that 71 percent of property owners' names in the sample had been updated. In urban areas most property owners register in order to seek protection. It is worthwhile noting that 81 percent of property owners in Peru's highest socio-economic sector have updated information; while among the poorest segment of the Peruvian population, the figure is only 60 percent. If we assume that registered properties from the lowest socio-economic levels correspond to the settlements formalized by COFOPRI during the last

13 years, it is alarming that 40 percent of those recently formalized properties have already slipped back into informality.

The main reasons for such registration lags include the high cost of formalizing property transactions, registering inherited goods, subdividing properties, or building expansions to their houses. A secondary cause is the lack of a "registration culture" due to scarce information about the advantages of preserving registration and distrust of government, particularly among poor citizens. Peruvians outside of the economic mainstream have little incentive to update records and prefer to opt out of official registry schemes to protect their property.

Registry information, according to Peruvian law, is open to any citizen—without a specific statement of the reason for the request. The oversight body, SUNARP, is a modern, service-driven organization that must meet specific goals in opening access to users. In practice, however, most poor Peruvians are not aware of such registries; nor can they afford the cost of keeping their properties registered.

Efficiency and Transparency of Land Administration Services (Based on LGI-18 and LGI-19)

The LGAF indicators revealed that the cost for registering a property transfer is between 2 percent and less than 5 percent of the property value. We also found that a clear schedule of fees for different services is publicly available and receipts are issued for all transactions. SUNARP's modernization has permitted greater transparency in fees and introduced schemes to prevent corruption. Rate schedules are fixed by an official decision from SUNARP and are published at all the agency's offices. Registrars are required to explicitly account for the procedures used in setting the rates they apply to individual cases. To fight corruption, property registry office managers continuously evaluate performance and service quality. An electronic system distributes files among registrars to balance their work loads. Users cannot choose the registrar who will process their files.

A panel confirmed that while there has, in fact, been a capital investment in the system to record land rights, it is insufficient to ensure that the system is sustainable. The poor also have limited access to the recording system. SUNARP's fee-based revenues pay for its overall operation costs and leave a balance (about 25 percent of revenues) for technology research and staff training. Most decentralized offices are not financially self-sustainable and the six largest among them, located in the most densely populated cities, cross-subsidize operations in the remaining offices where small demand does not create a revenue base to pay for the facility's infrastructure. SUNARP is still unavailable in 131 provinces throughout Peru, resulting in even higher costs to users living far away from available services.[35]

The registry's long-term sustainability will depend on creating greater efficiencies so users can pay registration services and create revenue streams. LGAF features an indicator to assess the cost to register a property transfer. In Peru, cost calculations must also include the fees for the attorney and notary. If all the costs considered in the different laws are met (3 percent transfer tax, property tax, costs of lawyer, notary, surveyors, registration fees) the user should pay more than 5 percent of the property's value, excluding indirect costs, such as the opportunity cost of time used in visiting registration offices.[36]

In societies like Peru without a widespread registration culture, high cost is a major disincentive and thus a significant obstacle to accessing registration services. SUNARP's efforts to improve its services do not ensure that they will be available to all, because the cost of access is not determined only by registration rates but rather by the lack of comprehensive strategies to tackle the sources of exclusion.

Dispute Resolution and Conflict Management

Access to Conflict Resolution Mechanisms (Based on LGI-20)

According to panel experts, both formal and informal arrangements are in place in Peru to address land related conflicts. Formal justice administration is available principally in the capitals of Peru's "departamentos," the nation's primary governmental subdivisions that are home to about 50 percent of the total population. This formal system is comprised of the Judiciary, COFOPRI's Property Administrative Court, the courts of the public registries, and other government agencies charged with addressing land administration functions, such as municipalities' urban land regulatory bodies.

When formal justice is not available or when the importance of the conflict does not warrant the expense involved, other recognized and legitimate informal institutions come into play, such as the Peasant Farming and Native Indigenous Communities' Assembly, the Peasant Civil Squads (*Rondas Campesinas*), the City Civil Squads, and the "neighborhood presidents".

The LGAF confirmed that Peru has an informal or community-based system that resolves disputes in an equitable manner. Its verdicts, however, have little or no recognition in the formal judicial system. The Peruvian Constitution recognizes the right to legal pluralism. If backed by their respective citizen squads, peasant farming communities in the Andes and indigenous Amazonian communities can perform judicial functions within their respective territories, provided they are not in breach of fundamental rights and follow their customary law. As a result, crimes or faults within a community's jurisdiction may be tried in compliance with internal law; the State's courts have a mandate to acknowledge those decisions.

Nevertheless, discrimination against these "informal judiciary decisions" and refusal to recognize a separate juridical jurisdiction permeate the Peruvian Judiciary. Professional judges do not acknowledge decisions from community authorities. Worse still, because people are aware that the formal system will not typically acknowledge the community court decisions, they opt for the local Justice of the Peace or a Combined Court. When a conflict is settled in a peasant or native community, for example, and the losing party is not satisfied with the verdict, the latter may resort to the formal Judiciary, disregarding the decision of community authorities.

Efficiency of Conflict Resolution Mechanisms (Based on LGI-21)

In Peru, clear regulations are in place to determine when one should appeal to either the judiciary or an administrative system. However, errors in the way the justice system has been set up open the way for a parallel procedure. Moreover, the parties can manipulate the system to identify a judge that will best fit their interests.

The panels came up with three main factors affecting access to justice:

- Lack of a centralized information system: Court data bases do not exchange information on files, creating an opportunity for court "shopping".
- The existing justice system allows aggrieved parties to file suit in several jurisdictions simultaneously, leading to shopping for the tribunal that will best suit their interests.
- Lack of penalties imposed for malpractice sends a signal of impunity to lawyers who are not constrained to act in good faith.

Policy Conclusions and the Way Forward

An evaluation of LGAF findings shows Peruvian land management governance laws are comprehensive and generally address—within the context of Peruvian decentralization—the principles of equity, predictability, and protection of public goods. However, institutional weaknesses and lack of resources prevent fully enforcing such principles. To this we must add the lack of coordination of multiple land governance agencies that follow their own sector and local agendas and priorities.

The system thus works well for some groups of people but not for others. Formalization programs, for example, have made significant progress in awarding individual property titles, but are far behind in titling for Andean peasant and Amazon indigenous communities. Urban land planning regulations and property tax collection operate efficiently in a handful of wealthier neighborhoods, but not in most local governments. Very modern property registry services are available in provincial capitals, but are unknown to the neediest citizens, who, even if they were aware of the importance of registering their property, would be unable to afford the costs.

Limited institutional capacity is linked to scarce resources. The obvious response is to increase the agencies' budgets, an option worth considering—but only if accompanied by strategies aimed at directing scarce resources to policy objectives that foster inclusion.

Specifically, the panel recommended:

- Prioritize the completion of mass-scale formalization in both urban and rural areas.
  - For urban areas it is necessary to preclude government's traditional response to extend the deadlines for formalization: Delay will only create incentives for new invasions. Encouraging new housing strategies for the neediest Peruvians seems a more efficient—and peaceful—way to provide adequate, safe housing to the poor.
  - In rural areas, to fulfill the promise of recognizing the tenure rights of Andean peasant and Amazonian native communities is a sine qua non to clearly defining the boundaries of their territories. To this end, it is important to ascertain whether the existing land tenure typologies are sufficient to capture the dynamic realities of the rural areas. If not, new typologies must be devised.
- Create within COFOPRI, Peru's formalization agency, in coordination with local governments, indicators about the remaining formalization demands according to land tenure type, and then monitor progress over time.

- Encourage the design of land use planning tools at the provincial level, and include specific criteria and provisions in provincial plans to streamline district-level government decision-making on land use within their respective jurisdictions.
- Design strategies for poor municipalities to build property tax collection capacities, including mechanisms to link the devolution of central government's role to provincial and local services that legitimize tax collection, update land assessment, and provide tax breaks to poor households.
- Include measures to reward regional governments that have made progress in improving property in the State-owned inventory where the government is in the process of handing over the land management role to regional authorities.
- Design strategies to encourage the poor to register their property. Such strategies could combine a reduction of transaction costs along with the standardization of assessment of registration by registrars.
- Provide new momentum for the National Cadastral System and strengthen its links to the Property Registry.
- Encourage the comprehensive land policy component of the property rights consolidation project funded by the World Bank.

The key to creating an equitable, inclusive land rights system in Peru that would promote economic development and sustainable use of resources is designing land policies that coordinate efforts by the land governance agencies in various government areas and levels. Such efforts should involve not only central, regional, and local government agencies in the definition of their policy priorities, but also the other actors such professional associations, civil society organizations, and academia. A shared vision of policy priorities should pave the way for more mutually supportive interventions and more efficient investment.

Is it possible to develop a land sector policy agenda articulating disparate—and often times competing—interests in such contentious issues as use of land and natural resources? Well, a good starting point would be having facts and needs objectively ascertained. A true democratic consensus will only emerge from an open discussion where vague perceptions and ideologies do not blind the debate.

An important outcome of this study is the realization that a community of actors with various points of view and often times disagreeing in their visions of what is relevant or a priority can share a panel discussion in order to contribute to improving land governance. Although this pilot study tested the applicability of LGAF tools, and limited resources have prevented providing more accurate indicators and restricted the study's geographic scope, it has nonetheless created a valuable information and experience base on which to build.

An institutionalized LGAF survey has the potential to bring together a wide range of government and private professionals, entrepreneurs, academics, NGOs and other civil society organizations. The strategy to institutionalize the LGAF would entail presenting the study to official representatives of participating organizations; organizing a public dissemination and debate event to obtain feedback from wider audiences; and building partnerships with government agencies, NGOs, advocacy groups for minorities, and private sector organizations (chambers of construction, and other industries advocacy groups). It is hoped that this would allow willing actors to take ownership of certain indicators and regularly monitor progress. Ideally, they could draw on administrative data in line with those obtained through sampling in this exercise, and that are put together by government. They would provide supporting indicator data, deepen the analysis, and create information for regular monitoring.

7.3:   Moving from Land Titling to Land Governance: The Case of the Kyrgyz Republic

ASYL UNDELAND, Independent Consultant, Kyrgyz Republic

Introduction

There is a growing recognition that well-defined and enforceable property rights to land are important for a range of economic and social functions. To assess land governance at the country level, the World Bank has elaborated a diagnostic tool based on empirical indicators that aims to identify areas for improvement and that could be used to monitor progress in the land sector. This tool, the Land Governance Assessment Framework (LGAF), was first tested in Ethiopia, Indonesia, the Kyrgyz Republic, Peru, and Tanzania, and is currently being implemented in a number of other countries worldwide. This paper summarizes the main results obtained from the Kyrgyz pilot to illustrate the case of land governance issues that arise in a post-transition economy formerly influenced by Soviet-style land administration and which made the transition towards private ownership of land over a decade ago. Policy recommendations are derived based on the assessment. This paper also highlights some of the challenges encountered in formulating a land governance indicator, and then uses the case of the Kyrgyz Republic to analyze the results in a specific country context.

LGAF Application to the Kyrgyz Republic

Background and Rationale

The Kyrgyz Republic was chosen as a representative case to illustrate land governance issues arising in a post-transition economy that, after having been strongly influenced by Soviet-style land administration, made the transition towards private ownership of land in 1998. With low population density, communal land ownership remains widespread, and management of such lands remains a major challenge. Large sections of land continue to be held by the public sector and it is not clear how efficient this is and what may need to be done to improve efficiency. Finally, the country has implemented a major foreign funded project to improve land administration.

The transition process involved major land reforms, starting with the restructuring of large collective farms and the liquidation of the state monopoly in land ownership to address the inefficiency of big farms and the difficulties stemming from the cut in subsidies coming from Moscow. About 600 collective and state farms were dismantled and the land shares transferred to rural citizens. Given the agrarian economic structure, and predominantly rural nature of the country, the transfer of arable agricultural land into private ownership was a key step in the country's social and economic transformation. Introduction of private land ownership implied that indefinite-term use rights were converted to ownership, and public land was provided to other entities. At the same time, state land has not been completely disposed of, and the overwhelming majority of the land remains state owned. In rural areas, the most important change was the distribution of arable land, but the process remains incomplete to this day. Twenty-five percent of the land was left in state ownership in order to establish a temporary land reserve that would deal with claims arising in the transition[37] and cater to the expansion of settlements. Although the need for such a large reserve no longer exists, reserve land continues to be held in an Agricultural Land Redistribution Fund (LRF) managed by local governments and leased out (for a maximum period of 10 years) in a process that is often less than transparent and fails to provide much-needed government revenue or convey incentives for optimum use of the affected land.

In the initial stages of the land privatization process in the early 1990s, land was allocated to members of collective and state farms notionally, without giving out certificates of title or physically identifying the land plots. These allocations were converted into actual land parcels only where land was withdrawn from state control to enable the commencement of independent farming, which was also to result in the issuance of formal documentation of land ownership. In many of these cases, land titles were issued either without any description of the location of the land or with highly inaccurate descriptions of the land. While the transition from state to individual ownership is now largely complete, the efficiency and equity of the process varied widely across regions. The legal procedures and mechanisms for the individualization of land rights by those who want to exit agricultural cooperatives, peasant farms or joint stock companies are lacking.[38] Also, with mass emigration from rural areas and from the Kyrgyz Republic in general, informal land sales were frequent. These problems were addressed through a systematic land registration project, with World Bank support.

Rights Recognition, Policy and Institutional Framework

Use rights to individual parcels regardless of gender are guaranteed by law. A low-cost and far-reaching process of systematic as well as sporadic titling has covered some 80 percent of the land parcels in the country so far. A clear and practical process for the formal recognition of long-term unchallenged possession is in place and implemented effectively, consistently and transparently, with the possibility of relying on non-documentary forms of evidence where needed.[39] The Kyrgyz Republic also has laws that recognize condominium property and make appropriate arrangements for the management of common property.

Several laws aim to ensure protection of women's land rights.[40] While the registration system does not disaggregate rights holders by gender, studies show that 35 to 45 percent of land registered to individuals is in the name of women. Women's real estate ownership is higher in regions with active land markets as opposed to remote areas. In rural areas the women's rights are registered basically to agricultural land allotted during the land reform and, although legislation recognizes female rights, customary law often prevails. This implies that women rarely inherit land from their parents or spouses or retain a share of the household plot in case of divorce.

While much land is individually owned, the state remains the Kyrgyz Republic's biggest landowner. For reasons to be discussed below, state land is often under-used or not managed effectively. A total of 9 million hectares, or 85 percent of agricultural land, is devoted to pastures. Although *de jure*, rights to such land had to be allocated through competitively awarded leases, pastures near villages remained in common use while the more distant so-called intensive and remote pastures were leased out. A non-transparent process of awarding leases led to negative equity consequences whereby the best pasture land was often leased by big farmers or well-connected businessmen who then entered into sub-leases with shepherds and villagers. This implied that the majority of small livestock holders had no access to good quality pastures, prompting them to graze their animals on the communal areas in the immediate proximity of villages, leading to a dramatic degradation of this type of land. To arrest this trend, and in the context of overall decentralization, the 2009 Pasture Law replaces leases with recognition of traditional use rights to pastures and allows these to be registered at the village level, with responsibility decentralized to pasture users' associations. By transforming leases into use rights with allowance for seasonal mobility and providing for retention of revenues generated from pastures at the village level, this law is expected to mark an important step that will foster decentralization and the sustainable use of natural resources. Implementing regulations are currently being drafted.

Policy explicitly accounts for equity goals with the Land Code stipulating that every citizen has a one-time right to receive a kitchen plot or land plot for housing for free. However, this provision has had unintended consequences, and has led to large-scale squatting and internal migration. Big waves of squatting are linked to political upheavals in 1989, 1998, and 2005. This created pressure for discretionary application of formalization processes on public land.

Forest land remains under state ownership, managed by the state agency for forestry and environmental protection at the national level and by forestry enterprises at the local level. Before being transferred to the national government in 1996, forests were used and managed by collective and state farms. The Forestry Code allows farmers to obtain long-term leases (up to 50 years) of rangeland for grazing purposes from forestry enterprises (*leskhozes*). The different procedures for obtaining use rights for grazing in forests and pastures has led to confusion on the ground and corruption in forestry enterprises.

In rural areas, legal restrictions prevent non-villagers, foreigners, and legal entities from purchasing land. Ownership of agricultural land may be transferred only to residents of the same rural area and not to legal entities such as banks or foreigners. Land in settlements may be owned only by Kyrgyz natural persons or legal entities with at least 80 percent ownership by Kyrgyz persons or legal entities. In rural areas, maximum holding size is set at 50 ha or the equivalent of 20 land shares within the village, whichever is smaller. The minimum size of a holding is the share size established in each village during land privatization. Because banks cannot own agricultural land, and must dispose of any land holdings within one year or risk its transference to the government, they seldom accept land as collateral.

Major strides have been made in the decentralization process to give greater responsibility to elected bodies at the local level and to build up their capacity. The agencies responsible for managing land and enforcing restrictions are clearly identified and efficient. As a result, land set aside for specific uses is largely used for the intended purpose. Functional distribution of institutional responsibilities (agriculture, environment, urban) is reasonably clear, with the possible exception of forest pastures. To increase transparency, the government annually approves and formally publishes a report on implementation of land policy.[41] Institutions dealing with land management, however, are not appropriately staffed and funded, implying that there are only limited resources to fulfill the mandates of institutions for the management of public land.

Land Use Planning and Taxation

In light of significant urbanization and in-migration, failure to allocate any land to new individual housing in the main cities (including Bishkek) over the past five years has led to serious shortcomings in housing supply and general public dissatisfaction. Town plans are often severely outdated. The main document for town-planning is the city's general plan. In most cases, this plan dates back to Soviet times; it is based on outdated specifications and is out of touch with current realities. Although participation by the public is legally required, such rules are largely ignored in practice. This leads to a very top-down process of planning and land management that is a major source of conflict and dissatisfaction. Information on changes to land use, modifications to the general city plan, or detailed layout designs and other architectural and town-planning documents that regulate land use are not available publicly. A project to establish town-planning maps and zoning regulations was only partly successful in accomplishing these goals, since urban land use plans are only partially implemented and the planning process/authority is struggling to cope with the increasing demand for housing units and land.

Land tax rates vary depending on land use categories[42], but a failure to take into account market values makes the process arbitrary and non-transparent, while at the same time constraining budgets. Although the proportion of properties covered by the land tax is reasonably high; infrequent adjustment of rates constrains land tax revenues. The Tax Code allows local governments to vary rates only to adjust for inflation; the fact that these adjustments are undertaken in an *ad hoc* and infrequent manner limits the buoyancy of land tax revenue. Nonetheless, especially in urban areas, the rate of tax collection is high and costs reasonably low. For example, in Bishkek, close to or even more than 100 percent of planned tax collections were realized in 2007 and 2008, due to both good tax administration and the inclusion of new sources of revenue from recent developments and residential areas as well as from lessors of municipal lands. In secondary cities, revenues from tax collection are lower—the average over the past five years is 72 percent and 63 percent in Karakol and Kichi-Kemin, respectively—indicating considerable potential for higher local revenue. Furthermore, in a process that gave rise to considerable debate, land tax was recently complemented by a property tax that will become effective in 2010.

Public Land Management

According to most observers, the 25 percent of total land that is vested in the State Land Redistribution Fund (LRF) is managed in a very inefficient way, giving rise to rent seeking and corruption on a large scale. This makes the LRF one of the major sources of corruption and lost revenue opportunities in the country. By law, the maximum duration of leases for LRF land is 10 years, but in most cases, leases are much shorter and without clear procedure for renewal. This undermines incentives for long-term improvements. Legally, land from LRF should be allocated through auction with priority of land access given to women, the poor and disadvantaged groups. In practice, unclear rules for auctions, lack of transparency and local involvement have led to allocation of the best lands to local elites.

Expropriation is limited and confined to public uses, with very few cases (only two or three for the entire country) of expropriated land being transferred to private uses. The Land Code also provides for the purchase of land for public needs, requiring written agreement between authorized state body and land user/owner. Appeals processes are available if any one of the parties is dissatisfied. Compensation is fair and paid in a timely manner. Compensation must include the market price for land and structures and any losses to the owner from termination of rights. The owner has the option of requesting the allocation of a new parcel of land of equal or higher value. At the same time, only registered rights are eligible for compensation, implying that informal or secondary rights (e.g. for grazing) will not be compensated.

The Land Code requires public auctions for the disposition of public land. However, the code contains a provision that allows land to be given for free without a competitive process that is frequently misused. While the majority of urban land plots are distributed through auctions, most leases of use rights for pastures and some of the leases for LRF land have been allocated using this provision. Local registry data show that 2008 rental income from the LRF and pasture leases was 87.6 and 13.3 million soms (US $2.2 and $0.33 million), or some 68 to 70 percent of projected revenue, respectively. A key gap, and possible area for policy action, is that even though the location of public lands as well as the conditions under which they are leased is recorded, the information is not publicly available and in practice almost impossible to obtain.

Public Provision of Land Information

A cost effective process for the first-time registration of individual rights has been implemented successfully, resulting in more than 80 percent of land parcels being registered; there are plans to complete the registration of the remaining land. Relevant private encumbrances are included in the records and more than 90 percent of registry records are mapped. While access to records is limited to intermediaries with demonstrated interest, searches can be conducted without restrictions after payment of a fee. Updating of registry records is satisfactory, fee schedules as well as meaningful service standards are published, receipts are used to discourage informal payments, and the registry operates in a sustainable and self-financing manner with reasonably high levels of customer satisfaction as assessed through independent surveys.

While information on individual land is available with the registry, this does not extend to information about public land. In particular, municipal land is defined residually as all land within settlement area borders, which is not in private or state ownership, and is thus difficult to identify. There is no inventory of municipal land, making it impossible to monitor how effectively this valuable resource is being used. Also, while the quality and coverage of land information has greatly improved, huge potential benefits from sharing are foregone because of very weak coordination among relevant institutions. Improving access to information could greatly increase returns from this investment.

Documents attesting to a transaction must be submitted for registration within 30 days, and unregistered transactions are considered invalid. Although registration is very affordable,[43] fee collections by Kyrgyz registries in areas with at least average levels of real estate market activity exceed operating costs, implying that most registration offices are self-financing. Still, the fact that there is no distribution of revenue among registries may imply that in areas with low levels of real estate market activity, offices will either have to close or merge to reduce costs. In areas with high real estate market activity, systematic registration provides a significant source of revenue that can be used to fund, for example, external loan payments to finance capital investment. Price lists and service standards for operation of all registration services are publicly displayed in each of the offices. Each action is supported by proper receipts and other documents. Boxes to register complaints are available in each of the offices to provide customers with a mechanism to register complaints about improper behavior (e.g., exaction of informal payments) by employees. Access to these boxes is restricted to high-level staff outside the agency. While insufficient on their own, it is felt that, if complemented by internal vigilance, such mechanisms can help address the challenge of corruption; which is an issue especially in areas where property values are high.

Dispute Resolution and Conflict Management

The Kyrgyz constitution provides for the possibility of establishing a court of elders (*aksakal court*) in each village with authority to make decisions regarding property conflicts within families. These courts are readily accessible and their decisions are implemented through peer pressure. While recent changes that allow participation by women may make them more representative, these courts are not always independent or fully representative, and the extent to which their verdicts are recognized by the formal system varies. At the same time, clear assignment of responsibilities limits forum shopping and aggrieved parties can apply to the local government (*rayon*) or city court to have the *aksakal court* decision enforced.

With development of land markets and housing construction, land conflicts are on the increase. Private conflicts regarding location of boundaries, overlapping claims to the same plot, and privatization of land plots by owners of buildings located on them make up some 10 to 30 percent of total court cases. Unresolved cases older than five years represent about 5 to 10 percent of total pending court cases. Also, with a relatively well-functioning and accessible system for resolving disputes among individuals, a large share of disputes concerns conflicts with the state regarding allocation of land plots and the cancellation of allocation of land plots. Mechanisms to appeal against rulings on land are available, although court fees for accessing them are, at 10 percent of any damages awarded, very high.

Policy Recommendations

Norms stipulating the right of each citizen to a residential land plot, while apparently attractive from an equity perspective, are difficult to apply, as land is not available. Instead, they encourage squatting. They will therefore need to be rethought and revised. Similarly, it may be time to rethink the size of and the overall justification for the LRF, as the reasons that led to its formation no longer seem to apply. This is even more urgent as the state appears to be unable to efficiently manage these lands, causing the country to score poorly on transparency and competition in the disposition of public land.

Although the distribution of collective land and state farms to the population played an important role in the transition, the small size of individual land plots limits the income that can be generated from such plots. As the economy develops, land markets will need to play an increasingly important function. It will be important to eliminate obstacles to allow land markets function efficiently. Pasture management will need to be improved based on the recently passed law that decentralizes responsibility to pasture users' associations and allows use rights to be registered.

With decentralization, the ability to derive revenue from land assumes increasing importance for the supply of local public goods. However, local governments' ability to set the land tax rates remains limited. Together with improved tax administration and better definition of municipal lands, this provides a major opportunity for greater autonomy by local governments. Such autonomy should then be used to establish transparent and participatory processes and to build local capacity for land use planning and public land management. This capacity can then replace the rigid land use regimes that are no longer in line with reality, but continue to provide opportunities for rent-seeking and decrease land values. Effective local land management will also require the closing of loopholes that allow the disposal of public land for free and without any auction.

While the land administration project in the Kyrgyz Republic provides many important lessons, it has yet to overcome barriers to information sharing among different land-related agencies in Government to ensure that the intended benefits are fully realized. A first step in this direction will be providing appropriate incentives to the registry for making information available to other bodies, possibly by allowing it to charge modest fees for such services. Similarly, development of ways to register lands that are not held individually and to make sure that such information is publicly available will be of great importance.

Conclusion and Next Steps

Instead of repeating the advantages and disadvantages of the framework and the substantive findings for the case of the Kyrgyz Republic, we conclude by highlighting three ways in which the LGAF can help to promote the policy dialogue in different settings. The first and most immediate use is the application of the LGAF as a diagnostic tool to help identify areas for intervention. If applied in a way that draws on existing expertise and broad participation by relevant stakeholders (including governments) from the beginning, the LGAF can not only help to broaden the range of issues to be covered in such analysis but also improve the relevance of the resulting analysis and the credibility of resulting recommendations for policy or further study.

A second use of the LGAF is to monitor discrete (rule-based) indicators for policy reform. This follows immediately, and can provide an excellent opportunity for a broad-based coalition of actors (including the private sector and chambers of commerce) to monitor the extent to which recommendations are followed through.

Finally, and possibly most importantly, the LGAF points toward a number of quantitative indicators which, together with the initial diagnostic, are essential to continually monitor land governance. Key variables include (i) the coverage of the land administration system and the registration of different types of transfers, especially for women; (ii) receipts of land tax revenue; (iii) the total area of public or private land that is mapped with information publicly available; (iv) the number of expropriations and the modalities of compensation (including delay in payment receipts); and (v) the number of conflicts of different types entering the formal system. The fact that each of these indicators is related to one or more core areas of the land administration system suggests that collection and publication of these indicators on a regular basis, and in a way that accommodates wide variations of these indicators over space in a way that can be easily disaggregated, should be routine in any land administration system.

7.4:   Rangeland Administration in (Post) Conflict Conditions: The Case of Afghanistan

J. DAVID STANFIELD, Terra Institute, University of Wisconsin, U.S.
M.Y. SAFAR, Terra Institute, University of Wisconsin, U.S.
AKRAM SALAM, Cooperation for the Reconstruction of Afghanistan, Afghanistan
JENNIFER BRICK MURTAZASVHILI, University of Pittsburgh, U.S.

Summary

Nearly all of the pastures in Afghanistan are officially owned by the state, but used by families, clans, or tribes, including nomadic groups who herd sheep, goats, cattle and camels across semi-arid lands. Under the traditional informal arrangements which have existed for the use of these lands, differences of opinion about use rights can emerge. Also with security of tenure not assured, the users are not motivated to invest in the improvement of these lands. To address these issues, procedures have been developed to draft agreements among the village leaders and elders as well as leaders of nomadic groups as to who are the legitimate users of pasture parcels.

Following the formalization of these agreements among the legitimate users of these pastures, their signing and witnessing by village leaders, and delineation of pasture parcels to which the agreements refer on satellite imagery, these documents are archived in the care of a villager named by the elders in a safe house or room in the village. Copies are filed with provincial government land administration institutions.

The District Governors and the Pasture Land Specialists of the Ministry of Agriculture, Irrigation and Livestock review the community crafted agreements as to the legitimate users of rangelands, and then work with the community identified pasture managers on designing and implementing pasture improvement plans for each pasture parcel.

Introduction

Afghanistan has a population estimated to be about 26 million people[44] and a total area of approximately 653,000 km². It is bordered on the north by Turkmenistan, Uzbekistan, and Tajikistan, on the extreme northeast by China, on the east and south by Pakistan, and by Iran on the west. The country is split east to west by the Hindu Kush mountain range, rising in the east to heights of over 24,000 feet. With the exception of the southwest, most of the country is covered by high mountains and is traversed by deep valleys. About 12 percent of the land area of the country is cultivated. The literacy rate is estimated to be 36 percent, and the per capita GDP is estimated to be about $800 per year.[45]

More than five years after the Bonn Agreement, peace cannot be said to have been restored in Afghanistan. The effectiveness of state institutions for improving the lives of Afghans and for making democracy work has not been restored. In most areas of the country, the institutional relations between community and state are borderline dysfunctional if not hostile. The state building efforts since the overthrow of the Taliban regime in 2001-2002 have focused in the main on national elections, national parliamentary legislation, and executive administration, but to date have not been successful. Rather than such a top down approach, a community based development strategy should be explored as the cornerstone of efforts to rebuild community-state relations. One component of such a strategy could be the community based administration of rangeland user records described in this chapter.

The information presented in this study comes from the efforts of a Rural Land Administration Project (RLAP) team which functioned between June 2006 and September 2007. That team included representatives from the Natural Resources Directorate of the Ministry of Agriculture, Irrigation and Livestock (MAIL), as well as cadastral survey specialists, community organizers from an Afghan NGO(Cooperation for the Reconstruction of Afghanistan), and two international advisors. This team developed procedures in four test sites for documenting and archiving legitimate rights to communal pasture lands and the incorporation of these documents into governmental agencies.[46]

Millions of Afghan rural households—including nomads—depend very heavily on rangeland[47] to survive. Rangeland, however, is legally defined as public land and cannot be privately owned.[48] Families, clans and tribes, as well as nomadic groups, use rangeland for feeding livestock, for gathering fuel, as a source of herbs for medicinal and cooking purposes, and a passage ways for moving livestock from one place to another. Rangelands also represent crucial water catchment systems, which supply water for valley settlements and farming. The degradation of such lands can lead to erosion and drops in the levels of aquifers, negatively affecting cultivated agricultural areas and water sources for urban uses.

Rangelands have been deteriorating in recent decades. Many formerly viable rangelands have become virtually barren wastelands. The degradation of rangelands has also been accompanied by the conversion of some areas formerly used for pastures into rain-fed agricultural cultivation. This conversion in drought years and in low rainfall areas severely weakens the capability of the land to regenerate a stabilizing plant cover. Figure 7.1 shows a typical rural ecology, with irrigated agricultural land and housing along the river, and with the lands above the irrigated perimeter being used for rain fed agriculture and pastures.

Figure 7.1. Typical Village Ecology

Photo by David Stanfield.

An important phenomenon accompanying the degradation of rangelands is the increase in conflicts among farming and livestock dependent families for a decreasing supply of adequate rangeland. As the supply of rangeland declines, and with a constant or increasing demand for areas to pasture livestock, competition for this increasingly scarce resource inevitably results. Evidence suggests that pastures are the principal focus of conflict in Afghanistan because they involve and affect more people than conflicts over farms or urban housing, often inflaming ethnic problems and cross-cutting with unresolved conflicting arable and pastoral land needs (Wily 2004).

A main cause of rangeland degradation and resulting social problems is the web of conflicts about how rural people hold and use rangelands. This web has three dimensions: *first*, a longstanding history of conflict over rights to rangelands among groups of village residents and nomadic groups;[49] *second*, differences of opinion about the preservation of rangeland between farming families with access to agricultural land and families without access to agricultural land but with a dependence on livestock; and *third*, contradictions between governmental agencies (empowered by formal law establishing state ownership of pasture land) and local communities which, by custom and necessity, use the rangelands.

According to the Land Management Law of 2000, the villagers can have the exclusive right of use to their community pastures, which is the pasture area directly surrounding the village. In the 2000 law (Article 9), such community pastures were defined as 'the area from where the loud voice of someone standing at the edge of the village can still be heard'. Lands used principally for grazing which are beyond the boundary of the community pasture, are called public pastures.

In the past, village elders and tribal leaders met and agreed about the users of both types of pastures (Barfield 2004). In some instances of public pastures, anyone can use them at any time. In general the customs and traditions about the uses of community and public pastures are more tentative today than they were prior to the 1980s, that is, rights are often not clear and the confidence people have in exercising these rights is often not high—which is fertile ground for social conflicts.

New Government Policy/Strategy for Rangelands

The Ministry of Agriculture, Irrigation and Livestock (MAIL) introduced a significant new policy/strategy in 2006, which advocates "the transfer of effective management responsibilities for forestry and range resources within defined community geographical areas to communities." The objective of this community based management of forestry and range resources is to create "value for community members (both in the form of productive resources—timber, firewood, better pasture, and as means of protecting natural resources from erosion)."[50]

This policy/strategy formalizes the de facto situation in most communities whose residents use rangeland. For decades, families, clans, and tribes through their elders and leaders have arrived at rules for deciding who has the rights to use particular pasture areas for what times of the year. This local administration of rights to rangelands has evolved regardless of the provisions of the formal law that pastures and forests are state owned and under the authority of state institutions. The theoretical notion has been that the state through its land management and administration[51] institutions would decide who could use state owned rangelands, would monitor their use and sanction unauthorized use, and would administer the records pertaining to rangeland. However, in practice the decisions about who uses rangeland and how they use rangeland have been negotiated among clans, families, and nomadic families at the local level. Under such de facto arrangements, there have been verbal agreements arrived at through often extended discussions among elders and other community leaders.

A major complication to this de facto traditional system of rangeland and forest management has been the turmoil of the past 25 years and the resulting displacement of populations and damage to local leadership structures. The emergence of local warlords using the threat of force to influence local people has led in many cases to the breakdown of the informal rules governing how communities and families get access to, and use, rangelands. Another complicating factor has been the sporadic attempts of governmental representatives to assert their legal authority over the use of rangelands, also with the threat of the use of force to influence local people. The result in many places is increased insecurity of tenure among people whose lives depend on secure access to these resources.

The Ministry of Agriculture's new Policy/Strategy for recognizing community based management of rangelands is an initial response to this problem. The state does not have the capacity for managing rangelands or for maintaining records about the use and conditions of rangeland, which it claims to own under legal provisions for state ownership of rangelands.

Sporadic attempts to enforce state management of rangelands ironically frequently serve to drive even more wedges between government and communities, and to weaken the local resolves to effectively manage rangelands. Identification and recording of the legitimate community users of rangeland are first steps in the implementation of the new Policy/Strategy[52] which recognizes the responsibilities of communities to manage rangelands.

This MAIL Policy/Strategy of 2006 has been updated and incorporated into the National Land Policy prepared by a multi-ministerial commission in early 2007 (figure 7.2).[53]

Figure 7.2. Excerpt from the Draft Land Policy

Section 2.2.6: Issue: Regulation of Pasture Land

Section 2.2.6: Policy

- It is a national policy that access to land resources be clarified and secured as part of an integrated natural resource management which springs from local community based resource management. Such community based resource management must be conducted under the strict supervision and guidance of the Ministry of Agriculture.

- It is national policy that community-based natural resource management strives to ensure environmental protection and usage for all public owned pasture users.

- It is national policy that the resolution to complex issues of ownership and access rights to pasture lands be examined at the provincial level and traditional use rights of settled farmers and pastoralists established and respected.

- It is national policy that the Ministry of Agriculture reactivates land surveying in order to clarify rights to land.

Source: Islamic Republic of Afghanistan, Land Policy, January, 2007.

The Ministry of Urban Development and the Municipality of Kabul have developed a similar community based approach for regularizing the tenure of some informal settlements in Kabul as part of the upgrading of those settlements.[54]

In a review of land registration options for Afghanistan, McEwen and Nolan (2007:23) make the following recommendation:

> Any future system for land registration should be rooted at the community level. The system will be able to draw upon community knowledge, practical understanding of local issues, and tried and tested (if sometimes imperfect) systems to resolve disputes. By directly engaging the community, the system will be viewed as transparent, equitable and legitimate. Also, implementation costs can be kept to a minimum and public access to records will be improved.

There are also important historical precedents for community administration of property records. The royal acts, which allotted land to families at the time of establishment of the communities, have typically been kept by an *arbab/malik* or by a respected elder of the village in their village homes.[55] Most of the 20,000 villages incorporated in the National Solidarity Program (NSP)[56] the NSP Community Development Councils have developed systems of producing and archiving accounting records and notes of council meetings, even though they are often rudimentary (Barakat 2006).

The problem of land tenure insecurity[57] derives from the disruption of customary arrangements concerning access to land due to population displacements, warlords demanding control over community lands, destruction of documents proving rights to real property, and land acquisition by influential individuals in the context of a weak State. Such actions include outright land grabbing, acquisition of immovable property from land grabbers through informal market transactions, and improper State allocation of land. Under these conditions, land holders perceive their rights to land to be tentative and insecure.

Perceptions of insecurity can be positively modified when rights to land are made both "legitimate" and "legally valid." As Camilla Toulmin (2006:4) has observed:

> Secure rights to land and property depend on a combination of two key elements. The rights being claimed must be seen, first, as legitimate by the local population; and second, they must also be ascribed legality by the state.

The customs and local traditions of Afghan communities provide rules which are often more effective in guiding the everyday lives of people than the laws and regulations emanating from the state's institutions. In such conditions, rights to land may be viewed as legitimate in terms of being locally recognized in the customary deeds. These describe transactions in land, but are not prepared in accordance with legally defined procedures.[58]

Similarly, government officials may issue apparently valid legal documents about rights to land, such as an allotment of land to a land developer, despite strong local opposition. Under such conditions, the rights to land may be legally valid yet not be considered socially legitimate, a situation potentially leading to long-running local conflict.

Improving the security with which people have rights to rangeland should result from having those land rights be both "legitimate" and "legally valid." But how can the country move toward that situation?

The state is weak in Afghanistan. The popular perception is that wealth and power influence the creation and application of state defined laws more than do dispassionate legal procedures administered by a transparent bureaucracy. Under these conditions, an approach to improving rangeland tenure security can be first to define legitimate rights through community consultations about customary rules concerning access to rangeland, and then appeal to institutions of the state for confirmation of the legal validity of these community legitimized rights to land. This approach reverses the usual focus of first establishing state policies, then crafting laws in line with those policies, and then enforcing those laws across the land. The "community first" approach means that rules about the use and improvement of rangelands have to be established in community consultations, community by community.

Delville (2006: 2) suggests that two questions must be answered in these local consultations in order to pull people out of the morass of insecurity; at least as far as reducing land tenure insecurity is concerned:

- What is the nature of the recognized rights to land: is the implicit model one of legally defined private property, or is the model one which starts with locally defined rights and rules?
- Is the system to administer the documentation of these rights capable of ensuring reliable management and be at the service of the general population?

The clarification of legitimate rights to rangeland through community consultations requires additional steps to confirm these rights through state review of the local decisions to verify that community claims to rangeland do not conflict with neighboring community claims. There should also be clear procedures defined in law for community decision making to avoid the illegitimate grabbing of land by powerful individuals or families within communities. This dual focus on documenting legitimate and legal rights to rangeland should have the added benefit of reconstructing the relations of community and state around the administration of rights to rangeland. This is an enormous task, but one that is necessary and appropriate to Afghan conditions.

Community Administration of Records

In many countries the answers to both of Delville's questions have focused on applying formal law to adjudicate claims to land through technically trained field teams, in some instances giving a role to community involvement in the adjudication process in the final stages of validating the findings of the field teams.[59] This approach also tends to focus on equipping and training field adjudication teams, and the developing of cadastral agencies for producing accurate parcel maps and the promotion of specialized governmental land registries for administering the legal documents which define property rights. These institutions of cadastre and registry must be equipped and trained to do their jobs properly, extending their services to the community typically through the use of information and communication technologies.

In the Afghan context a "community consultation" approach may be a more feasible way to try and answer both questions about how to establish more secure rights to at least one type of land, rangeland. Community based preparation of agreements and the administration of these agreements about legitimate users of rangeland could encourage their use and maintenance, and could strengthen the security with which these users hold and manage the land. Such a system is hypothesized to be speedier and generally more efficient than a solely government administered system (Wily 2003: 1–2).

Such a system also already has some support from the Judiciary. The RLAP field teams presented examples of rangeland user agreements to Provincial Appeals Court Judges in Kunduz and Herat. In both provinces the judges concluded that the agreements would have great value should disputes be presented to their courts pertaining to the lands covered by the agreements. In both provinces, appeals court judges observed that their present procedure is to refer disputes among villagers concerning land back to the village elders for their opinion on the dispute. The signed agreements represent evidence already gathered of these opinions.

Pertaining to the administration of property records, the RLAP field teams worked with community leaders to negotiate consensus as to the legitimate users of rangeland, including community families and nomads, the documentation of these agreements validated by the signatures of family and clan leaders and *arbabs*, and the archiving of these agreements in a secure place in the villages under the supervision of a trusted person. Community administration meant the actual administration by community people of property records, and not administration solely by a district office of a central land registry receiving petitions for land information or for recording transactions, nor a district office sending a team once in a while to communities to gather evidence of transactions.

This community based administration should function, but it requires training and technical support. As in the case of land tenure security, people should feel more secure in the documentation of their rights to land when they "own" their land records, that is, when they produce and control access to these records. When this security exists, people invest in the maintenance and usefulness of land records. As Liz Alden Wily states:

> only when land administration and management is fully devolved to the community level... is there likely to be significant success in bringing the majority of land interests under useful and lasting record-centered management.... (2003: abstract)

Wily describes this approach as the "empowerment of people at the local level to manage their land relations themselves" (2003: 35).

Bruce and Knox (2009) observe in their review of community based land administration experiences in the African context:

> ...community-based and user-friendly means of recording land rights which allow land administration to be managed at community level,

taking advantage of the community's remarkable collective memory
of things having to do with land but providing written record.

Community consultations are about who the community leaders recognize as the
legitimate users of rangeland. This method is at once a recognition of the customary
means for identifying these users, and an improvement on this custom through making
the user agreements written and signed by family heads and community elders and
prestigious persons, accompanied by community rangeland parcel boundary
delineations, and at least procedural support from the Judiciary and local
governmental entities (District *Woluswals* and the Provincial Cadastral Service).

The Community

The definition of the concept "community" is complicated in the Afghan context.
Various terms regarding the loci of rural community life exist in Afghanistan, such as
the village (*qarya*), the settlement (*qishlāq*), and the area (*manteqa*).

None of these concepts have a standard administrative definition in that the most
local unit of local government defined in Afghanistan is the District (*Woluswali*), which
contains many *qarya*, *qishlaq* and perhaps even *manteqa*. The Woluswali has a Head[60]
and Council, and its municipal center normally contains offices of national level
ministries and agencies.

Despite not having administrative designation, there are traditional institutional
structures of *qarya* and *qishlaq* that the RLAP field teams used to focus "community
consultations" about rangeland and agricultural land rights. Of basic importance is the
formation of *qarya* or *qishlaq* "shuras" (local councils) from time to time, which
traditionally are composed of family or clan elders, typically to resolve conflicts of one
sort or another.[61] Moreover, the National Solidarity Program (NSP) launched in 2002
has stimulated the formation of Community Development Councils to administer
infrastructure grants at the local level for settlements or villages. These NSP councils
encompass approximately 25-300 families, and are more formally constituted than the
traditional community shura.

In at least some Kuchi communities, the basic concept of organizing access to and
usage of pasture is the '*Yurt*'. Literally referring to a round dwelling place constructed
of portable materials, in Kuchi communities like that of Naw Abad this term also refers
to a defined geographic area of rangeland that is used by a specific family of herdsmen.
In the Kuchi village of Naw Abad, the shape of these geographic '*Yurts*' evolves over
time, and the location of their boundaries is established through family consultations,
and orally transferred from generation to generation. Originally, the size of each '*Yurt*'
is determined by the size of an individual herd. The number of animals belonging to a
specific user also influences who is allowed to use the area in question. The number of
500 animals is the standard size of a herd. In a given year, one herdsman family may
not be able to acquire that number of animals and thus will allow some related family
to use the grazing area of their '*Yurt*' so that its capacity is being used. However, the
shape and size of the '*Yurt*' does not usually change significantly through this practice,
and the use-rights are still exclusively assigned to the family in question.

In the view of Kuchis of Naw Abad, a *yurt* is not only a specified geographic area,
but also an essential element in a system of rights to pasture land collectively agreed
upon between all potential Kuchi community users. Villagers do not claim ownership

of the land in question, although in their view the long duration of well defined usage stretching over many generations does give them strong rights to control access to that land. Rather than talking about pasture land ownership, Kuchi families refer to the right of use which they claim to those areas. But since a *yurt*'s geographical space can change depending on size of herd, rainfall, stage in the family cycle, the Naw Abad community did not wish to delineate existing *yurt* boundaries, but rather the boundaries of the family/clan rangelands, containing several *yurts*.

In regard to defining the legitimate users of public pastures[62] whose users come from more than one *qarya* or *qishlaq*, the *manteqa* may become the relevant definition of local community, with the governance structure of a *manteqa shura* or *jirga* called into action under specific conditions.

Another community institution revolves around the person identified as the *arbab*.[63] *Arbabs*, also known as *maliks* in some regions, are respected villagers who are educated and have the political and social skills needed to deal with government agencies and other outside organizations about the needs of villages. Villagers also consult with these individuals for advice when disputes arise which cannot be resolved by the parties to the disputes or their families. An *arbab/malik* may serve more than one village. Their services are usually remunerated by villagers at the time of harvest, in the form and amount as defined in each village by the elders of the village, including contributions from each family. The *arbab/malik* typically has an official stamp to use for validating the documents that he prepares. One result of this role is that *arbabs/maliks* often keep community records, such as royal land grants and other written documents pertaining to community activities.

Since *arbabs/maliks* tend to be powerful people in the community, often from large landholding families, it seems likely that communities choose someone with economic or social power to represent them at least in part because such people could get governmental officials to listen to them. Whatever the case may be, as time passes, the position is either inherited or a new *arbab/malik* is re-appointed through community consensus.

The field teams defined a community as a settlement with a locally known name which had participated in the NSP and had a functioning NSP Community Development Council (CDC), although this CDC served only as an initial point of contact in order to identify the heads of families and clans and other influential people in the community who had the respect of the various village factions. This group of influential people, which the field team called a "rangeland consultative council" were the interlocutors of the RLAP field teams in order to reach consensus about legitimate rights to rangelands. Typically the community also had the services of an *arbab* (since the test sites were in the north and west of the country), although the function of linking the community with outside agencies also is frequently done by an influential *mullah*,[64] or by the head of a local cooperative. These individuals were also included in the "rangeland consultative council" with which the field teams worked to produce the agreements about legitimate users of rangelands.

Households that did not have their own livestock did not participate in this rangeland council, except when they had special knowledge of traditional usage, or when they were caring for livestock owned by others. In two of the test sites, there was a tribe or group which had been settled by a previous regime on lands near the target village. In one case, the "new group" was allowed to pasture their animals on some rangeland also used by the village families, but were not allowed to have agricultural land, only working as laborers. In that village the four main clan heads agreed to note in the legitimate user agreements the arrangements made with the "outsiders." In the second site, all that was agreed was that certain pastures were used exclusively by the settled group, but with lingering determination by the original villagers to one day recover "their lands". While the user agreements cannot be expected to overcome deep resentments, they can function for a time to calm expectations, and can always be changed should conditions change.

The task of the RLAP field team was to forge a consensus among existing community leaders about the boundaries of rangelands used by community families, and to document those leaders' opinions about the legitimate users of those rangelands; it did not involve planning for the actual use of these lands. This planning exercise is to occur at a later stage, and could involve the community action planning methods used in urban areas. In terms of gender roles, the field teams' community mobilizer had experience in urban informal settlements with organizing men's community planning councils, initially separate from women's planning councils, to ensure that women's opinions were adequately heard. However, in this exercise the RLAP field teams accepted family decisions on who should participate in the rangeland councils for the forging of community agreements about the legitimate family users of rangeland.

Community Consultations to Identify Legitimate Users of Rangeland

The hypothesis of this study is that where a local consensus or near consensus can be crafted about who are the legitimate users of rangeland at different times of the year, and if that consensus is expressed in written agreements, that local community agreement should be the starting point to define rights to land. This community focus, however, does not mean that the governmental agencies or the legal framework are irrelevant. On the contrary, the re-establishment of positive community-state relations is of critical importance. The community can and should be a locus for land administration and management, but a national program has to strengthen the capacities of communities and state agencies to promote and support these efforts for the country to achieve a viable and effective land administration system.

The hypothesis can be divided into five parts:

1. Community consultations can produce agreements as to the legitimate users of rangeland at various times of the year.
2. These agreements can be based on satellite imagery for delineating rangeland parcels used by community members.
3. These signed agreements and delineated imagery, which allow for changes from year to year, can be archived and administered in communities.
4. Governmental representatives can review the agreements as to their preparation according to regulations and can maintain back-up copies in district or provincial offices.
5. Governmental agencies and NGOs can use these agreements to identify families with legitimate use rights in order to work with them to improve the management of rangelands.

To develop and test these ideas, the RLAP team consulted with a variety of organizations in Afghanistan with community development experience or with an interest in supporting such efforts.[65] A RLAP team of land specialists and community organizers was formed in mid-2006 through the Rural Land Administration Project of MAIL. The RLAP was financially supported by the Asian Development Bank, and logistically supported by an international NGO—Mercy Corps—which had a watershed management improvement program in some of the RLAP areas of interest. RLAP also received significant support from International Security Assistance Force (ISAF) in the form of plotted satellite imagery at a scale of 1:5,000 to 1:50,000[66] showing the rangeland parcels used by community families.

The project team included Ministerial rangeland specialists, cadastral survey specialists including provincial AGCHO staff where appropriate, community organizers from an Afghan NGO—Cooperation for the Reconstruction of Afghanistan and two international advisors. This team developed procedures for documenting legitimate rights to communal pasture lands through agreements among community leaders in four test sites, focusing on these four target villages,[67] and the incorporation of these records into governmental agencies:

1. Village Dara-e-Kalan in Ishkamish District, Takhar Province, with rain-fed agriculture and 14 separate clan-based communal pastures, and limited use by Kuchis.
2. Village Safar Khan in Zindajan District, Herat Province, with irrigated agriculture and limited communal pastures close to the settlement, with annual Kuchi use.
3. Village Saghari in Karokh District, Herat Province, basically rain-fed agriculture, with communally managed pastures (rarely used by Kuchis) close to the settlement area.
4. Village Naw Abad in Chardara District, Kunduz Province, a Kuchi[68] settlement based on irrigated agriculture and large tribally managed pastures close to the settlement and tribally allocated public pastures in the distant mountains.

The four sites selected for the field work are shown in figure 7.3, which also shows the number of rangeland user agreements produced in each site. By "site" we mean a target village and the rangelands used by its residents. The target villages were selected through consultations with MAIL provincial staff, with NGOs working to implement the National Solidarity Program's Community Development Councils in each major village, and with other donor supported community development programs active in the RLAP areas. The villages selected had demonstrated during the previous two years an organizational capacity to make collective decisions.[69] In addition to the target villages, the "sites" included neighboring villages which the RLAP teams consulted about the boundaries of community used rangeland.

Figure 7.3. Locations of Program Sites

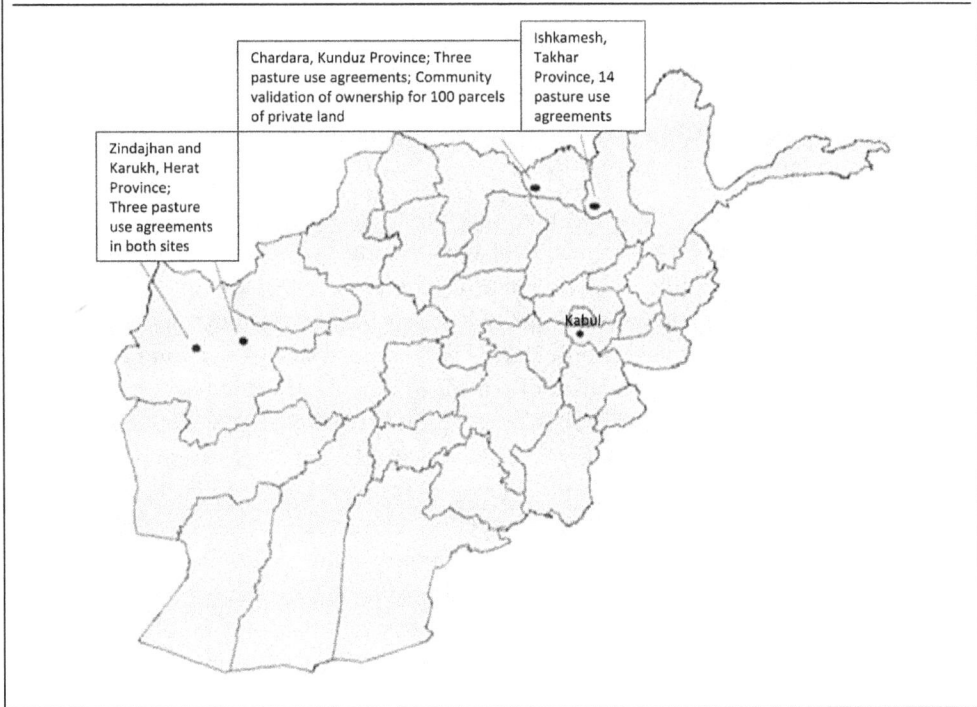

Zindajhan and Karukh, Herat Province; Three pasture use agreements in both sites

Chardara, Kunduz Province; Three pasture use agreements; Community validation of ownership for 100 parcels of private land

Ishkamesh, Takhar Province, 14 pasture use agreements

Kabul

Source: DFID/ADB Technical Assistance Consultant Report (2008).

Community Rights to Rangeland

In light of the legal ambivalence about the ownership of rangeland, the field teams avoided using the word "ownership" in the community consultations. Rather, the consultations generated community views on who legitimately holds what rights to use particular rangeland parcels during what times of the year. Villagers and Kuchis had no difficulty with this terminology, although reaching consensus about legitimate users often took substantial time, and for some parcels consensus was not possible. The RLAP teams explicitly recognized the authority of local people to define these rights in the first instance, based on the Ministry's new Policy/Strategy for community based management of rangeland, but subject to review and approval by the formal organs of government, particularly the Woluswal. Villagers repeatedly asked for this governmental review and formal approval of their rangeland use agreements.[70]

To protect the interests of the state in rangelands, the Ministry insisted on inserting the following paragraph into the rangeland user agreements, which was discussed and accepted in all community consultations without explicit objections from either the villagers or Kuchis:

"Obligations of the Users of the Parcel":

> We use the pasture only for grazing animals. We protect the pasture from converting to agricultural or residential uses and we work to improve the productivity and of the pasture/forest land parcel, in

collaboration with Ministry of Agriculture and other stakeholders. Since according to the Land Management Law and Pasture Law all pasture and the forest lands are government property; therefore, with the agreement of the local community, the government may establish large agricultural farms, livestock and industrial parks, roads and other infrastructure for the welfare and promotion of the living standard of the people.

The meaning of the phrase "pasture and forest lands are government property" in village discourse is more a recognition of the sovereignty of the State in reference to rangeland and forests, rather than an identification of state ownership[71] with all of the rights normally included in "ownership" of land, such as the right to sell or to develop.

In any case, for the villagers and Kuchis in the four test sites, reaching agreements about who has rights to specific uses of parcels of rangeland during specified times of the year seemed to be the critical issue to be settled in the consultations. Neither government officials nor the villagers considered as relevant a discussion of who holds the unilateral right to sell rangeland or develop it for other uses, which are typically rights encompassed within the concept of ownership. The clarification and documentation of legitimate users by the community is the critical element, at least for the present time and conditions. Also the "obligations" paragraph of the agreement contains the statement about governmental investments that may be done "with the agreement of the local community." This statement gives the community a right to negotiate with the government should government want to use rangeland for other purposes than the pasturing of animals by local people. Presumably, this right to negotiate includes the possibility for community rangeland management groups to be compensated for community financed improvements in pastures under their management, should the government wish to acquire those lands for other purposes.

A Pasture Act is being drafted to replace the legislation presently in place, which may clarify or may complicate community-government relations concerning the management of rangelands.[72] At present, the rangeland user agreement is a statement by community rangeland users and village elders about their understanding of who the legitimate users are. The agreement is not expressly authorized in legislation. However, it is in accord with the draft Land Policy, and with the MAIL's Policy/Strategy on community based management of rangeland. Moreover, the Herat and Kunduz Appeals Court Head Judges have reviewed the wording of completed agreements, and they indicated that such documents would have significant legal relevance in their courts, should a dispute be presented to them involving rangelands covered by the agreements. Their normal procedure when village land disputes come to them is to refer the parties involved back to the community elders to get their recommendations. In the case of a dispute involving rangelands with an agreement signed by these very elders, an important step in the resolution of the dispute has already been taken.

The field teams have also recommended that the Minister authorize rangeland specialists from the Land Resources Department to review rangeland user agreements and indicate on the agreements in writing when they find the agreements to be complete (all the relevant parties have signed) and clearly presented. The "legality" of the rangeland user agreements seems sufficient, but certainly more explicit authorization in law would be useful.

The local mullahs often participated in the crafting of the user agreements. Another source of "legality" for the agreements could be their consideration by religious leaders in each province. In Kunduz, there is a functioning council of religious scholars (*Shura-e-Ulama*) which could consider the "legality" of the agreements, especially since the majority of religious leaders in Kunduz expressed that they are constructively engaged in the effort to rebuild the country (Wardak et al. 2007). In other provinces, however, the *Shura-e-Ulama* may be largely defunct. The RLAP field teams considered that the Provincial Appeals Court Judges who were consulted represented the views of the *Shura-e-Ulama*, but in future efforts it would be helpful to consult them directly.

Other Experiences with Community as the Origin of Legitimate Rights to Land

In other countries, community keeping of land records has also been common, particularly in communities established through settlement programs. For example, the initial settlement of some parts of the United States by white settlers, who displaced the native peoples from their lands, was done with the formal adjudication of land rights by the state but without a governmental involvement in the administration of property records, at least initially. Settlers themselves set up organizations to recognize and enforce informally established claims to land (Murtazashvili 2008). Subsequently, as state institutions began to be established, the preference across the U.S. for the administration of property rights documents, normally without benefit of systematic cadastral surveys of property boundaries, was the multi-purpose local governmental unit (township or county) (Stanfield 2003).

In Norway, while the administration of a Land Registry has been done by a specialized government agency, no cadastral surveys were done in rural areas until 1980. New boundaries/parcels were set out in the field by three lay men appointed by the local "sheriff". New boundaries were demarcated using materials found at the spot, crosses in rock/stones, etc. Verbal descriptions and rather simple sketches were included in the documents supporting opening a new lot in the Land Register.[73]

In more recent times in the country of Benin, Village Land Tenure Management Committees have been adjudicating title and are administering the resulting property records (Delville 2006: 4-5). In Tanzania, Village Land Committees validate claims to land, and Village Land Registries administer the land records, in coordination with District Land Registries.[74] In Mozambique, communities present claims to the government for the lands that they have traditionally used, and apply for a certification from government as to the community having legal rights to such lands.[75]

Building Records about Rangeland Tenure

To deal with tenure insecurity on rangelands, the field teams designed a simple system for getting local stakeholders to agree about the legitimate users of community and public pasture lands, write down the agreements, delineate boundaries of the pasture parcels on satellite imagery, and develop plans for improving their productivity. Figure 7.4 shows a portion of a satellite image on which the boundaries of forest and pasture parcel boundaries have been delineated.

Figure 7.4. A Satellite Image with Pasture Parcel Boundaries

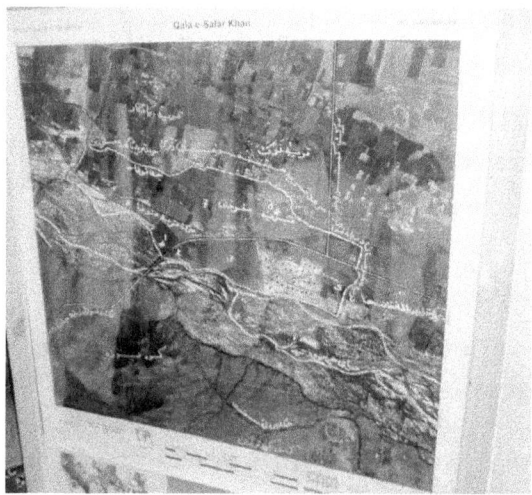

Photo by David Stanfield.
Note: Scale 1:5,000

Figure 7.5. A Signed Pasture Land Agreement

Photo by David Stanfield.

Where it is possible to reach agreements about legitimate rights to pastures, representatives of the families, clans, and tribes who are parties to the agreements sign the written agreements, along with the village elders, *arbabs*, *mulas*, and other respected local people who also sign as witnesses.[76] Figure 7.5 shows the signature page of one such pasture land agreement.

For large public pastures used by families from two or more villages as well as by nomadic groups where users and uses can be defined, a meeting is called of all interested parties and the agreement forged, signed, and witnessed as in the cases of the community pastures. In the Naw Abad community, distant public pastures are important to village families and are exclusively used by the two distinctive tribal groups (*Khel*) of Nau Abad village (*Baluch, Ashakehl*). In this instance, the description of these lands was a simple sketch, shown in figure 7.6, with two large parcels delineated.

Once the agreements and delineated images are completed, they are made available to the villagers and nomads for examination, to be finalized typically in a public meeting (*shura/jirga*)[77] or a series of public meetings. Figure 7.7 shows a group of villagers reviewing a delineated satellite image showing the boundaries of pasture land parcels.

Figure 7.6. Two Delineated Public Pasture Areas

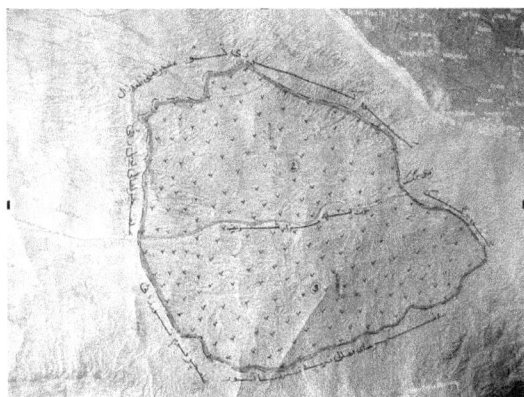

Photo by David Stanfield.

Figure 7.7. Villagers Reviewing Delineated Satellite Image

Photo by David Stanfield.

These pasture land agreements and parcel boundaries on images are "recorded" in the villages where the families which use the rangeland parcels reside. Typically, the village elders appoint an individual to be responsible for storing the agreements and images, a Village Recording Secretary (VRS). The VRS uses simple cabinets, which are placed in a secure room designated by the village elders. In one village of the RLAP the records were given to the headmaster of the village school for safekeeping.

If no agreements are possible or even desired about an identified area of rangeland, that situation is noted on the "summary rangeland situation" report for the village.

One suggestion for coordinating the use of large public pastures is for a management committee to be formed from the representatives of the main stakeholders for each public pasture to enforce the agreement and to oversee the efforts to improve the productivity of the public pasture. Another suggestion is for the preparation of the agreement to be subject to a *shura/jirga*, and any enforcement of the agreement and improvement plan, or resolution of disputes to be handled by elders and if needed by reconvening the *shura/jirga*.

The procedures devised by the RLAP for consultations and agreement formalization about the legitimate users of rangeland at the community level (called ADAMAP)[78] can be summarized by the following:

Ask for community cooperation

Delineate the boundaries of rangeland parcels

Agreements are prepared concerning the legitimate users of the rangeland parcels.

Meet, discuss, and approve the agreements and delineations

Archive the agreements and delineated images

Plan for the improvement of the rangeland parcels

The field tests yielded evidence that a national rangeland program with the following features is desirable and feasible:

- Community rangeland agreements and delineated images recorded and maintained in the village where the resident users live, with copies filed with the Regional Cadastre (the delineated image) and with the Provincial Amlak.[79]
- The public pasture agreements and delineated images are recorded in the village designated for that responsibility by the *manteqa jirga*, with copies recorded with the Regional Cadastral Survey and Provincial Amlak(s).
- Once the rangeland agreements have been reviewed and discussed locally, they are reviewed by the Woluswali officials, including Rangeland specialists as well as specialists from the Amlak and Cadastral Survey, monitored and reviewed by the Head of the Woluswali administration.
- Particularly important to the ADAMAP methodology is the preparation of a plan for the improvement of each of the rangeland parcels for which agreements are devised, and the continued interaction of community rangeland users and government officials led by specialists from the Rangelands Department of the Ministry of Agriculture, Irrigation and Livestock (MAIL) for the implementation of such plans.

In four test sites the following outputs pertaining to rangeland legitimate user agreements have been produced:[80]

- 17 village pasture land signed agreements for 17 pasture parcels, covering approx. 28,210 Jeribs (5,642 hectares) in three villages, and over 110,000 Jeribs (in a large Kuchi community pasture and two public pastures in the fourth test site in Kunduz (3 agreements).[81]
- 39 satellite images, ortho-rectified, scale 1:5,000 and 1:50,000, printed in 4 paper copies, each showing 4.5 km x 4 km on paper images of 84.1 cm x 76.2 cm, with 20 pasture land parcels delineated. In the Kunduz site, satellite images of smaller scale were used to delineate the very large public pasture parcel boundaries.
- The agreements and delineated images showing pasture land parcels are archived in the four test sites, and copies are archived with Cadastral Survey Department of the Afghan Geodetic and Cartographic Head Office (AGCHO) in Kabul.

In addition to the agreements and delineated imagery, another important output was the introduction of the community based rangeland administration concepts and procedures to villagers, Kuchi leaders, Provincial and District AMLAK and Rangeland specialists, and MAIL staff.In KABUL, Department Heads in the MAIL, the Minister and his advisors, and the implementers of other rangeland improvement programs were introduced to the same concepts and procedures. This introduction was done through workshops in each Province and in Kabul, where villagers, District and Provincial officials, and representatives of NGOs met and discussed the achievements and implications of community based administration of rangelands.

While this community recording and maintaining of records about rights to rangeland is a new idea in Afghanistan, it appears to be well received by villagers, nomadic groups, and many government officials. Further monitoring and adjusting of the ADAMAP procedures to produce and administer these records is certainly needed to fit this concept into the expectations of villagers and governmental officials.

Figure 7.8 shows a RLAP recommendation about how the rangeland parcel-based information concerning rights and boundaries is generated and archived. The capacities of Amlak, Cadastral Survey, the Land Resources Directorate, and Woluswali officials require attention for assuring that they will be able to fulfill their responsibilities in a significant modification of the property records administration system.

This experience with community based rangeland administration could be extended to a more general community based land records system being introduced into the existing land records administration system, including agricultural land parcels and other types of parcels in villages. In one of the test sites, after the community leaders had seen and understood the procedures for producing community agreements as to the legitimate users of rangeland, they spontaneously asked the RLAP team to help include agricultural land parcels into their records system. That idea is more fully developed in Stanfield et al., 2010 (forthcoming).

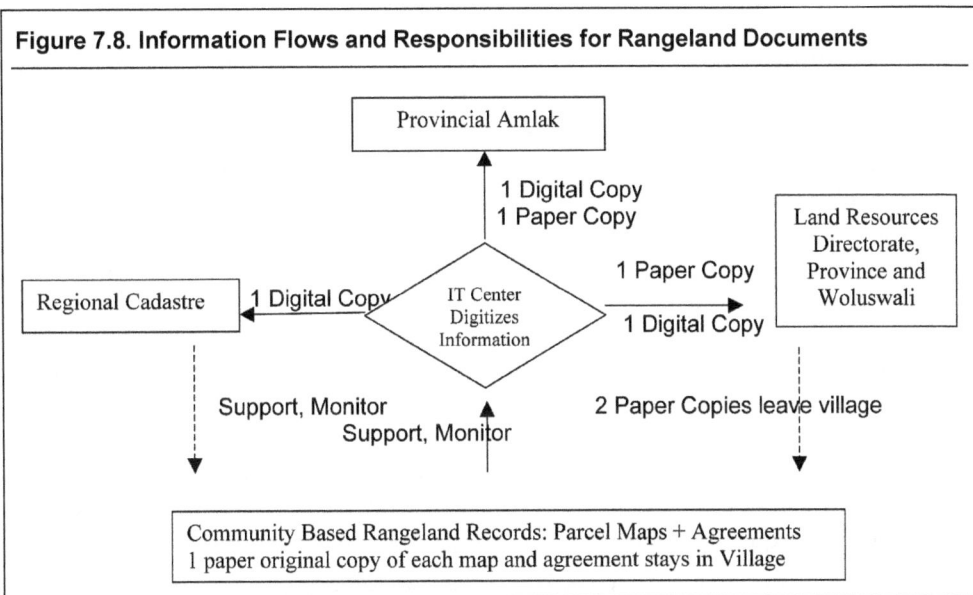

Figure 7.8. Information Flows and Responsibilities for Rangeland Documents

Source: DFID/ADB (2007).

Conclusions

The ADAMAP procedure for producing and archiving community approved agreements about the legitimate users of rangeland has proven popular in the four test sites, with community residents and with Kuchi seasonal users of rangelands. Community based administration of these records seems feasible, at least in the four sites of the study.

Not every settlement can operate its own rangeland use agreements registry, or else the system would be inordinately expensive, so the geographic definition of "community" has to be negotiated in each case. The administration of this community based system should be more effective in avoiding conflicts and misunderstandings, since traditional leaders in villages have the authority for confirming legitimate users that governmental officials do not have.

The setting up of this community based rangeland administration system will involve as many as 20,000 villages, and will require good organization, sizeable budget, and policy directives to Provincial judges and governmental agencies to support such an effort. Under Afghan conditions, where the institutions of the State are not well connected to the population, reestablishing the confidence of the people in its governing institutions and re-defining the roles of government to be supportive of the legitimate land users are fundamental to peace building. Special and often relatively costly efforts for the re-linking of community and State, in particular concerning property rights, will be necessary at least for a period of years. Making the record of rights to land transparent and observable at the community level is of fundamental importance and an area where government could redefine its societal roles with cooperative villagers. While District staff in the MAIL and Woluswali offices were quite supportive of the community administration idea, there is undoubtedly resistance to such an approach among staff and high officials in Provincial and Kabul government agencies. Exploring the roots of such resistance and dealing with legitimate issues for the more extensive implementation of this model will be essential, as has been observed in other situations where central administrative authority has been devolved to local authorities.[82]

The experiences of the field teams with the local legitimization of rights to pasture lands, a potentially very complicated process, show that community definition of such rights is entirely feasible, relatively simple, and normally quickly accomplished. Moreover, village leaders are quite willing to keep those records, and they readily commit to updating the agreements when the conditions change and require changes in the written agreements and/or pasture parcel boundaries.

Despite the positive results of this experiment showing how community-state relations can be rebuilt, village by village, district by district around the administration of rangeland records, any extension of the community based rangeland administration approach will require additional testing and careful monitoring:

- The ADAMAP methodology starts with "asking" community leaders whether they want to participate in the program. All communities contacted by the RLAP teams were positive, although in some cases only following extensive explanation. There may be communities which would not agree. A procedure is needed for continued dialogue with such communities.

- Further testing is needed of methodologies suitable for community land administration, such as refining the role of 'Village Recording Secretaries' designated by the community council assembled for this rangeland exercise, who shall be responsible for the management and archiving of delineated satellite images and rangeland parcel forms and who need training in the procedures for maintaining and updating records about legitimate users of rangeland parcels and maps of those parcels.

▪ Questions remain pertaining to the amount of review needed of the field teams' work on boundary delineation and parcel register forms and how to control unauthorized changing of parcel records.

▪ There are many governance issues which need consideration before the rolling out of a large community based land administration program. Central government officials in Kabul are very suspicious of a community oriented program, despite the relative successes of the NSP program. Changing these perceptions will require concerted efforts at dealing with legitimate concerns.

▪ The means for incorporating Kuchi input into the rangeland agreements have to be refined to fit with their seasonal presence in villages.

▪ The mobilization of community consultations about legitimate rights to land has to find ways of incorporating the various community segments, and not be limited to the input from just the heads of families with the largest herds of livestock.

▪ The capacities of Amlak, Cadastral Survey, Land Resources, and *Woluswali* Heads to perform new functions of supporting community land administration have to be strengthened. People in these government agencies have to be convinced to support this community rangeland user agreements initiative by helping to build the capacities of communities to administer these records, by monitoring their work, by providing backup digital archiving, by providing plotted satellite images, and by assisting with the formulation and implementation of rangeland improvement plans.

▪ A fundamental need is for a more supportive formal legal framework, although the RLAP showed that a program that operates in alignment with *shar'ia* law and custom is quite acceptable at least among Provincial judges and community leaders.

The conclusions of this study are cautiously optimistic, but conditioned on continuing efforts to resolve several complex issues. Nonetheless, a proposal has been prepared for expanding this study into a multi-province project, called the Land Administration and Management Program (LAMP).[83]

Notes

[1] Most household surveys indicate that land constitutes between half and two thirds of the asset endowment by the poorest households.

[2] The World Bank alone currently has a portfolio of dedicated land projects totaling $1.5 billion under supervision. Other donors provide large amounts of support as well.

[3] Recently, the importance of land policy for economic development from the country level has been highlighted by African Heads of State who endorsed, at their July 2009 summit, a framework and guidelines for land policy, with an explicit mandate to effectively monitor and regularly report on progress with implementation. This implies a need for technical input to help to translate these principles into practice and to make the transition from problem identification to actionable policy and institutional reforms, and to generate resources for implementing them. Similarly, the EU has adopted a set of land policy guidelines.

4 MCC's inclusion of the 'doing business' indicator for the cost and time required to register a property together with the IFAD land sub-indicator illustrates the political advantages of having an explicit reference to land at this level—although more input is needed to translate it into action (as in Liberia).

5 For example, in all 41 countries covered by the World Bank's 2006 Governance Indicators, taking a bribe is officially considered as legal and all but three (Brazil, Liberia, and Lebanon) had anti-corruption commissions (Kaufmann and Kraay 2008).

6 The World Bank's CPIA, used to determine the allocation of IDA resources, includes property rights as one of 16 areas (macroeconomic management, fiscal policy, debt policy, trade, financial sector, business regulatory environment, gender equality, equity of public resource use, building human resources, social protection and labor, policies and institutions for environmental sustainability, property rights and rule-based governance, quality of budgetary and financial management, efficiency of revenue mobilization, quality of public administration, transparency, accountability, and corruption in the public sector). *See* http://go.worldbank.org/F5531ZQHT0 for details. IFAD's performance-based allocation system is targeted more specifically to rural areas and includes an explicit indicator for access to land under its five broad headings. These are A. Strengthening the capacity of the rural poor and their organizations (ROs), including (i) policy and legal framework for ROs; and (ii) dialogue between government and ROs. B. Improving equitable access to productive natural resources and technology, including (i) access to land; (ii) access to water for agriculture; and (iii) access to agric. research and extension services. C. Increasing access to financial services and markets, including (i) enabling conditions for rural financial services development; (ii) investment climate for rural business; and (iii) access to agricultural input and produce markets. D. Gender issues, including (i) access to education in rural areas; and (ii) women representatives. E. Resource management and accountability, including (i) allocation and management of public resources for rural development; and (ii) accountability, transparency and corruption in rural areas (IFAD 2009).

7 We will need to make reference to the UN Habitat's urban indicators, USAID's blueprint, and the Bank's Real Estate Assessment.

8 Global indicators on the cost and time required to register land, collected since 2004 by IFC for the main city in any given country based on expert opinion have received a considerable attention by policy-makers and development partners. Several extensions are currently underway.

9 Classic examples are laws that were written without considering the technical feasibility or affordability of implementation, survey standards that are out of line with the capacity and time available for implementation, land use or planning regulations that, with the stroke of a pen push most existing land users into informality, or large scale efforts at surveying without an appropriate policy framework, a clear, transparent and well-publicized process for adjudicating rights, or a functioning system of registration to ensure that information can be maintained current.

10 One example that has received great publicity is the attempt to acquire land for building a Tata car factory by in West Bengal. As expropriation proceedings became highly politicized, this failed to materialize. Tight limits on expropriation in Peru are supported by entrepreneurs who prefer to directly negotiate with land users rather than having the public sector drag out the process.

11 With modern technology, deeds systems can also provide reliable information that allows checking for possible pre-existing claims and includes protection against malfeasance.

12 While data on reversion to informality after systematic titling campaigns are limited, the few cases where such information is available suggest that the magnitudes involved can be large (Barnes and Griffith-Charles 2007). More rigorous quantitative assessment of this issue would be highly desirable.

[13] Having realistic fee schedules and paying employees competitive wages is important to prevent middlemen and registry officials rely on bribes for provision of quick or high quality services, therefore leading to a culture of corruption that is one of the reasons why land administration ranks so highly in any independent assessments of governance.

[14] A good example that has gained considerable publicity is the attempted acquisition of land for building a car factory by Tata in West Bengal that eventually was not realized because expropriation proceedings became highly politicized. In fact, the tight limits on expropriation in Peru are supported by entrepreneurs who prefer to directly negotiate with land users rather than having the public sector drag out the process.

[15] Systematic documentation on the trade-offs involved would be highly desirable.

[16] PEFA is a partnership between the World Bank, the European Commission, the UK's Department for International Development, the Swiss State Secretariat for Economic Affairs, the French Ministry of Foreign Affairs, the Royal Norwegian Ministry of Foreign Affairs, and the International Monetary Fund that aims to support integrated and harmonized approaches to assessment and reform in the field of public expenditure, procurement and financial accountability. It aims to strengthen recipient and donor ability to (i) assess the condition of country public expenditure, procurement and financial accountability systems, and (ii) develop a practical sequence of reform and capacity-building actions, in a manner that encourages country ownership, reduces the transaction costs to countries, enhances donor harmonization, allows monitoring of progress of country public finance management performance over time., better addresses developmental and fiduciary concerns, and leads to improved impact of reforms. The partnership started in 2001 and, since finalization of the assessment framework in 2005, has conducted 127 assessments in 105 countries. See www.pefa.org for details.

[17] Procedures varied slightly across pilot countries, partly in response to local practices and country coordinator characteristics. Based on this experience, it seems that it will be most effective to provide written information to panel members together with the invitation for a first meeting to explain the general methodology, present the results (including the preliminary ranking) from the expert investigation, and ask panel members to identify sources of additional information which the country coordinator can collect in advance of a second meeting. Results from doing so, together with tentative policy recommendation, if circulated in advance, will then provide a basis for panel members to have a meaningful discussion that will allow them to come up with a consensus view (or note any dissenting views) during a second meeting. In this way, the Aide Memoire can evolve over time and be reviewed by panel members more than once. Providing a honorarium for such efforts is appropriate to compensate panel members for the time spent on this, help equalize input across members, and ensure accountability for results.

[18] In a number of instances during the pilot, involvement of mid-level government officials unwilling to admit to shortcomings in the way the system operated made it impossible for the panel to come to a consensus view. If there is a danger of this happening, it would probably be useful to have the panel present a user view of the system and get consolidated Government comments thereafter but before a public workshop is held.

[19] The Framework has since been applied in a number of other countries, including Benin (on-going).

[20] Panelists suggested that these field studies should include provincial cities—one main city of the north coast (Chiclayo, Trujillo or Piura); one Andean city (Arequipa or Cusco); and one city in the jungle area (Iquitos or Tarapoto). Because of limited funding, our field studies were conducted only in Lima and two other provinces, i.e. Chiclayo and Cusco. A total 356 surveys on registries were conducted, in addition to visits to 15 municipal agencies and interviews with 33 judges, lawyers, architects, and construction and business owners.

[21] Alan Garcia, "El Síndrome del Perro del Hortelano. Poner en Valor los Recursos no Utilizados." (The Dog in the Manger Syndrome. How to develop non-utilized resources). El Comercio daily. October 28, 2007.

[22] National Housing Plan 2006–2015 "Housing for All."

[23] Strategic Multi-annual Sector Plan of Agriculture 2007 – 2011.

[24] In the Lima- Callao conurbation, 70% of districts have a city cadastre but only half as many are complete and updated. Out of Peru's 26 main cities, only 45% have a city cadastre and 30% have a complete cadastre. Source: Report from the National Urban Development Director, June 2008.

[25] Goods in the public domain include such properties as government buildings, prisons, museums, cemeteries, ports, airports and others used to provide a public service and to meet State obligations towards its citizens. Supreme Decree 007-2008-VIVIENDA, Article 2.2.

[26] Law 29151 article 23.

[27] Law 29151 also includes in the State-owned goods system those State entities, projects and programs that carry out activities by virtue of a legal administrative mandate.

[28] Article 7 under Law 29151creates the Guarantees of the National Goods System. In article 62 it rules conveyance among public entities may be for no valuable consideration provided the good is used in development or investment programs and projects.

[29] Constitution of Peru, Article 70. *Ownership rights are inviolable and are guaranteed by the State. They must be exercised in harmony with the common good and within the rule of law. Nobody can be forced to surrender his property except for reasons of national security or public need acknowledged by the law and after payment of a fair valuable consideration that compensates the eventual damage incurred. The Judiciary may be invoked to challenge the value of the property set by the State for the expropriation.*

[30] Law 29320 was approved on February 10, 2009 and has as its background Organic Municipalities Law 27972 where a similar provision was included. Curiously, approval of the Municipalities Law failed to spark any public debate.

[31] The National Public Registries System is comprised of the Natural Persons Registry, the Juridical Persons Registry, the Real Estate Registry, the Movable Goods Registry, and the Movable Guarantees Registry.

[32] SUNARP has started a Nationwide Registry Project to create an IT-based decentralized back office so a registrar in Tumbes state can assess a deed filed in Tacna, at the other end of the country. As a result, workloads could be better balanced and specialized units would tackle complex issues.

[33] An ordinary user cannot know the file's registration number and if he does not know the owner's name, there is no way to access the registry's information.

[34] The registration docket is the document by means of which the good is registered and where all legally relevant information is included, such as property owner, record of transactions, liens and other facts encumbering the property. The registration docket is prepared by the Registrar who, based on the titles submitted by the user, prepares a summary of all legally relevant facts.

[35] At present, registration services are provided at SUNARP's 58 registration offices and 23 windows (branch offices that act as front desks only to receive request for services that are processed in the main registration offices). Residents in 131 underserved provinces must incur additional expenses for these services, including transportation, room and board, and time. Such steep cost increase clearly discourages registration despite the potential benefit (Prefeasibility study, Immovable Property Right Consolidation Project, Ministry of Justice—SUNARP—COFOPRI. January 2006, p.186). The Nationwide Property Registration Project sponsored by SUNARP will provide real time access to registration services from anywhere across Peru.

[36] According to estimations from SUNARP the average value of registered properties is S/. 30,000.

[37] Only those who lived in rural area at the time of land privatization, and who worked in collective and state farms were entitled to agricultural land share. However, in the beginning of

the land reform, many people in rural areas who were entitled to a right to land, refused to claim their land shares so as to avoid paying taxes, or because they migrated to cities or out of the country.

[38] Difficulties arise regarding the so-called 'unified' farms, where the conversion from state to individual lots was subverted and new collective entities were directly created, especially in the country's North.

[39] During systematic first time registration, 34% of all registered property units were registered based on non-documentary forms of evidence.

[40] These include the Law of the Kyrgyz Republic on the Foundation of the State Guarantees for Gender Equality (March 2003, N 60), which was followed by the amendment to this law (State Guarantees of Equal Rights and Equal Opportunities for Men and Women, Aug, 2008, No184), and others. According to the Article 13 of this law the right to land is equally reserved for persons of both sexes.

[41] This report is available on the Gosregister website (www.gosreg.kg) and at the National Statistics Committee.

[42] These include agricultural (arable land, irrigated and dry land, perennial plantings, hay land, pastures) land, land plots near the house, and land plots of settlement areas and land for commercial purposes.

[43] As of April 30, 2009, a uniform fee for conducting a registration of somewhat less than US$4.00 has been adopted.

[44] Afghanistan Web Site. The CIA World Fact Book estimates the population to be closer to 32 million.

[45] http://www.iaea.org/inisnkm/nkm/aws/eedrb/data/AF-gdpc.html.

[46] For a detailed discussion of the results of this effort, see Asian Development Bank, Final Report, September, 2007, which can be found at: www.terrainstitute.org.

[47] The English terms "pastures", "rangeland" and "pasture land" are translations of the same Farsi term used in various English language documents, and are used interchangeably in this chapter. People use such lands for grazing of livestock, gathering of fuelwood, house, and fence making materials, and medicinal herbs.

[48] The Land Management Law of 2008, Article 82 (1) basically repeats Article 84 (1) in the Land Management Law of 2000, and neither is clear: "(1) Pastures are virgin and arid lands, on which state and individual possession has not been proved legally and they are deemed public property. An individual or the Emirate (State) can not possess pasture lands, unless otherwise stipulated by the *Shari'a*." A Pasture Law approved in 1971 which holds in Article 3, "Pasture land is owned by the government and people can use it in accordance with provisions of this law" seems to be the operative principle for most government officials.

[49] Frauke de Weijer estimated that "the total number of (semi-)nomads currently lies between 1.5 and 2.0 million, including those that settled recently and possibly temporarily." p. 6.

[50] Ministry of Agriculture, Irrigation and Livestock, "Policy and Strategy for Forest and Rangeland Management Sub-Sector," 2006, p. 2.

[51] In this study we use the term "land management" to mean the actions taken by the owners of the land, the persons, or organizations with rights to the use land and to enjoy the benefits produced from that use. By the term "land administration" we refer to the activities of governance structures and associated private individuals pertaining to assembling and making available information about the ownership, use, and value of land. Land administration functions include the "identification of landholdings, confirming boundaries, certifying rights, and recording transactions and inheritances" (Bruce and Knox, p. 1362). Land administration entities provide services to land managers and to land regulators, taxation agencies, public utilities, as

well as developers. *See also* UN Economic Council for Europe, 1996. *See also* the FIG elaboration of a land management paradigm (Enmark, 2005), as distinct from land management.

[52] The new Policy/Strategy for a community based management paradigm of rangeland (and forests) faces many implementation issues, including the resistance of governmental land management officials. For an analysis of such resistance to the devolution of management to communities in various countries *see* Marshall 2007 and Bruce and Knox 2009. Even at the highest political levels in Afghanistan and also within the donor community, there are few leaders committed to a community based land management paradigm without a clear specification of the responsibilities of communities and higher levels of government and the capacities of each to make such a paradigm work. This study is a step toward that specification.

[53] Islamic Republic of Afghanistan, "Draft Land Policy," Section 2.2.6, January, 2007.

[54] *See* USAID Land Titling and Economic Restructuring in Afghanistan, January 2006.

[55] From discussions with community leaders in the RLAP test sites.

[56] The NSP is a nationwide effort begun in 2003 through the Ministry of Rural Rehabilitation and Development to target the needs of rural communities by employing community-driven development, delivered through a collaborative partnership, encompassing central government, local and international non-governmental organizations (NGOs), and the communities—represented by specially devised Community Development Councils (CDCs). *See* Bakarat 2006.

[57] Land tenure security is defined as landholders' confidence that neither the State nor other people will interfere with the landholder's possession or use of the land for an extended period of time (*see* Bruce 1998). Tenure insecurity can be defined as the extent to which holders of land lack such confidence. Some conditions for reducing the perceptions of insecurity are discussed in the text.

[58] *See* Sheleff (2000) for an introduction to the literature on customary law.

[59] For a review of the various approaches to land administration, including property records administration, *see* Burns et. al. 2006.

[60] "*Woluswals* (District Governors) are appointed by the President and represent the Ministry of Interior at the district level. District Governors report to the provincial governor and their role is primarily to represent the government at the district level and to coordinate ministry activities. They are also responsible for civil registration of births, deaths, and marriages. They may also assist in conflict resolution, through referral to the police or the local *shura*." *See* World Bank, 2007, page 8.

[61] Also known as "jirgas" in Pashtun areas, these institutions have played important roles in resolving community, regional or national conflicts or in establishing agreements about general policies. *See* Wardak 2003.

[62] Subsequently in the text we discuss the concepts of community/specific pastures and public pastures.

[63] *See* Brick (2008) for a more complete discussion.

[64] *See* Wardak, et al. (2007) for a useful discussion of the importance of local and regional religious leaders.

[65] *See* Scanagri/Terra Institute (2006), Sections 2.3 through 2.6 for a discussion of these institutional consultations.

[66] ISAF accessed Quickbird satellite imagery, for plotting the images on paper sheets of 84.1 cm x 76.2 cm, using coordinates which the RLAP team and village elders gathered using GPS units from site visits to rangelands. ISAF also plotted image maps which were tested to delineate smaller rangeland parcels and even agricultural parcels in the Kuchi settlement, at a scale of 1:5,000.

[67] The four test sites were selected through the consideration of several factors: 1) What provinces have a substantial area of rangeland? 2) In which of these provinces is the security situation

favorable for doing field work; 3) What villages in those provinces have had three years of experience with the National Solidarity Program of village council strengthening? 4) Out of those villages which ones were recommended by Ministry provincial staff and by NGOs involved in rural development as being relatively well organized? 5) Following meetings with village councils, which ones agreed to participate in the RLAP? A test site included the selected core village plus neighboring villages with rangeland parcels bordering on those used by villagers of the core village.

[68] In this paper the terms "Kuchi" and "nomad" are used as having the same meaning.

[69] The time constraints on the RLAP did not allow time for building this local capacity. At the same time, the RLAP did not insist on the villages using the NSP CDCs, but allowed village leaders to set up a special committee for defining the legitimate users of rangeland, if they so desired.

[70] This study involved team members who were experienced in the mobilization of communities for the upgrading of informal settlements in Kabul. They were highly skilled in finding ways to motivate people to work together on complicated and at times contentious issues in that urban context. Their community mobilization skills were complimented by those of cadastral land survey specialists with years of experience dealing with land tenure issues in rural villages. The definition of boundaries of community pastures was comparatively easy to agree upon, once the neighboring villagers joined the discussions. Agreeing upon the legitimate users of each rangeland parcel took more time, and for some parcels disputes remained even after two month community discussions. Those parcels without agreements were identified on the images and a report prepared as to the nature of the remaining disputes. There were only two such parcels in the four test sites. Special mediation efforts were planned for these remaining disputes, but the time limitations on the present study did not permit dedication of resources to this longer term mediation effort.

[71] For more on this distinction between "sovereignty" and "ownership" see Kadouf, cxxi-cxxix.

[72] See Gebremedhin for a comprehensive discussion of pasture related legislation as well as other aspects of the legal framework affecting rural land tenure and administration.

[73] Personal communication from Helge Onsrud, March, 2007.

[74] Government of Tanzania's Village Land Act of 1999.

[75] Norfolk and Tanner, 2007.

[76] The content of the standard agreement form, and instructions for completing the form, are found in the Asian Development Bank, Final Report, 2007.

[77] Community councils are called "shuras" in the north and "jirgas" mostly in the south.

[78] See Asian Development Bank/ Department for International Development, for a description of the ADAMAP methodology for arriving at signed agreements as to the legitimate users of parcels whose boundaries are described on delineated satellite imagery.

[79] The Cadastral Survey Department of AGCHO has 16 regional offices which administer cadastral maps produced mainly in the 1960s and 1970s. See Safar and Stanfield (2007). The "Amlak" is the main state land management institution, which also maintains records about the ownership of agricultural land based on a comprehensive survey in the mid 1970s. For details on the structure and operations of the Amlak, see Stanfield and Safar (2007).

[80] See Stanfield (August, 2007), and also Asian Development Bank, Final Report, op. cit. for more details concerning the four test sites and the outputs produced by the project.

[81] The RLAP field team in the five months of field work, used a budget of US$348,000 for the regional and Kabul workshops, the preparation of training manuals for the field team and for the ADAMAP procedures, in addition to the five month field work needed to produce these 20 agreements covering 27,642 hectares. A more adequate estimate of future costs of a program of this sort is contained in Scanagri/Terra, 2007

[82] Marshal, 2007; Bruce and Knox, 2009.

[83] *See* Scanagri/Terra Institute, 2007, for a proposed program description, including an estimated five year budget.

References

Chapter 1

Chiu, Amanda. 2009. The Changing Climate and a Warming World. http://www.peopleandplanet.net/doc.php?id=754&section=8

Communities and Local Government. 2008. Place Matters: the Location Strategy for the United Kingdom. http://www.communities.gov.uk/publications/communities/locationstrategy

Enmark, S. 2001. Land Administration Infrastructures for Sustainable Development. Paper presented at the UN/FIG International Conference on Spatial Information for Sustainable Development. Nairobi, Kenya. October 2–5.

Enemark, S. 2004. Building Land Information Policies. Proceedings of the Special Forum on Building Land Information Policies in the Americas. Aguascalientes, Mexico, October 26-27. http://www.fig.net/pub/mexico/papers_eng/ts2_enemark_eng.pdf.

Enemark, S. 2006. People, Politics, and Places—responding to the Millennium Development Goals. Proceedings of international conference on Land Policies & Legal Empowerment of the Poor. World Bank, Washington, November 2-3. http://www.fig.net/council/enemark_papers/2006/wb_workshop_enemark_nov_2006_paper.pdf

Enemark, S. and R. McLaren. 2008. Preventing Informal Development—Through Means of Sustainable Land Use Control. Proceedings of FIG Working Week, Stockholm, June 14-19. http://www.fig.net/pub/fig2008/papers/ts08a/ts08a_01_enemark_mclaren_2734.pdf.

FAO. 2007. "Good Governance in Land Tenure and Administration". *FAO Land Tenure Series no 9*. Rome. ftp://ftp.fao.org/docrep/fao/010/a1179e/a1179e00.pdf

FIG. 2006. "The Contribution of the Surveying Profession to Disaster Risk Management." FIG Publication No. 38. FIG Office, Copenhagen, Denmark. http://www.fig.net/pub/figpub/pub38/figpub38.htm

Government of Kenya. 2004. "Report of the Commission of Inquiry into the Illegal/Irregular Allocation of Public Land." Nairobi: Government Printer.

IPCC. 2007. "Climate Change 2007." *Fourth Assessment Report*. Cambridge: Cambridge University Press.

Molen, Paul v. d. 2009. Cadastres and Climate Change. Proceedings of FIG Working Week, Eilat, Israel, 3-8 May 2009. FIG Article of the Month, August 2009. http://www.fig.net/pub/monthly_articles/august_2009/august_2009_vandermolen.html.

RICS. 2009. The Built Environment Professions in Disaster Risk Reduction and Response. London. http://www.rics.org/NR/rdonlyres/8810B119-367D-46AE-B5A7-A2F099C5BA39/0/BEProfessionsGuide.pdf

Transparency International. 2009. "Global corruption barometer 2009." Berlin: Transparency International.

Transparency International India. 2005. "India corruption study 2005." New Delhi: Transparency International.

United Nations. 2000. "United Nations Millennium Declaration." Millennium Summit, New York, 6-8 September 2000. UN, New York. http://www.un.org/millennium/declaration/ares552e.pdf.

UNEP. 2009. "The Role of Ecosystem management in Climate Change Adaptation and Disaster Risk Reduction." Copenhagen Dicussion Series. http://www.unep.org/climatechange/LinkClick.aspx?fileticket=rPyahT90aL4%3d&tabid=129&language=en-US.

UN-Habitat. 2008a. "State of the World's Cities 2008/2009." *Harmonious Cities. Overview and Key Findings*. Nairobi, Kenya.

UN-Habitat. 2008b. "Secure Land Rights for All." UN-Habitat, Global Land Tools Network. http://www.gltn.net/en/e-library/land-rights-and-records/secure-land-rights-for-all/details.html.

UN/ISDR. 2004. "Living with Risks: A Global Review of Disaster Reduction Initiatives." United Nations publications. http://www.unisdr.org/eng/about_isdr/basic_docs/LwR2004/ch1_Section1.pdf.

Williamson, Enemark, Wallace, and Rajabifard. 2009. "Land Administration Systems for Sustainable Development." ESRI Press. In press.

Chapter 2.1

Alchian, A. and H. Demsetz. 1973. "The Property Right Paradigm". *Journal of Economic History* 33(1): 16-27.

Bassett, T. 1995. "L'introduction de la propriété de la terre" in: Blanc-Pamard, C. & L. Cambrézy (coord.) *Terre, terroir, territoire, les tensions foncières*, coll. "Dynamique des systèmes agraires", Paris, ORSTOM: 395-420.

Berry, S. 1989. "Social institutions and acces to resources," *Africa* 59 (1): 41-55.

Bini, K.K. 1999. "Gestion publique du foncier rural", communication à l'atelier *Reconnaissance et formalisation des droits fonciers en Afrique rurale*, GRET/APREFA/MAE.

Binswanger, H.P., K. Deininger and G. Feder. 1995. "Power, distortions and reform in agricultural land markets" in Behrman J., Srinivasan T.N. and Chenery H. eds. *Handbook of Development Economics*, vol III., Amsterdam, New York and Oxford: Elsevier Science, North Holland, pp.2659-2772.

Bruce, J.W. and S.E. Migot-Adholla, eds. 1994. *Searching for land tenure security in Africa.* Kendall/Hunt publishing company, p. 282.

Chauveau, J.P. 1998. "La logique des systèmes coutumiers" in Lavigne Delville (dir). *Quelles politiques foncières en Afrique rurale?* Ministère de la Coopération/Karthala, Paris.

Chauveau, J.P. 2003. "Rural Land Plans, Establishing Relevant Systems for Identifying and Registering Rights" in Lavigne Delville, P., H. Ouedraogo, C. Toulmin, eds,

Making Land Rights More Secure, Proceedings of the International Workshop for Researchers and Policy Makers, 19-21 March 2002, Ouagadougou, GRAF/GRET/IIED.

Chauveau J.P., P.M. Bosc and M. Pescay. 1998. "Le plan foncier rural en Côte d'Ivoire." In Lavigne Delville (dir). *Quelles politiques foncières en Afrique rurale?* Ministère de la Coopération/Karthala, Paris.

Chauveau, J.P., J.P. Colin, J.P. Jacob, P. Lavigne Delville, and P.Y. Le Meur. 2006. *Changes in land access and governance in West Africa: markets, social mediations and public policies.* Results of the CLAIMS research project, London, IIED, 86 p.

Codjia, X., C. Dossou-Yovo, M. Gandounou, and P. Lavigne Delville. 2008. *Renforcement des capacités des maîtres d'œuvre pour la conduite des enquêtes socio-foncières PFR.* Rapport de la formation, Ouidah, 13-17 mai 2008, GRET/GTZ.

Colin, J.P. 2005. "Droits fonciers, pratiques foncières et relations intra-familiales : les bases conceptuelles et méthodologiques d'une approche comprehensive", *Land Reform and Cooperatives,* FAO.

Colin, J.P. 2006. "Disentangling Property Rights in Land. An Economic Ethnography of Intra-family Access to Land in Lower Côte d'Ivoire". Paper presented at the International Society for New Institutional Economics (ISNIE) *Conference "Economic, Political and Social Behavior",* Boulder, Colorado, September 21-24, 2006.

Colin, J.P. 2008. "Disentangling Intra-Kinship Property Rights in Land: A Contribution of Economic Ethnography to Land Economics in Africa". *Journal of Institutional Economics* 4(2): 231-254.

Colin, J.P., P.Y. Le Meur, and E. Léonard. 2009. "Introduction générale: Identifier les droits et dicter le droit. La politique des programmes de formalisation des droits fonciers", in Colin J.P., P.Y. Le Meur, E. Léonard (eds.), *Les politiques d'enregistrement des droits fonciers. Du cadre légal aux pratiques locales,* Paris, Karthala,

Comby, J. 1998. "La gestation de la propriété", in : Lavigne Delville, Philippe (dir.) *Quelles politiques foncières pour l'Afrique rurale? Réconcilier pratiques, légitimité et légalité,* Paris, Karthala-Coopération française : 692-707.

D'Aquino, Patrick. 1998. "Le traitement et la gestion de l'information foncière". In: Lavigne Delville, Philippe (ed.) *Quelles politiques foncières pour l'Afrique rurale? Réconcilier pratiques, légitimité et légalité,* Paris, Karthala-Coopération française.

De Soto, H. 2000. *The Mystery of Capital. Why Capitalism Triumphs in the West and Fails Everywhere Else.* New York: Basic Books, London: Bantam Press, Randam House.

Durand-Lasserve, A. and H. Selod. 2009. "The Formalization of Urban Land Tenure in Developing Countries", in Lall S.V. *et al.* (eds)., *Urban Land Markets. Improving Land Management for Successful Urbanization,* Dordrecht, Springer.

Edja H., P.Y. Le Meur with the collab. of P. Lavigne Delville. 2003.*Les enquêtes socio-foncières dans la perspectives de la future loi foncière rurale au Bénin, second rapport d'étape,* GRET/PGTRN/AFD/GTZ, mars 2003, 111 p.

Edja, H. and P.Y. Le Meur. 2009. "Le Plan Foncier Rural au Bénin: connaissance, reconnaissance et participation", in Colin J.-Ph., P.-Y. Le Meur, E. Léonard (eds.), *Les politiques d'enregistrement des droits fonciers. Du cadre légal aux pratiques locales,* Paris, Karthala,

Fitzpatrick, D. 2005. "'Best Practice' Options for the Legal recognition of Customary Tenure". *Development and Change* 36 (3): 449-475.

Gastaldi, J. 1998. "Les plans fonciers ruraux en Côte d'Ivoire, au Bénin et en Guinée", In: Lavigne Delville (dir). *Quelles politiques foncières en Afrique rurale?* Ministère de la Coopération/Karthala, Paris.

Hounkpodote, R.M. 2000. "L'opération pilote du plan foncier rural au Bénin : acquis et perspectives", Lavigne Delville Ph., Toulmin C., Traore S. dir., 2000, *Gérer le foncier rural en Afrique de l'ouest*, Paris/Saint-Louis, Karthala/URED.

Hounkpodote, R.M. 2007. *Manuel de procédures pour l'établissement du plan foncier rural*, Cellule opérationnelle Plan foncier rural, MCA-Bénin/GTZ.

Jacob, J.P. 2005. *Sécurité foncière, bien commun, citoyenneté. Quelques réflexions à partir du cas burkinabé*, Etude n° 6, Ouagadougou, ACE/RECIT, 26 p.

Jacob, J.P. 2009. "La brousse ne peut pas bouffer un fils de la terre!". Droits sur la terre et sociologie du développement dans le cadre d'une opération de sécurisation foncière. Le Plan foncier rural dans le Ganzourgou (Burkina Faso)". In: Colin, J.-P., Le Meur, P.-Y. & E. Léonard (dir.) *Les politiques d'enregistrement des droits fonciers. Du cadre légal aux pratiques locales*, Paris, IRD.

Land Tenure Committee. 2009. *Land Governance and Security of Tenure in Developing Countries*, Summary. AFD/French Ministry for Foreign and European Affairs, 120 p.

Lavigne Delville, P. 1998. *Rural land tenure, renewable resources and development in Africa*, Coll. Rapports d'études, Ministère des Affaires Etrangères—Coopération et francophonie, Paris, 131 p.

Lavigne Delville, P. 2002. *Towards an articulation of land regulation modes? Recent progress and issues at stake (French-speaking West Africa)*, Contribution to the regional meeting on land issues, World Bank, Kampala, April 29th - Mai 2nd 2002 (available on the CD-ROM Proceedings and on the World Bank Website)

Lavigne Delville, P. 2006a. "Conclusions", in Chauveau J.P., Colin J.P., Jacob J.P., Lavigne Delville Ph., Le Meur P.Y., 2006, *Changes in land access and governance in West Africa: markets, social mediations and public policies, Results of the CLAIMS research project*, London, IIED/CLAIMS, pp. 64-73.

Lavigne Delville, P. 2006b. "Sécurité, insécurités, et sécurisation foncières: un cadre conceptuel", *Réforme agraire et coopératives* 2006/2, FAO, pp.18-25.

Lavigne Delville, P. forthcoming. "La réforme foncière rurale au Bénin: émergence et mise en question d'une politique instituante dans un pays sous régime d'aide", *Revue Française de Science Politique* 60 (4).

Lavigne Delville, P., R. Mongbo and A. Mansion, coord. 2009. *Vers une gestion foncière communale : stratégies, outils et conditions de réussite (Afrique de l'Ouest et Madagascar)*. Actes de l'atelier d'échanges de pratiques (Cotonou, 20-25 octobre 2008). Gret/CEBEDES, 96 p.

Le Meur, P.Y. 2006. "Governing land, translating rights: The Rural Land Plan in Benin". In: Lewis, D. & D. Mosse (eds.) *Development Brokers and Translators*, New York & Houndmills, Palgrave MacMillan.

Le Roy, E. 1997. "La sécurité foncière dans un contexte africain de marchandisation imparfaite de la terre" in Blanc-Pamard et Cambrézy coord. *Terre, terroir, territoire, les tensions foncières*, Coll. Dynamique des systèmes agraires, Paris, Orstom, pp. 455-472.

Le Roy, E. 1998. "Les orientations des réformes foncières depuis le début des années quatre-vingt dix." In Lavigne Delville (dir). *Quelles politiques foncières en Afrique rurale?* Ministère de la Coopération/Karthala, Paris.

Le Roy, E. 2003. "Actualité des droits dits 'coutumiers' dans les pratiques et les politiques foncières en Afrique et dans l'Océan Indien à l'orée du XXIᵉ siècle", *Cahiers d'Anthropologie du Droit*, cahier thématique "Retour au foncier", LAJP/Karthala ; pp. 237-263.

Lund, C. 1998. *Land, Power and Politics. Land Struggles and the Rural Code.* Hamburg: APAD-Lit Verlag.

Lund, C. 2001. "Les réformes foncières dans un contexte de pluralisme juridique et institutionnel : Burkina Faso et Niger", in Winter G. ed, *Inégalités et politiques publiques en Afrique, pluralité des normes et jeux d'acteurs*, Paris: Karthala/IRD.

Lund ,C. 2002. "Negociating Property Institutions: On the Symbiosis of Property and Authority in Africa" in Juul K. and Lund C. eds. 2002, *Negociating Property in Africa*, Porthsmouth, Heinemann, pp.11-44.

Ouedraogo, H. 2005. "Étude comparative de la mise en oeuvre des Plans Fonciers Ruraux en Afrique de l'Ouest: Bénin, Burkina Faso, Côte d'Ivoire", *Études juridiques en ligne* 42, FAO, 41 p.

PGTRN. 2000. *Manuel de procédures du Plan Foncier Rural*, PGTRN/GTZ/AFD.

Platteau, J.P. 1996. "The evolutionnary theory of land rights as applied to sub-Saharan Africa: a critical assesment, *Development and change* 27 (1): 29-86.

Platteau, J.P. 1998. "Droits fonciers, enregistrement des terres et accès au crédit", in Lavigne Delville, Philippe (dir.) *Quelles politiques foncières pour l'Afrique rurale? Réconcilier pratiques, légitimité et légalité*, Paris: Karthala-Coopération française: 293-201.

Schlager, E. and E. Ostrom. 1992. "Property-rights regimes and natural resources: a conceptual analysis." *Land Economics* 68 (3): 249-262.

Shipton, P. 1988. "The Kenyan land tenure reform: misunderstandings in the public creation of private property" in Downs and Reyna eds., *Land and society in contemporary Africa*, Univ. Press of New England: 91-135.

Shipton, P. and M. Goheen. 1992. "Understanding African Land-holding: Power, Wealth and Meaning". *Africa* 62 (3): 307-325.

Soro, D. and J.P. Colin. 2004. *Droits et gestion intra-familiale de la terre chez les migrants sénoufo en zone forestière de Côte d'Ivoire. Le cas de Kongodjan (sous-préfecture d'Adiaké).* Document de travail de l'Unité de Recherche 095 n°11, IRD, UR-REFO.

World Bank. 2003. Land policy for growth and poverty reduction, Policy Research Report, Washington, DC: World Bank.

Chapter 2.2

Adams, M. and R. Palmer. 2007. 'Independent Review of Land Issues' *Volume 111 2006-2007 Eastern and Southern Africa* (June).

Deininger, K. and G. Feder, on behalf of the World Bank. 2008. "Land Registration, Economic Development and Poverty Reduction." World Bank. July.

Government of Rwanda (MINECOFIN). 2000 'Rwanda Vision 2020', MINECOFIN, Kigali.

Government of Rwanda (MINECOFIN). 2007. "'Economic Development and Poverty Reduction Strategy," Kigali.

Government of Rwanda (MINIRENA). 2008. "Draft Strategic Road Map for Land Tenure Reform in Rwanda." November.

Pagiola, S. on behalf of the World Bank.1999. "Economic Analysis of Rural Land Administration Projects," World Bank.

Payne, G et al. 2007. "Social and Economic Impacts of Land Titling Programmes in Urban and Peri-urban Areas: a Review of the Literature," presented at the World Bank Urban Research Symposium, Washington DC, May.

Smith, R. 2004. "Land Tenure, Fixed Investment and Farm Productivity: Evidence from Zambia's Southern Province."

UNESCO Institute for Statistics in EdStats. 2009. http://web.worldbank.org/WBSITE/ EXTERNAL/TOPICS/EXTEDUCATION/EXTDATASTATISTICS/.

Chapter 2.3

Division of Land Board Tenure and Advise. 2006. Operational Manual for Communal Land Boards, (second edition). Windhoek, Namibia, Ministry of Lands and Resettlement.

Kapitango, D., M. Meijs, P. Saers, and R. Witmer. 2008. Registration of Customary Land Rights with Aerial Photos in the Olukonda Constituency, project report, Windhoek, Namibia. Ministry of Lands and Resettlement.

Lemmen, C., J. Zevenbergen, M. Lengoiboni, K. Deininger, and T. Burns. 2009. First experiences with High Resolution Imagery Based Adjudication Approach for Social Tenure Domain Model in Ethiopia, Proceeding of the FIG – World Bank Conference on Land Governance in Support of the Millennium Development Goals – Responding to New Challenges, Washington, DC. March 9–10.

Malan, Johann. 2003. Guide to the Communal Land Reform Act, No. 5 of 2002. Windhoek, Namibia. Legal Assistance Center and Namibia National Farmers Union.

Rattanabirabongse,V., R. A. Eddington, A. E. Burns and K. G. Nettle. 1998. The Thailand land titling project—thirteen years of experience, Great Britain, *Land Use Policy* 15: 3-23.

Republic of Namibia. Communal Land Reform Act, No 5 of 2002. Windhoek, Namibia. Government Gazette, 2002.

Republic of Namibia. National Land Policy. Windhoek, Namibia. Government Gazette, 1998.

Sagashya, D. and C. English. 2009. Designing and Establishing a Land Administration System for Rwanda: Technical and Economic Analysis, Proceeding of the FIG - World Bank Conference on Land Governance in Support of the MDGs - Responding to New Challenges, Washington, DC. March 9–10.

Wubbe, M. 2008. Draft Roadmap For the Land Registration of the Communal Areas 2009-2013 (v0.3). Windhoek, Namibia: Ministry of Lands and Resettlement.

Chapter 3.1

Allen Consulting Group. 2008. Economic Benefits of High Resolution Positioning Services, Final Report. Prepared for Victorian Department of Sustainability and Environment and the Cooperative Research Centre for Spatial Information, November 2008.

Altamimi, Z., X. Collilieux, J. Legrand, B. Garayt, and C. Boucher. 2007. ITRF2005: A new release of the International Terrestrial Reference Frame based on time series of station positions and Earth Orientation Parameters. *J. Geophys. Res.* 112, B09401.

Dow, J.M., R.E. Neilan, and C. Rizos. 2008. The International GNSS Service in a Changing Landscape of Global Navigation Satellite Systems. *Journal of Geodesy* 83 (3-4): 191-198 (March).

Enemark, S. 2008. Towards a Sustainable Future—Building the Capacity. Opening Speech FIG Working Week, 14–19 June, Stockholm, Sweden.

Higgins, M. 2007. Delivering Precise Positioning Services in Regional Areas. Proceedings of IGNSS 2007 Symposium on GPS/GNSS. December. Sydney, Australia.

Higgins, M.B. 2008. An Organisational Model for a Unified GNSS Reference Station Network for Australia. *Journal of Spatial Science* 53 (2) (December).

Lateral Economics. 2009. Nation Building for the Information Age: The economic case for governments leading the development of a national high accuracy positioning network. An unpublished report prepared by Lateral Economics for the Australian Spatial Consortium.

Ong Kim Sun, G. and P. Gibbings. 2005. "How Well Does the Virtual Reference Station (VRS) System of GPS Base Stations Perform in Comparison to Conventional RTK?" *Journal of Spatial Science* 50 (1).

Picco, J., M.B. Higgins, R. Sarib, G. Johnston, and G. Blick. 2006. Streamlining the Exchange of Geodetic Data in Australia and New Zealand. XXIII FIG International Congress, International Federation of Surveyors (FIG), Munich, Germany, 13–18 October. www.fig.net/pub/fig2006/techprog.htm (Paper 0502).

Rizos, C. 2008. "Multi-Constellation GNSS/RNSS from the Perspective of High Accuracy Users in Australia." *Journal of Spatial Science*, 53 (2) (December).

Rummel, R., M. Rothacher and G. Beutler. 2005. "Integrated Global Geodetic Observing System (IGGOS)—Science Rationale," *Journal of Geodynamics* 40 (4–5) (November-December): 357–362.

Tullberg, J.N. 2008. Paddock Change for Climate Change. ed. M. J. Unkovich. Proceedings of the 14th Australian Agronomy Conference, September, Adelaide, South Australia. Australian Society of Agronomy.

UN/FIG. 1999. The Bathurst Declaration on Land Administration for Sustainable Development. Published by The International Federation of Surveyors (FIG), FIG PublicationNo. 21, December. Available at: www.fig.net/pub/figpub/pubindex.htm.

UN/FIG. 2005. The Aguascalientes Statement: The Inter-regional Special Forum on Development of Land Information Policies in the Americas. Published by The

International Federation of Surveyors (FIG), FIG Publication No. 34, January. Available at: www.fig.net/pub/figpub/pubindex.htm.

Wirola, L. 2008. High-Accuracy Positioning for the Mass Market. FIG Working Week 2008, International Federation of Surveyors (FIG), Stockholm, Sweden, 14–19 June. Available at: www.fig.net/pub/fig2008/techprog.htm (Paper 3167, Presentation only).

World Bank. 2009. Agriculture and Rural Development, Infrastructure. Available at http://go.worldbank.org/L44T63B830 as at 6 March 2009).

Chapter 3.2

Dhal, N., R. S. Madame, and Y. V. N. Krishna Murthy. 1994. Cadastral Mapping and LIS. Proceedings, 14th INCA Congress, Bangalore, India.

GOI. 1985. Government of India. 73rd and 74th Amendment Acts. India.

Gopala Rao, M. 2000. LIS in India—Perspective and Retrospective. Proceedings, National Conference on Land Information System, New Delhi.

Krishna Murthy, Y.V.N., Srinivasa Rao, S., Srinivasan, D. S. and Adiga, S., "A Land Information System (LIS) for rural development", Technical proceedings, Geomatics-2000.

Krishna Murthy, Y.V.N, Srinivasa Rao, S., Srinivasan, D. S., and Radhakrishnan K. 1996. "Land Information Systems (LIS) for Rural Development" IX INCA conference, New Delhi.

Williamson, I.P., L. Ting, and D. M. Grant. 2000. The Evolving Role of Land Administration in Support of Sustainable Development—A review of the United Nations. *The Australian Surveyor* 44 (2):126–135.

Chapter 3.3

Augustinus, C., Lemmen, C. H. J. and van Oosterom, P. J. M. 2006. Social Tenure Domain Model Requirements from the Perspective of Pro-poor Land Management. In: proceedings of the Fifth FIG Regional Conference for Africa: Promoting Land Administration and Good Governance, Accra, Ghana.

Belay, Gebeyehu. 2009. The Procedure Followed and the Results Achieved from CIM Piloting. Presentation at the International Workshop on Cadastral Index Mapping, Bahir Dar (Ethiopia). (online at World Bank: http://web.worldbank.org/WBSITE/EXTERNAL/TOPICS/EXTARD/0,,contentM DK:22196904~pagePK:148956~piPK:216618~theSitePK:336682,00.html)

Deininger, Klaus, Jaap Zevenbergen, Daniel Ayalew Ali. 2006, Assessing the Certification Process of Ethiopia's Rural Lands. Colloque International, At the Frontier of Land Issues: Social Embeddedness of Rights and Public Policy, Montpellier, France.

Deininger, Klaus, Daniel Ayalew Ali, Stein Holden, and Jaap Zevenbergen. 2008. Rural land certification in Ethiopia: Process, initial impact, and implications for other African countries. *World Development* 36(10):1786–1812.

Haile, Solomon Abebe. 2005. Bridging the Land Rights Demarcation Gap in Ethiopia: Usefulness of High Resolution Satellite Image (HRSI) Data. Dissertation, BOKU, Vienna, October.

Kansu, Oguz and Sezgin Gazioglu. 2006. The Availability of the Satellite Image Data in Digital Cadastral Map Production. XXIII International FIG Congress: Shaping the Change, Munich, Germany.

Kapitango, D and M. Meijs. 2009. Land Registration Using Aerial Photography in Namibia: Costs and Lessons. FIG-WB Conference. Land Governance in Support of the Millennium Development Goals: Responding to New Challenges. World Bank, Washington, D.C.

Konstantinos, Christodoulou. 2003. Combination of Satellite Omage Pan IKONOS-2 with GPS in Cadastral Applications. UN/ECE WPLA Workshop on Spatial Information Management for Sustainable Real Estate Market Best Practice Guidelines on Nationwide Land Administration, Athens, Greece.

Lemmen, C.H.J., C. Augustinus, P. J. M. van Oosterom, and P. van der Molen. 2007. The Social Tenure Domain Model: Design of a First Draft Model. In: FIG Working Week 2007: Strategic Integration of Surveying Services. Hong Kong SAR, China. Copenhagen: International Federation of Surveyors (FIG).

Ondulo, Joe-Duncan and William Kalande. 2006. High Spatial Resolution Satellite Imagery for PID Improvement in Kenya. Shaping the Change, XXIII FIG Congress, Munich, Germany.

Palm, Lars. 2006. Comparison of Total Station/Advanced GPS Survey and High Resolution Satellite Imagers. The National Conference on Standardization of Rural Land Registration and Cadastral Survey Methodologies. https://webmail.itc.nl/exchange/lemmen/Inbox/Re:Yourpaper-2.EML/-_ftn1#_ftn1. United Nations Conference Centre, Addis Ababa, Ethiopia.

Paudyal, Dev Raj and Nab Raj Subedi. 2005. Identification of Informal Settlement by Integration of Cadastral Information and Remote Sensing Satellite Imagery. A Seminar on Space Technology Application and Recent Development In Geospatial Products in Kathmandu, Nepal.

Sagashya, D. and C. English. 2009. Designing and Establishing a Land Administration System for Rwanda: Technical and Economic Analysis. FIG - WB Conference, Land Governance in Support of the Millennium Development Goals: Responding to New Challenges. World Bank, Washington D.C.

Tuladhar, Arbind Man. 2005. Innovative use of remote sensing images for pro-poor land management. FIG Expert Group Meeting on Secure Land Tenure: New Legal Frameworks and Tools, Bangkok, Thailand.

Zahir, Ali. 2009. Second Fieldwork Report (Part 2), Assessing Usefulness of High-Resolution Satellite Imagery (HRSI) in GIS-based Cadastral Land Information System. Internal Report, ITC. November (unpublished).

Chapter 4.1

Agarwal, B. 1994. *A Field of One's Own: Gender and Land Rights in South Asia*. Cambridge University Press

Agarwal, B. 1995. "Women's Legal Rights in Agricultural Land in India". *Economic and Political Weekly*. March 1.

Ambrus, A., E. Field and M. Torero, M. 2009. *Muslim Family Law, Prenuptial Agreements and the Emergence of Dowry in Bangladesh*. Harvard University Working Paper, January.

Anderson, S. 2003. "Why Dowry Payments Declined with Modernization in Europe but Are Rising in India". *Journal of Political Economy* 111 (2): 269–310.

Anderson, S. and M. Eswaran. 2009. Determinants Female Autonomy: Evidence from Bangladesh. forthcoming *Journal of Development Economics*.

Arnold, J. E. M. 2001. "Devolution of Control of Common Pool Resources to Local Communities: Experiences in Forestry." in A. de Janvry, G. Gordillo, J. P. Plateau and E. Sadoulet (eds.), *Access to Land Rural Poverty and Public Action*, OUP, Oxford.

Behrman, J. R. and M. R. Rosenzweig. 2004. "Parental Allocations to Children: New Evidence on Bequest Differences among Siblings." *Review of Economics and Statistics*, 86 2, 637-640.

Bloch, F. and V. Rao. 2002. "Terror as a Bargaining Instrument: A Case-Study of Dowry Violence in Rural India." *American Economic Review* 92 (4): 1029–1043.

Caldwell, J., P. H. Reddy and P. Caldwell. 1983. "The Causes of Marriage Change in South India". Population Studies. 37 (3):343–361, November.

Carroll, L. 1991. Daughters Right of Inheritance in India—A Perspective on the Problem of Dowry. *Modern Asian Studies* 25: 791–809.

Chiappori, P. A., B. Fortin and G. Lacroix. 2002. "Marriage Market, Divorce Legislation, and Household Labor Supply". *Journal of Political Economy* 110 (1): 37–72.

Deere, Carmen Diana, and Cheryl Doss. 2006. "The gender asset gap: What do we know and why does it matter?," *Feminist Economics*, 1-2, 1-50.

Duflo, E. 2003. "Grandmothers and Granddaughters: Old-Age Pensions and Intrahousehold Allocation in South Africa". *World Bank Economic Review* 17 (1): 1–25.

Duflo, E. and P. Topalova. 2004. Unappreciated Service: Performance, Perceptions, and Women Leaders in India. Mimeo, Massachusetts Institute of Technology.

Dyson, T. and M. Moore. 1983. "Kinship Structure, Female Autonomy, and Demographic Behavior in India". *Population and Development Review* 9 (1): 35–60.

Estudillo, J. P., A. R. Quisumbing and K. Otsuka. 2001. "Gender Differences in Land Inheritance and Schooling Investments in the Rural Philippines". *Land Economics* 77 (1): 130–143.

Eswaran, M. 2002. "The Empowerment of Women, Fertility, and Child Mortality: Towards a Theoretical Analysis." *Journal of Population Economics* 15: 433–454.

Goldstein, M. and C. Udry. 2008. "The Profits of Power: Land Rights and Agricultural Investment in Ghana." *Journal of Political Economy* 116 (6): 980–1022.

Jensen, R., and R. Thornton. 2003. "Early Female Marriage in the Developing World." *Gender and Development* 11(2): 9–19.

Luke, N. and K. Munshi. 2007. *Women As Agents of Change: Female Income and Mobility in Developing Countries*. Providence, RI: Brown University.

Marimuthu, P. 2008. "Effects of Female Age at Marriage on Birth Order and Utilisation of Motherhood Services: A District Level Analysis." *Journal of Family Welfare* 54 (1):79–84

Munshi, K. and M. Rosenzweig. 2008. The Efficacy of Parochial Politics: Caste, Commitment, and Competence in Indian Local Governments. Economics Department, Working Paper 53. New Haven, CT: Yale University.

Panda, P. and B. Agarwal. 2005. "Marital Violence, Human Development and Women's Property Status In India." *World Development* 33 (5): 823–50.

Platteau, J. P. and J. M. Baland. 2001. "Impartial Inheritance Versus Equal Division: A Comparative Perspective Centered on Europe and Sub-Saharan Africa." in A. de Janvry, G. Gordillo, J.-P. Platteau and E. Sadoulet (eds.), *Access to Land Rural Poverty and Public Action*, Oxford University Press.

Qian, Nancy. 2008. "Missing Women and the Price of Tea in China: The Effect of Sex-Specific Earnings on Sex Imbalance." *Quarterly Journal of Economics* 123, (3): 1251–1285.

Roy, S. 2008. Female Empowerment through Inheritance Rights: Evidence from India. Working Paper, LSE.

Stevenson, B. 2007. "The Impact of Divorce Laws on Marriage-Specific Capital." *Journal of Labor Economics* 25 (1): 75–94.

Strauss, J., G. Mwabu, and K. Beegle. 2000. "Intrahousehold Allocations: a Review of Theories, Empirical Evidence and Policy Issues", *Journal of African Economics*, 9, pp.83-143.

Thomas, D. 1990. "Intrahousehold Resource Allocation: An Inferential Approach." *Journal of Human Resources* 25 (4): 635–664.

Udry, C. 1996. "Gender, Agricultural Production, and the Theory of the Household." *Journal of Political Economy* 104 (5): 1010–46.

Walker, C. 2002. Ensuring Women's Land Access. World Bank Regional Land Workshop in Kampala, Uganda.

World Bank. 2001. *Engendering Development: Through Gender Equality in Rights, Resources, and Voice.* Oxford: Oxford University Press.

Chapter 4.2

Alemu, T. 1999. Land Tenure and Soil Conservation: Evidence from Ethiopia. Unpublished PhD dissertation, Göteborg University, Göteborg.

Arellano, M. and R. Carrasco. 2003. "Binary Choice Panel Data Models with Predetermined Variables." *Journal of Econometrics* 115: 125–157.

Bell, C. and C. Sussangkarn. 1988. "Rationing and Adjustment in the Market for Tenancies: The Behavior of Landowning Households in Thanjavur District." *American Journal of Agricultural Economics* 70(4): 779–789.

Besley, T. 1995. "Property Rights and Investment Incentives: Theory and Evidence from Ghana." *Journal of Political Economy* 103(5): 903–37.

Besley, T. and R. Burgess. 2000. "Land Reform, Poverty Reduction, and Growth: Evidence from India." *The Quarterly Journal of Economics* 115(2): 389–430.

Bliss, C.J. and N.H. Stern. 1982. *Palanpur: The Economy of an Indian Village.* Delhi and New York: Oxford University Press.

Blundell, R.W. and S. Bond. 1998. "Initial Conditions and Moment Restrictions in Dynamic Panel Data Models." *Journal of Econometrics* 87: 115–143.

Brasselle, A.S., F. Gaspart and J.-P.Platteau. 2002. "Land Tenure Security and Investment Incentives: Puzzling Evidence From Burkina Fasso." *Journal of Development Economics* 67: 373–418.

Carter, M., K.D. Weibe and B. Blarel. 1994. Tenure Security for Whom? Differential Effects of Land Policy in Kenya. in J.W. Bruce and Migot-Adholla. *Searching for Tenure Insecurity in Africa.* Dubuque, Iowa, Kendall/Hunt, 141–168.

Cotula, L., C. Toulmin and C. Hesse. 2004. *Land Tenure and Administration in Africa: Lessons of Experience and Emerging Issues.* International Institute for Environment and Development, London.

Deaton, A. 1997. *The Analysis of Household Surveys: A Microeconometric Approach to Development Policy.* Washington, D.C.: World Bank Publications.

Deininger, K. 2003. *Land Policies for Growth and Poverty Reduction.* Washington, D.C.: The World Bank.

Deininger , K. and S. Jin. 2006. "Tenure Security and Land-Related Investment: Evidence from Ethiopia." *European Economic Review* 50: 1245–1277.

Deininger, K., D.A. Ali, S. T. Holden and J. Zevenbergen. 2008. "Rural Land Certification in Ethiopia: Process, Initial Impact, and Implications for Other African Countries." *World Development 36: 1786–1812.*

Fafchamps, M. 2004. *Market Institutions in Sub-Saharan Africa.* Cambridge, Massachusettes: The MIT Press.

Ghebru, H. and S. T. Holden. 2008. Factor Market Imperfections and Rural Land Rental Markets in Northern Ethiopian Highlands. in Holden, S.T., Otsuka, K., Place, F. (eds). *The Emergence of Land Markets in Africa: Assessing the Impacts on Poverty, Equity and Efficiency,* Washington, D.C.: Resources for the Future Press. 74–92.

Hagos, F., and S.T. Holden. 2003. Incentives for Conservation in Tigray, Ethiopia: Findings from a Household Survey. Unpublished. Department of Economics and Social Sciences, Agricultural University of Norway.

Haile, M., W. Witten, K. Abraha, S. Fissha, A. Kebede, G. Kassa, and G. Redda. 2005. Land Registration in Tigray, Northern Ethiopia. Research Report 2. Mekelle, University, Mekelle, Tigray.

Holden, S.T. and M. Bezabih. 2008. Gender and Land Productivity on Rented Out Land: Evidence from Ethiopia. in Holden S. T., Otsuka K., Place F. eds. *The Emergence of Land Markets in Africa: Assessing the Impacts on Poverty, Equity and Efficiency.* Washington, D.C.: Resources For the Future Press. 179–196

Holden, S. and H. Ghebru, H. 2006. Kinship, Transaction Costs and Land Rental Market Participation. Working Paper, Norwegian University of Life Sciences, Ås.

Holden, S.T. and H. Yohannes. 2002. "Land Redistribution, Tenure Insecurity, and Intensity of Production: A Study of Farm Households in Southern Ethiopia." *Land Economics* 78(4): 573–590.

Holden, S.T., K. Deininger and H. Ghebru. 2009. "Impacts of Low-Cost Land Certification on Investment and Productivity." *American Journal of Agricultural Economics* 912): 359–373.

Holden, S., K. Deininger, and H. Ghebru. In press. "Tenure Insecurity, Gender, Low-cost Land Certification, and Land Rental Market Participation." *Journal of Development Studies* (Forthcoming).

Holden S.T., K. Otsuka, F. Place, eds. 2008. *The Emergence of Land Markets in Africa: Assessing the Impacts on Poverty, Equity and Efficiency,* Washington, D.C.: Resources For the Future Press.

Honoré, B.E. (1993). "Orthogonality Conditions for Tobit Models with Fixed Effects and Lagged Dependent Variables." *Journal of Econometrics* 59: 35–61.

Honoré, B.E. and E. Kyriazidou. 2000). "Panel Data Discrete Choice Models with Lagged Dependent Variables." *Econometrica* 68: 839–874.

Jacoby, H.G. and B. Minten. 2007. "Is Land Titling in Sub-Saharan Africa Cost-Effective? Evicence from Madagascar." *The World Bank Economic Review* 21(3): 461–485.

Jacoby, H.G. and B. Minten. 2006. *Land Titles, Investment, and Agricultural Productivity in Madagascar: A Poverty and Social Impact Analysis.* Washington, D.C.: The World Bank.

Moor, G.M. 1998. "Tenure Security and Productivity in the Zimbabwean Small Farm Sector: Implications for South Africa." *Development Southern Africa* 15(4): 609–620.

MUT. (2003). Securing Land Rights in Africa: Can Land Registration serve the Poor? Interim Report of Mekelle University Team. Mekelle, Tigray, Ethiopia.

Pender, J. and M. Fafchamps. 2006. "Land Lease Markets and Agricultural Efficiency in Ethiopia." *Journal of African Economies* 15(2): 251–284.

Place, F. and S. Migot-Adholla. 1998. "The Economic Effects of Land Registration on Smallholder Farms In Kenya: Evidence from Nyeri and Kakamega Districts." *Land Economics.* 74: 360–373.

Rahmato, D. 1984. *Agrarian Reform in Ethiopia.* Uppsala: Scandinavian Institute of African Studies.

Skoufias, E. (1995). "Household Resources, Transactions Costs, and Adjustment Through Land Tenancy." *Land Economics* 71(1), pp. 42-56.

Tadesse, M., S.T. Holden and R. Øygard. 2008. Contract Choice and Poverty in Southern Highlands of Ethiopia. In Holden, S. T., K. Otsuka, and F. Place, eds. *The Emergence of Land Markets in Africa: Impacts on Poverty and Efficiency.* Resources For the Future Press, Washington, D.C.

Teklu, T. and A. Lemi. 2004. "Factors Affecting Entry and Intensity in Informal Rental Land Markets in Southern Ethiopian Highlands." *Agricultural Economics* 30: 117–128.

Tikabo, M.O., S.T. Holden and O. Bergland. 2007. Factor Market Imperfections and the Land Rental Market in the Highlands of Eritrea: Theory and Evidence. Unpublished. Department of Economics and Resource Management, Norwegian University of Life Sciences.

Wooldridge, J. 2005. "Simple Solutions to the Initial Conditions Problem in Dynamic, Nonlinear Panel Data Models with Unobserved Heterogeneity." *Journal of Applied Econometrics* 20: 39–54.

Chapter 5.1

Angel, S., S.C. Sheppard, and D. L. Civco. 2005. "The Dynamics of Global Urban Expansion," Washington, D.C.: Transport and Urban Development Department, World Bank.

Baker, J. 2008. "Urban Poverty: A Global View," The World Bank Group Urban Papers, Urban Sector Board.

Deininger, K. 2003. "Land Policies for Growth and Poverty Reduction," a World Bank Policy Research Report, World Bank and Oxford University Press.

Food and Agricultural Organization, 2007. "Land Reform, Land Settlement and Cooperatives," Vol. 2.

Food and Agricultural Organization and UN-HABITAT, Towards Good Land Governance (forthcoming), Rome.

Kessides, C. 2006. "The Urban Transition in Sub-Saharan Africa: Implications for Economic Growth and Poverty Reduction," World Bank.

Mangin, W.P. 1967. "Latin American Squatter Settlements: a Problem and a Solution," Latina American Research.

Martine, G., G. McGranahan, M. Montgomery, and R. Fernandez-Castilla, eds. 2008. "The New Global Frontier Urbanization, Poverty and Environment in the 21st Century," Earthscan, London.

Mitlin, D., and S. Patel. 2005. "Re-interpreting the Rights-Based Approach—A Grassroots Perspective on Rights and Development," Economic and Social Research Council, Global Poverty Research Group Working Paper Series.

Moreno. E., UN-HABITAT. "Living with Shelter Deprivations: Slums Dwellers in the World" (forthcoming), UN-DESA.

Roberts, B. and T. Kanaley, eds. (2006. "Urbanization and Sustainability in Asia Good Practice Approaches in Urban Region Development," Asian Development Bank and Cities Alliance.

Sietchiping, R. 2008. "Predicting and Preventing Slum Growth Theory, Method, Implementation and Evaluation," VDM Verlag Dr. Muller Aktiengesellscahft & Co., Saarbrucken, Germany.

The Norwegian Forum on Environment and Development. 2007. Beyond Formalisation, Briefing Paper.

United Nations. 2007. "The Millennium Development Goals Report 2007," New York.

United Nations Economic Commission for Europe 2008 "In Search for Sustainable Solutions for Informal Settlements in the ECE Region Challenges and Policy Responses" (unedited draft), Sixty-ninth session, Geneva, September 22-23.

UNFPA-United Nations Population Fund. 2007. "State of the World Population: Unleashing the Potential of Urban Growth."

UN-HABITAT. 1996. "The Habitat Agenda Goals and Principles, Commitments and the Global Plan of Action." Nairobi.

UN-HABITAT. 2001. *State of the World's Cities*. Nairobi.

UN-HABITAT. 2002. "Cities Without Slums," Paper presented to the World Urban Forum, Nairobi, April 29-May 3, 2002, HSP/WUF/DLG.1.

UN-HABITAT. 2003. *The Challenge of Slums Global Report on Human Settlements 2003*. London: Earthscan.

UN-HABITAT. 2005. Facts and Figures about Financing Urban Shelter.

UN-HABITAT. 2006a, "Reinventing Planning: A New Governance Paradigm for Managing Human Settlements," a Position Paper developing themes from the Draft Vancouver Declaration for debate leading into the World Planners Congress, Vancouver, June 17-20, 2006.

UN-HABITAT. 2006b. *State of the World's Cities 2006-7: The Millennium Development Goals and Urban Sustainabilty*. London.

UN-HABITAT. 2006c. *Enabling Shelter Strategies: Review of Experience from Two Decades of Implementation.* Nairobi, UN-HABITAT.

UN-HABITAT. 2007. *Global Report on Human Settlements: Enhancing Urban Safety and Security.* London: Earthscan.

UN-HABITAT. 2008a. *State of the World's Cities 2008-9: Harmonious Cities.* London: Earthscan.

UN-HABITAT. 2008b. "Secure Land Rights for All," UN-HABITAT, Nairobi.

UN-HABITAT. "Medium-Term Strategic and Institutional Plan." (forthcoming). Focus Area 3 Policy, Strategy and Programme document on Pro Poor Land and Housing (internal document).

UN-HABITAT. Policy Guide to Rental Housing in Developing Countries. (forthcoming), Nairobi.

World Bank. 2007. "Responses to the Problem of Informal Development: Current Projects and Future Action." Paper presented at "Informal Settlements—Real Estate Markets Needs Related to Good Land Administration and Planning," FIG Commission 3 Workshop, Athens March 28-31.

Chapter 5.2

Eppli, M. J., and J.D. Benjamin. 1994. "The Evolution of Shopping Center Research: A Review and Analysis." *The Journal of Real Estate Research* 9 (1): 5-32.

Gatzlaff, D.H., G.S. Sirmans, and B.A. Diskin. 1994. "The Effect of Anchor Tenant Loss on Shopping Center Rents." *The Journal of Real Estate Research* 9 (1): 99-110.

Ghosh, A. 1986. "The Value of a Shopping Center and Other Insights from a Revised Central Place Model." *Journal of Retailing* 62: 79-97.

Hendriks, D. 2005. "Apportionment in Property Valuation: Should We Separate the Inseparable?" *Journal of Property Investment & Finance* 23 (5): 455-70.

Ingene, C. A., and A. Ghosh. 1990. "Consumer and Producer Behavior in a Multipurpose Shopping Environment." *Geographical Analysis* 22: 70-91.

Chapter 5.3

Adams, M., L. Steyn, C. Tanner, S. Turner, and R. White . 2004. "Case Studies on Investment on Community Land in Southern Africa Foreign Investment Advisory Services" (FIAS), World Bank Group, Oxford, Mokoro Ltd.

Allen, T. 2000. "The Right to Property in Commonwealth Constitutions," Cambridge: Cambridge University Press, chapter 6: Acquisition and deprivation 162–200.

Blessings, Prof. 2009. "Sold Birthright: Illegal Taking of Land". Accessed 2009 at http://www.modernghana.com/news/ 199287/1/sold-birthright-illegal-taking-of-land.html, 20 Jan 2009.

Bruce, J.W. 2006. "Reform of Land Law in the Context of World Bank Lending", in J.W. Bruce, R Giovarelli, L.Rolfes Jr., D. Bledsoe, and R. Mitchell, *Land Law Reform: Achieving Development Policy Objectives.* Washington, DC: World Bank, 11–65.

Bruce, J.W. and Shem E. Migot-Adholla, eds. 1994. *Searching for Land Tenure Security in Africa,* Dubuque, Iowa: Kendall/Hunt Publishing Co.

Cotula, L., S. Vermeulen, R. Leonard, and J. Keeley. 2009. "Land Grab or Development Opportunity? Agricultural Investment and International Land Deals in Africa." London/Rome: IIED/FAO/IFAD.

FAO. 2008. "Compulsory Acquisition of Land and Compensation," FAO Land Tenure Studies, 10, Rome.

Gauri, V., D.M. Brinks. 2008. *Courting Social Justice: Judicial Enforcement of Social and Economic Rights in the Developing World*, Cambridge: Cambridge University Press.

Government of Alberta. 1979. "Alberta Regulation 160/79: Regulations Respecting the Ownership of Agricultural and Recreational Land in Alberta."

Government of Queensland. 1988. *Foreign Ownership of Land Register Act.*

Government of the United States of America. 2000. African Growth and Opportunity Act (AGOA) Title I, Trade and Development Act of 2000 (P.L. 106–200).

Harring, S.L. and W. Odendaal. 2008. "Kessl: A New Jurisprudence for Land Reform in Namibia," Land Environment and Development Project of the Legal Assistance Centre and Namibian Economic Policy Research Unit, Windhoek.

Hodgson, S, C. Cullinan, and K. Campbell. 1999. "Land Ownership and Foreigners: a Comparative Analysis of Regulatory Approaches to the Acquisition and Use of Land by Foreigners." Rome: FAO Legal Papers Online 86.

The Law and Development Partnership. 2009. "Republic of Sudan: Mini Diagnostic: State Level Barriers to Investment in Gedaref State, Gezira State, North Kordofan State, Red Sea State," a report for the International Finance Corporation, London.

Luttrell, C.B. 1979. "The 'Danger' From Foreign Ownership of U.S. Farmland". United States Federal Reserve Bank of St Louis, pages 2–9.January 1979.

McAuslan, P. 2006. Improving Tenure Security for the Poor in Africa, LEP Working Paper No.1, Rome, FAO

Migai Aketch, J.M. 2001. The African Growth and Opportunity Act: Implications for Kenya's Trade and Development, 33 New York University Review of International Law and Politics, 651–702.

Peterson, L.E. 2009. "Tribunal Orders Zimbabwe to Pay £7,3m to Dutch Farmers," posted April 28 at newsdesk@newzimbabwe.com.

Schreiberg, S.L. and H.A. Levy. 1993. "The Uniform State Law Movement in the United States as a Model for the Development of Land Privatization Legislation in the Newly Independent States" (unpublished manuscript), quoted in Burke, D.W. 1995. "Argument for the Allocation of Resources to the Development of a Well-Defined System of Real Property Law in the Czech Republic," *Vanderbilt Journal of Transnational Law* 29, 661–690.

Sparkes, P. 2007. *European Land Law*. Oxford: Hart Publishing.

Sulle, E., F. and Nelson. 2009. "Biofuels, Land Access and Rural Livelihoods in Tanzania", London: IIED.

Tesser, L.M. 2004. "East-Central Europe's New Security Concern: Foreign Land Ownership." Paper presented at annual meeting of the Midwest Political Science Association. Palmer House Hilton< Chicago, April 15, 2004.

van der Walt, A.J. 1999. *Constitutional Property Clauses*, Kenwyn, Juta & Co.

World Bank. 2003. *Financial Sector Assessment Report on Tanzania*. Washington, D.C.: World Bank.

Chapter 6.1

Barreto, P., A. Pinto, B. Brito, and S. Haiashy. 2008. 'Quem é Dono da Amazônia: Uma análise do recadastramento de imóveis rurais.' Belém, Imazon.

Brito, B. and P. Barreto. 2006. 'A eficácia da aplicação da lei de crimes ambientais pelo Ibama para proteção de florestas no Pará.' Revista de Direito Ambiental. São Paulo: Ed. *Revista dos Tribunais* 43: 35–65. (in Portuguese).

Ewers, R., W. Laurance, and C. Souza, Jr. 2008. "Temporal Fluctuations in Amazonian Deforestation Rates." *Environmental Conservation* 35(4): 303–310.

Fearnside, P. M. 2003. "Deforestation Control in Mato Grosso: A New Model for Slowing the Loss of Brazil's Amazon Forest." *AMBIO* 32(5): 343–345.

Haiashy, S., C. Souza, Jr., and A. Veríssimo. 2009. Forest Transparency for the Legal Amazon. Imazon. November. http://bit.ly/a2fSvo.

INPE. 2008. Monitoramento da Cobertura Florestal da Amazônia por Satélites. INPE. São José dos Campos, Brasil. http://www.obt.inpe.br/deter/metodologia_v2.pdf

ISA. 2005. Desmatamentos de florestas em propriedades rurais integradas ao Sistema de Licenciamento Ambiental Rural entre 2001 e 2004. Instituto Socioambiental—ISA, Brasília.

MMA (Ministério do Meio Ambiente)-SNUC (Sistema Nacional de Unidades de Conservação). 2000. MMA, SNUC, Brasília. http://www.mma.gov.br/port/snuc.pdf.

Morton, D.C., R.S. DeFries, Y.E. Shimabukuro, L.O. Anderson, E. Arai, FdB. Espirito-Santo, R. Freitas, and Morisette. 2006. "Cropland Expansion Changes Deforestation Dynamics in the Southern Brazilian Amazon." *J. Proc. Nat'l. Acad. Sci.* 103: 14637–14641.

Nepstad, D., C. Stickler, O. Almeida. 2006. "Globalization of the Amazon Beef and Soy Industries: Opportunities for Conservation." *Conservation Biology* 20 (6): 1595–1603.

PRODES. 2009. Monitoramento da Floresta Amazônica por Satélite. http://www.obt.inpe.br/prodes/.

Sales, M.H, C.M. Souza Jr., and P.C. Kyriakidis, (in review) Fusion of MODIS Images Using Kriging with External Drifts. *IEEE Transactions on Geoscience and Remote Sensing*.

Souza,Jr., C.M., P. Barreto. 2001. Sistema de fiscalização, licenciamento e monitoramento de propiedades rurais de Mato Grosso. In: Ministério do Meio Ambiente. Causas e dinâmicas do desmatamento da Amazônia. 307–341.

Souza, Jr., C.M., D. Roberts and M.A. Cochrane. 2005. "Combining Spectral and Spatial Information to Map Canopy Damages from Selective Logging and Forest Fires." *Remote Sensing of Environment* 98: 329–343.

Souza, Jr., C.M., A. Veríssimo, L. Micol and S. Guimarães. 2006. "Transparência Florestal do Estado de Mato Grosso." *Forest Transparency Bulletin* N. 2, September.

Souza, Jr., C.M., K. Pereira, V. Lins, S. Haiashy, and D. Souza. 2009. "Web-Oriented GIS Systems for Monitoring, Conservation and Law Enforcement of the Brazilian Amazon." *Earth Science Informatics* 2: 205–215.

Chapter 6.2

Arima, E., P. Barreto, and M. Brito. 2006. "Cattle Ranching in the Amazon: Trends and Implications for Environmental Conservation." http://www.imazon.org.br/ novo2008/arquivosdb/livro_pecuaria_ingles.pdf . (May 6, 2010).

Arima, E.Y., C.S. Simmons, R.T. Walker, and M.A. Cochrane. 2007. "Fire in the Brazilian Amazon: A Spatially Explicit Model for Policy Impact Analysis." *Journal of Regional Science* 47 (3): 541–567.

Barreto, P., A. Pinto, B. Brito, and S. Hayashi. 2008a. Quem é Dono da Amazônia: Uma análise do recadastramento de imóveis rurais. Belém, PA, Brazil. Imazon. http://www.imazon.org.br/novo2008/arquivosdb/QuemDonoAmazonia.pdf. (May 19, 2009)

Barreto, P., R. Pereira, and E. Arima. 2008b. Pecuária e o Desmatamento na Amazônia na Era das Mudanças Climáticas. Belém, PA, Brazil. Imazon. http://www.imazon.org.br/novo2008/arquivosdb/120849pecuaria_mudancas_cli maticas.pdf (May 19, 2009).

Brito, B. and P. Barreto. 2006. A eficácia da aplicação da lei de crimes ambientais pelo Ibama para proteção de florestas no Pará. Revista de Direito Ambiental. São Paulo: Ed. *Revista dos Tribunais* 43: 35–65. (in Portuguese).

Brito, B., and P. Barreto. 2009. "The Risks and the Principles for Landholding Regularization in the Amazon Imazon." *State of the Amazon* 10. Belém: Imazon. http://www.imazon.org.br/novo2008/arquivosdb/181120oea_march2009_10.pdf (May, 2010).

Brasil. 2008. Ministério do Desenvolvimento Agrário. Ministro anuncia recadastramento de imóveis rurais em fevereiro. 2008. Brasília, DF, Brazil. http://www.INCRA.gov.br (February 6, 2008).

Brasil. 2004. Ministério de Ciência e Tecnologia. Comunicação nacional inicial do Brasil à convenção-quadro das Nações Unidas sobre mudança do clima. Brasília, DF, Brazil.

CEA (California Environmental Associates). 2007. Design to Win: Philanthropy's Role in the Fight Against Global. San Francisco, CA, USA. http://www.hewlett.org/NR/rdonlyres/17FBB397-D9BB-46A2-819F-4B855430C29E/0/Design_to_Win_Final_Report.pdf. (March 8, 2008).

Ecodebate. 2008. BNDES diz que o Fundo mundial para Amazônia terá US$1 bilhão. 2 Aug. 2008. http://www.ecodebate.com.br/2008/08/02/bndes-diz-que-o-fundo-mundial-para-amazonia-tera-us1-bilhao/. (May 21, 2009).

Enkvist, Per-Anders, T. Nauclér, and J. Rosander. 2007. "A Cost Curve For Greenhouse Gas Reduction." *The McKinsey Quarterly* 1. McKinsey & Company.

IPCC. 2007a. Summary for Policymakers. In: Climate Change 2007: Mitigation. Contribution of Working Group III to the Fourth Assessment Report of the Intergovernmental Panel on Climate Change (B. Metz, O.R. Davidson, P.R. Bosch, R. Dave, L.A. Meyer, eds.). Cambridge and New York, USA: Cambridge University Press.

IPCC. 2007b. Summary for Policymakers. In: Climate Change 2007: Impacts, Adaptation and Vulnerability. Contribution of Working Group II to the Fourth Assessment Report of the Intergovernmental Panel on Climate Change. 7–22.

(M.L. Parry, O.F. Canziani, J.P. Palutikof, P.J. van der Linden and C.E. Hanson, eds.) Cambridge, UK: Cambridge University Press.

Instituto Socioambiental (ISA). 2006. "O desafio da regularização fundiária na Terra do Meio." http://www.socioambiental.org/nsa/detalhe?id=2336

Greenpeace. 2009. "A farra do boi na Amazônia" http://www.greenpeace.org/brasil/amazonia/gado

Lima, A. 2008. Plano de Ação para Prevenção e Controle dos Desmatamentos na Amazônia Brasileira—PPCDAm. Ações do Governo Federal em 2008. Director of Policies Against Deforestation of the Brazilian Ministry of Environment. (Microsoft PowerPoint presentation). Brasília, DF, Brazil.

Lopes, R. 2008. Noruega doará US$1 bilhão para o Fundo Amazônia. Agência Brasil. Brasília, Brazil. September 16, 2008. http://www.agenciabrasil.gov.br/noticias/2008/09/16/materia.2008-09-16.6549696579/. (May 21, 2009).

Norway, Ministry of Foreign Affairs. 2009. "Um bilhão de dólares para preservar a Amazônia brasileira" http://www.noruega.org.br/ARKIV/Old_web/indigenous2/Fundo_Amaz%C3%B4nia/fundo_amazonia/

Ribeiro, M. B. and A. Veríssimo. 2007. draft. Evolução das Áreas Protegidas na Amazônia Legal. Imazon. December.

Ribeiro, M. B., A. Veríssimo and K. Pereira. 2006. Deforestation in Protected Areas in the Brazilian Amazon: The Case of Rondônia. *State of the Amazon* 6. Belém: Imazon.

UN (United Nations). 2007. Bali Action Plan. Conference of the Parties. Thirteenth session Bali, December 13–14, 2007. http://unfccc.int/files/meetings/cop_13/application/pdf/cp_bali_act_p.pdf (December 30, 2007).

Chapter 6.3

Agrawal, A. 2001. Common Property Institutions and Sustainable Governance of Resources. *World Development* 29 (10): 1649–1672.

Allen, T. and K. Baylis. 2005. Who Owns Carbon? Property Rights Issues in a Market for Green House Gases. Unpublished Document, University of British Columbia, Canada.

Angelsen, A., ed. 2009. REDD+ National Strategy and Policy Options. CIFOR Publication, Denmark.

Ankersen, T. and G. Barnes. 2004. "Inside the Polygon: Emerging Community Tenure Systems and Forest Resource Extraction." *Working Forests in the Neotropics*, (D. Zarin, R. Janaki, F. Putz, and M. Schmink, eds), 156–177. New York: Columbia University Press.

Archer, D. 2005. "Fate of Fossil Fuel CO_2 in Geologic Time." *J. Geophysical Research* 110 (C09505).

Barry, D. and R. Meinzen-Dick. 2008. The Invisible Map: Community Tenure Rights. Proceedings of IASC, Cheltenham, UK. http://iasc2008.glos.ac.uk/conference%20papers/papers/B/Barry_138902.pdf.

Barnes, G. 2006. "Field Notes on Land Tenure Status and Dynamics in Madre de Dios (Peru)." Unpublished report. University of Florida, Gainesville.

Basnet-Parasai, R. 2007. Who Owns Carbon in Community Managed Forest? Paper prepared for Amsterdam Summer School. http://www.2007amsterdam conference.org/Downloads/AC2007_Basnet.pdf. (September 1, 2008).

BLD. 1979. *Black's Law Dictionary*. St. Paul, MN: West Publish Co.

Boydell, S., J. Sheehan, and J. Prior. 2008. Carbon Property Rights in Context. Draft paper submitted to *Environmental Practice*.

Chave et al. 2005. Tree Allometry and Improved Estimation of Carbon Stocks and Balance in Tropical Forests. *Oecologia* 145: 87–89.

Cronkleton, P., M. Albornoz, G. Barnes, K. Evans, and W. de Jong (in press). Social Geomatics: Participatory Forest Mapping to Mediate Resource Conflict in the Bolivian Amazon. Submitted to *Human Ecology Journal*.

Cronkleton, P., C. Gönner, K. Evans, M. Haug, W. de Jong, and M. Albornoz. 2007. Supporting Forest Communities in Times of Tenure Uncertainty: Participatory Mapping Experiences from Bolivia and Indonesia. Proceedings: International Conference on Poverty Reduction and Forests, Bangkok, September 2007.

De Jong, W., S. Ruiz and M. Becker. 2006. "Conflicts and communal forest management in northern Bolivia." *Forest Policy and Economics* 8: pp. 447– 457.

De Soto, H. 2000. *The Mystery of Capital: Why Capitalism Triumphs in the West and Fails Everywhere Else*. New York: Basic Books.

Duchelle, A. 2009. Conservation and Livelihood Development in Brazil Nut Producing Communities in a Tri-National Amazonian Frontier. PhD dissertation, University of Florida, Gainesville, FL.

Ecosecurities. 2009. The Forest Carbon Offsetting Survey 2009 http://www.ecosecurities.com/Registered/ECOForestry Survey2009.pdf.

Ecosystem Marketplace. 2009. State of the Voluntary Carbon Markets 2009, http://ecosystemmarketplace.com/documents/cms_documents/StateOfTheVolun taryCarbonMarkets_2009.

ELI. 1995. Brazil's Extractive Reserves: Fundamental Aspects of Their Implementation. Environmental Law Institute Research Report. Washington, DC.

Environmental Leader. 2009. Carbon Market Up 83 percent in 2008, Value Hits $125 Billion. http://www.environmentalleader.com/2009/01/14/carbon-market-up-83-in-2008-value-hits-125-billion/

Goldstein, E. 1995. *Economics and the Environment*. New Jersey: Prentice Hall.

Griffiths, T. 2007. Seeing "RED"? "Avoided Deforestation" and the Rights of Indigenous Peoples and Local Communities. http://www.forestpeoples.org/documents/ifi_igo/avoided_deforestation_red_jun07_eng.pdf

Hardin, G. 1968. Tragedy of the Commons. *Science* 162: 1243–1248

Houghton, R.A. 2007. Balancing the Global Carbon Budget. *Annual Review of Earth Planetary Sciences* 35: 313–47.

IPCC. 2001. Climate Change 2001: Impacts, Adaptation, and Vulnerability. Contribution of Working Group II to the Third Assessment Report of the Intergovernmental Panel on Climate Change. (J.J. McCarthy, O.F. Canziani, N.A. Leary, D.J.Dokken and K.S.White, eds.) Cambridge: Cambridge University Press. http://www.ipcc.ch/.

IPCC. 2003. IPCC Workshop Report on the Detection and Attribution of the Effects of Climate Change. (C. Rosenzweig and P.G. Neofotis, eds.) NASA/Goddard Institute for Space Studies, New York. http://www.ipcc.ch/.

IPCC. 2007. Climate Change 2007: The Physical Science Basis. Contribution of Working Group I to the Fourth Assessment Report of the Intergovernmental Panel on Climate Change. (S. Solomon, D. Qin, M. Manning, Z. Chen, M. Marquis, K.B. Averyt, M. Tignor and H.L.Miller, eds.). Cambridge: Cambridge University Press. http://www.ipcc.ch/.

Larson, A., P. Cronkleton, D. Barry, and P. Pacheco. 2008. Tenure Rights and Beyond: Community Access to Forest Resources in Latin America. Occassional Paper No. 50. CIFOR, Bogor, Indonesia.

Lewis, S.L., G. Lopez-Gonzales, B. Sonké, K. Affum-Baffoc, T. Baker, L. Ojo, O. Phillips, J. Reitsma, L. White, J. Comisky, et al. 2009. Increasing Carbon Storage in Intact African Tropic Forests. *Nature* 457: 1003–1006.

McCay, B.J. and J. Acheson, eds. 1987. *The Question of the Commons: The Culture and Economy of Communal Resources.* Tucson: University of Arizona Press.

Melone, M. (1993). The struggle of the *seingueiros*: Environmental action in the Amazon. (In J. Friedmann and H. Rangan, eds.) *In Defense of Livelihood: Comparative Studies on Environmental Action.* West Hartford: Kumarian Press. 106–126.

Monterroso, I. and D. Barry. 2008. Institutional Change and Community Forestry in the Mayan Biosphere Reserve Guatemala. Proceedings of 12th Biennial Conference of the International Association for the Study of Commons, Cheltenham, England.

Biosphere Reserve Guatemala. Proceedings of 12th Biennial Conference of the International Association for the Study of Commons, Cheltenham, England.

Murrieta, J. and R. Rueda. 1995. *Reservas extractivistas.* Gland, Switzerland.

OCC. 2008. Eliasch Report—Climate Change: Financing Global Forests. Office of Climate Change, UK.

Ostrom, E., J. Burger, C. Field, R. Norgaard, and D. Policansky. 1999. Revisiting the Commons: Local Lessons, Global Challenges. *Science* 284 (5412): 278–282.

Ostrom, E. 1990. *Governing the Commons: The Evolution of Institutions for Collective Action.* New York: Cambridge Univ. Press.

Pacheco, P. 2007. La economía política del desarrollo forestal en Bolivia: Políticas, actores e ideologías. *Revista Virtual REDESMA* (June), Centro Boliviano de Estudios Multidisciplinarios, Bolivia: 30–52.

Parker, C., A. Mitchell, M. Trivedi, and N. Mardas. 2008. The Little REDD Book: A Guide to Governmental and Non-governmental Proposals for Reducing Emissions from Deforestation and Degradation. Global Canopy Programme, Oxford, UK.

Pearson, Walker, and Brown. 2008. *Sourcebook for Land-Use, Land-Use Change and Forestry Projects.* BioCF Document Library, World Bank, Washington, DC.

Phillips, G. and A. Razzouk. 2007. A Trillion Dollar Marketplace. *Environmental Finance.*

Porrua, M. and A. Garcia-Guerrero. 2008. Case Study: The Noel Kempff Climate Action Project, Bolivia. In *Climate Change and Forests: Emerging Policy and Market*

Opportunities. (C. Streck, R. O'Sullivan, T. Janson-Smith, and R. Tarasofsky, eds.) Baltimore: Brookings Institution Press.

Randrianarisoa, J., B. Vitale, and S. Pandya. 2008. Case Study: Creative Financing and Multisector Partners in Madagascar. (C. Streck, R. O'Sullivan, T. Janson-Smith and R, Tarasofsky, eds.) *Climate Change and Forests: Emerging Policy and Market Opportunities*, Baltimore: Brookings Institution Press.

Robiedo, C. and H. Ok Ma. 2008. Why Are There So Few Forestry Projects Under CDM? *ITTO Tropical Forests Update Online Newsletter*, 18(3). http://www.itto.or.jp/live/PageDisplayHandler?padeld=243&id=4476.

Singer, J. 2000. Property and Social Relations: From Title to Entitlement. In *Property and Values: Alternatives to Public and Private Ownership* (C. Geisler and G. Daneker, eds.). Washington, DC: Island Press.

Stern, N. et al. 2007. Stern Review on the Economics of Climate Change. Cambridge: Cambridge University Press, UK.

Stickler, C. 2009. Defending Public Interests in Private Forests: Land-Use Policy Alternative for the Xingu River Headwaters Region of Southeastern Amazônia. PhD dissertation, University of Florida, Gainesville, FL.

Sunderlin, W., J. Hatcher and M. Liddle. 2008. From Exclusion to Ownership? Challenges and Opportunities in Advancing Forest Tenure Reform. Published by Rights and Resources Initiative. http://www.rightsandresources.org/documents/index.php?pubID=736, (March 3, 2009).

Takacs, David. 2009. Forest Carbon: Law and Property Rights. Conservation International, Arlington, VA.

UNDP. n.d. UN-REDD Program Fund. http://www.undp.org/mdtf/UN-REDD/overview.shtml.

UNFCC. 2009. CDM Projects by Sector. http://cdm.unfccc.int/Statistics/Registration/RegisteredProjByScopePieChart.html.

UNFCC. 2008. CDM Statistics. http://cdm.unfcc.int/Statistics/index.html.

White, A., and Martin A. 2002. Who Owns the World's Forests? Report published by Forest Trends, Washington, DC.

Woods Hole Research Center. 2008. An Overview of Readiness for REDD: A Compilation of Readiness Activities Prepared on Behalf of the Forum on Readiness for REDD. (T. Johns and E. Johnson, eds.)

World Bank. 2009. State and Trends of the Carbon Markets. World Bank Institute, Washington DC. http://wbcarbonfinance.org/Router.cfm.

Chapter 7.1

African Union. 2009. "Land policy in Africa: A framework to strengthen land rights, enhance productivity and secure livelihoods." Addis Ababa: African Union and Economic Commission for Africa.

Arrunada, B. 2007. "Pitfalls to Avoid When Measuring Institutions: Is Doing Business Damaging Business?" *Journal of Comparative Economics* 35 (4): 729-47.

Barnes, G. and C. Griffith-Charles. 2007. "Assessing the formal land market and deformalization of property in St. Lucia." *Land Use Policy* 24 (2): 494-501.

FAO Land Tenure and Managment Unit. 2009. "Towards voluntary guidelines on responsible governance of tenure of land and other natural resources." Land

Tenure Working Paper 10. Rome: Food and Agricultural Organization of the UN.

IFAD. 2009. "Report on implementation of the performance based allocation system." Rome: International Fund for Agricultural Development.

Kaufmann, D. and A. Kraay. 2008. "Governance indicators: Where are we, where should we be going?" *World Bank Research Observer 23* (1): 1-30.

Palmer, D., S. Fricska, and B. Wehrmann. 2009. " Towards improved land governance." Land Tenure Working Paper 11. Rome: Food and Agriculture Organization of the United Nations and United Nations Human Settlements Programme.

Transparency International. 2009. "Global corruption barometer 2009." Berlin: Transparency International.

Transparency International India. 2005. "India corruption study 2005." New Delhi: Transparency International.

World Bank. 2007. "Strengthening World Bank Group Engagement on Governance and Anticorruption." Washington, DC: Joint Ministerial Committee of the Boards of Governors of the Bank and the Fund on the Transfer of Real Resources to Developing Countries.

World Bank. 2009. *Doing Business in 2010: Reforming through difficult times*. Washington, D.C.: World Bank, International Finance Corporation, and Oxford University Press.

Chapter 7.2

Afghanistan Web Site, December, 18, 2008.

Afghanistan, Government of, "The Land Management Law", Kabul, 2000.

Afghanistan, Government of, Ministry of Agriculture, Irrigation and Livestock. 2006. Kabul, "Policy and Strategy for Forest and Rangeland Management Sub-Sector."

Afghanistan, Government of. "Draft Land Policy", Land Commission headed by the Minister of Agriculture, Irrigation and Livestock, with representatives from the Ministry of Justice and the Minister of Urban Development and Housing, January, 2007.

Asian Development Bank/ Department for International Development, TA 4483-AFG, "Final Report, Capacity Building for Land Policy and Administration Reform, (September, 2007).

Barakat, Sultan, Evaluation Team Leader. 2006. "Mid-term Evaluation Report of the National Solidarity Program (NSP) Afghanistan". Post-war Reconstruction & Development Unit (PRDU), The University of York; and Ministry of Rural Rehabilitation and Development, Islamic Republic of Afghanistan.

Barfield, Thomas. 2004. "Nomadic Pastoralists in Afghanistan", World Bank, Washington, D.C., Bank Information Center.

Brick, Jennifer. 2008. "The Political Foundations of State-Building and Limited Government in Afghanistan", paper presented to the 66th Midwest Political Science Association Annual Meeting in Chicago, IL, April 3.

Bruce, John. 1998. "Review of Tenure Terminology", Land Tenure Center, University of Wisconsin-Madison.

Bruce, John and Anna Knox. 2009. "Structures and Stratagems: Making Decentralization of Authority over Land in Africa Cost-Effective", *World Development* 37 (8): 1368.

Burns, Tony, Chris Grant, Kevin Nettle, Anne-Marie Brits and Kate Dalrymple. 2006. "Land Administration Reform: Indicators of Success, Future Challenges", Land Equity Inc. 13 November.

de Weijer, Frauke. 2003. "Pastoralist Vulnerability Study", Kabul, World Food Program.

Delville, Philippe Lavigne. 2006. "Registering and Administering Customary Land Rights: PFRs in West Africa", World Bank Conference on Land Policies and Legal Empowerment of the Poor, Washington, DC.

Enemark, Stig. 2005. "Understanding the Land Management Paradigm", FIG Commission 7, Symposium on Innovative Technologies for Land Administration, 19–25 June 2005, Madison, Wisconsin, USA.

Gebremedhin, Yohannes. 2007. "Land Tenure and Administration in Rural Afghanistan: Legal Aspects", Project Report 7, Capacity Building for Land Policy and Administration Reform, Asian Development Bank, Manila/ Department for International Development, United Kingdom.

Islamic Republic of Afghanistan, "Draft Land Policy", approved by Multi-Ministerial Land Commission, January, 2007.

Kadouf, Hunud Abia. 1997. "The traditional Malay Ruler and the Land: Maxwell's Theory Revisited", *The Malayan Law Journal*, International Islamic University, Malaysia, 4 April.

Marshall, Graham R. 2007. "Nesting, Subsidiarity, and Community-Based Environmental Governance Beyond the Local Level", Occasional Paper 2007/01, Institute for Rural Futures, University of New England, Australia, June.

McEwen, Alec and Sharna Nolan. 2007. "Options for Land Registration," Afghanistan Research and Evaluation Unity, Working Paper Series, Kabul.

Murtazashvili, Ilia. 2008. "The Political Economy of Private-Order Property Systems: From Informal to Formal Property Rights on the American Frontier," Ph.D. Thesis, University of Wisconsin, Madison.

Norfolk, Simon and Christopher Tanner. 2007. "Improving Tenure Security for the Rural Poor," Food and Agriculture Organization, *Support to the Legal Empowerment of the Poor*. Rome.

Scanagri/Terra Institute. 2006. "Capacity Building for Land Policy and Administration Reform: Inception Report", Asian Development Bank. TA-4483-AFG. July.

———. 2007. "Project Report No. 6: A Proposal for a Land Administration and Management Program (LAMP)", prepared for the Ministry of Agriculture, Irrigation and Livestock, Kabul, November.

Safar, M. Yasin and David Stanfield. 2007. "Cadastral Survey in Afghanistan", Scanagri/Terra Institute, Capacity Building for Land Policy and Administration Reform, ADB / DFID, TA 4483-AFG.

Sheleff, Leon. 2000. *The Future of Tradition*, London: Frank Cass.

Stanfield, David. 2003. "A Town Model of Land Registration: The Case of Killingworth, Connecticut", Terra Institute, Mt. Horeb, Wisconsin.

Stanfield, J. David. 2007. "Project Brief", Capacity Building for Land Policy and Administration Reform, Project, Asian Development Bank/ DFID, TA 4483-AFG, August.

Stanfield, J. David and M. Yasin Safar. 2007. "A Study of the General Directorate of Land Management and Amlak of the Ministry of Agriculture, Irrigation and Livestock", Capacity Building for Land Policy and Administration Reform, Project, Asian Development Bank/ DFID, TA 4483-AFG.

Stanfield, J. David, Jennifer Brick, M.Y. Safar and Akram Salam, forthcoming. "Rebuilding the Afghan State: Community-State Cooperation for Documenting Land Tenures", chapter in Carl Bruch, Strengthening Post-Conflict Peacebuilding through Natural Resource Management. Environmental Law Institute, Washington, DC.

Tanzania, Government of. *Village Land Act 1999; s. 8, 54, 58 & Regulations 61-74 (2001).*

Toulmin, Camilla. 2006. "Securing land rights for the poor in Africa—Key to growth, peace and sustainable development", International Institute for the Environment and Development, paper prepared for the Commission on the Legal Empowerment of the Poor, January.

United Nations Economic Commission for Europe. 1996. "Land Administration Guidelines", New York and Geneva.

U.S. Agency for International Development—USAID. 2006. Land Titling and Economic Restructuring in Afghanistan Project, Kabul, "Informal Settlements and Tenure Issues", Kabul, January.

Wardak, Ali. 2003. "*Jirgas*: A Traditional Mechanism of Conflict Resolution in Afghanistan", http://unpan1.un.org/intradoc/groups/public/documents/APCITY/UNPAN017434.pdf.

Wardak, Mirwais, Idrees Zaman and Kanishka Nawabi. 2007. "The Role and Functions of Religious Civil Society in Afghanistan", Cooperation for Peace and Unity, Kabul, July. www.cpau.org.af

Wily, Liz Alden. 2003. "Governance and Land Relations: A Review of Decentralisation of Land Administration and Management in Africa." International Institute for Environment and Development. London.

Wily, Liz Alden. 2004. "Looking for Peace on the Pastures", Kabul, Afghanistan Research and Evaluation Unit.

World Bank. 2007. "Service Delivery and Governance at the Sub-National Level in Afghanistan." Washington, DC. July.

Chapter 7.3

DFID/ADB Technical Assistance Consultant Report. 2008. "Community Based Approaches for Rural Land Administration and Management in Afghanistan." Islamic Republic of Afghanistan: Capacity Building for Land Policy and Administration Reform. Kabul, April, 2008, p. 16.

DFID/ADB. 2007. "Capacity Building for Land Policy and Administrative Reform." Project Report No. 6. Kabul, November, 2007, p. 40.

Eco-Audit

Environmental Benefits Statement

The World Bank is committed to preserving Endangered Forests and natural resources. We print World Bank Working Papers and Country Studies on postconsumer recycled paper, processed chlorine free. The World Bank has formally agreed to follow the recommended standards for paper usage set by Green Press Initiative—a nonprofit program supporting publishers in using fiber that is not sourced from Endangered Forests. For more information, visit www.greenpressinitiative.org.

In 2008, the printing of these books on recycled paper saved the following:

Trees*	Solid Waste	Water	Net Greenhouse Gases	Total Energy
289	8,011	131,944	27,396	92 mil.
*40 feet in height and 6–8 inches in diameter	Pounds	Gallons	Pounds CO$_2$ Equivalent	BTUs

green press INITIATIVE

www.ingramcontent.com/pod-product-compliance
Lightning Source LLC
Chambersburg PA
CBHW082350270326
41935CB00013B/1572